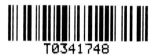

DUMBARTON OAKS TEXTS

I

CONSTANTINE PORPHYROGENITUS
DE ADMINISTRANDO IMPERIO

CORPUS FONTIUM
HISTORIAE BYZANTINAE

CONSILIO SOCIETATIS INTERNATIONALIS
STUDIIS BYZANTINIS PROVEHENDIS DESTINATAE
EDITUM

———————

VOLUMEN I

CONSTANTINUS PORPHYROGENITUS
DE ADMINISTRANDO IMPERIO

EDIDIT
GY. MORAVCSIK

ANGLICE VERTIT
R. J. H. JENKINS

CONSTANTINE PORPHYROGENITUS DE ADMINISTRANDO IMPERIO

GREEK TEXT EDITED

by

GY. MORAVCSIK

ENGLISH TRANSLATION

by

R. J. H. JENKINS

New, Revised Edition

Dumbarton Oaks
Center for Byzantine Studies
Trustees for Harvard University
Washington, District of Columbia
1967

Printed in the United States of America

Eighth Printing, 2020

LIBRARY OF CONGRESS CATALOGING-IN-PUBLICATION DATA
Constantine VII Porphyrogenitus, Emperor of the East, 905–959.
Constantine Porphyrogenitus De administrando imperio.
p. cm.
(Corpus fontium historiae Byzantinae; v. 1)
(Dumbarton Oaks texts ; 1)
Translation of: De administrando imperio.
English and Greek.
Includes index.
ISBN 978-0-88402-021-9 (hardcover : alk. paper)
ISBN 978-0-88402-343-2 (paperback : alk. paper)
1. Byzantine Empire—History—Constantine VII Porphyrogenitus, 913–959.
2. Byzantine Empire—History—To 527.
3. Byzantine Empire—History—527–1081.
4. Education of Princes.
I. Moravcsik, Gyula, 1892–1972.
II. Title. III. Series. IV. Series.
DF593.C6613 1985   949.5 85-6950
Library of Congress Catalog Number 68-24220

Cover: The Emperor Constantine with the facial features of Emperor Constantine
VII Porphyrogenitus, wing of an ivory triptych, Constantinople, mid-tenth century,
Dumbarton Oaks BZ.1947.11. Courtesy of the Byzantine Collection,
Dumbarton Oaks Research Library and Collection, Washington, D.C.

www.doaks.org/publications

TABLE OF CONTENTS

viii

DUMBARTON OAKS TEXTS
I.

CONSTANTINE PORPHYROGENITUS
DE ADMINISTRANDO IMPERIO

FOREWORD TO THE FIRST EDITION

In publishing this critical edition and translation of the text of the treatise *De Administrando Imperio*, compiled exactly one thousand years ago by the emperor Constantine VII, we feel that we should explain how our work began.

The editor of the Greek text started to work on it as long ago as 1926; but the carrying out of other academic projects interfered during many years with completing the collection of his material, and bringing it into final shape for publication. Then, the latter years of the world war made completion and publication alike impossible. Fortunately, however, the ms. survived the siege of Budapest; and immediately after the war efforts were again made to finish the work, and the question arose of bringing it out.

The first draft of the English translation was made independently. But while its publication was under consideration, chance brought it into relation with the publication of the Greek text. In the pursuit of our common purpose, we established contact with one another, and agreed that text and translation should be published together, believing that an edition of a Greek text is incomplete without a translation, and having in mind that, apart from the old Latin versions and those in the Russian and Croat languages, there is still no complete translation of the treatise in existence.

From the beginning of 1947 we have worked together, through the medium of correspondence, to bring text and translation into line with one another, and have thus been able to subject the work of each to the revision of the other. Doubtless both parts of the work have benefited from this revision. Certain deficiences came to light in the Greek text, and the editor owes some corrections to the translator, who has also contributed a few conjectural emendations to the apparatus. At the same time, the translator wishes to own a special debt to the editor, whose long study and deep knowledge of the text have assisted in solving many difficulties of interpretation; and though the translator takes responsibility for everything printed in the English version, he is happy to make this cordial acknowledgment to his senior colleague.

Edition and translation are complementary. For all that, their purposes are not quite identical; and it has been necessary that a few corruptions and errors which stand in the text of Constantine should be corrected in the version. We have therefore printed in italic those few words or phrases of the translation which do not correspond exactly with the text. References to the present edition are cited by *chapter* and *line of the chapter*; in such citations the letter «P» stands for «Proem» (Προοίμιον), *i. e.*, the introductory passage which precedes chapter 1.

Fifty years ago two scholars, the Hungarian R. Vári and the Englishman J. B. Bury, were already concerning themselves with the preparation of a new edition of Constantine. In bringing to fulfilment what they were compelled to abandon, we dedicate this work to the memory of both.

Budapest — London
15th of March, 1949.

GY. MORAVCSIK — R. J. H. JENKINS

FOREWORD TO THE SECOND EDITION

This re-edition of the Text and Translation of *D. A. I.*, which appeared in Budapest eighteen years ago, is published by the Harvard University Center for Byzantine Studies, Dumbarton Oaks, Washington, D. C., and is the first of a series of texts to be brought out by this institute. We wish to thank Dumbarton Oaks for its generosity; and also that large number of scholars whose suggestions have enlarged our apparatus and improved our translation.

Despite minor corrections, it has been possible to preserve the earlier pagination and alignment of the Greek text: so that the Commentary[1], which was arranged for use with the first edition, may equally well be used with the second.

Washington, D. C.
November, 1966   Gy. M. — R. J.

---

[1] Const. Porph. *De Adm. Imp.* Vol. II, Commentary (University of London, The Athlone Press, 1962).

GENERAL INTRODUCTION

The emperor Constantine VII Porphyrogenitus[1] (905—959) was the second and only surviving son[2] of the emperor Leo VI, surnamed the Wise, (866—912) by his mistress and later fourth wife, Zoë Carbunopsina.[3] Constantine's early life was clouded by a series of misfortunes for which he himself was in no way responsible. His constitution was sickly, and he was indeed invalid throughout his life.[4] His father's birth was doubtful; and he was himself born out of regular wedlock, although his legitimacy was afterwards grudgingly recognized. From his eighth to his sixteenth year he was the pawn by turns of his malignant uncle Alexander, of his mother, of the patriarch Nicholas and of the lord admiral Romanus Lecapenus. After the seizure of power by the last of these in the year 920, he was for the next twenty four years held in a degrading tutelage, cut off from all power and patronage, and, though married to the usurper's daughter Helen, demoted successively to second, third and perhaps fifth place in the hierarchy of co-emperors. It was not until January of the year 945, at the age of nearly forty, that, with the aid of a clique of guards officers devoted to his house, he was able to expel the Lecapenid usurpers and seat himself in sole majesty on the throne that was rightfully his.

For the next fourteen years he governed, or seemed to govern: for the substance of power appears to have been in the hands of the Augusta Helen, of the hetaeriarch Basil Peteinos, of the eparch Theophilus, of the sacellarius Joseph Bringas, and of the protovestiary Basil, the emperor's illegitimate

---

[1] Sources in A. Rambaud, *L'Empire grec au dixième siècle*, (Paris, 1870), pp. 1—4. For date of birth, see *Vita Euthymii*, (ed. de Boor, Berlin, 1888), pp. 116—118; R. J. H. Jenkins, *Dumbarton Oaks Papers* 19 (1965), pp. 108, 109.

[2] His elder brother, Basil, son of his father's third wife Eudocia, died in infancy; see *De Cer.*, (ed. Bonn.), I, p. 643.

[3] For her family, see Theoph. Cont., (ed. Bonn.), p. 370; *D. A. I.*, 22_{79}; *Vita Euthymii*, p. 58; and G. Kolias, *Léon Choerosphactès*, (Athens, 1939), p. 18.

[4] Theoph. Cont., pp. 212, 379, 459, 464, 465.

brother-in-law.[5] These made or marred — for the traditions are conflicting[6] — the internal administration. The church was scandalized by the impieties of the worldly patriarch Theophylact; he, dying in 956, was succeeded by the ascetic Polyeuctus, who soon showed that stiff-necked king Stork might be worse trouble than disreputable king Log. But abroad the imperial forces, under the leadership of Bardas Phocas and his two sons, and of the proto-vestiary Basil, continued, with occasional set-backs, that glorious career which had begun with the accession of Michael III and was to terminate only with the death of Basil II. The sole major disaster recorded of the reign was the failure of a costly but ill-led expedition against Crete in 949.[7]

During these years the emperor devoted himself with tireless zeal to the *minutiae* of every department of administration, and to the punctilious observance of every kind of imperial ritual.[8] His greatest personal contributions to the prosperity of his empire were externally, in the sphere of diplomacy,[9] and internally, in the encouragement of higher education.[10] His relaxations were the pursuits which had always lain next his heart, and which, during the long years of his enforced seclusion, he had been able to cultivate without interruption: art, literature, history and antiquities.[11] He found domestic happiness in the society of his three daughters, whom he tenderly loved;[12] nor is there evidence that his relations with his wife were other than uniformly affectionate, despite a difference of temperament.[13] With his only son Romanus he was not so fortunate. To fit the youth for his future lofty station, he lavished on him a wealth of minute instruction[14] which was probably excessive. The boy is said to have grown up weak and even vicious; but the accounts are conflicting, and he died at the age of 24.

By the age of fifty-four the emperor was old and worn out. His fourteen years of power had been years of ceaseless toil, and his infirmities grew fast upon him. A quarrel with the patriarch Polyeuctus, whom he seems to have had in mind to depose,[15] occasioned a journey to the monks and hermits of the Bithynian Olympus; and from them he learnt the mournful tidings of his own approaching dissolution. He dragged himself back to the City guarded of

---

[5] Cedrenus, (ed. Bonn.), II, p. 326.
[6] F. Hirsch, *Byzantinische Studien*, (Leipzig, 1876), pp. 286ff.
[7] Leo Diac., (ed. Bonn.), p. 7; Cedrenus, II, p. 336.
[8] Theoph. Cont., pp. 447, 449.
[9] Theoph. Cont., pp. 448, 455; *De Cer.*, I, pp. 570ff.; Liutprand, *Antapodosis*, VI, 5.
[10] Theoph. Cont., p. 446.
[11] See A. Stránsky, 'Costantino VII Porfirogenito, amante delle arti e collezio-nista', in *Atti del V Congresso Internazionale di Studi Bizantini*, (Rome, 1940), II, pp. 412ff.
[12] Theoph. Cont., p. 459.
[13] Theoph. Cont., p. 458.
[14] Theoph. Cont., p. 458.
[15] Cedrenus, II, p. 337; Theoph. Cont., pp. 463ff.

God; and there, on the 15th of November, 959, he died.[16] In person, he was tall, broad-shouldered and erect in bearing, with a long face, an aquiline nose, blue[17] eyes and a fair complexion. Of stainless morals, deep piety and unremitting devotion to duty, he was an emperor after the hearts of his people, who testified their affection by a spontaneous outburst of grief at his funeral.

The favourable and the unfavourable traditions concerning the character of Constantine VII provide no mutually incompatible elements.[18] They show him to have been a weak and retiring personality, artistic, studious and laborious. If he drank wine to excess, it was his antidote to shyness. If he had fits of severity, even of cruelty, they were the obverse of his diffidence. His love of learning was inherited from his father, and was confirmed by seclusion. His lack of self-confidence was inveterated by his long durance in the hands of the Lecapenids. Yet in those years he was amassing a wealth of historical and antiquarian knowledge which bore fruit in those encyclopedic manuals and historical studies to which we owe the chief part of our knowledge of the machinery and organization of the mediaeval empire of East Rome.

His achievements in the cultural field were indeed immense. Of his patronage of the manual arts this is no place to speak. But of his encouragement of learning and research a word must be said. Himself deeply versed in classical learning,[19] his liberal intelligence comprehended both the theoretical and the practical aspects of knowledge, the knowledge which was good in itself, and the knowledge which was necessary to enable the practical man to arrive at a correct decision in the affairs of life.[20] To the latter branch, which was principally concerned with the study of history,[21] he devoted especial attention; and from among the graduates of his university, of which he was, after the Caesar Bardas, second founder, he chose his higher bureaucrats and churchmen.[22] To this practical education he naturally subjected his son Romanus also. If such knowledge was important for the governed in the conduct of their individual, everyday lives, how much more important was it for him who should govern all![23] How essential was it that decisions which would affect the whole world should be dictated by the utmost practical wisdom, sharpened by the widest experience and knowledge of every similar decision or parallel set of circumstances in the past!

---

[16] The symptoms recorded (Theoph. Cont., p. 464) do not seem to support the later allegation that he was poisoned.

[17] Theoph. Cont., p. 468, if that is what χαροποιούς means here; but cf. Genesis 49, 12, where the reference is to wine-induced brightness, and may in Theoph. Cont. covertly refer to the emperor's φιλοινία.

[18] Rambaud, *op. cit.*, pp. 41, 42.

[19] Zonaras, (ed. Bonn.), III, p. 483.

[20] Theoph. Cont., p. 446; *D. A. I.*, P_6 ff.

[21] Theoph. Cont., p. 211.

[22] Theoph. Cont., pp. 446, 447; Cedrenus, II, p. 326.

[23] *D. A. I.*, 1_6.

This belief in the practical value of learning and education, which is set out at full in the preface to the *De Administrando Imperio* and repeated in many subsequent parts of the book, was, of course, derived through Plutarch[24] from Aristotle; and the method of education through the early inculcation of precept, which is illustrated in a long series of mediaeval manuals of gnomic wisdom, goes back ultimately to the *Ad Demonicum*[25] of the Pseudo-Isocrates, which, with the Latin *Disticha* of Cato, formed the basis of primary education throughout later mediaeval and renaissance Europe. But to Constantine may be given the credit for its revival at Byzantium; for, to teach practical wisdom, the material for such teaching is required, and was in his time extremely scanty. With tireless zeal he set about the enormous task of creating such material, and set about it in three ways: first, by diligent search for and collection of books, of which the supply was quite inadequate[26]; second, by the compilation of anthologies and encyclopedias from such books as existed but were too tedious or prolix for any but a scholar to read[27]; third, by writing or causing to be written histories of recent events and manuals of technical instruction on the various departments of business and administration.[28] A school of historians wrote beneath his eye, sometimes at his dictation.[29] Documents from the files of every branch of the administration, from the foreign ministry, the treasury, the offices of ceremonial, were scrutinized and abstracted.[30] Provincial governors and imperial envoys wrote historical and topographical reports on the areas of their jurisdiction or assignment.[31] Foreign ambassadors were diligently questioned as to the affairs of their respective countries.[32] From every quarter the tide of information rolled in, was co-ordinated and written down. Learning became the key to worldly advancement.[33] The principle

---

[24] Plutarch, *De Virtute Morali*, (ed. Bernardakis, Leipzig, 1891), pp. 154, 155. For this technical usage of σοφία and φρόνησις cf. *D. A. I.*, P₇; Romanus was of course to be σοφός as well as φρόνιμος, but practical wisdom is the end of our treatise.

[25] Cf. *Ad Demonicum*, p. 9 C, (βουλευόμενος παραδείγματα, κτλ.), with *D. A. I.*, 46₁₆₇ (ἄξιον γάρ, φίλτατε υἱέ, κτλ.); *ibid.* p. 11 E (ὥσπερ ἐκ ταμιείου προφέρῃς), with *ibid.* 13₁₃ (ὡς ἐκ πατρικῶν θησαυρῶν προφέρειν).

[26] *De Cer.*, I, p. 456; Theoph. Cont., p. 212; *Prooemium ad Excerpta de Legationibus* (M. P. G., vol. CXIII), c. 633.; *Exc. de leg.*, ed. de Boor, I, p. 1.

[27] *ibid.* pp. 633, 636.

[28] Theoph. Cont., pp. 3, 4; *D. A. I.*, P₂₅ (ἐσοφισάμην κατ' ἐμαυτόν). For Constantine's own works, see Rambaud, *op. cit.*, p. 73, and for those compiled under his aegis, *ibid.*, pp. 78 ff.; also Moravcsik, in *Atti del V Congresso Internazionale di Studi Bizantini*, (Rome, 1939), I, pp. 514—516, and *id.*, *Byzantinoturcica*, (Budapest, 1942), I, pp. 207ff. (2nd ed. pp. 358ff.).

[29] Rambaud, *op. cit.*, p. 65.

[30] Bury, in *Byzantinische Zeitschrift*, XV, 1905, pp. 539ff.

[31] Theoph. Cont., p. 448.

[32] Bury, *op. cit.*, pp. 553, 556.

[33] Theoph. Cont., p. 447.

laid down by the illiterate Basil I[34] found its ultimate fulfilment in the educational reforms of his scholarly grandson. This is the true glory of the Porphyrogenitus. Among the great emperors who enriched the middle-Byzantine heritage between A. D. 843 and 1204, none is to be compared with Constantine VII for depth of scholarship, catholicity of interest or fineness of taste. Of the last, his *Life* of his grandfather is a unique memorial. It was Constantine who amassed the libraries from which his successors acquired their learning. With him Byzantium, rapidly approaching the apex of its military glory, as rapidly approached the apex of its intellectual achievement, an achievement fostered by a princely patron of the arts whose like the world scarcely saw in the thirteen centuries which divided Hadrian from Lorenzo the Magnificent.

The *De Administrando Imperio*,[35] to give this nameless treatise the Latin title attached to it by Meursius,[36] was written and complied, as we know from internal evidence, between the years 948 and 952.[37] It is a manual of kingcraft addressed to the youthful Romanus, the emperor's son, and is in form, like numerous other contemporary manuals on various subjects, avowedly didactic. It aims at *teaching*[38] the youth to be a wise sovereign, first by a knowledge of past and present affairs, and second by giving him a summary of the experience of others in circumstances analogous to those likely to surround himself; so that, knowing what policies have succeeded or failed in the past, he may himself be able to act prudently and successfully in the future. The matter of this teaching is a political and historical survey of very wide extent, suitable to the training of one who is to rule the world. The preface divides it into four sections: the first, a key to *foreign policy* in the most dangerous and complicated area of the contemporary political scene, the area of the «northerners and Scythians»; the second, a lesson in the *diplomacy* to be pursued in dealing with the nations of this same area; the third and longest, a comprehensive *historical* and *geographical* survey of most of the nations surrounding the empire, starting with the Saracens to the southeast, fetching a compass round the Mediterranean and Black Seas, and ending with the Armenian states on the eastern frontier; the fourth, a summary of recent *internal history*, *politics* and *organization*, within the borders of the empire.[39] Upon the whole, these divisions are adhered to in the text as we have it.[40]

---

[34] Basilii Imp. *Paraenesis ad Leonem filium* (M. P. G., vol. CVII), p. XXI (περὶ παιδεύσεως; cf. *D. A. I.*, ch. 1); and *ibid.*, p. XLIX (περὶ μελέτης γραφῶν: cf. Theoph. Cont., p. 314).

[35] For full bibliography, see Moravcsik, *Byzantinoturcica*, I, pp. 215—221 (2nd ed. pp. 367—380).

[36] Johannes van Meurs (1579—1639); see below, p. 23.

[37] Bury, *op. cit.*, pp. 522 ff.

[38] *D. A. I.*, 1_{13}, (διδάξαι).

[39] *ibid.*, P_{14-24}.

[40] Bury, *op. cit.*, p. 574.

The method of compilation has been elucidated in detail in the General Introduction to the Commentary[41]. These findings can here be very briefly summarized. The work as we have it now is a *rifacimento* of an earlier work which corresponds to chapters 14—42 in the present arrangement. This earlier work was a historical and antiquarian treatise probably entitled Περὶ ἐθνῶν, which the emperor had compiled during the 940's as a companion volume to his Περὶ θεμάτων. As the Περὶ θεμάτων described the origins, antiquities and topography of the imperial provinces, so the Περὶ ἐθνῶν told the traditional, sometimes legendary, stories of how the territories surrounding the empire came in past centuries to be occupied by their present inhabitants (Saracens, Lombards, Venetians, Slavs, Magyars, Pechenegs). These chapters, then, are the earliest parts of *D. A. I.* The remaining parts of the book (except for a few chapters — 23—25, 48, 52, 53 and perhaps 9 and 30 — of source-material included by oversight) are notices of a different kind: they are *political directives*, illustrated by contemporary or nearly contemporary examples. Chapters 1—8, 10—12, explain imperial policy towards the Pechenegs and Turks. Chapter 13 is a general directive on foreign policy from the emperor's own pen. Chapters 43—46 deal with contemporary policy in the north-east (Armenia and Georgia). Chapters 49—52 are guides to the incorporation and taxation of new imperial provinces, and to some parts of civil and naval administration. These later parts of the book are designed to give *practical instruction* to the young emperor Romanus II, and were probably added to the Περὶ ἐθνῶν during the year 951—952, in order that the whole treatise might mark Romanus' fourteenth birthday (952). The book as it now stands is therefore an amalgam of two unequal parts: the first historical and antiquarian, the second political and diplomatic.

The sources of the various sections, where these are known, are noted in the apparatus to the present volume. But the peculiar construction of the book, with its diversity of styles and often careless expression, calls for a note of explanation regarding the English translation. The chief value of the treatise to the modern historian lies in its third section, which provides information not found elsewhere about the origins and early history of many nations established on the borders of the Byzantine empire in the tenth century of our era. This information, valuable as it is, is often given in a style so careless as to leave many statements open to more than one interpretation. Chapter 39 is a notable instance of this;[42] but there are several others. Now, these statements have been, are and probably will continue to be the subject of controversy between scholars of many nations; and it is therefore our duty as translators, at whatever cost to elegance or even in a few cases to sense, to render

---

[41] See *D. A. I.* Vol. II, Commentary (London, 1962), pp. 1—8; also Moravcsik, *Byzantinoturcica* (2nd ed.) I, pp. 361—367.

[42] *D. A. I.*, 39$_{3-5, 7-10}$.

as closely as possible what the text says rather than what we are disposed to think it means to say. Interpretations may be left to a commentary. If therefore our rendering is in some cases ambiguous, so is the original. If it often halts, so does the text. If it is often inelegant and uncouth, it is no more so than the Greek. Where our author is plain and even elegant, we have tried to preserve his idiom; where he has left his sources to tell their own stories in their own styles, we have left them too.

With all its inaccuracies and shortcomings,[43] the *De Administrando Imperio*, for the bulk and variety of its information on so much of foreign relations and internal administration, must be allowed to be one of the most important historical documents surviving from mediaeval Byzantium, even surpassing the great *Book of Ceremonies* compiled by the same indefatigable author. Its very omissions, the lack of any historical account of Bulgaria or of an up-to-date appreciation of the Saracen power, have their own historical lessons to teach us: for these two longstanding menaces to the empire had at length yielded, the one to the diplomacy of Romanus I, the other to the hammer of Gourgen. The first-hand information comes mainly from Italy, from the Balkans and Steppes, and from Armenia. In Armenia the advance of the Roman arms and the retreat of the Saracens involved a complicated Roman diplomacy in the numerous and jealous principalities beyond the eastern frontier. In a divided and enfeebled Italy, during the interim between the empires of Charlemagne and Otto, Byzantium was for the last time in its history a strong military and diplomatic influence. The only hint of anxiety comes from the north, where the watchful eyes of the foreign ministry observed intently the ever shifting kaleidoscope of the political scene, as Magyar and Slav, Russian and Pecheneg, Chazar and Alan made their complicated moves between the Caucasus and the Carpathians.

There is no doubt that the *De Administrando Imperio* was a secret and confidential document. It tells too much about the principles of imperial foreign policy and diplomacy, especially in the first thirteen chapters, to be safe for publication. Knowledge of these early chapters would have been worth untold sums in blackmail to the Pechenegs. Moreover, in the Armenian chapters there are several traces of information got through secret service channels,[44] which the government must have been most reluctant to divulge. Nor is it probable that the outspoken criticisms which the emperor passes on his father-in-law and colleague[45] were intended for general reading. These criticisms betray the justifiable resentment of a prince deprived of his throne by an interloper during a quarter of a century; but his strong regard for the imperial dignity would have debarred him from publishing this resentment to the world at

---

[43] Bury, *op. cit.*, p. 574.
[44] e. g.: *D. A. I.* 43_{13-16}, 46_{54-64}.
[45] *ibid.*, $13_{149-175}$, $51_{184-186}$.

large. This confidential character of the book, confirmed, if confirmation be required, by its manuscript history and by the circumstance that later writers betray no knowledge of it,[46] enhances its value. It is no partial document of propaganda, fudged up to impress domestic or foreign circles. Much of it is an honest appreciation of the contemporary political situation, compiled from information upon which the government based its day-to-day foreign policy. And, as such, it is unique.

R. J. H. JENKINS.

---

[46] See below, p. 32.

CRITICAL INTRODUCTION

1. MANUSCRIPTS

The *De Administrando Imperio* is preserved in four mss.[1] Three of these contain the full text, the fourth a part only. These mss. are:

P = *codex Parisinus gr. 2009*: codex on vellum, of 211 numbered leaves.[2] There are also some additional leaves, 4 at the beginning of the ms. (3 vellum, 1 paper), and 7 at the end (4 paper, 3 vellum). The leaves are of sizes varying between c. 23.8 cm — 24 cm × 15 cm. The first three of the additional leaves are blank. On the recto of the fourth is a Greek table of the contents of the codex, in a later hand;[3] on the verso of the same leaf is gummed a small slip of paper, inscribed with the table of contents in Latin.[4] On the first numbered page begins the first Greek text, which covers 4 pages (fol. 1ʳ—2ᵛ); it is entitled: Ἐπιστολὴ Πυθαγόρα πρὸς Λαΐδα («Letter of Pythagoras to Laïs»), and is followed, still on fol. 2ᵛ, by a table which relates to it. The «Letter» and table have been published from this ms. by P. Tannery.[5] At fol. 3ʳ begins the text of *D. A. I*, and it finishes at fol. 211ʳ. This text originally constituted an independent codex, with which the «Letter of Pythagoras» was subsequently bound up, as is clear from the facts, *a)* that the numeration of the quaternios

---

[1] See Gy. Moravcsik, ''Η χειρόγραφος παράδοσις τοῦ De administrando imperio', Ἐπετηρὶς Ἑταιρείας Βυζαντινῶν Σπουδῶν, 7 (1930), pp. 138—152.

[2] See H. Omont, *Inventaire sommaire des manuscrits grecs de la Bibliothèque Nationale*, vol. II (Paris, 1888), p. 178.

[3] «Κωνσταντίν(ου) βασιλέ(ως) Ῥωμαί(ων) πρὸς Ῥωμαν(ὸν) τὸν ἴδιον υἱὸν καὶ συμβασιλέα ἐθνογραφία κ(αὶ) χωρογραφία κ(αὶ) ποικίλη τὶς ἱστορία τείνουσα πρὸς ὀρθὴν διοίκησιν τ(ῆς) Ῥωμαί(ων) βασιλεί(ας) No. 21.»

[4] «Codex 1783. Membr. 13. saec. Epistola Pythagorae ad Laidem cum laterculo eiusdem de vita et morbo, victoria et clade aliisque rebus, inventione et amissione, lucro et damno, bona via et mala. Constantini Imperatoris ad Romanum filium Porphyrogenitum Imperatorem. Est liber de administrando imperio, quem edidit Meursius. Ms. 1240.»

[5] 'Notices sur des fragments d'onomatomancie arithmétique', *Notices et extraits des manuscrits de la Bibliothèque Nationale et autres bibliothèques*, vol. XXXI. 2. partie, (Paris, 1886), pp. 231—260; cf. K. I. Dyobuniotes, Ὀνοματομαντεία', Εἰς μνήμην Σπυρίδωνος Λάμπρου, (Athens, 1935), pp. 491—494.

begins only at fol. 3ʳ; and b) that the beginning of D. A. I., that is to say, the
first page (fol. 3ʳ) of the original codex, is so much worn, and the handwriting
so indistinct, as to require its mending in brown ink by a later hand. In any
case, the «Letter of Pythagoras» is copied in a different, and in all probability
a later, hand. The subsequent history of the codex gives us, as we shall see,
some clue as to when the «Letter» became attached to the ms. of D. A. I.

The text of D. A. I. ends in the middle of fol. 211ʳ. The rest of this page
and its verso, which, as it was the last page of the original codex, is very much
the worse for wear, contain a number of notes in different and, in some cases,
later hands. Of especial interest as casting light on the origin of the codex is
that written on the then blank fol. 211ᵛ by the actual copyist of D. A. I., in
the same red ink which he employed for the initial letters and headings of the
chapters. Some of the letters in this note are so much worn and so dim as to
render them now almost illegible. The text of this metrical epilogue is as
follows: ¹Βίβλος καίσ[αρ]ος ²Ἰωάννου τοῦ Δούκα ³γραφῆ(σα) χερσὶν ⁴οἰκογενοὺς
οἰκέτου ⁵Μιχα(ὴ)λ ὀνόματι ⁶τοῦ Ῥοϊζαίτου †, which makes it quite
clear that the ms. at one time belonged to the library of the Caesar John Ducas,
and that the copyist was his own confidential secretary, Michael.⁶ Unfortunately
there is no date, but the name of the Caesar John Ducas, references to whom
in Byzantine sources occur between the years 1059—1081, proves that the
ms. was copied towards the end of the XI century. This is confirmed by a
dated note in a later hand on the same page, which contains a reference to the
year 1098/9.⁷

Concerning the adventures of the codex during the Byzantine age we
have no other information, apart from the evidence of marginal notes to be
described lower down; it emerges again only towards the beginning of the
XVI century, when it was copied in 1509 by Antony Eparchus, very probably
in the island of Corfu (see ms. V below). By the middle of the century our ms.
was in Italy, whither it had been brought perhaps through the agency of
Janus Lascaris.⁸ The first mention of it in Italy is in the catalogue of the
library of Cardinal Niccolò Ridolfi.⁹ On the death of Ridolfi in 1550, it passed,

---

⁶ See G. Kolias, "Ὁ καῖσαρ Ἰωάννης Δούκας ἀντιγραφεὺς τοῦ cod. Par. Gr. 2009
τοῦ De administrando imperio', Ἐπετηρὶς Ἑταιρείας Βυζαντινῶν Σπουδῶν, 14 (1938),
pp. 300—305; Gy. Moravcsik, 'La provenance du manuscrit byzantin du «De administrando imperio»', Bulletin de la Société Historique Bulgare, 16—18 (1940), pp. 333—337;
B. Leib, 'Jean Doukas, César et moine', Analecta Bollandiana 68 (1950), pp. 163—180.
— In the deciphering of the text I was given valuable assistance by Prof. F. Dölger (Munich) and Dir. V. Laurent (Paris), to whom I express my sincere gratitude.

⁷ See Gy. Moravcsik, Ἐπετηρὶς Ἑταιρείας Βυζαντινῶν Σπουδῶν, 7 (1930), p. 141,
but cf. V. Laurent, Erasmus, 3 (1950) p. 766.

⁸ See B. Knös, Un ambassadeur de l'hellénisme — Janus Lascaris — et la tradition
greco-byzantine dans l'humanisme français, (Uppsala-Paris, 1945), pp. 213, 216.

⁹ «Num. 21. Constantini Romanorum Imperatoris ad Romanum filium descriptio
gentium et locorum, ac varia historia ad rectam administrationem tendens.» See B. Mont-
faucon, Bibliotheca bibliothecarum manuscriptorum nova II (Parisiis, 1739), p. 777.

τοῦτο τόπου αὐτῶν· καὶ καθελεῖναι
ἡμᾶς· ἦλθε γὰρ καὶ πρότερον ἐκεῖ
σε ἐκαθέζεσθαι· πρὸς τὸ εἶναι πλησίον τῆς ὠφελείας μου· καὶ ὅτε θέλω ἀποστέλλω καὶ ἐν τάχει εὑρίσκω
ἡμᾶς, πάντες οἱ ἄρχοντες τῶν
Τούρκων μὲ ἀφωνήθησαν σαν· ὅτι
ἡμεῖς μετὰ τοῦ πατζινακίτου
εἰς τὸ ἴσον οὐ μαλλόμεν· οὐ γὰρ δυνάμεθα πολεμεῖν πρὸς αὐτούς· ὅτι
καὶ χώρα μεγάλη καὶ λαὸς πολύς·
καὶ κακὰ παιδία εἰσὶ· καὶ τοῦ λοιποῦ τὸν λόγον τοῦτον πρὸς ἡμᾶς
μὴ στρέφῃς· οὐ γὰρ ἀγαπῶμεν αὐτόν·
Ὅτι καὶ οἱ πατζινακῖται ἐκεῖθεν τοῦ
δαναπρὲρ ποταμοῦ ποταμοῦ μου· μετὰ τὸ
βαρδ... ἔχονται· καὶ ἀεὶ ἐκεῖσε καλοκαιρίζουσιν:~

along with others of his books, into the possession of Pietro Strozzi, and later, in 1560, into the collection of Catherine de Medici. At this period some chapters from it were transcribed by Andrea Darmari (see ms. M below). From Catherine's library it passed in 1599 to the Bibliothèque Royale in Paris, where it was numbered 2661.[10] Now, since the relevant entry in the catalogue of Ridolfi's library is simply a Latin rendering of the Greek note on the recto of the fourth fly-leaf at the beginning of our ms. (see above), and since this entry notes *D. A. I.* only, we conclude that the «Letter of Pythagoras» was attached to our ms. subsequently to its being placed in the Bibliothèque Royale. This conclusion is confirmed by the circumstance that the present sumptuous binding of gilt red morocco bears the cypher of King Henry IV (1589—1610).

This manuscript, some pages of which have been published in facsimile,[11] I have studied by means of photographic reproductions in the Library of the Hungarian National Museum, and also by examination of the original in the Bibliothèque Nationale at Paris in 1936 and in 1948.

The text of *D. A. I.* was, as we have seen, copied by a certain Michael Roïzaïtes. Only in two passages (fol. 31^v—32^r = 14$_{22}$ συμψευδομαρτυροῦντος —15$_6$ πολέμους καὶ, and 35^v—36^r = 20$_6$ καὶ τὴν νῆσον — 21$_{13}$ γενέσθαι)[12] has another hand relieved him. The text is written in single columns, and the columns vary in dimension between c. 16—17 cm. deep × 11—12 cm. across. The medium is the usual dark brown Byzantine ink, save that initial letters and headings of chapters are in red, a detail which goes back to the original copyist. The script is a mixture of uncial and minuscule; γ, δ, ε, ζ, η, κ, λ, μ, ξ, π are written both ways indifferently; uncial forms of β, φ, ω are uncommon, and very rare are uncial forms af α, ν, σ, ψ. Here and there we find a cursive ϑ, while τ occasionally rises above the height of the other letters. Rough breathing is still angular in shape, but the smooth breathing is always round. The writing is either on the ruled lines or under them, but never above them. Ligature abbreviations are frequent; short-hand abbreviations and

[10] See H. Omont, 'Un premier catalogue des manuscrits grecs du cardinal Ridolfi', *Bibliothèque de l'École des Chartes*, 49 (1888), pp. 309—323; J. Haury, *Sitzungsberichte der philos.-philol. und der hist. Classe der bayer. Akademie der Wiss.* 1895. I, pp. 142—143, 147; V. Gardthausen, *Sammlungen und Cataloge griechischer Handschriften*, (Leipzig, 1903), p. 18; F. Dölger, 'Der Titel des sog. Suidaslexikons', *Sitzungsberichte der Bayerischen Akademie der Wissenschaften*, Philos.-hist. Abt. 1936. Heft 6., (München, 1936), pp. 36—37.

[11] See *Árpád és az Árpádok*, szerk. Csánky Dezső, (Budapest, 1908): fol. 111^r = p. 46/7., fol. 112^v = p. 168/9., fol. 113^r = p. 174/5., fol. 115^v = p. 140/1.; cf. Gy. Moravcsik, *Byzantinoturcica*, vol. II, (Budapest, 1943), p. 51 (2nd ed. pl. II, no. 4). See also the facsimile on the opposite page.

[12] For the principles which have been applied to the transcription of the mss. variants, see below p. 37.

abbreviations by suspension occur rarely, and mostly at the ends of lines. The copyist is fond of special ligatures for ατ, σσ, ττ, of kinds which occur in other contemporary mss.

In the orthography the most notable points are these: iota subscript is never found, iota adscript once only (53_{382} τῶι). As regards peculiarities of accentuation, we may note that proper names ending in -ῖται in many cases carry the paroxytone accent in nom. and gen. plural (e. g. 2_2 Πατζινακίται, 8_{14} Πατζινακίτων, 53_{535} Χερσωνίται, 53_{65} Χερσωνίτων); while the genitive plural of paroxytone racial names in -ος is sometimes perispomenon (e. g. 28_{43} Φραγγῶν, 32_2 Σερβλῶν). The word ἐπεί is occasionally accented with double stroke: ἐπεῒ (e. g. 48_{22}, 49_9, 49_{13}). With regard to misspellings due to pronunciation, it is particularly noticeable that the copyist makes the same error consistently through a series of particular words or forms. Characteristic examples of such regularly repeated misspellings are: αι for ε at the end of 2nd person plural verbs (e. g. 8_{27} ἐκαθέζεσθαι, 53_{70} μάθεται, 53_{477} ὑποδείξαται); ει for η commonly in the words εἴτις = ἥτις (e. g. 13_6, 26_{64}, 29_{234}), εἴπερ = ἤπερ (e. g. 38_{49}, 50_{192}) and εἷς = ἧς (e. g. 31_1, 35_1, 43_{187}); and in the augmented forms of the verb αἰτῶ (e. g. 29_{157} εἰτίσατο = ἠτήσατο, 42_{29} εἰτήσαντο = ἠτήσαντο, 50_{209} εἰτήσατο = ἠτήσατο); η for ει almost invariably in the infinitive forms -ειν and -εῖν (e. g. 1_8 πηδαλιουχὴν, 47_9 διαπεσὴν), and quite often also in the words ἤ and ἥ = εἰ (e. g. 13_{87}, 29_{148}, 41_{16}), δῆ = δεῖ (e. g. 13_{19}, 13_{146}), and in the verb ὑπήκω = ὑπείκω (e. g. 38_{38}, 50_{29}, 50_{81}). Some confusion is seen in the use of ει and η in the different forms of the verbs λαμβάνω and λείπω (e. g. P_{31} λείψεται = λήψεται, 25_{54} συνελείφθη = συνελήφθη, 29_{203} ἀπολείψεσθαι = ἀπολήψεσθε, 21_{26} ὑπελήφθησαν = ὑπελείφθησαν, 26_{30} καταληφθείς = καταλειφθείς, 46_{22} κατελήφθη = κατελείφθη). ω is found consistently for o in the -ονται termination of the 3rd person plur. pres. ind. pass. (e. g. 9_{111} κατέρχωνται, 31_{29} περισώζωνται, 37_{64} εὑρίσκωνται); and often also in the termination -ον of nom. neut. partic. act. (e. g. 9_{67} ἔχων, 13_{99} κατελθών, 37_{58} ἀποβλέπων). From verbs beginning with o the temporal augment is usually absent (e. g. 13_{51} διορίσατο, 26_{71} μετονομάσθη, 30_{46} ὅρμισαν). From the point of view of the history of Byzantine pronunciation it is significant that in our codex we frequently meet with υ for οι (e. g. 20_2 στυχήσας = στοιχήσας, 45_4 μυχευθήσης = μοιχευθείσης, 51_{120} ἤνυξαν = ἤνοιξαν), and *vice versa* (e. g. 9_{35} προίμναν = πρύμναν, 26_{52} ὁμοίοντες = ὀμνύοντες, 53_{191} φροιαττόμενος = φρυαττόμενος). This proves that at the period when the work was copied, the pronunciation of these two sounds was still identical (a modified *u*). An odd feature, which we meet here and elsewhere, is the frequent interchange between the forms ἡμεῖς and ὑμεῖς (e. g. 27_{35} 43_{15} 53_{69}). As regards consonants, we note uncertainty in the writing of double consonants (e. g. P_{27} ἀντιτάσεσθαι, 15_9 φοσάτον, 42_{23} ἐναλλασόμενοι, 9_{19} ἰουννίου, 28_{22} νησσῶν, 45_{39} σήμμερον); and the substitution of μθ, μπ for νθ, νπ (e. g. 13_{107} συμπεμθεριᾶσαι, 26_9 ἐμ Παλαιστίνη, 27_{76} ἐμπρώτοις); and of χν for γχν (e. g. 29_{97} σπλαχνησθεῖς = σπλαγχνισθείς). These details also throw light on contemporary pronunciation. There is a curious use of ν for γ before γ, κ, χ (e. g. 27₇₃ Κόνκορδα, 29₃₈ ἐνκρύμματα, 43₁₁₃ διαγονγγύζοντες, 52₁₁ κονχυλευταί); moreover, while on the one hand the accusative sing. in α of 3rd declension substantives and the -θη or -η of the 3rd pers. sing. aor. pass. indic. add a ν before a word beginning with a vowel (e. g. 13₃₂ βασιλέαν, 26₄₉ ῥίναν, 26₆₅ θυγατέραν, 53₃₁₇ νύκταν, 32₃₃ ἐγεννήθην, 43₁₇₇ ἀπεστάλην), on the other hand the ν of the acc. sing. of μέγας (e. g. 9₂₉, 41₆, 46₁₅₁), and of the 1st pers. sing. aor. pass. indic. drops off before words beginning with a consonant (e. g. 27₂₈ ἐνομίσθη, 29₁₆₈ ἐδιώχθη, 53₃₄₇ ἠναγκάσθη).

In the ms. we note several words erased, amended, completed or corrected. A detailed study of the original may identify traces of at least six different hands in the text and, besides, of five other hands which have added marginal notes. There is no doubt that the copyist himself made some erasures and corrections; but from the styles of the handwriting and from other evidence it can be established that many alterations have been made by hands in the XIV and later centuries. In one place a marginal gloss bears a date which proves it to have been written in 1361/2 (16₈). To determine the chronology of certain other alterations we may argue from the fact that in V, which was copied from P, we often find the true text as it was before correction, which proves that at least these alterations in P were done by a hand posterior to the date when V was copied, that is, posterior to 1509 (e. g. P₁₉ ἐθνῶν P V: ἐθῶν Pʸ ‖ 38₄₄ ὁ Ἀλμούτζης P V: Σαλμούτζης Pʸ ‖ 38₄₉ Ἀλμούτζη P V: Σαλμούτζη Pʸ).

In the margins of the ms. are notes, some of which are from the hand of the original copyist, but others, as the style of handwriting demonstrates, from those of later readers, principally of the XIV and XVI centuries. Some of these notes are in Latin. In the marginal notes, too, we may distinguish at least six hands. Those which go back to the hand of the copyist are mainly chapter-headings and citations of the contents, which were added to the text either by collaborators of the imperial author or by later scribes and readers. At least one of these original notes is not contemporary with the work itself, as is proved beyond doubt by its reference to the Abbot John Tornices as holder of the office of Syncellus, an office which, as we know, was conferred on him about the year 979;[13] this note, therefore, was written about three decades after the treatise was compiled.

A list of these original comments, and the passages to which they refer, is as follows: 1₁ Πε(ρὶ) τῶν Πατζινακιτῶν ‖ 2₁ Πε(ρὶ) τῶν Πατζινακιτῶν (καὶ) τῶν Ῥῶς ‖ 3₁ Πε(ρὶ) τῶν Πατζινακιτ(ῶν) (καὶ) Τούρκ(ων) ‖ 4₁ Πε(ρὶ) τῶν γ´ ἐθν(ῶν) ‖ 5₁ Πε(ρὶ) τῶν Πατζινακιτ(ῶν) (καὶ) τ(ῶν) Βουλγάρων ‖ 6₁ Πε(ρὶ) τῶν Πατζινακιτ(ῶν) (καὶ) Χερσωνιτῶν ‖ 7₁ Πε(ρὶ) τ(ῶν) ἀπὸ Χερσῶνος ἀποστελλομ(ένων) βασιλικ(ῶν) ἐν Πατζινακία ‖ 8₁

---

[13] N. Adontz, 'Tornik le moine', *Byzantion*, 13 (1938), pp. 148—149.

Πε(ρὶ) τοῦ ἀποστελλομ(ένου) βασιλικ(οῦ) ἐκ τ(ῆς) πόλ(εως) διὰ τ(ῶν) ποτ(α)μ(ῶν) ‖ 8_{23} Πε(ρὶ) τοῦ κληρικοῦ Γαβριήλ ‖ 9_1 Πε(ρὶ) τοῦ πῶς κατέρχωντ(αι) οἱ Ῥῶς ἐν Κωνσταντινουπό(λει) ‖ 9_{22} Πε(ρὶ) τῶν λεγομ(ένων) καταράκτ(ων) ‖ 9_{39} Πε(ρὶ) τοῦ β′ φραγμ(οῦ) ‖ 9_{43} Πε(ρὶ) τοῦ γ′ φραγμ(οῦ) ‖ 9_{45} Πε(ρὶ) τοῦ δ′ φραγμ(οῦ) ‖ 9_{57} Πε(ρὶ) τοῦ ε′ φραγμοῦ ‖ 9_{61} Πε(ρὶ) τοῦ ς′ φραγμοῦ ‖ 9_{64} Πε(ρὶ) τοῦ ζ′ φραγμοῦ ‖ 9_{72} Πε(ρὶ) τῆς νήσου καὶ τοῦ δρυὸς καὶ τῶν θυσιῶν ‖ 9_{114} Πε(ρὶ) τ(ῶν) Οὔζω(ν) ‖ 10_1 Πε(ρὶ) τῆς Χαζαρίας ‖ 11_1 Πε(ρὶ) τῆς Χερσῶνο(ς) και τ(ῆς) Βοοσπόρου ‖ 13_{73} Πε(ρὶ) τοῦ λαμπροῦ ‖ 16_1 Τὸ θεμάτιν τῶν Σαρακιν(ῶν) (καὶ) ποῖον χρό(νον) ἐξῆλθ(ον) ‖ 21_{16} Διέρε(σις) τῶν Ἀράβων ‖ 21_{37} ε′ ἀρχηγὸ(ς) Ἀράβων ‖ 21_{49} Οὗτος παρεκάθησε(ν) τὴν Κωνσταντινούπο(λιν) ‖ 22_9 ,Ϛρη′ ‖ 22_{40} Πε(ρὶ) τῆς νήσσου τῆς Κρήτης ‖ 22_{61} ,Ϛσπη′ ‖ 31_6 Διὰ τί λέγωνται Χρ(ω)- βάτοι ‖ 33_{10} Πόθ(εν) λέγω(ν)ται Ζαχλούμοι ‖ 34_1 Πε(ρὶ) ἑτέρ(ων) ἐθνῶν ‖ 36_{18} Πε(ρὶ) τοῦ ἁγίου ἀπο(στόλου) Λουκᾶ καὶ Παύλου ‖ 37_{15} Ὅτι ἡ ἄρχο(ν)- τες εἰσὶ(ν) ἐν Πατζιν(α)κία ‖ 37_{33} Ὅτι (καὶ) εἰς μ′ μέρη ἡ Παζινακί(α) ‖ 38_{10} Ὅτι οἱ Τοῦρ(κοι) εἰς ζ′ διαιροῦνται ‖ 42_1 Πε(ρι)ήγη(σις) γεωγρα(φικὴ) τῆς σκυθικῆς γῆς ‖ 43_{136} Οὗτο(ς) ἐστι(ν) ὁ π(ατ)ὴρ Νικο(λάου) μαγίστρου τοῦ Τορνίκη ‖ 44_1 Πε(ρὶ) τ(ῶν) κά(στρων) τ(ῆς) Ἀνατολῆς ‖ 45_1 Πε(ρὶ) τῶν Ἰβήρων ‖ 45_{56} Οὗτο(ς) (ἐστὶν) ὁ Τζιμισχ(ῆς) ἐπικληθεὶς ‖ 45_{100} Πε(ρὶ) τοῦ κά(στρου) τοῦ Ἀβνίκου ‖ 45_{103} Οὗτο(ς) (ἐστὶν) Ζουρβανέλ(ης) ὁ π(ατ)ὴρ τοῦ Τορνίκη τ(οῦ) ἀβᾶ τοῦ ἀρτ(ίως) συγκέλλου ‖ 46_1 Πόθ(εν) γεγόνα(σιν) οἱ Ἴβηρες ‖ 47_1 Πε(ρὶ) τ(ῶν) Κυπρίων ‖ 50_{235} Ποίου τιμήματ(ος) ἦν τοῦ (πρωτοσπαθαρίου) ἀξίωμα ‖ 51_1 Πε(ρὶ) τοῦ δρομωνίου ‖ 53_{10} Οὗτο(ς) (ἐστὶν) ὁ τοῦ μεγάλου Κωνσταντ(ίνου) π(ατ)ήρ.

The marginal notes appended by later hands consist principally of repetitions of words or names occuring in the text; but there are a few which are worth noting from the point of view of their content. These are: 3_1 Πατζινάκαι οἱ Δᾶκες πρότερον P^5 (cf. Suidas s. v. Δάκες, ed. Ada Adler, II, p. 2.) ‖ 5_1 Πατζινάκαι οἱ Δᾶκες, Βουλγάροι οἱ Μυσοί P^5 ‖ 16_8 νῦν δέ (ἐστιν) ,Ϛωσ′ (ἰνδικτιῶνος) ιε′ ὡς εἶναι ἀπὸ τότ(ε) ἕως νῦν χρόνοι ψμ′ P^3 ‖ 21_{69} Περὶ τοῦ Ἀλὴμ τοῦ γαμβροῦ τοῦ Μουάμεθ P^2 ‖ 21_{74} Πόλεμος Ἀλὴμ καὶ Μαβία P^8 ‖ 28_{25} Μαδαμα(ύκον) τὸ νῦν Μαλαμόκ(ον) P^8 ‖ 29_{258} Τραγούριον P^7 ‖ 30_{115} Ἀλβούνου P^7 Ἀλμπόνα P^8 ‖ 32_{11} Σέρβλια P^5 τὰ νῦν Σέρβοια ἐν τῇ Βεροία P^8 ‖ 32_{12} Σέρβλοι διὰ τί δοῦλοι ρωμαϊκ(ῶς) P^5 ‖ 36_{20} Φάρα νῆσος ἡ Λέζενα P^8 ‖ 36_{21} Βράτζης νῆσος τὰ Πράτζα P^8 ‖ 40_{24} Ἐτὲλ πο(ταμὸς) κ(αὶ) Κουζοῦ P^8.

Marginal notes and textual emendations are especially frequent in the chapters dealing with the Arabs (14—22), a fact which, like the gloss of the year 1361/2, mentioned above, suggests that this section of the treatise was at some time or another an object of peculiar interest to Byzantine readers.

The original text has not merely been subject to emendations and alterations by later hands, but has also been touched by the hand of time. We have said that the writing on the first and last pages of the originally independent ms. was so much worn and faded that it had to be rewritten. Traces of such rewriting are observable in other parts of the codex as well. Apart from these ravages of time, some leaves (fol. 59, 63, 75, 80) have received such material damage through clipping of the margins that the text itself is impaired and some letters are missing.

V = *codex Vaticanus—Palatinus gr. 126*: codex on paper of 271 number-ed leaves; 3 additional leaves at the beginning, 1 at the end. Leaves measure 21.2 × 15.4 cm. Ms. contains several works. After *D. A. I.*, which covers fol 2^r to 127^r, come works of Tzetzes, Theophrastus, Bessarion and Nicolas Secundinus, though these have been copied by other hands.[14] At the end of the text of *D. A. I.*, at the bottom of fol. 127^r, are two notes in the hand of the copyist: δόξα τῷ ϑ(ε)ῷ τῷ λόγον καὶ γνῶσιν τοῖς ἀν(ϑρώπ)οις δωρουμένῳ: ͵αφθ´: ἰου-ν(ίῳ) ε´^{η} ἐτελειώϑ(η): ͵αφνδ´^{ν} μαΐῳ ιϛ´^{η}. ἐγὼ ᾿Αντώνιος ὁ ῎Επαρχος παῖς ὢν κατὰ τὸ ͵αφϑ´^{ον} ἔτος ἔγραψα τὸ ἄνωϑ(εν) βιβλίον («Glory be to God who giveth understanding and knowledge to men: finished, 5th June 1509. — 16 May, 1554: I, Antony Eparchus, then a boy, wrote this book in the year 1509.») It was, then, the well-known humanist of Corfiot origin, Antony Eparchus (1491—1571), who copied the ms. — apart from a single passage at fol. 16^v (= 13$_{192—197}$), which is in another hand — in the 18th year of his age; three years before, in 1506, he had completed his ms. copy of the Gospels.[15] The ms. passed into the possession of John Egnatius (1473—1553),[16] probably very soon after it was copied, since Egnatius in the book which he published in 1516 refers to it as being already in his library.[17] It should seem that the second note, dated 16th May 1554, was penned when Eparchus, after the death of Egnatius, came across his own copy among the relics of the deceased. The codex next passed

[14] See H. Stevenson, *Codices manuscripti Palatini graeci bibliothecae Vaticanae*, (Romae, 1885), p. 60.

[15] See E. Legrand, *Bibliographie hellénique au 15e et 16e siècles*, I, (Paris, 1885), pp. CCX—CCXXVII; L. Dorez, 'Antoine Eparque', *Mélanges d'archéologie et d'histoire*, 13 (1893), pp. 281—364; M. Vogel—V. Gardthausen, *Die griechischen Schreiber des Mittelalters und der Renaissance*, (Leipzig, 1909), p. 35.

[16] Stevenson, *op. cit.*, p. 302; A. Firmin-Didot, *Alde Manuce et l'hellénisme à Venise*, (Paris, 1875), pp. 449—452.

[17] «... hic (sc. Constantinus) à literis, optimisque disciplinis non abhorrens, quas penè extinctas ab interitu uindicauit, librum Romano filio reliquit. in quo summam totius imperii, sociorum omnium foedera, hostium uires, rationes, consilia explicuit. quem nos in bibliotheca nostra tanquam thesaurum seruamus, in quo multa de Venetis etiam nostris imperator ipse disserat.» See J. B. Egnatius, *De Caesaribus libri III a dictatore Caesare ad Constantinum Palaeologum, hinc à Carolo Magno ad Maximilianum Caesarem*, (Venetiis, 1516) (sine numeris pag.); cf. *Romanorum principum ll. III*, ex recognitione Des. Erasmi Roterodami, (Basileae, 1518), p. 850.

to the Bibliotheca Palatina at Heidelberg, where it appears in the catalogue compiled by Fr. Sylburg about the year 1584.[18] From Heidelberg it was transferred in 1623, along with other mss., to the Vatican Library in Rome. In the margins of V, as of P, there is a number of notes in Greek and Latin, which are the additions of later readers. An exceptionally large proportion of these notes is appended to the chapters dealing with Venice (27, 28), which obviously were of particular interest to Italian readers. Some of these are worth our attention: 27_{69} μαστρομήλης ὁ καπετάνιος ‖ 27_{73} Κονκόρδια ‖ 27_{80} Κόγραδον vide ne Γράδον ‖ 27_{82} ῾Ριβαλένσης ‖ 27_{83} Λικέντζιά ‖ 27_{86} Μαδοῦκον ‖ 27_{87} Βρουνδουλον (*sine acc.*) ‖ 27_{88} Λαύριτον ‖ 27_{93} ῾Ρίβαλτον ‖ 28_{22} ᾽Αεϊβολας ‖ 29_{258} Τράγουρις ‖ 29_{263} Κάτερα.

I have studied this ms. partly by means of photographic reproductions in the library of the Hungarian National Museum, and partly by examination of the original in the Vatican Library in 1927 and in 1936.

F = *codex Parisinus gr. 2967*: codex on paper, of 241 numbered leaves and 11 additional leaves. Leaves measure 32 × 21.5 cm. Apart from the text of *D. A. I.*, which covers fol. 1ʳ to 80ᵛ, ms. includes several other works, such as compositions of Photius, Themistius, Choricius, Polybius and Apollodorus.[19] The first part of *D. A. I.* (fol. 1ʳ to 16ᵛ) was copied by Antony Eparchus, as appears from a comparison of the script with that of V; the remainder (fol. 17ʳ to 80ᵛ), together with the excerpts of Polybius and the work of Apollodorus, which are together at the end of the ms. (fol. 125ʳ to 241ʳ), is the work of another hand. Omont in his catalogue identified this copyist as the Cretan Michael Damascene, but in the index of the same catalogue we find instead the name of Valeriano de Forli.[20] A comparison with the script of the last named and with other mss. of Michael Damascene[21] shows that the copyist of the latter part of *D. A. I.* was not Valeriano de Forli, but Michael Damascene.

The first mention of F occurs in the catalogue of mss. sent by Jerome Fondulo to Fontainebleau in 1529.[22] That the ms. there mentioned is in fact

[18] «126. Constantini Imper. ad Romanum filium suum liber de Notitia utriusque Imperii, orientalis sc. et occidentalis in quo et de rebus Turcicis, aliisque nationibus hodiernis. Citatur in eodem Theophanis Chronographia bis ...» See Friderici Sylburgii *Catalogus codicum Graecorum M.SS. olim in Bibliotheca Palatina, nunc Vaticana asservatorum ...*, (Francofurti ad M., 1701), p. 40.

[19] See H. Omont, *Inventaire sommaire* ... III, (Paris, 1888), p. 76.

[20] *Introduction. Liste des copistes des manuscrits grecs*, (Paris, 1898), p. XXXIII; cf. M. Vogel—V. Gardthausen, *op. cit.*, pp. 311, 371.

[21] Cod. Paris. gr. 1926, 2937 (Michael Damascene); cod. Paris. gr. 1687, 1823, 1830, 2376 (Valeriano de Forli); cf. H. Omont, *Facsimilés des manuscrits grecs du XVᵉ et XVIᵉ siècles*, (Paris, 1887), II pl. 36., 48.; E. M. Thompson, *Handbook of Greek and Latin Palaeography*, (London, 1906), p. 178; E. Thompson—Sp. P. Lampros, ᾽Εγχειρίδιον ἑλληνικῆς καὶ λατινικῆς παλαιογραφίας, (Athens, 1903), p. 297.

[22] «No. 25. Κωνσταντίνου βασιλέως πρὸς υἱὸν ῾Ρωμανόν.» See H. Omont, *Catalogues des manuscrits grecs de Fontainebleau sous François Iᵉʳ et Henri II*, (Paris, 1889), p. 372.

our F is proved by later catalogues, which mention not only *D. A. I.*, but also
the other components of the same ms. These catalogues are: the catalogue of
1544;[23] that of 1550, by Angelo Vergetius and Constantine Palaeocappa;[24] and
that compiled in the reign of Charles IX (1550—1574).[25] Since, as we shall
see, F is a copy of V, it is certain that it was written between 1509—1529, to
which period are assignable also the water-marks of fol. 1—80.
I have studied this ms. both through photographic reproductions and
by examination of the original in the Bibliothèque Nationale at Paris in 1936
and in 1948.

M = *codex Mutinensis gr. 179 (III F 1)*: codex on paper, of 104 leaves.
Leaves measure 32.4 × 22.4 cm. Fol. 2^r to 6^v of the ms. contain text of chh.
15—21 of *D. A. I.* (15$_1$ Περὶ τοῦ γένους τῶν Φατεμιτῶν — 21$_{118}$ διὰ ξηρᾶς),
copied by Andrea Darmari.[26] As to chronology, we know only that the dated
mss. of this famous copyist fall between the years 1560—1586.[27] I have studied
the relevant portion of this ms. by means of photographic reproductions.

2. EDITIONS

Of the Greek text in its entirety seven editions have hitherto been
published. The first edition was published in 1611 by John Meursius (= **Me**)
under the title «*De administrando imperio*»[28] a title which he himself gave to
the work and which has been since then generally adopted. In his notes he
informs the reader that the basis of his edition was the Vatican ms. (= V),
which was at that time still in the Bibliotheca Palatina at Heidelberg. Meursius

---

[23] «No 199. Κωνσταντίνου βασιλέως πρὸς υἱὸν Ῥωμανὸν καὶ Φωτίου περὶ ι' ῥητόρων.»
See H. Omont, *op. cit.*, p. 365.
[24] «Κωνσταντίνου βασιλέως νουθεσίαι. Nᵒ 334. Βιβλίον α' μήκους, ἐνδεδυμένον
δέρματι λευκῷ, εἰσὶ δ' ἐν αὐτῷ ταῦτα· Κωνσταντίνου βασιλέως νουθεσίαι πρὸς τὸν ἴδιον
υἱὸν αὐτοῦ Ῥωμανὸν τὸν Πορφυρογέννητον, ὅπως δεῖ γινώσκειν παντὸς ἔθνους φύσεις
τε καὶ ἤθη καὶ ἰδιώματα, καὶ τόπων καὶ χωρῶν αὐτῶν, καὶ ποῖον ἐξ αὐτῶν δύναται ὠφελῆσαι
Ῥωμαίοις καὶ ποῖον οὐχί, καὶ ἱστορίας τινὰς νέας. Φωτίου πατριάρχου περὶ δέκα ῥητόρων.
Θεμιστίου . . .». See H. Omont, *op. cit.*, p. 113.
[25] «No 560. Κωνσταντίνου βασιλέως νουθεσίαι.» See H. Omont, *op. cit.*, p. 449.
[26] See V. Puntoni, 'Indice dei codici greci della biblioteca Estense di Modena',
Studi italiani di filologia classica, 4 (1896), p. 495.
[27] See Vogel—Gardthausen, *op. cit.*, pp. 16—27.
[28] *Constantini Imperatoris Porphyrogeniti, De Administrando Imperio, ad Romanum F. Liber nunquam antehac editus.* Ioannes Mevrsivs primus vulgavit, Latinam inter-
pretationem, ac Notas adjecit. Lvgdvni Batavorvm. Ex officinâ typographicâ Ioannis
Balduini, impensis verò Ludovici Elzeviri. CIↃ.IↃC.XI.

worked on it by favour of the then librarian, Janus Gruterus.[29] Six years later a new edition came out, but is was simply a literal copy of the first.[30] The text, with corrections from Bandur's edition, was also published by John Lami in his complete edition of the works of Meursius.[31]

A century after the first edition, that is, in 1711, the work was republished by Anselm Bandur (= **Ba**).[32] It appears from his introduction that Bandur collated the text of Meursius' edition of 1617 with the original Paris ms. (P), and was thus able to introduce several corrections into his text.[33] Bandur's edition was twice reprinted: an uncorrected reprint appeared in 1729, in the Venetian collection of the Byzantine Historians[34], and in 1864 Migne republished Bandur's text with a few corrections.[35]

The final edition was the work of Emmanuel Bekker (= **Be**),[36] who did not divulge his methods, though it is clear that he did not use any fresh ms. material.

Editions containing excerpted chapters only of *D. A. I.* have generally followed Bekker's text. Such are, e. g., the editions of Fr. Rački,[37] H. Marczali,[38]

---

[29] «Scias autem unde habeam. Descripsi ante quatuor amplius annos ex Codice qui est in Bibliothecâ Palatinâ, et Ioannis Baptistae Egnatii olim fuisse perhibetur ... Quin accessit huc quoque comitas V. C. Jani Gruteri, eius praefecti, per quem liber mihi quotidie ad eam accessus patuit.» See *ed. cit.*, Notae, p. 2.

[30] *Constantini Porphyrogennetae Imperatoris Opera. In quibus Tactica nunc primum prodeunt.* Ioannes Mevrsivs collegit, coniunxit, edidit. Lvgdvni Batavorum. Ex Officinâ Elzeviriana. Anno CIƆIƆCXVII.

[31] *Ioannis Meursi Operum volumen sextum* ex recensione Ioannis Lami, Florentiae, CIƆ.IƆ.CC.XLV., cc. 929—1132.

[32] *Imperium Orientale sive Antiquitates Constantinopolitanae in quatuor partes distributae* ... Operà et studio Domni Anselmi Banduri Ragusini, Presbyteri ac Monachi Benedictini è Congregatione Melitensi. Tomus primus. Parisiis. Typis et sumptibus Joannis Baptistae Coignard, Regis et Academiae Gallicae Architypographi. MDCCXI. (Corpus Byzantinae Historiae XXXIII.), pp. 53—157.

[33] «Imprimis textum Graecum contuli cum Codice MS. membranaceo Bibliothecae Regiae, optimae notae num. 2661. quem annis ab hinc circiter quingentis scriptum fuisse aiunt: innumerabiles mendas, quibus Meursiana editio undique scatebat, sustulimus, loca corrupta ac mutila quae plurima erant in textu Graeco edito ex eodem MS. Regio sarcivimus.» See *op. cit.*, p. IV.

[34] *Imperium Orientale sive Antiquitates Constantinopolitanae in quatuor partes distributae* ... opera et studio D. A. Banduri ... Venetiis 1729. (Corpus Historiae Byzantinae XV.) I., pp. 45—127.

[35] *Patrologiae cursus completus* ... Series Graeca posterior ... accurante J. P. Migne t. CXIII., Parisiis 1864, c. 158—422.

[36] *Constantinus Porphyrogenitus De thematibus et De administrando imperio. Accedit Hieroclis Synecdemus cum Banduri et Wesselingii commentariis.* Recognovit Immanuel Bekkerus, Bonnae MDCCCXL. (Corpus Scriptorum Historiae Byzantinae), pp. 65—270.

[37] Fr. Rački, *Documenta historiae Croaticae periodum antiquam illustrantia* (Monumenta spectantia historiam Slavorum meridionalium VII.) (Zagrabiae, 1877), pp. 264—419.

[38] Pauler-Szilágyi, *A magyar honfoglalás kútfói*, (Budapest, 1900), pp. 110—136; H. Marczali, *A magyar történet kútfőinek kézikönyve* (Enchiridion fontium historiae Hungarorum), (Budapest, 1902), pp. 27—55.

J. B. Bury,[39] St. Stanojević — V. Ćorović,[40] A. Gombos,[41] and G. Cankova-Petkova — P. Tivčev.[41bis] Only C. G. Cobet, who published a part of ch. 9 dealing with the Russians,[42] and E. Jakubovich, who published chh. 38—40 dealing with the Hungarians,[43] made a fresh collation of P. Certain variants in P are cited by V. Thomsen,[44] G. Fehér,[45] F. Šišić[46], H. Grégoire[47] and K. O. Falk[47bis] in their works. A new edition of the chh. on the Southern Slavs prepared by R. Vári was never published, and his ms. is in the archives of the Hungarian National Museum.[48]

The plan for a new critical edition of *D. A. I.* originated when the Hungarian scholar, R. Vári, at that time a young man, began preliminary researches in 1892 with a view to elucidating the ms. tradition.[49] The plan next engaged the English historian J. B. Bury, who proposed to include the work in his collection of Byzantine Texts. But these projects came to nothing. Bury, in a letter dated 5th October, 1925, announced that he had given up the plan of an edition, which he surrendered to me.

[39] J. B. Bury, *The early History of the Slavonic Settlements in Dalmatia, Croatia, & Serbia, Constantine Porphyrogennetos De administrando imperio*, Chapters 29—36. (Texts for Students No. 18.), (London, 1920).

[40] St. Stanojević—V. Ćorović, Одабрани извори за српску историју I, (Beograd, 1921), pp. 58—72.

[41] A. B. Gombos, *Catalogus fontium historiae Hungaricae aevo ducum et regum ex stirpe Arpad descendentium ab anno Christi DCCC usque ad annum MCCCI.* T. I, (Budapestini, 1937). pp. 720—727.

[41 bis] Гръцки извори за българската история V (Sofia, 1964), pp. 198—220.

[42] C. G. Cobet, 'Locus Constantini Porphyrogeniti ex codice archetypo Parisino descriptus', *Mnemosyne*, 4 (1876), pp. 378—382.

[43] E. Jakubovich—D. Pais, *Ó-magyar olvasókönyv* (Tudományos Gyüjtemény 30.), (Pécs, 1929), pp. 6—10.

[44] V. Thomsen, *Der Ursprung des russischen Staates*, (Gotha, 1879), p. 59.

[45] G. Fehér, 'Ungarns Gebietsgrenzen in der Mitte des 10. Jahrhunderts. Nach dem De administrando imperio des Konstantinos Porphyrogennetos', *Ungarische Jahrbücher*, 2 (1922), p. 46. = 'Magyarország területe a X. század közepe táján Konstantinos Porphyrogennetos De administrando imperioja alapján', *Századok*, 56 (1921—22), p. 354.

[46] F. Šišić, *Povijest Hrvata u vrijeme narodnih vladara*, (Zagreb, 1925), p. 239.

[47] H. Grégoire, *Annuaire de l'Institut de Philologie et d'Histoire Orientales et Slaves* V. *Mélanges Émile Boisacq*, (Bruxelles, 1937), p. 450.

[47 bis] *Dneprforsarnas namn i Kejsar Konstantin VII Porfyrogennetos' De administrando imperio* (Lund, 1951).

[48] 12. Quart. Graec. fol. 11—79, 99—105.

[49] R. Vári, 'Jeléntes Constantinus Porphyrogennitus De administrando imperio czimű munkájának kéziratairól', *Akadémiai Értesítő*, 6 (1895), pp. 710—712.

3. TRANSLATIONS

Of the full text of *D. A. I.* four translations have been published, two in Latin, one in Russian, and one in Croat.

The first Latin rendering, supplied by Meursius, was printed in his edition of 1611 and afterwards reprinted without alteration in the edition of 1617: it appeared side by side with the Greek text. It was reprinted by Lami in his collected works of Meursius, as an appendix.[50] The translation of Meursius was radically revised and amended by Anselm Bandur in his edition of 1711, and the revised version was published in the Venice edition of 1729. Bandur's rendering was also republished by Lami, side by side with the Greek text, in his collected works of Meursius. The same rendering was introduced, practically without alteration, by Bekker into his edition of 1840 and by Migne into the text of his *Patrologia* (1864).

D. A. I. was translated into Russian by G. Laskin,[51] and into Croat by N. Tomašić.[52]

Translation of select chapters or sections have been published in many works and in many languages. We may instance the following: several passages in Latin translation are to be found in Stritter's collection;[53] N. V. Malickij published a revised Russian translation of chh. 1—14, 38—40, 42—46 and 53, which was found in ms. among the papers of V. V. Latyšev[54]; Russian renderings of other passages are found in the works of E. Kunik, N. Protopopov, A. Zernin, V. Jurgevič, K. Grot, F. I. Uspenskij, S. P. Šestakov, F. Westberg, N. P. Kondakov and others. K. Dieterich turned some chapters into German.[55] German translations of select passages are found in the works of A. C. Lehrberg, E. Kunik, V. Thomsen and others; French translations in the work of M. Brosset; and English in that of C. A. Macartney. Serb and Croat renderings of select passages have been published in the works of Fr. Rački, A. Pavić, F. Šišić, G. Manojlović, Stanojević—Ćorović, B. Ferjančić and others; and

---

[50] See *ed. cit.*, c. 1133—1208.

[51] 'Сочиненія Константина Багрянороднаго: ,,О ѳемахъ'' (De thematibus) и ,,О народахъ'' (De administrando imperio)', Чтенія въ Имп. Обществѣ исторіи и древностей россійскихъ при Московскомъ Университетѣ 1899, I (188), (Moskva, 1899), pp. 1—262.

[52] *Vjesnik kr. Hrvatsko-Slavonsko-Dalmatinskoga Zemaljskog Arkiva*, 20 (1918), pp. 1—91; *Vjesnik kr. Državnog Arkiva u Zagrebu*, 3 (1928), pp. 1—70.

[53] J. G. Stritter, *Memoriae populorum olim ad Danubium, Pontum Euxinum, paludem Maeotidem, Caucasum, mare Caspium et inde magis ad septemtriones incolentium e scriptoribus historiae Byzantinae erutae et digestae* I—IV, Petropoli, 1771—1779.

[54] (V. V. Latyšev—N. V. Malickij), 'Константина Багрянородного Об управлении государством,' Известия Государственной Академии истории материальной культуры 91, Moskva—Leningrad, 1934.

[55] K. Dieterich, *Byzantinische Quellen zur Länder- und Völkerkunde* I—II, (Leipzig, 1912).

Bulgarian in the work of G. Cankova-Petkova—P. Tivčev. A Hungarian version of the chh. dealing with the Hungarians may be found both in the editions of H. Marczali and in the special study of K. Szabó.

4. MUTUAL RELATIONSHIP OF MANUSCRIPTS AND EDITIONS

A full collation of the four mss. (P, V, F, M) and of the three editions (Me, Ba, Be) shows their mutual relationship to have been as follows:

V is a simple transcript of P. This is clear from the following considerations:

1. V contains many orthographical errors, which are due to the peculiar and individual forms of letters employed by P, that is to say, they are due to palaeographical causes. Antony Eparchus imitated faithfully in many places the peculiarities and abbreviations in the script of P, but occasionally misread some of the letters and abbreviations, e. g.: 13_{183} περιγίνεσθαι P: περιήνεσθαι V || 29_{63} Χρωβάτοι P: Χρωμάτοι V || 30_{110} Βράτζα P: Βράτζω V || 42_{88} Χαράκουλ P: Χωράκουλ V || 43_{87} ἔγγραφον P: ἄγγραφον V || 43_{111} Κα^κι^κίου P: Κικίου V || 43 $_{169—170}$ α^θ′ Κρινίτ(ην) P: ἀκρινίτην V || 50_{199} προβληθέντας P: προκληθέντας V || 53_{425} ἔσπευσε(ν) P: ἔπεσεν V || 53_{429} λεληθότι P: λεμθότι V.

2. In other passages some letters of P are indistinct and were in consequence omitted by the copyist of V, e. g.: 13_{136} προσετρίψατο P: προετρέψατο V || 14_{16} συναναστρεφόμενος P: συνανατρεφόμενος V || 25_{14} μεταπεμφθεὶς P: μεταπεμφεὶς V.

3. Further, it is clear that in two places the copyist of V has written a passage twice over, just because the initial words of the duplicated passages happen in P to recur at the beginning of a line. These dittographies are: 50_{126} Μεσοποταμίαν — 50_{128} θέμα *iter.* V. || 51_{198} μαγίστρου — ὄντος *om. et a*^θ′ — ταξειδεύειν (cf. $51_{194—195}$) *iter.* V.

4. Basic corruptions of P recur in V. Common to both versions are: P_{19} αὐτῶν *om.* P V || 1_4 δεῖν *om.* P V || 9_{90} καιρὸς] ταρὸς P V || 13_{77} Θεοῦ *om.* P V || 26_{71} *post* ἔτη *lac. ind.* P V || 29_{47} ʽΡωμάνους] Κομάνους P V || 29_{50} τὰ Δεκάτερα] τάδε κάστρα P V || 32_{29} χριστιανῶν] χρόνων P V || 37_{22} Χαραβόη] Χαβόη P V || 38_{33} Λεβεδία] χελάνδια P V || 42_{23} τριακόσιοι] τὰ P V || 42_{27} ὁ καὶ P V || 53_{101} ἀθροίλους P V.

5. Antony Eparchus incorporated into his version additions and alterations made by later hands in P, among which is the note, already referred to, which bears the date 1361/2, e. g.: 16_8 *post* ͵ϛρλ′ *siglo* ·/. *adhibito* νῦν δέ (ἐστιν) ͵ϛωο′ (ἰνδικτιῶνος) ιε′, ὡς εἶναι ἀπὸ τότ(ε) ἕως νῦν χρόνοι ψμ′ *mg. add.* P^3: ͵ϛρλ′ νῦν δέ ἐστι ͵ϛωο′ (ἰνδικτιῶνος) ιε′, ὡς εἶναι ἀπὸ τότ(ε) ἕως νῦν χρόνοι ψμ′ V || 21_{55} *post* ἱκανόν *s. v. add.* ἤτι ζ′ ἔτη P^3: ἱκανὸν, ἤτοι ἔτη ζ′ V || 22_{81} *post* Βασιλείου *s. v. add.* τοῦ ἐκ Μακεδονίας P^3: Βασιλείου τοῦ ἐκ Μακεδονίας V.

6. In two passages of the text of P (22₅₃, 22₅₇: correction of the word Ἀράβων) we recognise unmistakably the handwriting of Antony Eparchus (= P⁴).

These examples prove indisputably that the youthful Antony Eparchus copied V from P in 1509. For all that, V is not a faithful, verbal transcript of P. The text of V, as compared with P, shows many significant variants, a large proportion of which has crept into the editions (Me, Ba, Be). It is unnecessary to detail all the errors of V; some examples are:

1. The copyist of V often omits words or phrases, e. g.: 9₁₅ καὶ ἀπέρχον-ται *om.* V (F Me) ‖ 13₄₉ βασιλέως *om.* V (F Me Ba Be) ‖ 21₄₉₋₅₀ τοῦ Μουάμεθ ἐκράτησεν τῆς ἀρχῆς τῶν Ἀράβων, οὐκ ἐκ τοῦ γένους ἦν *om.* V (F Me) ‖ 25₅₇₋₅₉ ἐν τῷ Βαγδάδ, ἔστιν δὲ ἐκ τῆς τοῦ Μουάμεθ γενεᾶς, ἤτοι τοῦ Μουχούμετ . ὁ δὲ δεύτερος καθέζεται *om.* V (F Me) ‖ 40₅₇ ἐποίησεν υἱὸν τὸν Ἐζέλεχ *om.* V (F Me) ‖ 45₁₁ χρηματισθῆναι *om.* V (F Me Ba Be) ‖ 50₉₀₋₉₁ Ἰστέον, ὅτι ἡ τοῦ Χαρσιανοῦ στρατηγὶς τοῦρμα ἦν τὸ παλαιὸν τῆς τῶν Ἀρμενιάκων στρατηγίδος *om.* V (F Me) ‖ 50₁₅₂ καὶ *om.* V (F Me Ba Be) ‖ 51₇₂₋₇₄ ὁ τοῦ πρωτοσπαθαρίου Ἀρσενίου καὶ μαγγλαβίτου πατήρ. Οὗτοι δέ, ὅ τε ὁ πρωτοσπαθάριος ὁ Ποδάρων καὶ ὁ πρωτοσπαθάριος Λέων ὁ Ἀρμένης *om.* V (F Me) ‖ 53₃₄₃₋₃₄₄ Καὶ λέγει τῇ παιδίσκῃ. «Πῶς εὖρες τὸ πρᾶγμα τοῦτο;» *om.* V (F Me).

2. The copyist of V read or transcribed some words incorrectly, e. g.: 9₆₉ φθάζειν P: φθάνειν V (F Me Ba Be) ‖ 25₅₀ κροτηθέντος P (Ba Be): κρατηθέντος V (F Me) ‖ 27₈₇ Βροῦνδον P (Ba Be): Βροῦδον V (F Me) ‖ 30₄₂ ἀρεσθέντες P: ἐρασθέντες V (F Me Ba Be) ‖ 32₉₄ ἔχοντας P (Be): ἔχοντες V (F Me Ba) ‖ 38₆₄ πρὸ ῥηθέντες P: προειρημένοι V (F Me Ba Be) ‖ 40₇ Κάβαροι P (Ba Be): Βάκαροι V (F Me) ‖ 40₃₄ Σφενδοπλόκος P (Ba Be): Σφενδονοπλόκος V (F Me) ‖ 42₁₀₆ Σπαταλοῦ P: ποταμοῦ V (F Me Ba Be) ‖ 43₂₆ ἐσκήπτετο P (Be): ἐσκέπτετο V (F Me Ba) ‖ 44₁₉ Ἀπελβάρτ P (Ba Be): Ἀπελκάρτ V (F Me) ‖ 50₁₄₈ Βαασακίου P (Me Ba Be): Κααcακίου V (F) ‖ 51₁₁₄ πλοκοὺς P: πλοκὰς V (F Me Ba Be) ‖ 53₂₇₁ Γυκίαν P: γυναῖκα V (F Me Ba Be) ‖ 53₄₀₃ βάλεται P: λάβετε V (F Me Ba Be) ‖ 53₅₂₅ πραγματείας P: πράγματος V (F Me Ba Be).

3. The copyist of V sometimes replaced the numerical cyphers of P by the verbal equivalents, or, conversely, rendered the numerals of P by numerical cyphers, e. g.: 9₃₆ α′ P: πρῶτον V (F Me Ba Be) ‖ 9₄₅ δ′ P: τέταρτον V (F Me Ba Be) ‖ 9₅₃ ἐξ P (Me Ba Be): ϛ′ V (F) ‖ 16₇ ιβ′ P: δωδέκατον V (F M Me Ba Be) ‖ 23₁₆ β′ P: δευτέρας V (F Me Ba Be) ‖ 26₂₈ α′ P: πρῶτον V (F Me Ba Be) ‖ 29₂₄₈ μιὰς P: α′ V (F Me Ba Be) ‖ 30₂₀ ,α P: χιλίων V (F Me Ba Be) ‖ 46₆ γ′ P: τρεῖς V (F Me Ba Be) ‖ 52₆ δύο P (Me Ba Be): β′ V F.

4. The copyist of V occasionally changed the word-order, e. g.: P₄₀ αἰώνιος καὶ ἀνώλεθρος P: ἀνώλεθρος καὶ αἰώνιος V (F Me Ba Be) ‖ 7₁₋₂ περὶ τῶν ἀπὸ Χερσῶνος ἀποστελλομένων βασιλικῶν P: περὶ τῶν ἀποστελλομέ-

νων βασιλικῶν ἀπὸ Χερσῶνος V (F Me Ba Be) ‖ 9₁₀₅₋₁₀₆ ἐξέρχωνται ἄρχοντες P: ἄρχοντες ἐξέρχονται V (F Me Ba Be) ‖ 13₅₀₋₅₁ διὰ τοῦ ἀγγέλου ὁ
Θ(εὸ)ς P: ὁ Θ(εὸ)ς διὰ τοῦ ἀγγέλου V (F Me Ba Be) ‖ 17₈ ἐσθίοντα ἀπὸ
καμήλου P (M): ἀπὸ καμήλου ἐσθίοντα V (F Me Ba Be) ‖ 29₂₅₈ νησίον
ἐστὶν μικρὸ(ν) P: μικρόν ἐστι νησίον V (F Me Ba Be) ‖ 32₉₂ ἐν τοῦτο
γενόμενος P: γενόμενος ἐν τούτῳ V (F Me Ba Be) ‖ 46₄₂ ἔστιν ὀχυρὸν
πάνυ P: ὀχυρόν ἐστι πάνυ V (F Me Ba Be) ‖ 49₅₀ ναὸν αὐτοῦ P: αὐτοῦ
ναόν V (F Me Ba Be) ‖ 50₂₂₆ τῆς αὐτοῦ P: αὐτοῦ τῆς V (F Me Ba Be).

5. The copyist of V occasionally made stylistic changes, e. g.: 16₄₋₅
καὶ τίς ὁ τὰ σκῆπτρα τῆς βασιλείας 'Ρωμαίων διέπω(ν) P (M): καὶ τίς ἦν
τότε ὁ βασιλ(εὺς) 'Ρωμαί(ων) V (F Me Ba Be) ‖ 29₃₇₋₃₈ διαπερασάντων
ποτὲ τῶν 'Ρωμανῶν, ποιήσαντες οὗτοι ἐνκρύμματα P (Ba Be): διαπεράσαντες ποτὲ οἱ 'Ρωμάνοι ἐποίησαν οὗτοι ἔγκρυμα V (F Me) ‖ 38₆₀₋₆₁ παρὰ
τῶν Πατζινακιτῶν οὐκ ἐδέξαντο P: μετὰ τῶν Πατζινακιτῶν οὐκ ἐποίησαν
V (F Me Ba Be) ‖ 46₁₁₀ βαλὼν αὐτὸ εἰς κοντάριον P: λαβὼν αὐτὸ εἰς
κοντάριον περιέθηκε καὶ V (F Me Ba Be) ‖ 50₆₇ τοῦ τελεῖν αὐτοὺς P: ἵνα
τελῶσι τὰ V (F Me Ba Be).

6. The copyist of V occasionally inserted words which are missing
in P, e. g.: 9₄₈ post ἅπαντα add. τὰ μονόξυλα τὰ V (F) ‖ 9₆₁ ante δεύτερον
add. εἰς τὸν V (F Me Ba Be) ‖ 9₁₀₆ post Κίαβον add. ποταμὸν V (F Me) ‖
18₁ post 'Αράβων add. ἀρχηγὸς V (F Me) ‖ 29₂₀₃ ante μέλλοντος add. τοῦ
V (F) ‖ 33₉ post βασιλέα add. 'Ρωμάνων V (F) ‖ 40₃₂ post ἐκεῖνο add.
τὸ V (F Me Ba Be) ‖ 42₆₆ post μέχρι add. τοῦ V (F Me Ba Be) ‖ 50₂₂₉ ante
πατρίκιος add. ὁ V (F Me Ba Be) ‖ 53₂₅ post Χερσωνιτῶν add. χώρας V
(F Me Ba Be) ‖ 53₃₀₈ ante παίδων add. τῶν V (F Me Ba Be) ‖ 53₃₉₀
post ἔθος add. μου V (F Me Ba Be) ‖ 53₄₈₀ post πόλεως² add. αὐτὴν V
(F Me Ba Be).

If we look more closely at the variants of V, we observe that they are
only in part oversights or slips of the copyist, while others of them represent
a deliberate attempt to emend the text. Antony Eparchus, like so many other
humanists, was, it should seem, no slavish copyist, but showed some indepen-
dence in his efforts to correct what he was copying. This is clear also from the
fact that in many places he has emended not only misspellings in P, but also
textual corruptions.

Comparison of the mss. makes it clear that F is copied immediately
from V. This is proved not only by the circumstance that at the end of the
text of F we discover the same chronological note which, as we saw, Antony
Eparchus appended to V in 1509, but also by the fact that all the omissions,
repetitions and variants of V recur in F; that is to say, where P and V disagree,
F invariably follows V to the letter. The copyist of F was faithful to the text
of V, but here and there introduced noteworthy corrections of his own.

It is also beyond question that in his transcription into M of the section
relating to the Saracens, Andrea Darmari copied from P. This is proved
indisputably by the fact that where P and V disagree, M always agrees with

P, and further that Darmari introduced into his text corrections and additions made by later hands in P. Numerous errors distort his text; and in two places the copyist has incorporated marginal notes from P as though they were chapter-headings.

As for the editions, Meursius, as he tells us himself, used V: but comparison shows that in many places he has diverged from his original. These divergences are in most cases blunders on the part of Meursius, and only in a few instances can be regarded as deliberate attempts at emendation. Some of his blunders Meursius himself corrected in the «Notae breves» and «Errata» appended to his edition, but most of them perpetuated themselves in the later editions, Ba and Be.

Discrepancies between the text of Meursius and V are:

1. Meursius omitted many words and phrases, e. g.: 2_3 πρὸς ἀλλήλους *om.* Me ‖ 13_{198} καὶ ἐθῶν *om.* Me ‖ 21_{91-92} Μαυΐου γέρων πρὸς τὸν γέροντα τοῦ *om.* Me ‖ 26_3 τοῦ *om.* Me (Ba) ‖ 26_{12} ἐστέφθη παρὰ τοῦ τότε πάπα. Καὶ *om.* Me ‖ 27_{79} κάστρου *om.* Me (Ba Be) ‖ 29_{16-17} καὶ καταμαθεῖν, τίνες κατοικοῦσιν ἐκεῖθεν τοῦ ποταμοῦ, διαπεράσαντες *om.* Me ‖ $29_{253-254}$ ὅλον καὶ ποιῆσαι τὰ παλάτια αὐτοῦ καὶ πάντα τὰ οἰκήματα τοῦ κάστρου *om.* Me ‖ 36_{11-12} 'ἀβάπτιστοι' ἑρμηνεύονται, τῇ τῶν Ρωμαίων δὲ διαλέκτῳ *om.* Me ‖ $43_{170-171}$ αὐτοῦ ἀναλαβέσθαι καὶ εἰσαγαγεῖν *om.* Me ‖ 44_{66} τὸ κάστρον *om.* Me (Ba Be) ‖ 46_{53} τὸ *om.* Me (Ba) ‖ 49_{63-65} καὶ ἀναστήσονται καὶ ἀπαγγελοῦσιν αὐτὸ τοῖς υἱοῖς αὐτῶν, ἵνα μὴ ἐπιλάθωνται τῶν εὐεργεσιῶν, ὧν ἐποίησεν ὁ Θεὸς διὰ πρεσβειῶν τοῦ ἀποστόλου *om.* Me ‖ 53_{65} παρὰ τῶν Χερσωνιτῶν *om.* Me ‖ 53_{129} αὐτοὺς *om.* Me (Ba Be) ‖ $53_{172-173}$ τόπῳ πολεμήσαντες τὸν Σαυρόματον ἐνίκησαν, ἐν ᾧ *om.* Me ‖ 53_{502} Ἰστέον, ὅτι καὶ ἑτέρα βρύσις ἔστιν ἐκεῖσε ἄφθαν ἀναδιδοῦσα *om.* Me.

2. Meursius misread or miscopied several words, and his edition has also typographical errors, e. g.: 1_{21} θεοφυλάκτῳ (P) V (F Be): θευφυλάκτῃ Me (Ba) ‖ 9_{10} αἱ λοιπαὶ Σκλαβινίαι (P) V (F): οἱ λοιποὶ Σκλαβίνιοι Me (Ba Be) ‖ 17_{17} ἀποκτενόμενος (P) V (F): ἀποκτεινόμενος (M) Me (Ba Be) ‖ 27_{30} Λαγούβαρδοι (P) V (F): Λογουβάρδοι Me (Ba Be) ‖ 37_{22} Κουρκοῦται (P) V (F): Κουρκοῦταν Me (Ba Be) ‖ 40_5 Κουρτουγερμάτου (P) V (F): Κουρτυγερμάτου Me (Ba Be) ‖ 43_{70} διατρίψας (P) V (F Be): ἐπιτρίψας Me (Ba) ‖ 43_{110} ἀνεβλάστησεν (P) V (F): ἐβλάστησε Me (Ba Be) ‖ 49_{73} τὸ τί (P) V (F Ba Be): τότε Me ‖ 50_5 τοῦ παρ' αὐτῶν τελουμένου πάκτου (P) V (F): τῶν παρ' αὐτῶν τελουμένων πάκτων Me (Ba Be) ‖ 53_{113} ἡμεῖς (P) V (F Ba Be): οὐδεὶς Me ‖ 53_{357} ἐκλεξάσθωσαν (P) V (F): ἐκλεξάτωσαν Me (Ba Be) ‖ 53_{428} ἐνεχθῆναι (P) V (F Be): ἠνεχθῆναι Me (Ba).

3. Meursius in most cases replaced the numerical cyphers of V by the verbal equivalents, e. g.: 9_{57} ε' (P) V (F): πέμπτον Me (Ba Be) ‖ 18_5 γ' (P) V (F M): τρία Me (Ba Be) ‖ 29_{98} ρ' (P) V (F): ἑκατόν Me (Ba Be) ‖ 29_{265} ιε' (P) V (F): δεκαπέντε Me (Ba Be) ‖ 30_{50} ͵α (P) V (F): χιλίων Me (Ba Be) ‖ 37_{33} μ' (P) V (F): τεσσαράκοντα Me (Ba Be) ‖ 40_{38} α' (P) V: πρῶτος (F) Me (Ba Be) ‖ 49_{39} γ' (P) V (F): τρίτη Me (Ba Be) ‖

51₂₁ β΄ (P) V (F): δεύτερον Me (Ba Be) ‖ 53₂₉₅ ι΄ ἤ ιβ΄ (P) V (F): δέκα ἤ δώδεκα Με (Ba Be).

4. Meursius made occasional changes in word-order, e. g.: 27₂₀ ἀποσταλῆναι μοι (P) V (F): μοι ἀποσταλῆναι Me (Ba Be) ‖ 29₂₁₁ σφαγῆς αὐτοῦ (P) V (F): αὐτοῦ σφαγῆς Me (Ba Be) ‖ 29₂₈₆ ἐκεῖσε κλύδωνα (P) V (F): κλύδωνα ἐκεῖσε Me (Ba Be) ‖ 32₁₃₆ τῶν Ῥωμαίων βασιλεὺς (P) V (F): βασιλεὺς Ῥωμαίων Me (Ba Be) ‖ 40₅₁ κύρια ὀνόματα (P) V (F): ὀνό-ματα κύρια Me (Ba Be) ‖ 45₁₄₁ γενέσθαι δοῦλος (P) V (F): δοῦλος γενέ-σθαι Me (Ba Be) ‖ 50₁₃₀₋₁₃₁ τῶν Ῥωμαίων ἐξουσίαν (P) V (F): ἐξουσίαν τῶν Ῥωμαίων Me (Ba Be) ‖ 51₁₂₅ βασιλικὸν δρομώνιον (P) V (F): δρομώ-νιον βασιλικὸν Me (Ba Be) ‖ 53₃₆₉ πληροφορῆσαι ἐν ὅρκῳ (P) V (F): ἐν ὅρκῳ πληροφορῆσαι Me (Ba Be).

5. Meursius here and there inserts words missing in V, and hence in P also, e. g.: 9₁ *ante* Ῥωσίας *add.* τῆς Me (Ba Be) ‖ 9₆₃ *post* τούτου *add.* καὶ Me ‖ 22₂₉ *ante* Ἰουστινιανὸν *add.* τὸν Me (Ba Be) ‖ 22₆₄ *ante* τήν¹ *add.* διὰ Me ‖ 25₃ *post* Βρεττανίαν *add.* ἀλλὰ Me ‖ 25₂₈ *post* ἑσπερίου *add.* Λιβύης Me (Ba Be) ‖ 25₆₃ *post* ὅτι *add.* ἐν τῷ Me (Ba Be) ‖ 27₄₄ *ante* τῶν *add.* διὰ Me (Ba Be) ‖ 40₆₀ *ante* υἱοὶ *add.* οἱ Me (Ba Be) ‖ 43₇₃ *post* εἰς *add.* τὴν Me (Ba Be) ‖ 46₁₅ *ante* Ῥωμανίας *add.* τῆς Me (Ba Be) ‖ 50₄ *post* κάστρου *add.* τοῦ Me (Ba Be) ‖ 50₂₂₉ *ante* βασιλέως *add.* τοῦ Me (Ba Be) ‖ 53₂₈₈ *post* ταῦτα *add.* τὰ Me (Ba Be).

If we take into consideration that the ms. V used by Meursius contains, as we have shown, innumerable errors, we can scarcely wonder that the first edition presents a sufficiently corrupted version of the original. It should, how-ever, be emphasized that Meursius, particularly in his notes, made a large number of emendations to the text, and of these emendations later editions have made use.

The edition of Bandur marks an advance on that of Meursius; Bandur, as he himself records, collated Meursius' text with P, and was thus able to correct, both in his text and in his notes, a large number of errors originating partly in V and partly in Me. But Bandur did not make his collation with the necessary care, with the result that many omissions and blunders escaped his attention. How many errors of Meursius were corrected by Bandur, and how many Bandur transferred to his own edition, may be easily discerned if we look at the examples given above in our examination of the relationship of V and Me, and note the proportion of the number of errors found in V Me and Me only to the number of errors found in V Me Ba or V Me Ba Be, and in Me Ba or Me Ba Be. To the number of inherited blunders Bandur added a fresh crop of his own, e. g.: 6₈ πέπερι Ba (Be) ‖ 29₆₁ ἐξ *om.* Ba ‖ 29₈₂ ἑρμηνεύονται Ba (Be) ‖ 30₉₄ οἱ λοιποὶ Σκλαβίνιοι Ba (Be) ‖ 40₁₂ Λιούντινα Ba (Be) ‖ 45₂₁ καί¹ *om.* Ba (Be) ‖ 46₁₁₁ Κωνσταντίνῳ *(per comp.* P)] Κώνσταντι Ba (Be) ‖ 46₁₄₄ Κωνσταντῖνος *(per comp.* P)] (Be) Κώνστας Ba ‖ 51₇₀ πρωτοσπαθάριος *om.* Ba (Be) ‖ 51₂₀₀ Λογουβαρδία Ba (Be) ‖ 53₂₁₈ ἐν τῷ τοῦ Φαρνάκου στρατῷ *om.* Ba (Be) ‖ 53₂₅₁ ἀρχομένου Ba (Be) ‖ 53₄₅₅ τῆς¹]τὴν Ba (Be).

Bekker's edition marks no considerable advance. He made no study of mss., and therefore made no use of fresh ms. material. He republished Bandur's text, which he occasionally emended by his own conjectures. Although he recorded in his critical apparatus the variants between the mss. used by Meursius and Bandur, and between their respective editions, yet he merely copied this information out of Bandur's notes, as is seen from the fact that he reproduces Bandur's typographical errors. Bekker's edition therefore repeats numerous errors of earlier editions, as appears in our examination above of the relationship between V Me and Ba; and he added to their number the slips and typographical errors of his own edition, e. g.: 21_{42} κροβάλλονται || 26_{16} τὸν] τὴν || 29_{26} κάστρον² om. || 30_{78} καὶ μόνον om. || 30_{88} καὶ om. || $30_{103-105}$ ordinem versuum permutavit || 37_2 οἱ om. || 37_{18} Κουλπέη || 37_{49} πλησιέστερον || 37_{55} κόντευρα || 45_{44} τὸν¹ om. || 45_{101} προσφασιζόμενος || 45_{145} Μασάτου′ || 46_{69} πᾶσας || 47_{19} ἐν om. || 49_{42} τἆλλα || 49_{60} παραδόττες || 50_{79} τὴν om. || 50_{213} Νικήτης || 51_{159} νήπιον τυγχάνειν τὸν βασιλέα, καθὼς εἴρηται, καὶ τὸ om. || 51_{174} τῷ βασιλεῖ || 53_{267} τε¹ om. || 53_{510} τὸ χωρίον om.

In the light of our examination of the mutual relationship of mss. and editions, we may summarize as follows the history of the text of *D. A. I.*

Of *D. A. I.*, as of the *De Cerimoniis*, only one ms. survives from the Byzantine age.[55bis] In view of the fact that none of the later Byzantine historians or chronographers makes use of the work, we must conclude that *D. A. I.*, which was a confidential, indeed a most secret, document, was never published, but only preserved at the imperial court. There, probably, it was discovered by a member of the imperial family, the Caesar John Ducas, who between 1059 and 1081 had it copied for his library. But P is not an immediate copy of the original. Since P exhibits so many corruptions, and one marginal note refers to the year 979, we must postulate, between the archetype and P, yet another copy, probably made towards the close of the X century after the death of the author. Marginal notes and emendations make it clear that P continued to be read during the Byzantine age; from the note of 1361/2 and from other corrections we may conclude that the chh. on the Saracens were of peculiar interest at the period when the Ottoman Turks had crossed the Hellespont (1360) and were threatening the capital.

After this the history of P is obscure. We do not know where it went from the library of John Ducas or what was its fate, until it came into the hands of Antony Eparchus. Certain it is that during the Renaissance the interest of Venetian humanists was aroused by the chh. of the work dealing with Venice, as is clear from the marginal notes to V; and that it is owing to this circumstance, not merely that the copy from the library of the Byzantine

---

[55 bis] But see now C. Mango—I. Ševčenko, 'A New MS of the *De Cerimoniis*', *Dumbarton Oaks Papers*, 14 (1960), pp. 247—249.

Caesar reached Italy, but also that, at the beginning of the XVI century, two other complete copies of the work were made there as well. Upon the copy of Antony Eparchus was based the first edition of Meursius, the errors of which Bandur endeavoured to correct by a collation with the Byzantine copy; but even so, many inherited errors were transmitted not only to his own edition but also to the final edition of Bekker, published more than a century ago.

The relationships of mss. and editions may be seen at a glance in the following tree:

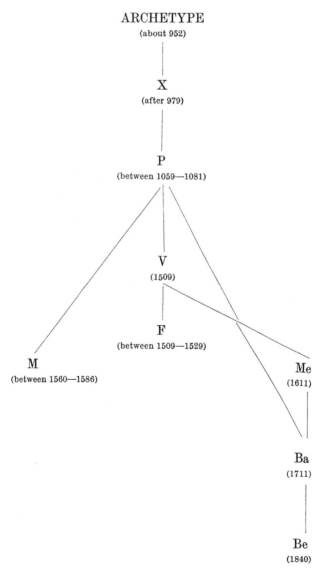

ARCHETYPE

(about 952)

X

(after 979)

P

(between 1059—1081)

V

(1509)

F

(between 1509—1529)

M

(between 1560—1586)

Me

(1611)

Ba

(1711)

Be

(1840)

5. METHOD FOLLOWED IN THE PRESENT EDITION

It will be clear from our examination of the relationship of mss. and editions that all the known mss. of _D. A. I._ derive from a Byzantine copy of the XI century, P, which is thus the source of the whole textual tradition. On this ms. therefore, a new edition must be based.[56] However, as we have emphasized, P exhibits additions, erasures and emendations which are partly the work of the copyist or a contemporary, and partly of various later hands. These last are again divisible into two categories: into those which were added to P before V and M were copied, and those which were added after V and M were copied. Insertions of the former class, which go back to the Byzantine age, are of unequal value: we find among them alterations which are mere arbitrary additions of later readers, such as the marginal note of 1361/2; but there are others, especially in the chh. dealing with the Arabs, which do emend errors which have occurred in the copying of P. Additions of the second category, dating from the post-Byzantine period and consisting of arbitrary alterations made by later readers, are of no value whatever; a characteristic specimen of these is the garbling from analogy of the original name 'Almoutzis' (see 38_{44}, 38_{49}). But, apart from the attentions of later hands, P has also, as we saw, sustained material damage; and to restore the occasionally faded or mutilated text we are compelled to have recourse to the copies of P, made when P was in better condition than it is to-day. For these reasons, then, to restore the original text of P, use must be made of its copies, V and M.

But even if the text of the Byzantine version preserved to us be purged of its later alterations and be restored, so far as may be, to its original state, the question remains whether P, thus restored, can be regarded as a faithful replica of the original text of Constantine. Since our new edition rests upon one ms. only, which cannot be checked by comparison with any other, the problem thus raised can be solved only by reference to internal evidence, that is, to the condition of the text as preserved in P and to the linguistic peculiarities of the work. There can be no doubt that copyist's errors have crept even into P. It can be demonstrated that in some passages the copyist has omitted words, as is seen is cases where the text is mutilated or unintelligible (e. g. 1_4, 9_{19}, 13_{77}, 22_{61}, 26_{71}, 46_{95}). It is also certain that, in other passages, we have to deal with more serious corruptions (e. g. 13_{177}, 29_{58}, 29_{229}, 38_{33}, 42_{23}, 53_{101}), which can only be conjecturally emended.

In correcting the text of P, we have to take into account the fact that _D. A. I._ is compiled from various sources of which the language is not uniform. In some chapters we find vulgarisms whose removal would distort the genuine

---

[56] See Gy. Moravcsik, 'L'édition critique du «De administrando imperio»', _Byzantion,_ 14 (1939), pp. 353—360.

form of the work.[57] But since, as we saw above, the orthography of P is extremely faulty, there are many places where it is not easy to determine which linguistic peculiarities are native to Constantine's text and which are to be put down to the copyist. So, for example, we see in P forms which indicate the amalgamation of the participles of οἶδα and εἶδον (e. g. 45_{140}, 49_{28}, 49_{34}, 53_{193}, 53_{419}, 53_{429}), a phenomenon exemplified also in papyri and other demotic texts.[58] Again, as is well known, in later Greek certain forms of indicative and subjunctive coincide in pronunciation; and since P often confuses the diphthong ει with the vowel η, these forms coincide and amalgamate in its text also. It is well known, too, that in the post-classical age the conjunction ἵνα is followed by indicative as well as subjunctive; and since the orthography of P is not consistent, we sometimes find after ἵνα indicative and subjunctive forms used alternately even in the same sentence (e. g. 13_{81}—$_{83}$, 53_{516}). All these and other confusions in the orthography of P (e. g. absence of the temporal augment) often make it hard to determine when we have, or have not, the right to correct it.

Again, it is common knowledge that Constantine drew one part of his material from written sources which have come down to us independently. Such sources are, apart from citations of Holy Scripture, the Chronicles of Theophanes and George Monachus, the *Ethnica* of Stephanus of Byzantium, the Acts of the Synod in Trullo, etc. Elsewhere, passages of *D. A. I.* agree so closely with parallel passages of the *De Thematibus*, attributed to the same imperial author, and of the work known as Theophanes Continuatus, that for these passages we must postulate a common source. Some passages, then, of *D. A. I.* have come down to us immediately, and do not depend on P. We can thus compare the text of P with the text of the sources of the work, which sources may be used to restore the text of *D. A. I.*

A comparison of the text of P with that of the sources and of other parallel passages shows that the author sometimes followed his originals faithfully, but at other times modified their styles, and occasionally supplemented his sources with others of unknown origin. But for our appraisal of the text of Constantine it is of great importance to realize that the text of *D. A. I.* preserved to us, when compared with the text of its sources, gives evidence in several places of serious corruption. At first sight we might conclude that

---

[57] See Gy. Moravcsik, Τὰ συγγράμματα Κωνσταντίνου τοῦ Πορφυρογεννήτου ἀπὸ γλωσσικῆς ἀπόψεως᾽, *Studi Bizantini e Neoellenici*, 5 (1938), pp. 514—520.

[58] See S. G. Kapsomenakis, *Voruntersuchungen zu einer Grammatik der Papyri der nachchristlichen Zeit*, (Munich, 1938), p. 91.

P is a faulty copy, and that these errors must be corrected from the sources. But this is not so. A more searching examination shows that these supposed corruptions were to be found already in some mss. of the sources themselves (e. g. 25_{30}, 42_{49}). It follows that, as Constantine or his collaborators copied the sources they used out of mss. which were themselves corrupt, it is incorrect to attribute these corruptions to the carelessness of the copyist of P or other copyists of *D. A. I.*; we must, on the contrary, suppose that these very corruptions stood even in the original ms. of Constantine. Recognition of this fact, and of its bearing on the restoration of the original form of *D. A. I.*, enjoins upon us the preservation of these corruptions in our text; since, if we emend P, we shall be disturbing the true text as Constantine wrote it. Of course, in the many cases where direct evidence is lacking, it is very hard to pronounce whether a corruption is of pre- or post-Constantinian origin, that is to say, whether it has been introduced by the copyist or existed already in the mss. of the sources and was thence transferred to the original ms. of Constantine. In this difficulty we derive some assistance from the fact that, considering the corruptions from the point of view of their nature and quantity, we note a great difference between those sections of *D. A. I.* which are based on contemporary information and those which the editor has derived from older, written sources. In the former sections we find fewer errors, mainly of a minor character; but in the latter, which had been subject to continual transcription over a period of a century or more, the corruptions are proportionately greater in numbers and importance. This principle cannot be used as an absolute criterion; we have in each case, according to the nature of the corruption, to judge whether the corruption in question is or is not anterior to the age of Constantine, and whether in consequence we may or may not retain it in his text.

In view of these facts, the principles applied to the new edition may thus be summarized:

The new edition is based on P, the text of which, however, in places where it is disturbed by material damage, erasures or alterations by later hands, is restored by reference to V and M. The critical text diverges from P when the text of P appears to be corrupt, that is to say, in places where it may be supposed that, owing to copyists' errors or alterations by later hands, the text of P does not correspond to the original text of Constantine's work. In such places we have taken into account the variants of the later transcripts (V, F, M) and editions (Me, Ba, Be) and the conjectural emendations of later researchers; and on the basis of these we have emended the text of P.

Besides, the critical text diverges from P in spelling also. Modern spelling has been adopted, which has involved the tacit correction of errors arising from itacism, of accentual errors (including the Byzantine system of enclitic accentuation) and of other irregularities. This has been done the more readily since in our description of P above we have pointed out its orthographical peculiarities. We have kept the forms of the codex for the *ephelcusticon* and for elision, although P is not consistent in their use. As regards numbers in the text, P uses verbal forms and cyphers indifferently, sometimes in the same sentence; we have substituted verbal forms for cyphers in the text only where consistency absolutely demanded it.

The apparatus criticus falls into two parts, and contains

1. references to sources and parallel passages (F);
2. variants of mss. and editions, and emendations and conjectures of scholars (V).

In the first section we have directed attention not merely to the immediate sources of Constantine but also to other, parallel passages which may assist the understanding of passages to which they are referred. But we have restricted ourselves to Greek sources only, because the enumeration of all parallels in the different Western and Eastern sources would have made the apparatus too bulky. In cases where there is no question of borrowing, but only of a common source, of similar sources of information, or simply of fortuitous concord, we cite the works in question with the symbol «cf.».

In the second section, the following principles have been adopted. In each case where, for reasons already set forth, we diverge from the text of P, or where traces of emendations or erasures appear in the text of P, the fact is noted *positively*; i. e. we indicate the origin of the variant adopted in the text, and the reading of P, and if necessary, the readings of the later transcripts V, F, M, and of the editions Me, Ba, Be. In all other cases, that is, where the form adopted in the text differs only in spelling from the form found in P, or when noteworthy variants are recorded in later transcripts or editions, we note *negatively*, that is, we confine ourselves to a reference to the variants in the transcripts or editions in question.

In its references to P, the apparatus records not only the corrections of the copyist himself (P[1]), but also the alterations and the marginal notes made by different later hands (P[2]—P[9]). By the symbol P[x] are noted the alterations or erasures which were made by an unrecognizable hand before V was copied, and by the symbol P[y] are noted the alterations or erasures which were made by another unrecognizable hand after V was copied. We have left unnoted erasures or alterations which are of a purely orthographical character, or those which occur in words whose meaning is obvious, though we note all erasures and alterations met with in uncommon proper names. Unnoted also are traces of occasional attempts by later hands to amend faded writing, unless such traces suggest that the text has been altered.

Orthographical irregularities of P are noted in the apparatus only when they occur in uncommon proper names, words of foreign derivation, colloquial words, or where the handwriting of P admits of more than one reading; and lastly where the accent falls on a syllable other than that which generally carries it. Abbreviations of P are noted only where their interpretation is doubtful, or when numerals are denoted by letters.

Variants found in V, an immediate transcript of P, are noted in the apparatus only in cases where the parallel passages of P have suffered from material damage, erasures or alterations by later hands, or where V gives a variant which differs from the variant of P and which may serve to elucidate or emend the text. Variants found in F, a transcript of V, are noted only in exceptional cases, i. e. when F supplies some emendation of substance, or where the parallel passages of both V and P show trades of alteration. Variants found in M, a transcript of P, are noted only when erasure or alteration is found in the parallel passage of P.

We regard it as unnecessary to note in the apparatus all the omissions, all the blunders and all the alterations of later transcripts and editions, especially as in our description of mss. and editions we have already given several examples. The apparatus, therefore, notes only the variants which are informative from the point of view of the restoration or history of the text (including the discrepancies between our new text and the text of Be). Note that where reference is made to the text of the editions, the abbreviations noted above (Me, Ba, Be) are employed; but where we refer to emendations or conjectures in the notes or apparatus of the editions, we cite them under the names of the respective editors (Meursius, Bandur, Bekker).

If a source copied word for word by Constantine has come down to us independently, our apparatus notes variations therefrom, but not omissions and arbitrary alterations made by Constantine, who often modified the wording of his sources. Where, however, the author has inserted anything into the text of his source, this is noted in the apparatus.

In respect to these sources, it has been found necessary in two cases to examine their mss., and make use of the results of the new collation. The relevant passages of the edition of Theophanes Continuatus I have collated with V (= codex Vaticanus gr. 167), and of *De Thematibus* with C (= codex Parisinus gr. 854); the variants are noted in the apparatus. Special treatment had to be applied to the text of George Monachus; for, as C. de Boor has shown, the emperor Constantine made use of that variant of his text which is represented by codex P (= cod. Coislin. gr. 305). We have therefore considered in the apparatus those variants especially which occur in this codex of George Monachus.

In the apparatus ms. variants are noted in all cases in the original spelling, omitting only the horizontal strokes above proper names and the dots over the ι and υ. Variant proper names are given an initial capital. Uncial numerical signs are replaced by the usual minuscule forms, and the horizontal stroke above them by the acute stroke universally employed to-day. Signs and technical details of the apparatus of our edition are generally in conformity with the ruling of the International Union of Academies.[59]

---

[59] *Emploi des signes critiques, disposition de l'apparat dans les éditions savantes de textes grecs et latins.* Conseils et recommandations par J. Bidez et A. B. Drachmann. Édition nouvelle par A. Delatte et A. Severyns, (Bruxelles-Paris, 1938).

Lastly, we have included in the apparatus most of the emendations and conjectures of scholars known to us, though they are not all of equal value.[60] This course is justified by the fact that the bibliography relating to *D. A. I.* is so rich and extensive that many individual conjectures are extraordinarily difficult to find. The work has in the past attracted so many different scholars, and their studies are published in so many different languages, that it is practically impossible for one who is not a specialist to know them all.[61] We hope that it will be of service to those who use this edition to find collected here all the resources of previous research directed towards critical examination of the text, and that they will be able to build further upon the foundations here laid; for research on *D. A. I.* is by no means exhausted yet, and the present edition aims at providing future research with a sure and reliable substructure.

GY. MORAVCSIK.

---

[60] I have also made use of some comments of Prof. Ph. Kukules (Athens) which he kindly communicated by letter, and for which I express my sincere gratitude.

[61] See the complete bibliography by Gy. Moravcsik, *Byzantinoturcica*, vol. I, (Budapest, 1942), pp. 215—221 (2nd ed. pp. 367—379). — The studies published since are as follows: M. Vasmer, *Die Slaven in Griechenland* (Abhandlungen der Preussischen Akademie der Wissenschaften, Jahrgang 1941., Philos.-hist. Klasse No. 12., Berlin, 1941); A. Vogt, 'Le protospathaire de la phiale et la marine byzantine', *Échos d'Orient*, 39 (1941—42), pp. 329—332; M. Laskaris, 'La rivalité bulgaro-byzantine en Serbie et la mission de Léon Rhabdouchos (917), (Constantin Porphyrogénète, De adm. imp. chap. 32)', *Revue historique du Sud-Est Européen*, 20 (1943), pp. 202—207; H. Grégoire, 'L'origine et le nom des Croates et des Serbes', *Byzantion*, 17 (1944—45), pp. 88—118; K. H. Menges, 'Etymological notes on some Päčänäg names', *Byzantion*, 17 (1944—45), pp. 256—279; K. Czeglédy, 'A IX. századi magyar történelem főbb kérdései', *Magyar Nyelv*, 41 (1945), pp. 33—55; G. Vernadsky, 'Great Moravia and White Chorvatia', *Journal of the American Oriental Society*, 65 (1945), pp. 357—359; J. Deér, 'A IX. századi magyar történet időrendjéhez', *Századok*, 79—80 (1945—46). pp. 2—30; J. Harmatta, 'Szines lovú népek', *Magyar Nyelv*, 42 (1946), pp. 26—34; G. Labuda, *Pierwsze państwo słowiańskie. Państwo Samona*, Poznań, 1949. pp. 194—262. For bibliography since 1949, see Gy. Moravcsik, *Byzantinoturcica* (2nd ed.) I, pp. 367—379; *D. A. I.* vol. II, Commentary (London, 1962); *Byzantinische Zeitschrift* 55 (1962) and subsequent volumes.

LIST OF SIGNS

F = Fontes et loci paralleli
V = Variae lectiones et coniecturae

MANUSCRIPTS:

P = cod. Parisinus gr. 2009 (cf. pp. 15—21.)
   P^1 = manus prima
   P^{2-9} = manus recentiores
   P^x = manus incerta (ante a. 1509)
   P^y = manus incerta (post a. 1509)
V = cod. Vaticanus-Palatinus gr. 126 (cf. pp. 21—22.)
   V^1 = manus prima
   V^2 = manus secunda
F = cod. Parisinus gr. 2967 (cf. pp. 22—23.)
   F^1 = manus prima
   F^2 = manus secunda
M = cod. Mutinensis gr. 179 [III F 1] (cf. p. 23.)

EDITIONS:

Me = editio Meursiana (cf. p. 24.)
   Meursius = notae Meursii
Ba = editio Banduriana (cf. p. 24.)
   Bandurius = animadversiones Bandurii
Be = editio Bekkeriana (cf. p. 24.)
   Bekker = apparatus criticus Bekkeri
edd. = editiones Me Ba Be
Migne = editio a Migne curata (cf. p. 24.)
Bury = editio cap. 29—36 a J. Bury facta (cf. p. 25.)

SOURCES AND PARALLEL PASSAGES:

Georg. Mon. = Georgius Monachus, ed. C. de Boor (Lipsiae, 1904)
   Georg. Mon. ^{BEPV} = codices B E P V a C. de Boor collati
De Them. = Constantinus Porphyrogenitus, De Thematibus, ed. I. Bekkerus
   (Bonnae, 1840); ed. A. Pertusi (Roma, 1952)
   De Them.^{c} = cod. Parisinus gr. 854 a me collatus
Theoph. = Theophanes, ed. C. de Boor (Lipsiae, 1883)
   Theoph. $^{codd.}$ = codices a. C. de Boor collati
   Theoph. ^{bcdefghm} = codices b c d f g h m a C. de Boor collati
Theoph. Cont. = Theophanes Continuatus, ed. I. Bekkerus (Bonnae, 1838)
   Theoph. Cont.^{v} = cod. Vaticanus gr. 167 a me collatus

TEXT AND TRANSLATION

ΚΩΝΣΤΑΝΤΙΝΟΥ

ΕΝ ΧΡΙΣΤΩΙ ΒΑΣΙΛΕΙ ΑΙΩΝΙΩΙ ΒΑΣΙΛΕΩΣ ΡΩΜΑΙΩΝ
ΠΡΟΣ ΤΟΝ ΙΔΙΟΝ ΥΙΟΝ ΡΩΜΑΝΟΝ
ΤΟΝ ΘΕΟΣΤΕΦΗ ΚΑΙ ΠΟΡΦΥΡΟΓΕΝΝΗΤΟΝ ΒΑΣΙΛΕΑ

⟨Π ρ ο ο ί μ ι ο ν.⟩

Υἱὸς σοφὸς εὐφραίνει πατέρα, καὶ πατὴρ φιλόστοργος ἐπὶ υἱῷ
τέρπεται φρονίμῳ. Κύριος γὰρ δίδωσι νοῦν, ἡνίκα δεῖ εἰπεῖν, καὶ προστί-
θησιν οὓς τοῦ ἀκούειν· παρ' αὐτῷ θησαυρὸς σοφίας, καὶ ἐξ αὐτοῦ δίδοται
πᾶν δώρημα τέλειον· καθιστᾷ βασιλεῖς ἐπὶ θρόνου καὶ κυρίαν τοῦ 5
παντὸς δίδωσιν αὐτοῖς. Νῦν οὖν ἄκουσόν μου, υἱέ, καὶ τήνδε μεμαθηκὼς
τὴν διδαχὴν ἔσῃ σοφὸς παρὰ φρονίμοις, καὶ φρόνιμος παρὰ σοφοῖς
3ᵛP λογισθήσῃ· εὐλογήσουσί σε οἱ λαοί, καὶ μακαριοῦσί σε πλήθη | ἐθνῶν.
Διδάχθητι, ἃ χρή σε πρὸ πάντων εἰδέναι, καὶ νουνεχῶς τῶν τῆς βασιλείας οἰάκων ἀντιλαβοῦ. Περὶ τῶν ἐνεστώτων μελέτησον, καὶ περὶ τῶν 10
μελλόντων διδάχθητι, ἵνα πεῖραν μετ' εὐβουλίας ἀθροίσῃς, καὶ μεγαλε-
66Be πήβολος ἔσῃ περὶ | τὰ πράγματα. Ἰδοὺ ἐκτίθημί σοι διδασκαλίαν,
ὥστε τῇ ἐκ ταύτης πείρᾳ καὶ γνώσει συνετισθέντα περὶ τὰς βελτίστας
βουλὰς καὶ {τῷ} τὸ κοινῇ συμφέρον μὴ διαμαρτάνειν· πρῶτα μὲν ποῖον
ἔθνος κατὰ τί μὲν ὠφελῆσαι δύναται Ῥωμαίους, κατὰ τί δὲ βλάψαι, 15
{καὶ ποῖον} καὶ πῶς ἕκαστον τούτων καὶ παρὰ ποίου δύναται ἔθνους
καὶ πολεμεῖσθαι καὶ ὑποτάσσεσθαι, ἔπειτα περὶ τῆς ἀπλήστου καὶ
4ʳP ἀκορέστου αὐτῶν γνώ|μης, καὶ ὧν παραλόγως ἐξαιτοῦνται λαμβάνειν,
εἶθ' οὕτως καὶ περὶ διαφορᾶς ἑτέρων ἐθνῶν, γενεαλογίας τε ⟨αὐτῶν⟩

F   P. 2 Υἱὸς — πατέρα: Prov. 10, 1.   2 ἐπὶ υἱῷ — 3 φρονίμῳ: cf.
Prov. 17, 21.   3 Κύριος — 4 ἀκούειν: Is. 50, 4.   4 παρ' αὐτῷ
— σοφίας: cf. Prov. 2, 6; Sir. 1, 25.   4 ἐξ αὐτοῦ — 5 τέλειον:
Iac. 1, 17.   5 καθιστᾷ — θρόνου: cf. II Paralip. 23, 20.   8 εὐλο-
γήσουσι — ἐθνῶν: cf. Psalm. 71, 17.

CONSTANTINE

IN CHRIST THE ETERNAL EMPEROR EMPEROR OF THE ROMANS
TO HIS SON ROMANUS
THE EMPEROR CROWNED OF GOD AND BORN IN THE PURPLE

P r o e m.

A wise son maketh glad a father, and an affectionate father taketh delight in a prudent son. For the Lord giveth wit to speak in season, and addeth thereto an ear to hear; with Him is the treasure of wisdom, and from Him cometh every perfect gift; He setteth kings upon the throne and giveth unto them the lordship over all. Now therefore hearken unto me, my son, and being adept in this my teaching thou shalt be wise among the prudent, and be accounted prudent among the wise; the peoples shall bless thee, and the multitudes of the nations shall call thee blessed. Be instructed in what it behoves thee before all else to know, and lay hold skilfully upon the helm of the rule. Study the things that are now, and be instructed concerning the things that are to be, so that thou mayest amass experience with sound judgment, and thou shalt be most competent in thine affairs. Lo, I set a doctrine before thee, so that being sharpened thereby in experience and knowledge, thou shalt not stumble concerning the best counsels and the common good: first, in what each nation has power to advantage the Romans, and in what to hurt, and how and by what other nation each severally may be encountered in arms and subdued; then, concerning their ravenous and insatiate temper and the gifts they demand inordinately; next, concerning also the difference between other nations, *their* origins

V   **Tit. 1** *post* Κωνσταντίνου *add.* τοῦ edd. ‖ 4 πορφυρογέννητον] *litteras* φυρ *s. v. add.* P¹ ‖ *post* βασιλέα *add.* νουθεσίαι F².

      P. 1 Προοίμιον *add.* Moravcsik ‖ 8 εὐλογήσουσί F¹ edd.: εὐλογήσωσί P ‖ 11/12 μεγαλεπήβολος Meursius Ba Be: μεγαλεπίβολος P ‖ 13 συνετισθέντα Meursius Ba Be: συνετισθέντι P ‖ 14 τῷ *secl.* Be ‖ 16 καί ποῖον *secl.* Be ‖ 19 τε F¹ Meursius Ba Be: δὲ P ‖ αὐτῶν *add.* Moravcsik ‖

καὶ ἐθῶν καὶ βίου διαγωγῆς καὶ θέσεως καὶ κράσεως τῆς κατοικουμένης 20
παρ' αὐτῶν γῆς καὶ περιηγήσεως αὐτῆς καὶ σταδιασμοῦ, πρὸς τούτοις
καὶ περὶ τῶν ἔν τινι καιρῷ μεταξὺ Ῥωμαίων καὶ διαφόρων ἐθνῶν
συμβεβηκότων, καὶ μετὰ ταῦτα, ὅσα ἐν τῇ καθ' ἡμᾶς πολιτείᾳ, ἀλλὰ καὶ
ἐν πάσῃ τῇ Ῥωμαίων ἀρχῇ κατά τινας χρόνους ἐκαινοτομήθη. Ταῦτα
ἐσοφισάμην κατ' ἐμαυτόν, καὶ εἶπα γνωστά σοι ποιῆσαι, τῷ ἠγαπημένῳ 25
μου υἱῷ, ἵν' ἔχῃς εἰδέναι τὴν ἑκάστου τούτων διαφοράν, καὶ πῶς ἢ
4ᵛP μεταχειρίζεσθαι ταῦτα καὶ οἰκειοῦσθαι ἢ πολεμεῖν | καὶ ἀντιτάσσεσθαι.
Πτοηθήσονται γάρ σε ὡς μεγαλοφυῆ, καὶ ὡς ἀπὸ πυρὸς φεύξονται ἀπὸ
σοῦ· φιμωθήσονται τὰ χείλη αὐτῶν, καὶ ὡς ὑπὸ βελῶν τοῖς σοῖς κατα-
τρωθήσονται ῥήμασιν. Ὀφθήσῃ αὐτοῖς φοβερός, καὶ ἀπὸ προσώπου 30
σου τρόμος λήψεται αὐτούς. Καί σου ὁ Παντοκράτωρ ὑπερασπιεῖ, καὶ
συνετιεῖ σε ὁ πλάσας σε· κατευθυνεῖ σου τὰ διαβήματα, καὶ ἑδράσει
67Be σε ἐπὶ βάσιν ἀσάλευτον. Ὁ θρόνος σου ὡς ὁ ἥλιος ἐναντίον | αὐτοῦ,
καὶ οἱ ὀφθαλμοὶ αὐτοῦ ἔσονται βλέποντες ἐπί σε, καὶ οὐδὲν οὐ μὴ ἅψηταί
σου τῶν χαλεπῶν, καθότι αὐτός σε ἐξελέξατο καὶ ἀπὸ μήτρας ἀφώρισεν, 35
καὶ τὴν αὐτοῦ βασιλείαν ὡς ἀγαθῷ ὑπέρ πάντας σοι ἔδωκεν, καὶ τέθεικε
5ʳP ὡς σκέ|πην ἐπὶ βουνοῦ καὶ ὡς χρυσοῦν ἀνδριάντα ἐφ' ὑψηλοῦ, καὶ ὡς
πόλιν ἐπ' ὄρους ἀνύψωσεν, ὥστε δωροφορεῖσθαι ὑπὸ ἐθνῶν καὶ προσκυνεῖσθαι ὑπὸ τῶν κατοικούντων τὴν γῆν. Ἀλλὰ σύ, Κύριε ὁ Θεός μου,
οὗ ἡ βασιλεία αἰώνιος καὶ ἀνώλεθρος, εἴης κατευοδῶν τὸν διὰ σοῦ ἐξ 40
ἐμοῦ γεννηθέντα, καὶ ἔστω ἡ ἐπισκοπὴ τοῦ προσώπου σου ἐπ' αὐτόν, καὶ
τὸ οὖς σου ἐπικλινέσθω ταῖς τούτου δεήσεσιν. Σκεπασάτω αὐτὸν ἡ χείρ
σου, καὶ βασιλευέτω ἕνεκεν ἀληθείας, καὶ ὁδηγήσει αὐτὸν ἡ δεξία σου·
κατευθυνθείησαν αἱ ὁδοὶ αὐτοῦ ἐνώπιόν σου τοῦ φυλάξασθαι τὰ δικαιώματά σου. Πρὸ προσώπου αὐτοῦ πεσοῦνται πολέμιοι, καὶ λείξουσι 45
5ᵛP χοῦν οἱ ἐχθροὶ αὐτοῦ. Κατασκιασθείη τὸ στέλεχος τοῦ γένους | αὐτοῦ
πολυγονίας φύλλοις, καὶ ἡ σκιὰ τοῦ καρποῦ αὐτοῦ ἐπικαλύψαι ὄρη
βασίλεια, ὅτι διὰ σοῦ βασιλεύουσι βασιλεῖς δοξάζοντές σε εἰς τὸν αἰῶνα.

F   28 ὡς ἀπό — 29 ἀπὸ σοῦ: cf. Deut. 28, 7; Is. 10, 18.   31 τρόμος
λήψεται: Is. 33, 14.   31 ὁ Παντοκράτωρ ὑπερασπιεῖ: Zach. 9, 15.   32
κατευθυνεῖ σου τὰ διαβήματα: cf. Psalm. 39, 3; 118, 133.   32 ἑδράσει —
33 ἀσάλευτον: cf. Sap. 4, 3.   33 Ὁ θρόνος — αὐτοῦ: Psalm. 88,
37.   34 οἱ ὀφθαλμοὶ — βλέποντες cf. I Paralip. 21, 3.   34 οὐδὲν — 35
χαλεπῶν: cf. Iob 5, 19; Sap. 3, 1.   35 σε ἐξελέξατο: Deut. 14,
2.   35 ἀπὸ μήτρας ἀφώρισεν: cf. Galat. 1, 15.   36
τὴν αὐτοῦ — ἔδωκεν: cf. Esd. 1, 2.   36 τέθεικεν — 37 ἐφ' ὑψηλοῦ:
cf. Psalm. 17, 34; Ezech. 40, 2.   37 ὡς πόλιν — 38 ἀνύψωσεν:
cf. Matth. 5, 14.   38 ὥστε — ἐθνῶν: cf. Psalm. 71,
10.   38 προσκυνεῖσθαι — 39 γῆν: cf. Psalm. 32, 14; 71, 11.   40
κατευοδῶν: cf. Psalm. 67, 20,   41 ἔστω — ἐπ'αὐτόν: cf. Exod. 13,
19.   42 Σκεπασάτω — 43 χείρ σου: cf. Exod. 33, 22; Sap. 19, 8.

and customs and manner of life, and the position and climate of the land they dwell in, its geographical description and measurement, and moreover concerning events which have occurred at various times between the Romans and different nations; and thereafter, what reforms have been introduced from time to time in our state, and also throughout the Roman empire. These things have I discovered of my own wisdom, and have decreed that they shall be made known unto thee, my beloved son, in order that thou mayest know the difference between each of these *nations*, and how either to treat with and conciliate them, or to make war upon and oppose. For so shall they quake before thee as one mighty in wisdom, and as from fire shall they flee from thee; their lips shall be bridled, and as darts shall thy words wound them unto death. Thou shalt appear terrible unto them, and at thy face shall trembling take hold upon them. And the Almighty shall cover thee with his shield, and thy Creator shall endue thee with understanding; He shall direct thy steps, and shall establish thee upon a sure foundation. Thy throne shall be as the sun before Him, and His eyes shall be looking towards thee, and naught of harm shall touch thee, for He hath chosen thee and set thee apart from thy mother's womb, and hath given unto thee His rule as unto one excellent above all men, and hath set thee as a refuge upon a hill and as a statue of gold upon an high place, and as a city upon a mountain hath He raised thee up, that the nations may bring to thee their gifts and thou mayest be adored of them that dwell upon the earth. But Thou, O Lord my God, whose rule abideth unharmed for ever, prosper him in his ways who through Thee was begotten of me, and may the visitation of Thy face be toward him, and Thine ear be inclined to his supplications. May Thy hand cover him, and may he rule because of truth, and may Thy right hand guide him; may his ways be made straight before Thee to keep thy statutes. May foes fall before his face, and his enemies lick the dust. May the stem of his race be shady with leaves of many offspring, and the shadow of his fruit cover the kingly mountains; for by Thee do kings rule, glorifying Thee for ever and ever.

---

43 βασιλευέτω — ἡ δεξιά σου: Psalm. 44, 5.   44 κατευθυνθείησαν — 45 τὰ δικαιώματά σου: Psalm. 118, 5; cf. Psalm. 5, 9.   45
Πρὸ προσώπου—πολέμιοι: cf. Psalm. 71, 9; Lev. 26, 8.   45 λείξουσι —
46 αὐτοῦ Psalm. 71, 9; Is. 49, 23.   48 διὰ σοῦ — βασιλεῖς Prov. 8, 15.

V 20 καί¹ *om.* V edd. ‖ ἐθ-ῶν (*littera* ν *erasa*) Pᵞ: ἐθνῶν P V edd. ‖ 22 τινι V edd.: τισι P ‖ 24 πάσῃ edd. πάσῃ V: πᾶσι P ‖ κατα τίνας P ‖ 31 καὶ σοῦ P ‖ 35 ἀφόρησεν P ‖ 36 αὐτοῦ Migne ‖ τέθηκεν P ‖ 37 σκέπην *coni.* Moravcsik: σκέπων P   σκοπὴν Meursius Ba Be ‖ 38 δωροφορεῖθαι V F edd.   δορ   φορεῖ-σθαι P   δορυφορεῖσθαι F¹ ‖ 40 ἀνώλεθρος καὶ αἰώνιος V edd. ‖ 43 ὁδηγήσει V Me: ὁδιγήσῃ P ὁδηγήσῃ Meursius Ba Be

48

1, 2

1. Περὶ τῶν Πατζινακιτῶν, καὶ πρὸς πόσα συμ-
βάλλονται μετὰ τοῦ βασιλέως 'Ρωμαίων
εἰρηνεύοντες.

"Ακουσον τοίνυν, υἱέ, ἅ μοι δοκεῖ ⟨δεῖν⟩ σε μή ἀγνοεῖν, καὶ
68Be νοήμων γενοῦ, ἵνα κτήσῃ κυβέρνησιν. Φημὶ γὰρ καὶ τοῖς ἄλλοις | ἅπασιν 5
εἶναι καλὸν τῶν ὑποτεταγμένων τὴν μάθησιν, διαφερόντως δὲ σοί, τῷ
ὑπὲρ τῆς πάντων σωτηρίας ὀφείλοντι διαμεριμνᾶν καὶ πὴν κοσμικὴν
ὁλκάδα πηδαλιουχεῖν τε καὶ κυβερνᾶν. Εἰ δὲ σαφεῖ καὶ κατημαξευμένῳ
6ʳP λόγῳ καὶ οἷον εἰκῇ ῥέοντι πεζῷ καὶ ἀπλοϊκῷ πρὸς τὴν τῶν | προκειμένων
ἐχρησάμην δήλωσιν, μηδὲν θαυμάσῃς, υἱέ. Οὐ γὰρ ἐπίδειξιν καλλιγρα- 10
φίας ἢ φράσεως ἠττικισμένης καὶ τὸ διηρμένον διογκούσης καὶ ὑψηλὸν
ποιῆσαι ἐσπούδασα, ἀλλὰ μᾶλλον διὰ κοινῆς καὶ καθωμιλημένης ἀπαγ-
γελίας διδάξαι σοι ἔσπευσα, ἅπερ οἴομαι δεῖν σε μὴ ἀγνοεῖν, καὶ ἃ τὴν
ἐκ μακρᾶς ἐμπειρίας σύνεσίν τε καὶ φρόνησιν εὐμαρῶς σοι δύναται
προξενεῖν. 15
'Ψπολαμβάνω γὰρ κατὰ πολὺ συμφέρειν ἀεὶ τῷ βασιλεῖ 'Ρωμαίων
εἰρήνην ἐθέλειν ἔχειν μετὰ τοῦ ἔθνους τῶν Πατζινακιτῶν καὶ φιλικὰς
πρὸς αὐτοὺς ποιεῖσθαι συνθήκας τε καὶ σπονδὰς καὶ ἀποστέλλειν καθ᾽
ἕκαστον χρόνον ἐντεῦθεν πρὸς αὐτοὺς ἀποκρισιάριον μετὰ ξενίων ἁρμο-
6ᵛP ζόντων | καὶ πρὸς τὸ ἔθνος ἐπιτηδείων καὶ ἀναλαμβάνεσθαι ἐκεῖθεν 20
ὁμήρους, ἤτοι ὄψιδας καὶ ἀποκρισιάριον, οἵτινες ἐν τῇ θεοφυλάκτῳ
ταύτῃ πόλει μετὰ τοῦ καθυπουργοῦντος εἰς ταῦτα συνελεύσονται, καὶ
βασιλικῶν εὐεργεσιῶν καὶ φιλοτιμιῶν τῶν ἐπαξίων πάντων τοῦ βασιλεύοντος ἀπολαύσουσιν.

"Οτι γειτνιάζει τὸ τοιοῦτον ἔθνος τῶν Πατζινακιτῶν τῷ μέρει 25
τῆς Χερσῶνος, καὶ εἰ μὴ φιλίως ἔχουσι πρὸς ἡμᾶς, δύνανται κατὰ τῆς
Χερσῶνος ἐξέρχεσθαι καὶ κουρσεύειν καὶ ληΐζεσθαι αὐτήν τε τὴν Χερσῶνα καὶ τὰ λεγόμενα κλίματα.

69Be   2. Περὶ τῶν Πατζινακιτῶν καὶ τῶν 'Ρῶς.

"Οτι καὶ τοῖς 'Ρῶς οἱ Πατζινακῖται γείτονες καὶ ὅμοροι καθε-
7ʳP στήκασιν, καὶ πολλάκις, ὅταν μὴ πρὸς ἀλ|λήλους εἰρηνεύουσι, πραιδεύουσι
τὴν 'Ρωσίαν, καὶ ἱκανῶς αὐτὴν παραβλάπτουσι καὶ λυμαίνονται.
"Οτι καὶ οἱ 'Ρῶς διὰ σπουδῆς ἔχουσιν εἰρήνην ἔχειν μετὰ τῶν 5

F   1. 4 "Ακουσον — ἀγνοεῖν: cf. Prov. 1, 8; De cerim., ed. Bonn. p.
456, 3—4.   5 νοήμων — κυβέρνησιν Prov. 1, 5.   8 Εἰ δὲ —
13 ἔσπευσα: cf. De cerim., ed. Bonn. p. 5, 2—4. = ed. Vogt I. p. 2, 15 — 17.

1. Of the Pechenegs, and how many advantages accrue from their being at peace with the emperor of the Romans.

Hear now, my son, those things of which I think you *should* not be ignorant, and be wise that you may attain to government. For I maintain that while learning is a good thing for all the rest as well, who are subjects, yet it is especially so for you, who are bound to take thought for the safety of all, and to steer and guide the laden ship of the world. And if in setting out my subject I have followed the plain and beaten track of speech and, so to say, idly running and simple prose, do not wonder at that, my son. For I have not been studious to make a display of fine writing or of an Atticizing style, swollen with the sublime and lofty, but rather have been eager by means of every-day and conversational narrative to teach you those things of which I think you should not be ignorant, and which may without difficulty provide that intelligence and prudence which are the fruit of long experience.

I conceive, then, that it is always greatly to the advantage of the emperor of the Romans to be minded to keep the peace with the nation of the Pechenegs and to conclude conventions and treaties of friendship with them and to send every year to them from our side a diplomatic agent with presents befitting and suitable to that nation, and to take from their side sureties, that is, hostages and a diplomatic agent, who shall be collected together under charge of the competent minister in this city protected of God, and shall enjoy all imperial benefits and gifts suitable for the emperor to bestow.

This nation of the Pechenegs is neighbour to the district of Cherson, and if they are not friendly disposed towards us, they may make excursions and plundering raids against Cherson, and may ravage Cherson itself and the so-called Regions.

2. Of the Pechenegs and the Russians.

The Pechenegs are neighbours to and march with the Russians also, and often, when the two are not at peace with one another, raid Russia, and do her considerable harm and outrage.

The Russians also are much concerned to keep the peace with the

---

V   1. 4 δεῖν *add.* Moravcsik || 6 τῷ V edd.: τὸ P || 11 διῃρημένον V
διηρημένον Me || ὑψηλοῦ Meursius Ba Be || 12 καθομηλιμένης P || 13 σοι:
σε V edd. || 21 ὄψηδας P || 28 κλήματα P.
      2. 2 Πατζινακίται P ||

Πατζινακιτῶν. Ἀγοράζουσι γὰρ ἐξ αὐτῶν βόας καὶ ἵππους καὶ πρόβατα, καὶ ἐκ τούτων εὐμαρέστερον διαζῶσι καὶ τρυφερώτερον, ἐπεὶ μηδὲν τῶν προειρημένων ζώων ἐν τῇ Ῥωσίᾳ καθέστηκεν. Ἀλλ’ οὐδὲ πρὸς ὑπερορίους πολέμους ἀπέρχεσθαι δύνανται ὅλως οἱ Ῥῶς, εἰ μὴ μετὰ τῶν Πατζι- νακιτῶν εἰρηνεύοντες, διότι δύνανται — ἐν τῷ ἐκείνους τῶν οἰκείων 10 ὑποχωρεῖν — αὐτοὶ ἐπερχόμενοι τὰ ἐκείνων ἀφανίζειν τε καὶ λυμαίνεσθαι. Διὸ μᾶλλον ἀεὶ σπουδὴν οἱ Ῥῶς τίθενται — διά τε τὸ μὴ παραβλάπτεσθαι 7ᵛP παρ’ αὐτῶν καὶ διὰ τὸ ἰσχυ|ρὸν εἶναι τὸ τοιοῦτον ἔθνος — συμμαχίαν παρ’ αὐτῶν λαμβάνειν καὶ ἔχειν αὐτοὺς εἰς βοήθειαν, ὡς ἂν καὶ τῆς ἔχθρας αὐτῶν ἀπαλλάττωνται καὶ τῆς βοηθείας καταπολαύοιεν. 15

Ὅτι οὐδὲ πρὸς τὴν βασιλεύουσαν ταύτην τῶν Ῥωμαίων πόλιν οἱ Ῥῶς παραγίνεσθαι δύνανται, εἰ μὴ μετὰ τῶν Πατζινακιτῶν εἰρηνεύον- τες, οὔτε πολέμου χάριν, οὔτε πραγματείας, ἐπειδή — ἐν τῷ μετὰ τῶν πλοίων εἰς τοὺς φραγμοὺς τοῦ ποταμοῦ γίνεσθαι τοὺς Ῥῶς καὶ μὴ δύνασθαι διελθεῖν, εἰ μὴ ἐξαγάγωσι τοῦ ποταμοῦ τὰ πλοῖα αὐτῶν, καὶ 20 70Be ἐπὶ τῶν ὤμων βαστάζοντες διαβάσωσιν, — ἐπιτί|θενται τότε αὐτοῖς 8ʳP οἱ τοῦ τοιούτου ἔθνους τῶν Πατζινακιτῶν, καὶ | ῥᾳδίως, ἅτε πρὸς δύο πόνους ἀντέχειν μὴ δύνανται, τροποῦνται καὶ κατασφάζονται.

3. Περὶ τῶν Πατζινακιτῶν καὶ Τούρκων.

Ὅτι καὶ τὸ τῶν Τούρκων γένος μεγάλως πτοεῖται καὶ δέδιε τοὺς εἰρημένους Πατζινακίτας διὰ τὸ πολλάκις ἡττηθῆναι παρ’ αὐτῶν καὶ τελείως σχεδὸν παραδοθῆναι ἀφανισμῷ. Καὶ διὰ τοῦτο ἀεὶ φοβεροὶ τοῖς Τούρκοις οἱ Πατζινακῖται νομίζονται, καὶ συστέλλονται ἀπ’ αὐτῶν. 5

4. Περὶ τῶν Πατζινακιτῶν καὶ Ῥῶς καὶ Τούρκων.

Ὅτι τοῦ βασιλέως Ῥωμαίων μετὰ τῶν Πατζινακιτῶν εἰρηνεύον- τος, οὔτε ⟨οἱ⟩ Ῥῶς πολέμου νόμῳ κατὰ τῆς Ῥωμαίων ἐπικρατείας, 8ᵛP οὔτε οἱ Τοῦρκοι δύνανται ἐπελθεῖν, ἀλλ’ οὔτε | ὑπὲρ τῆς εἰρήνης μεγάλα 5 καὶ ὑπέρογκα χρήματά τε καὶ πράγματα παρὰ τῶν Ῥωμαίων δύνανται ἀπαιτεῖν, δεδιότες τὴν διὰ τοῦ τοιούτου ἔθνους παρὰ τοῦ βασιλέως κατ’ αὐτῶν ἰσχὺν ἐν τῷ ἐκείνους κατὰ Ῥωμαίων ἐκστρατεύειν. Οἱ ⟨γὰρ⟩ Πατζινακῖται, καὶ τῇ πρὸς τὸν βασιλέα φιλίᾳ συνδούμενοι καὶ παρ’ ἐκείνου διὰ γραμμάτων καὶ δώρων ἀναπειθόμενοι, δύνανται ῥᾳδίως 10

V 21 τῶν V edd.: τὸν P ‖ διαβήσωσιν edd.

2, 3, 4

Pechenegs. For they buy of them horned cattle and horses and sheep, whereby they live more easily and comfortably, since none of the aforesaid animals is found in Russia. Moreover, the Russians are quite unable to set out for wars beyond their borders unless they are at peace with the Pechenegs, because while they are away from their homes, these may come upon them and destroy and outrage their property. And so the Russians, both to avoid being harmed by them and because of the strength of that nation, are the more concerned always to be in alliance with them and to have them for support, so as both to be rid of their enmity and to enjoy the advantage of their assistance.

Nor can the Russians come at this imperial city of the Romans, either for war or for trade, unless they are at peace with the Pechenegs, because when the Russians come with their ships to the barrages of the river and cannot pass through unless they lift their ships off the river and carry them past by portaging them on their shoulders, then the men of this nation of the Pechenegs set upon them, and, as they cannot do two things at once, they are easily routed and cut to pieces.

3. Of the Pechenegs and Turks.

The tribe of the Turks, too, trembles greatly at and fears the said Pechenegs, because they have often been defeated by them and brought to the verge of complete annihilation. Therefore the Turks always look on the Pechenegs with dread, and are held in check by them.

4. Of the Pechenegs and Russians and Turks.

So long as the emperor of the Romans is at peace with the Pechenegs, neither Russians nor Turks can come upon the Roman dominions by force of arms, nor can they exact from the Romans large and inflated sums in money and goods as the price of peace, for they fear the strength of this nation which the emperor can turn against them while they are campaigning against the Romans. *For* the Pechenegs, if they are leagued in friendship with the emperor and won over by him through letters and gifts, can easily

---

3. 5 Πατζινακῖται Be Πατζινακίται F¹ Me Ba: Πατζινάκαι P ‖ ἀπ': ὑπ' edd.
4. 4 οἱ *add.* Jenkins ‖ 5 Τούρκοι P ‖ 8 *post* ἰσχὺν *punctum posuerunt* P V Me Ba Migne ‖ *post* ἐκστρατεύειν *punctum posuerunt* P V F Be *comma posuerunt* Ba Migne ‖ 9 γὰρ *add.* Moravcsik: δὲ *add.* F¹ Be ‖ Πατζινακίται P.

4, 5, 6

κατὰ τῆς χώρας τῶν τε ῾Ρῶς καὶ τῶν Τούρκων ἐπέρχεσθαι καὶ ἐξανδρα-
ποδίζεσθαι τὰ τούτων γύναια καὶ παιδάρια καὶ ληΐζεσθαι τὴν χώραν
αὐτῶν.

71Be   5. Π ε ρ ὶ τ ῶ ν Π α τ ζ ι ν α κ ι τ ῶ ν κ α ὶ τ ῶ ν
Β ο υ λ γ ά ρ ω ν.

"Οτι καὶ τοῖς Βουλγάροις φοβερώτερος ἂν εἶναι δόξειεν ὁ τῶν
9ʳP ῾Ρωμαί|ων βασιλεύς, καὶ ἀνάγκην ἡσυχίας ἐπιτιθέναι τούτοις δύναται
ἐκ τοῦ μετὰ τῶν Πατζινακιτῶν εἰρηνεύειν, ἐπειδὴ καὶ πρὸς αὐτοὺς 5
τοὺς Βουλγάρους οἱ εἰρημένοι Πατζινακῖται πλησιάζουσιν, καὶ ἡνίκα
βουληθῶσιν, ἢ δι᾿ οἰκεῖον κέρδος ἢ τῇ πρὸς τὸν βασιλέα ῾Ρωμαίων
χάριτι εὐχερῶς δύνανται κατὰ Βουλγαρίας ἐκστρατεύειν καὶ ἀπὸ τοῦ
περιόντος πλήθους καὶ τῆς ἰσχύος αὐτῶν ὑπερνικᾶν αὐτοὺς καὶ ἡττᾶν.
Διὰ τοῦτο καὶ οἱ Βούλγαροι ἀγῶνα καὶ σπουδὴν διηνεκῶς ἔχουσι τοῦ 10
εἰρηνεύειν καὶ ὁμονοεῖν μετὰ τῶν Πατζινακιτῶν. ᾿Εκ τοῦ γὰρ πολλάκις
ὑπ᾿ αὐτῶν καταπολεμηθῆναι καὶ πραιδευθῆναι τῇ πείρᾳ ἐγνώκασι
9ᵛP καλὸν καὶ συμφέρον | εἶναι τὸ εἰρηνεύειν ἀεὶ πρὸς αὐτούς.

6. Π ε ρ ὶ τ ῶ ν Π α τ ζ ι ν α κ ι τ ῶ ν κ α ὶ Χ ε ρ σ ω ν ι τ ῶ ν.

"Οτι καὶ ἕτερος λαὸς τῶν τοιούτων Πατζινακιτῶν τῷ μέρει
τῆς Χερσῶνος παράκεινται, οἵτινες καὶ πραγματεύονται μετὰ τῶν
Χερσωνιτῶν, καὶ ποιοῦσι τὰς δουλείας αὐτῶν τε καὶ τοῦ βασιλέως εἴς
τε τὴν ῾Ρωσίαν καὶ Χαζαρίαν καὶ τὴν Ζιχίαν καὶ εἰς πάντα τὰ ἐκεῖθεν 5
μέρη, δηλονότι λαμβάνοντες παρὰ τῶν Χερσωνιτῶν τὸν προσυμπεφωνη-
72Be μένον μισθὸν ὑπὲρ τῆς τοιαύτης διακονίας κατὰ τὸ | ἀνῆκον τῆς δουλείας
καὶ τοῦ κόπου αὐτῶν, οἷον βλαττία, πράνδια, χαρέρια, σημέντα, πέπεριν,
10ʳP δερμάτια ἀληθινὰ Πάρ|θικα καὶ ἕτερα εἴδη τὰ ὑπ᾿ αὐτῶν ἐπιζητούμενα,
καθὼς ἂν ἕκαστος Χερσωνίτης ἕκαστον Πατζινακίτην πείσῃ συμφωνῶν 10
ἢ πεισθῇ. ᾿Ελεύθεροι γὰρ ὄντες καὶ οἷον αὐτόνομοι οἱ τοιοῦτοι Πατζινακῖται οὐδεμίαν δουλείαν ἄνευ μισθοῦ ποιοῦσί ποτε.

F   6. 8 οἷον — 9 ἐπιζητούμενα cf. Eparch. bibl. IX. 6., ed. I. et P. Zepos,
Jus Graecoromanum II. p. 382.   9 Πάρθικα: cf. Ioannes Lydus,
De magistr. II. 13., ed. Wuensch p. 68, 23—24.

4, 5, 6

come upon the country both of the Russians and of the Turks, and enslave their women and children and ravage their country.

5. Of the Pechenegs and the Bulgarians.

To the Bulgarians also the emperor of the Romans will appear more formidable, and can impose on them the need for tranquillity, if he is at peace with the Pechenegs, because the said Pechenegs are neighbours to these Bulgarians also, and when they wish, either for private gain or to do a favour to the emperor of the Romans, they can easily march against Bulgaria, and with their preponderating multitude and their strength overwhelm and defeat them. And so the Bulgarians also continually struggle and strive to maintain peace and harmony with the Pechenegs. For from having frequently been crushingly defeated and plundered by them, they have learned by experience the value and advantage of being always at peace with them.

6. Of the Pechenegs and Chersonites.

Yet another folk of these Pechenegs lies over against the district of Cherson; they trade with the Chersonites, and perform services for them and for the emperor in Russia and Chazaria and Zichia and all the parts beyond: that is to say, they receive from the Chersonites a prearranged remuneration in respect of this service proportionate to their labour and trouble, in the form of pieces of purple cloth, ribbons, loosely woven cloths, gold brocade, pepper, scarlet or «Parthian» leather, and other commodities which they require, according to a contract which each Chersonite may make or agree to with an individual Pecheneg. For these Pechenegs are free men and, so to say, independent, and never perform any service without remuneration.

V   5. 1 τῶν² om. V edd. ‖ 6 Πατζινακῖται P.
       6. 1 Χερσωνίτων P ‖ 4 Χερσωνίτων P ‖ 6 Χερσωνίτων P ‖ 8 χεράρια Meursius ‖ σήμεντα edd. ‖ πέπερι Ba Be ‖ 9 post ἀληθινὰ et πάρδικα punctum posuit P Πάρθικα scr. Moravcsik Παρθικὰ coni. Bekker Šestakov: πάρδικα P edd. ‖ 11/2 Πατζινακῖται P.

54

7. Περὶ τῶν ἀπὸ Χερσῶνος ἀποστελλομένων
βασιλικῶν ἐν Πατζινακίᾳ.

Ὅτι ἡνίκα περάσῃ βασιλικὸς εἰς Χερσῶνα ἕνεκα τῆς τοιαύτης
διακονίας, ὀφείλει εὐθὺς ἀποστέλλειν εἰς Πατζινακίαν καὶ ἐπιζητεῖν
ὄψιδας παρ᾽ αὐτῶν καὶ διασώστας, καὶ ἐρχομένων αὐτῶν, τοὺς μὲν 5
ὄψιδας εἰς τὸ κάστρον Χερσῶνος κρατουμένους καταλιμπάνειν, αὐτὸς
10ᵛP δὲ μετὰ | τῶν διασωστῶν πρὸς Πατζινακίαν ἀπέρχεσθαι καὶ τὰ ἐντε-
ταλμένα ἐπιτελεῖν. Οἱ δὲ τοιοῦτοι Πατζινακῖται ἄπληστοι ὄντες καὶ
τῶν παρ᾽ αὐτοῖς σπανίων ὀξεῖς ἐπιθυμηταὶ ἀνέδην ἐπιζητοῦσιν ξενάλια
ἱκανά, οἱ μὲν ὄψιδες ἄλλα μὲν λόγῳ αὐτῶν καὶ ἄλλα λόγῳ τῶν αὐτῶν 10
γυναικῶν, οἱ δὲ ἀποσῶσται τὰ μὲν ὑπὲρ τοῦ κόπου αὐτῶν, τὰ δὲ ὑπὲρ
τοῦ κόπου τῶν ἀλόγων αὐτῶν. Εἶτα, εἰσερχομένου τοῦ βασιλικοῦ εἰς
τὴν χώραν αὐτῶν, ζητοῦσι πρότερον τὰ τοῦ βασιλέως δῶρα, καὶ πάλιν,
ὅτε κορέσουσι τοὺς ἀνθρώπους αὐτῶν, ζητοῦσι τὰ τῶν γυναικῶν αὐτῶν
καὶ τῶν γονέων αὐτῶν. Ἀλλὰ καὶ ὅσοι ἐν τῷ ἀποσώζειν αὐτὸν ὑποστρέ- 15
73Be
φοντα πρὸς Χερσῶνα κατέλθωσι | μετ᾽ αὐτοῦ, ζητοῦσι παρ᾽ αὐτοῦ
11ʳP
ῥογευθῆναι διὰ τὸν κόπον αὐτῶν τε καὶ τῶν ἀλόγων αὐτῶν.

8. Περὶ τῶν ἀπὸ τῆς θεοφυλάκτου πόλεως ἀποστελλομένων βασιλικῶν μετὰ χελανδίων διά τε
τοῦ Δανουβίου καὶ Δάναπρι καὶ Δάναστρι
ποταμοῦ ἐν Πατζινακίᾳ.

Ὅτι καὶ εἰς τὸ μέρος τῆς Βουλγαρίας καθέζεται λαὸς τῶν Πατζι- 5
νακιτῶν, ἐπὶ τὸ μέρος τοῦ Δάναπρι καὶ τοῦ Δάναστρι καὶ τῶν ἑτέρων
τῶν ἐκεῖσε ὄντων ποταμῶν. Καὶ βασιλικοῦ ἀποστελλομένου ἐντεῦθεν
μετὰ χελανδίων, δύναται καὶ χωρὶς τοῦ εἰς Χερσῶνα ἀπελθεῖν ἐνταῦθα
11ᵛP συντόμως καὶ ταχέως εὑρίσκειν τοὺς αὐτοὺς | Πατζινακίτας, οὓς καὶ
εὑρὼν μηνύει διὰ ἀνθρώπου αὐτοῦ ὁ βασιλικός, ἐντὸς τῶν χελανδίων 10
μένων καὶ μεθ᾽ ἑαυτοῦ τὰ βασιλικὰ ἐπιφερόμενος καὶ φυλάττων ἐν τοῖς
χελανδίοις πράγματα. Καὶ κατέρχονται πρὸς αὐτόν, καὶ ὅτε κατέλθωσιν,
δίδωσι πρὸς αὐτοὺς ὁ βασιλικὸς ἀνθρώπους αὐτοῦ ὄψιδας, καὶ λαμβάνει
καὶ αὐτὸς ἀπὸ τῶν τοιούτων Πατζινακιτῶν ἑτέρους ὄψιδας, καὶ κρατεῖ
αὐτοὺς εἰς τὰ χελάνδια, καὶ τότε συμφωνεῖ μετ᾽ αὐτῶν· καὶ ὅτε 15

V   7. 1/2 τῶν ἀποστελλομένων βασιλικῶν ἀπὸ Χερσῶνος V edd. ‖ 5 ὄψηδας
P ‖ 8 Πατζινακίται P ‖ 9 σπανιῶν P ‖ ἀναίδην P edd. ‖ 14 κορέσουσι
versionem Laskin secutus coni. Moravcsik: χωρήσουσι P χωρίσουσι coni.
Kukules.

7. Of the dispatch of imperial agents from Cherson to Patzinacia.

When an imperial agent goes over to Cherson on this service, he must at once send to Patzinacia and demand of them hostages and an escort, and on their arrival he must leave the hostages under guard in the city of Cherson, and himself go off with the escort to Patzinacia and carry out his instructions. Now these Pechenegs, who are ravenous and keenly covetous of articles rare among them, are shameless in their demands for generous gifts, the hostages demanding this for themselves and that for their wives, and the escort something for their own trouble and some more for the wear and tear of their cattle. Then, when the imperial agent enters their country, they first ask for the emperor's gifts, and then again, when these have glutted the menfolk, they ask for the presents for their wives and parents. Also, all who come with him to escort him on his way back to Cherson demand payment from him for their trouble and the wear and tear of their cattle.

8. Of the dispatch of imperial agents with ships of war from the city protected of God to Patzinacia along the Danube and Dnieper and Dniester river.

In the region of Bulgaria also is settled a folk of the Pechenegs, toward the region of the Dnieper and the Dniester and the other rivers of those parts. And when an imperial agent is dispatched from here with ships of war, he may, without going to Cherson, shortly and swiftly find these same Pechenegs here; and when he has found them, the imperial agent sends a message to them by his man, himself remaining on board the ships of war, carrying along with him and guarding in the ships of war the imperial goods. And they come down to him, and when they come down, the imperial agent gives them hostages of his men, and himself takes other hostages of these Pechenegs, and holds them in the ships of war, and then he makes

---

8. 5/6 Πατζινακίτων P ‖ 8 Χερσῶνα Be: Χερσῶνος P Me Ba ‖ 14 Πατζινακίτων P ‖

8, 9

ποιήσουσιν οἱ Πατζινακῖται πρὸς τὸν βασιλικὸν τοὺς ὅρκους κατὰ τὰ
12ʳP ζάκανα αὐτῶν, ἐπιδίδωσιν αὐτοῖς τὰς βασιλικὰς δωρεάς, καὶ ἀ|ναλαμβά-
νεται φίλους ἐξ αὐτῶν, ὅσους βούλεται, καὶ ὑποστρέφει.

Οὕτω δὲ χρὴ
συμφωνεῖν μετ' αὐτῶν, ὥστε, ὅπου ἂν χρεωποιηθῇ αὐτοὺς ὁ βασιλεύς,
ποιήσωσι δουλείαν, εἴτε εἰς τοὺς Ῥῶς, εἴτε εἰς τοὺς Βουλγάρους, εἴτε 20
74Be καὶ εἰς τοὺς Τούρκους. Εἰσὶ γὰρ δυνατοὶ | τοῦ πάντας τούτους πολεμεῖν,
καὶ πολλάκις κατ' αὐτῶν ἐλθόντες, φοβεροὶ νῦν καθεστήκασιν. Καὶ
τοῦτο δῆλον καὶ ἐντεῦθέν ἐστιν. Τοῦ γὰρ κληρικοῦ Γαβριὴλ ποτε πρὸς
τοὺς Τούρκους ἀποσταλέντος ἀπὸ κελεύσεως βασιλικῆς καὶ πρὸς αὐτοὺς
εἰπόντος, ὅτι· «Ὁ βασιλεὺς δηλοποιεῖ ὑμᾶς ἀπελθεῖν καὶ ἀποδιῶξαι 25
12ᵛP τοὺς Πατζινακίτας ἀπὸ | τοῦ τόπου αὐτῶν καὶ καθεσθῆναι ὑμᾶς (ὑμεῖς
γὰρ καὶ πρότερον ἐκεῖσε ἐκαθέζεσθε) πρὸς τὸ εἶναι πλησίον τῆς βασιλείας μου, καὶ ὅτε θέλω, ἀποστέλλω, καὶ ἐν τάχει εὑρίσκω ὑμᾶς»,
πάντες οἱ ἄρχοντες τῶν Τούρκων μιᾷ φωνῇ ἐξεβόησαν, ὅτι· «Ἡμεῖς
μετὰ τοὺς Πατζινακίτας ἑαυτοὺς οὐ βάλλομεν· οὐ γὰρ δυνάμεθα πολε- 30
μεῖν πρὸς αὐτούς, ὅτι καὶ χώρα μεγάλη καὶ λαὸς πολὺς καὶ κακὰ παιδία
εἰσί· καὶ τοῦ λοιποῦ τὸν λόγον τοῦτον πρὸς ἡμᾶς μὴ εἴπῃς· οὐ γὰρ
ἀγαπῶμεν αὐτόν.»

Ὅτι καὶ οἱ Πατζινακῖται ἐκεῖθεν τοῦ Δανάπρεως ποταμοῦ μετὰ
τὸ ἔαρ διέρχονται, καὶ ἀεὶ ἐκεῖσε καλοκαιρίζουσιν. 35

13ʳP 9. Περὶ τῶν ἀπὸ Ῥωσίας ἐρχομένων Ῥῶς
μετὰ τῶν μονοξύλων ἐν Κωνσταντινουπόλει.

Ὅτι τὰ ἀπὸ τῆς ἔξω Ῥωσίας μονόξυλα κατερχόμενα ἐν Κωνσταντινουπόλει εἰσὶ μὲν ἀπὸ τοῦ Νεμογαρδάς, ἐν ᾧ Σφενδοσθλάβος,
ὁ υἱὸς Ἴγγωρ, τοῦ ἄρχοντος Ῥωσίας, ἐκαθέζετο, εἰσὶ δὲ καὶ ἀπὸ τὸ 5
κάστρον τὴν Μιλινίσκαν καὶ ἀπὸ Τελιούτζαν καὶ Τζερνιγῶγαν καὶ
ἀπὸ τοῦ Βουσεγραδέ. Ταῦτα οὖν ἅπαντα διὰ τοῦ ποταμοῦ κατέρχονται
75Be Δανάπρεως, καὶ ἐπισυνάγονται εἰς τὸ κάστρον | τὸ Κιοάβα, τὸ ἐπονομα-
ζόμενον Σαμβατάς. Οἱ δὲ Σκλάβοι, οἱ πακτιῶται αὐτῶν, οἱ Κριβηταιη-
13ᵛP νοὶ λεγόμενοι, καὶ οἱ Λενζανῆνοι καὶ αἱ λοιπαὶ | Σκλαβηνίαι εἰς τὰ ὄρη 10
αὐτῶν κόπτουσι τὰ μονόξυλα ἐν τῷ τοῦ χειμῶνος καιρῷ, καὶ καταρτί-
σαντες αὐτά, τοῦ καιροῦ ἀνοιγομένου, ἡνίκα διαλυθῇ ὁ παγετός, εἰς
τὰς πλησίον οὔσας λίμνας εἰσάγουσιν αὐτά. Καὶ ἐπειδὴ ἐκεῖναι εἰσβάλ-
λουσιν εἰς τὸν ποταμὸν τὸν Δάναπριν, ἀπὸ τῶν ἐκεῖσε οὗτοι εἰς τὸν

V 16 Πατζινακίται P ‖ 34 Πατζινακίται P.
9. 1 ante Ῥωσίας add. τῆς edd. ‖ 4 Νεμογαρδάς: Νεογαρδα (sine acc.)
coni. Bayer Νεύογαρδα (sic) coni. Rački Νεβογαρδάς coni. Bury Obolensky
Νευογαρδάς Kukules ‖

8, 9

agreement with them; and when the Pechenegs have taken their oaths to the imperial agent according to their 'zakana', he presents them with the imperial gifts, and takes from among them as many 'friends' as he sees fit, and returns. Agreement must be made with them on this condition, that wherever the emperor calls upon them, they are to serve him, whether against the Russians, or against the Bulgarians, or again against the Turks. For they are able to make war upon all these, and as they have often come against them, are now regarded by them with dread. And this is clear from what follows. For once when the cleric Gabriel was dispatched by imperial mandate to the Turks and said to them, «The emperor declares that you are to go and expel the Pechenegs from their place and settle yourselves there (for in former days you used to be settled there yourselves) so that you may be near to my imperial majesty, and when I wish, I may send and find you speedily», then all the chief men of the Turks cried aloud with one voice, «We are not putting ourselves on the track of the Pechenegs; for we cannot fight them, because their country is great and their people numerous and they are the devil's brats; and do not say this to us again; for we do not like it!»

When spring is over, the Pechenegs cross to the far side of the Dnieper river, and always pass the summer there.

9. Of the coming of the Russians in 'monoxyla' from Russia to Constantinople.

The 'monoxyla' which come down from outer Russia to Constantinople are from Novgorod, where Sviatoslav, son of Igor, prince of Russia, had his seat, and others from the city of Smolensk and from Teliutza and Chernigov and from Vyshegrad. All these come down the river Dnieper, and are collected together at the city of Kiev, also called Sambatas. Their Slav tributaries, the so-called Krivichians and the Lenzanenes and the rest of the Slavonic regions, cut the 'monoxyla' on their mountains in time of winter, and when they have prepared them, as spring approaches, and the ice melts, they bring them on to the neighbouring lakes. And since these *lakes* debouch into the river Dnieper, they enter thence on to this same

---

6 Μιλινίσκαν: ⟨Σ⟩μιλινίσκαν *coni.* Rački ‖ Τελιούτζαν: τε Λιούτζαν *coni.* Šafarik Manojlović τε Λιού⟨β⟩τζαν *coni.* Rački ‖ Τζερνιγώγαν V edd. Τζερνιγώϋαν *coni.* Rački ‖ 8 εἰς (*etiam* Bandurius): ἐπὶ edd. ‖ 10 οἱ λοιποὶ Σκλαβίνιοι edd. ‖ Σκλαβινίαι P ‖ 11/2 καταρτήσαντες P edd. ‖ 12 αὐτά *corr.* Moravcsik: αὐτῶν P edd. ‖ 13 ἐκεῖνα edd. ‖ 14 τὸν¹ *om.* edd. ‖

58

9

αὐτὸν ποταμὸν εἰσέρχονται, καὶ ἀπέρχονται εἰς τὸν Κίοβα, καὶ σύρουσιν 15
εἰς τὴν ἐξάρτισιν, καὶ ἀπεμπολοῦσιν αὐτὰ εἰς τοὺς Ῥῶς. Οἱ δὲ Ῥῶς
σκαφίδια καὶ μόνα ταῦτα ἀγοράζοντες, τὰ παλαιὰ αὐτῶν μονόξυλα
καταλύοντες, ἐξ αὐτῶν βάλλουσιν πέλλας καὶ σκαρμοὺς εἰς αὐτὰ καὶ
14ʳP λοιπὰς | χρείας * * * ἐξοπλίζουσιν αὐτά. Καὶ Ἰουνίου μηνὸς διὰ τοῦ
ποταμοῦ Δανάπρεως ἀποκινοῦντες, κατέρχονται εἰς τὸ Βιτετζέβη, 20
ὅπερ ἐστί πακτιωτικὸν κάστρον τῶν Ῥῶς, καὶ συναθροιζόμενοι ἐκεῖσε
μέχρι δύο καὶ τριῶν ἡμερῶν, ἡνίκα ἂν ἅπαντα ἀποσυναχθῶσι τὰ μονόξυλα, τότε ἀποκινοῦσιν, καὶ κατέρχονται διὰ τοῦ εἰρημένου Δανάπρεως
ποταμοῦ. Καὶ πρῶτον μὲν ἔρχονται εἰς τὸν πρῶτον φραγμόν, τὸν ἐπονομαζόμενον Ἐσσουπῆ, ὃ ἑρμηνεύεται Ῥωσιστὶ καὶ Σκλαβηνιστὶ ʽμὴ κοιμᾶ- 25
σαι'· ὁ δὲ τούτου φραγμὸς τοσοῦτόν ἐστιν στενός, ὅσον τὸ πλάτος τοῦ
14ᵛP τζυκανιστηρίου· μέσον δὲ αὐτοῦ πέτραι εἰσὶ ῥιζιμαῖαι | ὑψηλαὶ νησίων
76Be δίκην ἀποφαινόμεναι. Πρὸς αὐτὰς οὖν ἐρχόμενον τὸ ὕδωρ καὶ | πλημμυ-
ροῦν κἀκεῖθεν ἀποκρημνιζόμενον πρὸς τὸ κάτω μέρος ἦχον μέγαν καὶ
φόβον ἀποτελεῖ. Καὶ διὰ τοῦτο μέσον αὐτῶν οὐ τολμῶσιν οἱ Ῥῶς διελ- 30
θεῖν, ἀλλὰ πλησίον σκαλώσαντες καὶ τοὺς μὲν ἀνθρώπους ἐκβαλόντες
εἰς τὴν ξηράν, τὰ δὲ λοιπὰ πράγματα ἐάσαντες εἰς τὰ μονόξυλα, εἶθ'
οὕτως γυμνοὶ τοῖς ποσὶν αὐτῶν ψηλαφοῦντες * * *, ἵνα μή τινι λίθῳ
προσκρούσωσιν. Τοῦτο δὲ ποιοῦσιν οἱ μὲν πλώρᾳ, οἱ δὲ μέσον, οἱ δὲ
καὶ εἰς τὴν πρύμναν μετὰ κονταρίων κοντοβευόμενοι, καὶ μετὰ τοιαύτης 35
ἁπάσης ἀκριβείας διέρχονται τὸν τοιοῦτον πρῶτον φραγμὸν διὰ τῆς
15ʳP γωνίας καὶ τῆς ὄχθης τοῦ ποταμοῦ. Ἡνίκα δὲ διέλθωσι | τὸν τοιοῦτον
φραγμόν, πάλιν ἀπὸ τῆς ξηρᾶς ἀναλαμβανόμενοι τοὺς λοιποὺς ἀποπλέουσι, καὶ κατέρχονται εἰς τὸν ἕτερον φραγμόν, τὸν ἐπιλεγόμενον
Ῥωσιστὶ μὲν Οὐλβορσί, Σκλαβηνιστὶ δὲ Ὀστροβουνιπράχ, ὅπερ ἑρμη- 40
νεύεται ʽτὸ νησίον τοῦ φραγμοῦ'. Ἔστιν κἀκεῖνος ὅμοιος τῷ πρώτῳ,
χαλεπός τε καὶ δυσδιέξοδος. Καὶ πάλιν ἐκβαλόντες τὸν λαὸν διαβιβάζουσι
τὰ μονόξυλα, καθὼς καὶ πρότερον. Ὁμοίως δὲ διέρχονται καὶ τὸν τρίτον
φραγμόν, τὸν λεγόμενον Γελανδρί, ὃ ἑρμηνεύεται Σκλαβηνιστὶ ʽἦχος
φραγμοῦ', εἶθ' οὕτως τὸν τέταρτον φραγμόν, τὸν μέγαν, τὸν ἐπιλεγόμε- 45
νον Ῥωσιστὶ μὲν Ἀειφόρ, Σκλαβηνιστὶ δὲ Νεασήτ, διότι φωλεύουσιν
οἱ πελεκᾶνοι εἰς τὰ λιθάρια τοῦ φραγμοῦ. Ἐν τούτῳ οὖν τῷ φραγμῷ
15ᵛP σκαλώνουσιν ἅπαντα | εἰς τὴν γῆν ὀρθόπλωρα, καὶ ἐξέρχονται οἱ ὡρι-

---

V 15 τὸν: τὸ Meursius Ba Be ǁ Κιόβα edd. ǁ 16 ἐξάρτησιν P edd. ǁ 18 ante
πέλλας add. καὶ edd. ǁ 19 lac. ind. Moravcsik καὶ οὕτως addendum coni. Bekker ǁ 24/5 τὸν ἐπονομαζόμενον Ῥωσιστὶ ⟨μὲν...⟩, Σκλαβινιστὶ ⟨δὲ⟩ Νεσσουπῆ, ὃ
ἑρμηνεύεται coni. Kunik aliquid excidisse susp. Thomsen ǁ 25 Ἐσσουπῆ: Νεσσουπί
coni. Bandurius   Νεσσουπῆ coni. Bayer Thunmann Safarik Kunik Gedeonov
Thomsen Hruševskyj ǁ Σκλαβινιστῇ P ǁ 25/6 κοιμᾶσαι (etiam Cobet):

9

river, and come down to Kiev, and draw *the ships* along to be finished and sell them to the Russians. The Russians buy these bottoms only, furnishing them with oars and rowlocks and other tackle from their old 'monoxyla', which they dismantle; *and so* they fit them out. And in the month of June they move off down the river Dnieper and come to Vitichev, which is a tributary city of the Russians, and there they gather during two or three days; and when all the 'monoxyla' are collected together, then they set out, and come down the said Dnieper river. And first they come to the first barrage, called Essoupi, which means in Russian and Slavonic 'Do not sleep!'; the barrage itself is as narrow as the width of the Polo-ground; in the middle of it are rooted high rocks, which stand out like islands. Against these, then, comes the water and wells up and dashes down over the other side, with a mighty and terrific din. Therefore the Russians do not venture to pass between them, but put in to the bank hard by, disembarking the men on to dry land leaving the rest of the goods on board the 'monoxyla'; they then strip and, feeling with their feet to avoid striking on a rock, ***. This they do, some at the prow, some amidships, while others again, in the stern, punt with poles; and with all this careful procedure they pass this first barrage, edging round under the river-bank. When they have passed this barrage, they re-embark the others from the dry land and sail away, and come down to the second barrage, called in Russian Oulvorsi, and in Slavonic Ostrovouniprach, which means 'the Island of the Barrage'. This one is like the first, awkward and not to be passed through. Once again they disembark the men and convey the 'monoxyla' past, as on the first occasion. Similarly they pass the third barrage also, called Gelandri, which means in Slavonic 'Noise of the Barrage', and then the fourth barrage, the big one, called in Russian Aeifor, and in Slavonic Neasit, because the pelicans nest in the stones of the barrage. At this barrage all put into land prow foremost,

---

κοιμάσαι Me Ba κοιμᾶσθαι Be ‖ 27 ῥιζημαῖαι P Me Ba Cobet: ῥιζικαῖαι Du Cange Be ‖ 29 μέγαν edd.: μέγα P ‖ 33 *lac. ind.* διέρχονται *vel* διαβάζουσιν *excidisse coniciens* Moravcsik σύρουσιν *coni.* Kyriakides σύρουσιν αὐτά *coni.* Dujčev ‖ 34 Τοῦτο δὲ ποιοῦσιν: ταῦτα, ὁδοποιοῦσιν *coni.* Jenkins ‖ πλώρᾳ *coni.* Jenkins πλῶρα P: πλῶραν Ba Be πρῶραν Meursius ‖ 35 κοντοβευόμενοι: κοντο- βολούμενοι *vel* κοντευόμενοι *coni.* Meursius ‖ 36 πρῶτον V edd.: α΄ P ‖ 40 Οὐλβοροί: Οὐλμβοροί *seu* Οὐλμοροί *coni.* Thunmann Οὐλμφόρς *coni.* Zeuss ‖ 41 ὅμοιως P ‖ 42 χαλεπῶς P ‖ δυσδιέξοδος P¹ V¹ edd.: δισδιέξοδος P ‖ 44 τὸν λεγόμενον ⟨'Ρωσιστὶ μὲν⟩ Γελανδ {ρ }ί, Σκλαβινιστὶ ⟨δὲ...⟩, ὃ ἑρμηνεύεται *coni.* Kunik *aliquid excidisse susp.* Thomsen ‖ Γελανδρὶ: Γελανδί *coni.* Kunik Gedeonov ‖ 44/5 Σκλα- βινιστὶ ⟨σβόνετζ ὅ ἐστι⟩ ἦχος φραγμοῦ *coni.* Lehrberg ‖ 45 τέταρτον V edd.: δ΄ P ‖ μέγαν edd.: μέγα P ‖ 46 'Αειφόρ (*etiam* V¹ F Cobet): 'Αειφάρ V edd. ‖ Νεασήτ: Νενασήτ *coni.* Thomsen ‖ 48 *post* ἅπαντα *add.* τὰ μονόξυλα τὰ V ‖ ὀρθόπρωρα Meursius ‖ 48/9 ὁρισμενοι (*sine acc.*) P ‖

9

σμένοι ἄνδρες φυλάττειν τὴν βίγλαν μετ' αὐτῶν, καὶ ἀπέρχονται, καὶ
τὰς βίγλας οὗτοι διὰ τοὺς Πατζινακίτας ἀγρύπνως φυλάττουσιν. Οἱ δὲ 50
77Be λοιποὶ τὰ | πράγματα, ἅπερ ἔχουσιν εἰς τὰ μονόξυλα, ἀναλαμβανόμενοι,
τὰ ψυχάρια μετὰ τῶν ἁλύσεων διὰ τοῦ ξηροῦ αὐτὰ διαβιβάζουσι
μίλια ἕξ, ἕως ἂν διέλθωσι τὸν φραγμόν. Εἶθ' οὕτως οἱ μὲν σύροντες,
οἱ δὲ καὶ εἰς τοὺς ὤμους βαστάζοντες τὰ αὐτῶν μονόξυλα εἰς τὸ τοῦ
φραγμοῦ ἐκεῖθεν μέρος διαβιβάζουσιν· καὶ οὕτως ῥίπτοντες αὐτὰ εἰς 55
τὸν ποταμὸν καὶ τὰ πετζιμέντα αὐτῶν ἐμβλησκόμενοι, εἰσέρχονται,
16ʳP καὶ αὖθις ἐναποπλέουσιν. Ἀπερχόμε|νοι δὲ εἰς τὸν πέμπτον φραγμόν,
τὸν ἐπονομαζόμενον Ῥωσιστὶ μὲν Βαρουφόρος, Σκλαβηνιστὶ δὲ Βουλνηπράχ, διότι μεγάλην λίμνην ἀποτελεῖ, πάλιν εἰς τὰς τοῦ ποταμοῦ γωνίας
τὰ αὐτῶν μονόξυλα διαβιβάσαντες, καθὼς καὶ εἰς τὸν πρῶτον φραγμὸν 60
καὶ δεύτερον, καταλαμβάνουσι τὸν ἕκτον φραγμόν, λεγόμενον μὲν
Ῥωσιστὶ Λεάντι, Σκλαβηνιστὶ δὲ Βερούτζη, ὅ ἐστιν 'βράσμα νεροῦ',
καὶ διαβαίνουσι καὶ αὐτὸν ὁμοίως. Καὶ ἀπὸ τούτου ἀποπλέουσι καὶ
πρὸς τὸν ἕβδομον φραγμόν, τὸν ἐπιλεγόμενον Ῥωσιστὶ μὲν Στρούκουν,
Σκλαβηνιστὶ δὲ Ναπρεζή, ὃ ἑρμηνεύεται 'μικρὸς φραγμός'. Καὶ διαβαί- 65
νουσιν εἰς τὸ λεγόμενον πέραμα τοῦ Κραρίου, ἐν ᾧ διαπερῶσιν ἀπὸ
16ᵛP Ῥωσίας οἱ Χερσωνῖται | καὶ οἱ Πατζινακῖται ἐπὶ Χερσῶνα, ἔχον τὸ
αὐτὸ πέραμα τὸ μὲν πλάτος, ὅσον τοῦ ἱπποδρομίου, τὸ δὲ ὕψος ἀπὸ κάτω
ἕως ὅτου προκύπτουσιν ὕφαλοι, ὅσον καὶ φθάζειν σαγίτταν τοῦ τοξεύον-
τος ἔνθεν ἐκεῖσε. Ὅθεν καὶ εἰς τὸν τοιοῦτον τόπον κατέρχονται οἱ 70
Πατζινακῖται, καὶ πολεμοῦσι τοὺς Ῥῶς. Μετὰ δὲ τὸ διελθεῖν τὸν
78Be τοιοῦτον τόπον τὴν νῆσον, τὴν ἐπιλεγομένην | ὁ Ἅγιος Γρηγόριος
καταλαμβάνουσιν, ἐν ᾗ νήσῳ καὶ τὰς θυσίας αὐτῶν ἐπιτελοῦσιν διὰ τὸ
ἐκεῖσε ἵστασθαι παμμεγέθη δρῦν, καὶ θύουσι πετεινοὺς ζῶντας. Πηγνύουσι δὲ καὶ σαγίττας γυρόθεν, ἄλλοι δὲ καὶ ψωμία καὶ κρέατα, καὶ 75
ἐξ ὧν ἔχει ἕκαστος, ὡς τὸ ἔθος αὐτῶν ἐπικρατεῖ. Ῥίπτουσι δὲ καὶ
17ʳP σκαρφία περὶ τῶν πετεινῶν, εἴτε σφάξαι αὐτούς, | εἴτε καὶ φαγεῖν, εἴτε
καὶ ζῶντας ἐάσειν αὐτούς. Ἀπὸ δὲ τοῦ νησίου τούτου Πατζινακίτην οἱ
Ῥῶς οὐ φοβοῦνται, ἕως ἂν φθάσωσιν εἰς τὸν ποταμὸν τὸν Σελινάν.
Εἶθ' οὕτως ἀποκινοῦντες ἐξ αὐτοῦ μέχρι τεσσάρων ἡμερῶν ἀποπλέουσιν, 80
ἕως οὗ καταλάβωσιν εἰς τὴν λίμνην τοῦ ποταμοῦ στόμιον οὖσαν, ἐν ᾗ
ἐστιν καὶ ἡ νῆσος τοῦ Ἁγίου Αἰθερίου. Καταλαβόντες οὖν οὗτοι τὴν
τοιαύτην νῆσον, προσαναπαύουσιν ἑαυτοὺς ἐκεῖσε ἕως δύο καὶ τριῶν
ἡμερῶν. Καὶ πάλιν τὰ αὐτῶν μονόξυλα, εἰς ὅσας ἂν λίπωνται χρείας,
περιποιοῦνται, τά τε ἄρμενα καὶ τὰ κατάρτια καὶ τὰ αὐχένια, ἅπερ 85

F   72 τὴν νῆσον — Γρηγόριος: cf. Not. episc. (s. XIV.), ed. G. Parthey
p. 130. No 3, 754.

9

and those who are deputed to keep the watch with them get out, and off they go, these men, and keep vigilant watch for the Pechenegs. The remainder, taking up the goods which they have on board the 'monoxyla', conduct the slaves in their chains past by land, six miles, until they are through the barrage. Then, partly dragging their 'monoxyla', partly portaging them on their shoulders, they convey them to the far side of the barrage; and then, putting them on the river and loading up their baggage, they embark themselves, and again sail off in them. When they come to the fifth barrage, called in Russian Varouforos, and in Slavonic Voulniprach, because it forms a large lake, they again convey their 'monoxyla' through at the edges of the river, as at the first and second barrages, and arrive at the sixth barrage, called in Russian Leanti, and in Slavonic Veroutzi, that is 'the Boiling of the Water', and this too they pass similarly. And thence they sail away to the seventh barrage, called in Russian Stroukoun, and in Slavonic Naprezi, which means 'Little Barrage'. This they pass at the so-called ford of *Vrar*, where the Chersonites cross over from Russia and the Pechenegs to Cherson; which ford is as wide as the Hippodrome, and, measured upstream from the bottom as far as the rocks break surface, a bow-shot in length. It is at this point, therefore, that the Pechenegs come down and attack the Russians. After traversing this place, they reach the island called St. Gregory, on which island they perform their sacrifices because a gigantic oak-tree stands there; and they sacrifice live cocks. Arrows, too, they peg in round about, and others bread and meat, or something of whatever each may have, as is their custom. They also throw lots regarding the cocks, whether to slaughter them, or to eat them as well, or to leave them alive. From this island onwards the Russians do not fear the Pecheneg until they reach the river Selinas. So then they start off thence and sail for four days, until they reach the lake which forms the mouth of the river, on which is the island of St. Aitherios. Arrived at this island, they rest themselves there for two or three days. And they re-equip their 'monoxyla' with such tackle as is needed, sails and masts and rudders, which they bring with them. Since this

---

V 51 ἀναλαβόμενοι V edd. ‖ 57 πέμπτον edd.: ε′ P ‖ 58 Σκλαβινιστὶ P ‖ 58/9 Βουλνηπράχ: Βολνοῦτ πράχ *coni.* Zeuss ‖ 59 λίμνην: δίνην *coni.* Lehrberg Zeuss Thomsen Hruševskyj ‖ 61 *ante* δεύτερον *add.* εἰς τὸν V edd. ‖ 62 Λεάντι: Λωάντι *seu* Λωάνδι *coni.* Zeuss ‖ Σκλαβινιστὶ P ‖ 64 ἕβδομον edd.: ζ′ P ‖ Στρούκουν (*etiam* Cobet): Στρούβουν V edd. ‖ 65 Σκλαβινιστὶ P ‖ Ναστρεζή *coni.* Falk ‖ 65/6 διαβαίνοντες Me Be διαβαίνονται Meursius Ba ‖ 66 Κριαρίου *coni.* Vasmer Βραρίου *coni.* Falk ‖ 67 Χερσωνίται P ‖ Πατζινακίται P ‖ 69 προκύπτουσιν ὕφαλοι *coni.* Jenkins: παρακύπτουσιν οἱ φίλοι P edd. ‖ φίλοι: ὀφθαλμοί Ba ‖ φθάνειν V edd. ‖ 71 Πατζινακίται P ‖ πολεμοῦσι V edd.: πολεμῶσι P ‖ 77 εἴτε καὶ φαγεῖν εἴτε καὶ σφάξαι αὐτούς V Me Ba ‖ 78 αὐτούς (*add. etiam* Bandurius): *om.* V edd. ‖ 79 οὐ *om.* Me ‖ 82 Ἐθαιρίου P ‖ 84 αὐτῶν: ἑαυτῶν V edd. ‖ λίπωνται *scr.* Moravcsik λίπονται P: λείπωνται Be ‖

ἐπιφέρονται. Ἐπεὶ δὲ τὸ στόμιον τοῦ τοιούτου ποταμοῦ ἐστιν ἡ τοιαύτη
17ᵛP λίμνη, καθὼς εἴρηται, καὶ | κρατεῖ μέχρι τῆς θαλάσσης, καὶ πρὸς τὴν
θάλασσαν κεῖται ἡ νῆσος τοῦ Ἁγίου Αἰθερίου, ἐκ τῶν ἐκεῖσε ἀπέρχονται
πρὸς τὸν Δάναστριν ποταμόν, καὶ διασωθέντες ἐκεῖσε πάλιν ἀναπαύον-
ται. Ἡνίκα δὲ γένηται καιρὸς ἐπιτήδειος, ἀποσκαλώσαντες ἔρχονται 90
εἰς τὸν ποταμὸν τὸν ἐπιλεγόμενον Ἄσπρον, καὶ ὁμοίως κἀκεῖσε ἀνα-
παυσάμενοι, πάλιν ἀποκινοῦντες ἔρχονται εἰς τὸν Σελινάν, εἰς τὸ τοῦ
Δανουβίου ποταμοῦ λεγόμενον παρακλάδιον. Καὶ ἕως οὗ διέλθωσι τὸν
79Be Σελινὰν | ποταμόν, παρατρέχουσιν αὐτοῖς οἱ Πατζινακῖται. Καὶ ἐὰν
πολλάκις ἡ θάλασσα μονόξυλον εἰς τὴν γῆν ἀπορρίψῃ, σκαλώνουσιν 95
18ʳP ὅλα, ἵνα τοῖς Πατζινακίταις ἀντιπαρα|ταχθῶσιν ὁμοῦ. Ἀπὸ δὲ τὸν
Σελινὰν οὐ φοβοῦνταί τινα, ἀλλὰ τὴν τῆς Βουλγαρίας γῆν ἐνδυσάμενοι,
εἰς τὸ τοῦ Δανουβίου στόμιον ἔρχονται. Ἀπὸ δὲ τοῦ Δανουβίου καταλαμβάνουσιν εἰς τὸν Κωνοπάν, καὶ ἀπὸ τοῦ Κωνοπᾶ εἰς Κωνστάντιαν
* * * εἰς τὸν ποταμὸν Βάρνας, καὶ ἀπὸ Βάρνας ἔρχονται εἰς τὸν ποταμὸν100
τὴν Διτζίναν, ἅπερ πάντα εἰσὶ γῆ τῆς Βουλγαρίας. Ἀπὸ δὲ τῆς Διτζίνας
εἰς τὰ τῆς Μεσημβρίας μέρη καταλαμβάνουσιν, καὶ οὕτως μέχρι τούτων
ὁ πολυώδυνος αὐτῶν καὶ περίφοβος, δυσδιέξοδός τε καὶ χαλεπὸς ἀπο-
περαίνεται πλοῦς. Ἡ δὲ χειμέριος τῶν αὐτῶν Ῥῶς καὶ σκληρὰ διαγωγὴ
ἐστιν αὕτη. Ἡνίκα ὁ Νοέμβριος μὴν εἰσέλθῃ, εὐθέως οἱ αὐτῶν ἐξέρχον-105
18ᵛP ται ἄρχοντες | μετὰ πάντων τῶν Ῥῶς ἀπὸ τὸν Κίαβον, καὶ ἀπέρχονται
εἰς τὰ πολύδια, ὃ λέγεται γύρα, ἤγουν εἰς τὰς Σκλαβηνίας τῶν τε Βερβιάνων καὶ τῶν Δρουγουβιτῶν καὶ Κριβιτζῶν καὶ τῶν Σεβερίων καὶ λοιπῶν
Σκλάβων, οἵτινές εἰσιν πακτιῶται τῶν Ῥῶς. Δι' ὅλου δὲ τοῦ χειμῶνος
ἐκεῖσε διατρεφόμενοι, πάλιν ἀπὸ μηνὸς Ἀπριλίου, διαλυομένου τοῦ110
πάγους τοῦ Δανάπρεως ποταμοῦ, κατέρχονται πρὸς τὸν Κίαβον. Καὶ
εἶθ' οὕτως ἀπολαμβάνονται τὰ αὐτῶν μονόξυλα, καθὼς προείρηται, καὶ
ἐξοπλίζονται, καὶ πρὸς Ῥωμανίαν κατέρχονται.

Ὅτι οἱ Οὖζοι δύνανται τοῖς Πατζινακίταις πολεμεῖν.

80Be 10. Π ε ρ ὶ   τ ῆ ς   Χ α ζ α ρ ί α ς ,   π ῶ ς   δ ε ῖ   π ο λ ε μ ε ῖ σ θ α ι
κ α ὶ   π α ρ ὰ   τ ί ν ω ν .

19ʳP Ὅτι οἱ Οὖζοι δύνανται πολεμεῖν τοὺς Χαζάρους, ὡς αὐτοῖς
πλησιάζοντες, ὁμοίως καὶ ὁ ἐξουσιοκράτωρ Ἀλανίας.

V 88 Ἐθαιρίου P ‖ 89 Δάναστριν coni. Laskin: Δάναπριν P edd. ‖ 90 καιρὸς
Meursius Ba Be: ταρὸς P ‖ 94 Πατζινακῖται P ‖ 95 μονόξυλα edd. ‖
99 Κωνοπά P ‖ Κωνσταντίαν edd. ‖ 100 lac. ind. καὶ ἀπὸ Κωνσταντίας
excidisse coniciens Jenkins ‖ 101 γῆς edd. ‖ Δίτζινας P ‖ 105/6 ἄρχοντες
ἐξέρχονται V edd. ‖ 106 post Κίαβον add. ποταμὸν V Me ‖ 107 πολύδρια

9, 10

lake is the mouth of this river, as has been said, and carries on down to the sea, and the island of St. Aitherios lies on the sea, they come thence to the Dniester river, and having got safely there they rest again. But when the weather is propitious, they put to sea and come to the river called Aspros, and after resting there too in like manner, they again set out and come to the Selinas, to the so-called branch of the Danube river. And until they are past the river Selinas, the Pechenegs keep pace with them. And if it happens that the sea casts a 'monoxylon' on shore, they all put in to land, in order to present a united opposition to the Pechenegs. But after the Selinas they fear nobody, but, entering the territory of Bulgaria, they come to the mouth of the Danube. From the Danube they proceed to the Konopas, and from the Konopas to Constantia, *and from Constantia* to the river of Varna, and from Varna they come to the river Ditzina, all of which are Bulgarian territory. From the Ditzina they reach the district of Mesembria, and there at last their voyage, fraught with such travail and terror, such difficulty and danger, is at an end. The severe manner of life of these same Russians in winter-time is as follows. When the month of November begins, their chiefs together with all the Russians at once leave Kiev and go off on the 'poliudia', which means 'rounds', that is, to the Slavonic regions of the Vervians and Drugovichians and Krivichians and Severians and the rest of the Slavs who are tributaries of the Russians. There they are maintained throughout the winter, but then once more, starting from the month of April, when the ice of the Dnieper river melts, they come back to Kiev. They then pick up their 'monoxyla', as has been said above, and fit them out, and come down to Romania.

The Uzes can attack the Pechenegs.

10. Of Chazaria, how and by whom war must be made upon it.

The Uzes can attack the Chazars, for they are their neighbours, and so can the ruler of Alania.

Meursius ‖ ὅ (*coni. etiam* Schlözer Nevolin): ᾅ edd. ‖ 107 Σκλαβινίας P ‖ 107/8 τε Βερβιάνων: Τεβερβιάνων *coni.* Šafarik τε Δερβιάνων *coni.* Marquart Šachmatov ‖ 108 Σεβερίων V *coni.* Šachmatov Σευερίων P: Σεβέρων *coni.* Rački Σεβίρων *coni.* Marquart Σερβίων edd. ‖ 112 ἀπολαμβάνονται edd.: ἐπιλαμβάνωνται P ‖ 114 Οὔζοι P.
    10. 2 παρά τινων Be ‖ 3 Οὔζοι P ‖ 4/5 ᾽Αλανίας· ὅτι Ba Migne

10, 11, 12, 13

῞Οτι τὰ ἐννέα κλίματα τῆς Χαζαρίας τῇ ᾽Αλανίᾳ παράκεινται, 5
καὶ δύναται ὁ ᾽Αλανός, εἰ ἄρα καὶ βούλεται, ταῦτα πραιδεύειν καὶ μεγάλην βλάβην καὶ ἔνδειαν ἐντεῦθεν τοῖς Χαζάροις ποιεῖν· ἐκ γὰρ τῶν ἐννέα
τούτων κλιμάτων ἡ πᾶσα ζωὴ καὶ ἀφθονία τῆς Χαζαρίας καθέστηκεν.

**11. Περὶ τοῦ κάστρου Χερσῶνος καὶ τοῦ
κάστρου Βοσπόρου.**

῞Οτι τοῦ ἐξουσιοκράτορος ᾽Αλανίας μετὰ τῶν Χαζάρων μὴ εἰρη-
νεύοντος, ἀλλὰ μᾶλλον προτιμοτέραν τιθεμένου τὴν φιλίαν τοῦ βασι-
19ᵛP λέως ῾Ρωμαίων, ἐὰν οἱ Χάζαροι οὐ βούλωνται τὴν | πρὸς τὸν βασιλέα 5
φιλίαν καὶ εἰρήνην τηρεῖν, δύναται μεγάλως αὐτοὺς κακοῦν, τάς τε
ὁδοὺς ἐνεδρεύων καὶ ἀφυλάκτως αὐτοῖς ἐπιτιθέμενος ἐν τῷ διέρχεσθαι
πρὸς τε τὸ Σάρκελ καὶ τὰ κλίματα καὶ τὴν Χερσῶνα. Καὶ εἰ ποιήσηται
σπουδὴν ὁ τοιοῦτος ἐξουσιοκράτωρ τοῦ κωλύειν αὐτούς, μεγάλης καὶ
βαθείας εἰρήνης μετέχουσιν ἥ τε Χερσὼν καὶ τὰ κλίματα· φοβούμενοι 10
γὰρ οἱ Χάζαροι τὴν τῶν ᾽Αλανῶν ἐπίθεσιν καὶ μὴ εὑρίσκοντες ἄδειαν
μετὰ φοσσάτου ἐπιτίθεσθαι τῇ Χερσῶνι καὶ τοῖς κλίμασιν, ὡς μὴ πρὸς
ἀμφοτέρους ἐν ταὐτῷ πολεμεῖν ἐξισχύοντες, εἰρηνεύειν ἀναγκασθήσονται.

81Be
20ʳP
**12. Περὶ τῆς μαύρης Βουλγαρίας καὶ τῆς
Χαζαρίας.**

῞Οτι καὶ ἡ μαύρη λεγομένη Βουλγαρία δύναται τοῖς Χαζάροις
πολεμεῖν.

**13. Περὶ τῶν πλησιαζόντων ἐθνῶν τοῖς
Τούρκοις.**

῞Οτι τοῖς Τούρκοις τὰ τοιαῦτα ἔθνη παράκεινται· πρὸς μὲν τὸ
δυτικώτερον μέρος αὐτῶν ἡ Φραγγία, πρὸς δὲ τὸ βορειότερον οἱ Πατζινακῖται, καὶ πρὸς τὸ μεσημβρινὸν μέρος ἡ μεγάλη Μοραβία, ἤτοι ἡ 5
χώρα τοῦ Σφενδοπλόκου, ἥτις καὶ παντελῶς ἠφανίσθη παρὰ τῶν τοιούτων
Τούρκων, καὶ παρ᾽ αὐτῶν κατεσχέθη. Οἱ δὲ Χρωβάτοι πρὸς τὰ ὄρη
τοῖς Τούρκοις παράκεινται.

20ᵛP ῞Οτι δύνανται καὶ οἱ Πατζινακῖται | τοῖς Τούρκοις ἐπιτίθεσθαι
καὶ μεγάλως πραιδεύειν καὶ παραβλάπτειν αὐτούς, καθὼς καὶ ἐν τῷ 10
περὶ Πατζινακιτῶν κεφαλαίῳ προείρηται.

V ᾽Αλανίας, ὅτι Be ‖ 5 ἐννέα edd.: ϑ′ P ‖ κλήματα P ‖ 7 ἐννέα edd.: ϑ′ P ‖
8 κλημάτων τούτων V Me Ba κλιμάτων τούτων Be ‖ κλημάτων P.

10, 11, 12, 13

Nine regions of Chazaria are adjacent to Alania, and the Alan can, if he be so minded, plunder these and so cause great damage and dearth among the Chazars: for from these nine regions come all the livelihood and plenty of Chazaria.

11. Of the city of Cherson and the city of Bosporus.

If the ruler of Alania is not at peace with the Chazars, but thinks preferable the friendship of the emperor of the Romans, then, if the Chazars are not minded to preserve friendship and peace with the emperor, he, *the Alan*, may do them great hurt by ambushing their routes and setting upon them when they are off their guard, in their passage to Sarkel and the Regions and Cherson. And if this ruler will act zealously to check them, then Cherson and the Regions may enjoy great and profound peace; for the Chazars, afraid of the attack of the Alans and consequently not being free to attack Cherson and the Regions with an army, since they are not strong enough to fight both at once, will be compelled to remain at peace.

12. Of black Bulgaria and Chazaria.

The so-called black Bulgaria can also attack the Chazars.

13. Of the nations that are neighbours to the Turks.

These nations are adjacent to the Turks: on their western side Francia; on their northern the Pechenegs; and on the south side great Moravia, the country of Sphendoplokos, which has now been totally devastated by these Turks, and occupied by them. On the side of the mountains the Croats are adjacent to the Turks.

The Pechenegs too can attack the Turks, and plunder and harm them greatly, as has been said above in the chapter on the Pechenegs.

---

11. 2 Βοοσπόρου P ‖ 7 ἀφυλάκτοις *coni.* Kyriakides ‖ 8 κλήματα P ‖ ποιήσεται edd. ‖ 10 Χερσῶν P ‖ κλήματα P ‖ 12 κλήμασιν P.

12. 1 τῆς² *om.* V edd.

13. 4/5 Πατζινακῖται P ‖ 5 *post* μέρος ἡ *lac. ind.* Jenkins *excidisse suspiciens* Χρωβατία ἦν δέ ποτε ὁ τόπος ἡ *vel hujusmodi aliquid* ‖ 9 Πατζι-νακῖται P ‖

66

13

Ἐπίστησον, υἱέ, διανοίας ὄμμα τῆς σῆς λόγοις ἐμοῖς, καὶ γνῶθι, ἅ σοι ἐντέλλομαι, καὶ ἕξεις ἐν καιρῷ ὡς ἐκ πατρικῶν θησαυρῶν προφέρειν πλοῦτον φρονήσεως καὶ ἐπιδείκνυσθαι χύμα συνέσεως. Ἴσθι οὖν, ὅτι τοῖς βορείοις ἅπασι γένεσι φύσις ὥσπερ καθέστηκεν τὸ ἐν χρήμασι 15 λίχνον καὶ ἄπληστον καὶ μηδέποτε κορεννύμενον, ὅθεν πάντα ἐπιζητεῖ καὶ πάντων ἐφίεται, καὶ οὐκ ἔχει τὰς ἐπιθυμίας ὅρῳ περιγραφομένας, ἀλλ᾽ ἀεὶ τοῦ πλείονος ἐπιθυμεῖ, καὶ ἀντὶ μικρᾶς ὠφελείας μεγάλα κέρδη 21ʳP προσ|πορίζεσθαι | βούλεται. Διὸ δεῖ τὰς τούτων ἀκαίρους αἰτήσεις 82Be καὶ παρρησιαστικὰς ἀξιώσεις διὰ λόγων πιθανῶν καὶ φρονίμων καὶ 20 συνετῶν ἀπολογιῶν ἀνατρέπειν καὶ ἀποκρούεσθαι, αἵτινες, ὅσον ἀπὸ τῆς πείρας ἡμεῖς καταλαβεῖν ἠδυνήθημεν, ὡς ἐν τύπῳ περιλαβεῖν, τοιαῦταί τινες ἔσονται.

Εἰ ἀξιώσουσί ποτε καὶ αἰτήσονται εἴτε Χάζαροι, εἴτε Τοῦρκοι, εἴτε καὶ Ῥῶς, ἢ ἕτερόν τι ἔθνος τῶν βορείων καὶ Σκυθικῶν, οἷα πολλὰ 25 συμβαίνει, ἐκ τῶν βασιλείων ἐσθήτων ἢ στεμμάτων ἢ στολῶν ἕνεκά τινος δουλείας καὶ ὑπουργίας αὐτῶν ἀποσταλῆναι αὐτοῖς, οὕτως χρή σε ἀπολογήσασθαι, ὅτι· «Αἱ τοιαῦται στολαὶ καὶ τὰ στέμματα, ἃ παρ᾽ 21ᵛP ὑμῶν καμε|λαύκια ὀνομάζεται, οὔτε παρὰ ἀνθρώπων κατεσκευάσθησαν, οὔτε ἐξ ἀνθρωπίνων τεχνῶν ἐπενοήθησαν ἢ ἐξηργάσθησαν, ἀλλ᾽ ὡς 30 ἀπὸ παλαιᾶς ἱστορίας ἐν ἀπορρήτοις λόγοις γεγραμμένον εὑρίσκομεν, ἡνίκα ὁ Θεὸς βασιλέα ἐποίησεν Κωνσταντῖνον ἐκεῖνον τὸν μέγαν, τὸν πρῶτον Χριστιανὸν βασιλεύσαντα, δι᾽ ἀγγέλου αὐτῷ τὰς τοιαύτας στολὰς ἐξαπέστειλεν καὶ τὰ στέμματα, ἅπερ ὑμεῖς καμελαύκια λέγετε, καὶ διωρίσατο αὐτῷ θεῖναι ταῦτα ἐν τῇ μεγάλῃ τοῦ Θεοῦ ἁγίᾳ ἐκκλησίᾳ, 35 ἥτις ἐπ᾽ ὀνόματι αὐτῆς τῆς ἐνυποστάτου σοφίας Θεοῦ Ἁγία Σοφία κατονομάζεται, καὶ μὴ καθ᾽ ἑκάστην αὐτὰ ἀμφιέννυσθαι, ἀλλ᾽ ὅτε 22ʳP δημοτελὴς καὶ με|γάλη τυγχάνῃ δεσποτικὴ ἑορτή. Διὸ δὴ Θεοῦ προστάγματι ταῦτα ἀπέθετο, ἅτινα καὶ ἄνωθεν τῆς ἁγίας τραπέζης ἐν τῷ θυσιαστηρίῳ τοῦ αὐτοῦ ναοῦ ἀποκρέμαται, καὶ εἰς κόσμον τῆς ἐκκλη- 40 83Be σίας καθέστηκεν. Τὰ δὲ λοιπὰ ἱμάτια καὶ σαγία βασιλικὰ τῆς ἱερᾶς | ταύτης τραπέζης ἄνωθεν ἐπίκεινται ἐφαπλούμενα. Ἡνίκα δὲ καταλάβῃ τοῦ Κυρίου ἡμῶν καὶ Θεοῦ Ἰησοῦ Χριστοῦ ἑορτή, ἀναλαμβάνεται ἐκ τῶν τοιούτων στολῶν καὶ στεμμάτων τὰ πρὸς τὸν καιρὸν ἐπιτήδεια καὶ ἁρμόζοντα ὁ πατριάρχης, καὶ ἀποστέλλει πρὸς τὸν βασιλέα, καὶ 45 ἀμφιέννυται αὐτὰ ἐκεῖνος, ὡς ὑπηρέτης Θεοῦ καὶ διάκονος, ἐν τῇ προελεύ- 22ᵛP σει καὶ μόνον, καὶ πάλιν μετὰ τὴν χρείαν ἀν|τιστρέφει αὐτὰ πρὸς τὴν ἐκκλησίαν, καὶ ἀπόκεινται ἐν αὐτῇ. Ἀλλὰ καὶ κατάρα τοῦ ἁγίου καὶ

F   12 Ἐπίστησον — σῆς cf. Prov. 23, 5.   13 ἅ σοι ἐντέλλομαι
Prov. 6, 3.

13

Fix, my son, your minds's eye upon my words, and learn those things which I command you, and you will be able in due season as from ancestral treasures to bring forth the wealth of wisdom, and to display the abundance of wit. Know therefore that all the tribes of the north have, as it were implanted in them by nature, a ravening greed of money, never satiated, and so they demand everything and hanker after everything and have desires that know no limit or circumscription, but are always eager for more, and desirous to acquire great profits in exchange for a small service. And so these importunate demands and brazenly submitted claims must be turned back and rebutted by plausible speeches and prudent and clever excuses, which, in so far as our experience has enabled us to arrive at them, will, to speak summarily, run more or less as follows:

Should they ever require and demand, whether they be Chazars, or Turks, or again Russians, or any other nation of the northerners and Scythians, as frequently happens, that some of the imperial vesture or diadems or state robes should be sent to them in return for some service or office performed by them, then thus you shall excuse yourself: «These robes of state and the diadems, which you call 'kamelaukia', were not fashioned by men, nor by human arts devised or elaborated, but, as we find it written in secret stories of old history, when God made emperor the former Constantine the great, who was the first Christian emperor, He sent him these robes of state by the hand of His angel, and the diadems which you call 'kamelaukia', and charged him to lay them in the great and holy church of God, which, after the name of that very wisdom which is the property of God, is called St.Sophia; and not to clothe himself in them every day, but *only* when it is a great public festival of the Lord. And so by God's command he laid them up, and they hang above the holy table in the sanctuary of this same church, and are for the ornament of the church. And the rest of the imperial vestments and cloaks lie spread out upon this holy table. And when a festival of our Lord and God Jesus Christ comes round, the patriarch takes up such of these robes of state and diadems as are suitable and appropriated to that occasion, and sends them to the emperor, and he wears them in the procession, and only in it, as the servant and minister of God, and after use returns them again to the church, and they are laid up in it. Moreover, there is a curse of the holy and great emperor Constantine en-

---

μεγάλου βασιλέως Κωνσταντίνου ἐστὶν ἐν τῇ ἁγίᾳ ταύτῃ τραπέζῃ τῆς
τοῦ Θεοῦ ἐκκλησίας ἐγγεγραμμένη, καθὼς αὐτῷ διὰ τοῦ ἀγγέλου ὁ 50
Θεὸς διωρίσατο, ἵνα, ἐὰν βουληθῇ βασιλεὺς διά τινα χρείαν ἢ περίστασιν
ἢ ἐπιθυμίαν ἄκαιρον ἐξ αὐτῶν ἐπᾶραι καὶ ἢ αὐτὸς καταχρήσασθαι ἢ
ἑτέροις χαρίσασθαι, ὡς πολέμιος καὶ τῶν τοῦ Θεοῦ προσταγμάτων
ἐχθρός, ἀναθεματίζεται καὶ τῆς ἐκκλησίας ἀποκηρύττεται· εἰ δὲ καὶ
αὐτὸς ἕτερα ὅμοια καμεῖν βουληθῇ, ἵνα καὶ αὐτὰ ἡ τοῦ Θεοῦ ἐκκλησία 55
ἀναλαμβάνηται, τῶν ἀρχιερέων πάντων εἰς ταῦτα παρρησιαζομένων
23ʳP καὶ τῆς συγκλήτου· | καὶ μὴ ἔχειν ἐξουσίαν μήτε τὸν βασιλέα, μήτε
τὸν πατριάρχην, μήτε ἕτερόν τινα τὰς τοιαύτας ἀναλαμβάνεσθαι στολὰς
ἢ τὰ στέμματα ἀπὸ τῆς ἁγίας τοῦ Θεοῦ ἐκκλησίας. Καὶ φόβος μέγας
ἐπήρτηται τοῖς βουλομένοις ἀνατρέπειν τι τῶν τοιούτων θεϊκῶν διατά- 60
ξεων. Εἷς γάρ τις τῶν βασιλέων, Λέων ὀνόματι, ὃς καὶ ἀπὸ Χαζαρίας
γυναῖκα ἠγάγετο, ἀβούλῳ τόλμῃ χρησάμενος ἐν τῶν τοιούτων ἀνελάβετο
84Be στεμμάτων, δεσποτικῆς μὴ παρούσης | ἑορτῆς, καὶ δίχα γνώμης τοῦ
πατριάρχου τοῦτο περιεβάλετο. Καὶ εὐθέως ἄνθρακα ἐπὶ τοῦ μετώπου
ἐκβαλὼν καὶ ταῖς ἐκ τούτου ὀδύναις κατατρυχόμενος κακιγκάκως ἀπέρ- 65
23ᵛP ρηξεν τὸ ζῆν, | καὶ πρὸ καιροῦ τὸν θάνατον ἐπεσπάσατο. Καὶ τοῦ τοιούτου
συντόμως ἐκδικηθέντος τολμήματος, ἔκτοτε τύπος ἐγένετο, ὥστε ἐν
τῷ μέλλειν στέφεσθαι τὸν βασιλέα πρότερον ὀμνύειν καὶ ἀσφαλίζεσθαι,
ὅτι οὐδὲν ἐναντίον τῶν προστεταγμένων καὶ ἐκ παλαιοῦ φυλαττομένων
τολμήσει ποιήσειν ἢ ἐννοήσασθαι καὶ οὕτως ὑπὸ τοῦ πατριάρχου στέ- 70
φεσθαι καὶ τὰ ἁρμόζοντα τῇ καθεστώσῃ ἑορτῇ ἐπιτελεῖν τε καὶ δια-
πράττεσθαι.»

Ὡσαύτως χρή σε καὶ περὶ τοῦ ὑγροῦ πυρός, τοῦ διὰ τῶν σιφώνων
ἐκφερομένου μεριμνᾶν τε καὶ μελετᾶν, ὡς εἴπερ ποτὲ τολμήσωσί τινες
24ʳP καὶ αὐτὸ ἐπιζητῆσαι, καθὼς καὶ παρ' ἡμῶν πολλάκις ἐ|ζήτησαν, τοιού- 75
τοις αὐτοὺς ἔχεις ἀποκρούεσθαι καὶ ἀποπέμπεσθαι ῥήμασιν, ὅτι· «Καὶ
αὐτὸ ἀπὸ τοῦ ⟨Θεοῦ⟩ δι' ἀγγέλου τῷ μεγάλῳ καὶ πρώτῳ βασιλεῖ Χριστιανῷ, ἁγίῳ Κωνσταντίνῳ ἐφανερώθη καὶ ἐδιδάχθη. Παραγγελίας δὲ
μεγάλας καὶ περὶ τούτου παρὰ τοῦ αὐτοῦ ἀγγέλου ἐδέξατο, ὡς παρὰ
πατέρων καὶ πάππων πιστωθέντες πληροφορούμεθα, ἵνα ἐν μόνοις 80
τοῖς Χριστιανοῖς καὶ τῇ ὑπ' αὐτῶν βασιλευομένῃ πόλει κατασκευάζηται,
ἀλλαχοῦ δὲ μηδαμῶς, μήτε εἰς ἕτερον ἔθνος τὸ οἱονδήποτε παραπέμπηται,
μήτε διδάσκηται. Ὅθεν καὶ τοῖς μετ' αὐτὸν ὁ μέγας οὗτος βασιλεὺς
85Be ἐξασφαλιζόμενος περὶ τούτου ἐν τῇ ἁγίᾳ τραπέζῃ τῆς τοῦ Θεοῦ | ἐκκλη-
24ᵛP σίας ἀρὰς ἐγγραφῆναι πεποίηκεν, ἵνα ὁ ἐκ τοῦ | τοιούτου πυρὸς εἰς 85

F   61 Εἷς — 66 ἐπεσπάσατο: cf. Theoph. p. 453, 25—30; Georg. Mon.
p. 765, 8—14.

13

graved upon this holy table of the church of God, according as he was charged by God through the angel, that if an emperor for any use or occasion or unseasonable desire be minded to take of them and either himself misuse them or give them to others, he shall be anathematized as the foe and enemy of the commands of God, and shall be excommunicated from the church; moreover, if he himself be minded to make others like them, these too the church of God must take, with the freely expressed approval of all the archbishops and of the senate; and it shall not be in the authority either of the emperor, or of the patriarch, or of any other, to take these robes of state or the diadems from the holy church of God. And mighty dread hangs over them who are minded to transgress any of these divine ordinances. For one of the emperors, Leo by name, who also married a wife from Chazaria, out of his folly and rashness took up one of these diadems when no festival of the Lord was toward, and without the approval of the patriarch put it about his head. And straightway a carbuncle came forth upon his forehead so that in torment at the pains of it he evilly departed his evil life, and ran upon death untimely. And, this rash act being summarily avenged, thereafter a rule was made, that when he is about to be crowned the emperor must first swear and give surety that he will neither do nor conceive anything against what has been ordained and kept from ancient times, and then may he be crowned by the patriarch and perform and execute the rites appropriate to the established festival.»

Similar care and thought you must take in the matter of the liquid fire which is discharged through tubes, so that if any shall ever venture to demand this too, as they have often made demands of us also, you may rebut and dismiss them in words like these: «This too was revealed and taught by *God* through an angel to the great and holy Constantine, the first Christian emperor, and concerning this too he received great charges from the same angel, as we are assured by the faithful witness of our fathers and grandfathers, that it should be manufactured among the Christians only and in the city ruled by them, and nowhere else at all, nor should it be sent nor taught to any other nation whatsoever. And so, for the confirmation of this among those who should come after him, this great emperor caused curses to be inscribed on the holy table of the church of God, that he who

---

V 49 βασιλέως *om.* V edd. ‖ 50/1 ὁ Θεὸς διὰ τοῦ ἀγγέλου V edd. ‖ 51 διορίσατο P ‖ 54 ἀναθεματίζηται Meursius Ba Be ‖ ἀποκηρύττηται Meursius Ba Be ‖ 65 κακὴν κάκος P ‖ 69 φυλαττομένων edd.: φυλαττομένοις P ‖ 70 τολμήσῃ Ba Be ‖ 73 χρῆσαι P ‖ σιφόνων P ‖ 76 αὐτοὺς edd.: αὐτοῖς P ‖ ἔχοις V edd. ‖ 77 ἀπὸ τοῦ *om.* edd. ‖ Θεοῦ *add.* Moravcsik ‖ 77/8 Χριστιανῷ Meursius Ba Be: Χριστιανῶν P ‖ 82 παραπέμπηται edd.: παραπέμπεται P ‖

ἕτερον ἔθνος δοῦναι τολμήσας μήτε Χριστιανὸς ὀνομάζεται, μήτε ἀξίας
τινὸς ἢ ἀρχῆς ἀξιοῦται· ἀλλ' εἴ τινα καὶ ἔχων τύχῃ, καὶ ἀπὸ ταύτης
ἐκβάληται καὶ εἰς αἰῶνας αἰώνων ἀναθεματίζηται καὶ παραδειγματίζη-
ται, εἴτε βασιλεύς, εἴτε πατριάρχης, εἴτε τις ἄλλος ὁ οἱοσοῦν ἄνθρωπος,
εἴτε ἄρχων, εἴτε ἀρχόμενος τυγχάνοι ὁ τὴν τοιαύτην ἐντολὴν παραβαίνειν 90
πειρώμενος. Καὶ προετρέψατο πάντας τοὺς ζῆλον καὶ φόβον Θεοῦ
ἔχοντας, ὡς κοινὸν ἐχθρὸν καὶ παραβάτην τῆς μεγάλης ταύτης ἐντολῆς,
τὸν τοιοῦτον ἐπιχειροῦντα ποιεῖν ἀναιρεῖν σπουδάζειν, καὶ ἐχθίστῳ
⟨καὶ⟩ χαλεπῷ παραπέμπεσθαι θανάτῳ. Συνέβη δέ ποτε, τῆς κακίας
25ʳP ἀεὶ χώραν εὑρισκούσης, τινὰ τῶν ἡμετέρων στρατηγῶν δῶ|ρα παρά 95
τινων ἐθνικῶν πάμπολλα εἰληφότα μεταδοῦναι αὐτοῖς ἐκ τοῦ τοιούτου
πυρός, καὶ μὴ ἀνεχομένου τοῦ Θεοῦ ἀνεκδίκητον καταλιπεῖν τὴν παρά-
βασιν, ἐν τῷ μέλλειν αὐτὸν ἐν τῇ ἁγίᾳ τοῦ Θεοῦ εἰσιέναι ἐκκλησίᾳ πῦρ
ἐκ τοῦ οὐρανοῦ κατελθὸν τοῦτον κατέφαγε καὶ ἀνάλωσεν. Καὶ ἀπὸ τότε
φόβος μέγας καὶ τρόμος ἐν ταῖς ἁπάντων ἐνετέθη ψυχαῖς, καὶ οὐκέτι 100
οὐδεὶς τοῦ λοιποῦ, οὔτε βασιλεύς, οὔτε ἄρχων, οὔτε ἰδιώτης, οὔτε στρατηγός, οὔτε ὁ οἱοσοῦν ὅλως ἄνθρωπος κατετόλμησέ τι τοιοῦτον ἐνθυμη-
θῆναι, μήτι γε καὶ ἔργῳ ἐπιχειρῆσαι ποιῆσαι ἢ διαπράξασθαι.»
86Be
25ᵛP
Ἀλλ' ἄγε δὴ μετάβηθι, καὶ πρὸς ἕτερον εἶδος αἰτήσεως παραλόγου
καὶ ἀπρεποῦς εὐπρεπεῖς καὶ ἁρμόζοντας λόγους ἀνα|ζήτει |καὶ ἀναμάν-105
θανε. Εἰ γάρ ποτε ἔθνος τι ἀπὸ τῶν ἀπίστων τούτων καὶ ἀτίμων βορείων
γενῶν αἰτήσηται συμπενθεριάσαι μετὰ τοῦ βασιλέως Ῥωμαίων καὶ ἢ
θυγατέρα αὐτοῦ εἰς νύμφην λαβεῖν ἢ ἐπιδοῦναι οἰκείαν θυγατέρα εἰς
γυναῖκα χρηματίσαι βασιλέως ἢ βασιλέως υἱοῦ, χρή σε τοιούτοις ῥήμασι
καὶ τὴν τοιαύτην αὐτῶν παράλογον ἀποκρούσασθαι αἴτησιν, λέγοντα,110
ὅτι· «Καὶ περὶ ταύτης τῆς ὑποθέσεως παραγγελία καὶ διάταξις φοβερὰ
καὶ ἀπαραποίητος τοῦ μεγάλου καὶ ἁγίου Κωνσταντίνου ἐναπογέγραπται
ἐν τῇ ἱερᾷ τραπέζῃ τῆς καθολικῆς τῶν Χριστιανῶν ἐκκλησίας τῆς Ἁγίας
Σοφίας· τοῦ μηδέποτε βασιλέα Ῥωμαίων συμπενθεριάσαι μετὰ ἔθνους
26ʳP παρηλ|λαγμένοις καὶ ξένοις ἔθεσι χρωμένου τῆς Ῥωμαϊκῆς καταστάσεως,115
μάλιστα δὲ ἀλλοπίστου καὶ ἀβαπτίστου, εἰ μὴ μετὰ μόνων τῶν Φράγγων·
τούτους γὰρ μόνους ὑπεξείλετο ὁ μέγας ἐκεῖνος ἀνήρ, Κωνσταντῖνος
ὁ ἅγιος, ὅτι καὶ αὐτὸς τὴν γένεσιν ἀπὸ τῶν τοιούτων ἔσχε μερῶν, ὡς
συγγενείας καὶ ἐπιμιξίας πολλῆς τυγχανούσης Φράγγοις τε καὶ Ῥωμαίοις.
Καὶ διὰ τί μετὰ τούτων μόνων προετρέψατο συνιστᾶν γαμικὰ συναλ-120

F   98 πῦρ — 99 ἀνάλωσεν: cf. IV Reg. 1, 10—12; Apoc. 20, 9; Socrates,
Hist. eccl. VII. 43.   100 φόβος — τρόμος: cf. Exod. 15, 16; Psalm.
54, 6.   104 Ἀλλ' ἄγε δὴ μετάβηθι: Homeri Od. VIII. 492.

V   86 ὀνομάζηται edd. ‖ 88 ἐκβάλληται Be ‖ αἰῶνα V edd. ‖ ἀναθεματί-

13

should dare to give of this fire to another nation should neither be called a Christian, not be held worthy of any rank or office; and if he should be the holder of any such, he should be expelled therefrom and be anathematized and made an example for ever and ever, whether he were emperor, or patriarch, or any other man whatever, either ruler or subject, who should seek to transgress this commandment. And he adjured all who had the zeal and fear of God to be prompt to make away with him who attempted to do this, as a common enemy and a transgressor of this great commandment, and to dismiss him to a death most hateful *and* cruel. And it happened once, as wickedness will still find room, that one of our military governors, who had been most heavily bribed by certain foreigners, handed over some of this fire to them; and, since God could not endure to leave unavenged this transgression, as he was about to enter the holy church of God, fire came down out of heaven and devoured and consumed him utterly. And thereafter mighty dread and terror were implanted in the hearts of all men, and never since then has anyone, whether emperor, or noble, or private citizen, or military governor, or any man of any sort whatever, ventured to think of such a thing, far less to attempt to do it or bring it to pass.»

'But come, now, turn', and to meet another sort of demand, monstrous and unseemly, seemly and appropriate words discover and seek out. For if any nation of these infidel and dishonourable tribes of the north shall ever demand a marriage alliance with the emperor of the Romans, and either to take his daughter to wife, or to give a daughter of their own to be wife to the emperor or to the emperor's son, this monstrous demand of theirs also you shall rebut with these words, saying: «Concerning this matter also a dread and authentic charge and ordinance of the great and holy Constantine is engraved upon the sacred table of the universal church of the Christians, St. Sophia, that never shall an emperor of the Romans ally himself in marriage with a nation of customs differing from and alien to those of the Roman order, especially with one that is infidel and unbaptized, unless it be with the Franks alone; for they alone were excepted by that great man, the holy Constantine, because he himself drew his origin from those parts; for there is much relationship and converse between Franks and Romans. And why did he order that with them alone the emperors of the Romans should

ζεται V ǁ 88/9 παραδειγματίζεται V ǁ 89 ὁ om. edd. ǁ 90 παραβαίνειν V edd.: παραβαίνον P /ǁ 91 προυτρέψατο edd. ǁ 93 τοιοῦτο Ba Be   τοῦτο Meursius ǁ 93/4 ἐχθίστῳ ⟨καὶ⟩ χαλεπῷ coni. Moravcsik: ἐκτίστῳ χαλεπῶ P ἐκτίστῳ τῷ χαλεπῷ Ba Be   εὐθὺς τῷ χαλεπῷ Meursius   ἐκτίστῳ καὶ χαλεπῷ Bandurius   an ἐχθίστῳ vel οἰκτίστῳ omissis τῷ χαλεπῷ? Bekker ǁ 99 κατελθὸν ἐκ τοῦ οὐρανοῦ V Me ǁ ἀνήλωσεν V edd. ǁ 102 ὁ om. edd. ǁ 104 ᾿Αλλ᾿ ἄγε Be: ἀλλάγε P ǁ 107 αἰτήσεται edd. ǁ συμπεμφθεριᾶσαι P ǁ 108 εἰς corr. Kyriakides: ἢ P edd. ǁ 109 χρῆσαι P ǁ 114 συμπεμφθεριᾶσαι P ǁ 115 ἤθεσι V Me Ba ǁ 120 τί: τοῦτο edd. ǁ προυτρέψατο Be ǁ 120/1 συναλλαγία P ǁ

13

λάγια τοὺς βασιλεῖς Ῥωμαίων; Διὰ τὴν ἄνωθεν τῶν μερῶν ἐκείνων
καὶ γενῶν περιφάνειαν καὶ εὐγένειαν. Μετ' ἄλλου δέ του οἱουδήποτε
ἔθνους μὴ δυναμένους τοῦτο ποιεῖν, ἀλλ' ὁ τοῦτο ποιῆσαι τολμήσας
ἵνα, ὡς παραβάτης πατρικῶν εἰσηγήσεων καὶ βασιλείων θεσμῶν, ἀλλό-
26ᵛP τριος κρί|νοιτο τῶν Χριστιανῶν καταλόγων καὶ τῷ ἀναθέματι παραδί-125
87Be δοιτο. Ὁ δὲ προμνημονευθεὶς Λέων ἐκεῖνος ὁ βασιλεύς, ὁ καὶ |τὸ στέμμα,
καθὼς ἀνωτέρω προείρηται, παρανόμως καὶ τολμηρῶς ἀπὸ τῆς ἐκκλησίας δίχα γνώμης τοῦ τότε πατριαρχοῦντος λαβὼν καὶ περιθέμενος
καὶ τὴν δίκην συντόμως δοὺς ἀξίαν τῆς αὐτοῦ πονηρᾶς ἐγχειρήσεως,
ἐτόλμησε καὶ τὴν τοιαύτην ἐντολὴν τοῦ ἁγίου βασιλέως ἐκείνου, ἥτις,130
ὡς ἤδη δεδήλωται, ἐν τῇ ἁγίᾳ τραπέζῃ ἀναγεγραμμένη καθέστηκεν,
παρὰ φαῦλον θέσθαι καὶ ὡς μηδὲν λογίσασθαι, καὶ ὡς ἅπαξ ἔξω τοῦ
θείου φόβου καὶ τῶν ἐντολῶν αὐτοῦ πεποίηκεν ἑαυτόν, συνεστήσατο
27ʳP καὶ μετὰ τοῦ χαγάνου Χαζαρίας | γαμικὸν συναλλάγιον, καὶ τὴν θυγα-
τέρα αὐτοῦ εἰς γυναῖκα ἐδέξατο, καὶ μέγα ἐκ τούτου ὄνειδος καὶ τῇ135
Ῥωμαίων ἀρχῇ καὶ ἑαυτῷ προσετρίψατο, ὡς τὰ προγονικὰ παραγγέλ-
ματα ἀκυρώσας καὶ παρ' οὐδὲν λογισάμενος· πλὴν οὐδὲ ὀρθόδοξος
ἐκεῖνος Χριστιανὸς ἦν, ἀλλ' αἱρετικὸς καὶ εἰκονομάχος. Διὸ χάριν τῶν
τοιούτων αὐτοῦ παρανόμων ἀσεβημάτων ἐν τῇ τοῦ Θεοῦ ἐκκλησίᾳ
διηνεκῶς ἀποκηρύττεται καὶ ἀναθεματίζεται, ὡς καὶ τῆς τοῦ Θεοῦ140
καὶ τῆς τοῦ ἁγίου καὶ μεγάλου βασιλέως Κωνσταντίνου διατάξεως
παραβάτης καὶ ἀνατροπεύς. Πῶς γάρ ἐστιν τῶν ἐνδεχομένων Χριστιανοὺς μετὰ ἀπίστων γαμικὰς κοινωνίας ποιεῖν καὶ συμπενθεριάζειν, τοῦ
27ᵛP κανόνος τοῦτο κωλύ|οντος καὶ τῆς ἐκκλησίας ἁπάσης ἀλλότριον αὐτὸ
λογιζομένης καὶ ἔξω τῆς Χριστιανικῆς καταστάσεως; Ἢ τίς τῶν ἐγκρί-145
των καὶ εὐγενῶν καὶ σοφῶν βασιλέων Ῥωμαίων κατεδέξατο;» Εἰ δὲ
ἀντείπωσιν· «Πῶς ὁ κύρις Ῥωμανὸς ὁ βασιλεὺς μετὰ Βουλγάρων
88Be συνεπενθερίασεν, καὶ τὴν ἰδίαν | ἐκγόνην δέδωκεν τῷ κυρῷ Πέτρῳ τῷ
Βουλγάρῳ;», δεῖ ἀπολογήσασθαι, ὅτι· «Ὁ κύρις Ῥωμανός, ὁ βασιλεύς,
ἰδιώτης καὶ ἀγράμματος ἄνθρωπος ἦν, καὶ οὔτε τῶν ἄνωθεν ἐν βασιλείοις150
τεθραμμένων, οὔτε τῶν παρηκολουθηκότων ἐξ ἀρχῆς τοῖς Ῥωμαϊκοῖς
ἐθισμοῖς, οὔτε ἀπὸ γένους βασιλείου καὶ εὐγενοῦς, καὶ διὰ τοῦτο
28ʳP αὐθαδέστερον καὶ ἐξουσιαστικώτερον τὰ πολλὰ κατεπράττετο, | καὶ ἐν
τούτῳ οὔτε τῇ ἐκκλησίᾳ ἀπαγορευούσῃ ὑπήκουσεν, οὔτε τῇ ἐντολῇ καὶ
διαταγῇ τοῦ μεγάλου Κωνσταντίνου κατηκολούθησεν, ἀλλ' ἐκ γνώμης155
αὐθάδους καὶ αὐτοβούλου καὶ τῶν καλῶν ἀμαθοῦς καὶ μὴ βουλομένης

F   142 Πῶς γάρ ἐστιν — 145 καταστάσεως: cf. can. XIV. IV. Concilii, can.
LXXII. VII. Concilii, ed. Mansi VII. 364, XI. 976. = Ralles-Potles II, 251,
471. 147 Πῶς ὁ κύρις — 149 Βουλγάρῳ: cf. Georg. Mon. (cont.), ed. Bonn,
p. 905, 19—907, 5; 913, 6—8; Georg. Mon. (cont.), ed. Istrin II. p. 56,
8—34; 60, 6—8; Theoph. Cont. p. 414, 1—415, 9; 422, 10—13. 150 ἰδιώτης καὶ
ἀγράμματος: cf. Acta 4, 13.

intermarry? Because of the traditional fame and nobility of those lands and races. But with any other nation whatsoever it was not to be in their power to do this, and he who dared to do it was to be condemned as an alien from the ranks of the Christians and subject to the anathema, as a transgressor of ancestral laws and imperial ordinances. And that emperor Leo aforesaid, who also, as has been described above, unlawfully and rashly, without the consent of him who was then patriarch, took from the church the diadem and put it about his head and was summarily punished in full for his wicked attempt, dared to make light of and to disregard this commandment also of that holy emperor, which, as has already been made clear, is engraved on the holy table; and as he had once put himself outside the fear of God and His commandments, so also he contracted an alliance in marriage with the chagan of Chazaria, and received his daughter to be his wife, and thereby attached great shame to the empire of the Romans and to himself, because he annulled and disregarded the ancestral injunctions; yet he, however, was not even an orthodox Christian, but an heretic and a destroyer of images. And so for these his unlawful impieties he is continually excommunicated and anathematized in the church of God, as a transgressor and perverter of the ordinance of God and of the holy and great emperor Constantine. For how can it be admissible that Christians should form marriage associations and ally themselves by marriage with infidels, when the canon forbids it and the whole church regards it as alien to and outside the Christian order? Or which of the illustrious or noble or wise emperors of the Romans has admitted it?» But if they reply: «How then did the lord Romanus, the emperor, ally himself in marriage with the Bulgarians, and give his grand-daughter to the lord Peter the Bulgarian?», this must be the defence: «The lord Romanus, the emperor, was a common, illiterate fellow, and not from among those who have been bred up in the palace, and have followed the Roman national customs from the beginning; nor was he of imperial and noble stock, and for this reason in most of his actions he was too arrogant and despotic, and in this instance he neither heeded the prohibition of the church, nor followed the commandment and ordinance of the great Constantine, but out of a temper arrogant and self-willed and untaught in virtue and refusing to follow what was

---

V 121 *post* Ῥωμαίων *signum interrogationis posuit* Moravcsik: Ῥωμαίων διὰ Be ‖ 122 τοῦ οἵου δήποτε edd.: τοιουδήποτε P ‖ 123 δυναμένους edd.: δυναμένου P δύνασθαι *coni.* Kyriakides ‖ 124 παραβάτης edd.: παραβάτην P ‖ 128 πατριαρχεύοντος edd. ‖ 129 ἐγχειρίσεως P ‖ 138 Χριστιανὸς ἦν ἐκεῖνος edd. ‖ 143 συμπεμφεριάζειν P ‖ 144 αὐτὸ Ba Be: αὐτῶ P ‖ 145/6 ἐκκρίτων Meursius Ba ‖ 147 κῦρης P: κύριος edd. ‖ 148 συνεπεμφερίασεν P ‖ κυρίῳ edd. ‖ 149 κῦρης P: κύριος edd. ‖ 151 τεθραμμένων Be: τετραμμένων P ‖

ἕπεσθαι τῷ πρέποντι καὶ καλῷ, μηδὲ ταῖς πατροπαραδότοις στοιχεῖν
διατάξεσιν τοῦτο ποιῆσαι τετόλμηκεν, ταύτην μόνην εὔλογον δηλονότι
προβαλλόμενος πρόφασιν, τοσοῦτον πλῆθος αἰχμαλώτων Χριστιανῶν
διὰ τῆς τοιαύτης πράξεως ἀναρρύεσθαι, καὶ τὸ Χριστιανοὺς εἶναι καὶ τοὺς160
Βουλγάρους ⟨καὶ⟩ ὁμοπίστους ἡμῶν, ἄλλως τε καὶ ὅτι οὐδὲ αὐτοκράτορος
καὶ ἐνθέσμου βασιλέως θυγάτηρ ἡ ἐκδιδομένη ἐτύγχανεν, ἀλλὰ τρίτου
28ᵛP καὶ ἐσχάτου καὶ ἔτι ὑποχει|ρίου καὶ μηδεμίαν ἐξουσίαν ἐν τοῖς τῆς ἀρχῆς
μετέχοντος πράγμασι· καὶ οὐδὲν διέφερεν τὸ τοιοῦτον τοῦ καὶ ἄλλην
τινὰ τῶν βασιλικῶν συγγενίδων, τῶν πορρωτέρω τε καὶ ἐγγὺς τῆς βασι-165
λείας εὐγενείας τυγχανουσῶν, καὶ διά τινα κοινωφελῆ δουλείαν, καὶ τοῦ
ἐσχάτου καὶ μηδὲν σχεδὸν ἐξουσιάζοντος. Ἐπεὶ ἔξω τοῦ κανόνος καὶ τῆς
ἐκκλησιαστικῆς παραδόσεως καὶ τῆς τοῦ μεγάλου καὶ ἁγίου βασιλέως,
Κωνσταντίνου διαταγῆς τε καὶ ἐντολῆς τοῦτο πεποίηκεν, πολλὰ καὶ
89Be ζῶν ὠνειδίσθη ὁ προρρηθεὶς κύρις Ῥωμανός, καὶ διε|βλήθη καὶ ἐμι-170
σήθη παρά τε τῆς συγκλήτου βουλῆς καὶ τοῦ δήμου παντὸς καὶ τῆς
ἐκκλησίας αὐτῆς, ὡς καὶ τὸ μῖσος ἀπὸ τοῦ τέλους γενέσθαι καταφανές,
29ʳP καὶ μετὰ θάνατον | ὁμοίως ἐξουθενεῖται καὶ διαβάλλεται καὶ ὑπὸ κατα-
γνώμην τίθεται καὶ οὗτος, ἀνάξιον πρᾶγμα καὶ ἀπρεπὲς εἰς τὴν εὐγενῆ
πολιτείαν Ῥωμαίων καινοτομήσας.» Ἕκαστον γὰρ ἔθνος διάφορα ἔχον175
ἔθη καὶ διαλλάττοντας νόμους τε καὶ θεσμοὺς ὀφείλει τὰ οἰκεῖα κρατύνειν καὶ ἀπὸ τοῦ αὐτοῦ ἔθνους τὰς πρὸς ἀνάκρασιν βίου κοινωνίας ποιεῖσθαι καὶ ἐνεργεῖν. Ὥσπερ γὰρ ἕκαστον ζῶον μετὰ τῶν ὁμογενῶν τὰς
μίξεις ἐργάζεται, οὕτω καὶ ἕκαστον ἔθνος οὐκ ἐξ ἀλλοφύλων καὶ ἀλλο-
γλώσσων, ἀλλ' ἐκ τῶν ὁμογενῶν τε καὶ ὁμοφώνων τὰ συνοικέσια τῶν180
γάμων ποιεῖσθαι καθέστηκεν δίκαιον. Ἐντεῦθεν γὰρ καὶ ἡ πρὸς ἀλλή-
29ᵛP λους ὁμοφροσύνη καὶ συνομιλία καὶ προσφιλὴς συνδιατριβὴ καὶ συμβί|ωσις
περιγίνεσθαι πέφυκεν· τὰ δὲ ἀλλότρια ἔθη καὶ διαλλάττοντα νόμιμα
ἀπεχθείας μᾶλλον καὶ προσκρούσεις καὶ μίση καὶ στάσεις εἴωθεν ἀπο-
γεννᾶν, ἅπερ οὐ φιλίας καὶ κοινωνίας, ἀλλ' ἔχθρας καὶ διαστάσεις φιλεῖ185
ἀπεργάζεσθαι. Καὶ ὅτι μὴ δεῖ τὰ κακῶς παρά τινων ἐξ ἀμαθείας ἢ
αὐθαδείας καταπραχθέντα τοὺς ἐννόμως ἄρχειν βουλομένους μιμεῖσθαί
τε καὶ ζηλοῦν, ἀλλὰ τῶν ἐννόμως καὶ δικαίως βεβασιλευκότων τὰς
ἀοιδίμους πράξεις ἔχειν, ὡς εἰκόνας ἀγαθὰς εἰς παράδειγμα προκειμένας
μιμήσεως, καὶ κατ' ἐκείνας πειρᾶσθαι καὶ αὐτὸν ἀπευθύνειν πάντα τὰ190
παρ' αὐτοῦ ἐνεργούμενα, ἐπεὶ καὶ τὸ διὰ τὰς τοιαύτας αὐτοβούλους
30ʳP
90Be πρά|ξεις αὐτοῦ ἐπελθὸν αὐτῷ τέλος, φημὶ δὴ τῷ κυρῷ Ῥωμανῷ,

---

V 157 στοιχεῖν Ba Be: τυχεῖν P ‖ 158 δηλονότι edd.: δηλόθεν P ‖
162 καὶ add. Jenkins ‖ 167 Ἐπεὶ δ' coni. Bekker ‖ 168 καὶ² om. edd. ‖

right and good, or to submit to the ordinances handed down by our fore-
fathers, he dared to do this thing; offering, that is, this alone by way of
specious excuse, that by this action so many Christian prisoners were ran-
somed, and that the Bulgarians too are Christians *and* of like faith with us,
and that in any case she who was given in marriage was not daughter of
the chief and lawful emperor, but of the third and most junior, who was
still subordinate and had no share of authority in matters of government;
but this was no different from *giving* any other of the ladies of the imperial family, whether more distantly or closely related to the imperial
nobility, nor did it make any difference that she was given for some service
to the commonweal, or was daughter of the most junior, who had no authority to speak of. And because he did this thing contrary to the canon and
to ecclesiastical tradition and the ordinance and commandment of the
great and holy emperor Constantine, the aforesaid lord Romanus was in
his lifetime much abused, and was slandered and hated by the senatorial
council and all the commons and the church herself, so that their hatred
became abundantly clear in the end to which he came; and after his death
he is in the same way vilified and slandered and condemned inasmuch as
he too introduced an unworthy and unseemly innovation into the noble
polity of the Romans.» For each nation has different customs and divergent
laws and institutions, and should consolidate those things that are proper
to it, and should form and develop out of the same nation the associations
for the fusion of its life. For just as each animal mates with its own tribe,
so it is right that each nation also should marry and cohabit not with those
of other race and tongue but of the same tribe and speech. For hence arise
naturally harmony of thought and intercourse among one another and
friendly converse and living together; but alien customs and divergent
laws are likely on the contrary to engender enmities and quarrels and hatreds
and broils, which tend to beget not friendship and association but spite
and division. Mark, too, that it is not for those who wish to govern lawfully
to copy and emulate what has been ill done by some out of ignorance or
arrogance, but rather to have the glorious deeds of those who have ruled
lawfully and righteously as noble pictures set up for an example to be copied,
and after their pattern to strive himself also to direct all that he does; since
the end which came upon him, I mean, the lord Romanus, through these

---

170 ὀνειδίσθη P ‖ κῦρης P ‖ 172 ἀπὸ: ἐπὶ edd. ‖ 176/7 κρατύνειν *scr.* Moravcsik
κρατοίνην P: κρατεῖν edd.   ‖ 177 ἀνάκρασιν *coni.* Jenkins: ἀνάκρισην P
ἀνάκρισιν edd. ‖ 183 πέφυκεν Pʸ   πέφυκε Ba Be: πέφοικεν P V   πεφίληκε
Meursius ‖ ἔθη edd.: ἤθη P ‖ 185 φιλεῖ (*littera* ν *erasa*) Pʸ Ba Be: φιλεῖν P V
φιλῶν Meursius   ‖ 186 ἀπεργάζεσθαι (*littera* σ *inserta et littera* τ *in* ϑ *correcta*)
Pʸ Ba Be: ἀπεργάζεται P V Me ‖ 187 ἐννόμως Meursius Ba Be: ἐννόμοις
P ἐν νόμοις *coni.* Kyriakides ‖ 192 δὴ V δῆ P: δὲ edd. ‖

13, 14

ἱκανόν ἐστιν πρὸς σωφρονισμὸν παράδειγμα τῷ βουλομένῳ τὰ κακῶς
παρ᾽ ἐκείνου πραχθέντα ζηλοῦν.

Χρεὼν δὲ μετὰ τῶν ἄλλων καὶ ταῦτά σε γινώσκειν, υἱὲ πολυέραστε,195
ἅτε τῆς τούτων γνώσεως μεγάλα σοι συμβαλέσθαι δυναμένης καὶ θαυ-
μαστότερον ἀποδεῖξαι. Τὰ δέ ἐστιν περὶ διαφορᾶς πάλιν ἑτέρων ἐθνῶν,
γενεαλογίας τε αὐτῶν καὶ ἐθῶν καὶ βίου διαγωγῆς καὶ θέσεως καὶ
κράσεως τῆς παρ᾽ αὐτῶν κατοικουμένης γῆς καὶ περιηγήσεως αὐτῆς
καὶ σταδιασμοῦ, καθὼς ἑξῆς πλατύτερον διηρμήνευται.   200

14. Περὶ τῆς γενεαλογίας τοῦ Μουχούμετ.

30ᵛP   Γενεαλογεῖται ὁ δυσσεβὴς καὶ ἀκάθαρ|τος Μουχούμετ, ὃν λέγου-
σιν οἱ Σαρακηνοὶ προφήτην αὐτῶν εἶναι, ἐκ φυλῆς γενικωτάτης Ἰσμαήλ,
υἱοῦ Ἀβραάμ, καταγόμενος. Ζιναρὸς γάρ, ὁ τοῦ Ἰσμαὴλ ἀπόγονος,
πατὴρ αὐτῶν ἀναγορεύεται πάντων. Οὗτος οὖν γεννᾷ υἱοὺς δύο, Μούνδα- 5
ρον καὶ Ῥαβίαν, ὁ δὲ Μούνδαρος τίκτει Κούσαρον καὶ Κάϊσον καὶ Θεμίμην
καὶ Ἄσανδον καὶ ἄλλους τινὰς ἀνωνύμους, οἳ καὶ τὴν Μαδιανῖτιν ἔρημον
κληρωσάμενοι, ἐκτηνοτρόφουν ἐν σκηναῖς κατοικοῦντες. Εἰσὶ δὲ καὶ
ἐνδότεροι τούτων οὐκ ἐκ τῆς φυλῆς αὐτῶν, ἀλλὰ τοῦ Ἰεκτάν, οἱ λεγόμε-
91Be νοι | Ὁμηρῖται, τουτέστιν Ἀμανῖται. Ἀναδείκνυται δὲ οὕτως. Ἀπόρου 10
ὄντος αὐτοῦ τοῦ Μουχούμετ καὶ ὀρφανοῦ, ἔδοξεν αὐτῷ μισθωτεύσασθαι
31ʳP γυναικί τινι πλουσίᾳ καὶ συγγε|νεῖ αὐτοῦ, καλουμένῃ Χαδιγᾷ, πρὸς
τὸ καμηλεύειν καὶ πραγματεύεσθαι ἐν Αἰγύπτῳ μετὰ τῶν ἀλλοφύλων
καὶ ἐν Παλαιστίνῃ. Εἶτα κατὰ μικρὸν παρρησιασάμενος καὶ ὑπελθὼν
τῇ γυναικὶ χήρᾳ οὔσῃ, λαμβάνει αὐτὴν εἰς γυναῖκα. Καὶ δὴ ἐπιχωριάζων 15
ἐν Παλαιστίνῃ καὶ συναναστρεφόμενος Ἰουδαίοις τε καὶ Χριστιανοῖς,
ἐθηρᾶτο λόγους καὶ γραφικὰς λύσεις τινάς. Ἔχων δὲ τὸ πάθος τῆς
ἐπιληψίας, ἐλυπεῖτο σφόδρα ἡ γυνὴ αὐτοῦ, ὡς περιφανὴς καὶ πλουσία
καὶ τῷ τοιούτῳ ἀνδρὶ συναφθεῖσα, οὐ μόνον ἀπόρῳ, ἀλλὰ καὶ ἐπιληπτικῷ,
ἣν καὶ τροπωσάμενος φάσκων, ὅτι· «Φοβερὰν ὀπτασίαν ἀγγέλου θεωρῶ 20

F   **14.** 2 Γενεαλογεῖται — 28 Αἰθρίβου: Georg. Mon. p. 697, 13—699, 10
(cf. textum codicis P); cf. Theoph. p. 333, 14—334, 19; Leo Gramm., ed.
Bonn. p. 153, 4—154, 7; Theod. Melit., ed. Tafel p. 105, 24—106, 21;
Cedr., ed. Bonn. I. p. 738, 12—739, 15; Excerpta cod. Harl. 5624. (s. XV.)
fol. 418ʳ sqq., ed. Sp. Lampros, Νέος Ἑλληνομνήμων XV. p. 359.

V 196 μεγάλας V μεγάλως edd. ‖ 197 τάδε P ‖ 198 γενεαλογίας edd.:
γενεθλεαλογίας P ‖ ἐθνῶν V ‖ 200 διερμηνεύσεται Meursius Ba Be.
     14. 2 Γενεαλογεῖται (etiam Migne): Γενεαλογῆται edd. ‖ Μουχούμετ
(etiam Georg. Mon.ᴮᴱⱽ)· Μουχούμεδ Georg. Mon. ‖ 4 Ἀβραάμ Georg. Mon. ‖
καταγόμενος V Georg. Mon.: καταγομένου P καταγόμενον edd. ‖ Ζηναρὸς P:
Νίζαρος Meursius Georg. Mon. Theoph. ‖ 5/6 Μούνδαρον (etiam Theoph.ᶜᵒᵈᵈ·):

13, 14

his headstrong acts is a sufficient warning to restrain anyone who is minded to emulate his evil deeds.

But now, with the rest, you must know also what follows, my well-loved son, since knowledge of it may greatly advantage you and render you the object of greater admiration. That is, once again, knowledge 'of the difference between other nations, their origins and customs and manner of life, and the position and climate of the land they dwell in, and its geographical description and measurement', as they are more widely expounded hereafter.

14. Of the genealogy of Mahomet.

The blasphemous and obscene Mahomet, whom the Saracens claim for their prophet, traces his genealogy by descent from the most widespread race of Ishmael, son of Abraham. For *Nizaros*, the descendant of Ishmael, is proclaimed the father of them all. Now he begat two sons, Moundaros and Rabias, and Moundaros begat Kousaros and Kaïsos and Themimes and Asandos and various others whose names are unknown, who were allotted the Madianite desert and reared their flocks, dwelling in tents. And there are others further off in the interior who are not of the same tribe, but of Iektan, the so-called Homerites, that is, Amanites. And the story is published abroad thus. This Mahomet, being destitute and an orphan, thought fit to hire himself out to a certain wealthy woman, his relative, Chadiga by name, to tend her camels and to trade for her in Egypt among the foreigners and in Palestine. Thereafter by little and little he grew more free in converse and ingratiated himself with the woman, who was a widow, and took her to wife. Now, during his visits to Palestine and intercourse with Jews and Christians he used to follow up certain of their doctrines and interpretations of scripture. But as he had the disease of epilepsy, his wife, a noble and wealthy lady, was greatly cast down at being united to this man, who was not only destitute but an epileptic into the bargain, and so he deceived her by alleging: «I behold a dreadful vision of an angel called Gabriel, and

---

Μούδαρον Georg. Mon. Theoph. ‖ 6 'Ραβείαν P ‖ Μούνδαρος (*etiam* Theoph.^(codd.)): Μούδαρος Georg. Mon. Theoph. ‖ Κούσαρον (*etiam* Georg. Mon.): Κούρασον Georg. Mon.^P Theoph. ‖ Θεμίμην Georg. Mon. Theoph.: Θυμίμην P edd. ‖ 7 'Ασανδὸν Cod. Harl. "Ασαδον Georg. Mon. Theoph. ‖ ἀνωνύμους Meursius Be Georg. Mon.: ὁμωνύμους P ἀγνώστους Theoph. ‖ Μαδιανίτην P ‖ 9 'Ιεκτᾶν P ‖ 10 'Ομηρεῖται P ‖ 'Αμανῖται (*etiam* Theoph.): 'Αμμανῖται Georg. Mon. ‖ 'Αναδείκνυται δὲ οὕτως *deest in* Georg. Mon. ‖ 11 αὐτοῦ τοῦ: τοῦ προειρημένου Georg. Mon.^P Theoph. ‖ Μουχούμεδ Georg. Mon. ‖ μισθοτεύσασθαι P: μισθωτεῦσαι Georg. Mon. μισθοδοτήσεσθαι edd. ‖ 12 Χαδιγᾷ Georg. Mon..: Χάδιγα P Χαδίγα edd. Χαδίγαν Theoph. ‖ 13 ἀλλοφύλων: ὁμοφύλων Georg. Mon. ‖ 16 συνανατρεφόμενος V Me Ba ‖ 17 λύσεις: ῥήσεις Georg. Mon. ‖

14, 15

Γαβριὴλ ὀνόματι, καὶ μὴ ὑποφέρων αὐτοῦ τὴν θέαν ὀλιγωρῶ καὶ πίπτω»,
31ᵛP ἐπιστεύθη, | συμψευδομαρτυροῦντος αὐτῷ 'Αρειανοῦ τινος μοναχοῦ
ψευδωνύμου δι' αἰσχροκέρδειαν. Καὶ οὕτως ἡ γυνὴ πλανηθεῖσα καὶ
ἄλλαις γυναιξὶν ὁμοφύλαις κηρύξασα προφήτην αὐτὸν εἶναι, προῆλθεν
τὸ ψεῦδος τῆς ἀπάτης καὶ εἰς ἄνδρα φύλαρχον τοὔνομα Βουβάχαρ. 25
Ἡ οὖν γυνὴ θανοῦσα καὶ τοῦτον διάδοχον καὶ κληρονόμον καταλείψασα
τῶν ἑαυτῆς, ἐγένετο περιφανὴς καὶ ἄγαν ὑπερούσιος, καὶ κατέσχεν
ἡ πονηρὰ πλάνη τε καὶ αἵρεσις αὐτοῦ τὰ μέρη τῆς Αἰθρίβου. Καὶ ἐδίδαξεν
οὗτος ὁ παράφρων καὶ πεφενακισμένος τοὺς αὐτῷ πειθομένους, ὅτι ὁ
92Be φονεύων ἐχθρὸν | ἢ ὑπὸ ἐχθροῦ φονευόμενος εἰς τὸν παράδεισον 30
32ʳP εἰσέρχεται καὶ ἄλλα, ὅσα φλυ|αρεῖ. Προσεύχονται δὲ καὶ εἰς τὸ τῆς
'Αφροδίτης ἄστρον, ὃ καλοῦσι Κουβάρ, καὶ ἀναφωνοῦσιν ἐν τῇ
προσευχῇ αὐτῶν οὕτως· «'Αλλὰ οὐὰ Κουβάρ», ὅ ἐστιν 'ὁ θεὸς καὶ
'Αφροδίτη'. Τὸν γὰρ θεὸν ''Αλλά' προσονομάζουσι, τὸ δὲ 'οὐά' ἀντὶ
τοῦ 'καί' συνδέσμου τιθέασιν, καὶ τὸ 'Κουβάρ' καλοῦσι τὸ ἄστρον, καὶ 35
λέγουσιν οὕτως· «'Αλλὰ οὐὰ Κουβάρ.»

15. Π ε ρ ὶ τ ο ῦ γ έ ν ο υ ς τ ῶ ν Φ α τ ε μ ι τ ῶ ν.

'Ιστέον, ὅτι ἡ Φατὲμ θυγάτηρ ἦν τοῦ Μουχούμετ, καὶ ἀπ' ἐκείνης
γεννῶνται οἱ Φατεμῖται. Οὐκ εἰσὶ δὲ οὗτοι ἐκ τοῦ Φατέμη ἀπὸ τῆς
Λιβύης χώρας, ἀλλὰ κατοικοῦσι πρὸς τὰ βορειότερα μέρη τοῦ Μέκε,
βαθύτερα τοῦ τάφου τοῦ Μουχούμετ. Εἰσὶ δὲ ἔθνος 'Αραβικόν, πρὸς 5
32ᵛP πολέμους καὶ | μάχας ἀκριβῶς ἐξησκημένον· μετὰ γὰρ τοῦ τοιούτου
γένους ἐπολέμησεν ὁ Μουχούμετ, καὶ πολλὰς πόλεις καὶ χώρας ἐπόρθη-
σεν καὶ καθυπέταξεν. Εἰσὶ γὰρ ἠνδρειωμένοι καὶ πολεμισταί, ὅτι εἰ
εὑρεθῶσι μέχρι μιᾶς χιλιάδος εἰς φοσσᾶτον, τὸ τοιοῦτον φοσσᾶτον
ἄηττητον καὶ ἀκαταμάχητον γίνεται. Οὐ καβαλλικεύουσι δὲ ἵππους, 10
ἀλλὰ καμήλους, ἐν δὲ τῷ καιρῷ τοῦ πολέμου οὐκ ἐνδύονται θώρακας,
οὔτε κλιβάνια, ἀλλὰ περιβόλαια ῥοδωτά, καὶ ἔχουσι δόρατα μακρὰ καὶ
ἀσπίδας ἀνδρομήκεις καὶ τόξα ξύλινα παμμεγέθη, σχεδὸν μὴ δυνάμενα
τείνεσθαι παρ' ὀλίγων ἀνδρῶν.

F   28 Καὶ ἐδίδαξεν — 31 εἰσέρχεται: Georg. Mon. (cod. P) app. ad p.
699, 10; cf. Theoph. p. 334, 20—22.   31 Προσεύχονται — 36 Κουβάρ:
cf. Georg. Mon. p. 706, 1—13; Cedr. ed. Bonn. I. p. 744, 9—21; Exc. cod.
Harl. 5624. I. c. p. 362.
15. 10 Οὐ καβαλλικεύουσι — 14 ἀνδρῶν: cf. Leo, Tact. XVIII. 112—115.,
ed. Migne, P. G. 107. c. 972 D—973 B.

being unable to endure his sight, I faint and fall»; and he was believed because a certain Arian, who pretended to be a monk, testified falsely in his support for love of gain. The woman being in this manner imposed on and proclaiming to other women of her tribe that he was a prophet, the lying fraud reached also the ears of a head-man whose name was Boubachar. Well, the woman died and left her husband behind to succeed her and to be heir of her estate, and he became a notable and very wealthy man, and his wicked imposture and heresy took hold on the district of Ethribos. And the crazy and deluded fellow taught those who believed on him, that he who slays an enemy or is slain by an enemy enters into paradise, and all the rest of his nonsense. And they pray, moreover, to the star of Aphrodite, which they call Koubar, and in their supplication cry out: «Alla wa Koubar», that is, 'God and Aphrodite'. For they call God 'Alla', and 'wa' they use for the conjunction 'and', and they call the star 'Koubar', and so they say 'Alla wa Koubar'.

15. Of the tribe of the Fatemites.

Fatem was a daughter of Mahomet, and from her are begotten the Fatemites. But these are not from Fatemi, from the country of Libya, but dwell in the district north of Mecca, away behind the tomb of Mahomet. They are an Arab nation, carefully trained to wars and battles; for with the aid of this tribe Mahomet went to war, and took many cities and subdued many countries. For they are brave men and warriors, so that if they be found to the number of a thousand in an army, that army cannot be defeated or worsted. They ride not horses but camels, and in time of war they do not put on corselets or coats of mail but pink-coloured cloaks, and have long spears and shields as tall as a man and enormous wooden bows which few can bend, and that with difficulty.

V 22 'Αριανοῦ P ‖ 24 ὁμοφύλαις (etiam Theoph.ᵈ): ὁμοφύλοις Be Georg. Mon. Theoph. ‖ 25 φύλαρχον Meursius Ba Be Georg. Mon.: φίλαρχον P ‖ Βουβάχαρ: 'Αβουβάχαρ coni. Thunmann ‖ 27 ἄγαν καὶ Georg. Mon.ᴾ ‖ ὑπερούσιος: περιούσιος Georg. Mon. ὑπερπλούσιος coni. Stephanus ‖ 28 Αἰθρίβου Be Theoph.ᵍ Αἰθρήβου P: 'Εθρίβου Georg. Mon. Theoph. ‖ 31 καὶ ἄλλα, ὅσα φλυαρεῖ deest in Georg. Mon. Theoph. ‖ φλυαρεῖ Be: φλυαρῇ P ‖ 33 ὅ V edd.: οὔ P ‖ καὶ Meursius Ba Be: ἡ P ‖ 34 Τὸν (littera ν addita) P² V edd.: τὸ P ‖ 'Αλλά V: 'Αλλα (sine acc.) P ‖ 34/5 ἀντὶ τοῦ καὶ συνδέσμου τιθέασιν V edd.: ἀντι καὶ συνδ' τιθέασιν P   accentum supra ἀντὶ add. itemque τοῦ et μου s. v. add. P²   ἀντὶ τοῦ καὶ συνδέσμου mg. iter. P².

15. 1 incipit cod. Mutin. gr. 179 [= M]‖ 3 Φατεμεῖται P ‖ Φατέμη edd.: Φάτεμη P ‖ 5 τοῦ¹ om. edd. ‖ 9 φοσάτον P ‖ φοσάτον P ‖ 12 ῥόδωτά edd. ῥοδοτά P: ῥυτιδωτά coni. Meursius ‖ 14 τείνεσθαι ⟨εἰ μή⟩ coni. Kyriakides.

16, 17

93Be 16. Ἐκ τοῦ κανόνος, οὗ ἐθεμάτισεν Στέφανος ὁ
33rP μαθηματικὸς περὶ τῆς τῶν Σαρακηνῶν | ἐξόδου,
ἐν ποίῳ χρόνῳ τῆς τοῦ κόσμου συστάσεως
ἐγένετο, καὶ τίς ὁ τὰ σκῆπτρα τῆς βασιλείας
Ῥωμαίων διέπων. 5

Ἐξῆλθον οἱ Σαρακηνοὶ μηνὶ Σεπτεμβρίῳ τρίτῃ, ἰνδικτιῶνος
δεκάτης, εἰς τὸ δωδέκατον ἔτος Ἡρακλείου, ἔτος ἀπὸ κτίσεως κόσμου
,ϛρλ΄. Τὸ δὲ θεμάτιν τῶν αὐτῶν Σαρακηνῶν ἐγένετο εἰς μῆνα Σεπτέμ-
βριον τρίτην, ἡμέρᾳ πέμπτῃ. Εἰς τοὺς αὐτοὺς χρόνους πρῶτος ἀρχηγὸς
τῶν Ἀράβων Μουάμεθ, ὃν οἱ Ἄραβες καλοῦσι Μουχούμετ, ὁ καὶ προ- 10
φήτης αὐτῶν χρηματίσας, ἐκράτησε δὲ τῆς ἀρχῆς τῶν Ἀράβων ἔτη
ἐννέα.

17. Ἐκ τοῦ Χρονικοῦ τοῦ μακαρίου Θεοφάνους.

Τούτῳ τῷ ἔτει, ἤγουν ,ϛρλθ΄, ἀπεβίω Μουάμεθ, ὁ τῶν Σαρακηνῶν
33vP ἀρχηγὸς καὶ ψευδοπροφήτης, προχειρισάμενος ἀν|τ᾽ αὐτοῦ Ἀβουβάχα-
ρον, τὸν καὶ Βουπάκτωρα, συγγενῆ αὐτοῦ. Οἱ δὲ πεπλανημένοι Ἑβραῖοι
ἐν ἀρχῇ τῆς παρουσίας αὐτοῦ ἐνόμισαν εἶναι τοῦτον τὸν παρ᾽ αὐτοῖς 5
προσδοκώμενον Χριστόν, ὡς καί τινας τῶν προυχόντων αὐτῶν προσ-
ελθεῖν αὐτῷ, καὶ δέξασθαι τὴν αὐτοῦ θρησκείαν, καὶ καταλιπεῖν τὴν
τοῦ θεόπτου Μωσέως. Θεωρήσαντες δὲ αὐτὸν ἐσθίοντα ἀπὸ καμήλου,
ἔγνωσαν, ὅτι οὐκ ἔστιν, ὃν ἐνόμισαν. Ἐδίδασκον δὲ αὐτὸν ἀθέμιτα
94Be κατὰ τῶν Χριστιανῶν, | καὶ διῆγον σὺν αὐτῷ. Οὗτοί εἰσιν οἱ διδάξαντες 10
αὐτὸν παραδέχεσθαι μέρη τινὰ τοῦ νόμου, τήν τε περιτομὴν καὶ ἄλλα
τινά, ἅπερ παραφυλάττονται οἱ Σαρακηνοί. Πρῶτος οὖν Ἀβουβάχαρ
34rP ἠκολούθησεν αὐτὸν καὶ προφήτην | ἐκήρυξεν, διὸ καὶ διάδοχον αὐτὸν
κατέλιπεν. Ἐκράτησεν δὲ ἡ αἵρεσις αὐτοῦ τὰ μέρη τῆς Αἰθρίβου, πρώην
μὲν ἐν κρυπτῷ ἔτη δέκα, τὸ δὲ ἔσχατον διὰ πολέμου ὁμοίως ἔτη δέκα, 15

F   16. 1 Ἐκ τοῦ — 5 διέπων: cf. H. Usener, De Stephano Alexandrino,
Index lect. Bonn. 1879. p. 3—16., 1879/80. p. 15—22, Notae Bullialdi
ad Ducae Historiam, ed. Bonn. pp. 622—626.   6 Ἐξῆλθον — 9
πέμπτῃ: cf. Leo Gramm., ed. Bonn. p. 152, 20—153, 3; Cedr., ed. Bonn.
I. p. 717, 7—17; Excerpta cod. Bruxellensis II 4836. (s. XIII.) fol. 90v,
ed. J. Davreux, Byzantion X. p. 99.
    17. 2 Τούτῳ — 10 αὐτῷ: Theoph. p. 333, 1—13; cf. Cedr., ed. Bonn. I.
p. 738, 3—11; Exc. cod. Harl. 5624., l. c. p. 358—359.   10 Οὗτοι
— 11 περιτομὴν: cf. Georg. Mon. p. 700, 5—6; Cedr. I. p. 739, 22.   14
Ἐκράτησεν — 23 ἀδικουμένοις: Theoph. p. 334, 17—27; cf. Cedr. I. p.
739, 15—17; Exc. cod. Harl. 5624., l. c. p. 359.

16. From the canon which Stephen the astrologer cast from the stars concerning the Exodus of the Saracens, in what year of the foundation of the world it took place, and who then held the sceptre of the empire of the Romans.

The Exodus of the Saracens took place on the third day of the month of September of the tenth indiction, in the twelfth year of Heraclius, in the year from the creation of the world 6130. And the horoscope of these same Saracens was cast in the month of September, on the third day of the month, the fifth day of the week. At this same time Mouameth was first chief of the Arabs, whom the Arabs call Mahomet, who was also their prophet, and he held rule over the Arabs nine years.

17. From the Chronicle of Theophanes, of blessed memory.

In this year 6139, died Mouameth, chief and false prophet of the Saracens, having appointed in his stead Aboubacharos, or Boupaktor, his kinsman. And the deluded Jews at his first appearance had taken him for the Christ whom they expect, so that some of their leading men approached him and received his religion and forsook that of Moses who beheld God. But when they saw him eating camel's flesh, they realized that he was not what they had thought him. But they taught him to do nefarious crimes against the Christians and continued in his company. These are they who taught him to accept some parts of the Law, both the circumcision and other matters, which the Saracens observe. The first to come after him, then, was Aboubachar, who had proclaimed him to be a prophet and was for that reason left behind to succeed him. And his heresy prevailed in the district of Ethribos, at first in secret ten years, and at last through

---

V   **16.** 1 οὗ: ὄν edd. || 4/5 καὶ τίς ὁ τὰ σκῆπτρα τῆς βασιλείας ῾Ρωμαίων διέπων: καὶ τίς ἦν τότε ὁ βασιλεὺς ῾Ρωμαίων V edd. || 7 δωδέκατον V M edd.: ιβ′ P   τῷ ιβ′ ἔτει (sc. ῾Ηρακλείου) Cedr. τῷ ... δωδεκάτῳ τοῦ Μωάμεθ χρόνῳ Leo Gramm. || 8 post ͵ϛρλ′ siglo ./. adhibito νῦν δὲ (ἐστιν) ͵ϛωσ′ (ἰνδικτιῶνος) ιε′, ὡς εἶναι ἀπὸ τότ(ε) ἕως νῦν χρόνοι ψμ′ mg. add. P³, quae omnia in textum receperunt V M Me, qua de causa caput hoc insiticium esse suspicatus est Meursius || 10/1 προφήτης P¹ V M edd.: προφήτην P || 11 αὐτῶν P¹ V M edd.: αὐτὸν P || δὲ om. V edd. || 12 ἐννέα edd.: θ′ P.
      17. 2 ἤγουν ͵ϛρλθ′ deest in Theoph. || Μουάμεδ Theoph. || 3 ἀντ' αὐτοῦ deest in Theoph. || 4 τὸν καὶ Βουπάκτωρα deest in Theoph. || Βουτάκτωρα V edd. || 5 τοῦτον: αὐτὸν Theoph. || 7 καταλιπεῖν: ἀφῆσαι Theoph. || 8 ἀπὸ καμήλου ἐσθίοντα V edd. || 9 δὲ deest in Theoph. || 10 διδάσκοντες edd. || 14 δὲ deest in Theoph. || Αἰθρίβου P² V edd. Theoph.ᵍ: Αἰθρίου P ᾿Εθρίβου Theoph. || 15 δέκα¹ edd.: ι′ P || δὲ deest in Theoph. || δέκα² edd.: ι′ P ||

καὶ φανερῶς ἔτη ἐννέα. Ἐδίδαξεν δὲ τοὺς ἑαυτοῦ ὑπηκόους, ὅτι ὁ ἀποκτείνας ἐχθρὸν ἢ ἀπὸ ἐχθροῦ ἀποκτεννόμενος ἀκωλύτως εἰς τὸν παράδεισον
εἰσέρχεται, τὸν δὲ παράδεισον σαρκικῆς βρώσεως καὶ πόσεως καὶ
μίξεως γυναικῶν ἔλεγεν, ποταμὸν δὲ οἴνου καὶ μέλιτος καὶ γάλακτος
καταρρεῖν, καὶ γυναικῶν τὴν ὅρασιν ἀσύγκριτον, οὐ τῶν παρόντων, 20
ἀλλ' ἄλλων, καὶ τὴν μῖξιν πολυχρόνιον ἔφασκεν καὶ διαρκῆ τὴν ἡδονὴν
καὶ ἄλλα τινὰ ἀσωτίας καὶ μωρίας ἔμπλεα, συμπαθεῖν τε ἀλλήλοις καὶ
34ᵛP βοηθεῖν | ἀδικουμένοις.

18. Δ ε ύ τ ε ρ ο ς ἀ ρ χ η γ ὸ ς τ ῶ ν Ἀ ρ ά β ω ν, Ἀ β ο υ-
β ά χ α ρ, ἔ τ η τ ρ ί α.

Οὗτος ὁ Ἀβουβάχαρ πρῶτος λαμβάνει τὴν πόλιν Γάζαν καὶ
πᾶσαν αὐτῆς τὴν περίχωρον. Τελευτᾷ δὲ ὁ αὐτὸς Ἀβουβάχαρ ἀμηρεύσας
ἔτη τρία, καὶ παραλαμβάνει τὴν ἀρχὴν Οὔμαρ, καὶ κρατεῖ τῶν Ἀράβων 5
ἔτη δώδεκα.

95Be 19. Τ ρ ί τ ο ς ἀ ρ χ η γ ὸ ς Ἀ ρ ά β ω ν, Ο ὔ μ α ρ.

Ὁ αὐτὸς οὖν Οὔμαρ ἐπεστράτευσε κατὰ τῆς Παλαιστίνης, καὶ
παρακαθίσας ἐν αὐτῇ ἐπολιόρκησεν τὴν Ἱερουσαλὴμ διετῆ χρόνον,
καὶ παρέλαβεν αὐτὴν δόλῳ. Σωφρόνιος γάρ, ὁ Ἱεροσολύμων ἐπίσκοπος,
θείῳ κινούμενος ζήλῳ καὶ ἀγχινοίᾳ διαπρέπων, λόγον ἔλαβεν παρ' 5
αὐτοῦ ὑπὲρ τῶν ἐκκλησιῶν τῆς πάσης Παλαιστίνης ἀσφαλέστατον, ὥστε
35ʳP ἀκαθαιρέτους | μεῖναι τὰς ἐκκλησίας καὶ ἀπορθήτους. Τοῦτον ἰδὼν ὁ
Σωφρόνιος ἔφη· «Ἐπ' ἀληθείας τοῦτό ἐστιν τὸ βδέλυγμα τῆς ἐρημώ-
σεως, τὸ ῥηθὲν διὰ Δανιὴλ τοῦ προφήτου ἑστὸς ἐν τόπῳ ἁγίῳ.» Οὗτος
τὸν ναὸν ἐζήτησεν τῶν Ἰουδαίων, ὃν ᾠκοδόμησε Σολομών, πρὸς τὸ ποιῆσαι 10
αὐτὸν προσκυνητήριον τῆς αὐτοῦ βλασφημίας. Καὶ ἔστι ἕως τῆς σήμερον.

F 18. 1 Δεύτερος — 6 δώδεκα: cf. Theoph. p. 336, 4—8, 14—16, 28—29;
337, 13—17; Exc. cod. Harl. 5624., l. c. p. 363.
19, 2 Ὁ αὐτὸς — 11 βλασφημίας: Theoph. p. 339, 15—24; cf. Cedr., ed.
Bonn. I. p. 746, 8—15.   8 τὸ βδέλυγμα — 9 ἁγίῳ: Matth. 24, 15;
cf. Dan. 9, 27; Vita Sophronii, ed. A. Papadopulos-Kerameus, Ἀνάλεκτα
Ἱεροσολυμιτικῆς σταχυολογίας V. p. 144.

V 16 ἔτη deest in Theoph. ‖ ἐννέα edd.: ϑ' P ‖ 17 ἀπὸ (etiam Theoph.ᶜᵈᵉᶠᵐ):
ὑπὸ V edd. Theoph. ‖ ἀποκτεννόμενος Theoph. ἀποκτενόμενος P: ἀποκτεινόμενος edd. ‖ ἀκωλύτως deest in Theoph. ‖ τὸν deest in Theoph. ‖ 19 δὲ
(etiam Theoph.ʰ): τε Theoph. ‖ 20 καταρρεῖν deest in Theoph. ‖ τὴν ὅρασιν
ἀσύγκριτον deest in Theoph. ‖ παρόντων (etiam Theoph.ᵉᶠᵍʰᵐ): παρουσῶν V

17, 18, 19

war another ten years, and openly nine years. And he taught his subjects that he who has slain an enemy or is slain by an enemy enters unhindered into paradise, and said that it is a paradise of carnal eating and drinking and lying with women, and that a river of wine and honey and milk flows down it and the women are incomparable to look upon, not such as we know here but other, and he fabled that intercourse with them is of long duration and the pleasure continuous, and other matters replete with libertinism and folly; and they are to forgive one another and aid one another when wronged.

18. The second chief of the Arabs, Aboubachar, three years.

This Aboubachar first took the city of Gaza and all the territory round about it. And the same Aboubachar died after ruling as emir three years, and Oumar succeeded to the rule and governed the Arabs twelve years.

19. The third chief of the Arabs, Oumar.

This same Oumar marched against Palestine, and laid siege in it and blockaded Jerusalem for the space of two years, and took it by guile. For Spohronius, bishop of Jerusalem, one moved with divine zeal and excellent in sagacity, received from him a most sure undertaking concerning the churches throughout Palestine, so that the churches were neither destroyed nor sacked. When Sophronius saw him, he said: «Of a truth this is the abomination of desolation spoken of by Daniel the prophet, that standeth in the holy place.» He demanded the temple of the Jews that Solomon built, to make it the place of worship of his blasphemy. And it is so to this day.

Theoph. ‖ 21 ἔφασκεν: εἶναι Theoph. ‖ διαρκῆ τὴν Be Theoph.: διαρκιτικὴν P ‖ 22 ἔμπλεα V edd.: ἔμπλεω P   μεστὰ Theoph. ‖ τε: δὲ Theoph.

18. 2 τρία scr. Moravcsik: γ′ P Ba Be ‖ 3 Ἀβουβάχαρ (etiam Theoph.ef): Ἀβουβάχαρος Theoph. ‖ 5 τρία edd.: γ′ P   δύο ἥμισυ hic, sed alio loco γ′ Theoph. ‖ 5 Οὔμαρος Theoph. ‖ 6 δώδεκα edd.: ιβ′ P.

19. 1 Οὔμαρ] litteras rest. P² ‖ 2 Οὔμαρος Theoph. ‖ ἐπεστράτευσε (etiam Meursius Migne Theoph.): ἀπεστράτευσε V edd. ‖ τῆς deest in Theoph. ‖ 3 ἐν αὐτῇ ἐπολιόρκησεν deest in Theoph. ‖ τὴν Ἱερουσαλήμ: τὴν ἁγίαν πόλιν Theoph. ‖ 4 καὶ deest in Theoph. ‖ αὐτὴν δόλῳ] litteras ἣν δόλῳ rest. P² ‖ δόλῳ: λόγῳ Theoph. ‖ ἐπίσκοπος: ἀρχιερεὺς Theoph ‖ 5 θείῳ κινούμενος ζήλῳ καὶ ἀγχινοίᾳ διαπρέπων deest in Theoph. ‖ 5/6 παρ' αὐτοῦ ὑπὲρ τῶν ἐκκλησιῶν τῆς deest in Theoph. ‖ 6 ἀσφαλέστατον (etiam Theoph.codd.): ἀσφαλείας Theoph. ‖ 6 ὥστε — 7 ἀπορθήτους deest in Theoph. ‖ 7 ὁ deest in Theoph. ‖ 9 ἑστῶς P   ἑστὼς Theoph.cdg ‖ Οὗτος: Οὔμαρος Theoph. ‖ 10 πρὸς τὸ deest in Theoph.

20. Τέταρτος Ἀράβων ἀρχηγός, Οὐθμάν.

Οὗτος λαμβάνει τὴν Ἀφρικὴν πολέμῳ, καὶ στοιχήσας φόρους μετὰ τῶν Ἄφρων ὑπέστρεψεν. Τούτου στρατηγὸς χρηματίζει Μαυίας, ὁ παραλύσας τὸν κολοσσὸν Ῥόδου καὶ πορθήσας Κύπρον τὴν νῆσον καὶ πάσας τὰς πόλεις αὐτῆς. Οὗτος παραλαμβάνει καὶ νῆσον τὴν Ἄραδον, 5
35ᵛP καὶ τὴν πόλιν αὐτῆς ἐνέπρησεν, | καὶ τὴν νῆσον ἀοίκητον κατέστησεν ἕως τοῦ νῦν. Οὗτος τὴν νῆσον Ῥόδον καταλαβὼν καθεῖλε τὸν ἐν αὐτῇ
96Be κολοσσὸν μετὰ χίλια τζ΄ ἔτη τῆς αὐτοῦ | ἱδρύσεως, ὃν Ἰουδαῖός τις ἔμπορος ὠνησάμενος Ἐδεσσηνός, Θ΄ καμήλους ἐφόρτωσεν αὐτοῦ τὸν χαλκόν. Οὗτος ὁ Μαυίας ἐπεστράτευσε καὶ κατὰ Κωνσταντινουπόλεως, 10 καὶ ἐλυμήνατο τήν τε Ἔφεσον καὶ Ἁλικαρνασσὸν καὶ Σμύρνην καὶ τὰς λοιπὰς πόλεις Ἰωνίας, ὃς καὶ γέγονεν τῶν Ἀράβων ἀρχηγὸς πέμπτος μετὰ τὴν Οὐθμὰν τελευτὴν ἔτη εἴκοσι τέσσαρα.

21. Ἐκ τοῦ Χρονικοῦ Θεοφάνους· ἔτος ἀπὸ κτίσεως κόσμου ϛροα΄.

Ἰστέον, ὅτι πρὸς τῇ τελευτῇ Μαυίου, τῶν Ἀράβων ἀρχηγοῦ,
36ʳP εἰσῆλθον οἱ Μαρδαῖται εἰς τὸν Λίβανον, καὶ ἐκράτησαν ἀπὸ | τοῦ Μαύρου ὄρους ἕως τῆς ἁγίας πόλεως, καὶ ἐχειρώσαντο τὰς τοῦ Λιβάνου περιωπάς· 5 καὶ πολλοὶ δοῦλοι καὶ αὐτόχθονες πρὸς αὐτοὺς κατέφυγον, ὥστε δι᾽ ὀλίγου χρόνου εἰς πολλὰς χιλιάδας γενέσθαι. Καὶ τοῦτο μαθὼν Μαυίας καὶ οἱ σύμβουλοι αὐτοῦ, ἐφοβήθησαν σφόδρα. Καὶ ἀποστέλλει πρέσβεις πρὸς τὸν αὐτοκράτορα Κωνσταντῖνον ζητῶν εἰρήνην. Ἐπὶ ταύτῃ τῇ προφάσει πέμπεται παρὰ τοῦ βασιλέως Κωνσταντίνου, τοῦ ὀρθοδόξου, 10 υἱοῦ τοῦ Πωγωνάτου, Ἰωάννης ὁ ἐπίκλην Πιτζηκαύδης. Τούτου δὲ καταλαβόντος ἐν Συρίᾳ, Μαυίας ἐδέξατο αὐτὸν μετὰ μεγάλης τιμῆς,

F   20. 2 Οὗτος — 3 ὑπέστρεψεν: cf. Theoph. p. 343, 17—20, 24—28.   3
Μαυίας — 5 αὐτῆς: cf. Theoph. p. 345, 8—9; 343, 30—31; Cedr., ed.
Bonn. I. p. 755, 1—2, 8—9.   5 Οὗτος — 7 νῦν: Theoph. p. 344,
12—15; cf. Cedr. I. p. 755, 3—5.   7 Οὗτος — 10 χαλκόν: Theoph.
p. 345, 8—11; cf. Cedr. I. p. 755, 8—10; Zon. XIV. 19., ed. Bonn. III. p.
219, 7—10.   10 Οὗτος — Κωνσταντινουπόλεως: cf. Theoph. p. 345,
16—18.   11 ἐλυμήνατο — 12 Ἰωνίας: cf. Theoph. p. 353, 14—16;
Cedr. I. p. 764, 18—20.   12 ὃς — 13 τέσσαρα: cf. Theoph. p. 346,
20—21, 25; 355, 1—5.
        21. 4 εἰσῆλθον — 16 εὐγενεῖς ν΄: Theoph. p. 355, 6—25; cf. Niceph.,
ed. de Boor p. 32, 23—33, 6; Cedr., ed. Bonn. I. p. 765, 19—766, 6; Zon.
XIV. 20., ed. Bonn. III. p. 224, 11—225, 7.

20, 21
20. The fourth chief of the Arabs, Outhman.

He took Africa by war, and arranged imposts with the Africans and returned. His general was Mauias, who pulled down the colossus of Rhodes and took the island of Cyprus and all its cities. He took the island of Arados also and burnt its city, and made the island desolate to this day. When he came to the island of Rhodes, he demolished the colossus in it, one thousand 360 years after it had been set up, and a Jewish merchant of Edessa bought it and loaded 900 camels with the bronze of it. This Mauias also made an expedition against Constantinople and ravaged Ephesus and Halicarnassus and Smyrna and the rest of the cities of Ionia, and after the death of Outhman was fifth chief of the Arabs for twenty-four years.

21. From the Chronicle of Theophanes: the year from the creation of the world 6171.

At the end of the life of Mauias, chief of the Arabs, the Mardaïtes entered the Lebanon and took possession of it from the Black mountain to the holy city, and made themselves masters of the summits of the Lebanon; and many slaves and natives ran to them for refuge, in numbers which shortly amounted to many thousands. On learning this, Mauias was greatly alarmed, and his counsellors with him. And he sent envoys to the emperor Constantine, seeking for peace. Therefore, the emperor Constantine, the orthodox, son of Pogonatus, dispatched John surnamed Pitzikaudis. And when he arrived in Syria, Mauias received him with great honour, and it

---

V   **20.** 1 ἀρχηγὸς ᾿Αράβων V edd. || 3 Μαυίας P Theoph.: Μαβίας P² V M || 6 καὶ τὴν² *bis* P || 7 νῆσον *deest in* Theoph. || ἐν αὐτῇ *corr.* Moravcsik: ἑαυτῇ P   ἑαυτῆς V M Me Ba   αὐτῆς Be   ἐν αὐτῇ *deest in* Theoph. || 8 χίλια τξ': ͵ατξ' Theoph. || 9 ᾿Εδεσινὸς P || ͵θ' *corr.* Moravcsik   ἐννακοσίας Ba Be Theoph.: ͵λ P   τριάκοντα χιλιάδας *s. v. add.* P³ V M Me || 10 Μαυίας P Theoph.: Μαβίας P² V M || 11 Σμύρνην *corr.* Moravcsik: Σμύρνης P M   Σμύρναν P² V edd. || 12 πέμπτος V edd.: ε' *s. v. add.* P¹   *in textum recepit* M || 13 Οὐθμὰν] *litteras rest.* P².
21. 3 Μαυίου P: Μαβίου P² V M || 3 *post* ᾿Αράβων *s. v. add.* πέμπτου P³ *in textum receperunt* V M edd. || 4 οἱ (*habet etiam* Cedr.): *deest in* Theoph. || Μαρδαΐται P || 7 τοῦτο: ταῦτα Theoph. || Μαυίας P Theoph.: Μαβίας P² V M || 8 πρέσβεις P³ V M edd.: πρέσβης P || 9/10/᾿Επὶ ταύτη τῇ προφάσει *deest in* Theoph. || 10 πέμπεται: ἀπέστειλε Theoph. || 10/1 Κωνσταντίνου, τοῦ ὀρθοδόξου, υἱοῦ τοῦ Πωγωνάτου *deest in* Theoph. || 11 υἱοῦ *omittendum coni.* Meursius Bandurius   *secl.* Be   *post* υἱοῦ *comma posuit* Migne || τοῦ *om.* V Me || ὁ: τὸ Theoph. || Πιτζηκαύδης: Πιτζικαύδην Cedr.   Πιτζιγαῦδιν Theoph. ||

36ᵛP καὶ συνεφωνήθη πρὸς ἀμφοτέρους ἔγγραφον γενέσθαι | εἰρήνης μεθ᾽
ὅρκου λόγον ἐπὶ συμφώνου ἐτησίου πάκτου, παρέχεσθαι τῷ τῶν Ῥω-
97Be μαίων βασιλεῖ παρὰ τῶν Ἀγαρηνῶν χρυσίου | χιλιάδας τρεῖς καὶ 15
ἄνδρας αἰχμαλώτους ω΄ καὶ ἵππους εὐγενεῖς ν΄. Ἐπὶ τούτου διῃρέθη
ἡ τῶν Ἀράβων ἀρχὴ εἰς μέρη δύο. Καὶ εἰς μὲν τὴν Αἴθριβου ἐκράτησε
τὴν ἀρχὴν ὁ Ἀλή, τὴν δὲ Αἴγυπτον καὶ Παλαιστίνην καὶ Δαμασκὸν
ἐκράτει ὁ Μαυίας. Καὶ οἱ μὲν τὴν Αἴθριβον οἰκοῦντες μετὰ τῶν υἱῶν
τοῦ Ἀλὴ ἐστράτευσαν κατὰ τοῦ Μαυίου. Ὁ δὲ Μαυίας ἀνθωπλίσατο 20
κατ᾽ αὐτῶν, καὶ συνῆψεν πόλεμον παρὰ τὸν ποταμὸν Εὐφράτην, καὶ
ἡττήθη τὸ μέρος Ἀλή, καὶ παρέλαβεν ὁ Μαυίας τὴν Αἴθριβον καὶ
πᾶσαν τὴν γῆν τῆς Συρίας. Ἐκράτησεν δὲ ἡ αὐτοῦ γενεὰ ἔτη πε΄. Καὶ
37ʳP μετ᾽ αὐτὸν ἐξῆλθον οἱ λεγόμε|νοι Μαυροφόροι ἀπὸ Περσίδος, | οἱ κρατοῦν-
τες ἕως τῆς σήμερον, καὶ ἐπολέμησαν τὴν γενεὰν τοῦ Μαυίου καὶ ἠφάνι- 25
σαν αὐτήν. Ἔσφαξαν δὲ καὶ Μαρουάμ, τὴν κεφαλὴν αὐτῶν. Ὑπελείφθησαν δὲ ὀλίγοι τοῦ Μαυίου, καὶ ἐδιώχθησαν παρὰ τῶν Μαυροφόρων
ἕως τῆς Ἀφρικῆς μετὰ καὶ ἑνὸς ἐκγόνου τοῦ Μαυίου. Ὁ δὲ αὐτὸς ἔκγονος τοῦ Μαυίου μετ᾽ ὀλίγων τινῶν διεπέρασεν εἰς τὴν Ἰσπανίαν ἐν
ταῖς ἡμέραις Ἰουστινιανοῦ τοῦ Ῥινοτμήτου, οὐχὶ δὲ τοῦ Πωγωνάτου. 30
Τοῦτο δὲ παρὰ τοῖς ἡμετέροις ἱστορικοῖς οὐ γέγραπται. Ἀφ᾽ οὗ γὰρ
παρελήφθη ἡ μεγάλη Ῥώμη παρὰ τῶν Γότθων, ἤρξατο ἀκρωτηριάζεσθαι
τὰ Ῥωμαϊκὰ πράγματα, καὶ οὐδεὶς τῶν ἱστορικῶν τῶν τῆς Ἰσπανίας
37ᵛP
98Be μερῶν ἐποιήσατο μνείαν, οὔτε τῆς γενεᾶς | τοῦ Μαυίου. Ἔχει | δὲ τοῦ
μακαρίου Θεοφάνους ἡ ἱστορία οὕτως. Ἀπεβίω οὖν ὁ Μαυίας, ὁ τῶν 35
Σαρακηνῶν ἀρχηγός, γεγονὼς στρατηγὸς ἔτη κς΄, ἀμηρεύσας δὲ ἔτη
κδ΄. Καὶ ἐκράτησεν τῆς ἀρχῆς τῶν Ἀράβων Ἰζίδ, ὁ υἱὸς αὐτοῦ, ἔτη ς΄.
Τούτου τελευτήσαντος, ἐταράχθησαν οἱ Ἄραβες τῆς Αἰθρίβου, καὶ
διεγερθέντες κατέστησαν ἑαυτοῖς ἀρχηγὸν Ἀβδελᾶν, τὸν υἱὸν Ζουβέρ.
Τοῦτο ἀκούσαντες οἱ τὴν Φοινίκην καὶ Παλαιστίνην καὶ Δαμασκὸν 40
κατοικοῦντες Ἀγαρηνοί, ἔρχονται πρὸς Οὐσάν, ἀμηρᾶν Παλαιστίνης, καὶ
προβάλλονται Μαρουάμ, καὶ ἱστῶσιν αὐτὸν ἀρχηγόν, καὶ κρατεῖ τῆς
ἀρχῆς μῆνας θ΄. Τούτου δὲ τελευτήσαντος, Ἀβιμέλεχ, ὁ υἱὸς αὐτοῦ

F   16 Ἐπὶ τούτου — 23 Συρίας: cf. Theoph. p. 346, 20—347, 4;
347, 26—28.   23 Καὶ μετ᾽ αὐτὸν — 30 Πωγωνάτου: cf. Theoph.
p. 403, 12—13; 424, 12—16; 425, 13—15; 426, 1—7.   35 Ἀπεβίω
— 37 ἔτη ς΄: Theoph. p. 356, 15—17; 360, 13—17.   38 Τούτου —
46 διάδοχος: Theoph. p. 360, 27—361, 3.

V 13 καὶ deest in Theoph.   ‖   ἀμφοτέρους: ἑκατέρους Theoph.   ‖   14 λόγον
V edd. Theoph.: λόγων P Theoph.ᵈᵍ   ‖   14/15 τῷ τῶν Ῥωμαίων βασιλεῖ:
τῇ Ῥωμαϊκῇ πολιτείᾳ Theoph.   ‖   15 χρυσίου (etiam Niceph. Cedr. Zon.):

21

was agreed on both sides that a convention of peace should be drawn up
in writing and sworn to, on the basis of an agreed annual tribute, the Agarenes
to pay to the emperor of the Romans three thousand pieces of gold and 800
prisoners and 50 thoroughbred horses. At this time the empire of the Arabs
was divided in two parts. In Ethribos Ali held rule, but Mauias held Egypt
and Palestine and Damascus. And the dwellers in Ethribos marched with
the sons of Ali against Mauias. And Mauias armed himself against them
and joined battle by the river Euphrates, and the party of Ali was defeated,
and Mauias took Ethribos and all the land of Syria. And his family held rule
85 years. And after him came forth the so-called Black-robed out of Persia,
who hold rule to this day, and they fought with the clan of Mauias and
utterly destroyed it. And they slew Marouam also, who was its head. And
few of the party of Mauias were left, and they, together with one grandson
of Mauias, were pursued by the Black-robed as far as Africa. Now this
same grandson of Mauias with a few followers crossed over into Spain in
the days of Justinian Rhinotmetus, not of Pogonatus. But this has not
been written by our historians. For from the time of the capture of old
Rome by the Goths, the Roman possessions began to be lopped off, and
none of the historians has made mention of the region of Spain, nor of the
clan of Mauias. But the history of Theophanes, of blessed memory, has the
following account: And so Mauias, chief of the Saracens, died, who had been
general 26 years, and had ruled as emir 24 years. And Izid, his son, held rule
over the Arabs 6 years. On his death the Arabs of Ethribos were disturbed,
and they arose and set up Abdelas, son of Zouber, to be their chief. When they
heard this, the Arabs who dwelt in Phoenicia and Palestine and Damascus
came to Ousan, the emir of Palestine, and appointed Marouam and set
him up to be chief, and he held the rule 9 months. On his death, his son
Abimelech succeeded to the rule and held it 22 years and 6 months. And

---

χρυσοῦ Theoph. ‖ 16 ω': ν' Theoph. ‖ τούτου Be: τούτω P ‖ 19 Μαυίας P:
Μαβίας Pʸ mg. P⁷ V M ‖ 20 Μαυίου P V: Μαβίου Pʸ M ‖ Μαυίας P V: Μαβίας
Pʸ M ‖ ἀνθοπλήσατο P ‖ 22 Μαυίας P V: Μαβίας Pʸ M ‖ 23 τῆς om. V edd. ‖
πε' P V M: ο' (littera π ex dimidia parte, ε autem penitus erasa) Pʸ Ba Be ‖
24 αὐτὸν V edd.: αὐτῶν P ‖ 25 ἐπολέμισαν P ‖ Μαυίου P V: Μαβίου Pʸ M ‖
27 Μαυίου P V: Μαβίου Pʸ M ‖ 28 Μαυίου P V: Μαβίου Pʸ M ‖ 29 Μαυίου
P V: Μαβίου Pʸ M ‖ 34 Μαυίου P V: Μαβίου Pʸ M ‖ 35 ἡ inser. Pˣ in
textum receperunt V M Ba Be ‖ οὖν ὁ deest in Theoph. ‖ Μαυίας P V: Μαβίας
Pʸ M ‖ 36 ἀρχηγός: πρωτοσύμβουλος Theoph. ‖ κς' (etiam Theoph.ᵉᶠᵐ):
κ' Theoph. ‖ 37 Ἀράβων Ἰζίδ: post Ἀράβων mg. ἔτη, post ιζ s. v. καὶ, post
ιδ s. v. ἡως λα' add. P² ἔτη ιζ' καὶ ιδ' ἡὸς λα' in textum recepit M ‖ ς': γ'
Theoph. ‖ 38 τῆς Ba Be: τοῦ P Theoph. ‖ Αἰθρίβου (etiam Theoph.ᵍ):
Ἐθρίβου Theoph. ‖ 39 Ἀβδελὰν P ‖ τὸν: τινα Theoph. ‖ 40 Τοῦτο ἀκούσαντες
deest in Theoph. ‖ 40/1 οἱ τὴν Φοινίκην καὶ Παλαιστίνην καὶ Δαμασκὸν
κατοικοῦντες Ἀγαρηνοί: Οἱ Φοίνικες καὶ οἱ Παλαιστίνης ἐπὶ τὴν Δαμασκὸν
Theoph. ‖ 41 Οὐσάν: Ἀσὰν Theoph. ‖ ἀμηρὰν P ‖ 42 προβάλλονται: δίδουσι
χεῖρας δεξιὰς τῷ Theoph. ‖ 42/3 κρατεῖ τῆς ἀρχῆς: ἀμηρεύει Theoph. ‖
43 Ἀβιμέλεχ] litteras rest. P² ‖

21

διαδέχεται τὴν ἀρχήν, καὶ κρατεῖ ἔτη κβ' καὶ μῆνας ς'. Καί χειροῦται
38ʳᴾ τοὺς | τυράννους, καὶ ἀποκτέννει τὸν Ἀβδελᾶν, υἱὸν Ζουβὲρ καὶ διά- 45
δοχον. Ἐν τούτοις τελευτᾷ Κωνσταντῖνος ὁ βασιλεύς, ὁ υἱὸς τοῦ Πωγωνάτου, κρατήσας τῆς Ῥωμαίων ἀρχῆς ἔτη ιζ'· καὶ ἐβασίλευσεν ἀντ'
αὐτοῦ Ἰουστινιανός, ὁ υἱὸς αὐτοῦ.

Ἰστέον, ὅτι ὁ τῶν Ἀράβων ἀρχηγός, ⟨ὃς⟩ πέμπτος ἀπὸ τοῦ
Μουάμεθ ἐκράτησεν τῆς ἀρχῆς τῶν Ἀράβων, οὐκ ἐκ τοῦ γένους ἦν τοῦ 50
Μουάμεθ, ἀλλ' ἐξ ἑτέρας φυλῆς. Καὶ πρῶτον μὲν ἐχειροτονήθη στρατηγὸς
καὶ ναύαρχος παρὰ Οὐθμάν, ἀρχηγοῦ τῶν Ἀράβων, καὶ ἀπεστάλη κατὰ
τῆς Ῥωμαίων πολιτείας μετὰ χειρὸς ἰσχυρᾶς καὶ καταφράκτων νηῶν
99Be ασ'. Καὶ | εἰσῆλθεν ἕως τῆς Ῥόδου, κἀκεῖθεν ἐξοπλισάμενος ἀνῆλθεν
38ᵛᴾ ἕως Κωνσταντινούπολιν, καὶ διατρίψας χρόνον | ἱκανόν, λεηλατήσας 55
τε τὰ ἔξω τοῦ Βυζαντίου, ὑπέστρεψεν ἄπρακτος. Ἐλθὼν δὲ ἐν τῇ
Ῥόδῳ καθεῖλεν τὸν κολοσσὸν τὸν ἐν αὐτῇ ἱστάμενον. Ἄγαλμα δὲ ἦν
τοῦ ἡλίου χαλκοῦν, κεχρυσωμένον ἀπὸ κεφαλῆς ἕως ποδῶν, ἔχον ὕψος
πήχεις π' καὶ πλάτος ἀναλόγως τοῦ ὕψους, καθὼς μαρτυρεῖ τὸ ἐπίγραμμα
τὸ πρὸς τὴν βάσιν τῶν ποδῶν αὐτοῦ γεγραμμένον, ἔχον οὕτως·   60
      Τὸν ἐν Ῥόδῳ κολοσσὸν ὀκτάκις δέκα
      Λάχης ἐποίει πηχέων, ὁ Λίνδιος.
Ἔλαβεν δὲ τὸν χαλκὸν αὐτοῦ καὶ διεπέρασεν αὐτὸν ἐν Συρίᾳ, καὶ ἔστησεν
αὐτὸν εἰς ἀγορὰν παντὶ τῷ βουλομένῳ· ὠνήσατο δὲ αὐτὸν Ἑβραῖος
Ἐδεσσηνός, ἐπιφορτώσας αὐτὸν ἀπὸ θαλάσσης καμήλους ϡπ'. Τελευτή- 65
39ʳᴾ σαντος οὖν τοῦ Οὐθμάν, διεδέξατο τὴν τῶν Ἀράβων | ἀρχὴν αὐτὸς ὁ
Μαυίας. Ἐκράτησεν δὲ τῆς ἁγίας πόλεως καὶ τῶν τῆς Παλαιστίνης
μερῶν, τήν τε Δαμασκὸν καὶ Ἀντιόχειαν καὶ πάσας τὰς τῆς Αἰγύπτου
πόλεις. Ὁ δὲ Ἀλήμ, ὃς ἦν γαμβρὸς τοῦ Μουάμεθ ἐπὶ θυγατρί, καλου-
μένη Φατιμέ, ἐκράτησεν τῆς Αἰθρίβου καὶ πάσης τῆς τραχείας Ἀραβίας. 70
Ἐν ταύταις οὖν ταῖς ἡμέραις διηγέρθησαν πρὸς πόλεμον κατ' ἀλλήλων

F   46 Ἐν τούτοις — 48 υἱὸς αὐτοῦ: Theoph. p. 361, 15—16; cf.
Cedr. I. p. 770, 22—24.   51 Καὶ πρῶτον — 54 ,ασ': cf. Theoph.
p. 343, 30—31; Cedr. I. p. 755, 1—2.   54 Καὶ εἰσῆλθεν — Ῥόδου:
cf. Theoph. p. 345, 8; Cedr. I. p. 755, 8.   54 κἀκεῖθεν — 55
Κωνσταντινούπολιν: cf. Theoph. p. 345, 16—18; Cedr. I. p. 755,
17—18.   56 Ἐλθὼν— 57 ἱστάμενον: cf. Theoph. p. 345, 8—9; Cedr. I. p.
755, 8—9.   57 Ἄγαλμα — 62 Λίνδιος: cf. Cedr. I. p. 755,
10—16.   61 Τὸν ἐν — 62 Λίνδιος: cf. Simonidis epigr. 165., ed. Diehl, A. L.
Gr. II². 5. p. 143; Strabo XIV. 2, 5., p. 652; Ps.—Draco, De metris,
ed. Hermann p. 99.   64 ὠνήσατο — 65 ϡπ': Theoph. p. 345,
9—11; cf. Cedr. I. p. 755, 9—10; Zon. XIV. 19., ed. Bonn. III. p. 219,
9—10.   65 Τελευτήσαντος— 69 πόλεις: cf. Theoph. p. 346, 20—25.   71
Ἐν ταύταις — 74 ἀλλήλων: cf. Theoph. p. 346, 27—347, 4; 347,
27—28.

21

he overcame the rebels, and slew Abdelas, son and successor of Zouber. Meanwhile, the emperor Constantine, son of Pogonatus, died, having held rule over the Romans 17 years; and his son Justinian reigned in his stead. The chief of the Arabs *who* was fifth after Mouameth to hold rule over the Arabs was not of the family of Mouameth, but of another tribe. And first he was appointed general and admiral by Outhman, chief of the Arabs, and was sent against the state of the Romans with a strong force and 1200 decked ships. He proceeded to Rhodes, and thence, after fitting out his expedition, came up to Constantinople, and lingered a long time, and laid waste the environs of Byzantium, but returned with his purpose unachieved. When he came to Rhodes, he pulled down the colossus that stood in it. It was a brazen statue of the sun, gilded from head to foot, 80 cubits in height and broad in proportion, as witness the inscription written on the base of its feet, running like this:

The Rhodian colossus, eight times ten
Cubits in height, Laches of Lindos made.

He took the bronze of it and carried it over into Syria, and put it up for sale to any who wanted it; and a Hebrew of Edessa bought it and brought it up from the sea laden on 980 camels. On the death of Outhman, then, this Mauias succeeded to the rule of the Arabs. And he ruled over the holy city and the regions of Palestine, over Damascus and Antioch and all the cities of Egypt. But Alim, who was son-in-law of Mouameth, having married his daughter called Fatime, ruled over Ethribos and all Arabia Tracheia. Now, in these days Alim and Mauias were roused up to war against one

---

V 44 κρατεῖ ἔτη κβ' καὶ μῆνας ϛ': ἀμηρεύσας ἔτη κα' ἥμισυ Theoph. ‖ 45 ἀποκτέννει Theoph. ἀποκτενεῖ P: ἀποκτείνει V edd. ‖ 'Αβδελὰν P ‖ Ζουβὲρ] litteras ζου rest. P² ‖ 45/6 διάδοχον (etiam Theoph.cefghm): Δάδαχον Theoph. ‖ 46 τελευτᾷ: ἀνεπάη Theoph. ‖ 46/7 ὁ βασιλεύς, ὁ υἱὸς τοῦ Πωγωνάτου deest in Theoph. ‖ 47 τῆς 'Ρωμαίων ἀρχῆς deest in Theoph. τὴν 'Ρωμαίων ἀρχὴν edd. ‖ ιζ'] litteras rest. P² ‖ 47/8 ἀντ' αὐτοῦ deest in Theoph. ‖ 48 'Ιουστινιανὸς V M edd.: 'Ιουστιανὸς P ‖ 49 post ἀρχηγός s. v. add. Μαβίας P³ in textum receperunt V M edd. ‖ ὃς addendum coni. Bekker ‖ 50 ἦν s. v. add. P³ in textum receperunt M Ba Be ‖ 53 καταφράκτων νηῶν: σκάφη Theoph. ‖ 54 ,ασ': ,αψ' Theoph. ‖ 55 post ἱκανόν s. v. add. ἥτι ζ' ἔτη P³ ἤτοι ἔτη ζ' in textum receperunt V edd. ‖ 61 Τὸν ἐν 'Ρόδῳ κολοσσὸν: 'τὸν 'Ηλίου κ. vel ὃν εἰσορᾶις κ. (sic Robert l. c.) fuit in statua ' Diehl ‖ ὀκτάκις (etiam Simonides Ps.-Draco): ἑπτάκις Strabo ‖ 62 Λάχης: Χάρης Simonides Strabo Ps.-Draco ‖ ὀλίνδιος P ‖ 63 αὐτὸν om. edd. ‖ post ἐν add. τῇ edd. ‖ 64 ὀνήσατο P ‖ 65 'Εδεσσηνός coni. Meursius 'Εδεσηνὸς Theoph. coni. Bandurius: 'Εμησινὸς P ὁ 'Εμεσηνός Be ‖ Ꙃπ' P ἐννακοσίας καὶ ὀγδοήκοντα Ba Be: ,λπ' (littera Ꙃ partim erasa) Pˣ V Me τριάκοντα χιλιάδας καὶ ὀγδοήκοντα mg. P² ἐννακοσίας Theoph. ‖ 66 Οὐθμάν] litteras θμὰν in ras. scr. P² ‖ αὐτὸς om. edd. ‖ 67 Μαυίας P V: Μαβίας Pʸ M ‖ 69 'Αλήμ: 'Αλή Theoph. ‖ ὃς ἦν] litteras ϛ ἦν in ras. scr. P² ‖ post θυγατρὶ add. τῇ edd. ‖ 70 Αἰθρίβου P² V edd.: Αἰθρίου P ‖

ὅ τε Ἀλὴμ καὶ ὁ Μαυίας ἐρίζοντες περὶ τῆς ἀρχῆς, τίς αὐτῶν κυριεύσει
100Be πά|σης Συρίας. Συνήχθησαν δὲ παρὰ τὸν Εὐφράτην ποταμόν, καὶ συνά-
πτουσι πόλεμον ἰσχυρὸν μετ᾽ ἀλλήλων. Τοῦ δὲ πολέμου κρατοῦντος, καὶ
πολλῶν ἐξ ἀμφοτέρων πιπτόντων, ἔκραξαν τὰ πλήθη τῶν Ἀγαρηνῶν 75
39ᵛP ἀμφοτέρων τῶν {δύο} μερῶν· | «Τίνι τρόπῳ σφάζομεν καὶ σφαζόμεθα,
καὶ ἀφανίζεται τὸ γένος ἡμῶν ἐκ τῆς τῶν ἀνθρώπων βιοτῆς; Ἀλλὰ
χωρισθήτωσαν δύο γέροντες ἐξ ἀμφοτέρων τῶν μερῶν, καὶ ὃν ἂν προκρίνωσιν, ἐχέτω τὴν ἀρχήν.» Ὁ δὲ Ἀλὴμ καὶ ὁ Μαυίας ἠρέσθησαν
ἐπὶ τῷ λόγῳ αὐτῶν, καὶ ἐκβαλόντες ἐκ τῶν χειρῶν τοὺς ἑαυτῶν δακτυ- 80
λίους, δεδώκασι τοῖς δυσὶ γέρουσιν, ὅπερ ἐστὶ σημεῖον τῆς ἀρχῆς τῶν
Ἀγαρηνῶν, καὶ παρέσχον τὴν ἐξουσίαν αὐτῶν εἰς τὴν θέλησιν τῶν δύο
γερόντων, τὸ πρᾶγμα ἔνορκον ποιησάμενοι καὶ τοῦτο στοιχήσαντες,
ἵνα ὃν ἂν προκρίνωσιν οἱ γέροντες, ἐκεῖνος ἔσται κύριος καὶ ἀρχηγὸς
40ʳP πάντων τῶν Σαρακηνῶν. Καὶ εἰσελθόντων τῶν δύο γερόντων | ἀναμέσον 85
τῆς παρεμβολῆς τοῦ πολέμου τῶν δύο μερῶν καὶ σταθέντων ἐν τῷ
μεταιχμίῳ τοῦ στρατοπέδου ἀντιπροσώπων, τοῦ μὲν Ἀλὴμ ὁ γέρων
ὑπῆρχεν κατὰ τὸ τῶν Σαρακηνῶν ἔθνος εὐλαβής, οἵους ἐκεῖνοι λέγουσι
καδῆς, τουτέστιν πιστοὺς καὶ ἡγιασμένους· ὁ δὲ τοῦ Μαυίου γέρων
ἐν σχήματι μόνῳ ἦν εὐλαβής, τὰ δ᾽ ἄλλα δολερὸς καὶ αὐθάδης καὶ πονηρίᾳ 90
πάντας ὑπερβάλλων ἀνθρώπους. Εἶπεν δὲ ὁ τοῦ Μαυίου γέρων πρὸς
101Be τὸν γέροντα τοῦ Ἀλήμ, ὅτι· «Σὺ πρῶτος εἰπέ, ὅπερ βούλῃ, | ὃς εἶ τε
φρόνιμος καὶ εὐλαβὴς καὶ μακρὰ τοὺς ἐμοὺς χρόνους ὑπερβαλλόμενος.»
Καὶ ἀπεκρίθη ὁ γέρων τοῦ Ἀλὴμ τοῦτο, ὅτι· «Ἐξέβαλον τὸν Ἀλὴμ
40ᵛP ἐκ τῆς ἀρχῆς, ὡς ἐξήγαγον τὸν δακτύ|λιον αὐτοῦ ἐκ τῆς χειρὸς αὐτοῦ 95
καὶ εἰσήγαγον εἰς τὸν ἐμὸν δάκτυλον· ἐκβάλω καὶ τὸν δακτύλιον τοῦ
Ἀλὴμ ἐκ τοῦ δακτύλου μου, συνεκβαλὼν αὐτὸν καὶ τῆς ἀρχῆς αὐτοῦ.»
Καὶ ἀνταπεκρίθη ὁ τοῦ Μαυίου γέρων, ὡς ὅτι· «Εἰσήγαγον τὸν Μαυίαν
εἰς τὴν ἀρχήν, ὥσπερ εἰσήγαγον τὸν δακτύλιον αὐτοῦ εἰς τὸν δάκτυλόν
μου· εἰσαγάγω καὶ τὸν δακτύλιον τοῦ Μαυίου εἰς τὸν δάκτυλον αὐτοῦ.»100
Καὶ τότε διεχωρίσθησαν ἀπ᾽ ἀλλήλων. Παραλαμβάνει οὖν ὁ Μαυίας
πᾶσαν τὴν ἐξουσίαν Συρίας, ἐπειδὴ ὁμωμόκεσαν ἀλλήλοις οἱ ἀμηραῖοι
πάντες, ὡς· «Ὅ τι ἂν εἴπωσιν οἱ γέροντες, ἵνα ἐπώμεθα εἰς τοὺς λόγους
αὐτῶν.» Ὁ γοῦν Ἀλὴμ παραλαβὼν τὸν λαὸν αὐτοῦ, ἀπῆλθεν εἰς τὰ μέρη
41ʳP Αἰθρίβου μετὰ πάσης τῆς συγγε|νείας αὐτοῦ, κἀκεῖσε τελευτᾷ105

F   81 ὅπερ — 82 Ἀγαρηνῶν: cf. Achmet, Oneirocriticon, ed. ˙ Drexl.
p. 212, 20.

V 72 Μαυίας P: Μαβίας Pʸ V M ‖ κυριεύσει V M edd.: κυριεύσῃ P ‖
73 Ἐφράτην P ‖ 76 ἀμφοτέρων om. Me secl. Be ‖ δύο secl. Moravcsik ‖
79 Ἀλεὶμ P ‖ ἠρέσθησαν (coni. etiam Bekker): ἠρέσκησαν edd. ‖ 80 ἐκβάλλοντες

21

another, disputing over the rule, which of them should be lord of all Syria. They encountered one another by the river Euphrates, and joined in fierce battle one against the other. But when the battle was at its height and many were falling on either side, the multitudes of the Agarenes of both parties cried out: «Why is this, that we slay and are slain, and our tribe perishes from among living men? But let two elders be chosen apart from both the parties, and whomsoever they prefer, let him have the rule.» Alim and Mauias were pleased at this saying of theirs, and, drawing off from their hands their rings, which are a token of rule of the Agarenes, they gave them to the two elders, and placed their authority at the disposal of the two elders, confirming the matter by an oath and settling it so that whomsoever the elders might prefer, he should be lord and chief of all the Saracens. The two elders entered into the middle of the battle array of the two parties, and took their stand face to face in the space between the armies; the elder of Alim was a man devout according to the nation of the Saracens, one such as they call 'cadi', that is, faithful and sanctified; but the elder of Mauias was devout only in appearance, but in all else deceitful and arrogant and surpassing all men in mischief. The elder of Mauias said to the elder of Alim: «Do you speak first what you will, for you are prudent and devout, and far surpassing my years.» And the elder of Alim answered thus: «I cast Alim off from the rule, as I drew his ring from his hand and drew it on to my own finger; now will I cast off the ring of Alim from my finger and therewith cast him off from his rule also.» The elder of Mauias made answer again: «I drew Mauias into the rule, as I drew his ring on to my finger; now will I draw the ring of Mauias on to his finger.» And then they parted one from the other. So Mauias took all the dominion of Syria, since all the emirs had sworn to each other, saying: «Whatever the elders say, we will be obedient to their words.» And so Alim took his army and departed to the region of Ethribos with all his kin, and there ended his life. After

---

edd. ‖ 81 τοῖς] *litteras* οι *in ras. scr.* P² ‖ 87 ἀντιπροσώπως *coni.* Moravcsik: ἀντιπρόσωπον P   ἀντιπροσώπου edd. ‖ 92 ὅς εἴ τε *coni.* Moravcsik: ὥστε Ba Be   ὥς τε (*litteris* ἔσ *erasis*) Pʸ   ὡς ἔστε P V Me   ὅς ς τε M   ὡσεί τε Meursius ‖ 93 τοὺς ἐμοὺς χρόνους *coni.* Jenkins: τοῖς ἐμοῖς χρόνοις P edd. ‖ 95 δακτύλιον P² V M edd.: δάκτυλον P ‖ 96 ἐκβάλω V: ἐκβάλλω edd. ἐκβαλὼν M ἔκβαλων P ‖ 97 δακτύλου Meursius Ba Be: δακτυλίου P ‖ μου P V edd.: Μαβίου (*litteris* ου *in* α *correctis et litteris* βίου *s. v. additis*) Pʸ ‖ 99 αὐτοῦ *s. v. add.* P²   *in textum receperunt* V M edd. ‖ 100 εἰσαγάγω Meursius Ba Be: εἰσαγαγὸν P   εἰσαγαγὼν V Me ‖ 101 ἀπ'] *litteram* α *in ras. scr.* P² ‖ Μαυίας P: Μαβίας P² V M ‖ 102 πᾶσαν *om.* edd. ‖

21, 22

τὸν βίον. Μετὰ δὲ τὸν θάνατον τοῦ Ἀλὴμ λῆρον ἡγησάμενοι οἱ τούτου
υἱοὶ τὴν τοῦ πατρὸς αὐτῶν βουλήν, ἐπανέστησαν κατὰ τοῦ Μαυίου, καὶ
συνῆψαν πόλεμον ἰσχυρὸν μετὰ τοῦ Μαυίου, καὶ ἡττηθέντες ἔφυγον ἀπὸ
προσώπου αὐτοῦ, καὶ ἀποστείλας Μαυίας ἀπέκτεινεν ἅπαντας. Καὶ
ἔκτοτε ἦλθε πᾶσα ἡ ἀρχὴ τῶν Ἀράβων εἰς τὸν Μαυίαν.   110
Ἰστέον δέ, ὅτι οὗτος ὁ Μαυίας ἔκγονος ἦν τοῦ Σοφιάμ. Ἔκγονος
δὲ τοῦ Μαυίου ὑπῆρχεν ὁ Μάσαλμας, ὁ κατὰ Κωνσταντινουπόλεως
ἐκστρατεύσας, οὗτινος καὶ δι᾽ αἰτήσεως ἐκτίσθη τὸ τῶν Σαρακηνῶν
102Be| μαγίσδιον ἐν τῷ βασιλικῷ πραιτωρίῳ. Οὐκ ἦν δὲ οὗτος ἀρχηγὸς τῶν
41ᵛP Ἀράβων, ἀλλὰ Σουλεϊμὰν ὑπῆρχεν ἀρχηγὸς τῶν Σαρακηνῶν, | ὁ δὲ115
Μάσαλμας ἐν τάξει στρατηγοῦ ἐχρημάτιζεν. Ἦλθεν δὲ Σουλεϊμὰν
μετὰ τοῦ στόλου αὐτοῦ κατὰ Κωνσταντινουπόλεως, ὁ δὲ Μάσαλμας
διὰ ξηρᾶς, καὶ διεπέρασεν ἐν Λαμψάκῳ ἐπὶ τὰ μέρη τῆς Θράκης, ἄγων
μεθ᾽ ἑαυτοῦ στρατιώτας χιλιάδας π′. Καὶ διὰ τῆς τοῦ Θεοῦ προνοίας ὅ τε
στόλος Σουλεϊμάν, τοῦ ἀρχηγοῦ τῶν Ἀράβων καὶ ὁ πεζὸς στρατὸς120
τοῦ Μάσαλμα ὑπέστρεψαν ἅπαντες μετ᾽ αἰσχύνης, ἡττηθέντες καὶ
καταπολεμηθέντες παρά τε τοῦ στόλου καὶ τῶν στρατιωτῶν τοῦ βασιλέως. Καὶ εἰρήνευσεν ἡ καθ᾽ ἡμᾶς πολιτεία ἐπὶ μήκιστον χρόνον, στρατη-
γούσης καὶ περιεπούσης τῆς δεσποίνης ἡμῶν καὶ ἀειπαρθένου Μαρίας
42ʳP τῆς Θεοτόκου τήνδε τὴν πόλιν, ἧς καὶ τὴν ἄχραντον καὶ ἁγίαν εἰκόνα|καὶ125
αὐτὸς ⟨ὁ⟩ Σουλεϊμὰν ᾐδέσθη καὶ ἐνετράπη καὶ τοῦ ἵππου κατέπεσεν.

22. Ἐκ τοῦ Χρονογράφου τοῦ μακαρίου Θεοφάνους περὶ τῶν αὐτῶν καὶ περὶ Μαυίου καὶ
τῆς γενεᾶς αὐτοῦ, ὅπως διεπέρασεν ἐν Ἰσπα-
νίᾳ. Ῥωμαίων βασιλεὺς Ἰουστινιανὸς ὁ Ῥινό-
τμητος.   5

Αὕτη ἐστὶν ἀρχὴ τῆς βασιλείας αὐτοῦ, καὶ μετὰ ταῦτα ἐξεβλήθη
ὑπὸ Λεοντίου, καὶ πάλιν ἀντεισῆλθεν ἐκβαλὼν τὸν Λεόντιον καὶ Ἀψίμα-
103Βeρον, καὶ ἀμφοτέρους αὐτοὺς ἐν τῇ ἱπ|ποδρομίᾳ θριαμβεύσας καὶ ἀποκτεί-
νας. Τούτῳ τῷ ἔτει ἀποστέλλει Ἀβιμέλεχ πρὸς Ἰουστινιανὸν βεβαιῶσαι

F   106 Μετὰ — 110 Μαυίαν: cf. Theoph. p. 347, 26—27.   112 ὁ
Μάσαλμας — 113 ἐκστρατεύσας: cf. Theoph. p. 386, 25—26.   115
Σουλεϊμὰν — Σαρακηνῶν: cf. Theoph. p. 386, 20—24.   116 Ἦλθεν
— 125 πόλιν: cf. Theoph. p. 395, 13—396, 23; Niceph., ed. de Boor p.
53, 10—54, 1; Zon. XV. 1., ed. Bonn. III. p. 252, 9—253, 6.
22. 6 μετὰ — 9 ἀποκτείνας: cf. Theoph. p. 361, 26—28; 374, 28—375,
13.   9 Τούτῳ — 22 νῦν: Theoph. p. 363, 1—20; cf. Cedr., ed. Bonn.
I. p. 771, 4—15.

V 107 υἱοὶ τὴν τοῦ s. v. add. P²   in textum receperunt V M edd. ‖ 108 post
ἀπὸ add. τοῦ edd. ‖ 110 Μαυίαν V: Μαυία P   Μαβίαν edd. ‖ 112 Μάσαλμας

21, 22

the death of Alim, his sons, regarding their father's counsel as nonsense, rebelled against Mauias, and joined fierce battle with Mauias, and being worsted fled from before his face, and Mauias sent after and put them all to death. And thereafter the rule over all the Arabs came into the hands of Mauias.

Now, this Mauias was grandson of Sophiam. And Mauias' grandson was Masalmas, who made an expedition against Constantinople, and at whose request was built the mosque of the Saracens in the imperial praetorium. He was not chief of the Arabs; Souleiman was chief of the Saracens, and Masalmas held the rank of general. Souleiman came with his fleet against Constantinople, and Masalmas came overland, and crossed over at Lampsacus into the region of Thrace, carrying with him 80 thousand troops. And through the Providence of God both the fleet of Souleiman and the infantry army of Masalmas all retired with ignominy, being worsted and utterly overthrown by the fleet and soldiers of the emperor. And our state was at peace for many a long year, for this city was guided and guarded by Our Lady the ever-virgin Mary, the Mother of God, by whose inviolate and holy image Souleiman himself was awed and put to shame, and he fell from his horse.

22. From the Chronicle of Theophanes, of blessed memory, concerning the same events and concerning Mauias and his clan, how it crossed over into Spain. Emperor of the Romans, Justinian Rhinotmetus.

This is the beginning of his reign; and thereafter he was expelled by Leontius, and then in his turn came back again and expelled Leontius and Apsimarus, and held his triumph over them both in the hippodrome, and put them to death. In this year Abimelech sent to Justinian to ratify the

(etiam Theoph.ᶜᵈᶠʰ): Μασαλμᾶς Theoph. ‖ Κωνσταντινουπόλεως corr. Moravcsik: Κωνσταντινούπολιν P edd. ‖ 114 μαγίσδιον: μασγίδιον coni. Meursius ‖ 115 Σουλεημᾶν P ‖ ante ἀρχηγὸς add. ὁ V edd. ‖ 116 Σουλεημᾶν P ‖ 117 Κωνσταντινουπόλεως corr. Moravcsik: Κωνσταντινούπολιν P edd. ‖ Μάσαλμας (etiam Theoph.ᵈʰ): Μασαλμᾶς Theoph. ‖ 118 desinit cod. Mutin. gr. 179 [= M] ‖ 119 χιλιάδας π': λαὸν ἱκανὸν Theoph. ‖ 120 Σουλεημᾶν P ‖ τῶν: τοῦ Ba Be ‖ 121 Μασάλμα edd. ‖ 125 τῆς Θεοτόκου per comp. s. v. add. P² in textum receperunt V edd. ‖ ῆς] litteram ς in ras. scr. P² ‖ 126 ὁ add. V edd. ‖ Σουλεημᾶν P ‖ ἠδέσθη] litteram ἠ in ras. scr. P².
   22. 2 τῶν αὐτῶν: τῶν ⟨Μαρδ⟩αϊτῶν coni. Bury ‖ 4 Ἰουστινιανὸς coni. Laskin: Ἰουστῖνος P edd. ‖ 9 post ἔτει rubro atramento mg. add. ͵ϛρη' P¹ τῷ ͵ϛρη' mg. iter. P² in textum receperunt V Me ͵ϛροη' Theoph. ‖

22

τὴν εἰρήνην οὕτως, ἵνα ὁ βασιλεὺς παύσῃ τὸ τῶν Μαρδαϊτῶν τάγμα 10
42ᵛP ἐκ τοῦ Λιβάνου καὶ διακωλύσῃ τὰς ἐπιδρομὰς αὐτῶν, καὶ 'Αβι|μέλεχ
δώσῃ τοῖς 'Ρωμαίοις καθ' ἑκάστην νομίσματα χίλια καὶ ἵππον εὐγενῆ
ἕνα καὶ Αἰθίοπα δοῦλον ἕνα, καὶ ἵνα ἔχωσι κοινὰ κατὰ τὸ ἴσον τοὺς
φόρους τῆς Κύπρου καὶ 'Αρμενίας καὶ 'Ιβηρίας. Καὶ ἔπεμψεν ὁ βασιλεὺς Παῦλον τὸν μαγιστριανὸν πρὸς 'Αβιμέλεχ ἀσφαλίσασθαι τὰ στοιχη- 15
θέντα, καὶ γέγονεν ἔγγραφος ἀσφάλεια μετὰ μαρτύρων. Καὶ φιλοτιμηθεὶς
ὁ μαγιστριανὸς ὑπέστρεψεν. Καὶ πέμψας ὁ βασιλεὺς προσελάβετο τοὺς
Μαρδαΐτας χιλιάδας ιβ', τὴν 'Ρωμαϊκὴν δυναστείαν ἀκρωτηριάσας.
Πᾶσαι γὰρ αἱ νῦν οἰκούμεναι παρὰ τῶν 'Αράβων εἰς τὰ ἄκρα πόλεις
ἀπὸ Μομψουεστίας καὶ ἕως τετάρτης 'Αρμενίας ἀνίσχυροι καὶ ἀοίκητοι 20
43ʳP ἐτύγχανον διὰ τὴν ἔφοδον τῶν Μαρδαϊτῶν, ὧν πα|ρασταλέντων, πάνδεινα
κακὰ πέπονθεν ἡ 'Ρωμανία ὑπὸ τῶν 'Αράβων μέχρι τοῦ νῦν. Τῷ δ'
αὐτῷ ἔτει εἰσελθὼν ὁ βασιλεὺς εἰς 'Αρμενίαν, ἐκεῖ ἐδέξατο τοὺς ἐν τῷ
Λιβάνῳ Μαρδαΐτας, χάλκεον τεῖχος διαλύσας. Παρέλυσε δὲ καὶ τὴν
μετὰ τῶν Βουλγάρων παγιωθεῖσαν εἰρήνην, διαταράξας τοὺς ὑπὸ τοῦ 25
οἰκείου πατρὸς ἐνορδίνους γεγονότας τύπους.
104Be Ἔτι κρατοῦντος τοῦ 'Αβιμέλεχ, ἐπεστρά|τευσαν οἱ Ἄραβες
τῇ 'Αφρικῇ καὶ ταύτην παρέλαβον, καὶ ἐκ τοῦ οἰκείου στρατοῦ ταξατιῶνα
ἐν αὐτῇ κατέστησαν. Λεόντιος δὲ ἦν τῷ τότε χρόνῳ ἐκβαλὼν 'Ιουστινια-
νὸν τῆς 'Ρωμαίων ἀρχῆς, καὶ ἐξορίσας αὐτὸν ἐν Χερσῶνι, τῆς βασιλείας 30
43ᵛP ἐκράτησεν. 'Αψιμάρου δὲ τοῦ Τιβερίου τὸν Λεόντιον διαδεξα|μένου
τῆς βασιλείας καὶ τὰ τῶν 'Ρωμαίων σκῆπτρα κρατήσαντος, τέθνηκεν
'Αβιμέλεχ, ὁ τῶν 'Αράβων ἀρχηγός, καὶ ἐκράτησεν Οὐαλίδ, ὁ υἱὸς
αὐτοῦ, ἔτη ἐννέα. Τῷ δ' αὐτῷ ἔτει πάλιν ὑπέστρεψεν 'Ιουστινιανὸς
εἰς τὴν βασιλείαν, καὶ ῥαθύμως καὶ ἀμελῶς ταύτην διακυβερνῶν, τῆς 35
'Αφρικῆς ἐπεκράτησαν ὁλοσχερῶς οἱ 'Αγαρηνοί. Τότε ὁ τοῦ Μαυίου
ἔγγονος μετὰ ὀλιγοστοῦ τινος λαοῦ διεπέρασεν ἐν 'Ισπανίᾳ, καὶ ἐπισυν-
άξας πάντας τοὺς ἐκ τοῦ γένους αὐτοῦ, ἐκράτησεν τὴν 'Ισπανίαν μέχρι
τῆς σήμερον, ὅθεν οἱ τὴν 'Ισπανίαν κατοικοῦντες 'Αγαρηνοὶ Μαυιᾶται
κατονομάζονται. Τούτων ἀπόγονοι τυγχάνουσιν οἱ τὴν Κρήτην οἰκοῦντες 40
44ʳP 'Αγαρηνοί. Ὅτε γὰρ Μιχαὴλ ὁ Τραυ|λὸς τῆς τῶν 'Ρωμαίων ἀρχῆς
ἐπεκράτησεν, καὶ ἡ τοῦ Θωμᾶ ἀνταρσία ἐγένετο μέχρι τριετοῦς χρόνου

F   22 Τῷ δ' αὐτῷ — 26 τύπους: Theoph. p. 364, 4—7; cf. Niceph.,
ed. de Boor p. 36, 16—17; Cedr. I. p. 771, 18—21.   27 Ἔτι
— 29 κατέστησαν: Theoph. p. 370, 6—8; cf. Niceph. p. 39,
12—14.   29 Λεόντιος — 31 ἐκράτησεν: cf. Theoph. p. 368, 15; 369,
26.   31 'Αψιμάρου — 32 κρατήσαντος: cf. Theoph. p. 371, 19.
32 τέθνηκεν — 34 ἐννέα: cf. Theoph. p. 374, 14—15, 25.   34 Τῷ
δ' αὐτῷ — 35 βασιλείαν: cf. Theoph. p. 374, 16, 28.   35 τῆς 'Αφρικῆς

22

peace on these conditions: the emperor to withdraw the Mardaïte legion from the Lebanon and check their incursions, and Abimelech to give the Romans daily a thousand nomismata and one thoroughbred horse and one Ethiopian slave, and the taxes of Cyprus and Armenia and Iberia to be held commonly and in equal shares by both parties. The emperor dispatched Paul the imperial agent to Abimelech, to confirm the terms agreed upon, and a confirmation was drawn up in writing and attested. The imperial agent was presented with gifts, and returned. And the emperor sent and took in the Mardaïtes, 12 thousand of them, thereby crippling the Roman power. For all the frontier cities now inhabited by the Arabs from Mopsouestia and as far as Armenia Quarta were defenceless and uninhabited because of the incursion of the Mardaïtes, by whose drawing away Romania has suffered terrible damage at the hands of the Arabs, and suffers it still. And in the same year the emperor went to Armenia and there took in the Mardaïtes of the Lebanon, thus destroying his brazen wall. Moreover, he broke the pledge of peace with the Bulgarians, disturbing the treaty made by his own father.

It was also during the reign of Abimelech that the Arabs marched against Africa and took it, and placed in it a garrison of their troops. At that time Leontius had expelled Justinian from the rule over the Romans, and had exiled him to Cherson and had possessed himself of the empire. But after Apsimarus Tiberius had ousted Leontius from the throne and had possessed himself of the sceptre of the Romans, Abimelech, chief of the Arabs, died, and Oualid his son ruled nine years. In the same year Justinian returned once more to his throne, and during his slack and careless government the Agarenes obtained complete control of Africa. Then, the grandson of Mauias with a very few men crossed over into Spain, and, having collected together all of his tribe, gained control of Spain even to this day, and that is why the Agarenes who dwell in Spain are called Mauiates. Their descendants are the Agarenes who live in Crete. For when Michael the Lisper had got possession of the rule over the Romans, and the rebellion of Thomas broke out and lasted three years, then, while the emperor was

---

— 36 Ἀγαρηνοί: cf. Theoph. p. 370. 6—7.   36 Τότε — 39 σήμερον:
cf. Theoph. p. 403, 12—13; 426, 4—5.   40 Τούτων — 48 σήμερον: cf.
Theoph. Cont. p. 73, 13—76, 7; 474, 1—7.

V   12 χίλια V edd. Theoph.: ‚α P ‖ 12/3 εὐγενῆ ἕνα deest in Theoph. ‖
13 Αἰθίοπα deest in Theoph. ‖ ἕνα deest in Theoph. ‖ 19 γὰρ αἱ νῦν Theoph.
coni. Bekker νῦν γὰρ (omisso αἱ) Theoph.ᵉᶠᵐ γὰρ νῦν αἱ P edd. ‖ οἰκουμέναι P ‖
τὰ ἄκρα πόλεις Theoph. τὰς ἀκροπόλεις P edd. ‖ 20 ἀοίκητοι] ἀοίκητι (litteris τι
insertis) P¹ ‖ 22 post νῦν aliquid excidisse susp. Bury ‖ 23 εἰσελθών: ἐλθών Theoph.
‖ 26 ἐνορδίνους Theoph.: ἐνορδίνος P   ἐνορδίνως V edd. ‖ 27 Ἔτι: Ὅτι Me ‖
28 τῇ Ἀφρικῇ: τὴν Ἀφρικὴν Theoph. ‖ ταξατίωνα edd. ‖ 29 ante Ἰουστινιανὸν
add. τὸν edd. ‖ 34 ἐννέα edd.: θ′ P ‖ 38 τῆς Ἰσπανίας edd. ‖

ἐπικρατήσασα, τότε τοῦ βασιλέως ἀσχολουμένου ἐπὶ τοῖς συμβεβηκόσι
πράγμασιν, εὑρόντες διωρίαν οἱ τὴν Ἰσπανίαν οἰκοῦντες Ἀγαρηνοί,
στόλον ἱκανὸν ἐξαρτύσαντες καὶ ἀρξάμενοι ἀπὸ τῶν τῆς Σικελίας μερῶν 45
πάσας τὰς Κυκλάδας νήσους ἠρήμωσαν, καὶ ἐλθόντες ἐν Κρήτῃ καὶ
105Βεταύτην εὔκαι|ρον καὶ ἀνειμένην εὑρόντες, μηδενὸς ἀνταίροντος ἢ μαχο-
μένου, ταύτην παρέλαβον, καὶ διακρατοῦσιν ἕως τὴν σήμερον. Τὸν δὲ
Οὐαλὶδ διαδέχεται Σουλεϊμάν, καὶ κρατεῖ ἔτη τρία. Ἐπὶ τούτου ἐπεστράτευσε Μάσαλμας, ὁ στρατηγὸς Σουλεϊμάν, μετὰ στρατοῦ διὰ ξηρᾶς, 50
44ᵛΡ Οὖμαρ δὲ διὰ θαλάττης, | καὶ τῇ τοῦ Θεοῦ συνεργείᾳ ἄπρακτοι μετ'
αἰσχύνης ὑπέστρεψαν. Τὸν δὲ Σουλεϊμὰν διαδέχεται Οὖμαρ, καὶ κρατεῖ
τῆς τῶν Ἀράβων ἀρχῆς ἔτη δύο. Τὸν δὲ Οὖμαρ διαδέχεται Ἀζίδ, καὶ
κρατεῖ τῆς ἀρχῆς ἐπὶ ἐνιαυτοὺς τέσσαρας. Τοῦτον δὲ διαδέχεται Ἰσάμ,
καὶ κρατεῖ τῆς ἀρχῆς ἐπὶ ἔτη ιθ'. Τούτου τελευτήσαντος, κρατεῖ τῆς 55
ἀρχῆς Μαρουὰμ ἔτη ἕξ. Μαρουὰμ δὲ τελευτήσαντος, Ἀβδελᾶς τῆς
τῶν Ἀράβων ἀρχῆς κύριος γίνεται, καὶ κρατεῖ ἔτη κα'. Τούτου τελευτήσαντος, Μαδὶς ἀρχηγὸς Ἀράβων γίνεται, καὶ κρατεῖ τῆς ἀρχῆς ἔτη
ἐννέα. Τούτου παρελθόντος, Ἀαρὼν τῆς τῶν Ἀράβων ἀρχῆς κύριος
γίνεται, καὶ κρατεῖ τῆς ἀρχῆς ἔτη κγ'. 60
Ἐν τούτῳ τῷ χρόνῳ, ἤγουν τῆς τῶν Ῥωμαίων ἀρχῆς * * * Εἰρή-
45ʳΡ νης καὶ Κωνσταντίνου, ἔτους ἀπὸ κτί|σεως κόσμου ͵Ϛσπη'. Τῷ δ' αὐτῷ
ἔτει Ἀαρών, ὁ τῶν Ἀράβων ἀρχηγός, τέθνηκεν εἰς τὴν ἐνδοτέραν Περσίδα,
τὴν καλουμένην Χωρασάν, καὶ διεδέξατο τὴν ἀρχὴν Μοάμεδ, ὁ υἱὸς
αὐτοῦ, ἀφυὴς κατὰ πάντα καὶ ἀσυνάρτητος ὑπάρχων, πρὸς ὃν Ἀβδελᾶς, 65
106Βεὸ ἀδελφὸς αὐτοῦ, στασιάσας ἐκ | τῆς αὐτῆς χώρας τοῦ Χωρασὰν ἅμα
ταῖς πατρικαῖς δυνάμεσιν, ἐμφυλίου πολέμου γέγονεν αἴτιος. Κἀντεῦθεν
οἱ κατὰ τὴν Συρίαν καὶ Αἴγυπτον καὶ Λιβύην εἰς διαφόρους κατατμηθέν-
τες ἀρχὰς τά τε δημόσια πράγματα καὶ ἀλλήλους κατέστρεψαν, σφαγαῖς
καὶ ἁρπαγαῖς καὶ παντοίαις ἀτοπίαις πρός τε ἑαυτοὺς καὶ τοὺς ὑπ' 70
αὐτοὺς Χριστιανοὺς συγκεχυμένοι. Ἔνθα δὴ καὶ αἱ κατὰ τὴν ἁγίαν

F   48 Τὸν δὲ — 49 τρία: cf. Theoph. p. 384, 15—19; 386;
20—24.   49 Ἐπὶ τούτου — 51 θαλάττης: cf. Theoph. p. 386,
25—27.   52 Τὸν δὲ — 53 δύο: cf. Theoph. p. 396, 23—24; 398, 5; 401,
13—14.   53 Τὸν δὲ — 54 τέσσαρας: cf. Theoph. p. 401, 4—8, 14; 403,
24—25.   54 Τοῦτον — 55 ιθ': cf. Theoph. p. 402, 19; 403,
25.   55 Τούτου — 56 ἕξ: cf. Theoph. p. 421, 7—10.   56 Μαρουὰμ
— 57 κα': cf. Theoph. p. 429, 15.   57 Τούτου — 59 ἐννέα: cf. Theoph.
p. 448, 28; 449, 1, 4—8.   59 Τούτου — 60 κγ': cf. Theoph. p. 461,
7, 10; 465, 27—30.   62 Τῷ δ' αὐτῷ — 76 πέντε: Theoph. p. 484, 5—19.

V 44 διορίαν V edd.   ‖   47 ἀνταίροντος coni. Moravcsik: ἀντεροῦντος P
ἀνταιρομένου Be ‖ 48 τὴν: τῆς V edd. ‖ Τὸν edd.: τοῦ P ‖ 49 ante Σουλεϊμὰν
add. ὁ edd. ‖ Σουλεημᾶν P   Σολεημὰν Be ‖ τρία edd.: γ' P ‖ τούτου corr.

22

engrossed with the troubles which had arisen, the Agarenes who lived in Spain saw their chance had come, fitted out a large fleet and started out from the region of Sicily and desolated all the islands of the Cyclades, and, coming to Crete and finding it rich and carelessly guarded, since none opposed or engaged them, they took it, and hold it to this day. Oualid was succeeded by Souleiman, who ruled three years. In his time Masalmas, the general of Souleiman, made an expedition with an army overland, and Oumar by sea, and by God's aid they returned with shame, their purpose unachieved. Souleiman was succeeded by Oumar, who held the rule over the Arabs two years. Oumar was succeeded by Azid, who held the rule for four years. He was succeeded by Isam, who held rule for 19 years. On his death Marouam held the rule six years. On the death of Marouam Abdelas became master of the rule over the Arabs, and held it 21 years. On his death Madis became chief of the Arabs, and held the rule nine years. When he had passed away Aaron became master of the rule over the Arabs, and held the rule 23 years.

In this year, that is to say, when the rule over the Romans *** Irene and Constantine, the year from the creation of the world 6288. In the same year Aaron, the chief of the Arabs, died in inner Persia, that is called Chorasan, and Moamed his son succeeded to the rule, a stupid, unbalanced man in every way, against whom his brother Abdelas came in revolt out of that same country of Chorasan together with the powers that had been his father's, and brought about a civil war. And thereafter those who dwelt in Syria and Egypt and Libya were split up under different governments, and destroyed the public weal and one another, in a welter of slaughter and rapine and outrage of every sort against themselves and their Christian subjects. Then it was that the churches in the holy city of Christ our God

---

Moravcsik: τούτω P   τούτῳ edd. ‖ 50 Μάσαλμας Pˣ mg. P⁸ V edd. Theoph.ᶜᵈᶠʰ: Μασαλμὰς P   Μασαλμᾶς Theoph. ‖ Σουλεημὰν P ‖ 51 Οὔμαρ P: Οὔμαρος P² mg. P⁸ V edd. ‖ θαλάττης (etiam Theoph.ᵉᶠ): θαλάσσης Theoph. ‖ 53 Ἀράβων] litteras ἀράβ in ras. scr. P⁴ ‖ Ἀζῆδ P: Ἀζὶδ Theoph.ᵉᶠᵐ Ἰζὶδ Theoph. ‖ 55 ἐπὶ om. V edd. ‖ 56 Μαρούαμ edd. ‖ Μαρούαμ edd. ‖ Ἀβδελὰς P ‖ τῆς: τις V Me Ba Migne ‖ 57 Ἀράβων] litteras ραβ in ras. scr. P ‖ 58 Μαδὶς (etiam Theoph.ʰ): Μαδί Theoph. ‖ 59 ἐννέα edd.: θ' P ‖ τῆς: τις V Me Ba Migne ‖ 61 ad χρόνῳ rubro atramento ,ϛσπη' mg. add. P¹ post ἤγουν s. v. τῷ ,ϛσπη' iter. P² in textum receperunt V Me ‖ post ἀρχῆς lac. ind. Bury Laskin ‖ 61/2 Εἰρήνης P² V edd.: Εἰρήνη P ‖ 62 Κωνσταντίνου corr. Moravcsik: Κώνσταντος P edd. ‖ ἔτος V edd. ‖ 64 Μουάμεδ Theoph. Μοάμεθ edd. ‖ 65 καὶ ἀσυνάρτητος ὑπάρχων deest in Theoph. ‖ ἀσυνάρτητος Be: ἀσυνάρτιστος P ‖ Ἀβδελὰς P ‖ 71 Ἔνθα (etiam Theoph.ᶜᵒᵈᵈ·): ἔνθεν Me Be Theoph. ‖ κατὰ om. Me Be ‖ τὴν ἁγίαν P Theoph.: τῆς ἁγίας P¹ V edd. ‖

45ᵛP Χριστοῦ τοῦ Θεοῦ ἡμῶν πόλιν | ἐκκλησίαι ἠρήμωνται, τά τε μοναστήρια
τῶν δύο μεγάλων λαυρῶν, τοῦ ἐν ἁγίοις Χαρίτωνος καὶ Κυριακοῦ καὶ
τοῦ ἁγίου Σάβα, καὶ τὰ λοιπὰ κοινόβια τῶν ἁγίων Εὐθυμίου καὶ Θεοδοσίου. Ἐπεκράτησεν δὲ τῆς τοιαύτης ἀναρχίας ἡ κατ' ἀλλήλων καὶ 75
ἡμῶν μιαιφονία ἔτη πέντε.

Ἕως ὧδε ἐκανόνισεν τοὺς χρόνους τῶν Ἀράβων ὁ ἐν ἁγίοις
Θεοφάνης, ὁ τὴν μονὴν συστήσας τοῦ καλουμένου μεγάλου Ἀγροῦ,
μητρόθειος τυγχάνων τοῦ μεγάλου καὶ εὐσεβοῦς καὶ χριστιανικωτάτου
βασιλέως Κωνσταντίνου, υἱοῦ Λέοντος, τοῦ σοφωτάτου καὶ ἀγαθοῦ 80
βασιλέως, ἐγγόνου δὲ Βασιλείου, τοῦ ἐν μακαρίᾳ τῇ μνήμῃ τὰ σκῆπτρα
τῆς τῶν Ῥωμαίων βασιλείας κρατήσαντος.

46ʳP   23. Π ε ρ ὶ Ἰ β η ρ ί α ς κ α ὶ Ἰ σ π α ν ί α ς.

107Be   Ἰβηρίαι δύο· ἡ μὲν πρὸς ταῖς Ἡρακλείαις στήλαις, ἀπὸ | Ἴβηρος
ποταμοῦ, οὗ μέμνηται Ἀπολλόδωρος ἐν τῇ Περὶ γῆς β'· «Ἐντὸς δὲ
Πυρήνης Ἴβηρ τ' ἐστὶ μέγας ποταμὸς φερόμενος ἐνδοτέρω.» Ταύτης
δὲ πολλά φασιν ἔθνη διαιρεῖσθαι, καθάπερ † Ἡρόδοτος † ἐν τῇ ιʹ Τῇ 5
καθ' Ἡρακλέα γέγραφεν ἱστορίᾳ οὕτως· «Τὸ δὲ Ἰβηρικὸν γένος τοῦτο,
ὅπερ φημὶ οἰκεῖν τὰ παράλια τοῦ διάπλου, διώρισται ὀνόμασιν ἐν γένος
ἐὸν κατὰ φῦλα· πρῶτον μὲν οἱ ἐπὶ τοῖς ἐσχάτοις οἰκοῦντες τὰ πρὸς
δυσμέων Κύνητες ὀνομάζονται (ἀπ' ἐκείνων δὲ ἤδη πρὸς βορέαν ἰόντι
Γλῆτες)· μετὰ δὲ Ταρτήσιοι· μετὰ δὲ Ἐλευσίνιοι· μετὰ δὲ Μαστινοί· 10
46ᵛP | μετὰ δὲ Κελκιανοί· ἔπειτα δὲ † ἠδιορόδανος †.» Ἀρτεμίδωρος δὲ ἐν
τῇ βʹ τῶν Γεωγραφουμένων οὕτως διαιρεῖσθαί φησιν· «Ἀπὸ δὲ τῶν
Πυρηναίων ὀρῶν ἕως τῶν κατὰ Γάδειρα τόπων ἐνδοτέρω καὶ συνωνύμως
Ἰβηρία τε καὶ Ἰσπανία καλεῖται. Διήρηται δὲ ὑπὸ Ῥωμαίων εἰς δύο
ἐπαρχίας * * * διατείνουσα ἀπὸ τῶν Πυρηναίων ὀρῶν ἅπασα {καὶ} μέχρι 15

F   77 ὁ ἐν — 78 Ἀγροῦ: cf. Vita Theophanis, ed. de Boor p. 30, 11—12.
23. 2 Ἰβηρίαι — 44 πολυτελεστάτας: cf. Steph. Byz., ed. Meineke
s. v. Ἰβηρίαι.   2 Ἰβηρίαι — 4 ἐνδοτέρω: cf. Apollodori fr. 324., ed.
Jacoby F. Gr. Hist. II B. p. 119.   4 Ταύτης — 11 ἠδιορόδανος: cf.
Herodori fr. 2 a., ed. Jacoby, F. Gr. Hist. I. p. 215.   11 Ἀρτεμίδωρος
— 17 Λυσιτανίας: cf. Artemidori fr. 21., ed. R. Stiehle, Philologus XI. p. 203.

V 72 πόλιν Theoph.: πόλεως P edd.   ‖ 76 πέντε edd.: εʹ P ‖ 78 Θεοφάνης (litteris
ης s. v. additis) P² mg. P⁸ Ba Be: Θεοφάνιος P ‖ μεγάλου s. v. add. P² in textum
receperunt V edd.   ‖ 81 post Βασιλείου s. v. τοῦ ἐκ Μακεδονίας add. P³ in textum
receperunt V edd.
23. 3 Ἀπολλόδωρος Ba Be Ἀπολλόδορος per comp. P: Ἀπολλόνιος
coni. Meursius ‖ 4 Πυρήνης P ‖ ἐστὶν Meineke Jacoby ‖ ἐνδοτέρωθεν coni.
Meineke ‖ ταύτην Ba Berkel ‖ 5 post δὲ add. εἰς Ba Berkel ‖ Ἡρόδοτος

22, 23

were desolated, and the monasteries of the two great Laurai, those of SS. Charito and Cyriac and of St. Sabas, and the other coenobite monasteries of SS. Euthymius and Theodosius. This anarchy, during which they murdered one another and us, lasted five years.

Up to this point the history of the Arabs is set in order chronologically by St. Theophanes, who founded the monastery of the so-called Megas Agros and was uncle on the mother's side of the great and pious and most Christian emperor Constantine, son of Leo, the most wise and virtuous emperor, and grandson of Basil, of blessed memory for his tenure of the sceptre over the empire of the Romans.

23. Of Iberia and Spain.

There are two Iberias: one, at the Pillars of Hercules, is *so called* from the river Iber, mentioned by Apollodorus in 'Concerning the Earth', II: «Within the Pyrenees is the Iber, a great river running towards the interior.» In this country are said to be many distinct nations, as *Herodorus* has written in the Xth book of his 'History Relating to Herakles': «This Iberian race, which, I say, lives on the shores of the strait, though one race, is distinguished by names according to its tribes: first, those who inhabit the western parts at the farthest verge are called Kynetes (and after them, if one travels northward, are the Gletes); then, Tartessians; then, *Elbusinians*; then, *Mastienoi*; then, Kelkianoi; and *then*, thereafter, *the Rhône.*» Artemidorus, in book II of the 'Geography', says that *the country* is divided thus: «The interior between the Pyrenees mountains and the district about Gadara is denominated alternatively Iberia and Spain. It has been divided by the Romans into two provinces *** the whole extending

---

V Me ἡ ῥόδοτος P: ʽΗρόδωρος Ba Be Berkel Meineke Jacoby ‖ ι′: δεκάτη Ba Be Meineke Jacoby ‖ Τῇ: τῶν Ba Be Meineke Jacoby ‖ 6 ἱστορίᾳ: ἱστοριῶν *coni.* Meineke ἱστορῶν Jacoby ‖ 7 οἰκέειν Meineke ‖ διάπλου Ba Be Meineke Jacoby:: διαπλοῦ P διαροῦ V Me ὠκεανοῦ *coni.* Bekker ‖ οὐνόμασι *coni.* Meineke ‖ 8 οἰκέοντες Meineke ‖ 9 Κύνιταις P ‖ οὐνομάζονται *coni.* Meineke ‖ 9 ἀπ᾽ — 10 Γλῆτες *in parenthesi posuit* Schulten ‖ 9 βορέην Meineke ‖ 10 Γλήτες P ‖ ʼΕλευσίνιοι: ʼΕλβυσίνιοι Ba Be Berkel Meineke Jacoby ‖ Μαστινοί: Μαστιηνοί Ba Be Berkel Meineke Jacoby ‖ 11 Κελκιανοί: Καλπιανοί Ba Be Berkel Κέλται *coni.* Bandurius Κελτικοί *coni.* Meineke ‖ ἠδιορόδανος P Me † ηδιοροδανος Jacoby: ἤδη ὁ ʽΡοδανός Be Berkel Meineke ἤδη ὁ ʽΡόδανος Ba ἤδη ὁ Σαρδόνιος Unger ἤδη ὁ πορθμός Schulten ‖ ʼΑρτεμίδωρος] *litteras* τε ί *rest.* P² ‖ 13 Πυρinαίων P ‖ Γάδειρα] *litteras* ει *in ras. scr.* P¹ ‖ καὶ ἐνδοτέρω Schubart Meineke ‖ 14 ʽΙσπανία (*etiam* Thunmann Meineke): Σπανία edd. ‖ 15 *post* ἐπαρχίας *lac. ind.* Be Meineke πρώτη μὲν ἐπαρχία *suppl.* Ba Berkel ‖ Πυρinαίων P ‖ καὶ *om.* Ba Be Meineke Stiehle *secl.* Moravcsik ‖

100

23

τῆς Καινῆς Καρχηδόνος καὶ τῶν τοῦ Βαίτιος πηγῶν, τῆς δὲ δευτέρας
ἐπαρχίας τὰ μέχρι Γαδείρων καὶ Λυσιτανίας.» Λέγεται δὲ καὶ Ἰβηρίτης.
Παρθένιος ἐν Λευκαδίαις· «Ἰβηρίτη πλεύσει ἐν αἰγιαλῷ.» Ἡ δ' ἑτέρα
108Be'Ἰβηρία | πρὸς Πέρσας ἐστίν. Τὸ ἔθνος Ἴβηρες, ὡς Πίερες, Βύζηρες.
47ʳP Διονύσιος· | «Ἀγχοῦ στηλάων μεγαθύμων ἔθνος Ἰβήρων.» Καὶ Ἀριστο- 20
φάνης Τριφάλητι· «Μανθάνοντες τοὺς Ἴβηρας τοὺς Ἀριστάρχου πάλαι»
καὶ «Τοὺς Ἴβηρας, οὓς χορηγεῖς μοι, βοηθῆσαι δρόμῳ.» Καὶ Ἀρτεμίδωρος ἐν δευτέρῳ Γεωγραφουμένων· «Γραμματικῇ δὲ χρῶνται τῇ τῶν
Ἰταλῶν οἱ παρὰ θάλατταν οἰκοῦντες τῶν Ἰβήρων.» Καὶ ἀπὸ τῆς Ἴβηρος
γενικῆς Ἰβηρὶς τὸ θηλυκόν. «Ἑλληνίς, οὐκ Ἰβηρίς» Μένανδρος Ἀσπίδι. 25
Λέγεται καὶ Ἰβηρικός· «† Πρῶτος μὲν πρός τινος † Ἰβηρικὸς ἀρχομένοισι.» Διηρεῖτο δὲ ἡ Ἰβηρία εἰς δύο, νῦν δὲ εἰς τρεῖς, ὡς Μαρκιανὸς ἐν
Περίπλῳ αὐτῆς · «Πρότερον μὲν οὖν ἡ Ἰβηρία εἰς δύο διηρεῖτο ὑπὸ
Ῥωμαίων, νυνὶ δὲ εἰς τρεῖς· Βαιτικὴν Σπανίαν καὶ Σπανίαν καὶ Ταρρα-
47ᵛP |κωνησίαν.» Ἀπὸ τῆς γενικῆς Ἴβηρος εὐθεῖαν Ἀπολλώνιος, ὡς τῆς 30
φύλακος ὁ φύλακος. Ἐν τοῖς Παρωνύμοις φησίν· «Ἀπὸ γενικῶν εὐθεῖαι
παράγονται, † τὸ μὲν ὕδωρ † δύο συλλαβὰς ὁμοίως τῇ εὐθείᾳ κατὰ τὸν
τόνον παροξυνόμενον, καὶ ἢ ἐν ἁπλῷ σχήματι ἢ ἐν συνθέτῳ. Ἁπλὸν
μὲν οὖν ⟨μάρτυρ⟩, μάρτυρος, ὁ μάρτυς, Χάροψ, Χάροπος, ὁ Χάροπος,
109Be'Χαρόποιό τ' ἄνακτος', Τροίζην, Τροίζη|νος, ὁ Τροίζηνος, υἱὸς Τροι- 35
ζήνοιο', Ἴβηρ, Ἴβηρος, ὁ Ἴβηρος», ἀφ' οὗ παρὰ Κουαδράτῳ ἐν Ῥωμαϊ-

---

F   18 Παρθένιος — αἰγιαλῷ: cf. Parthenii fr. 10., ed. Martini,
Mythographi Graeci II. 1. suppl. p. 17; Herodianus, ed. Lentz I. p. 76,
29—30.   20 Ἀγχοῦ — Ἰβήρων: Dionys. Perieg. v. 282., ed. Müller,
G. G. M. II. p. 117.   20 Ἀριστοφάνης — 22 δρόμῳ: cf. Aristoph. fr.
550., 551., ed. Kock, C. A. Fr. I. p. 531.   22 Ἀρτεμίδωρος — 24
Ἰβήρων: cf. Artemidori fr. 22., ed R. Stiehle, Philologus XI. p. 203.   25
Ἑλληνίς — Ἀσπίδι: cf. Menandri fr. 79., ed. Kock, C. A. Fr. III. p.
25.   26 Πρῶτος — 27 ἀρχομενοισι: Dionys. Perieg. v. 69., ed. Müller,
G. G. M. II. p. 108.   28 Πρότερον — 30 Ταρρακωνησίαν: Marcian.
Peripl. II. 7., ed. Müller G. G. M. I. p. 544.   30 Ἀπολλώνιος — 36
Ἴβηρος: cf. Apollonii Dyscoli fr., ed. Schneider p. 47.; Herodianus, ed.
Lentz I. p. 196, 22—29; II. p. 854, 1—9.   35 Χαρόποιό τ' ἄνακτος:
Hom. ll. II. 672.   35 υἱὸς Τροιζήνοιο: Hom. Il. II. 847.   36 παρὰ
Κουαδράτῳ — 38 πολεμέοντες: cf. Asinii Quadrati fr. 2., ed. Jacoby, F. Gr.
Hist. II A. p. 448.

V 16 δευτέρας V edd. Meineke: β′ P ‖ 17 Γαδείρων] litteras ει in ras. scr. P¹ ‖
Λουσιτανίας Ba Be Meineke ‖ Ἰβηρίτης Ba Be Meineke: Βηρίτις P ‖ 18
Παρθένιος Ba Be Meineke Lentz Martini: Παρθύνιος P ‖ Λευκαδίαις Ba Be
Martini: Λευκαδίας P   Λευκαδίᾳ Meineke Lentz ‖ Ἰβήριτι P ‖ πλεύσει ἐν
Meineke Lentz Martini: πλεύσειεν P edd.   πλεύσῃ ἐν coni. Bekker ‖ δ': δὲ

23

from the Pyrenees mountains as far as New Carthage and the sources of the Baetis, while the second province *comprehends* the area reaching to Gadara and Lusitania.» *The form* 'Iberite' is also found. Parthenius in 'Leucadiae': «Thou shalt coast along the 'Iberite' shore.» The other Iberia is over toward the Persians. The ethnic term is 'Iberians', like 'Pierians', 'Byzerians'. Dionysius: «Nigh unto the Pillars the nation of great-hearted 'Iberians'.» And Aristophanes, 'Triphales': «Learning that the 'Iberians', who anciently of Aristarchus», and, «The 'Iberians', whom thou lendest me, to run to my aid.» And Artemidorus in part two of 'Geography': «Those of the 'Iberians' who live on the coast use the alphabet of the Italians.» Also, from genitive 'Iberos' *is formed* the feminine 'Iberis'. «A Greek woman, not an 'Iberis'», Menander, 'Aspis'. The form 'Iberic' is also found: «The first *sea* is the 'Iberic' at the outset.» Iberia used to be divided in two, but now in three, as Marcian says in its 'Circumnavigation': «Now of old Iberia was divided in two by the Romans, but now in three: Baetic Spain and *Lusitanian* Spain and Tarragonese *Spain.*» From genitive 'Iberos' Apollonius *derives* a nominative, as 'phylakos' from genitive 'phylakos'. In 'Paronyma' he says: «Nominatives are derived from genitives *of more than* two syllables which, like the *derivative* nominative, carry the *pro*paroxytone accent, whether *these are* in simple or compound form. Simple are: martyr, martyros, nominative *martyros*; Charops, Charopos, nominative Charopos, 'of king Charopos'; Troezen, Troezenos, nominative Troezenos, 'son of Troezenos'; Iber, Iberos, nominative Iberos»; whence in Quadratus, 'Roman Millennium',

---

Ba Be Epitome Steph. Byz. ‖ 19 ἔθνος: ἐθνικὸν Meineke Epitome Steph. Byz. ‖ Ἴβηρες] *litteras* ἴβη *rest.* P² ‖ 20 ἔθνος] *litteras rest.* P² ‖ Ἰβήρων] *litteras* ἰβή *rest.* P² ‖ 21 Τριφάλιτι P ‖ 23 *post* δευτέρῳ *add.* τῶν edd. Meineke ‖ Γραμματικῇ Ba Be Meineke: γραμματικοὶ P ‖ 24 θάλατται P V edd. Meineke: θάλατται (*littera* ν *ex dimidia parte erasa*) P^ᵛ ‖ 24 Καὶ — 26/7 ἀρχομένοισι *secl.* V ‖ 25 Ἀσπίδη P ‖ 26 *post* Ἰβηρικός¹ *add.* Διονύσιος Ba Be Berkel Meineke ‖ 26 Πρῶτος μὲν πρός τινος: πόντος μὲν πρώτιστος Ba Be Berkel Meineke Dionysios ‖ 26/7 ἀρχομένοισοι P ‖ 27 ἡ Ἰβηρία Meineke: Ἰβηρία Ba Be ἡ Ἴβηρις P ‖ *post* εἰς¹ *add.* ἐπαρχίας Berkel Meineke ‖ τρεῖς Meineke γ′ P: τρία V edd. ‖ 28 *post* δύο *add.* ἐπαρχίας Meineke ‖ 28/9 διήρητο ὑπὸ Ῥωμαίων εἰς ἐπαρχίας δύο Marcianus ‖ 28 διήρητο Meineke ‖ 29 τρεῖς Meineke Marcianus γ′ P: τρία edd. ‖ 29/30 εἰς Ἱσπανίαν Βαιτικὴν καὶ εἰς Ἱσπανίαν Λουσιτανίαν καὶ Ἱσπανίαν Ταρρακωνησίαν Marcianus ‖ 29 Βαιτίκην Meineke ‖ Σπανίαν¹ *om.* Be Meineke ‖ καὶ¹ *om.* V Me Be Meineke ‖ Σπανίαν² *om.* V Me Λουσιτανίαν Be Salmasius Meineke ‖ 30 Ἀπὸ — 38 φησί *secl.* V ‖ 30 εὐθεῖα Meineke ‖ *post* εὐθεῖαν *add.* παράγει Ba Berkel ‖ 30/1 ὡς τῆς φύλακος ὁ φύλακος. Ἀπολλώνιος Bastius Meineke ‖ 30 τῆς² (*etiam* Meineke): τοῦ Ba Be ‖ 32 τὸ μὲν ὕδωρ: τῶν μὲν ὑπὲρ Meineke Apollonius τὸ μὲν Ἴβηρ Ba Berkel ‖ μὲν *delendum coni.* Meineke ‖ 33 παροξυνόμενον: προπαροξυνόμεναι Meineke Apollonius ‖ ἁπλοῦν Meineke Apollonius ‖ 34 μάρτυρ *add.* Ba Be Meineke ‖ μάρτυρ μάρτυρος ὁ μάρτυρος Apollonius ‖ ὁ μάρτυς: ὁ μάρτυρος edd. Meineke ‖ 35 Χαρόποιό τ᾽ ἄνακτος Ba Be Meineke Apollonius: χαροποιότης ἄνακτος P ‖ Τρύζειν Τρύζηνος ὁ Τρύζηνος P ‖ 35/6 Τρυζήνοιο P ‖

23, 24, 25

κῆς χιλιάδος ⟨ε′⟩ ἔστιν Ἰβήροισιν οὕτως· «Καί τοι Λίγυσί θ’ ἅμα καὶ Ἰβήροισι πολεμέοντες.» Τὸ αὐτὸ καὶ Ἄβρων ἐν Παρωνύμοις φησί.

48ʳP Καὶ «αὐτὸς Ἴβηρος τραγοπώγων» ἐν Μαλθακοῖς εἴρη|ται Κρατίνου.

Λέγονται οἱ Ἴβηρες ὑδροποτεῖν, ὡς Ἀθήναιος ἐν Δειπνοσοφιστῶν β′ 40 οὕτως· «Φύλαρχος μὲν ἐν τῇ ζ′ καὶ τοὺς Ἴβηράς φησι ὑδροποτεῖν πάντας, καίτοι πλουσιωτάτους πάντων ἀνθρώπων τυγχάνοντας (κέκτηνται γὰρ καὶ ἄργυρον καὶ χρυσὸν πλεῖστον), μονοσιτεῖν τε αὐτοὺς ἀεὶ λέγει διὰ μικρολογίαν, ἐσθῆτάς τε φορεῖν πολυτελεστάτας.»

24. Περὶ Ἰσπανίας.

Πόθεν εἴρηται Ἰσπανία; Ἀπὸ Ἰσπάνου γίγαντος οὕτω καλουμένου. Ἰσπανίαι δύο τῆς Ἰταλίας ἐπαρχίαι· ἡ μὲν μεγάλη, ἡ δὲ μικρά. Ταύτης ἐμνήσθη Χάραξ ἐν ι′ Χρονικῶν· «Ἐν Ἰσπανίᾳ τῇ μικρᾷ τῇ 48ᵛP ἔξω Λουσιτανῶν πάλιν ἀποστάντων, ἐπέμφθη ὑπὸ Ῥω|μαίων στρατη- 5 γὸς ἐπ’ αὐτοὺς Κύιντος.» Ὁ αὐτὸς ὁμοῦ περὶ τῶν δύο· «Κύιντος ὁ τῶν Ῥωμαίων πολέμαρχος ἐν ἀμφοτέραις ταῖς Ἰσπανίαις. Ἡσσώμενος δὲ ὑπὸ Οὐιριάθου σπονδὰς πρὸς αὐτὸν ἐποιήσατο.» Ταύτην κεκλῆσθαί 110Be φησιν Ἰβηρίαν ἐν Ἑλληνικῶν γ′· «Τὴν δὲ Ἰσπανίαν Ἕλληνες τὰ | πρῶτα Ἰβηρίαν ἐκάλουν, οὔπω ξύμπαντος τοῦ ἔθνους τὴν προσηγορίαν μεμαθη- 10 κότες, ἀλλ’ ἀπὸ μέρους τῆς γῆς, ὅ ἐστιν πρὸς ποταμὸν Ἴβηρα, καὶ ἀπ’ ἐκείνου ὀνομάζεται, τὴν πᾶσαν οὕτω καλοῦντες·» Ὕστερον δέ φασιν αὐτὴν μετακεκλῆσθαι Πανωνίαν.

25. Ἐκ τῆς ἱστορίας τοῦ ὁσίου Θεοφάνους τῆς Σιγριανῆς.

Τούτῳ τῷ ἔτει Οὐαλεντινιανὸς οὐ μόνον Βρεττανίαν καὶ Γαλλίαν 49ʳP καὶ Ἰσπανίαν | ἀνασώσασθαι οὐκ ἴσχυσεν, ἀλλὰ καὶ τὴν ἑσπέριον Λιβύην,

---

F   38 Τὸ αὐτὸ — φησί: cf. Habronis fr., ed R. Berndt, Berl. Phil. Wochenschrift XXXV. p. 1454; Herodianus, ed. Lentz I. p. 196, 29; II. p. 854, 9.   39 αὐτὸς — Κρατίνου: cf. Cratini fr. 101., ed. Kock, C. A. Fr. I. p. 46; Herodianus, ed. Lentz I. p. 196, 22—23; II. p. 854, 1—3.   40 Λέγονται — 44 πολυτελεστάτας: Athen. Dipnosoph. II. 44 b., ed. Kaibel I. p. 102, 15—19.   24. 2 Πόθεν — 13 Πανωνίαν: cf. Steph. Byz., ed. Meineke s. v. Ἰσπανίαι.   4 Χάραξ — 8 ἐποιήσατο: cf. Characis fr. 26., 27., ed. Jacoby, F. Gr. Hist. II A. p. 488.   9 ἐν Ἑλληνικῶν — 13 Πανωνίαν: cf. Characis fr. 3., ed. Jacoby. F. Gr. Hist. II A. p. 483.   25. 3 Τούτῳ — 55 βασιλεύσας: Theoph. p. 93, 31—95, 25; cf. Procop., De bello Vand. I. 2—4., ed. Haury I. p. 320, 18—322, 4; 311, 5—313, 1; 317, 9—20; 322, 4—326, 4.

23, 24, 25

V, occurs *the dative plural* 'Iberoisin', thus: «Though warring at once with the Ligurians and 'Iberoisi'.» Habro says the same in 'Paronyma'. And «the goat-bearded 'Iberos' himself» is found in the 'Effeminates' of Cratinus. The Iberians are said to drink water, as Athenaeus says in 'Deipnosophists', II: «Phylarchus in book VII says that all the Iberians too drink water, though they are the wealthiest of mankind (for they possess very great quantities of silver and gold), and he says that they never eat but once in the day out of their parsimony, and wear the most magnificent clothes.»

24. Of Spain.

Whence is the name Spain? From Hispanus, a giant so called. The Spains are two provinces of Italy: one is large, the other small. The country is referred to by Charax in 'Chronicles', X: «In Little, or Outer, Spain the Lusitanians again revolted, and the Romans sent against them their general Quintus». And, of the two *provinces* together, the same *author writes*: «Quintus, the Roman commander-in-chief in both the Spains. He was defeated by Viriathus and made a truce with him.» He says the country is called Iberia, in 'Greek History', III: «Spain the Greeks originally called Iberia, not yet having learnt the title of the whole nation but calling it all after that part of the country which is near the river Iber and derives its name therefrom.» Afterwards, they say, the name was changed to *Spain*.

25. From the history of the holy Theophanes of Sigriane.

In this year Valentinian was not merely too weak to recover Britain and Gaul and Spain, but also lost western Libya as well, the so-called land

---

V 37 ε' add. Ba Be Meineke Jacoby ‖ ἔστιν Jacoby: ἐστὶν P edd. Meineke ‖ Καί τοι Λίγυσί ϑ' ἅμα Ba Be Meineke Jacoby χαὶ τολίγοισι τ' αμα (*sine acc.*) P ‖ 38 'Αβρῶν P ‖ 39 αὐτὸς: οὗτος Meineke ‖ 40 'Αϑηναῖος P ‖ δείπνῳ σοφιστῶν P ‖ 41 Φίλαρχος P edd. ‖ 41/2 φησὶ δὲ χαὶ ⟨ἐν τῇ ζ'⟩ τοὺς Ἴβηρας πάντας ὑδροποτεῖν καίτοι πλουσιωτάτους ἀνϑρώπων ὄντας Athenaeus ‖ 42 χέχτηνται — 43 πλεῖστον *deest apud* Athenaeum *in parenthesi posuit* Moravcsik ‖ 43 χαὶ¹ om. edd. Meineke ‖ 44 τε (*etiam* Athenaeus^CE): δὲ Athenaeus.

24. 2/3 χαλουμένου: λεγομένου Meineke ‖ 5 ἐπέμφϑη edd.: ἐπέμφη P ‖ 7 Ἰσπανίαις ⟨ἠγωνίσατο⟩ *coni.* Jacoby ‖ 8 Οὐιριάϑου Meineke Jacoby: Οὐριάϑου P edd. ‖ 11 Ἴβηρα Müller Jacoby: Ἰβηρίαν V edd. Ἰβηρία P ⟨Ἴβηρα⟩ Ἰβηρίαν Meineke ‖ 11/2 Ἰβηρίαν ἀπ' ἐκείνου ὠνόμαζον καὶ τὴν πᾶσαν *coni.* Meineke ‖ 12 ὀνομάζεται Müller Jacoby: ὀνομάζονται P Meineke ‖ 13 Πανωνίαν (*etiam* Epitome Steph. Byz.): Πα{νω}νίαν Jacoby Πανίαν Ba Be Meineke Σπανίαν *coni.* Kyriakides 'Ισπανίαν *coni.* Dujčev.

25. 3 Οὐαλεντινιανὸς P² *mg.* P⁸ edd. Theoph.: Οὐαλεντιανὸς P ‖ 4

τὴν τῶν Ἄφρων καλουμένην χώραν προσαπώλεσε τρόπῳ τοιῷδε. Δύο 5
στρατηγοὶ ἦσαν, Ἀέτιος καὶ Βονιφάτιος, οὓς Θεοδόσιος κατὰ αἴτησιν
Οὐαλεντινιανοῦ εἰς Ῥώμην ἀπέστειλεν. Βονιφάτιος δὲ τὴν ἀρχὴν τῆς
ἑσπερίου Λιβύης λαβών, φθονήσας Ἀέτιος διαβολὴν ποιεῖται κατ'
αὐτοῦ, ὡς ἀνταρσίαν μελετῶντος καὶ τῆς Λιβύης κρατῆσαι σπεύδοντος.
Καὶ ταῦτα μὲν πρὸς Πλακιδίαν ἔλεγε, τὴν τοῦ Οὐαλεντινιανοῦ μητέρα. 10
Γράφει δὲ καὶ Βονιφατίῳ, ὅτι· «Ἐὰν μεταπεμφθῇς, παραγενέσθαι μὴ
θελήσῃς· διεβλήθης γάρ, καὶ δόλῳ σε οἱ βασιλεῖς βούλονται χειρώσα-
49ᵛP σθαι.» Ταῦτα δεξάμενος Βονιφάτιος | καὶ ὡς γνησίῳ φίλῳ Ἀετίῳ πιστεύ-
σας, μεταπεμφθεὶς οὐ παρεγένετο. Τότε οἱ βασιλεῖς ὡς εὐνοοῦντα τὸν
111Be | Ἀέτιον ἀπεδέξαντο. Ἦσαν δὲ τῷ τότε Γότθοι καὶ ἔθνη πολλά τε καὶ 15
μέγιστα μέχρι τοῦ Δανουβίου ἐν τοῖς ὑπερβορείοις τόποις κατῳκισμένα.
Τούτων δὲ ἀξιολογώτερά εἰσι Γότθοι, Ἰσίγοτθοι, Γήπαιδες καὶ Οὐανδῆλοι, ἐν ὀνόμασι μόνον καὶ οὐδενὶ ἑτέρῳ διαλλάττοντες, μιᾷ διαλέκτῳ
κεχρημένοι· πάντες δὲ τῆς Ἀρείου ὑπάρχουσι κακοπιστίας. Οὗτοι ἐπ'
Ἀρκαδίου καὶ Ὀνωρίου τὸν Δανούβιν διαβάντες, ἐν τῇ τῶν Ῥωμαίων 20
γῇ κατῳκίσθησαν. Καὶ οἱ μὲν Γήπαιδες, ἐξ ὧν ὕστερον διῃρέθησαν
50ʳP Λογγίβαρδοι καὶ Ἄβαρεις, τὰ περὶ Σιγγιδῶνα καὶ Σέρ|μιον χωρία
ᾤκησαν. Οἱ δὲ Ἰσίγοτθοι μετὰ Ἀλάριχον τὴν Ῥώμην πορθήσαντες,
εἰς Γαλλίας ἐχώρησαν καὶ τῶν ἐκεῖ ἐκράτησαν. Γότθοι δὲ Παννονίαν
ἔχοντες πρῶτον, ἔπειτα ιθ' ἔτει τῆς βασιλείας Θεοδοσίου τοῦ νέου, 25
ἐπιτρέψαντος, τὰ τῆς Θρᾴκης χωρία ᾤκησαν, καὶ ἐπὶ νη' χρόνους ἐν τῇ
Θρᾴκῃ διατρίψαντες, Θευδερίχου ἡγεμονεύοντος αὐτῶν πατρικίου καὶ
ὑπάτου, Ζήνωνος αὐτοῖς ἐπιτρέψαντος, τῆς ἑσπερίου βασιλείας ἐκράτησαν. Οἱ δὲ Οὐανδῆλοι Ἀλανοὺς ἑταιρισάμενοι καὶ Γερμανούς, τοὺς
νῦν καλουμένους Φράγγους, διαβάντες τὸν †Νῖνον† ποταμόν, ἡγούμενον 30
50ᵛP ἔχοντες Γογίδισκλον, κατῴκησαν ἐν Ἱσπανίᾳ, πρώτῃ οὔσῃ χώ|ρᾳ τῆς
112Be Εὐρώπης ἀπὸ | τοῦ ἑσπερίου Ὠκεανοῦ. Βονιφάτιος δὲ φοβηθεὶς τοὺς
τῶν Ῥωμαίων βασιλεῖς, περάσας ἀπὸ Λιβύης, εἰς Ἱσπανίαν πρὸς τοὺς

V ἴσχυσεν (etiam Theoph.): ἴσχυεν edd. ‖ 5 προσαπόλεσε P ‖ 7 Οὐαλεντινιανοῦ
edd. Theoph.: Οὐαλεντιανὸς P   Οὐαλεντινιανὸς P² ‖ Βονηφάτιος P: Βονιφατίου
Ba Be Theoph. ‖ 8 λαβών (etiam Theoph.ᵇ): λαβόντος Ba Be Theoph. ‖ ante
Ἀέτιος add. ὁ Ba Be Theoph. ‖ 10 Οὐαλεντινιανοῦ P² edd.: Οὐαλεντιανοῦ P ‖
11 καὶ deest in Theoph. ‖ μεταπεμφθῇς Be Theoph.: παραπεμφθῇς Ba
παραπεμφθεὶς P ‖ 14 εὐνοοῦντα Theoph.: εὐνοῦντα P   εὐνοῦνστατον (accentu
mutato, littera σ inserta et s. v. τὸν addito) P²   εὐνοῦστατον V edd. ‖ 15 τῷ
deest in Theoph. ‖ Γότθοι καὶ (etiam Theoph.ᶜᵒᵈᵈ·): Γοτθικὰ Theoph. ‖ 16
μέχρι: πέραν Theoph. ‖ 17 Ἰσίγοτθοι mg. add. P¹: om. V edd.   Ἰσι mg.
iter. P² ‖ Γήπεδες P ‖ 20 Δανούβιν P V: Δάνουβιν Pˣ Theoph.ᵍ Δανοῦβιν
Theoph. Δανούβιον edd. ‖ 22 Ἄβαρεις (etiam Theoph.): Ἀβάρεις edd. ‖
Σιγγιδῶνα P ‖ Σέρμιον Theoph.: Σερμίων P   Σερμίω Theoph.ᵍʰ Σερμείω

25

of the Africans; it happened like this. There were two generals, Aëtius and Boniface, whom Theodosius had sent to Rome at the request of Valentinian. Boniface was given the command over western Libya, and Aëtius out of jealousy slanderously accused him of meditating rebellion and working to seize Libya. This he communicated to Placidia, the mother of Valentinian. But he wrote also to Boniface, saying: «If you are sent for, do not come, for you have been slanderously accused, and the emperor and empress are trying to get you into their hands by a trick.» This message Boniface received and, trusting in Aëtius as in a true friend, did not go when he was sent for. Then the emperor and empress accepted Aëtius as a loyal servant. At that time the Goths and many very large nations were settled in the regions of the far north down as far as the Danube. Of these the most notable are the Goths, Visigoths, Gepedes and Vandals, who differ from one another in name only and in nothing else, and speak one and the same tongue; and all are of the misbelief of Arius. These in the time of Arcadius and Honorius crossed the Danube and settled in the territory of the Romans. The Gepedes, from whom were later divided off the Lombards and Avars, lived in the territories about Singidunum and Sirmium. The Visigoths, under Alaric, after taking Rome, went off to the Gallic provinces and possessed themselves of those regions. The Goths first held Pannonia, but afterwards were permitted by Theodosius the younger, in the 19th year of his reign, to dwell in the territories of Thrace, and after remaining 58 years in Thrace they obtained permission of Zeno to possess themselves of the western kingdom, with their leader the patrician and consul Theodoric. The Vandals, joining up with the Alans and Germans, who are now called Franks, crossed the river *Rhine*, and, under the leadership of Gogidisclus, settled in Spain, the first country of Europe from the side of the western Ocean. Now, Boniface, fearing the emperor and empress of the Romans, crossed over from

---

Theoph.^{cefm}   Σερμεῖον Ba Be ‖ 23 Ἡσίγοτθοι P ‖ Ἀλάριχον P V Me Theoph.: Ἀλαρίχου (*littera* ν *ex dimidia parte erasa accentuque correcto*) P^y Meursius Ba Be ‖ 24 Πανωνίαν P edd.: Πανονίαν Theoph. ‖ 25 ἔχοντες: ἔσχον Theoph. ‖ *post* ἔπειτα *add.* τῷ Theoph.: *om.* Theoph.^{efm} ‖ ἔτη P ‖ 27 διατρίψαντες Meursius Ba Be Theoph.: διατρίψαντος P ‖ 28 αὐτοῖς Ba Be Theoph.: αὐτὰρ P ‖ ἐπιτρέψαντος F Ba Be Theoph.: ἐπιστρέψαντος P ‖ *post* ἑσπερίου *add.* Λιβύης edd.: *deest in* Theoph. ‖ 29 Οὐανδῆλοι P V: Οὐανδήλοι P^y *mg.* P⁸ ‖ 30 Νῖνον (*etiam* Theoph.^{bcg}) Νεῖνον Theoph.^{efm}   νῖνος *mg.* P⁸: Ῥῆνον Ba Be Theoph. ‖ 31 Γογίδισκλον (*litteris* γί *in ras. scriptis*) P² V edd. Γοδιγίσκλον Theoph. ‖ 33 εἰς (*habet etiam* Theoph.) *s. v. add.* P³   *in textum receperunt* V edd. ‖

25

Οὐανδήλους ἦλθεν, καὶ εὑρὼν τὸν μὲν Γογίδισκλον τελευτήσαντα, τοὺς
δὲ ἐκείνου παῖδας, Γότθαρόν τε καὶ Γηζέριχον τὴν ἀρχὴν διέποντας, 35
τούτους προτρεψάμενος τὴν ἑσπέριον Λιβύην εἰς τρία μέρη διελεῖν
ὑπέσχετο, ἐφ' ᾧ ἕκαστον τοῦ τρίτου μέρους ἄρχειν σὺν αὐτῷ, κοινῇ δὲ
ἀμύνεσθαι τὸν οἱονδήποτε πολέμιον. Ἐπὶ ταύταις ταῖς ὁμολογίαις
Οὐανδῆλοι τὸν πορθμὸν διαβάντες, τὴν Λιβύην κατῴκησαν ἀπὸ τοῦ
51ʳP Ὠκεανοῦ μέχρι Τριπόλεως τῆς κατὰ Κυρήνην. Οἱ δὲ Ἰσί|γοτθοι ἀνα- 40
στάντες ἀπὸ Γαλλίας, ἐκράτησαν καὶ τὴν Ἱσπανίαν. Τινὲς δὲ τῆς συγκλήτου Ῥωμαίων, φίλοι Βονιφατίου, τὴν Ἀετίου ψευδοκατηγορίαν ἀνήγγειλαν τῇ Πλακιδίᾳ, ἐμφανῆ ποιήσαντες καὶ τὴν πρὸς Βονιφάτιον Ἀετίου
ἐπιστολήν, τοῦ Βονιφατίου ταύτην αὐτοῖς ἀποστείλαντος. Ἡ δὲ Πλακι-
δία ἐκπλαγεῖσα τὸν μὲν Ἀέτιον οὐδὲν ἠδίκησεν, Βονιφατίῳ δὲ λόγον 45
προτρεπτικὸν μεθ' ὅρκων ἀπέστειλεν. Τοῦ δὲ Γοτθαρίου τελευτήσαντος,
Γηζέριχος τῶν Οὐανδήλων γέγονεν αὐτοκράτωρ. Βονιφάτιος δὲ τὸν
λόγον δεξάμενος τῶν Οὐανδήλων κατεστράτευσεν, στρατοῦ μεγάλου
51ᵛP ἐλθόντος αὐτῷ ἀπό τε Ῥώμης καὶ τοῦ Βυ|ζαντίου, στρατηγοῦντος
Ἄσπαρος. Πολέμου δὲ κροτηθέντος πρὸς Γηζέριχον, ἡττήθη ὁ τῶν 50
113Be Ῥωμαίων στρατός. Καὶ οὕτω | Βονιφάτιος μετὰ Ἄσπαρος εἰς Ῥώμην
ἐλθών, τὴν ὑποψίαν διέλυσεν, ἀποδείξας τὴν ἀλήθειαν. Ἡ δὲ Ἀφρικὴ
ὑπὸ Οὐανδήλοις γέγονεν. Τότε καὶ Μαρκιανὸς στρατιώτης ὢν καὶ δου-
λεύων Ἄσπαρα ζῶν συνελήφθη ὑπὸ Γηζερίχου, ὁ μετὰ ταῦτα βασιλεύσας. 55

Ἰστέον, ὅτι τρεῖς ἀμερμουμνεῖς εἰσιν ἐν ὅλῃ τῇ Συρίᾳ, ἤγουν
⟨ἐν⟩ τῇ τῶν Ἀράβων ἀρχῇ, ὧν ὁ μὲν πρῶτος καθέζεται ἐν τῷ Βαγδάδ,
ἔστιν δὲ ἐκ τῆς τοῦ Μουάμεθ γενεᾶς, ἤτοι τοῦ Μουχούμετ· ὁ δὲ δεύτερος
52ʳP καθέζεται ἐν Ἀφρικῇ, καὶ ἔστι ἐκ τῆς τοῦ Ἀλήμ γενεᾶς καὶ Φα|τιμέ,
τῆς θυγατρὸς Μουάμεθ, ἤτοι τοῦ Μουχούμετ, ἐξ οὗ καὶ Φατεμῖται 60
ὀνομάζονται· ὁ δὲ τρίτος καθέζεται ἐν Ἱσπανίᾳ, ἔστιν δὲ ἀπὸ τῆς γενεᾶς
τοῦ Μαυίου.

Ἰστέον, ὅτι κατ' ἀρχὰς ἐν τῷ κατακυριεῦσαι τοὺς Σαρακηνοὺς
πάσης τῆς Συρίας ἐκαθέσθη ἀμερμουμνῆς εἰς τὸ Βαγδάδ. Ἐδέσποζεν δὲ
πάσης τῆς Περσίας καὶ τῆς Ἀφρικῆς καὶ τῆς Αἰγύπτου καὶ τῆς εὐδαί- 65
μονος Ἀραβίας. Καὶ εἶχεν ἀμηραδίας μεγάλας, ἤτοι στρατηγίδας ταύ-
τας· πρώτην ἀμηραδίαν τὴν Περσίαν, ἤγουν τὸ Χωρασάν, δευτέραν
ἀμηραδίαν τὴν Ἀφρικήν, τρίτην ἀμηραδίαν τὴν Αἴγυπτον, τετάρτην

V 34 Γογίδισκλον: Γοδιγίσκλον Theoph. ‖ 35 Γότθαρον: Γότθαριν Theoph.ᶜ
Γόνθαριν Theoph. ‖ Γηζέριχον (etiam Theoph.ᶜ): Γιζέριχον Theoph. ‖
36 τρία edd. Theoph.: γ' P ‖ 39 Οὐανδῆλοι edd. Theoph.: Οὐάνδηλοι P ‖
40 Κυρήνην Ba Be Theoph.: Κυρίνης P ‖ 42 ante Ἀετίου add. τοῦ edd.:
deest in Theoph. ‖ 46 μεθόρκον P ‖ Γοτθαρίου (etiam Theoph.ᶜ): Γονθαρίου

25

Libya into Spain and came to the Vandals, and finding that Gogidisclus was dead and that his sons Gottharus and Gezerichus held the rule, he incited them by a promise to divide western Libya in three parts, so that each of them, with himself, should rule over a third part, but should unite to repel any enemy whoever he might be. These terms being agreed upon, the Vandals crossed the strait and settled in Libya, from the Ocean as far as Tripolis by Cyrene. The Visigoths, advancing from Gaul, took possession of Spain also. Now, some Roman senators who were friends to Boniface exposed to Placidia the falsity of Aëtius' accusation, and showed her also the letter of Aëtius to Boniface, which Boniface had sent them. Placidia, much amazed, forbore to injure Aëtius, but dispatched to Boniface a message recalling him to his duty, together with promises on oath. Now, on the death of Gottharius Gezerichus had become sole chief of the Vandals. Boniface, then, on receipt of the message, marched against the Vandals, with a large force which had come to him from Rome and Byzantium under the command of Aspar. Battle was joined with Gezerichus and the army of the Romans was defeated. So Boniface, accompanied by Aspar, came to Rome and dispelled suspicion by exposing the truth. But Africa fell beneath the Vandals. It was then that Marcian, the future emperor, who was a soldier in the service of Aspar, was taken alive by Gezerichus.

There are three commanders of the faithful in the whole of Syria, that is, in the empire of the Arabs, the first of whom has his seat at Bagdad and is of the family of Mouameth, or Mahomet; the second has his seat in Africa, and is of the family of Alim and Fatime, daughter of Mouameth, or Mahomet, whence the Fatemites are so called; the third has his seat in Spain, and he is of the family of Mauias.

Originally, when the Saracens made themselves masters over all Syria, the commander of the faithful had his seat at Bagdad. He was absolute ruler over Persia and Africa and Egypt and Arabia Felix. He had beneath him mighty emirates, or military provinces, as follows: first, the emirate of Persia, or Chorasan; second, the emirate of Africa; third, the emirate

---

Theoph. ‖ 47 Γηζέριχος (etiam Theoph.ᶜ): Γιζέριχος Theoph. ‖ δὲ: οὖν Theoph. ‖ 50 Γηζέριχον (etiam Theoph.ᶜ): Γιζέριχον Theoph. ‖ 52 ᾽Αφρικὴ Pˣ V mg. P⁸: ᾽Αφρικῇ P ‖ 54 ῎Ασπαρα: τὸν ῎Ασπαρα Theoph.ᵇᵉᶠᵐ ῎Ασπαρον P τῷ ῎Ασπαρι Ba Be Theoph. ‖ Γηζερίχου F edd. Theoph.ᶜ: Γιζερίχου Theoph. Γεζερίχου P ‖ 56 ἀμερμουμνεῖς Meursius: ἀμερουμνεῖς P edd. ‖ 57 ἐν add. edd. ‖ Βαγδάδ (littera β in ras. scripta) Pʸ Ba Be: Γαγδάδ P mg. P⁸ ‖ 58 δεύτερος scr. Moravcsik: β′ P Ba Be ‖ 60 Φατεμῖται V: Φατιμῖται Be Φατουμῖται P ‖ 61 τρίτος V edd.: γ′ P ‖ 63 post ὅτι add. ἐν τῷ edd. ‖ κατα-κυριεῦσαι: κυριεῦσαι V edd. ‖ 64 Συρίας] litteras υρίας rest. P² ‖ ἀμερμουμνεῖς P: ἀμερουμνῆς Be ‖ εἰς (litteris restitutis) P²: ἐν Be ‖ τὸ scr. Moravcsik: τῶ (litteris restitutis) P² τῷ Ba Be ‖ Βαγδάδ] litteras rest. P² ‖ 67 Χωρασάν scr. Moravcsik: Χωρασσάν mg. P⁸ Χωροσσάν P Χωροσάν Be ‖ δευτέραν edd.: β′ P ‖

108

25, 26

52ᵛP ἀμηραδίαν τὴν Φιλιστίημ, ἤτοι | τὸ 'Ράμβλε, πέμπτην ἀμηραδίαν τὴν
Δαμασκόν, ἕκτην ἀμηραδίαν τὸ Χέμψ, ἤτοι τὸ "Εμεσα, ἑβδόμην ἀμη- 70
114Be ραδίαν τὸ Χάλεπ, ὀγδόην ἀμηραδίαν τὴν 'Αν|τιόχειαν, ἐνάτην ἀμηρα-
δίαν τὸ Χαράν, δεκάτην ἀμηραδίαν τὸ "Εμετ, ἑνδεκάτην ἀμηραδίαν
τὴν 'Εσιβή, δωδεκάτην ἀμηραδίαν τὸ Μούσελ, τρισκαιδεκάτην ἀμηραδίαν
τὸ Τικρίτ. Τῆς δὲ 'Αφρικῆς ἀποσπασθείσης ἀπὸ τῆς τοῦ ἀμερμουμνῆ
ἐν τῷ Βαγδὰδ ἐξουσίας καὶ ἰδιοκρατησάσης καὶ ἀμηρᾶν ἴδιον ἀναγορευ- 75
σάσης, γέγονεν, καθὼς καὶ προϋπῆρχεν, πρώτη ἀμηραδία ἡ Περσία,
δευτέρα ἡ Αἴγυπτος καὶ καθεξῆς αἱ λοιπαί, καθὼς προείρηται. 'Αρτίως
δὲ πάλιν τοῦ ἀμερμουμνῆ τοῦ ἐν τῷ Βαγδὰδ ἀδυνατήσαντος, γέγονεν
53ʳP ἰδιόρρυθμος | ὁ τῆς Περσίας ἀμηρᾶς, ἤγουν τοῦ Χωρασάν· καὶ ἀπεκάλε-
σεν ἑαυτὸν ἀμερμουμνῆν, φορῶν καὶ τὸ κουρὰν διὰ πινακιδίων εἰς τὸν 80
τράχηλον αὐτοῦ δίκην μανιακίου. Λέγει δὲ ἑαυτὸν εἶναι ⟨ἐκ⟩ τῆς γενεᾶς
τοῦ 'Αλήμ. Ὁ δὲ ἀμηρᾶς τῆς εὐδαίμονος 'Αραβίας ὑπῆρχεν ἀεὶ καὶ
πάντοτε ὑπὸ τὴν ἐξουσίαν τοῦ ἀμηρᾶ Αἰγύπτου. Γέγονεν δὲ καὶ αὐτὸς
ἰδιόρρυθμος, καὶ ἀπεκάλεσεν καὶ αὐτὸς ἑαυτὸν ἀμερμουμνῆν· λέγει δὲ
καὶ αὐτὸς ἑαυτὸν εἶναι ἐκ τῆς τοῦ 'Αλήμ γενεᾶς. 85

26. Ἡ γενεαλογία τοῦ περιβλέπτου ῥηγὸς Οὔγωνος.

Ἰστέον, ὅτι ὁ ῥὴξ 'Ιταλίας, ὁ μέγας Λωθάριος, ὁ πάππος τοῦ
53ᵛP περιβλέπτου ῥηγὸς Οὔγωνος, ἀπὸ | τῆς γενεᾶς τοῦ μεγάλου Καρούλου
κατήγετο, περὶ οὗ πολὺς ἔπαινος, ἐγκώμιά τε καὶ διηγήματα καὶ περὶ
115Be πολέμους ἀνδραγαθήματα. Οὗτος οὖν ὁ Κάρουλος | ἦν μονοκράτωρ 5
πάντων τῶν ῥηγάτων, ἐβασίλευσε δὲ εἰς τὴν μεγάλην Φραγγίαν. 'Εν δὲ
ταῖς ἡμέραις αὐτοῦ οὐδεὶς τῶν ὑπολοίπων ῥηγῶν ἐτόλμησε ῥῆγα ἑαυτὸν
καλέσαι, ἀλλὰ πάντες ὑπῆρχον ὑπόσπονδοι αὐτοῦ, ὅστις χρήματα ἱκανὰ
καὶ πλοῦτον ἄφθονον ἐν Παλαιστίνῃ ἀποστείλας, ἐδείματο μοναστήρια
πάμπολλα. Ὁ τοίνυν Λωθάριος οὗτος ἀναλαβόμενος τὰ ἑαυτοῦ στρατεύ- 10
54ʳP ματα, κατὰ 'Ρώμης ἐκστρατεύσας, ἀπὸ πολέμου | ταύτην ἐκράτησεν,
καὶ ἐστέφθη παρὰ τοῦ τότε πάπα. Καὶ ἡνίκα ὑπέστρεφεν εἰς τὴν ἑαυτοῦ
ἐξουσίαν, ἤγουν εἰς Πάπιαν, κατήντησεν εἰς τὸ κάστρον Πλαζέντα,
τὸ ὂν ἀπὸ τριάκοντα μιλίων τῆς Παπίας. Κἀκεῖσε μὲν οὗτος τελευτᾷ,
ἔτεκεν δὲ υἱόν, ὀνόματι 'Αδέλβερτον, ὃς ἔγημεν γυναῖκα τὴν μεγάλην 15
Βέρταν, καὶ ἐξ αὐτῆς τὸν προρρηθέντα ῥῆγα, τὸν Οὔγωνα ἔτεκεν. Μετὰ
δὲ τὸ τελευτῆσαι τὸν μέγαν Λωθάριον Λοδόϊκος, ὁ ἴδιος τοῦ Λοδόϊκου,

---

V 69 Φιλιστίημ V edd. ‖ πέμπτην edd.: ε′ P ‖ 70 ἕκτην V edd.: ς′ P ‖
"Εμεσσα P edd. ‖ ἑβδόμην edd.: ζ′ P ‖ 71 ὀγδόην edd.: η′ P ‖ ἐνάτην
Be: θ′ P ‖ 72 δεκάτην edd.: ι′ P ‖ ἑνδεκάτην edd.: ια′ P ‖ 73 δωδεκάτην edd.:
ιβ′ P ‖ τρισκαιδεκάτην Moravcsik: ιγ′ P τρισδεκάτην edd. ‖ 75 ante ἐν adden-

25, 26

of Egypt; fourth, the emirate of Philistiem, or Rambleh; fifth, the emirate of Damascus; sixth, the emirate of Homs, or Emesa; seventh, the emirate of Aleppo; eighth, the emirate of Antioch; ninth, the emirate of Harran; tenth, the emirate of Emet; eleventh, the emirate of Esibe; twelfth, the emirate of Mosul; thirteenth, the emirate of Tikrit. But after Africa was torn away from the dominion of the commander of the faithful at Bagdad and had become self-governing and had proclaimed an emir of its own, then Persia was the first emirate, as it had been before, and Egypt became the second, and the rest thereafter in the order given above. But now, again, owing to the impotence of the commander of the faithful at Bagdad, the emir of Persia, or Chorasan, has become independent; and he has usurped the style of commander of the faithful, wearing the koran on tablets about his neck like a necklace. And he says he is *from* the family of Alim. Moreover the emir of Arabia Felix used always invariably to be beneath the dominion of the emir of Egypt. But he too has become independent, and he too has usurped the style of commander of the faithful; and he too says he is of the family of Alim.

26. The genealogy of the illustrious king Hugh.

The elder Lothair, king of Italy, grandfather of the illustrious king Hugh, was by descent of the family of the elder Charles, a man much celebrated in song and story and author of heroic deeds in war. This Charles was sole ruler over all the kingdoms, and reigned as emperor in great Francia. And in his days none of the other kings dared call himself a king, but all were his vassals; and he sent much money and abundant treasure to Palestine and built a very large number of monasteries. Well, this Lothair took his forces and marched against Rome and assaulted and got possession of it, and was crowned by the pope of that time. And when he was on his way back to his domain, that is, to Papia, he got as far as the city of Piacenza, thirty miles distant from Papia, and there he died; he begat a son called Adalbert, who took to wife the elder Bertha, and begat on her the aforesaid king Hugh. Now, after the death of the elder Lothair, Lewis, kinsman

---

dum τοῦ *coni.* Bekker ‖ ἀμηρὰν P ‖ 75/6 ἀναγορευσάσης Meursius Ba Be: ἀναγορεύσασα P ‖ 76 πρώτη edd.: α' P ‖ 77 δευτέρα edd.: β' P ‖ 79 ἀμηρὰς P ‖ τοῦ Be: τὸ P ‖ Χορασάν edd. ‖ 80 ἀμερμουμνὴν P ‖ 81 ἑαυτὸν *coni.* Moravcsik: αὐτὸν F edd. αὐτὸν P ‖ ἐκ *add.* Moravcsik: ἀπὸ *add.* edd. ‖ 82 ἀμηρὰς P ‖ 83 ἀμηρὰ P ‖ 84 ἀμερμουμνὴν P.

26. 1 ῥηγῶς P ‖ 2 ῥὶξ P ‖ 3 ῥιγὼς P ‖ Καρούλλου P ‖ 5 ὁ *om.* edd. ‖ Κάρουλλος P ‖ 6 ῥηγατῶν P ‖ 7 ῥιγῶν P ‖ ῥίγα P ‖ 9 ἐν: ἐμ P ‖ 13 Παπίαν edd. ‖ 16 ῥήγα P ‖ 17 μέγαν edd.: μέγα P ‖ Λοδόϊκου: Λωθαρίου *coni.* Ohnsorge ‖

110

26

ἀπὸ τῆς μεγάλης Φραγγίας ἐλθών, ἐκράτησεν τὴν Πάπιαν. Καὶ ἦν μὲν
54ᵛP ἄστεπτος. Ὕστερον δὲ ἦλθεν εἰς Βερῶναν, εἰς τὸ κάστρον, τὸ ὂν | ἀπὸ ρκ′
μιλίων τῆς Παπίας, καὶ ἐλθόντος αὐτοῦ ἐκεῖσε, ἐπανέστησαν αὐτῷ οἱ 20
τοῦ αὐτοῦ κάστρου, καὶ κρατήσαντες ἐτύφλωσαν. Καὶ τότε ἐκράτησεν
Βεριγγέριος, ὁ πάππος τοῦ νυνὶ Βεριγγέρη, καὶ εἰσελθὼν ἐν Ῥώμῃ
ἐστέφθη. Καὶ μετὰ τοῦτο ἐδηλοποίησεν λαὸς πολὺς τῷ Ῥοδούλφῳ
εἰς Βεργώνιαν ὄντι, λέγοντες, ὅτι· «Ἐλθὲ ἐνταῦθα, καὶ παραδίδομέν σοι
116Be τὸ ῥηγᾶτον καὶ ἀποκτενοῦμεν τὸν Βεριγγέ|ριον.» Ὁ δὲ ἦλθεν ἀπὸ 25
Βεργώνιαν πρὸς τὰ μέρη τῆς Παπίας, καὶ ὁ μὲν ἥμισυς λαὸς ἦν μετὰ
τοῦ Βεριγγέρη, ὁ δὲ λοιπὸς μετὰ τοῦ Ῥοδούλφου. Καὶ πολεμήσαντες,
ἐνίκησεν ὁ Βεριγγέρης τὸν πρῶτον πόλεμον, καὶ πάλιν πολεμήσαντες,
55ʳP ἐνίκη|σεν ὁ Ῥοδοῦλφος. Καὶ ἔφυγεν ὁ λαὸς τοῦ Βεριγγέρη, καὶ μόνος
καταλειφθεὶς ὁ Βεριγγέρης ἐποίησεν ἑαυτὸν ὡς τεθνεῶτα, καὶ ἔπεσεν 30
μέσον τῶν τεθνεώτων, σκεπάσας αὐτὸν μετὰ τῆς δόρκας αὐτοῦ, τὸν
δὲ πόδα αὐτοῦ εἶχεν ἔξω. Ἐλθὼν δὲ εἷς ἐκ τῶν στρατιωτῶν τοῦ Ῥοδούλφου, δέδωκεν αὐτῷ μετὰ μεναύλου εἰς τὸν πόδα, αὐτὸς δὲ τὸ σύνολον
οὐκ ἐσαλεύθη· τοῦ δὲ μὴ σαλευθέντος, ἀφῆσεν αὐτὸν ὡς δῆθεν νεκρὸν
ὄντα. Ἠγνόει δὲ ὁ τοῦ Ῥοδούλφου λαός, ὅτι ὁ Βεριγγέρης ἐστίν. Καὶ 35
παύσαντος τοῦ πολέμου, ἠγέρθη ὁ Βεριγγέρης καὶ ἦλθεν εἰς τὸ παλάτιον αὐτοῦ μόνος, καὶ πάλιν ἐκράτησεν τῆς βασιλείας, καὶ ἐπολέμησεν
55ᵛP τὸν Ῥοδοῦλφον καὶ ἐνίκησεν αὐτόν. Μετὰ δὲ | τοῦτο συνεβιβάσθησαν
εἰς ἀλλήλους, καὶ ἐμερίσθησαν τὴν χώραν εἰς δύο· καὶ ὁ μὲν εἷς ἀνελάβετο τὸ ἓν μέρος τῆς χώρας, ὁ δὲ ἕτερος τὸ ἕτερον. Ἦν δὲ ὁ Ῥοδοῦλφος 40
ὑπὸ τὴν βουλὴν καὶ ἐξουσίαν τοῦ Βεριγγέρη. Καὶ μετὰ τοῦτο ἦλθον
ἀπὸ Βεργώνιαν τρεῖς μαρκήσιοι πρὸς Πάπιαν τοῦ ἐκδιῶξαι τοὺς κρατοῦν-
τας καὶ κρατῆσαι αὐτοί· ἦσαν δὲ οὗτοι· Οὔγων ὁ Ταλιαφέρνου καὶ
Βόζος καὶ Οὔγων, ὁ ἀδελφὸς τοῦ Βόζου, ὁ προρρηθεὶς εὐγενέστατος
117Be ῥήξ. Ἦλθεν δὲ μετὰ λαοῦ ἱκανοῦ. Καὶ | μαθὼν ὁ Βεριγγέρης ἡτοιμάσθη, 45
καὶ ἀπῆλθεν εἰς συνάντησιν αὐτοῦ πρὸς πόλεμον, καὶ παρακαθίσας
ἐστενοχώρησεν αὐτοὺς ἀπὸ λιμοῦ, καὶ ὥρισεν τὸν λαὸν αὐτοῦ τοῦ
56ʳP μὴ φονεύειν | τινά, ἀλλ' ὅπου ἂν κρατήσωσί τινα ἐξ αὐτῶν, κόπτωσιν
τὴν ῥῖνα αὐτοῦ καὶ τὰ δύο ὠτία καὶ ἀπολύωσιν, ὃ δὴ καὶ ἐποίουν. Θεασά-
μενοι οὖν τοῦτο αἱ προρρηθεῖσαι τρεῖς κεφαλαί, ἄραντες ἀνυπόδετοι 50
τὰ θεῖα εὐαγγέλια εἰς τὰς χεῖρας αὐτῶν, ἦλθον πρὸς τὸν Βεριγγέρην,
αἰτούμενοι συγχώρησιν καὶ ὀμνύοντες τοῦ μηκέτι ἐλθεῖν ἐνθάδε μέχρι
τέλους ζωῆς αὐτοῦ, καὶ τότε εἴασεν αὐτοὺς ἀπελθεῖν εἰς τὴν ἰδίαν χώραν.

V 18 Παπίαν F edd. ‖ 22 Βεριγγέρι V edd. ‖ 25 ῥιγᾶτον P ‖ 26 Παπίας V
edd.: Πάπιας P ‖ ἥμισυς Be: ἥμισυ P ‖ 27 Βεριγγέρι Be ‖ Ῥοδούλφου edd.:
Ῥοδόλφου P ‖ πολεμίσαντες P ‖ 28 Βεριγγέρις Be ‖ πρῶτον V edd.: α′ P ‖

26

of Lewis, came from great Francia and took possession of Papia. He was not crowned. And afterwards he came to Verona, a city 120 miles from Papia, and on his arrival there the folk of that same city rose up against him and seized and blinded him. Then the rule was seized by Berengar, grandfather of the present Berengar, and he entered Rome and was crowned. After this, a large body of the folk made a declaration to Rodolf, who was in Burgundy, saying: «Come here, and we will give the kingdom over to you and will kill Berengar.» So he came from Burgundy to the region of Papia, and one half of the folk sided with Berengar, and the rest with Rodolf. They fought and Berengar was victorious in the first battle, and they fought again and Rodolf gained the victory. And the army of Berengar fled, and Berengar, left alone by himself, made as though he were dead, and fell down among the dead and covered himself with his shield, but left his leg protruding. One of Rodolf's soldiers came up and stabbed him in the leg with a spear, but he never stirred a muscle; and when he did not stir, he let him alone, supposing him in truth to be a corpse. And the army of Rodolf did not know that he was Berengar. When the battle was over, Berengar got up and came to his palace alone, and again got possession of his throne and fought with Rodolf and gained the victory over him. Thereafter they came to terms with one another and divided the country in two; and one of them took one part of the country, and the other the other. But Rodolf was subject to the counsel and authority of Berengar. After this, again, three marquises came from Burgundy to Papia with intent to expel its possessors and possess it themselves; they were Hugh Tagliaferro, and Boso, and Boso's brother Hugh, the most noble king aforesaid. And he came with a large army. When Berengar heard of it, he made ready and advanced to meet him in battle, and began to blockade and to reduce them by hunger, and gave orders to his army not to kill any, but if they should take any of them prisoner, to cut off his nose and his two ears and let him go; and so they did. When they saw this, the three chiefs aforesaid took the holy gospels in their hands and came barefoot to Berengar and begged his pardon and swore that they would never more come there so long as he should live; and then he let them depart to their

---

πολεμίσαντες P || 29 Ῥοδοῦλφος V edd.: Ῥουδοῦλφος P || Βεριγγέρι Be || 30 Βεριγγέρις Be || 31 αὐτὸν V edd.: αὐτὸν P || δόρκας scr. Moravcsik: δορκὰς P δορκᾶς edd. || αὐτοῦ (etiam Bandurius): αὐτοῦ edd. || 32 αὐτοῦ edd. || 32/3 Ῥοδούλφου Pᵞ: Ῥοδοῦλφου P V || 34 ἀφίησιν V edd. || 35 Ῥοδούλφου Pᵞ: Ῥοδούλφου P V || Βεριγγέρις Be || 36 Βεριγγέρις Be || 37 ἐπολέμισεν P || 41 Βεριγγέρι Be || 42 Βεργώνια edd. || μαρκέσιοι Meursius || Παπίαν F edd. || 44 Βόζος mg. Pˢ: Βόζον P Βόζων V edd. || Οὔγων V edd. Οὔγον P || 45 ῥίξ P || Βεριγγέρις Be || 47 ὥρισεν P || τοῦ om. edd. || 49 ῥῖνα Be: ῥίναν P || ἀπολύωσιν edd.: ἀπολύουσιν P || 51 Βεριγγέριν P ||

26, 27

Ὕστερον δὲ τοῦ Βεριγγέρη ἀπελθόντος εἰς Βερῶναν, ἀπέκτεινεν αὐτὸν
Φαλεμβέρτος, ὁ σύντεκνος αὐτοῦ, καὶ τότε ἐκράτησεν ὅλον τὸ ῥηγᾶτον 55
56ᵛP ὁ 'Ροδοῦλφος. Καὶ μετὰ τοῦτο ἐμήνυσεν ὁ λαὸς τῆς χώρας ὅλης | εἰς
Βεργώνιαν τῷ Οὔγωνι, τῷ προρρηθέντι ῥηγί, λέγοντες, ὅτι· «Ἐλθέ,
καὶ παραδίδομέν σοι τὴν χώραν.» Καὶ ἐλθόντος αὐτοῦ, ἐπῆρεν αὐτὸν
ὁ λαός, καὶ ἀπήγαγον εἰς τὸ παλάτιον, καὶ ἀπεκατέστησεν αὐτὸν ῥῆγα.
Τὸν δὲ 'Ροδοῦλφον εἶπον, ὅτι· «Ἄπελθε μετὰ τοῦ πλούτου σου, θέλῃς, 60
εἰς τὴν χώραν σου, θέλῃς, ἀλλαχοῦ.» Ὁ δὲ ἀπῆλθεν εἰς Βεργώνιαν, εἰς
τὴν χώραν αὐτοῦ, καὶ κατεῖχεν ἐκεῖσε λαὸν ἱκανόν. Καὶ τελευτήσαντος
αὐτοῦ, ἀπῆλθεν Οὔγων, ὁ προρρηθεὶς ῥήξ, εἰς Βεργώνιαν, καὶ τὴν γυναῖκα τοῦ 'Ροδούλφου, ἥτις καὶ Βέρτα ὠνομάζετο, ἔλαβεν εἰς γυναῖκα.
118Be Τὴν δὲ θυγατέρα αὐτῆς, ὀνόματι Ἀδέλεσαν, δέ|δωκεν Λωθαρίῳ, τῷ 65
57ʳP υἱῷ αὐ|τοῦ, τῷ νυνὶ ὄντι Ἰταλίας ῥηγί. Ἡ δὲ ἀνελθοῦσα ἐν Κωνσταντι-
νουπόλει καὶ συναφθεῖσα 'Ρωμανῷ τῷ πορφυρογεννήτῳ, υἱῷ Κωνσταντίνου, τοῦ φιλοχρίστου δεσπότου, ἤτοι ἡ θυγάτηρ τοῦ αὐτοῦ περιβλέπτου
ῥηγὸς Οὔγωνος, ἣ ὠνομάζετο Βέρτα κατὰ τὸ ὄνομα τῆς μάμμης αὐτῆς,
ἤγουν τῆς μεγάλης Βέρτας, ἥτις μετὰ θάνατον τοῦ Ἀδελβέρτου, ἀνδρὸς 70
αὐτῆς, ἐβασίλευσεν ἔτη * * *, μετωνομάσθη δὲ Εὐδοκία κατὰ τὸ ὄνομα
τῆς τε μάμμης καὶ ἀδελφῆς Κωνσταντίνου, τοῦ φιλοχρίστου δεσπότου.

27. Π ε ρ ὶ τ ο ῦ θ έ μ α τ ο ς Λ α γ ο υ β α ρ δ ί α ς κ α ὶ τ ῶ ν
ἐ ν α ὐ τ ῇ π ρ ι γ κ ι π ά τ ω ν κ α ὶ ἀ ρ χ ο ν τ ι ῶ ν.

Ἰστέον, ὅτι ἐν τοῖς παλαιοῖς χρόνοις κατεκρατεῖτο ἡ πᾶσα ἐξουσία
57ᵛP Ἰταλίας, ἥ τε Νεά|πολις καὶ Κάπυα καὶ ἡ Βενεβενδός, τό τε Σαλερινὸν
καὶ ἡ Ἀμάλφη καὶ Γαϊτὴ καὶ πᾶσα ἡ Λαγουβαρδία παρὰ τῶν 'Ρωμαίων, 5
δηλονότι βασιλευομένης τῆς 'Ρώμης. Μετὰ δὲ τὸ ἀνελθεῖν τὸ βασίλειον
ἐν Κωνσταντινουπόλει διεμερίσθησαν ταῦτα πάντα εἰς ἀρχὰς δύο, ἐξ
οὗ καὶ παρὰ τοῦ βασιλεύοντος ἐν Κωνσταντινουπόλει ἀπεστέλλοντο
πατρίκιοι δύο· καὶ ὁ μὲν εἷς πατρίκιος ἐκράτει τὴν Σικελίαν καὶ τὴν
Καλαβρίαν καὶ τὴν Νεάπολιν καὶ Ἀμάλφην, ὁ δὲ ἕτερος πατρίκιος 10
ἐκαθέζετο εἰς Βενεβενδόν, καὶ ἐκράτει τὴν Πάπιαν καὶ τὴν Κάπυαν καὶ
58ʳP τὰ λοιπὰ πάντα. Καὶ ἐτέλουν κατ' ἔτος τῷ βασιλεῖ τὰ νενομισμένα | τῷ

F 66 Ἡ δὲ — 72 δεσπότου: cf. Georg. Mon. (cont.), ed. Bonn. p. 917,
11—18; Georg. Mon. (cont.), ed. Istrin II. p. 62, 15—21; Theoph. Cont.,
ed. Bonn. p. 431, 11—19.

V 54 Βεριγγέρι Be ‖ Βερῶναν P ‖ 55 Φαλαμβέρτος V mg. P⁸ Φαλάμβερτος
edd. ‖ ῥιγάτον P ‖ 56 ὅ¹ om. edd. ‖ 57 Βεργωνίαν edd. ‖ ῥιγί P ‖ 58 ἐπεῖραν P:
ἐπῆρον Be ἐπῆραν Migne ‖ 59 ἀπεκατέστησαν Be ‖ ῥίγα P ‖ 61 Βεργώνειαν P:

26, 27

own country. But afterwards, when Berengar had gone to Verona, he was slain by Flambert, whose child he had held at the font, and then Rodolf became possessed of the whole kingdom. And after that the folk of the whole country sent a message to Burgundy, to the aforesaid king Hugh, saying: «Come, and we will give the country over to you.» And when he came, the folk raised him up, and brought him away to the palace and made him king again. But to Rodolf they said: «Depart with your treasure, either to your country or elsewhere, as you will.» So he went off to Burgundy, to his country, and there ruled over a large folk. And when he died, the aforesaid king Hugh went off to Burgundy and took to wife the widow of Rodolf, who was also called Bertha. And her daughter, Adelesa by name, he gave to Lothair his son, who is now king of Italy. Now, she who came up to Constantinople and was joined in marriage to Romanus, the son born in the purple of Constantine, the Christ-loving sovereign, *was* the daughter of the same illustrious king Hugh, and she was called Bertha after the name of her grandmother, I mean the elder Bertha, who after the death of Adalbert her husband reigned *ten* years; but she, *the young Bertha*, changed her name to Eudocia, after that of the grandmother and sister of Constantine, the Christ-loving sovereign.

27. Of the province of Lombardy and of the principalities and governorships therein.

In ancient times the whole domain of Italy, both Naples and Capua and Beneventum, Salerno and Amalfi and Gaëta and all of Lombardy, was in the possession of the Romans, I mean, when Rome was the imperial capital. But after the seat of empire was removed to Constantinople, all these territories were divided into two governments, and therefore two patricians used to be dispatched by the emperor in Constantinople; one patrician would govern Sicily and Calabria and Naples and Amalfi, and the other, with his seat at Beneventum, would govern Papia and Capua and all the rest. They used to remit annually to the emperor the sums due to the treasury.

Βεργωνίαν edd. || 63 ῥίξ P || Βεργωνίαν edd. || 64 'Ροδούλφου Pᵛ 'Ροδούλφου P V || ὀνομάζετο P || 65 θυγατέρα edd.: θυγατέραν P || 66 ῥιγί P || 68 ἥτοι: ἥτον coni. Bekker ἥτο coni. Jenkins εἴτουν coni. Kukules || 69 ῥιγὸς P || ὀνομάζετο P || 70 ἤγουν om. V edd. || 71 post ἔτη lac. 4 litt. ind. P lac ind. edd. αὐτῆς *** ἐβασίλευσεν ἔτη ⟨πέντε⟩ vel αὐτῆς ἐβασίλευσεν ἔτη ⟨δέκα⟩ coni. Jenkins || μετονομάσθη P || 72 μάμης P.
  27. 1 Λογουβαρδίας edd. || 2 πριγκηπάτων P || 4 ante 'Ι- λίας add. τῆς edd. || Κάπυα scr. Moravcsik: Καπύα P Καπύη V edd. || Σαλερινὸν Be: Σαλερῆνον P || 5 Γαϊτὴ Ba Be: Γαϊπῆ P Γαϊτη sive Γαιήτη Meursius || Λογουβαρδία edd. || 6 βασιλευομένων Me Ba || 10 Καλαυρίαν P || 'Αμάλφην Be: 'Αμαλφὴν P || 11 Παπίαν edd. ||

114

119Be δημοσίῳ. Αὗται δὲ πᾶσαι αἱ προρρηθεῖσαι χῶραι κατω|κοῦντο παρὰ
τῶν Ῥωμαίων. Ἐν δὲ τοῖς καιροῖς Εἰρήνης τῆς βασιλίδος ἀποσταλεὶς
ὁ πατρίκιος Ναρσῆς ἐκράτει τὴν Βενεβενδὸν καὶ τὴν Πάπιαν· καὶ Ζαχα- 15
ρίας, ὁ πάπας Ἀθηναῖος, ἐκράτει τὴν Ῥώμην. Συνέβη δὲ πολέμους
γενέσθαι εἰς τὰ τῆς Παπίας μέρη, καὶ ἐξωδίασεν ὁ πατρίκιος Ναρσῆς
εἰς τὸν στρατὸν τὰ εἰσκομιζόμενα πάκτα τῷ δημοσίῳ, καὶ οὐκ ἀπεστάλη
ἡ κατὰ τύπον εἰσκομιδὴ παρ᾽ αὐτοῦ. Ὁ δὲ Ναρσῆς ἀντεμήνυσεν, ὅτι·
«Ἀπὸ τῶν αὐτόθι μᾶλλον ἐλπίζω ἀποσταλῆναί μοι χρήματα, ἐπειδὴ 20
58ᵛP πᾶσαν τὴν ἀπὸ τῶν ὧδε εἰσκομιζομένην εἰσκο|μιδὴν εἰς τοὺς ἀνακύψαντας
πολέμους κατηνάλωσα, καὶ μᾶλλον ὑμεῖς ἀπὸ τῶν ὧδε ἐπιζητεῖτε εἰσκομι-
δάς.» Ταῦτα ἀκούσασα ἡ βασίλισσα Εἰρήνη καὶ ὀργισθεῖσα, ἀπέστειλεν
αὐτῷ ἄτρακτον καὶ ἠλακάτην, γράψασα πρὸς αὐτόν, ὅτι· «Λάβε ταῦτα,
ἃ καὶ ἁρμόζει σοι· νήθειν σε γὰρ μᾶλλον ἐκρίναμεν δίκαιον, ἢ μετὰ 25
ὅπλων ὡς ἄνδρα διεκδικεῖν καὶ διευθύνειν καὶ ὑπερπολεμεῖν Ῥωμαίων.»
Ταῦτα ἀκούσας ὁ πατρίκιος Ναρσῆς ἀντέγραψε πρὸς τὴν βασιλίδα, ὅτι·
«Ἐπεὶ οὕτως παρ᾽ ὑμῖν ἐνομίσθην νήθειν καὶ κλώθειν, καθάπερ γυνή,
59ʳP κλῶσαι ἔχω νήματα μετὰ τῆς ἀτράκτου καὶ ἠλακάτης, ἵνα, μέχρις ἂν | ζῶ-
σιν οἱ Ῥωμαῖοι, μὴ δυνηθῶσιν ἐξυφᾶναι ταῦτα.» Οἱ δὲ Λαγούβαρδοι τῷ 30
τότε καιρῷ κατῴκουν εἰς Παννονίαν, ἔνθα ἀρτίως οἰκοῦσιν οἱ Τοῦρκοι.
Καὶ ἀποστείλας ὁ πατρίκιος Ναρσῆς πρὸς αὐτοὺς ὀπώρας παντοίας,
120Be ἐδηλοποίησεν αὐτοῖς, ὅτι· «Δεῦτε ἐνταῦθα καὶ θεάσασθε | γῆν ῥέουσαν
κατὰ τὸ εἰρημένον μέλι καὶ γάλα, ἧς, ὡς οἶμαι, ὁ Θεὸς κρείττονα οὐκ
ἔχει· καὶ εἰ ἔστιν ὑμῖν ἀρεστόν, κατοικήσατε ἐν αὐτῇ, ὅπως εἰς αἰῶνας 35
αἰώνων μακαρίζητέ με». Ταῦτα δὲ ἀκούσαντες οἱ Λαγούβαρδοι καὶ
πεισθέντες, ἀναλαβόμενοι τὰς φαμιλίας αὐτῶν, ἦλθον εἰς Βενεβενδόν.
59ᵛP Οἱ δὲ τοῦ κάστρου Βενεβενδοῦ οὐκ εἴασαν αὐτοὺς | ἔνδον τοῦ κάστρου
εἰσελθεῖν, ᾤκησαν δὲ ἔξωθεν τοῦ κάστρου πλησίον τοῦ τείχους εἰς τὸν
ποταμόν, οἰκοδομήσαντες ἐκεῖσε κάστρον μικρόν, ἐξ οὗ καὶ ὀνομάζεται 40
Τζιβιτανόβα, τουτέστιν νεόκαστρον, ὃ καὶ μέχρι τῆς σήμερον συνίσταται.
Εἰσήρχοντο δὲ καὶ ἔνδοθεν τοῦ κάστρου καὶ ἐν τῇ ἐκκλησίᾳ, καὶ διὰ
μηχανῆς κυριεύσαντες τοὺς οἰκήτορας τοῦ κάστρου Βενεβενδοῦ, ἀνεῖλον
πάντας καὶ κατέσχον τὸ κάστρον. Ἔσωθεν γὰρ τῶν ῥάβδων αὐτῶν
σπαθία βαστάζοντες καὶ ἐν τῇ ἐκκλησίᾳ ὑπότροπον ποιήσαντες ἐπὶ τὸ 45
αὐτὸ μάχην, πάντας, ὡς εἴρηται, ἀπέκτειναν. Καὶ ἔκτοτε ἐκστρατεύσαν-

---

F   33 γῆν — 34 γάλα: Exod. 3, 8; Lev. 20, 24; Num. 13, 28; Deut.
6, 3 etc.; cf. Theoph. cont. p. 74, 21—22.

V 13 κατῳκοῦντο Ba Be: κατοικοῦντο P ‖ 15 Ναρσῆς edd.: Νάρσης P ‖
Πάπιαν scr. Moravcsik: Παπίαν P edd. ‖ 17 ἐξοδίασεν P ‖ 19 post παρ᾽ αὐτοῦ
lac. ind. Kyriakides ‖ 20 μοι ἀποσταλῆναι edd. ‖ 22 ἐπιζητεῖτε: ζητεῖτε F Be ‖

27

All these countries aforesaid used to be inhabited by the Romans. But in the time of the empress Irene the patrician Narses was sent out and was governing Beneventum and Papia; and pope Zacharias, the Athenian, was governing Rome. It happened that fighting had been going on in the region of Papia, and the patrician Narses had expended on the army the tribute collected for the treasury, and the regular revenue was not remitted by him. Narses sent back a reply, saying: «I expect, rather, that money should be sent to me from your side, since I have exhausted all the revenues incoming from here upon the fighting that has broken out; but, on the contrary, it is you who are demanding revenues from here.» When the empress Irene heard this she was angry and sent him a spindle and distaff, and wrote to him: «Take these, your proper instruments; for we have judged it fit that you should spin, rather than that as a man at arms you should defend and guide and do battle for the Romans.» On hearing this the patrician Narses wrote in reply to the empress: «Since I am thus judged by you fit to spin and twist like a woman, I will twist you hanks with spindle and distaff such as the Romans shall never be able to unravel so long as they endure». Now, at that time the Lombards were dwelling in Pannonia, where now the Turks live. And the patrician Narses sent to them fruits of all kinds and made them this declaration: «Come hither and behold a land flowing with honey and milk, as the saying is, which, I think, God has none to surpass; and if it please you, settle in it, that you may call me blessed for the ages of ages.» The Lombards heard and obeyed and took their families and came to Beneventum. The inhabitants of the city of Beneventum did not allow them to come inside the city, and they settled outside the city, near the wall and by the river, where they built a small city, which for that reason is called Civita Nova, that is, New City, and it stands to this day. But they began to come inside the city also and into the church, and having by a stratagem gained the upper hand of the inhabitants of the city of Beneventum, they made away with them all and took possession of the city. For they carried swords inside their staves, and in the church they wheeled round and attacked all together and, as has been said, killed everyone. And thereafter they marched out and sub-

---

28 ἐνομίσθην Be: ἐνομίσθη P ‖ 30 ταῦτα P² V edd.: τοῦτα P ‖ Λογουβάρδοι edd. ‖ 31 κατῴκουν edd.: κατοίκουν P ‖ Πανωνείαν P   Πανωνίαν V edd. ‖ Τούρκοι P ‖ 34 ἧς ὡς (littera ἦ in ras. scripta et ο in ω correcta) P¹ V edd.: ισος (?) P ‖ 35 ὑμῖν F Ba Be: ἡμῖν P ‖ 35/6 αἰῶνα αἰῶνος V edd. ‖ 36 μακαρίζητέ coni. Bekker: μακαρίζεταί P μακαρίζετέ F Ba Be ‖ Λογούβαρδοι edd. ‖ 40 οὗ V edd.: ο[ὕ] P ‖ 41 Τζιβιτανόβα: Τζιτανόβα V Τζιτὰ νόβα F Me ‖ 43 κυριεύσαντες V edd.: κυριεύσαντ[ες] P ‖ 44 κατέσχον Ba Be: κατέχουν P ‖ ante τῶν add. διὰ edd. ‖ 45 ὑπὸ τρόπον P ‖ ποιήσαντες V edd.: πο[ι]ήσαντες P ‖ 46 ἔκτοτε V edd.: ἔκτοτ[ε] P ‖

116

27

60ʳP τες πᾶσαν τὴν γῆν ἐκείνην ὑπέταξαν τοῦ τε θέματος Λαγου|βαρδίας
καὶ Καλαβρίας καὶ ἕως Παπίας ἄνευ τῆς Ὑδρεντοῦ καὶ Καλλιπόλεως
καὶ τοῦ Ῥουσιάνου καὶ τῆς Νεαπόλεως καὶ τῆς Γαϊτῆς καὶ Συρεντοῦ
καὶ Ἀμάλφης. Πρῶτον δὲ κάστρον ὑπῆρχεν ἀρχαῖον καὶ μέγα ἡ Κάπυα, 50
δεύτερον ἡ Νεάπολις, τρίτον ἡ Βενεβενδός, τέταρτον ἡ Γαϊτή, πέμπτον
ἡ Ἀμάλφη. Τὸ δὲ Σαλερινὸν ᾠκίσθη ἐπὶ τοῦ Σικάρδου, ὅτε διεμέρισαν
οἱ Λαγούβαρδοι τὰ πριγκιπᾶτα. Εἰσὶ δὲ μέχρι τῆς σήμερον, ἥτις ἐστὶν
121Be ἰνδικτιὼν ζ', ἔτη ἀπὸ κτίσεως κόσμου ,ϛυνζ', ἀφ' | οὗ ἐμερίσθη ἡ Λαγου-
βαρδία, ἔτη σ'. Ὑπῆρχον δὲ ἀδελφοὶ δύο, ὁ Σίκων καὶ ὁ Σίκαρδος. Καὶ 55
ὁ μὲν Σίκων ἐκράτησε τὴν Βενεβενδὸν καὶ τὰ μέρη τῆς Βάρεως καὶ τῆς
60ᵛP Σιπενδοῦ, ὁ δὲ Σί|καρδος τὸ Σαλερινὸν καὶ τὴν Κάπυαν καὶ τὰ μέρη
τῆς Καλαβρίας. Ἡ δὲ Νεάπολις ἦν ἀρχαῖον πραιτώριον τῶν κατερχομέ-
νων πατρικίων, καὶ ὁ κρατῶν τὴν Νεάπολιν κατεῖχεν καὶ τὴν Σικελίαν,
καὶ ἡνίκα κατέλαβεν ὁ πατρίκιος ἐν Νεαπόλει, ἀπήρχετο ὁ δοὺξ Νεαπό- 60
λεως ἐν Σικελίᾳ. Ἡ δὲ Κάπυα ἦν πόλις ὑπερμεγέθης, καὶ ἑάλω ὑπὸ
τῶν Οὐανδήλων, ἤτοι τῶν Ἀφρικῶν, καὶ κατέλυσαν αὐτήν. Ἐρημοκά-
στρου δὲ οὔσης, ᾤκουν ἐν αὐτῇ οἱ Λαγούβαρδοι. Καὶ πάλιν τῶν Ἀφρικῶν
ἐπερχομένων κατ᾽ αὐτῶν, ᾠκοδόμησεν ὁ ἐπίσκοπος Λανδοῦλφος κάστρον
61ʳP εἰς τὴν γέφυραν τοῦ ποταμοῦ, καὶ ἐπωνόμασεν αὐτὸ | Κάπυαν νέαν, 65
τὴν καὶ νῦν οὖσαν. Ἀφ᾽ οὗ δὲ ἐκτίσθη ἡ αὐτὴ Κάπυα, εἰσὶν ἔτη ογ'.
Ἡ δὲ Νεάπολις καὶ ἡ Ἀμάλφη καὶ ἡ Συρεντὸς ὑπῆρχον ἀεὶ ὑπὸ τὸν
βασιλέα Ῥωμαίων.

Ἰστέον, ὅτι μαστρομίλης ἑρμηνεύεται τῇ Ῥωμαίων διαλέκτῳ
'κατεπάνω τοῦ στρατοῦ'. 70

Ἰστέον, ὅτι πρὸ τοῦ περᾶσαι τοὺς Βενετίκους καὶ οἰκῆσαι εἰς τὰ
νησία, εἰς ἃ νῦν οἰκοῦσιν, ἐκαλοῦντο Ἐνετικοί, καὶ κατῴκουν εἰς τὴν
ξηρὰν εἰς αὐτὰ τὰ κάστρα· κάστρον Κόγκορδα, κάστρον Ἰουστινιάνα,
κάστρον τοῦ Νούνου καὶ ἕτερα πλεῖστα κάστρα.

122Be Ἰστέον, ὅτι περασάντων τῶν νῦν καλουμένων Βενετίκων, πρῶτον 75
61ᵛP δὲ Ἐνετικῶν, ἔκτισαν ἐν πρώτοις κάστρον ὀχυρόν, ἐν ᾧ καὶ σή|μερον
καθέζεται ὁ δοὺξ Βενετίας, ἔχον κυκλόθεν θάλασσαν ὡσεὶ μιλίων ἕξ,
εἰς ἣν καὶ εἰσέρχονται ποταμοὶ κζ'. Ὑπάρχουσι δὲ καὶ νῆσοι κατὰ
ἀνατολὰς τοῦ αὐτοῦ κάστρου. Ἔκτισαν δὲ καὶ ἐν ταῖς αὐταῖς νήσοις οἱ
νῦν Βενέτικοι καλούμενοι κάστρα· κάστρον Κογράδον, ἐν ᾧ καὶ μητρό- 80

F   69 Ἰστέον — 70 στρατοῦ: cf. De cerim., ed. Bonn. scholion ad p.
690, 23.

V 47 Λογουβαρδίας edd. ‖ 51 δεύτερον Moravcsik: β' P δευτέρα edd. ‖ τρίτον
Moravcsik: γ' P τρίτη edd. ‖ τέταρτον Moravcsik: δ' P τετάρτη edd. ‖

27

dued all that land, both the province of Lombardy and Calabria and as far as Papia, except for Otranto and Gallipoli and Rossano and Naples and Gaëta and Sorrento and Amalfi. The first city, ancient and mighty, was Capua, the second, Naples, the third, Beneventum, the fourth, Gaëta, the fifth, Amalfi. Salerno was settled in the time of Sicardus, when the Lombards divided the principalities. From the division of Lombardy until to-day, the 7th indiction, the year 6457 from the creation of the world, it is 200 years. There were two brothers, Sicon and Sicardus. Sicon governed Beneventum and the districts of Bari and Sipontum, and Sicardus governed Salerno and Capua and the district of Calabria. Naples was anciently the praetorium of the patricians who came out, and the governor of Naples had Sicily beneath him as well, and when the patrician arrived in Naples, the duke of Naples would go off to Sicily. Capua was a very large city indeed, and was captured by the Vandals, or Africans, who demolished it. When it was lying a deserted city, the Lombards settled in it. When the Africans came against them once more, bishop Landulf built a city at the bridge over the river and called it New Capua, and it still survives. From the foundation of this Capua, it is 73 years. Naples and Amalfi and Sorrento have always been subject to the emperor of the Romans.

'Mastromilis' means in the Roman tongue captain-general of the army.

Before the Venetians crossed over and settled in the islands in which they live now, they were called Enetikoi, and used to dwell on the mainland in these cities: the city of Concordia, the city of Justiniana, the city of Nonum and very many other cities.

When those who are now called Venetians, but were originally called Enetikoi, crossed over, they began by constructing a strongly fortified city, in which the doge of Venice still has his seat to-day, a city surrounded by some six miles of sea, into which 27 rivers also debouch. There are other islands also to the east of this same city. And upon these same islands also they who are now called Venetians built cities: the city of Cogradon, in

---

Γαϊτή Ba Be: Γαΐτης P ‖ πέμπτον Moravcsik: ε′ P πέμπτη edd. ‖ 53 Λογούβαρδοι edd. ‖ πριγκηπάτα P ‖ 54 ζ′: ἑβδόμη edd. ‖ 54/5 Λογουβαρδία edd. ‖ 55 σ′: ρ′ coni. Bury ‖ 61 Καπύη mg. V² ‖ 62 'Αφρίκων P ‖ 63 οἱ om. edd. ‖ Λογούβαρδοι edd. ‖ 63/4 τῶν 'Αφρικῶν ἐπερχομένων Meursius Ba Be: τὴν 'Αφρικὴν ἐπερχομένην (ultima littera η in ras. scripta) P¹ V ‖ 65 ἐπονόμασεν P ‖ 65/6 Κάπυαν νέαν τὴν coni. Be: Κάπυαν νέαν coni. Bandurius Καπαντὴν P Καπάντην F mg. V² ‖ 67 'Αμαλφή mg. V² ‖ 69 μαστρομήλης P ‖ 72 'Ενετικοί Meursius Ba Be: Αἰτίκιοι P ‖ 73 αὐτὰ: ταῦτα coni. Bekker ‖ Κόκκορδα P Κονκόρδια mg. V² ‖ 76 'Ενετικῶν Meursius Ba Be: Αἰτικίων P ‖ ἔκτισαν Meursius Ba Be: ἔκτησεν P ‖ ἐν¹: ἐμ P ‖ 77 κυκλῶθεν P: κύκλωθεν edd. ‖ 78 εἰς ἣν] litteras ς et η in ras. scr. P¹ ‖ 79 κάστρου om. edd. ‖ 80 Βενετίκοι P ‖ Κογράδον (etiam V): Γράδον V² mg. V² κ′ (= κάστρον) Γράδον coni. Skok ‖ 80/1 μητρόπολις: ἀκρόπολις coni. Meursius ‖

118

πολις ἔστιν μεγάλη καὶ πολλὰ λείψανα ἁγίων ἐν ταύτῃ ἀπόκεινται·
κάστρον Ῥιβαλενσῆς, κάστρον Λουλιανόν, κάστρον Ἄψανον, κάστρον
Ῥωματινά, κάστρον Λικεντζία, κάστρον Πίνεται, ὅπερ λέγεται Στρόβι-
λος, κάστρον Βινίολα, κάστρον Βόες, ἐν ᾧ ὑπάρχει ναὸς τοῦ ἁγίου
ἀποστόλου Πέτρου, κάστρον Ἡλιτούαλβα, κάστρον Λιτουμαγκέρσης, 85
62ʳP |κάστρον Βρόνιον, κάστρον Μαδαῦκον, κάστρον Ἡβόλα, κάστρον Πριστῆ-
ναι, κάστρον Κλουγία, κάστρον Βροῦνδον, κάστρον Φοσαῶν, κάστρον
Λαυριτῶν.

Ἰστέον, ὅτι εἰσὶ καὶ ἔτεραι νῆσοι ἐν τῇ αὐτῇ χώρᾳ Βενετίας.

Ἰστέον, ὅτι καὶ ἐν τῇ στερεᾷ εἰς τὸ μέρος τῆς Ἰταλίας ὑπάρχουσι 90
κάστρα τῶν Βενετίκων, ἅτινά εἰσιν ταῦτα· κάστρον Κάπρε, κάστρον
Νεόκαστρον, κάστρον Φινές, κάστρον Αἴκυλον, κάστρον Ἀειμάνας,
ἐμπόριον μέγα τὸ Τορτζελῶν, κάστρον Μουράν, κάστρον Ῥίβαλτον,
ὃ ἑρμηνεύεται 'τόπος ὑψηλότατος', ἐν ᾧ καθέζεται ὁ δοὺξ Βενετίας,
κάστρον Καβερτζέντζης. 95

Ἰστέον, ὅτι καὶ ἐμπόρια εἰσὶ καὶ καστέλλια.

123Be 28. Δ ι ή γ η σ ι ς, π ῶ ς κ α τ ῳ κ ί σ θ η ἡ ν ῦ ν κ α λ ο υ μ έ ν η
Β ε ν ε τ ί α.

62ᵛP   Ἰστέον, ὅτι ἡ Βενετία τὸ μὲν παλαιὸν ἦν τόπος ἔρημός τις ἀοίκη-
τος καὶ βαλτώδης. Οἱ δὲ νῦν καλούμενοι Βενέτικοι ὑπῆρχον Φράγγοι
ἀπὸ Ἀκουϊλεγίας καὶ ἀπὸ τῶν ἑτέρων τόπων τῆς Φραγγίας, καὶ κατῴ- 5
κουν εἰς τὴν ξηρὰν ἄντικρυ τῆς Βενετίας. Τοῦ δὲ Ἀττίλα, τοῦ βασιλέως
τῶν Ἀβάρων, ἐλθόντος καὶ πάσας τὰς Φραγγίας καταληϊσαμένου καὶ
ἀφανίσαντος, ἤρξαντο φεύγειν μὲν πάντες οἱ Φράγγοι ἀπὸ Ἀκουϊλεγίας
καὶ ἀπὸ τῶν ἑτέρων τῆς Φραγγίας κάστρων, ἔρχεσθαι δὲ πρὸς τὰς
ἀοικήτους νήσους τῆς Βενετίας καὶ ποιεῖν ἐκεῖσε καλύβια διὰ τὸν τοῦ 10
βασιλέως Ἀττίλα φόβον. Αὐτοῦ οὖν τοῦ βασιλέως Ἀττίλα ληϊσαμένου
6 3ʳP πᾶ|σαν τὴν χώραν τῆς ξηρᾶς καὶ μέχρι Ῥώμης καὶ Καλαβρίας ἐλθόντος
καὶ τὴν Βενετίαν μακρόθεν καταλιπόντος, ἄδειαν εὑρόντες οἱ προσπεφευ-
γότες ἐν ταῖς νήσοις τῆς Βενετίας καὶ οἷον τὴν δειλίαν ἀποσεισάμενοι,
ἅπαντες ἐβουλεύσαντο τοῦ κατοικῆσαι ἐκεῖσε, ὅπερ καὶ ἐποίησαν, 15
κατοικήσαντες ἐκεῖσε μέχρι τῆς σήμερον. Μετὰ δὲ τὸ ἀναχωρῆσαι τὸν
Ἀττίλαν, μετὰ χρόνους πολλοὺς παρεγένετο πάλιν Πιπῖνος ὁ ῥήξ, ὃς
ἦρχε τότε τῆς τε Παπίας καὶ ἑτέρων ῥηγάτων. Εἶχεν γὰρ οὗτος ὁ Πιπῖνος

V 82 Ῥιβαλενσῆς V edd. Ῥιβαλένσης mg. V² || 83 Ῥωμαντινά mg. Pᵃ ||
Λικέντζιά mg. V² || 85 Ἡλιτουάλβα edd. || Λιτουμανκέρσης P mg. Pᵃ:
Λιτουμανκέρσες edd. || 86 Μαδαῦκος mg. Pᵃ Μαδοῦκον mg. V² || 86/7 Πριστῆνα

27, 28

which is a great metropolitan church with many relics of saints laid up in it; the city of Rivalensis, the city of Lulianon, the city of Apsanon, the city of Romatina, the city of Licenzia, the city of Pinetai, which is called Strobilos, the city of Biniola, the city of Boes, in which is a church of the holy apostle Peter, the city of Ilitoualba, the city of Litoumangersis, the city of Bronion, the city of Madaucon, the city of Ebola, the city of Pristinai, the city of Clugia, the city of Brundon, the city of Phosaon, the city of Lauriton.

There are other islands also in the same country of Venice.

On the mainland, also, in the land of Italy, there are cities of the Venetians, as follows: the city of Capre, the city of Neokastron, the city of Phines, the city of Aikylon, the city of Aeimanas, the great trading station of Torcello, the city of Mouran, the city of Rivalto, which means 'highest point', where the doge of Venice has his seat; the city of Caverzenzis.

There are also trading stations and forts.

28. Story of the settlement of what is now called Venice.

Of old, Venice was a desert place, uninhabited and swampy. Those who are now called Venetians were Franks from Aquileia and from the other places in Francia, and they used to dwell on the mainland opposite Venice. But when Attila, the king of the Avars, came and utterly devastated and depopulated all the parts of Francia, all the Franks from Aquileia and from the other cities of Francia began to take to flight, and to go to the uninhabited islands of Venice and to built huts there, out of their dread of king Attila. Now when this king Attila had devastated all the country of the mainland and had advanced as far as Rome and Calabria and had left Venice far behind, those who had fled for refuge to the islands of Venice, having obtained a breathing-space and, as it were, shaken off their faintness of heart, took counsel jointly to settle there, which they did, and have been settled there till this day. But again, many years after the withdrawal of Attila, king Pippin arrived, who at that time was ruling over

edd. ‖ 87 Βροῦδον V Βρουνδουλον (*sine acc.*) *mg.* V² ‖ 88 Λαύριτον *mg.* V² ‖ 89 καὶ εἰσὶν edd. ‖ αὐτῇ *corr.* Moravcsik: αὐτῶν P edd. ‖ Βενετίᾳ *coni.* Kukules ‖ 92 Ἄκουλον *mg.* P⁸ ‖ 93 ἐμπορίου P ‖ τὸ *om.* edd. ‖ Ῥίβαλτον *mg.* V²: Ῥίβαντόν P V   Ῥίβαντον Ba Be ‖ 96 ἐμπορία P.

28. 5 Ἀκουηλεγίας P ‖ 6 ἀντικρὺ edd. ‖ Ἀτίλα P ‖ 8 Ἀκουηλεγίας P ‖ 10 ἀοικήτους V edd.: ἀοίκους P ‖ 11 Ἀτίλα P ‖ Ἀτίλα P ‖ 14 ἀποσεισάμενοι] *litteras* ει *in ras. scr.* P¹ ‖ 17 Ἀτίλαν P ‖ πάλιν παρεγένετο edd. ‖

28

ἀδελφοὺς τρεῖς, οἵτινες ἦρχον πασῶν τῶν Φραγγιῶν καὶ Σκλαβηνιῶν.
124Be Τοῦ δὲ ῥηγὸς | Πιπίνου ἐλθόντος κατὰ τῶν Βενετίκων μετὰ δυνάμεως 20
63ᵛP | καὶ λαοῦ πολλοῦ, παρεκάθισεν διὰ τῆς ξηρᾶς ἐκεῖθεν τοῦ περάματος
τῶν νήσων τῆς Βενετίας εἰς τόπον λεγόμενον ᾽Αειβόλας. Οἱ οὖν Βενέτικοι
ἰδόντες τὸν ῥῆγα Πιπῖνον μετὰ τῆς ἑαυτοῦ δυνάμεως κατ᾽ αὐτῶν ἐπερχό-
μενον καὶ μέλλοντα μετὰ τῶν ἵππων ἀποπλεῦσαι πρὸς τὴν νῆσον τοῦ
Μαδαμαύκου (ἔστιν γὰρ αὕτη ἡ νῆσος πλησίον τῆς ξηρᾶς), βαλόντες 25
κερατάρια, ἅπαν τὸ πέραμα ἐναπέφραξαν. Εἰς ἀμηχανίαν οὖν ἐλθὼν ὁ
τοῦ ῥηγὸς Πιπίνου λαὸς (οὐδὲ γὰρ ἦν δυνατὸν αὐτοὺς ἀλλαχοῦ περᾶσαι),
παρεκάθισαν αὐτοῖς διὰ τῆς ξηρᾶς μῆνας ἕξ, πολεμοῦντες καθ᾽ ἑκάστην
64ʳP ἡμέραν μετ᾽ αὐτῶν. Καὶ | οἱ μὲν Βενέτικοι εἰσήρχοντο εἰς τὰ πλοῖα
αὐτῶν, καὶ ἵσταντο ὄπισθεν τῶν παρ᾽ αὐτῶν ῥιφέντων κερατερίων, 30
ὁ δὲ ῥὴξ Πιπῖνος ἵστατο μετὰ τοῦ λαοῦ αὐτοῦ ἐν τῷ αἰγιαλῷ. Καὶ οἱ
μὲν Βενέτικοι μετὰ τοξείας καὶ ῥιππαρίων ἐπολέμουν, μὴ ἐῶντες αὐτοὺς
πρὸς τὴν νῆσον διαπερᾶσαι. ᾽Απορήσας οὖν ὁ ῥὴξ Πιπῖνος, εἶπεν πρὸς
τοὺς Βενετίκους, ὅτι· «῾Υπὸ τὴν ἐμὴν χεῖρα καὶ πρόνοιαν γίνεσθε, ἐπειδὴ
ἀπὸ τῆς ἐμῆς χώρας καὶ ἐξουσίας ἐστέ». Οἱ δὲ Βενέτικοι ἀντέλεγον 35
αὐτῷ, ὅτι· «῾Ημεῖς δοῦλοι θέλομεν εἶναι τοῦ βασιλέως ῾Ρωμαίων καὶ
οὐχὶ σοῦ.» ᾽Επὶ πολὺ δὲ βιασθέντες οἱ Βενέτικοι ἀπὸ τῆς γεγονυίας
64ᵛP ὀχλήσεως πρὸς αὐτούς, | ἐποιήσαντο εἰρηνικὰς σπονδὰς πρὸς τὸν ῥῆγα
Πιπῖνον τοῦ παρέχειν αὐτῷ πλεῖστα πάκτα. ῎Εκτοτε δὲ καθ᾽ ἕκαστον
125Be χρόνον ἠλαττοῦτο τὸ πάκτον, ὅπερ καὶ μέχρι τῆς σήμερον δια|σώζεται. 40
Τελοῦσι γὰρ οἱ Βενέτικοι τῷ κατέχοντι τὸ ῥηγᾶτον ᾽Ιταλίας, ἤτοι Παπίας,
διβάρια ἀσήμιν λίτρας λϛ΄ καθ᾽ ἕκαστον χρόνον. Καὶ τούτῳ τῷ τρόπῳ
ἔπαυσεν ὁ μεταξὺ Φράγγων καὶ Βενετίκων πόλεμος. ῞Οτε δὲ ἤρξατο
ἀποφεύγειν ὁ λαὸς πρὸς Βενετίαν καὶ ἀποσυνάγεσθαι, ὥστε πολλοὺς
γίνεσθαι, ἀνηγόρευσαν ἑαυτοὺς δοῦκα τὸν εὐγενείᾳ τῶν ἄλλων διαφέροντα. 45
᾽Εγεγόνει δὲ ὁ πρῶτος δοὺξ ἐν αὐτοῖς, πρὶν ἢ ἐλθεῖν κατ᾽ αὐτῶν ὁ ῥὴξ
65ʳP Πιπῖ|νος. ῏Ην δὲ τῷ τότε καιρῷ τὸ δουκᾶτον εἰς τόπον λεγόμενον Τζιβιτά-
νουβα, ὅπερ ἑρμηνεύεται ῾νεόκαστρον᾽. Διὰ δὲ τὸ εἶναι τὸ προειρημένον
νησίον πλησίον τῆς ξηρᾶς κοινῇ βουλῇ μετέθηκαν τὸ δουκᾶτον εἰς ἕτερον
νησίον, ἐν ᾧ καὶ νῦν ἔστιν σήμερον, διὰ τὸ εἶναι μήκοθεν τῆς ξηρᾶς, 50
ὅσον βλέπει τις ἄνδρα ἵππῳ ἐφεζόμενον.

V ῥίξ P ‖ 19 Φραγγιῶν P V edd.: Φραγγῶν (littera ι erasa) Pʸ ‖ Σκλαβινίων
P ‖ 20 ῥιγὸς P ‖ δυνάμεως V edd.: δυνάμεω[ς] P ‖ 22 νησσῶν P ‖
᾽Αείβολας mg. V² ‖ 23 ῥίγα P ‖ 27 ῥιγὸς P ‖ 33 ῥίξ P ‖ 36 θέλομεν V edd.:

28

Papia and other kingdoms. For this Pippin had three brothers, and they were ruling over all the Frank and Slavonic regions. Now when king Pippin came against the Venetians with power and a large army, he blockaded them along the mainland, on the far side of the crossing between it and the islands of Venice, at a place called Aeibolas. Well, when the Venetians saw king Pippin coming against them with his power and preparing to take ship with the horses to the island of Madamaucon (for this is an island near the mainland), they laid down spars and fenced off the whole crossing. The army of king Pippin, being brought to a stand (for it was not possible for them to cross at any other point), blockaded them along the mainland six months, fighting with them daily. The Venetians would man their ships and take up position behind the spars they had laid down, and king Pippin would take up position with his army along the shore. The Venetians assailed them with arrows and javelins, and stopped them from crossing over to the island. So then king Pippin, at a loss, said to the Venetians: «You are beneath my hand and my providence, since you are of my country and domain.» But the Venetians answered him: «We want to be servants of the emperor of the Romans, and not of you.» When, however, they had for long been straitened by the trouble that had come upon them, the Venetians made a treaty of peace with king Pippin, agreeing to pay him a very considerable tribute. But since that time the tribute has gone on diminishing year by year, though it is paid even to this day. For the Venetians pay to him who rules over the kingdom of Italy, that is, Papia, a twopenny fee of 36 pounds of uncoined silver annually. So ended the war between Franks and Venetians. When the folk began to flee away to Venice and to collect there in numbers, they proclaimed as their doge him who surpassed the rest in nobility. The first doge among them had been appointed before king Pippin came against them. At that time the doge's residence was at a place called Civitanova, which means 'new city'. But because this island aforesaid is close to the mainland, by common consent they moved the doge's residence to another island, where it now is at this present, because it is at a distance from the mainland, as far off as one may see a man on horseback.

θέλωμεν P ‖ 37 σοῦ Be: σοί P ‖ 38 ῥήγα P ‖ 40 ἠλάττωτο edd. ‖ 41 ῥιγάτον P ‖ Παπιας (sine acc.) P ‖ 42 ἀσίμιν P edd. ‖ 43 Φραγγῶν P ‖ 45 ἑαυτοῖς V edd. ‖ 46 ῥίξ P ‖ 47 δουκάτον P ‖ 47/8 Τζιβιτᾶ νούβα V   Τζιβιτὰ νόβα Ba Be ‖ 49 δουκάτον] litteras δουκ in ras. scr. P¹ ‖ 50 μηκόθεν edd.

122

29. Περὶ τῆς Δελματίας καὶ τῶν ἐν αὐτῇ
παρακειμένων ἐθνῶν.

Ὅτι Διοκλητιανὸς ὁ βασιλεὺς πάνυ τῆς χώρας Δελματίας ἠράσθη,
διὸ καὶ ἀπὸ τῆς 'Ρώμης λαὸν ἀγαγὼν μετὰ τὰς φαμιλίας αὐτῶν, ἐν τῇ
αὐτῇ τῆς Δελματίας χώρᾳ τούτους κατεσκήνωσεν, οἳ καὶ 'Ρωμᾶνοι 5
προσηγορεύθησαν διὰ τὸ ἀπὸ 'Ρώμης μετοικισθῆναι, καὶ ταύτην μέχρι
65ᵛP τῆς σήμερον | τὴν ἐπωνυμίαν ἐναποφέρονται. Οὗτος οὖν ὁ βασιλεὺς
126Be Διοκλητιανὸς καὶ τὸ τοῦ 'Ασπαλάθου κάστρον ᾠκοδόμησεν, καὶ | ἐν αὐτῷ
παλάτια ἐδείματο λόγου καὶ γραφῆς ἀπάσης ἐπέκεινα, ὧν καὶ μέχρι
τῆς σήμερον τῆς παλαιᾶς εὐδαιμονίας λείψανα φέρονται, κἂν ὁ πολὺς 10
χρόνος αὐτὰ κατηνάλωσεν. 'Αλλὰ καὶ τὸ κάστρον Διόκλεια, τὸ νῦν παρὰ
τῶν Διοκλητιανῶν κατεχόμενον, ὁ αὐτὸς βασιλεὺς Διοκλητιανὸς ᾠκοδόμησεν, ὅθεν καὶ τὴν ἐπωνυμίαν 'Διοκλητιανοὶ' καλεῖσθαι οἱ τῆς χώρας
ἐκείνης ἐναπειλήφασιν. Ἡ δὲ καὶ τῶν αὐτῶν 'Ρωμάνων διακράτησις
66ʳP ἦν μέχρι τοῦ Δανούβεως ποταμοῦ, οἳ καί ποτε θελή|σαντες τὸν ποταμὸν 15
διαπερᾶσαι καὶ καταμαθεῖν, τίνες κατοικοῦσιν ἐκεῖθεν τοῦ ποταμοῦ,
διαπεράσαντες εὗρον ἔθνη Σκλαβήνικα ἄοπλα ὄντα, ἅτινα καὶ "Αβαροι
ἐκαλοῦντο. Καὶ οὔτε οὗτοι ἤλπιζον ἐκεῖθεν τοῦ ποταμοῦ κατοικεῖν
τινας, οὔτε ἐκεῖνοι ἔνθεν τοῦ ποταμοῦ. Διὰ οὖν τὸ ἀόπλους εὑρεῖν αὐτοὺς
τοὺς 'Αβάρους οἱ 'Ρωμᾶνοι καὶ πρὸς πόλεμον ἀπαρασκευάστους 20
καταπολεμήσαντες, ἀνελάβοντο πραῖδαν καὶ αἰχμαλωσίαν καὶ ἀνεχώρη-
σαν. Καὶ ἔκτοτε ποιήσαντες ἀλλάγια δύο οἱ 'Ρωμᾶνοι ἀπὸ πάσχα ἕως
πάσχα τὸν λαὸν αὐτῶν ἐνήλλασσον, ὥστε τῷ μεγάλῳ καὶ ἁγίῳ σαββάτῳ
66ᵛP ἀλλήλοις συναντᾶν, | τοὺς μὲν ἀποστρεφομένους ἀπὸ τοῦ παραμονίμου,
τοὺς δὲ εἰς τὴν τοιαύτην δουλείαν ἀπερχομένους. Καὶ γὰρ πλησίον τῆς 25
θαλάσσης ὑπὸ τὸ αὐτὸ κάστρον κάστρον ἔστιν, τὸ ἐπιλεγόμενον Σαλῶνα,
μέγεθος ἔχον τὸ ἥμισυ Κωνσταντινουπόλεως, ἐν ᾧ πάντες οἱ 'Ρωμᾶνοι
127Be συνήγοντο καὶ καθωπλίζοντο καὶ | προσαπεκίνουν ἐκ τῶν ἐκεῖσε, καὶ
πρὸς τὴν κλεισοῦραν ἀπήρχοντο, τὴν ἀπὸ τοῦ αὐτοῦ κάστρου ὑπάρχουσαν
μίλια τέσσαρα, ἥτις καὶ μέχρι τοῦ νῦν καλεῖται Κλεῖσα διὰ τὸ συγκλείειν 30
τοὺς διερχομένους ἐκεῖθεν. Καὶ ἐκ τῶν ἐκεῖσε ἀπήρχοντο πρὸς τὸν
67ʳP ποταμόν. Τὸ οὖν τοιοῦτον ἀλλάγιον ἐπὶ πολλοὺς χρόνους γινόμε|νον,
οἱ ἐκεῖθεν τοῦ ποταμοῦ Σκλάβοι, οἱ καὶ "Αβαροι καλούμενοι, καθ'
ἑαυτοὺς ἐσκόπησαν λέγοντες, ὅτι· «Οὗτοι οἱ 'Ρωμᾶνοι, ἐπεὶ ἐπέρασαν
καὶ εὗρον πραῖδαν, ἀπὸ τοῦ νῦν καθ' ἡμῶν οὐ μὴ παύσονται διαπερῶντες, 35
καὶ διὰ τοῦτο μηχανησόμεθα κατ' αὐτῶν.» Οὕτως οὖν οἱ Σκλάβοι, οἱ
⟨καὶ⟩ "Αβαροι, βουλευσάμενοι, καὶ διαπερασάντων ποτὲ τῶν 'Ρωμάνων,

---

V   29. 4 φαμηλίας P ‖ 5 'Ρωμάνοι P ‖ 8 τοῦ *om.* Bury ‖ 9 παλάτια

29. Of Dalmatia and of the adjacent nations in it.

The emperor Diocletian was much enamoured of the country of Dalmatia, and so he brought folk with their families from Rome and settled them in this same country of Dalmatia, and they were called 'Romani' from their having been removed from Rome, and this title attaches to them until this day. Now this emperor Diocletian founded the city of Spalato and built therein a palace beyond the power of any tongue or pen to describe, and remains of its ancient luxury are still preserved to-day, though the long lapse of time has played havoc with them. Moreover, the city of Diocleia, now occupied by the Diocletians, was built by the same emperor Diocletian, for which reason those of that country have come to be called by the name of 'Diocletians'. The territory possessed by these Romani used to extend as far as the river Danube, and once on a time, being minded to cross the river and discover who dwelt beyond the river, they crossed it and came upon unarmed Slavonic nations, who were also called Avars. The former had not expected that any dwelt beyond the river, nor the latter that any dwelt on the hither side. And so, finding these Avars unarmed and unprepared for war, the Romani overcame them and took booty and prisoners and returned. And from that time the Romani formed two alternating garrisons, serving from Easter to Easter, and used to change their men about so that on Great and Holy Saturday they who were coming back from the station and they who were going out to that service would meet one another. For near the sea, beneath that same city, lies a city called Salona, which is half as large as Constantinople, and here all the Romani would muster and be equipped and thence start out and come to the frontier pass, which is four miles from this same city, and is called Kleisa to this day, from its closing in those who pass that way. And from there they would advance to the river. This exchange of garrisons went on for a number of years and the Slavs on the far side of the river, who were also called Avars, thought it over among themselves, and said: «These Romani, now that they have crossed over and found booty, will in future not cease coming over against us, and so we will devise a plan against them.» And so, therefore, the Slavs, or Avars, took counsel, and on one occasion when the Romani had crossed over, they laid ambushes

F edd.: πλάτεια P   παλάτεια P¹ V ‖ 13/4 ἐκείνης χώρης edd. ‖ 17 Σκλαβίνικα
P: Σκλαβινικὰ edd. ‖ 20 'Ρωμάνοι P ‖ post ἀπαρασκευάστους add. καὶ V edd. ‖
21 καταπολεμίσαντες P ‖ 22 'Ρωμάνοι P ‖ 26 κάστρον ² om. Be ‖ 27 'Ρωμάνοι P ‖
28 καθοπλίζοντο P ‖ 29 κλησοῦραν P ‖ 30 τέσσαρα edd.: δ' P ‖ 32 πολλοὺς corr.
Moravcsik πολλὺς P: πολλοῖς V edd. ‖ χρόνους corr. Moravcsik: χρόνοις P edd. ‖
γινόμενον χρόνοις V edd. ‖ 34 'Ρωμάνοι P ‖ 35 μὴ om. edd. ‖ 36 μηχανησώμεθα
Migne ‖ 37 καὶ add. Bury ‖ 37 διαπερασάντων — 38 ἐγκρύμματα:

29

ποιήσαντες οὗτοι ἐγκρύμματα καὶ πολεμήσαντες, ἐνίκησαν αὐτούς. Καὶ
ἀναλαβόμενοι τά τε ὅπλα αὐτῶν καὶ τὰ φλάμμουλα καὶ τὰ λοιπὰ πολεμικὰ σημεῖα, διαπεράσαντες οἱ προειρημένοι Σκλάβοι τὸν ποταμόν, ἦλθον 40
67ᵛP εἰς τὴν | κλεισοῦραν, οὓς καὶ ἰδόντες οἱ ἐκεῖσε ὄντες Ῥωμᾶνοι, θεασάμε-
νοι δὲ τὰ φλάμμουλα καὶ τὴν ἐξόπλισιν τῶν ὁμοφύλων αὐτῶν, τοὺς
αὐτῶν ὁμοφύλους εἶναι νομίσαντες, ἡνίκα κατέλαβον οἱ Σκλάβοι οἱ προρρηθέντες εἰς τὴν κλεισοῦραν, παρεχώρησαν αὐτοῖς διελθεῖν. Διελθόντων
δέ, εὐθὺς τοὺς Ῥωμάνους οὗτοι ἐξήλασαν, καὶ τὴν Σαλῶνα, τὸ προειρημέ- 45
νον κάστρον ἐκράτησαν. Καὶ κατοικήσαντες ἐκεῖσε, ἔκτοτε κατὰ μικρὸν
ἀρξάμενοι πραιδεύειν τοὺς Ῥωμάνους, τοὺς εἰς τοὺς κάμπους καὶ εἰς
128Be ὑψηλότερα μέρη | κατοικοῦντας, ἠφάνισαν καὶ τοὺς τόπους αὐτῶν κατε-
κράτησαν. Οἱ δὲ λοιποὶ Ῥωμᾶνοι εἰς τὰ τῆς παραλίας κάστρα διεσώθη-
68ʳP |σαν, καὶ μέχρι τοῦ νῦν κρατοῦσιν αὐτά, ἅτινά εἰσιν τὰ Δεκάτερα, τὸ 50
Ῥαούσιν, τὸ Ἀσπάλαθον, τὸ Τετραγγούριν, τὰ Διάδωρα, ἡ Ἄρβη, ἡ
Βέκλα καὶ τὰ Ὄψαρα, ὧντινων καὶ οἰκήτορες μέχρι τοῦ νῦν Ῥωμᾶνοι
κολοῦνται.

Ὅτι ἀπὸ τῆς βασιλείας Ἡρακλείου, τοῦ βασιλέως Ῥωμαίων,
καθ᾽ ὃν μέλλει τρόπον ῥηθήσεσθαι ἐν τῇ περὶ τῶν Χρωβάτων καὶ Σέρβλων 55
συγγραφῇ, πᾶσα ἡ Δελματία καὶ τὰ περὶ αὐτὴν ἔθνη, οἷον Χρωβάτοι,
Σέρβλοι, Ζαχλοῦμοι, Τερβουνιῶται, Καναλῖται, Διοκλητιανοὶ καὶ Ἀρεντανοί, οἱ καὶ Παγανοὶ προσαγορευόμενοι, * * *. Τῆς δὲ τῶν Ῥωμαίων
βασιλείας διὰ τὴν τῶν τότε κρατούντων νωθρότητα καὶ ἀφέλειαν εἰς τὸ
68ᵛP μηδὲν πα|ράπαν μικροῦ δεῖν ἐναπονευσάσης, καὶ μάλιστα δὲ ἐπὶ Μιχαὴλ 60
τοῦ ἐξ Ἀμορίου, τοῦ Τραυλοῦ, οἱ τὰ τῆς Δελματίας κάστρα οἰκοῦντες
γεγόνασιν αὐτοκέφαλοι, μήτε τῷ βασιλεῖ Ῥωμαίων, μήτε ἑτέρῳ τινὶ
ὑποκείμενοι, ἀλλὰ καὶ τὰ ἐκεῖσε ἔθνη, οἵ τε Χρωβάτοι καὶ Σέρβλοι καὶ
Ζαχλοῦμοι καὶ Τερβουνιῶται τε καὶ Καναλῖται καὶ Διοκλητιανοὶ καὶ
οἱ Παγανοί, τῆς τῶν Ῥωμαίων βασιλείας ἀφηνιάσαντες γεγόνασιν 65
ἰδιόρρυθμοι καὶ αὐτοκέφαλοι, τινὶ μὴ ὑποκείμενοι. Ἄρχοντας δέ, ὥς
φασι, ταῦτα τὰ ἔθνη μὴ ἔχειν, πλὴν ζουπάνους γέροντας, καθὼς καὶ αἱ
129Be λοιπαὶ Σκλαβηνίαι ἔχουσι τύπον. Ἀλλὰ καὶ οἱ | πλείονες τῶν τοιούτων
69ʳP Σκλάβων οὐ|δὲ ἐβαπτίζοντο, ἀλλὰ μέχρι πολλοῦ ἔμενον ἀβάπτιστοι.

F   56 πᾶσα — 69 ἀβάπτιστοι: cf. Theoph. Cont. p. 288, 18—289, 2;
Cedr., ed. Bonn. II. p. 218, 22—219, 3.

V διαπεράσαντες ποτὲ οἱ Ῥωμάνοι ἐποίησαν οὗτοι ἔγκρυμα (ἔγκρυμα V)
V Me ‖ 39 φλάμουλα P ‖ 41 κλεισούραν P ‖ Ῥωμάνοι P ‖ 42 φλάμουλα
P ‖ ἐξόπλησιν P ‖ 43 αὐτῶν: αὐτῶν coni. Bury ‖ 44 κλεισούραν P ‖ διελθόντες
V edd. ‖ 47 Ῥωμάνους V² edd.: Κομάνους P V¹ F ‖ post εἰς² add. τὰ
edd. ‖ 49 Ῥωμάνοι P ‖ 50 τὰ Δεκάτερα coni. Moravcsik: τάδε κάστρα P Ba
Be τὰ ι′ κάστρα F ‖ 51 Ῥαοῦσιν P ‖ Τετραγγούρην P ‖ 52 ante Ῥωμάνοι add.

29

and attacked and defeated them. The aforesaid Slavs took the *Roman* arms and standards and the rest of their military insignia and crossed the river and came to the frontier pass, and when the Romani who were there saw them and beheld the standards and accoutrements of their own men they thought they were their own men, and so, when the aforesaid Slavs reached the pass, they let them through. Once through, they instantly expelled the Romani and took possession of the aforesaid city of Salona. There they settled and thereafter began gradually to make plundering raids and destroyed the Romani who dwelt in the plains and on the higher ground and took possession of their lands. The remnant of the Romani escaped to the cities of the coast and possess them still, namely, Decatera, Ragusa, Spalato, Tetrangourin, Diadora, Arbe, Vekla and Opsara, the inhabitants of which are called Romani to this day.

Since the reign of Heraclius, emperor of the Romans, as will be related in the narrative concerning the Croats and Serbs, the whole of Dalmatia and the nations about it, such as Croats, Serbs, Zachlumi, Terbouniotes, Kanalites, Diocletians and Arentani, who are also called Pagani ✳✳✳. But when the Roman empire, through the sloth and inexperience of those who then governed it and especially in the time of Michael from Amorion, the Lisper, had declined to the verge of total extinction, the inhabitants of the cities of Dalmatia became independent, subject neither to the emperor of the Romans nor to anybody else, and, what is more, the nations of those parts, the Croats and Serbs and Zachlumites, Terbuniotes and Kanalites and Diocletians and the Pagani, shook off the reins of the empire of the Romans and became self-governing and independent, subject to none. Princes, as they say, these nations had none, but only 'zupans', elders, as is the rule in the other Slavonic regions. Moreover, the majority of these Slavs were not even baptized, and remained unbaptized for long enough. But

---

οἱ edd. ‖ Ῥωμάνοι P ‖ 55 καθ᾽ ὅν — 56 συγγραφῇ *expunxit* Rački ‖ 55 περὶ *om.* V edd. ‖ 56 *post* συγγραφῇ *inserenda* ὑπήκοα τοῖς Ῥωμαίοις ἐγένετο *coni.* Tomašić ‖ Δαλματίᾳ Theoph. Cont. ‖ Κρωβάτοι Theoph. Cont. Χρωβάτων Cedr. ‖ 57 Ζαχλούμοι P Ζαχλουμοὶ Theoph. Cont. ‖ Καναλεῖται P ‖ Διοκλειτιανοὶ P ‖ 57/8 Ἀρεντανοί: Ῥεντανοί Theoph. Cont. ‖ 58 οἱ καὶ Παγανοὶ *coni.* Bury: καὶ οἱ Παγανοὶ Meursius Ba Be καὶ Ὑπαγανοὶ P ‖ οἱ καὶ Παγανοὶ προσαγορευόμενοι *deest in* Theoph. Cont. ‖ *post* προσαγορευόμενοι *lac. ind.* δουλικῶς εἰσιν ὑποτεταγμένοι τῷ βασιλεῖ Ῥωμαίων *excidisse coniciens* Grot *lac. ind.* δουλικῶς ἦσαν τῷ βασιλεῖ Ῥωμαίων ὑποτεταγμένοι *vel talia excidisse coniciens* Bury ‖ 59 ἀφελείαν P ‖ 60 ἐναποπνευσάσης *coni.* Bury ‖ 61 Δελματείας P ‖ 63 Κρωβάτοι Theoph. Cont. Χρωβάτων Cedr. ‖ 64 Ζαχλοῦμοι καὶ Be: Ζαχλουμεῖται P Ζαχλουμοὶ Theoph. Cont. ‖ τε (*habet etiam* Theoph. Cont.): *om.* edd. ‖ Καναλεῖται P ‖ Διοκλειτιανοὶ P ‖ 65 Παγανοὶ Be: Παγάνοι P ‖ ἀφηνιάσαντες (*littera* σ *erasa, spiritu addito primaque littera* ι *in* η *correcta*) P^y *mg.* P^9 Meursius Ba Be Theoph. Cont.: σαφινιάσαντες P σαφηνιάσαντες V ‖ 66 ἰδιόρρυθμοι καὶ αὐτοκέφαλοι: αὐτόνομοί τε καὶ αὐτοδέσποτοι Theoph. Cont. ‖ 67 ἔχει edd. εἶχεν *coni.* Gedeonov ‖ 68 Σκλαβινίαι P: Σκλαβίνιαι edd. ‖ καὶ *om.* edd. ‖

29

'Επὶ δὲ Βασιλείου, τοῦ φιλοχρίστου βασιλέως, ἀπέστειλαν ἀποκρισιαρίους, 70
ἐξαιτούμενοι καὶ παρακαλοῦντες αὐτὸν τοὺς ἐξ αὐτῶν ἀβαπτίστους
βαπτισθῆναι καὶ εἶναι, ὡς τὸ ἐξ ἀρχῆς, ὑποτεταγμένους τῇ βασιλείᾳ
τῶν 'Ρωμαίων, ὧντινων εἰσακούσας ὁ μακάριος ἐκεῖνος καὶ ἀοίδιμος
βασιλεύς, ἐξαπέστειλεν βασιλικὸν μετὰ καὶ ἱερέων, καὶ ἐβάπτισεν αὐτοὺς
πάντας τοὺς τῶν προρρηθέντων ἐθνῶν ἀβαπτίστους τυγχάνοντας, καὶ 75
μετὰ τὸ βαπτίσαι αὐτοὺς τότε προεβάλετο εἰς αὐτοὺς ἄρχοντας, οὓς
ἐκεῖνοι ἤθελον καὶ προέκριναν, ἀπὸ τῆς γενεᾶς, ἧς ἐκεῖνοι ἠγάπων καὶ
69ᵛP ἔστεργον. Καὶ ἔκτοτε | μέχρι τοῦ νῦν ἐκ τῶν αὐτῶν γενεῶν γίνονται
ἄρχοντες εἰς αὐτούς, καὶ οὐκ ἐξ ἑτέρας. Οἱ δὲ Παγανοί, οἱ καὶ τῇ 'Ρωμαίων διαλέκτῳ 'Αρεντανοὶ καλούμενοι, εἰς δυσβάτους τόπους καὶ 80
κρημνώδεις κατελείφθησαν ἀβάπτιστοι. Καὶ γὰρ Παγανοὶ κατὰ τὴν
τῶν Σκλάβων γλῶσσαν 'ἀβάπτιστοι' ἑρμηνεύεται. Μετὰ δὲ τοῦτο καὶ
αὐτοὶ ἀποστείλαντες εἰς τὸν αὐτὸν ἀοίδιμον βασιλέα, ἐξητήσαντο βαπτισθῆναι καὶ αὐτοί, καὶ ἀποστείλας ἐβάπτισεν καὶ αὐτούς. 'Επεὶ δέ, ὡς προέ-
φημεν, ὅτι διὰ τὴν τῶν κρατούντων νωθρότητα καὶ ἀφέλειαν εἰς κατόπιν 85
τὰ τῶν 'Ρωμαίων ἦλθον πράγματα, καὶ οἱ τὰ τῆς Δελματίας κάστρα
70ʳP οἰκοῦντες γεγόνασιν αὐτο|κέφαλοι, μήτε τῷ βασιλεῖ 'Ρωμαίων, μήτε
130Be ἄλλῳ τινὶ ὑποκείμενοι. Μετὰ δὲ χρό|νον τινὰ ἐπὶ τῆς βασιλείας Βασι-
λείου, τοῦ ἀοιδίμου καὶ ἀειμνήστου βασιλέως, ἐλθόντων Σαρακηνῶν
ἀπὸ 'Αφρικῆς, τοῦ τε Σολδανοῦ καὶ τοῦ Σάβα καὶ τοῦ Καλφοῦς, μετὰ 90
καραβίων λϛ', κατέλαβον ἐν Δελματίᾳ, καὶ ἐπόρθησαν τὸ κάστρον τὰ
Βούτοβα καὶ τὸ κάστρον τὴν 'Ρῶσσαν καὶ τὸ κάστρον τὰ Δεκάτερα, τὸ
κάτω. Καὶ ἦλθον καὶ εἰς τὸ κάστρον 'Ραουσίου, καὶ παρεκάθισαν αὐτῷ
μῆνας δεκαπέντε. Τότε βιασθέντες οἱ 'Ραουσαῖοι ἐδηλοποίησαν Βασι-
λείῳ, τῷ ἀειμνήστῳ βασιλεῖ 'Ρωμαίων, λέγοντες αὐτῷ οὕτως· «'Ελέησον 95
70ᵛP ἡμᾶς, καὶ μὴ ἐάσῃς ἀπολέσθαι πα|ρὰ τῶν ἀρνητῶν τοῦ Χριστοῦ.» 'Ο δὲ
βασιλεὺς σπλαγχνισθεὶς ἀπέστειλεν τὸν πατρίκιον Νικήτα, δρουγγάριον
τοῦ πλωΐμου, οὗ τὸ ἐπίκλην 'Ωορύφας, μετὰ χελανδίων ἑκατόν. Οἱ δὲ
Σαρακηνοὶ μαθόντες τὴν μετὰ τοῦ στόλου ἄφιξιν τοῦ πατρικίου δρουγγα-

---

F   70 'Επὶ δὲ — 79 ἑτέρας: cf. Theoph. Cont. 291, 1—292, 13; Cedr. II. p.
220, 9—15; Zon. XVI. 9., ed. Bonn. III. p. 425, 9—426, 2.   82 Μετὰ
δὲ — 84 αὐτούς: cf. Leo, Tact. XVIII. 101., ed. Migne, P. G. 107. c. 969
A—B.   88 Μετὰ δὲ — 116 'Ρωμαίων: cf. Theoph. Cont. p. 289, 2—290,
23; 292, 14—294, 2; De Them. p. 61, 11—62, 18 (= ed. Pertusi 97, 18—98, 42);
Cedr., ed. Bonn. II. p. 219, 4—220, 8; 220, 15—221, 7; Zon. XVI. 9., ed. Bonn.
III. p. 425, 1—9.

V 70 ἀποκρισιαρίους: πρέσβεις Theoph. Cont. ‖ 72 ὡς τὸ: ὥστε edd. ‖
73 εἰσακούσας: ἐπακούσας Theoph. Cont. ‖ 76 βαπτίσαι: βαπτισθῆναι
V edd. ‖ 77 προέκρινον V edd. ‖ τῆς om. edd. ‖ 81 κρημνώδεις ⟨κατοικοῦντες⟩
coni. Kyriakides ‖ ante Παγανοὶ addendum τὸ coni. Bury ‖ 82 ἑρμηνεύεται (etiam
Bury): ἑρμηνεύονται Ba Be ‖ 83 εἰς bis P ‖ 85 ὅτι om. V edd. ‖ εἰς ⟨μηδὲν⟩

29

in the time of Basil, the Christ-loving emperor, they sent diplomatic agents, begging and praying him that those of them who were unbaptized might receive baptism and that they might be, as they had originally been, subject to the empire of the Romans; and that glorious emperor, of blessed memory, gave ear to them and sent out an imperial agent and priests with him and baptized all of them that were unbaptized of the aforesaid nations, and after baptizing them he then appointed for them princes whom they themselves approved and chose, from the family which they themselves loved and favoured. And from that day to this their princes come from these same families, and from no other. But the Pagani, who are called Arentani in the Roman tongue, were left unbaptized, in an inaccessible and precipitous part of the country. For 'Pagani' means 'unbaptized' in the Slavonic tongue. But later, they too sent to the same glorious emperor and begged that they too might be baptized, and he sent and baptized them too. And since, as we said above, owing to the sloth and inexperience of those in power things had gone the wrong way for the Romans, the inhabitants of the cities of Dalmatia also had become independent, subject neither to the emperor of the Romans nor to anybody else. But after some time, in the reign of Basil the glorious and ever-memorable emperor, Saracens from Africa, Soldan and Saba and Kalphus, came with 36 ships and reached Dalmatia and took the city of Butova and the city of Rossa and the lower city of Decatera. And they came also to the city of Ragusa and blockaded it fifteen months. Then in their strait the Ragusans made a declaration to Basil, the ever-memorable emperor of the Romans, saying this to him: «Have pity on us and do not allow us to be destroyed by them that deny Christ.» The emperor was moved with compassion and sent the patrician Nicetas, admiral of the fleet, surnamed Ooryphas, with one hundred ships of war. When the Saracens learnt of the arrival of the patrician admiral of the fleet with

---

κατόπιν coni. Kyriakides || 88/9: ἐπὶ τῆς βασιλείας Βασιλείου: ἐπὶ δὲ τῆς βασιλείας Μιχαὴλ τοῦ υἱοῦ Θεοφίλου De Them. || 89/90 Σαρακηνῶν ἀπὸ Ἀφρικῆς: οἱ ἀπὸ Καρχηδόνος Ἀγαρηνοὶ Theoph. Cont. || 90 Σολδανοῦ: Σολδανὸν De Them. Σολδάνον Theoph. Cont. || Σάβα (littera μ partim erasa) Pˣ V edd. Σάβαν Cedr.: Σάμα P Σάμβαν Theoph. Cont. || Καλφοῦς De Them. Καλφοὺς Theoph. Cont.: Κλαφοὺς P Κλαφοῦς V edd. || 91 καραβίων: κομπαρίων De Them. πλοίων πολεμικῶν Theoph. Cont. || Δελματίᾳ: Δαλματίας De Them. Theoph. Cont. || 91/2 τὰ Βούτοβα Ba Be τὴν Βούτοβαν De Them.: τὰ Βούγοβα P Βούγοβα mg. P⁷ ἡ Βούτομα Theoph. Cont. || 92 Ῥῶσαν De Them. Ῥῶσα Theoph. Cont. || 92/3 τὰ Δεκάτερα, τὸ κάτω: τὰ κάτω Δεκάτερα De Them. Theoph Cont.ⱽ τὰ κάτω Δεκάτορα Theoph. Cont. || 93 κάστρον: μητρόπολιν De Them. Theoph. Cont. || παρεκάθισαν: ἐπολιόρκουν De Them. Theoph. Cont. || 94 δεκαπέντε Be: ιε′ P ἐπὶ χρόνον... ἱκανόν De Them. Theoph. Cont. || Ῥαουσαῖοι P || 97 σπλαγχνισθεὶς P || Νικήτα: Νικήταν Theoph. Cont. || 98 τὸ ἐπίκλην: κατ' ἐπωνυμίαν Theoph. Cont. || Ὀορύφας Be Theoph. Cont.: Ὀορύφας P || χελανδίων: νεῶν Theoph. Cont. || ἑκατόν edd. Theoph. Cont.: ρ′ P De Them. || 99 Σαρακηνοί:

29

ρίου τοῦ πλωΐμου, ἔφυγον καταλιπόντες τὸ κάστρον ῾Ραουσίου, καὶ100
ἀντεπέρασαν ἐν Λαγουβαρδίᾳ, καὶ πολιορκήσαντες τὸ κάστρον Βάρεως,
τοῦτο ἐπόρθησαν. Τότε ὁ Σολδανὸς κτίσας ἐκεῖσε παλάτια, κατεκράτησεν
τὴν πᾶσαν Λαγουβαρδίαν μέχρι ῾Ρώμης ἔτη τεσσαράκοντα. ῾Ο οὖν
βασιλεὺς διὰ τὴν αἰτίαν ταύτην ἀπέστειλεν πρός τε τὸν Λοδόϊχον, τὸν
71ʳP ῥῆγα Φραγγίας καὶ τὸν πάπα ῾Ρώμης, ἵνα συνεπαμύνηται τῷ πα|ρὰ105
τοῦ βασιλέως ἀποσταλέντι στρατῷ. Οἱ δὲ ὑπείξαντες τῇ τοῦ βασιλέως
αἰτήσει, ὅ τε ῥὴξ καὶ ὁ πάπας, ἦλθον ἀμφότεροι μετὰ δυνάμεως πολλῆς,
131Be καὶ ἑνωθέν|τες τῷ παρὰ τοῦ βασιλέως ἀποσταλέντι στρατῷ ἅμα τῷ
Χρωβάτῳ καὶ Σέρβλῳ καὶ Ζαχλούμῳ καὶ Τερβουνιώταις καὶ Καναλίταις
καὶ ῾Ραουσαίοις μετὰ πάντων τῶν ἀπὸ τῆς Δελματίας κάστρων (οὗτοι110
γὰρ πάντες βασιλικῇ κελεύσει παρῆσαν), καὶ περασάντων ἐν Λαγουβαρδίᾳ, παρεκάθισαν τὸ κάστρον Βάρεως καὶ ἐπόρθησαν αὐτό.

᾽Ιστέον, ὅτι τοὺς Χρωβάτους καὶ τοὺς λοιποὺς Σκλαβάρχοντας
71ᵛP οἱ τοῦ κάστρου ῾Ραουσίου οἰκήτορες μετὰ τῶν ἰδίων αὐτῶν καρα|βίων
διεπέρασαν ἐν Λαγουβαρδίᾳ. Καὶ τὸ μὲν κάστρον Βάρεως καὶ ·τὴν χώραν115
καὶ τὴν αἰχμαλωσίαν πᾶσαν ἀνελάβετο ὁ βασιλεὺς τῶν ῾Ρωμαίων, τὸν
δὲ Σολδανὸν καὶ τοὺς λοιποὺς Σαρακηνοὺς ἀνελάβετο Λοδόϊχος, ὁ ῥὴξ
Φραγγίας, καὶ ἀπήγαγεν αὐτοὺς ἐν τῷ κάστρῳ Καπύης καὶ ἐν τῷ κάστρῳ
Βενεβενδοῦ. Καὶ οὐδεὶς αὐτὸν εἶδεν γελῶντα. Εἶπεν δὲ ὁ ῥήξ, ὅτι· «Εἴ
τίς μοι τὸν Σολδανὸν μετὰ ἀληθείας ἀναγγείλῃ ἢ ὑποδείξῃ γελῶντα,120
δώσω αὐτῷ χρήματα πολλά.» Καὶ μετὰ τοῦτο εἶδέν τις αὐτὸν γελῶντα,
καὶ τῷ ῥηγὶ Λοδοΐχῳ ἀπήγγειλεν. ῾Ο δὲ προσκαλεσάμενος τὸν Σολδανὸν
72ʳP ἠρώτησεν αὐτόν, ποίῳ τρόπῳ ἐγέλασεν. ῾Ο δὲ εἶπεν· «῎Αμαξαν εἶδον | καὶ
τοὺς ἐν αὐτῇ τροχοὺς κυλιομένους, καὶ τούτου χάριν ἐγέλασα, ὅτι καὶ
ἐγώ ποτε κεφαλὴ ἐγενόμην, καὶ ἀρτίως εἰμὶ ὑποκάτω πάντων, καὶ πάλιν125
δύναται ὁ Θεὸς ὑψῶσαί με.» Καὶ ἀπὸ τότε προσεκαλεῖτο αὐτὸν ὁ Λοδόϊχος

F   116 τὸν δὲ — 216 εὐεργεσίαν.: cf. Theoph. Cont. p. 294, 3—297,
23; Cedr., ed. Bonn. II. p. 221, 8—225, 8; Zon. XVI. 9., ed. Bonn. III.
p. 426, 2—429, 6; (Ps.—) Symeon, ed. Bonn. p. 695, 3—697, 2.   123
῎Αμαξαν — 126 ὑψῶσαί με: cf. Menandri fr. 3., Exc. de leg., ed. de Boor
p. 177, 12—34; Theoph. Simoc., ed. de Boor p. 243, 10—244, 17; Theoph.
p. 273, 14—27; Basilius, Paraen., ed. Migne, P. G. 107. c. XL D. Cf. V.
Grecu, Byzantinoslavica 13 (1952—3). p. 259.

V ἐξ ᾽Αφρικῆς Σαρακηνοί Theoph. Cont. ῎Αφροι De Them. ‖ 101 ἀντεπέρασαν:
ἀνεπέρασαν De Them.   διαπεράσαντες Theoph. Cont. ‖ Λογουβαρδίᾳ edd.
Λαγοβαρδία Theoph. Cont. De Them.ᶜ ‖ Βάρεως: Βάρης De Them. ‖ 102 ἐπόρθησαν: ἐξεπόρθησαν Theoph. Cont. ‖ 103 τὴν om. edd. ‖ τὴν πᾶσαν (etiam

29

his squadron, they quitted the city of Ragusa and took to flight and crossed over into Lombardy and laid siege to the city of Bari and took it. Then Soldan built a palace there and was for forty years master of all Lombardy as far as Rome. On this account, therefore, the emperor sent to Lewis, king of Francia, and to the pope of Rome, asking their cooperation with the army which he, the emperor, had sent. The king and the pope acceded to the emperor's request, and both of them came with a large force and joined up with the army sent by the emperor and with the Croat and Serb and Zachlumian chiefs and the Terbouniotes and Kanalites and the men of Ragusa and all the cities of Dalmatia (for all these were present by imperial mandate); and they crossed over into Lombardy, and laid siege to the city of Bari and took it.

The Croats and the other chiefs of the Slavs were carried over into Lombardy by the inhabitants of the city of Ragusa in their own vessels. The city of Bari and the country and all the prisoners were taken by the emperor of the Romans, but Soldan and the rest of the Saracens were taken by Lewis, the king of Francia, who carried them off to the city of Capua and the city of Beneventum. And no one saw *Soldan* laughing. And the king said: «If anybody truly reports to me or shows me Soldan laughing, I will give him much money.» Later, someone saw him laughing and reported it to king Lewis. He summoned Soldan and asked him, how he had come to laugh? And he said: «I saw a cart and the wheels on it turning round and therefore I laughed because I too was once at the top and am now lowest of all, but God may raise me up again.» And thereafter Lewis would summon

---

De Them.): πᾶσαν τὴν   Theoph. Cont. ‖ Λογουβαρδίαν edd. Λαγοβαρδίαν
Theoph. Cont. Λογγιβαρδίαν De Them. ‖ ἔτη τεσσαράκοντα *deest in*
Theoph. Cont. De Them. ‖ τεσσαράκοντα V edd.: σαράκοντα P τέσσαρα *coni.*
Kyriakides ‖ 104 Λοδόηχον P Λοδοΐχον Theoph. Cont. Λοδοῦχον De Them.
Δολόϊχον Theoph. Cont.ᵛ ‖ 105 ῥῆγα Meursius Ba Be Theoph. Cont.
De Them.: δοῦκα P ‖ πάπα (*etiam* De Them.): πάπαν Theoph. Cont. ‖
συνεπαμύνεται Me Ba συνεπαμῦναι De Them. συνεπικουρῆσαι Theoph. Cont. ‖
107 αἰτήσει: ἐντεύξει De Them. ‖ ῥίξ P ‖ 108 ἅμα τῷ — 110
κάστρων: τὰς ὀλίγῳ πρόσθεν μνημονευθείσας χώρας τῶν Σκλαβηνῶν Theoph.
Cont. *deest in* De Them. ‖ 108/9 τοῖς Χρωβάτοις καὶ Σέρβλοις καὶ
Ζαχλούμοις *coni.* Bury ‖ 109 καὶ¹: τῷ edd. ‖ Τερβουνιῶτες P ‖
Καναλῖταις P ‖ 110 Ῥαουσαίοις Moravcsik: Ῥαουσίοις P edd. ‖ 111/2
Λογουβαρδίᾳ edd. ‖ 112 παρεκάθισαν *coni.* Bekker   παρεκάθησαν P:
ἐκάθησαν edd. ἐκάθισαν Migne   Βάρεως: Βάρης De Them. ‖ 114
Ῥαουσίου V edd.: Ῥαουσαίου P ‖ οἰκήτορες V edd.: οἰκηταὶ P ‖ 115
Λογουβαρδίᾳ edd. ‖ 116 τῶν *om.* edd. ‖ 117 Σολδανὸν edd. De Them.:
Σολδάνον P Theoph. Cont. ‖ Λοδόϊχος Be   Λοδοίχος Bury Λοδοῦχος De
Them.: Δολόηχος P   Δοδοῦχος De Them.ᶜ ‖ ῥίξ P ‖ 119 ῥίξ P ‖ 120
Σολδάνον Theoph. Cont. ‖ 121 αὐτὸν V¹ edd.: αὐτῶ P V ‖ 122 ριγὶ
P ‖ Λοδοΐχῳ Be: Δολόηχω P ‖ 125 ἐγενόμην: ἤμην V edd. ‖ 126
Λοδόϊχος Be: Δολόηχος P ‖

132Be εἰς τὴν τράπεζαν αὐτοῦ, καὶ συν|ήσθιεν αὐτῷ. Οἱ δὲ ἄρχοντες τῆς Καπύης καὶ Βενεβενδοῦ ἤρχοντο πρὸς τὸν Σολδανὸν ἐρωτῶντες αὐτὸν περὶ ἰατρειῶν καὶ θεραπείας ἀλόγων καὶ λοιπῶν ὑποθέσεων, ὡς γέροντα καὶ πεπειραμένον. Ὁ δὲ Σολδανὸς πανοῦργος ὢν καὶ σκολιὸς εἶπεν πρὸς130 αὐτούς, ὅτι· «Πρᾶγμα θέλω εἰπεῖν πρὸς ὑμᾶς, καὶ δέδοικα τοῦ μὴ παρ' 72ᵛP ὑμῶν κατάδηλον γενέσθαι πρὸς τὸν ῥῆγα, καὶ ἀπολέσω τὴν | ἐμαυτοῦ ζωήν.» Οἱ δὲ ὤμοσαν αὐτῷ, καὶ θαρρήσας εἶπεν πρὸς αὐτούς, ὅτι· «Ὁ ῥὴξ ἐξορίσαι θέλει πάντας ὑμᾶς ἐν τῇ μεγάλῃ Φραγγίᾳ, καὶ ἐὰν ἀπιστῆτε, ἐκδέξασθε μικρόν, κἀγὼ πληροφορῶ ὑμᾶς.» Καὶ ἀπελθὼν εἶπεν πρὸς135 τὸν Λοδόϊχον, ὅτι· «Οἱ ἄρχοντες τοῦ τόπου τούτου κακοί εἰσιν, καὶ σὺ οὐ δύνασαι κυριεῦσαι τὴν χώραν ταύτην, ἐὰν μὴ ἀφανίσῃς τοὺς δυνατούς, τοὺς ἀντιπίπτοντάς σε· ἀλλὰ δέσμευσον τοὺς πρώτους τοῦ κάστρου, καὶ ἀπόστειλον αὐτοὺς εἰς τὴν χώραν σου, καὶ τότε, ὡς θέλεις, οἱ λοιποὶ ὑποταγήσονταί σοι.» Καὶ ὅτε παρέπεισεν αὐτόν, ἵνα πληρώσῃ τὴν βουλὴν140 αὐτοῦ, καὶ ὥρισεν γενέσθαι ἁλύσεις σιδηρᾶς εἰς τὸ ἐξορίσαι αὐτούς, 73ʳP ἀπῆλθεν ὁ Σολδανὸς καὶ | εἶπεν πρὸς τοὺς ἄρχοντας, ὅτι· «Ἀκμὴν οὐ πιστεύετε, ὅτι ὁ ῥὴξ ἐξορίστους ὑμᾶς ποιεῖ, καὶ παντελῶς ἐξ ἀνθρώπων γίνεται τὸ μνημόσυνον ὑμῶν; Ὅμως εἰ θέλετε τελείως πληροφορηθῆναι, ἀπελθόντες θεάσασθε, τί ἄρα ἐργάζονται πάντες οἱ χαλκεῖς τῇ προστάξει145 133Be τοῦ ῥηγός. | Καὶ εἰ οὐχ εὕρητε αὐτοὺς ἐργαζομένους τὰς ἁλύσεις καὶ τὰ δεσμά, γινώσκετε, ὅτι πάντα τὰ παρ' ἐμοῦ λαλούμενα ὑμῖν ἐστιν ψευδῆ· εἰ δὲ ἀληθεύω, φροντίσατε τὴν σωτηρίαν ὑμῶν καὶ ἐμὲ εὐεργετήσατε, τὸν τὰ χρηστὰ καὶ σωτήρια ὑμῖν βουλευσάμενον.» Οἱ δὲ ἄρχοντες πεισθέντες τῷ τοῦ Σολδανοῦ λόγῳ, θεασάμενοι δὲ καὶ τὰς ἁλύσεις καὶ τὰ δεσμά,150 73ᵛP τελείαν πληροφορίαν ἔλαβον, καὶ ἔκτοτε ἐμελέτων | τὴν ἀπώλειαν τοῦ ῥηγὸς Λοδοΐχου. Ὁ δὲ ῥὴξ ταῦτα πάντα ἀγνοῶν ἐξῆλθε πρὸς τὸ κυνηγῆσαι. Ὑποστρέψαντος δέ, οἱ τούτου ἄρχοντες ἐκράτησαν τὸ κάστρον, μὴ ἐάσαντες αὐτὸν εἰσελθεῖν. Ὁ δὲ ῥὴξ Λοδόϊχος τὴν τῶν ἀρχόντων ἔνστασιν θεασάμενος, εἰς τὴν ἰδίαν χώραν ὑπέστρεψεν. Οἱ δὲ ἄρχοντες εἶπον155 πρὸς τὸν Σολδανόν· «Τί ἄρα θέλεις ἡμᾶς ποιῆσαί σοι περὶ τῆς γενομένης εἰς ἡμᾶς παρὰ σοῦ σωτηρίας;» Ὁ δὲ ᾐτήσατο ἐν τῇ ἰδίᾳ χώρᾳ ἀπολῦσαι αὐτόν, καὶ τούτου γενομένου, ἀπῆλθεν ἐν Ἀφρικῇ εἰς τὴν ἰδίαν αὐτοῦ χώραν. Μὴ ἐπιλαθόμενος δὲ τῆς ἀρχαίας αὐτοῦ κακίας ἐστρατοπέδευσεν, καὶ ἦλθεν μετὰ δυνάμεως ἐν Καπύῃ καὶ ἐν Βενεβενδῷ πρὸς τὸ πολιορκῆ-160 74ʳP σαι | καὶ ὑποτάξαι αὐτούς. Οἱ δὲ τὰ τοιαῦτα κάστρα κρατοῦντες ἀπέστειλαν πρέσβεις πρὸς τὸν ῥῆγα Λοδόϊχον ἐν Φραγγίᾳ, ἵνα ἐλθὼν συνεπαμύνηται αὐτοῖς κατὰ τοῦ Σολδανοῦ καὶ τῶν Ἀφρικῶν. Ὁ δὲ ῥὴξ

F   143 καὶ παντελῶς — 144 μνημόσυνον ἡμῶν: cf. Psalm. 9, 7; 108, 15; Job 9, 2.

V 127 αὐτοῦ Migne ‖ 128 αὐτὸν V¹ edd.: αὐτῶ P V ‖ 130 Σολδανὸς V Ba Be: Σουλδανὸς P ‖ σκολιὸς: δόλων Φοινικικῶν οὐκ ἀμέτοχος Theoph. Cont.   δόλιος Cedr. ‖

29

him to his table and would eat with him. And the nobles of Capua and Beneventum used to go to Soldan and ask him questions about the treatment and care of cattle and other matters, because of his age and experience. And Soldan, who was cunning and crooked, said to them: «I would like to say a thing to you, but I fear to be betrayed by you to the king and I shall lose my life.» But they swore to him, and he took heart and said to them: «The king is minded to banish all of you to great Francia, and if you disbelieve it, wait a little, and I will satisfy you.» And he went off and said to Lewis: «The nobles of this place are evil, and you cannot be master of this country unless you destroy the powerful men who oppose you; but do you bind the first men of the city and send them off to your country, and then the rest will be submissive to you, as you desire.» When he had won him to carrying out his advice, and *the king* had instructed that chains of iron should be made for their banishment, Soldan went off and said to the nobles: «Do you still not believe that the king is sending you into banishment, and that all remembrance of you will vanish from among men? Yet, if you will be perfectly satisfied, go and see what all the smiths are making by order of the king. And if you do not find them making the chains and fetters, know that all I have told you is lies; but if I speak truth, look to your safety and reward me for my valuable and salutary advice to you.» The nobles obeyed the word of Soldan, and when they had seen the chains and fetters, they were completely satisfied, and thereafter began to devise the destruction of king Lewis. The king, in ignorance of all this, went out hunting. But when he came back, his nobles had taken possession of the city and did not allow him to enter. King Lewis, seeing himself thus opposed by the nobles, went back to his own country. The nobles said to Soldan: «What, then, would you have us do for you, in return for the salvation wrought for us by you?» And he requested them to dismiss him to his own country, which they did, and he went off to Africa, to his own country. But, mindful of his ancient malice, he made an expedition and came with a force to Capua and to Beneventum, to lay siege to and subdue them. The rulers of these cities sent envoys to king Lewis in Francia, asking him to come and help them fight against Soldan and the Africans. But king Lewis, when he heard of it, having learnt

---

132 ῥῆγα Meursius Ba Be: δοῦκα P ‖ 133 ὄμωσαν P ‖ ῥίξ P ‖ 134 θέλει V edd.: θέλη P ‖ 136 Λοδόϊχον Be: Δολόηχον P ‖ τόπου om. V Me ‖ τούτου coni. Moravcsik: τοῦ P om. edd. ‖ 139 θέλεις Be: θέλης P ‖ 140 σοι V edd.; σε P ‖ πληρώσῃ edd.: πληρώσει P ‖ 141 ὄρησεν P ‖ 142 Σολδάνος Theoph. Cont. ‖ 143 ῥίξ P ‖ 149 σωτηρία P ‖ 150 Σολδανοῦ V Ba Be: Σουλδανοῦ P ‖ 152 ῥιγὸς P ‖ Λοδοήχου P ‖ ῥίξ P ‖ 154 ῥίξ P ‖ Λοδόηχος P ‖ 155 ὑπέστρεψεν: ἀνθυπενόστησε Theoph. Cont. ‖ 156 Σολδάνος Theoph. Cont. ‖ θέλεις V edd.: θέλης P ‖ ἡμᾶς V edd.: ὑμῖν P ‖ 158 ἐν ᾿Αφρικῇ: κατὰ Καρχηδόνα Theoph. Cont. ‖ 162 ῥίγα P ‖ Λοδόηχον P ‖ 163 ῥίξ P ‖

29

Λοδόϊχος ταῦτα μαθὼν καί, ὅνπερ ἐποίησεν τρόπον ὁ Σολδανός, πείσας
καὶ τοὺς ἄρχοντας, ὅτι· «Δεσμίους μέλλει ὑμᾶς ὁ ῥὴξ ἐν Φραγγίᾳ ἐξορί-165
134Be σαι», ἀντεδήλωσεν αὐτοῖς, ὅτι· | «Καὶ ἅπερ ἐποίησα πρότερον εἰς ὑμᾶς,
μεταμέλημαι, ὅτι ἔσωσα ὑμᾶς ἀπὸ τῶν ἐχθρῶν ὑμῶν, καὶ ἀνταπεδώ-
κατέ μοι πονηρὰ ἀντὶ ἀγαθῶν, καὶ καθὼς ἐδιώχθην παρ' ὑμῶν, ἀρτίως
χαίρω ἐπὶ τῇ ἀπωλείᾳ ὑμῶν.» Τότε ἀπορήσαντες ἀπὸ τοῦ ῥηγὸς Λοδοΐχου,
74ᵛP ἀπέστειλαν πρέσβεις πρὸς | τὸν βασιλέα Ῥωμαίων τοῦ δοῦναι αὐτοῖς170
βοήθειαν καὶ λυτρώσασθαι τοῦ τοιούτου κινδύνου. Ὁ δὲ βασιλεὺς
ὑπέσχετο βοηθῆσαι αὐτοῖς. Τοῦ δὲ ἀποκρισιαρίου ἀπὸ τῆς πόλεως
ὑποστρέψαντος καὶ ἀγαθὰς ἀγγελίας τοῖς πέμψασιν αὐτὸν ἀποκομίζοντος περὶ τῆς τοῦ βασιλέως συμμαχίας, μήπω τούτου ἀποσωθέντος ἐν
τῷ κάστρῳ, ἐκρατήθη παρὰ τῶν βιγλῶν τοῦ Σολδανοῦ. Προεγνώκει175
γὰρ ὁ Σολδανὸς τὴν γεγονυῖαν ἀποστολὴν πρὸς ἱκεσίαν τοῦ βασιλέως
Ῥωμαίων, καὶ ἐπύκτευσεν τοῦ τὸν ἀποκρισιάριον αὐτῶν κρατῆσαι,
75ʳP ὅπερ καὶ γέγονεν. Κρατηθέντος δὲ αὐτοῦ, ἔμαθεν τὴν ἀποτελεσθεῖ|σαν
παρ' αὐτοῦ δουλείαν, καὶ ὅτι δι' ὀλίγων ἡμερῶν καταλαμβάνει ἡ τοῦ
βασιλέως Ῥωμαίων βοήθεια. Ὁ δὲ Σολδανὸς εἶπεν τῷ αὐτῷ ἀποκρισιαρίῳ,180
ὅτι· «Εἰ ποιήσεις, ὅπερ σοι εἴπω, ἐλευθερίας καὶ δωρεῶν μεγίστων
ἀξιωθήσῃ· εἰ δὲ μή, πονηρῷ θανάτῳ τὴν ζωήν ἀπολέσεις.» Τοῦ δὲ
ὑποσχομένου ἐκπληρῶσαι τὰ κελευόμενα αὐτῷ, εἶπεν ὁ Σολδανὸς πρὸς
αὐτόν, ὅτι· «Κελεύω στῆναί σε πλησίον τοῦ τείχους καὶ προσκαλέσασθαι
τοὺς ἀποστείλαντάς σε καὶ εἰπεῖν πρὸς αὐτούς· ''Ἐγὼ μὲν τὴν δουλείαν,185
135Be ἣν ὤφειλον ποιῆ|σαι, πεποίηκα, καὶ τὸν βασιλέα Ῥωμαίων περὶ ὑμῶν
75ᵛP ἐδυσώπησα· πλὴν οὖν γινώσκετε, ὅτι | εἰς κενὸν ἐγένετο ἡ ὁδός μου, καὶ
ὁ βασιλεὺς πάμφαυλον ἔθετο τὴν παρ' ὑμῶν γεγονυῖαν ἱκεσίαν, καὶ ἀπὸ
τοῦ βασιλέως μὴ ἐλπίζετε βοήθειαν'.» Τοῦ δὲ ὑποσχομένου ταῦτα μετὰ
χαρᾶς ἐκπληρῶσαι, ἤγαγον αὐτὸν πλησίον τοῦ κάστρου, καὶ ἐν οὐδενὶ190
θέμενος τὰ παρὰ τοῦ Σολδανοῦ ῥηθέντα πάντα, μήτε τὰς ἀπειλὰς αὐτοῦ
φοβηθείς, μήτε ταῖς ὑποσχέσεσιν αὐτοῦ πεισθείς, ἀλλὰ τὸν τοῦ Θεοῦ
φόβον ἐν τῇ καρδίᾳ αὐτοῦ θέμενος, διελογίσατο ἐν ἑαυτῷ, ὅτι· «Συμφέρον
ἐστὶν ἐμὲ μόνον ἀποθανεῖν καὶ μὴ τοσαύτας ψυχὰς διὰ λόγου παγιδεῦσαι
καὶ προδοῦναι εἰς θάνατον.» Καὶ δὴ πλησίον τοῦ τείχους αὐτοῦ γενομένου195
76ʳP καὶ πάντας τοὺς ἄρχον|τας προσκαλεσαμένου, εἶπεν πρὸς τοὺς ἐξουσιάζον-
τας τοῦ τοιούτου κάστρου· «'Ἐγὼ μέν, κύριοί μου, τὴν διακονίαν μου
ἐξεπλήρωσα, καὶ τὰ παρὰ τοῦ βασιλέως Ῥωμαίων δηλωθέντα ὑμῖν
ἀπαγγελῶ, πλὴν ὁρκίζω ὑμᾶς εἰς τὸν υἱὸν τοῦ Θεοῦ καὶ εἰς τὴν σωτηρίαν
παντὸς τοῦ κάστρου καὶ αὐτῶν τῶν ψυχῶν ὑμῶν, ἵνα ἀντὶ ἐμοῦ εὐεργετῆ-200

F   167 ἀνταπεδώκατε — 168 ἀγαθῶν: cf. I Reg. 25, 21; Prov. 17, 13.

V 164 Λοδόηχος] litteras λο in ras. scr. P¹   ‖   167 μεταμεμέλημαι Ba Be   ‖
168 ἐδιώχθην Meursius Ba Be: ἐδιώχθη P   ‖   169 Λοδοήχου P   ‖   172 ἀπο-

29

how Soldan had acted in persuading the nobles that, «the king purposes to
send you in chains to banishment in Francia», declared in answer to them:
«I repent my former conduct towards you, when I saved you from your
enemies, and you returned me evil for good; and as I was cast out by you,
now I rejoice at your destruction.» Then, having failed with king Lewis,
they sent envoys to the emperor of the Romans, asking that he should
give them aid and deliver them out of this danger. The emperor promised
to aid them. But when the diplomatic agent had left Constantinople on his
homeward way, bringing back to them who had sent him fair tidings of
the alliance with the emperor, he was still short of the city when he was
captured by the scouts of Soldan. For Soldan had obtained previous intelligence of the sending of a mission of supplication to the emperor of the
Romans and had made efforts to capture their diplomatic agent, which
he did. From his captive he learnt of the service he had performed, and
that in a few days the succours of the emperor of the Romans would arrive.
So Soldan said to this same diplomatic agent: «If you do what I tell you,
you shall be awarded freedom and very great gifts; but if not, you shall
lose your life and your death shall be cruel.» The man promised to carry
out his orders, and Soldan said to him: «I order you to stand close to the
wall and to summon those who sent you and say to them: 'For my part,
I have carried out the service laid upon me, and have importuned the
emperor of the Romans on your behalf; however, know that my journey
was vain, and that the emperor has altogether spurned the supplication
you made, and do not expect succour from the emperor'.» When he had
promised to perform this gladly, they conducted him close to the city,
where, disregarding all that Soldan had said, neither fearing his threats
nor seduced by his promises, but setting the fear of God in his heart, he
communed thus with himself: «It is expedient that I alone should die, and
not by my word entrap and betray so many souls to their death.» So, when
he was near the wall and had summoned the nobles, he thus addressed
those who were in authority over that city: «I, my lords, have discharged
my office and will announce to you what was declared by the emperor
of the Romans; but I adjure you by the Son of God and the salvation
of all the city and of your very souls, to reward, instead of me, my children

---

κρισιαρίου: τῆς ἀγγελίας διάκονος Theoph. Cont. πρεσβευτὴς Cedr. ‖ 177
τοῦ τὸν V Me Be: τοῦτον P ‖ 180 βοήθεια V edd.: β[ο]ήθεια P ‖ αὐτῷ
V edd.: α[ὐ]τὸ P ‖ 181 ποιήσεις F edd.: ποιήσῃς P ‖ δωρεῶν V edd.:
δ[ω]ρεῶν P ‖ 182 ἀπολέσεις F edd.: ἀπολ[έ]σῃς P ἀπολέσῃς V ‖ 183
ἐκπληρῶσαι V edd.: ἐκπλ[η]ρῶσαι P ‖ εἶπεν V edd.: ε[ἶ]πεν P ‖ 184 ὅτι
V edd.: ὅτ[ι] P ‖ τείχους V edd.: τεῖχ[ους] P ‖ 185 ἀποστείλαντάς V edd.:
ἀποστ[εί]λαντάς P ‖ αὐτούς V edd.: αὐτού[ς] P ‖ 186 ὤφειλον V edd.:
ὄφειλο[ν] P ‖ 187 ὅτι V edd.: ὅτ[ι] P ‖ κενὸν F Meursius Ba Be: καινὸν P ‖
188 πάμφαυλον Migne: παμφαῦλον P edd. παρὰ φαῦλον coni. Bekker ‖
ἔθετο: ἔθηκε edd. ‖ 193 αὐτοῦ edd. ‖ 196/7 ἐξουσιάσαντας edd. ‖ 199 ὑμᾶς
V edd. Theoph. Cont.: ὑμῖν P ‖

29

σητε τὰ τέκνα μου καὶ τὴν ἐλπίζουσαν ἀπολαβεῖν με σύμβιόν μου· ὡς
γὰρ ποιήσητε μετὰ αὐτῶν, παρὰ τοῦ δικαίου καὶ μισθαποδότου ἀγαθοῦ
Θεοῦ, μέλλοντος κρῖναι ζῶντας καὶ νεκρούς, τὸν μισθὸν ἀπολήψεσθε.»
76ᵛP Καὶ ταῦτα εἰπὼν παρεθάρρυνεν αὐτοὺς λέγων· «Ἐγὼ μὲν ἀπὸ | τοῦ
136Be | Σολδανοῦ ἀπολοῦμαι καὶ περὶ τὴν ζωὴν κινδυνεύω, ὑμεῖς δὲ στῆτε205
ἑδραῖοι καὶ μὴ δειλανδρήσητε, ἀλλ᾽ ὑπομείνατε μικρόν, καὶ εἰς ὀλίγον
ἡμερῶν φθάζει ἡ ἀποσταλεῖσα ὑμῖν σωτηρία παρὰ τοῦ βασιλέως Ῥωμαίων». Ταῦτα δὲ αὐτοῦ εἰπόντος, οἱ κατέχοντες αὐτὸν οἰκεῖοι τοῦ
Σολδανοῦ παρὰ προσδοκίαν τὰ παρ᾽ αὐτοῦ λαληθέντα ἀκούσαντες,
ἔβρυξαν ἐπ᾽ αὐτὸν τοὺς ὀδόντας, καὶ εἷς τοῦ ἑτέρου προέτρεχον, τίς ἄρα210
τῆς σφαγῆς αὐτοῦ γέγονεν αὐτουργός. Τοῦ δὲ παρ᾽ αὐτῶν ἀναιρεθέντος, πτοηθεὶς ὁ Σολδανὸς τὴν τοῦ βασιλέως κατερχομένην δυναστείαν,
ὑπέστρεψεν εἰς τὴν ἰδίαν χώραν. Καὶ ἔκτοτε καὶ μέχρι τοῦ νῦν καὶ οἱ
77ʳP τῆς Καπύης | καὶ οἱ τῆς Βενεβενδοῦ εἰσὶν ὑπὸ τὴν ἐξουσίαν τῶν Ῥωμαίων
εἰς τελείαν δούλωσιν καὶ ὑποταγὴν διὰ τὴν εἰς αὐτοὺς γενομένην μεγάλην215
ταύτην εὐεργεσίαν.

Ὅτι τὸ κάστρον τοῦ Ῥαουσίου οὐ καλεῖται Ῥαοῦσι τῇ Ῥωμαίων
διαλέκτῳ, ἀλλ᾽ ἐπεὶ ἐπάνω τῶν κρημνῶν ἵσταται, λέγεται ῥωμαϊστὶ ᾽ὁ
κρημνὸς λαῦ᾽· ἐκλήθησαν δὲ ἐκ τούτου Λαυσαῖοι, ἤγουν ᾽οἱ καθεζόμενοι
εἰς τὸν κρημνόν᾽. Ἡ δὲ κοινὴ συνήθεια, ἡ πολλάκις μεταφθείρουσα220
τὰ ὀνόματα τῇ ἐναλλαγῇ τῶν γραμμάτων, μεταβαλοῦσα τὴν κλῆσιν
Ῥαουσαίους τούτους ἐκάλεσεν. Οἱ δὲ αὐτοὶ Ῥαουσαῖοι τὸ παλαιὸν
ἐκράτουν τὸ κάστρον τὸ ἐπιλεγόμενον Πίταυρα, καὶ ἐπειδή, ἡνίκα τὰ
77ᵛP λοιπὰ ἐκρατήθησαν | κάστρα παρὰ τῶν Σκλάβων τῶν ὄντων | ἐν τῷ θέ-
137Be ματι, ἐκρατήθη καὶ τὸ τοιοῦτον κάστρον, καὶ οἱ μὲν ἐσφάγησαν, οἱ δὲ225
ἠχμαλωτίσθησαν, οἱ δὲ δυνηθέντες ἐκφυγεῖν καὶ διασωθῆναι εἰς τοὺς
ὑποκρήμνους τόπους κατῴκησαν, ἐν ᾧ ἐστιν ἀρτίως τὸ κάστρον, οἰκοδομήσαντες αὐτὸ πρότερον μικρόν, καὶ πάλιν μετὰ ταῦτα μεῖζον, καὶ
μετὰ τοῦτο πάλιν τὸ τεῖχος αὐτοῦ αὐξήσαντες μέχρι † δ᾽ ἔχειν † τὸ
κάστρον διὰ τὸ πλατύνεσθαι αὐτοὺς κατ᾽ ὀλίγον καὶ πληθύνεσθαι. Ἐκ230
δὲ τῶν μετοικησάντων εἰς τὸ Ῥαούσιον εἰσὶν οὗτοι· Γρηγόριος, Ἀρσά-
φιος, Βικτωρῖνος, Βιτάλιος, Βαλεντῖνος, ὁ ἀρχιδιάκων, Βαλεντῖνος, ὁ
πατὴρ τοῦ πρωτοσπαθαρίου Στεφάνου. Ἀφ᾽ οὗ δὲ ἀπὸ Σαλῶνα μετῴκη-
78ʳP σαν εἰς τὸ Ῥαούσι|ον, εἰσὶν ἔτη φ᾽ μέχρι τῆς σήμερον, ἥτις ἰνδικτιὼν ζ᾽
ἔτους ͵ςυνζ᾽. Ἐν δὲ τῷ αὐτῷ κάστρῳ κεῖται ὁ ἅγιος Παγκράτιος ἐν τῷ235
ναῷ τοῦ ἁγίου Στεφάνου, τῷ ὄντι μέσον τοῦ αὐτοῦ κάστρου.

F 203   μέλλοντος — νεκρούς: II Timoth. 4, 1.   203 τὸν μισθὸν ἀπολήψεσθε: cf. II Ioh. 8.   210 ἔβρυξαν — ὀδόντας: cf. Acta 7, 54.

V 201   σύμβιόν: σύνευνον Theoph. Cont.   ‖   203 ante μέλλοντος add. τοῦ V   ‖

and her who is hoping to receive me back, my wife; for as you deal with them, so shall your reward be from God, the just and righteous rewarder, who shall judge the quick and the dead.» When he had so spoken, he fortified them with these words: «For my part I shall be destroyed by Soldan and the threat of death is upon me; but do you stand fast and be not fainthearted, but endure a little while, and in a few days shall arrive the salvation which has been sent to you by the emperor of the Romans». When he had so spoken, the servants of Soldan who had charge of him, hearing his unexpected message, gnashed with their teeth upon him, and each outran the other to be the author of his murder. But after he was made away by them, Soldan, dreading the powers of the emperor that were coming upon him, withdrew to his own country. And from that time until this day the men of Capua and the men of Beneventum have been under the authority of the Romans in perfect servitude and subjection, for that great benefit which was done to them.

The city of Ragusa is not called Ragusa in the tongue of the Romans but, because it stands on cliffs, it is called in Roman speech 'the cliff, lau'; whence they are called 'Lausaioi', i. e. 'those who have their seat on the cliff'. But vulgar usage, which frequently corrupts names by altering their letters, has changed the denomination and called them Rausaioi. These same Rausaioi used of old to possess the city that is called Pitaura; and since, when the other cities were captured by the Slavs that were in the province, this city too was captured, and some were slaughtered and others taken prisoner, those who were able to escape and reach safety settled in the almost precipitous spot where the city now is; they built it small to begin with, and afterwards enlarged it, and later still extended its wall until the city reached *its present size*, owing to their gradual spreading out and increase in population. Among those who migrated to Ragusa are: Gregory, Arsaphius, Victorinus, Vitalius, Valentine the archdeacon, Valentine the father of Stephen the protospatharius. From their migration from Salona to Ragusa, it is 500 years till this day, which is the 7th indiction, the year 6457. In this same city lies St. Pancratius, in the church of St. Stephen, which is in the middle of this same city.

206 ὀλίγον Ba Be: ὀλίγων P ‖ 207 φθάσει edd. ἔρχεται Theoph. Cont. ‖ 208 οἰκεῖοι: ὑπηρέται Theoph. Cont. ‖ 211 αὐτοῦ σφαγῆς edd. ‖ γέγονεν: γένειεν V edd. ‖ 212 κατερχομένην: ἐρχομένην edd. ‖ 217 Ῥαούση P ‖ 218 post λέγεται add. δὲ Be ‖ 219 λαῦ: λαοῦ Migne ‖ δὲ om. Be ‖ 222 Ῥαουσαῖοι P ‖ 223 Πίταυρα: Ἐπίδαυρον coni. Bandurius ‖ 226 δὲ secl. Jenkins ‖ 229 δ' ἔχειν: δ' ἔχει Me δ' ἔχειν Ba Be ⟨τοῦ⟩ ὧδ' ἔχειν coni. Bekker τοῦ ἔχειν ⟨τὸ μέγεθος ὁ ἀρτίως ἔχει⟩ coni. Bury ‖ 232 Βικτωρῆνος P ‖ Βαλεντῖνος² Bandurius Be: Βανεντῖνος P mg. P ‖ 233/4 μετοίκησαν P ‖ 234 τὸ om. edd. ‖ φ´: τ´ coni. Mikoczi Šišić χ´ coni. Labuda ‖ ἰνδικτιῶνος edd. ‖ ζ´: ἑβδόμης edd. ‖ 235 τῷ αὐτῷ V edd.: τὸ αὐτὸ P ‖

"Οτι τοῦ 'Ασπαλάθου κάστρον, ὅπερ 'παλάτιον μικρόν' ἑρμηνεύεται,
ὁ βασιλεὺς Διοκλητιανὸς τοῦτο ἔκτισεν· εἶχεν δὲ αὐτὸ ὡς ἴδιον οἶκον,
καὶ αὐλὴν οἰκοδομήσας ἔνδοθεν καὶ παλάτια, ἐξ ὧν τὰ πλείονα κατελύθη-
σαν. Σώζεται δὲ μέχρι τοῦ νῦν ὀλίγα, ἐξ ὧν ἐστιν τὸ ἐπισκοπεῖον τοῦ240
κάστρου καὶ ὁ ναὸς τοῦ ἁγίου Δόμνου, ἐν ᾧ κατάκειται ὁ αὐτὸς ἅγιος
Δόμνος, ὅπερ ἦν κοιτὼν τοῦ αὐτοῦ βασιλέως Διοκλητιανοῦ. Ὑποκάτω
78ᵛP
138Be δὲ αὐτοῦ ὑπάρχουσιν εἰληματικαὶ καμάραι, αἵτινες | ὑπῆρχον | φυλακαί,
ἐν αἷς τοὺς παρ' αὐτοῦ βασανιζομένους ἁγίους ἐναπέκλειεν ἀπηνῶς.
'Απόκειται δὲ ἐν αὐτῷ τῷ κάστρῳ καὶ ὁ ἅγιος 'Αναστάσιος.   245

"Οτι τὸ τεῖχος τοῦ τοιούτου κάστρου οὔτε ἀπὸ βησσάλων ἐστὶν
ἐκτισμένον, οὔτε ἀπὸ ἐγχορήγου, ἀλλ' ἀπὸ λίθων τετραπεδίκων, ἐχόντων
εἰς μῆκος ἀνὰ ὀργυιᾶς μιᾶς, πολλάκις καὶ ἀνὰ δύο, καὶ τὸ πλάτος ἀνὰ
ὀργυιᾶς μιᾶς, οἵτινές εἰσιν συνηρμοσμένοι καὶ συνδεδεμένοι εἰς ἀλλήλους
μετὰ σιδήρων ἐν μολύβδῳ ἐγχυλιασμένων. Ἵστανται δὲ εἰς τὸ τοιοῦτον250
κάστρον καὶ κίονες πυκνοί, ἔχοντες ἐπάνω κοσμήτας, ἐν οἷς ἔμελλεν
ὁ αὐτὸς βασιλεὺς Διοκλητιανὸς εἰλημματικὰς ἐγεῖραι καμάρας, καὶ
79ʳP σκεπάσαι τὸ κάστρον ὅλον, καὶ ποιῆ|σαι τὰ παλάτια αὐτοῦ καὶ πάντα
τὰ οἰκήματα τοῦ κάστρου ἐπάνω τῶν εἰλημάτων ἐκείνων διώροφα καὶ
τριώροφα, ὥστε καὶ ὀλίγον ἐκ τοῦ αὐτοῦ κάστρου ἐσκέπασεν. Τοῦ δὲ255
τοιούτου κάστρου τὸ τεῖχος οὔτε περίπατον ἔχει, οὔτε προμαχῶνας,
ἀλλὰ τοίχους μόνους ὑψηλοὺς καὶ τοξικὰς φωταγωγούς.

"Οτι τὸ κάστρον τὸ Τετραγγούριν νησίον ἐστὶν μικρὸν ἐν τῇ θαλάσσῃ,
ἔχον καὶ τράχηλον ἕως τῆς γῆς στενώτατον δίκην γεφυρίου, ἐν ᾧ
διέρχονται οἱ κατοικοῦντες εἰς τὸ αὐτὸ κάστρον. Τετραγγούριν δὲ καλεῖ-260
ται διὰ τὸ εἶναι αὐτὸ μικρὸν δίκην ἀγγουρίου. 'Εν δὲ τῷ αὐτῷ κάστρῳ
ἀπόκειται ὁ ἅγιος μάρτυς Λαυρέντιος, ὁ ἀρχιδιάκων.

139Be   "Οτι τὸ κάστρον τῶν Δεκατέρων ἑρμηνεύεται τῇ 'Ρωμαίων
79ᵛP διαλέκτῳ 'ἐστε|νωμένον καὶ πεπνιγμένον', διότι εἰσέρχεται ἡ θάλασσα
ὥσπερ γλῶσσα ἐστενωμένη μέχρι τῶν ιε' ⟨ἢ⟩ καὶ κ' μιλίων, καὶ εἰς τὸ τῆς265
θαλάσσης συμπλήρωμά ἐστιν τὸ κάστρον. Ἔχει δὲ τὸ τοιοῦτον κάστρον
κύκλῳ αὐτοῦ ὄρη ὑψηλά, ὥστε μόνῳ τῷ καλοκαιρίῳ βλέπειν τὸν ἥλιον
διὰ τὸ μεσουρανεῖν, τῷ δὲ χειμῶνι οὐδαμῶς. 'Εν δὲ τῷ αὐτῷ κάστρῳ
κεῖται ὁ ἅγιος Τρύφων ἀκέραιος πᾶσαν νόσον ἰώμενος, μάλιστα τοὺς
ὑπὸ πνευμάτων ἀκαθάρτων τυραννουμένους· ὁ δὲ ναὸς αὐτοῦ ἐστιν270
εἰλημματικός.

"Οτι τὸ κάστρον τῶν Διαδώρων καλεῖται τῇ 'Ρωμαίων διαλέκτῳ
'ἰὰμ ἔρα', ὅπερ ἑρμηνεύεται 'ἀπάρτι ἦτον'· δηλονότι ὅτε ἡ 'Ρώμη ἐκτίσθη,

---

V 237 τοῦ: τὸ Be   ⟨τὸ⟩ τοῦ Bury || 243 ἠλιματικαὶ P   εἰληματικαὶ
Meursius Ba Be || 245 *post* δὲ add. καὶ edd. || αὐτῷ V edd.: αὐτὸ P ||

29

The city of Spalato, which means 'little palace', was founded by the emperor Diocletian; he made it his own dwelling-place, and built within it a court and a palace, most part of which has been destroyed. But a few things remain to this day, e. g. the episcopal residence of the city and the church of St. Domnus, in which lies St. Domnus himself, and which was the resting-place of the same emperor Diocletian. Beneath it are arching vaults, which used to be prisons, in which he cruelly confined the saints whom he tormented. St. Anastasius also lies in this city.

The defence-wall of this city is constructed neither of bricks nor of concrete, but of ashlar blocks, one and often two fathoms in length by a fathom across, and these are fitted and joined to one another by iron cramps puddled into molten lead. In this city also stand close rows of columns, with entablatures above, on which this same emperor Diocletian proposed to erect arching vaults and to cover over the city throughout, and to build his palace and all the living-quarters of the city on the top of those vaults, to a height of two and three stories, so that they covered little *ground-space* in the same city. The defence-wall of this city has neither rampart nor bulwarks, but only lofty walls and arrow-slits.

The city of Tetrangourin is a little island in the sea, with a very narrow neck reaching to the land like a bridge, along which the inhabitants pass to the same city; and it is called Tetrangourin because it is *long-shaped* like a cucumber. In this same city lies the holy martyr Lawrence the archdeacon.

The city of Decatera means in the language of the Romans 'contracted and strangled', because the sea enters like a contracted tongue for 15 *or* 20 miles, and the city is on this marine appendix. This city has high mountains in a circle about it, so that the sun can be seen only in summer, because it is then in mid-heaven, and in winter it cannot be seen at all. In the same city lies St. Tryphon entire, who heals every disease, especially those who are tormented by unclean spirits; his church is domed.

The city of Diadora is called in the language of the Romans 'iam era', which means, 'it was already': that is to say, when Rome was founded,

246 βισάλων P ‖ 247 ἐγχωρήγου P: ἐγχωρύγου coni. Kukules ‖ τετραπεδίκων: τετραπέδων coni. Laskin ‖ 248 ὀργυᾶς P ‖ μιᾶς: α′ V edd. ‖ 249 ὀργυᾶς P ‖ 250 μολίβδω P ‖ ἐγχυλιασμένων edd.: ἐγχυλιασμένα P ‖ post δὲ add. καὶ edd. ‖ 251 κοσμίτας P ‖ 252 εἰλημματικὰς Meursius Ba Be ‖ 254 εἰλημάτων V edd. ‖ διόροφα P ‖ 255 τριόροφα P ‖ καὶ: μὴ edd. ‖ ὀλίγον edd.: ὀλίγων P ‖ 258 Τετραγγούριν: τε Τραγγουρίον coni. Šafarik   Τραγούριον mg. P¹   Τράγουρις mg. V² ‖ μικρόν ἐστι νησίον V edd. ‖ 261 μικρόν: μακρὸν coni. Jenkins ‖ τῷ αὐτῷ κάστρῳ V edd.: τὸ αὐτὸ κάστρον P ‖ 262 μάρτυρ edd. ‖ 263 Δεκατέρων: Κάτερα mg. V² ‖ 264 πεπνιγμένον coni. Jenkins: πεπληγμένον P edd. ‖ 265 ιε′: δεκαπέντε edd. ‖ ἢ addendum coni. Bury ‖ κ′: εἴκοσι edd. ‖ 267 κύκλον V edd. ‖ 268 τῷ αὐτῷ V edd.: τὸ αὐτὸ P ‖ 269 ἀκέραιος corr. Kukules Kyriakides: ἀκεραίως Meursius Ba Be: ἀκαίρεως P ‖ 271 ἡλιματικῶς P: εἰλημματικὸς V edd. ‖ 272 'Ρωμαίων V edd.: ῥΔ′ P ‖ 273 ἰὰμ ἔρα V Me   ἡαμερά P: ἰὰμ ἔρατ Meursius Ba Be ‖

138

80ʳP προεκτισμένον ἦν τὸ τοιοῦτον κάστρον· ἔστιν δὲ τὸ κά|στρον μέγα.
Ἡ δὲ κοινὴ συνήθεια καλεῖ αὐτὸ Διάδωρα. Ἐν δὲ τῷ αὐτῷ κάστρῳ275
κεῖται ἐν σαρκὶ ἡ ἁγία ᾿Αναστασία, ἡ παρθένος, θυγάτηρ γεγονυῖα
Εὐσταθίου τοῦ κατὰ τὸν καιρὸν ἐκεῖνον βασιλεύσαντος, καὶ ὁ ἅγιος
Χρυσόγονος μοναχὸς καὶ μάρτυς καὶ ἡ ἁγία ἅλυσις αὐτοῦ. Ὁ δὲ ναὸς
τῆς ἁγίας ᾿Αναστασίας ἐστὶν δρομικός, ὅμοιος ⟨τῷ⟩ τῶν Χαλκοπρατείων
ναῷ, μετὰ κιόνων πρασίνων καὶ λευκῶν, ὅλος εἰκονισμένος ἐξ ὑλογραφίας280
ἀρχαίας· ὁ δὲ πάτος αὐτοῦ ἐστιν ἀπὸ συγκοπῆς θαυμαστῆς. Ἔστιν
δὲ καὶ ἕτερος ναὸς πλησίον αὐτοῦ εἰληματικός, ἡ ῾Αγία Τριάς, καὶ
140Be ἐπάνω τοῦ ναοῦ αὐ|τοῦ πάλιν ἕτερος ναὸς δίκην κατηχουμένων, καὶ
80ᵛP αὐτὸς εἰληματικός, εἰς ὃν | καὶ ἀνέρχονται διὰ κοχλίου.

Ὅτι εἰσὶν νησία ὑπὸ τὴν ἐπικράτειαν τῆς Δελματίας μέχρι Βενε-285
βενδοῦ πυκνὰ καὶ πάμπολλα, ὥστε μηδέποτε φοβεῖσθαι ἐκεῖσε κλύδωνα
τὰ πλοῖα. Ἐξ αὐτῶν τῶν νησίων ἐστὶν τὸ κάστρον ἡ Βέκλα, καὶ εἰς
ἕτερον νησίον ἡ Ἄρβη, καὶ εἰς ἕτερον νησίον τὰ Ὄψαρα, καὶ εἰς ἕτερον
νησίον τὸ Λουμβρικάτον, ἅτινα κατοικοῦνται μέχρι τοῦ νῦν. Τὰ δὲ
λοιπὰ εἰσιν ἀοίκητα, ἔχοντα ἐρημόκαστρα, ὧν τὰ ὀνόματά εἰσιν οὕτως·290
Καταυτρεβενώ, Πιζούχ, Σελβώ, Σκερδά, ᾿Αλωήπ, Σκηρδάκισσα, Πυρό-
τιμα, Μελετᾶ, ᾿Εστιουνὴζ καὶ ἕτερα πάμπολλα, ὧν τὰ ὀνόματα οὐ νοοῦν-
81ʳP ται. Τὰ δὲ λοιπὰ κάστρα, τὰ ὄντα εἰς τὴν ξηρὰν τοῦ θέματος | καὶ κρατη-
θέντα παρὰ τῶν εἰρημένων Σκλάβων, ἀοίκητα καὶ ἔρημα ἵστανται,
μηδενὸς κατοικοῦντος ἐν αὐτοῖς. 295

30. Δ ι ή γ η σ ι ς π ε ρ ὶ τ ο ῦ θ έ μ α τ ο ς Δ ε λ μ α τ ί α ς.

Εἰ πᾶσιν ἡ γνῶσις καλόν, καὶ ἡμεῖς ἄρα τῶν πραγμάτων τὴν
γνῶσιν καταλαμβάνοντες οὐ πόρρω τούτου γινόμεθα. Ὅθεν καὶ πᾶσι
φανερὰν ποιοῦμεν τῶν μεθ' ἡμᾶς πῆ μὲν τούτων τὴν δήλωσιν, πῆ δὲ
ἑτέρων ἀξιολόγων τινῶν, ἵνα καὶ διπλοῦν ἐπακολουθῇ τὸ καλόν.   5
141Be Τοῖς οὖν καὶ τῆς Δελματίας | τὴν παράληψιν ζητοῦσιν, ὅπως
ἐλήφθη παρὰ τῶν Σκλαβικῶν ἐθνῶν, ἐντεῦθεν ἔστι μαθεῖν, ἀλλὰ πρότερον τὴν θέσιν αὐτῆς διηγητέον. Ἐκ παλαιοῦ τοίνυν ἡ Δελματία τὴν

F   30. 2 πᾶσιν — καλόν: cf. Prov. 1, 7; cf. De Cer. (ed. Bonn) 456, 4—5.

V 275 τῷ αὐτῷ V edd.: τὸ αὐτὸ P ‖ 277 post Εὐσταθίου aliquid excidisse
coni. Bury ‖ 279 ⟨τῷ⟩ τῶν coni. Bekker: τῶν P: τῷ V edd. ‖ Χαλκοπρατίων P ‖
280 ὑλογραφίας: στηλογραφίας coni. Meursius ‖ 282 εἰληματικῶς P: εἰλημα-
τικὸς edd. ‖ 284 εἰληματικῶς P: εἰλημᾶτικός V edd. ‖ κοχλίου coni.
Kukules: κοχλίας P κοχλείας V edd. ‖ 285 Ὅτι V edd.: ["Ο]τι P ‖ 286
κλύδωνα ἐκεῖσε edd. ‖ 288 τὰ: ἡ edd. ‖ 289 Λουμβρίκατον mg. V² ‖

29, 30

this city had already been founded before it; it is a big city. Vulgar usage gives it the name Diadora. In the same city lies in the flesh St. Anastasia, the virgin, daughter of Eustathius, who was on the throne at that time; and St. Chrysogonus, monk and martyr, and his holy chain. The church of St. Anastasia is a basilica like the church of the Chalcopratia, with green and white columns, and all decorated with encaustic pictures in the antique style; its floor is of wonderful mosaic. Near it is another church, a domed one, Holy Trinity, and above this church again is another church, like a triforium, domed also, into which they mount by a spiral staircase.

Under the control of Dalmatia is a close-set and very numerous archipelago, extending as far as Beneventum, so that ships never fear to be overwhelmed in those parts. One of these islands is the city of Vekla, and on another island Arbe, and on another island Opsara, and on another island Lumbricaton, and these are still inhabited. The rest are uninhabited and have upon them deserted cities, of which the names are as follows: Katautrebeno, Pizouch, Selbo, Skerda, Aloëp, Skirdakissa, Pyrotima, Meleta, Estiounez, and very many others of which the names are not intelligible. The remaining cities, on the mainland of the province, which were captured by the said Slavs, now stand uninhabited and deserted, and nobody lives in them.

30. Story of the province of Dalmatia.

If knowledge be a good thing for all, then we too are approaching it by arriving at the knowledge of events. For this reason we are giving, for the benefit of all who come after us, a plain account both of these matters and of certain others worthy of attention, so that the resulting good may be twofold.

They, then, who are inquiring into the taking of Dalmatia also, how it was taken by the nations of the Slavs, may learn of it from what follows; but first of all its geographical position must be told. In olden times, there-

---

290 ἔχοντα V edd.: ἔχων[τα] P ‖ 291 Καταυτρεβενῶ P Κατανγρεβενώ seu Καταυνγρεβενώ coni. Skok ‖ Πιζύχ edd. Γιζύχ coni. Rački ‖ Σελβῶ P ‖ Σκιρδάκισσα V edd. Σκιρδὰ Κίσσα coni. Šafarik ‖ 292 Μελετὰ V edd. ‖ Ἐστιουνὴζ: Σεστρουνήζ (= Σεστρουνήσιον seu Σεστρουν-νησίον?) coni. Rački Grot Ἐστρουνήζ coni. Skok.

30. 3 γινόμεθα (coni. etiam Bekker Bury): γινώμεθα V edd. ‖ 4 φανερὰν Be: φανερὰ P ‖ 5 τινῶν ἀξιολόγων edd. ‖ καὶ om. V edd. ‖ ἐπανακολουθῇ edd. ‖ 7 Σκλαβι{νι}κῶν Migne ‖ 8 ante τοίνυν add. μὲν edd. ‖

140

30

81ᵛP ἀρχὴν μὲν εἶχεν | ἀπὸ τῶν συνόρων Δυρραχίου, ἤγουν ἀπὸ Ἀντιβάρεως, καὶ παρετείνετο μὲν μέχρι τῶν τῆς Ἰστρίας ὁρῶν, ἐπλατύνετο δὲ μέχρι 10 τοῦ Δανουβίου ποταμοῦ. Ἦν δὲ ἅπασα ἡ τοιαύτη περίχωρος ὑπὸ τὴν Ῥωμαίων ἀρχήν, καὶ ἐνδοξότερον τῶν ἄλλων ἑσπερίων θεμάτων τὸ τοιοῦτον θέμα ἐτύγχανε, πλὴν παρελήφθη παρὰ τῶν Σκλαβικῶν ἐθνῶν τρόπῳ τοιῷδε. Κάστρον ἐστὶν πλησίον Ἀσπαλάθου, ὃ Σαλῶνα λέγεται, ἔργον Διοκλητιανοῦ τοῦ βασιλέως, ἀλλ' ἡ μὲν Ἀσπάλαθος καὶ αὐτὴ παρὰ 15 Διοκλητιανοῦ ἐκτίσθη, καὶ τὰ αὐτοῦ βασιλικὰ ἐκεῖσε ἐτύγχανον, εἰς 82ʳP δὲ Σαλῶνα κατῴκουν οἵ τε μεγιστᾶνες αὐτοῦ καὶ τῶν ὄχλων ἱ|κανοί. Ὑπῆρχε δὲ τὸ τοιοῦτον κάστρον κεφαλὴ πάσης τῆς Δελματίας. Ἠθροίζοντο οὖν ἀνὰ πᾶν ἔτος ἐκ τῶν λοιπῶν κάστρων Δελματίας στρατιῶται ἔφιπποι, καὶ ἀπεστέλλοντο ἀπὸ Σαλῶνος μέχρι τῶν χιλίων, καὶ ἐφύλαττον 20 εἰς τὸν Δανούβιν ποταμὸν ἕνεκεν τῶν Ἀβάρων. Οἱ γὰρ Ἄβαρεις ἐκεῖθεν τοῦ Δανουβίου ποταμοῦ τὰς διατριβὰς ἐποιοῦντο, ἔνθα ἀρτίως εἰσὶν οἱ Τοῦρκοι νομάδα βίον ζῶντες. Ἀπερχόμενοι δὲ οἱ Δελματίας κατ' ἔτος ἔβλεπον πολλάκις ἐκεῖθεν τοῦ ποταμοῦ τά τε κτήνη καὶ τοὺς ἀνθρώ-
142Be πους. Ἔδοξεν οὖν αὐτοῖς κατά τινα χρόνον διαπερᾶσαι | καὶ ἐρευνῆσαι, 25
82ᵛP τίνες εἰσὶν οἱ ἐκεῖσε τὴν δίαιταν ἔχοντες. Πε|ράσαντες οὖν εὗρον τὰς γυναῖκας τῶν Ἀβάρων καὶ τὰ παιδία μόνα, τοὺς ἄνδρας δὲ καὶ τὴν ἀκμάζουσαν ἡλικίαν ἐν ταξιδίῳ. Ἄφνω οὖν ἐπιπεσόντες ἠχμαλώτευσαν αὐτούς, καὶ ὑπέστρεψαν ἀταλαιπώρως, ἀποκομίσαντες τὴν τοιαύτην πραῖδαν εἰς Σαλῶνα. Ὡς οὖν ὑπέστρεψαν οἱ Ἄβαρεις ἐκ τοῦ ταξιδίου 30 καὶ τὸ γενόμενον, ἀφ' ὧν ἔπαθον, ἔμαθον, ἐταράχθησαν μέν, ἠγνόουν δέ, ὁπόθεν αὐτοῖς ἡ τοιαύτη πληγὴ προσεγένετο. Ἔδοξεν οὖν παραφυλάξαι αὐτοῖς τὸν καιρὸν καὶ μαθεῖν τὸ πᾶν ἐξ αὐτοῦ. Ἐπεὶ οὖν κατὰ τὸ σύνηθες αὖθις οἱ ταξεῶται ἀπεστάλησαν ἀπὸ Σαλῶνος, ἦσαν δὲ οὐκ ἐκεῖνοι,
83ʳP ἀλλ' ἕτεροι, ταὐτὰ ἐκείνοις | καὶ οὗτοι κατὰ βουλὰς ἔθεντο. Διεπέρασαν 35 οὖν κατ' αὐτῶν, ἐντυχόντες δὲ αὐτοῖς συνηγμένοις ὁμοῦ, οὐχ, ὡς τὸ πρότερον, ἐσκορπισμένοις, οὐ μόνον οὐδὲν οὐκ ἐποίησαν, ἀλλὰ καὶ τὰ πάντων δεινότατα ἔπαθον. Οἱ μὲν γὰρ αὐτῶν ἐσφάγησαν, οἱ δὲ λοιποὶ ἐχειρώθησαν ζῶντες, καὶ οὐδεὶς ἐκείνων τῶν χειρῶν ἐξέφυγεν. Ἐξετάσαντες δὲ αὐτούς, τίνες τε καὶ ὅθεν εἰσίν, καὶ ἀναμαθόντες, ὅτι ἐξ αὐτῶν ἔπαθον 40 τὴν εἰρημένην πληγήν, ἔτι δὲ καὶ περὶ τῆς ποιότητος τοῦ τόπου αὐτῶν ἐρευνήσαντες, καὶ ὅσον ἐξ ἀκοῆς ἀρεσθέντες, ἐκράτησαν τοὺς ζῶντας δεσμίους, καὶ ἐνεδύσαντο τὰ ἱμάτια αὐτῶν, καθὰ ἐκεῖνοι, καὶ δὴ τοὺς

V 10 Ἰστρίας Pˣ   V¹ edd.: ἱστορίας P V ‖ 13 Σκλαβινικῶν V edd. ‖ 14 Σαλῶνα edd.: Σάλωνα P ‖ 15 τοῦ om. V edd. ‖ 17 Σαλῶνα (coni. etiam Bury): Σαλῶναν Ba Be ‖ κατῴκουν V edd.: κατοίκουν P ‖ τε om. edd. ‖ μεγιστάνες P ‖ ἱκακανοί P   ‖ 19 ante Δελματίας add. τῆς V edd. ‖ 20 post ἀπὸ add.

30

fore, Dalmatia used to start at the confines of Dyrrachium, or Antibari, and used to extend as far as the mountains of Istria, and spread out as far as the river Danube. All this area was under the rule of the Romans, and this province was the most illustrious of all the provinces of the west; however, it was taken by the nations of the Slavs in the following manner. Near Spalato is a city called Salona, built by the emperor Diocletian; Spalato itself was also built by Diocletian, and his palace was there, but at Salona dwelt his nobles and large numbers of the common folk. This city was the head of all Dalmatia. Now, every year a force of cavalry from the other cities of Dalmatia used to collect at, and be despatched from Salona, to the number of a thousand, and they would keep guard on the river Danube, on account of the Avars. For the Avars had their haunts on the far side of the river Danube, where now are the Turks, and led a nomad life. The men of Dalmatia who went there every year would often see the beasts and men on the far side of the river. On one occasion, therefore, they decided to cross over and investigate who they were that had their abode there. So they crossed, and found only the women and children of the Avars, the men and youths being on a military expedition. Falling suddenly upon them, therefore, they made them prisoner, and returned unmolested, carrying off this booty to Salona. Now when the Avars came back from their military expedition and learnt from their losses what had happened, they were confounded, but know not from what quarter this blow had come upon them. They therefore decided to bide their time and in this way to discover the whole. And so, when according to custom the garrison was once more dispatched from Salona, not the same men as before but others, they too decided to do what their predecessors had done. So they crossed over against them, but finding them massed together, not scattered abroad as on the previous occasion, not merely did they achieve nothing but actually suffered the most frightful reverse. For some of them were slain, and the remainder taken alive, and not one escaped the hand of *the enemy. The latter* examined them as to who they were and whence they came, and having learnt that it was from them that they had suffered the blow aforesaid, and having moreover found out by enquiry the nature of their homeland and taken a fancy to it as far as they might from hearsay, they held the survivors captive and dressed themselves up in their clothes, just as the others *had worn them*, and then, mounting the horses and *taking*

τὴν Me   *add.* τῆς Ba Be ‖ Σαλῶνα V Me ‖ χιλίων V edd.: ͵α P ‖
21 Δανουβίου edd. ‖ ἔνεκα edd. ‖ "Αβαρεις V Me Ba: 'Αβάρεις Be Migne
"Αβαρης Pˣ 'Αβάρης P "Αβαροι *mg.* P⁸ ‖ 23 Τούρκοι P ‖ 28 ἐπιπέσοντες
edd. ‖ 30 "Αβαρες edd. 'Αβάρεις Migne ‖ 32/3 αὐτοῖς παραφυλάξαι edd. ‖
35 ταὐτὰ Be: ταῦτα P ‖ ἐκείνοις edd.: ἐκείνοι P ‖ 37 οὐκ *secl.* Be Bury ‖
38 αὐτῶν V edd.: αὐτοῖς P ‖ 40 τε *om.* edd. ‖ 42 ἀρεσθέντες: ἐρασθέντες
V edd. ‖

142

30

83ᵛP | ἵππους ἀναβάντες, ⟨λαβόντες⟩ ἐπὶ χεῖρας τά τε φλάμμουλα καὶ τὰ
143Be λοιπὰ σημεῖα, ἃ ἐπεφέροντο μετ' αὐτῶν, | ἀπῆραν πάντες φοσσατικῶς 45
καὶ κατὰ τῆς Σαλῶνος ὥρμησαν. Ὡς οὖν καὶ τὸν καιρὸν ἔμαθον ζητήσαν-
τες, καθ' ὃν οἱ ταξεῶται ἐκ τοῦ Δανουβίου ὑπέστρεφον (ἦν δὲ τὸ μέγα
καὶ ἅγιον σάββατον), ἦλθον καὶ κατὰ τὴν αὐτὴν ἡμέραν. Καὶ τὸ μὲν
πλῆθος, ὅτε δήπου πλησίον ἐγένοντο, τοῦ φοσσάτου ἀπεκρύβη, μέχρι
δὲ τῶν χιλίων, οἵτινες τούς τε ἵππους καὶ τὰς στολὰς εἰς ἀπάτην ἐκέκτηντο 50
τῶν Δελματινῶν, ἐξήλασαν. Ἀναγνωρίσαντες δὲ οἱ τοῦ κάστρου τά τε
σημεῖα καὶ τὴν ἀμφίασιν αὐτῶν, ἀλλὰ καὶ τὴν ἡμέραν, ὡς ἔθους ὄντος
84ʳP αὐτοῖς | τοῦ ὑποστρέφειν ἐν αὐτῇ, ἤνοιξαν τὰς πόρτας, καὶ ὑπεδέξαντο
αὐτοὺς μετὰ περιχαρείας. Ἐκεῖνοι δὲ ἅμα τῷ εἰσελθεῖν τάς τε πόρτας
ἐκράτησαν, καὶ δήλην διὰ σημείου τὴν πρᾶξιν τῷ φοσσάτῳ πεποιηκότες, 55
συνεισδραμεῖν καὶ συνεισελθεῖν παρεσκεύασαν. Κατέσφαξαν οὖν πάντας
τοὺς τῆς πόλεως, καὶ ἔκτοτε κατεκράτησαν πᾶσαν τὴν χώραν Δελματίας,
καὶ κατεσκήνωσαν ἐν αὐτῇ. Μόνα δὲ τὰ πρὸς θάλασσαν πολίχνια οὐ
συνέδωκαν αὐτοῖς, ἀλλὰ κατείχοντο παρὰ τῶν Ῥωμαίων διὰ τὸ εἶναι
τὸν πόρον τῆς ζωῆς αὐτῶν ἐκ τῆς θαλάσσης. Ἰδόντες οὖν οἱ Ἄβαρεις 60
καλλίστην οὖσαν τὴν τοιαύτην γῆν, κατεσκήνωσαν ἐν αὐτῇ. Οἱ δὲ Χρω-
84ᵛP βάτοι κα|τῴκουν τηνικαῦτα ἐκεῖθεν Βαγιβαρείας, ἔνθα εἰσὶν ἀρτίως
οἱ Βελοχρωβάτοι. Μία δὲ γενεὰ διαχωρισθεῖσα ἐξ αὐτῶν, ἤγουν ἀδελφοὶ
πέντε, ὅ τε Κλουκᾶς καὶ ὁ Λόβελος καὶ ὁ Κοσέντζης καὶ ὁ Μουχλὼ καὶ
144Be ὁ Χρωβάτος καὶ ἀδελφαὶ δύο, ἡ Τουγὰ καὶ ἡ Βουγά, μετὰ | τοῦ λαοῦ 65
αὐτῶν ἦλθον εἰς Δελματίαν, καὶ εὗρον τοὺς Ἄβαρεις κατέχοντας τὴν
τοιαύτην γῆν. Ἐπί τινας οὖν χρόνους πολεμοῦντες ἀλλήλους, ὑπερίσχυσαν
οἱ Χρωβάτοι, καὶ τοὺς μὲν τῶν Ἀβάρων κατέσφαξαν, τοὺς δὲ λοιποὺς
ὑποταγῆναι κατηνάγκασαν. Ἔκτοτε οὖν κατεκρατήθη ἡ τοιαύτη χώρα
παρὰ τῶν Χρωβάτων, καὶ εἰσὶν ἀκμὴν ἐν Χρωβατίᾳ ἐκ {τοὺς} τῶν Ἀβά- 70
85ʳP ρων, καὶ γινώσκονται Ἄβαρεις | ὄντες. Οἱ δὲ λοιποὶ Χρωβάτοι ἔμειναν
πρὸς Φραγγίαν, καὶ λέγονται ἀρτίως Βελοχρωβάτοι, ἤγουν ἄσπροι
Χρωβάτοι, ἔχοντες ἴδιον ἄρχοντα· ὑπόκεινται δὲ Ὄτῳ, τῷ μεγάλῳ
ῥηγὶ Φραγγίας, τῆς καὶ Σαξίας, καὶ ἀβάπτιστοι τυγχάνουσιν, συμπενθε-
ρίας μετὰ τοὺς Τούρκους καὶ ἀγάπας ἔχοντες. Ἀπὸ δὲ τῶν Χρωβάτων, τῶν 75
ἐλθόντων ἐν Δελματίᾳ, διεχωρίσθη μέρος τι, καὶ ἐκράτησεν τὸ Ἰλλυρικὸν
καὶ τὴν Παννονίαν· εἶχον δὲ καὶ αὐτοὶ ἄρχοντα αὐτεξούσιον, διαπεμπόμε-
νον καὶ μόνον πρὸς τὸν ἄρχοντα Χρωβατίας κατὰ φιλίαν. Μέχρι δὲ
χρόνων τινῶν ὑπετάσσοντο καὶ οἱ ἐν Δελματίᾳ ὄντες Χρωβάτοι τοῖς Φράγ-

V 44 λαβόντες add. Moravcsik   coni. Bekker || φλάμουλα P || 45 φοσατικῶς
P || 46 ὅρμισαν P || 50 χιλίων edd.: ͵α P || 51 Δελματινῶν edd.: Δαλματινῶν
P || 54 τῷ scr. Moravcsik: τὸ P   τοῦ V edd. || 55 τῷ φοσσάτῳ V edd.:

ff in military array and made
for Salona. And since they had learnt by enquiry also the time at which
the garrison was wont to return from the Danube (which was the Great
and Holy Saturday), they themselves arrived on that same day. When
they got near, the bulk of the army was placed in concealment, but up to
a thousand of them, those who, to play the trick, had acquired the horses
and uniforms of the Dalmatians, rode out in front. Those in the city, recogni-
zing their insignia and dress, and also the day, for upon this day it was
customary for them to return, opened the gates and received them with
delight. But they, as soon as they were inside, seized the gates and, signal-
ling their exploit to the army, gave it the cue to run in and enter with them.
And so they put to the sword all in the city and thereafter made themselves masters of all the country of Dalmatia and settled down in it. Only
the townships on the coast held out against them, and continued to be in
the hands of the Romans, because they obtained their livelihood from the
sea. The Avars, then, seeing this land to be most fair, settled down in it.
But the Croats at that time were dwelling beyond Bavaria, where the Belocroats are now. From them split off a family of five brothers, Kloukas and
Lobelos and Kosentzis and Mouchlo and Chrobatos, and two sisters, Touga
and Bouga, who came with their folk to Dalmatia and found the Avars in
possession of that land. After they had fought one another for some years,
the Croats prevailed and killed some of the Avars and the remainder they
compelled to be subject to them. And so from that time this land was possessed by the Croats, and there are still in Croatia some who are of Avar
descent and are recognized as Avars. The rest of the Croats stayed over
against Francia, and are now called Belocroats, that is, white Croats, and
have their own prince; they are subject to Otto, the great king of Francia,
or Saxony, and are unbaptized, and intermarry and are friendly with the
Turks. From the Croats who came to Dalmatia a part split off and possessed
themselves of Illyricum and Pannonia; they too had an independent prince,
who used to maintain friendly contact, though through envoys only, with
the prince of Croatia. For a number of years the Croats of Dalmatia also

τὸ φοσσάτο P ‖ 60 Ἄβαρεις V Me Ba: Ἄβαρης P Ἀβάρεις Be Migne ‖
62 κατῴκουν edd.: κατοίκουν P ‖ Βαγιβαρείας: Βαβιγαρείας coni. Pavić ‖ 63
Βελοχρωβάτοι edd.: Βελαχρωβάτοι P ‖ μιὰ P ‖ 64 πέντε V edd.: ε′ P ‖
Κλουκὰς P ‖ Μουχλῶ P ‖ 65 Χρωβάτος (coni. etiam Bury): Χρώβατος edd. ‖
δύο V edd.: β′ P ‖ Τουγᾶ P: Τοῦγα V edd. ‖ Βοῦγα edd. ‖ 66 Ἀβάρεις Be ‖ 67
ἀλλήλοις V edd. ‖ 68 κατέσφαξαν] litteras κατ in ras. scr. P¹ ‖ 70 ἐκ: ⟨τινες⟩ ἐκ
coni. Bury ‖ τοὺς secl. Migne Bury: τούτων coni. Dujčev Kyriakides ‖ 71
Ἀβάρεις Be ‖ 73 ante ἴδιον add. τὸν edd. ‖ 74 ῥιγὶ P ‖ τῆς: τε coni. Bandurius ‖
74/5 συμπεμθερίας P ‖ 75 τῶν¹ om. V edd. ‖ 77 Παννονίαν Ba Be: Παπωνίαν P
mg. P⁸ ‖ 78 καὶ μόνον om. Be ‖

30

85ᵛP γοις, καθώς καὶ πρότερον ἐν τῇ χώρᾳ αὐτῶν· τοσοῦτον δὲ ἐσκλήρύ|νοντο 80
οἱ Φράγγοι πρὸς αὐτούς, ὅτι τὰ ὑπομάσθια τῶν Χρωβάτων φονεύοντες
προσέρριπτον αὐτὰ σκύλαξιν. Μὴ δυνάμενοι δὲ οἱ Χρωβάτοι ταῦτα
παρὰ τῶν Φράγγων ὑφίστασθαι, διέστησαν ἀπ' αὐτῶν, φονεύσαντες
καὶ οὓς εἶχον ἄρχοντας ἐξ αὐτῶν. Ὅθεν ἐστράτευσαν κατ' αὐτῶν
ἀπὸ Φραγγίας φοσσᾶτον μέγα, καὶ ἐπὶ ἑπτὰ χρόνους πολεμήσαντες 85
145Be ἀλλήλοις, ὀψὲ καὶ μόγις ὑπερί|σχυσαν οἱ Χρωβάτοι, καὶ ἀνεῖλον τοὺς
Φράγγους πάντας καὶ τὸν ἄρχοντα αὐτῶν Κοτζίλιν καλούμενον. Ἔκτοτε
δὲ μείναντες αὐτοδέσποτοι καὶ αὐτόνομοι, ἐξητήσαντο τὸ ἅγιον βάπτισμα
παρὰ τοῦ Ῥώμης, καὶ ἀπεστάλησαν ἐπίσκοποι, καὶ ἐβάπτισαν αὐτοὺς
86ʳP ἐπὶ Πορίνου, τοῦ ἄρχοντος αὐτῶν. | Διεμερίσθη οὖν ἡ χώρα αὐτῶν εἰς 90
ζουπανίας ια', ἤγουν ἡ Χλεβίανα, ἡ Τζένζηνα, τὰ Ἥμοτα, ἡ Πλέβα,
ἡ Πεσέντα, ἡ Παραθαλασσία, ἡ Βρεβέρη, ἡ Νόνα, ἡ Τνήνα, ἡ Σίδραγα,
ἡ Νίνα· καὶ ὁ βοάνος αὐτῶν κρατεῖ τὴν Κρίβασαν, τὴν Λίτζαν καὶ τὴν
Γουτζησκά. Καὶ ἡ μὲν εἰρημένη Χρωβατία, ἀλλὰ καὶ αἱ λοιπαὶ Σκλαβη-
νίαι διάκεινται οὕτως· ἡ δὲ Διόκλεια πλησιάζει πρὸς τὰ καστέλλια τοῦ 95
Δυρραχίου, ἤγουν πρὸς τὸν Ἐλισσὸν καὶ πρὸς τὸ Ἑλκύνιον καὶ τὴν
Ἀντίβαριν, καὶ ἔρχεται μέχρι τῶν Δεκατέρων, πρὸς τὰ ὀρεινὰ δὲ πλησιάζει τῇ Σερβλίᾳ. Ἀπὸ δὲ τοῦ κάστρου τῶν Δεκατέρων ἄρχεται ἡ ἀρχοντία
86ᵛP Τερβουνίας, καὶ παρεκτείνεται μέχρι τοῦ Ῥαουσίου, πρὸς δὲ | τὰ ὀρεινὰ
αὐτῆς πλησιάζει τῇ Σερβλίᾳ. Ἀπὸ δὲ τοῦ Ῥαουσίου ἄρχεται ἡ ἀρχοντία 100
τῶν Ζαχλούμων, καὶ παρεκτείνεται μέχρι τοῦ Ὀροντίου ποταμοῦ,
καὶ πρὸς μὲν τὴν παραθαλασσίαν πλησιάζει τοῖς Παγανοῖς, πρὸς δὲ
τὰ ὀρεινὰ εἰς ἄρκτον μὲν πλησιάζει τοῖς Χρωβάτοις, εἰς κεφαλὴν δὲ τῇ
Σερβλίᾳ. Ἀπὸ δὲ τοῦ Ὀροντίου ποταμοῦ ἄρχεται ἡ Παγανία, καὶ
παρεκτείνεται μέχρι τοῦ ποταμοῦ τῆς Ζεντίνας, τρεῖς ἔχουσα ζουπανίας,105
146Be τὴν Ῥάστωτζαν καὶ τὸν Μοκρὸν καὶ τοῦ Δαλέν. | Καὶ αἱ μὲν δύο ζου-
πανίαι, ἤγουν ἡ Ῥάστωτζα καὶ ἡ τοῦ Μοκροῦ, πρόσκεινται τῇ θαλάσσῃ,
αἵτινες καὶ σαγήνας ἔχουσιν· ἡ δὲ τοῦ Δαλενοῦ μήκοθέν ἐστιν τῆς
87ʳP θαλάσσης, | καὶ ἐκ τῆς ἐργασίας ζῶσι τῆς γῆς. Πλησιάζουσιν δὲ αὐτοῖς
νῆσοι τέσσαρες, τὰ Μέλετα, τὰ Κούρκουρα, τὰ Βράτζα καὶ ὁ Φάρος,110
κάλλισται καὶ εὐφορώταται, ἐρημόκαστρα ἔχουσαι καὶ ἐλαιῶνας πολλούς·
οἰκοῦσι δὲ ἐν αὐταῖς, καὶ ἔχουσι τὰ κτήνη αὐτῶν, καὶ ἐξ αὐτῶν ζῶσιν.
Ἀπὸ δὲ τῆς Ζεντίνας τοῦ ποταμοῦ ἄρχεται ἡ χώρα Χρωβατίας, καὶ
παρεκτείνεται πρὸς μὲν τὴν παραθαλασσίαν μέχρι τῶν συνόρων Ἰστρίας,
ἤγουν τοῦ κάστρου Ἀλβούνου, πρὸς δὲ τὰ ὀρεινὰ καὶ ὑπέρκειται μέχρι115

V 85 φοσσάτον P ‖ ἑπτὰ V edd.: ζ′ P ‖ πολεμίσαντες P ‖ 87 αὐτῶν
V edd.: αὐτὸν P ‖ Κοτζίλιν: Κοδίλιν coni. Rački Grot ‖ 88 καὶ om. Be ‖
89 post τοῦ add. πάπα Bury ‖ 90 Πορίνου: Βορίνου coni. Rački ‖ ἄρχοντος
V edd.: ἄρχοστος P ‖ 91 Τζέντζηνα edd. Τζέντηνα coni. Šišić ‖ 92 Βρεβέρα

30

were subject to the Franks, as they had formerly been in their own country; but the Franks treated them with such brutality that they used to murder Croat infants at the breast and cast them to the dogs. The Croats, unable to endure such treatment from the Franks, revolted from them, and slew those of them whom they had for princes. On this, a large army from Francia marched against them, and after they had fought one another for seven years, at last the Croats managed to prevail and destroyed all the Franks with their leader, who was called Kotzilis. From that time they remained independent and autonomous, and they requested the holy baptism from the bishop of Rome, and bishops were sent who baptized them in the time of Porinos their prince. Their country was divided into 11 'zupanias', viz., Chlebiana, Tzenzina, Imota, Pleba, Pesenta, Parathalassia, Breberi, Nona, Tnina, Sidraga, Nina; and their ban possesses Kribasa, Litza and Goutziska. Now, the said Croatia and the rest of the Slavonic regions are situated thus: Diocleia is neighbour to the forts of Dyrrachium, I mean, to Elissus and to Helcynium and Antibari, and comes up as far as Decatera, and on the side of the mountain country it is neighbour to Serbia. From the city of Decatera begins the domain of Terbounia and stretches along as far as Ragusa, and on the side of its mountain country it is neighbour to Serbia. From Ragusa begins the domain of the Zachlumi and stretches along as far as the river Orontius; and on the side of the coast it is neighbour to the Pagani, but on the side of the mountain country it is neighbour to the Croats on the north and to Serbia at the front. From the river Orontius begins Pagania and stretches along as far as the river Zentina; it has three 'zupanias', Rhastotza and Mokros and that of Dalen. Two of these 'zupanias', viz., Rhastotza and that of Mokros, lie on the sea, and possess galleys; but that of Dalenos lies distant from the sea, and they live by agriculture. Neighbour to them are four islands, Meleta, Kourkoura, Bratza and Pharos, most fair and fertile, with deserted cities upon them and many olive-yards; on these they dwell and keep their flocks, from which they live. From the river Zentina begins the country of Croatia and stretches along, on the side of the coast as far as the frontiers of Istria, that is, to the city of Albunum, and on the side of the mountain country it encroaches some way upon

---

edd. ‖ 93 Νίνα: Σμίνα coni. Rački ‖ Κρίβασαν: Κρίβαυαν coni. Rački Κρίβαβαν coni. Šišić Skok ‖ 94 Γουτζησκά (etiam Bandurius Bury): Γουτζηκᾶ edd. ‖ 94/5 αἱ λοιπαὶ Σκλαβινίαι coni. Bury οἱ λοιποὶ Σκλαβίνιοι Ba Be ‖ Σκλαβινίαι P ‖ 95 Διόκλεα P Ba Be ‖ 96 Ἐλισσὸν Be ‖ τὸ: τὸν edd. ‖ Ἐλκύνιον P ‖ 97 Ἀντίβαριν V edd.: Ἀντιβάρην P ‖ 98 Σερβλεία P ‖ 103 μὲν πλησιάζει — 105 ἔχουσα ordinem versuum permutavit Be ‖ 103/4 τῇ Σερβλίᾳ edd.: τὴν Σερβλίαν P ‖ 106 τὸν: τὸ V edd. ‖ τοῦ: τὸ edd. ‖ Δαλέν: Δαλμέν coni. Novaković Rački ‖ 107 Ῥάστωτζα (littera α² erasa) Pᵛ Be: Ἀράστωτζα P V ‖ Μοκροῦ edd.: Μόκρου P ‖ 108 αἴτινες edd.: οἴτινες P ‖ σαγίνας P ‖ μηκόθεν Be ‖ 109 ζῶσι] litteram ζ in ras. scr. P¹ ‖ 110 τέσσαρες edd.: δ' P ‖ Βράτζα: Βράτζω V Βάρτζω edd. ‖ 111 ἐλαιῶνας coni. Bury: ἐλῶνας P ἐλῶνας edd. ἀμπελῶνας coni. Dujčev Kyriakides: ‖ 113 ante Χρωβατίας add. τῆς V edd. ‖

30, 31

τινὸς τῷ θέματι Ἰστρίας, πλησιάζει δὲ πρὸς τὴν Τζέντινα καὶ τὴν Χλέβενα τῇ χώρᾳ Σερβλίας. Ἡ γὰρ χώρα Σερβλίας εἰς κεφαλὴν μέν ἐστιν
87ᵛP πασῶν τῶν λοιπῶν χωρῶν, πρὸς | ἄρκτον δὲ πλησιάζει τῇ Χρωβατίᾳ, πρὸς μεσημβρίαν δὲ τῇ Βουλγαρίᾳ. Ἀφ' οὗ δὲ κατεσκήνωσαν οἱ εἰρημένοι Σκλάβοι, κατεκράτησαν πᾶσαν τὴν περίχωρον Δελματίας· ἠργάζοντο120 δὲ τὰ κάστρα τῶν Ῥωμάνων τὰς νήσους, καὶ ἔζουν ἐξ αὐτῶν· ὑπὸ δὲ τῶν Παγανῶν καθ' ἑκάστην ἐπαιχμαλωτιζόμενοι καὶ ἀφανιζόμενοι κατέλιπον τὰς τοιαύτας νήσους, βουλόμενοι εἰς τὴν ἤπειρον ἐργάζεσθαι. Ἐκωλύοντο δὲ παρὰ τῶν Χρωβάτων· οὔπω γὰρ ἐτέλουν αὐτοὺς φόρους, ἀλλὰ πάντα, ἅπερ ἀρτίως παρέχουσι τοῖς Σκλάβοις, τῷ στρατηγῷ125 ταῦτα παρεῖχον. Ἀδυνάτως δὲ ἔχοντες τοῦ ζῆν προσῆλθον Βασιλείῳ
147Be τῷ | ἀοιδίμῳ βα|σιλεῖ, ἀναδιδάξαντες τὰ εἰρημένα πάντα. Ὁ οὖν ἀοίδιμος
88ʳP ἐκεῖνος βασιλεὺς Βασίλειος προετρέψατο πάντα τὰ διδόμενα τῷ στρατηγῷ δίδοσθαι παρ' αὐτῶν τοῖς Σκλάβοις καὶ εἰρηνικῶς ζῆν μετ' αὐτῶν καὶ βραχύ τι δίδοσθαι τῷ στρατηγῷ, ἵνα μόνον δείκνυται ἡ πρὸς τοὺς130 βασιλεῖς τῶν Ῥωμαίων καὶ πρὸς τὸν στρατηγὸν αὐτῶν ὑποταγὴ καὶ δούλωσις. Καὶ ἔκτοτε ἐγένοντο πάντα τὰ τοιαῦτα κάστρα ὑπόφορα τῶν Σκλάβων, καὶ τελοῦσιν αὐτοῖς πάκτα, τὸ μὲν κάστρον ἡ Ἀσπάλαθος νομίσματα σ', τὸ κάστρον τὸ Τετραγγούριν νομίσματα ρ', τὸ κάστρον τὰ Διάδωρα νομίσματα ρι', τὸ κάστρον τὰ Ὄψαρα νομίσματα ρ', τὸ135 κάστρον ἡ Ἀρβὴ ⟨νομίσματα⟩ ρ', τὸ κάστρον ἡ Βέκλα ⟨νομίσματα⟩
88ᵛP ρ', ὡς ὁμοῦ νομίσματα ψι' | ἐκτὸς οἴνου καὶ ἑτέρων διαφόρων εἰδῶν· ταῦτα γὰρ πλείονά εἰσιν ὑπὲρ τὰ νομίσματα. Τὸ δὲ κάστρον τὸ Ῥαούσιον μέσον τῶν δύο χωρῶν πρόσκειται, τῶν τε Ζαχλούμων καὶ τῆς Τερβουνίας· ἔχουσι δὲ καὶ τοὺς ἀμπελῶνας αὐτῶν εἰς ἀμφοτέρας τὰς χώρας,140 καὶ τελοῦσι πρὸς μὲν τὸν ἄρχοντα τῶν Ζαχλούμων νομίσματα λϛ', πρὸς δὲ τὸν ἄρχοντα Τερβουνίας νομίσματα λϛ'.

31. Π ε ρ ὶ τ ῶ ν Χ ρ ω β ά τ ω ν κ α ὶ ἧ ς ν ῦ ν ο ἰ κ ο ῦ σ ι
χ ώ ρ α ς.

148Be   Ὅτι οἱ Χρωβάτοι, οἱ εἰς τὰ τῆς Δελματίας νῦν κατοικοῦντες | μέρη, ἀπὸ τῶν ἀβαπτίστων Χρωβάτων, τῶν καὶ ἄσπρων ἐπονομαζομένων, κατάγονται, οἵτινες Τουρκίας μὲν ἐκεῖθεν, Φραγγίας δὲ πλησίον κατοι- 5
89ʳP κοῦσι, καὶ | συνοροῦσι Σκλάβοις, τοῖς ἀβαπτίστοις Σέρβλοις. Τὸ δὲ Χρωβάτοι τῇ τῶν Σκλάβων διαλέκτῳ ἑρμηνεύεται, τουτέστιν 'οἱ πολλὴν χώραν κατέχοντες'. Οἱ δὲ αὐτοὶ Χρωβάτοι εἰς τὸν βασιλέα τῶν

V 120 ἐργάζοντο edd. ‖ 121 Ῥωμαίων edd. ‖ 122 ἐπιχμαλωτιζόμενοι P ‖ 124 αὐτούς: αὐτοῖς edd. ‖ 129 αὐτῶν¹ edd.: αὐτῷ P ‖ 130 διδόσθαι P ‖ 133 ἡ Be: ὁ P ‖ 135 νομίσματα¹ om. edd.: „ P ‖ νομίσματα² om. edd.: „ P ‖

the province of Istria, and at Tzentina and Chlebena becomes neighbour to the country of Serbia. For the country of Serbia is at the front of all the rest of the countries, but on the north is neighbour to Croatia, and on the south to Bulgaria. Now, after the said Slavs had settled down, they took possession of all the surrounding territory of Dalmatia; but the cities of the Romani took to cultivating the islands and living off them; since, however, they were daily enslaved and destroyed by the Pagani, they deserted these islands and resolved to cultivate the mainland. But they were stopped by the Croats; for they were not yet tributary to the Croats, and used to pay to the military governor all that they now pay to the Slavs. Finding it impossible to live, they approached the glorious emperor Basil and told him all the above. And so that glorious emperor Basil ordered that all that was then paid to the military governor they should pay to the Slavs, and live at peace with them, and that some slight payment should be made to the military governor, as a simple token of submission and servitude to the emperors of the Romans and their military governor. And from that time all these cities became tributary to the Slavs, and they pay them fixed sums: the city of Spalato, 200 nomismata; the city of Tetrangourin, 100 nomismata; the city of Diadora, 110 nomismata; the city of Opsara, 100 nomismata; the city of Arbe, 100 *nomismata;* the city of Vekla, 100 *nomismata;* so that the total amounts to 710 nomismata, exclusive of wine and various other commodities, which are in excess of the payments in cash. The city of Ragusa is situated between the two countries of the Zachlumi and of Terbounia; they have their vineyards in both countries, and pay to the prince of the Zachlumi 36 nomismata, and to the prince of Terbounia 36 nomismata.

31. Of the Croats and of the country they now dwell in.

The Croats who now live in the region of Dalmatia are descended from the unbaptized Croats, also called 'white', who live beyond Turkey and next to Francia, and have for Slav neighbours the unbaptized Serbs. 'Croats' in the Slav tongue means 'those who occupy much territory'. These same Croats arrived to claim the protection of the emperor of the Romans Heraclius

---

136 νομίσματα[1] *add.* Moravcsik ‖ νομίσματα[2] *add.* Moravcsik ‖ 137 νομίσματα Bandurius Be: ,, P ‖ 141 νομίσματα Be: ,, P.
    31. 3 τῆς *om.* edd. ‖ 4 τῶν καὶ *coni.* Marquart Bury: καὶ τῶν P edd. ‖ 8 *ante* πολλὴν *add.* τὴν edd. ‖

31

Ῥωμαίων, Ἡράκλειον πρόσφυγες παρεγένοντο πρὸ τοῦ τοὺς Σέρβλους προσφυγεῖν εἰς τὸν αὐτὸν βασιλέα, Ἡράκλειον κατὰ τὸν καιρόν, ὃν οἱ 10 Ἄβαρεις πολεμήσαντες, ἀπ᾽ ἐκεῖσε τοὺς Ῥωμάνους ἐναπεδίωξαν, οὓς ὁ βασιλεὺς Διοκλητιανὸς ἀπὸ Ῥώμης ἀγαγὼν ἐκεῖσε κατεσκήνωσεν, διὸ καὶ Ῥωμᾶνοι ἐκλήθησαν διὰ τὸ ἀπὸ Ῥώμης μετοίκους αὐτοὺς γενέσθαι ἐν ταῖς τοιαύταις χώραις, ἤγουν τῆς νῦν καλουμένης Χρωβατίας καὶ 89ᵛP Σερβλίας. Παρὰ | δὲ τῶν Ἀβάρων ἐκδιωχθέντες οἱ αὐτοὶ Ῥωμᾶνοι ἐν 15 ταῖς ἡμέραις τοῦ αὐτοῦ βασιλέως Ῥωμαίων, Ἡρακλείου, αἱ τούτων ἔρημοι καθεστή·ασιν χῶραι. Προστάξει οὖν τοῦ βασιλέως Ἡρακλείου οἱ αὐτοὶ Χρωβάτοι καταπολεμήσαντες καὶ ἀπὸ τῶν ἐκεῖσε τοὺς Ἀβάρους ἐκδιώξαντες, Ἡρακλείου τοῦ βασιλέως κελεύσει ἐν τῇ αὐτῇ τῶν Ἀβάρων χώρᾳ, εἰς ἣν νῦν οἰκοῦσιν, κατεσκήνωσαν. Εἶχον δὲ οἱ αὐτοὶ Χρωβάτοι τῷ 20 τότε καιρῷ ἄρχοντα τὸν πατέρα τοῦ Πόργα. Ὁ δὲ βασιλεὺς Ἡράκλειος ἀποστείλας καὶ ἀπὸ Ῥώμης ἀγαγὼν ἱερεῖς καὶ ἐξ αὐτῶν ποιήσας 149Be ἀρχιεπίσκοπον καὶ ἐπίσκοπον καὶ πρεσβυτέρους | καὶ διακόνους, τοὺς 90ʳP | Χρωβάτους ἐβάπτισεν· εἶχον δὲ τῷ τότε καιρῷ οἱ τοιοῦτοι Χρωβάτοι ἄρχοντα τὸν Πόργα. 25

Ὅτι ἡ τοιαύτη χώρα, εἰς ἣν οἱ Χρωβάτοι κατεσκηνώθησαν, ἐξ ἀρχῆς ὑπὸ τὴν ἐξουσίαν ἦν τοῦ βασιλέως τῶν Ῥωμαίων, ἐξ οὗ καὶ παλάτια καὶ ἱπποδρόμια τοῦ βασιλέως Διοκλητιανοῦ ἐν τῇ ⟨τῶν⟩ αὐτῶν Χρωβάτων χώρᾳ μέχρι τῆς νῦν περισώζονται εἰς τὸ κάστρον Σαλώνας πλησίον τοῦ κάστρου Ἀσπαλάθου. 30

Ὅτι οὗτοι οἱ βαπτισμένοι Χρωβάτοι ἔξωθεν τῆς ἰδίας αὐτῶν χώρας πολεμεῖν ἀλλοτρίας οὐ βούλονται· χρησμὸν γάρ τινα καὶ ὁρισμὸν ἔλαβον παρὰ τοῦ πάπα Ῥώμης, τοῦ ἐπὶ Ἡρακλείου, τοῦ βασιλέως 90ᵛP Ῥωμαίων, ἀποστείλαντος | ἱερεῖς καὶ τούτους βαπτίσαντος. Καὶ γὰρ οὗτοι οἱ Χρωβάτοι μετὰ τὸ αὐτοὺς βαπτισθῆναι συνθήκας καὶ ἰδιόχειρα 35 ἐποιήσαντο καὶ πρὸς τὸν ἅγιον Πέτρον, τὸν ἀπόστολον ὅρκους βεβαίους καὶ ἀσφαλεῖς, ἵνα μηδέποτε εἰς ἀλλοτρίαν χώραν ἀπέλθωσιν καὶ πολεμήσωσιν, ἀλλὰ μᾶλλον εἰρηνεύειν μετὰ πάντων τῶν βουλομένων, λαβόντες καὶ παρὰ τοῦ αὐτοῦ πάπα Ῥώμης εὐχὴν τοιάνδε, ὡς εἴ τινες ἄλλοι ἐθνικοὶ κατὰ τῆς τῶν αὐτῶν Χρωβάτων χώρας ἐπέλθωσιν καὶ πόλεμον 40 ἐπενέγκωσιν, ἵνα τῶν Χρωβάτων ὁ Θεὸς προπολεμεῖ καὶ προΐσταται, καὶ νίκας αὐτοῖς Πέτρος ὁ τοῦ Χριστοῦ μαθητὴς προξενεῖ. Μετὰ δὲ 91ʳP χρόνους πολλοὺς ἐν ταῖς ἡμέραις Τερπημέρη τοῦ | ἄρχον|τος, τοῦ πατρὸς 150Be τοῦ ἄρχοντος Κρασημέρη, ἐλθὼν ἀπὸ Φραγγίας, τῆς μεταξὺ Χρωβατίας καὶ Βενετίας, ἀνήρ τις τῶν πάνυ μὲν εὐλαβῶν, Μαρτῖνος ὀνόματι, σχῆμα 45 δὲ κοσμικὸν περιβεβλημένος, ὃν καὶ λέγουσιν οἱ αὐτοὶ Χρωβάτοι θαύ-

31

before the Serbs claimed the protection of the same emperor Heraclius, at that time when the Avars had fought and expelled from those parts the Romani whom the emperor Diocletian had brought from Rome and settled there, and who were therefore called 'Romani' from their having been translated from Rome to those countries, I mean, to those now called Croatia and Serbia. These same Romani having been expelled by the Avars in the days of this same emperor of the Romans Heraclius, their countries were made desolate. And so, by command of the emperor Heraclius these same Croats defeated and expelled the Avars from those parts, and by mandate of Heraclius the emperor they settled down in that same country of the Avars, where they now dwell. These same Croats had at that time for prince the father of Porgas. The emperor Heraclius sent and brought priests from Rome, and made of them an archbishop and a bishop and elders and deacons, and baptized the Croats; and at that time these Croats had Porgas for their prince.

This country in which the Croats settled themselves was originally under the dominion of the emperor of the Romans, and hence in the country of these same Croats the palace and hippodromes of the emperor Diocletian are still preserved, at the city of Salona, near the city of Spalato.

These baptized Croats will not fight foreign countries outside the borders of their own; for they received a kind of oracular response and injunction from the pope of Rome who in the time of Heraclius, emperor of the Romans, sent priests and baptized them. For after their baptism the Croats made a covenant, confirmed with their own hands and by oaths sure and binding in the name of St. Peter the apostle, that never would they go upon a foreign country and make war on it, but rather would live at peace with all who were willing to do so; and they received from the same pope of Rome a benediction to this effect, that if any other foreigners should come against the country of these same Croats and bring war upon it, then might God fight for the Croats and protect them, and Peter the disciple of Christ give them victories. And many years after, in the days of prince Terpimer, father of prince Krasimer, there came from Francia that lies between Croatia and Venice a man called Martin, of the utmost piety though clad in the garb of a layman, whom these same Croats

V 9 τοὺς Σέρβλους edd.: τοῖς Σέρβλοις P ‖ 11 Ἀβάρεις Be ‖ πολεμίσαντες P ‖ 13 Ῥωμάνοι P ‖ 15 Ῥωμάνοι P ‖ 18 καταπολεμίσαντες P ‖ 21 Ποργά P: Βοργά seu Βορκά coni. Rački ‖ 23 ἐπισκόπους coni. Bury ‖ 26 ἤ] in ras. scr. P¹ ‖ 28 τῶν add. edd. ‖ 29 Σαλῶνας P: Σαλῶνος F ‖ 31 Ὅτι οὗτοι — 57 Βενετίας interpolationem posterioris aetatis esse coni. Laskin ‖ 31 Χρωβατοι (sine acc.) P ‖ 32 ἀλλοτρίαις Me ἀλλοτρίοις Ba Be ‖ ὁρισμὸν Ba Be: ὁρισμένον P ‖ 33 ante Ἡρακλείου add. τοῦ edd. ‖ 37/8 πολεμίσωσιν P ‖ 41 τῶν Χρωβάτων ὁ coni. Dujčev Kyriakides: ὁ τῶν Χρωβάτων P edd. ‖ προπολεμεῖ coni. Dujčev Kukules Kyriakides: πρὸς πολεμεῖ P προσπολεμεῖ V edd. ‖ 42 προξενεῖ] litteras ει in ras. scr. P¹ ‖ 45 εὐλαβῶν: εὐσεβῶν coni. Meursius ‖

31

ματα ἱκανὰ ποιῆσαι· ἀσθενὴς δὲ ὢν ὁ τοιοῦτος εὐλαβὴς ἀνὴρ καὶ τοὺς πόδας ἠκρωτηριασμένος, ὥστε ὑπὸ τεσσάρων βαστάζεσθαι καὶ περιφέρεσθαι, ὅπου δ' ἂν καὶ βούλεται, τὴν τοιαύτην τοῦ ἁγιωτάτου πάπα ἐντολὴν τοῖς αὐτοῖς Χρωβάτοις διατηρεῖν μέχρι τέλους ζωῆς αὐτῶν 50 ἐπεθέσπισεν, ἐπευξάμενος δὲ καὶ αὐτὸς αὐτοῖς τὴν ὁμοίαν τοῦ πάπα εὐχήν. Διὰ τοῦτο οὔτε αἱ σαγῆναι τῶν τοιούτων Χρωβάτων, οὔτε αἱ
91ᵛP κον|δοῦραι οὐδέποτε κατά τινος πρὸς πόλεμον ἀπέρχονται, εἰ μὴ ἄρα τις κατ' αὐτῶν ἐπέλθοι. Πλὴν διὰ τῶν τοιούτων πλοίων ἀπέρχονται οἱ βουλόμενοι τῶν Χρωβάτων διοικεῖν ἐμπόρια, ἀπὸ κάστρον εἰς κάστρον 55 περιερχόμενοι τήν τε Παγανίαν καὶ τὸν κόλπον τῆς Δελματίας καὶ μέχρι Βενετίας.

Ὅτι ὁ ἄρχων Χρωβατίας ἐξ ἀρχῆς, ἤγουν ἀπὸ τῆς βασιλείας Ἡρακλείου τοῦ βασιλέως, δουλικῶς ἐστιν ὑποτεταγμένος τῷ βασιλεῖ Ῥωμαίων, καὶ οὐδέποτε τῷ ἄρχοντι Βουλγαρίας καθυπετάγη. Ἀλλ' 60 οὐδὲ Βούλγαρος ἀπῆλθεν πρὸς πόλεμον κατὰ τῶν Χρωβάτων, εἰ μὴ Μιχαήλ, ὁ ἄρχων Βουλγαρίας, ὁ Βορίσης, ἀπελθὼν καὶ πολεμήσας
92ʳP αὐτοῖς | καὶ μηδὲν ἀνύσαι δυνηθεὶς εἰρήνευσε μετ' αὐτῶν, ξενιάσας τοὺς Χρωβάτους καὶ ξενιασθεὶς παρὰ τῶν Χρωβάτων. Ἀλλ' οὐδὲ πώ-
151Be ποτε οἱ Χρω|βάτοι οὗτοι τοῖς Βουλγάροις πάκτον δεδώκασιν, εἰ μὴ 65 πολλάκις ἀμφότεροι ξένιά τινα πρὸς ἀλλήλους παρέσχον φιλοφρονήσεως ἕνεκα.

Ὅτι ⟨ἐν⟩ τῇ βαπτισμένῃ Χρωβατίᾳ εἰσὶν κάστρα οἰκούμενα· ἡ Νῶνα, τὸ Βελέγραδον, τὸ Βελίτζιν, τὸ Σκόρδονα, τὸ Χλεβένα, τὸ Στόλπον, τὸ Τενήν, τὸ Κόρι, τὸ Κλαβώκα. 70

Ὅτι ἡ βαπτισμένη Χρωβατία ἐκβάλλει καβαλλαρικὸν ἕως τῶν ξ' χιλιάδων, πεζικὸν δὲ ἕως χιλιάδων ρ' καὶ σαγήνας μέχρι τῶν π' καὶ κονδούρας μέχρι τῶν ρ'. Καὶ αἱ μὲν σαγῆναι ἔχουσιν ἀνὰ ἀνδρῶν μ',
92ᵛP αἱ | δὲ κονδοῦραι ἀνὰ ἀνδρῶν κ', αἱ δὲ μικρότεραι κονδοῦραι ἀνὰ ἀνδρῶν ι'.

Ὅτι τὴν πολλὴν ταύτην δύναμιν καὶ τὸ τοῦ λαοῦ πλῆθος εἶχεν 75 ἡ Χρωβατία μέχρι τοῦ ἄρχοντος Κρασημέρη. Κἀκείνου μὲν τελευτήσαντος, τοῦ δὲ υἱοῦ αὐτοῦ, Μιροσθλάβου ἄρξαντος ἔτη τέσσαρα καὶ ὑπὸ τοῦ Πριβουνία βοεάνου ἀναιρεθέντος, καὶ διχονοιῶν καὶ πολλῶν διχοστασιῶν εἰς τὴν χώραν γενομένων, ἠλάττωται καὶ τὸ καβαλλαρικὸν καὶ τὸ πεζικὸν καὶ αἱ σαγῆναι καὶ αἱ κονδοῦραι τῆς ἐξουσίας τῶν Χρωβά- 80 των. Ἀρτίως δὲ ἔχει σαγήνας λ', κονδούρας μεγάλας καὶ μικρὰς * * * καὶ καβαλλαρικὸν * * * καὶ πεζικὸν * * *.

V 47 εὐλαβὴς: εὐσεβὴς coni. Meursius ‖ 48 post τεσσάρων add. καὶ V edd. ‖ 49 βούληται edd. ‖ 50 διατηρεῖν] litteram ρ in ras. scr. P¹ ‖ 51 δὲ omittendum coni. Kukules ‖ καὶ om. V Me ‖ 53 κονδοῦραι scr. Moravcsik: κοντοῦραι P edd. ‖

31

declare to have wrought abundant miracles; this pious man, who was sick
and had had his feet amputated, so that he was carried by four bearers and
taken about wherever he wanted to go, confirmed upon these same Croats
this injunction of the most holy pope, that they should keep it so long as
their life should last; and he himself also pronounced on their behalf a benediction similar to that which the pope had made. For this reason neither
the galleys nor the cutters of these Croats ever go against anyone to
make war, unless of course he has come upon them. But in these vessels
go those of the Croats who wish to engage in commerce, travelling round
from city to city, in Pagania and the gulf of Dalmatia and as far as Venice.

The prince of Croatia has from the beginning, that is, ever since the
reign of Heraclius the emperor, been in servitude and submission to the
emperor of the Romans, and was never made subject to the prince of
Bulgaria. Nor has the Bulgarian ever gone to war with the Croats, except
when Michael Boris, prince of Bulgaria, went and fought them and, unable
to make any headway, concluded peace with them, and made presents
to the Croats and received presents from the Croats. But never yet have
these Croats paid tribute to the Bulgarians, although the two have often
made presents to one another in the way of friendship.

In baptized Croatia are the inhabited cities of Nona, Belgrade, Belitzin,
Skordona, Chlebena, Stolpon, Tenin, Kori, Klaboka.

Baptized Croatia musters as many as 60 thousand horse and 100
thousand foot, and galleys up to 80 and cutters up to 100. The galleys carry
40 men each, the cutters 20 each, and the smaller cutters 10 each.

This great power and multitude of men Croatia possessed until the
time of prince Krasimer. But when he was dead and his son Miroslav, after
ruling four years, was made away with by the ban Pribounias, and quarrels
and numerous dissensions broke out in the country, the horse and foot
and galleys and cutters of the Croat dominion were diminished. And now
it has 30 galleys and *** cutters, large and small, and *** horse
and *** foot.

55 ἐμπορεία P ‖ κάστρον¹ (*etiam* Bury): κάστρου edd. ‖ 62 Βορίσης *coni.* Meursius
Bandurius Bury: Βορώσης P edd. ‖ πολεμίσας P ‖ 66 ἀλλήλους V edd.: ἀλλήλοις P ‖
68 ἐν τῇ βαπτισμένῃ Χρωβατίᾳ *coni.* Bury: ἡ βαπτισμένη Χρωβατία P edd. ‖ 69
Νόνα V edd. ‖ Βελόγραδον edd. Βελάγραδον V *mg.* P⁵ ‖ Βελίτζειν V edd. ‖
70 Κόρι V edd.: Κόρη P Κόρι-νιον *coni.* Rački ‖ 71 τῶν *om.* V edd. ‖ 72
ξ′ χιλιάδων *scr.* Moravcsik: ξ ᾶ ᾶ P Ba Be ‖ χιλιάδων² *corr.* Moravcsik:
χιλιάδας P edd. ‖ σαγῆνας P ‖ 73 κονδούρας (*littera* τ *in* δ *correcta*) Pᵛ: κοντούρας
P V edd. κοντούρας *mg.* P⁸ ‖ 74 κονδοῦραι (*littera* τ *erasa et s. v. littera*
δ *addita*) P¹ *mg.* P⁸ V edd.: κοντοῦραι P ‖ 77 τέσσαρα edd.: δ′ P ‖ 78
Πριβουνία (*etiam* Bandurius Be): Πριβουνίου V Me Ba ‖ 80 κονδοῦραι V edd.:
κουνδοῦραι P ‖ 81 κονδοῦρας P ‖ *post* κονδούρας *addendum* μ′ *coni.* Bury ‖ *post*
μικρὰς *lac. ind.* P   *numerum condurarum excidisse coni.* Meursius Bandurius ‖ 82 *post* καβαλλαρικὸν et *post* πεζικὸν *numerum equitatus peditatusque*
excidisse coni. Meursius Bandurius ‖

31, 32

"Ότι ή μεγάλη Χρωβατία, ή καὶ ἄσπρη ἐπονομαζομένη, ἀβάπτιστος
93ʳP τυγχάνει μέχρι τῆς σήμερον, καθὼς καὶ οἱ πλη|σιάζοντες αὐτὴν Σέρβλοι.
152Be Ὀλιγώτερον δὲ καβαλλαρικὸν ἐκβάλ|λουσιν, ὁμοίως καὶ πεζικὸν παρὰ 85
τὴν βαπτισμένην Χρωβατίαν, ὡς συνεχέστερον πραιδευόμενοι παρά τε
τῶν Φράγγων καὶ Τούρκων καὶ Πατζινακιτῶν. Ἀλλ' οὐδὲ σαγήνας
κέκτηνται, οὔτε κονδούρας, οὔτε ἐμπορευτικὰ πλοῖα, ὡς μήκοθεν οὔσης
τῆς θαλάσσης· ἀπὸ γὰρ τῶν ἐκεῖσε μέχρι τῆς θαλάσσης ὁδός ἐστιν
ἡμερῶν λ'. Ἡ δὲ θάλασσα, εἰς ἣν διὰ τῶν λ' ἡμερῶν κατέρχονται, ἐστὶν 90
ἡ λεγομένη σκοτεινή.

32. Περὶ τῶν Σέρβλων καὶ ἧς νῦν οἰκοῦσι χώρας.

Ἰστέον, ὅτι οἱ Σέρβλοι ἀπὸ τῶν ἀβαπτίστων Σέρβλων, τῶν καὶ
ἄσπρων ἐπονομαζομένων, κατάγονται, τῶν τῆς Τουρκίας ἐκεῖθεν κατοι-
93ᵛP κούντων εἰς τὸν παρ' | αὐτοῖς Βοΐκι τόπον ἐπονομαζόμενον, ἐν οἷς πλη-
σιάζει καὶ ἡ Φραγγία, ὁμοίως καὶ ἡ μεγάλη Χρωβατία, ἡ ἀβάπτιστος, 5
ἡ καὶ ἄσπρη προσαγορευομένη· ἐκεῖσε τοίνυν καὶ οὗτοι οἱ Σέρβλοι τὸ
ἀπ' ἀρχῆς κατῴκουν. Δύο δὲ ἀδελφῶν τὴν ἀρχὴν τῆς Σερβλίας ἐκ τοῦ
πατρὸς διαδεξαμένων, ὁ εἷς αὐτῶν τὸ τοῦ λαοῦ ἀναλαβόμενος ἥμισυ,
εἰς Ἡράκλειον, τὸν βασιλέα Ῥωμαίων, προσέφυγεν, ὃν καὶ προσδεξά-
μενος ὁ αὐτὸς Ἡράκλειος βασιλεύς, παρέσχεν τόπον εἰς κατασκήνωσιν 10
ἐν τῷ θέματι Θεσσαλονίκης τὰ Σέρβλια, ἃ ἔκτοτε τὴν τοιαύτην προση-
γορίαν ἀπείληφεν. Σέρβλοι δὲ τῇ τῶν Ῥωμαίων διαλέκτῳ 'δοῦλοι'
153Be προσαγορεύονται, | ὅθεν καὶ 'σέρβυλα' ἡ κοινὴ συνήθεια τὰ δουλικὰ
94ʳP | φησιν ὑποδήματα, καὶ 'τζερβουλιανοὺς' τοὺς τὰ εὐτελῆ καὶ πενιχρὰ
ὑποδήματα φοροῦντας. Ταύτην δὲ τὴν ἐπωνυμίαν ἔσχον οἱ Σέρβλοι διὰ 15
τὸ δοῦλοι γενέσθαι τοῦ βασιλέως Ῥωμαίων. Μετὰ δὲ χρόνον τινὰ ἔδοξεν
τοὺς αὐτοὺς Σέρβλους εἰς τὰ ἴδια ἀπελθεῖν, καὶ τούτους ἀπέστειλεν ὁ
βασιλεύς. Ὅτε δὲ διεπέρασαν τὸν Δανούβιν ποταμόν, μετάμελοι γενό-
μενοι ἐμήνυσαν Ἡρακλείῳ τῷ βασιλεῖ διὰ τοῦ στρατηγοῦ, τοῦ τότε τὸ
Βελέγραδον κρατοῦντος, δοῦναι αὐτοῖς ἑτέραν γῆν εἰς κατασκήνωσιν. 20
Καὶ ἐπειδὴ ἡ νῦν Σερβλία καὶ Παγανία καὶ ἡ ὀνομασθεῖσα Ζαχλούμων
94ᵛP χώρα καὶ Τερβουνία καὶ ἡ τῶν Καναλιτῶν ὑπὸ | τὴν ἐξουσίαν τοῦ βασι-
λέως Ῥωμαίων ὑπῆρχον, ἐγένοντο δὲ αἱ τοιαῦται χῶραι ἔρημοι παρὰ
τῶν Ἀβάρων (ἀπὸ τῶν ἐκεῖσε γὰρ Ῥωμάνους τοὺς νῦν Δελματίαν καὶ
τὸ Δυρράχιον οἰκοῦντας ἀπέλασαν), {καὶ} κατεσκήνωσεν ὁ βασιλεὺς 25

V 83 ἡ καὶ (coni. etiam Marquart Bury): καὶ ἡ V edd. ‖ 85 δὲ om. V edd. ‖
87 σαγήνας P ‖ 88 κονδοῦρας P ‖ οὔσης V edd.: οὖσαν P ‖ 90 λ' ἡμερῶν:
ἡμερῶν λ' edd.

31, 32

Great Croatia, also called 'white', is still unbaptized to this day, as are also the Serbs who are its neighbours. They muster fewer horse and fewer foot than does baptized Croatia, because they are more constantly plundered, by the Franks and Turks and Pechenegs. Nor have they either galleys or cutters or merchant-ships, for the sea is far away; for from those parts to the sea it is a journey of 30 days. And the sea to which they come down after the 30 days is that which is called 'dark'.

32. Of the Serbs and of the country they now dwell in.

The Serbs are descended from the unbaptized Serbs, also called 'white', who live beyond Turkey in a place called by them Boïki, where their neighbour is Francia, as is also Great Croatia, the unbaptized, also called 'white'; in this place, then, these Serbs also originally dwelt. But when two brothers succeeded their father in the rule of Serbia, one of them, taking one half of the folk, claimed the protection of Heraclius, the emperor of the Romans, and the same emperor Heraclius received him and gave him a place in the province of Thessalonica to settle in, namely Serbia, which from that time has acquired this denomination. 'Serbs' in the tongue of the Romans is the word for 'slaves', whence the colloquial 'serbula' for menial shoes, and 'tzerboulianoi' for those who wear cheap, shoddy footgear. This name the Serbs acquired from their being slaves of the emperor of the Romans. Now, after some time these same Serbs decided to depart to their own homes, and the emperor sent them off. But when they had crossed the river Danube, they changed their minds and sent a request to the emperor Heraclius, through the military governor then holding Belgrade, that he would grant them other land to settle in. And since what is now Serbia and Pagania and the so-called country of the Zachlumi and Terbounia and the country of the Kanalites were under the dominion of the emperor of the Romans, and since these countries had been made desolate by the Avars (for they had expelled from those parts the Romani who now live in Dalmatia and

32. 2 Σερβλῶν P ‖ 4 Βόϊκι edd. Βοῖσκι coni. Marquart Βοῖοι coni. Skok Βόϊμι coni. Grégoire ‖ 6 τοίνυν: οὖν V edd. ‖ 12 ἀπείληφεν: παρείληφε edd. ‖ 13 σέρβουλα edd. ‖ δουλικά coni. Bekker: δουλικῶς P edd. δουλικῶς ⟨ἔχοντά⟩ coni. Bury ‖ 18 Δάνουβιν edd. ‖ 20 Βελέγραδον scr. Moravcsik: Βελάγραδον P Βελόγραδον Be ‖ 21 ὀνομασθεῖσα: ὀνομαζομένη V edd. ‖ 23 ἔρημαι Ba Be ‖ 25 ἀπήλασαν Be ‖ καὶ omittendum coni. Bury Kukules ‖

32

τοὺς αὐτοὺς Σέρβλους ἐν ταῖς τοιαύταις χώραις, καὶ ἦσαν τῷ βασιλεῖ
Ῥωμαίων ὑποτασσόμενοι, οὓς ὁ βασιλεὺς πρεσβύτας ἀπὸ Ῥώμης
ἀγαγὼν ἐβάπτισεν, καὶ διδάξας αὐτοὺς τὰ τῆς εὐσεβείας τελεῖν καλῶς,
αὐτοῖς τὴν τῶν Χριστιανῶν πίστιν ἐξέθετο. Ἐπεὶ δὲ ἡ Βουλγαρία ὑπὸ
τὴν ἐξουσίαν ἦν τῶν Ῥωμαίων, * * * αὐτοῦ οὖν τοῦ ἄρχοντος τοῦ 30
95ʳᴾ Σέρβλου, τοῦ εἰς τὸν βασιλέα προσφυγόντος, τελευτήσαντος, | κατὰ
διαδοχὴν ἦρξεν ὁ υἱὸς αὐτοῦ, καὶ πάλιν ὁ ἔγγων, καὶ οὕτως ἐκ τῆς γενεᾶς
154Be αὐτοῦ οἱ καθεξῆς ἄρχοντες. | Μετὰ δὲ χρόνους τινὰς ἐγεννήθη ἐξ αὐτῶν
ὁ Βοϊσέσθλαβος, καὶ ἐξ αὐτοῦ ὁ Ῥοδόσθλαβος, καὶ ἀπ' ἐκείνου ὁ Προ-
σηγόης, καὶ ἐξ ἐκείνου ὁ Βλαστίμηρος, καὶ μέχρις αὐτοῦ τοῦ Βλαστιμή- 35
ρου μετὰ τῶν Σέρβλων εἰρηνικῶς διετέλουν οἱ Βούλγαροι, ὡς γείτονες
καὶ συνορῖται ἀγαπῶντες ἀλλήλους, ἔχοντες δὲ δούλωσιν καὶ ὑποταγὴν
εἰς τοὺς βασιλεῖς τῶν Ῥωμαίων καὶ εὐεργετούμενοι παρ' αὐτῶν. Ἐπὶ
δὲ τῆς ἀρχῆς τοῦ αὐτοῦ Βλαστιμήρου ἦλθεν μετὰ πολέμου Πρεσιάμ,
ὁ ἄρχων Βουλγαρίας, κατὰ τῶν Σέρβλων θέλων αὐτοὺς ὑποτάξαι, 40
95ᵛᴾ ἀλλ' ἐπὶ τρι|ετίαν πολεμήσας, οὐ μόνον οὐδὲν ἤνυσεν, ἀλλὰ καὶ λαὸν
αὐτοῦ πλεῖστον ἀπώλεσεν. Μετὰ δὲ θάνατον Βλαστιμήρου τοῦ ἄρχοντος
διεδέξαντο τὴν ἀρχὴν τῆς Σερβλίας οἱ τρεῖς υἱοὶ αὐτοῦ, ὁ Μουντιμῆρος
καὶ ὁ Στροΐμηρος καὶ ὁ Γοΐνικος, μερισάμενοι τὴν χώραν. Ἐπὶ τούτων
παρεγένετο ὁ τῆς Βουλγαρίας ἄρχων, Μιχαὴλ ὁ Βορίσης, θέλων διεκδικῆ- 45
σαι τὴν ἧτταν Πρεσιάμ, τοῦ πατρὸς αὐτοῦ, καὶ πολεμήσας, εἰς τοσοῦτον
αὐτὸν ἐπτόησαν οἱ Σέρβλοι, ὥστε καὶ τὸν υἱὸν αὐτοῦ, Βλαδίμηρον
ἐκράτησαν δέσμιον μετὰ καὶ βοϊλάδων δώδεκα μεγάλων. Τότε δὴ τῇ
τοῦ υἱοῦ θλίψει καὶ μὴ θέλων ὁ Βορίσης εἰρήνευσε μετὰ τῶν Σέρβλων.
96ʳᴾ Μέλλων δὲ ὑποστρέφειν ἐν Βουλγαρίᾳ | καὶ φοβηθείς, μήποτε ἐνεδρεύσω- 50
σιν αὐτὸν οἱ Σέρβλοι καθ' ὁδόν, ἐπεζήτησεν εἰς διάσωσιν αὐτοῦ τὰ τοῦ
ἄρχοντος Μουντιμήρου παιδία, τὸν Βόρενα καὶ τὸν Στέφανον, οἳ καὶ
155Be διέσωσαν αὐτὸν ἀβλαβῆ μέχρι τῶν συνόρων, | ἕως τῆς Ῥάσης. Καὶ ὑπὲρ
τῆς τοιαύτης χάριτος δέδωκεν αὐτοῖς Μιχαὴλ ὁ Βορίσης δωρεὰς μεγάλας,
καὶ ἐκεῖνοι ἀντέδωκαν αὐτῷ χάριν ξενίων ψυχάρια δύο, φαλκώνια δύο, 55
σκυλία δύο καὶ γούνας ὀγδοήκοντα, ὅπερ λέγουσιν οἱ Βούλγαροι εἶναι
πάκτον. Μετὰ μικρὸν δὲ ἐγένοντο κατ' ἀλλήλων οἱ αὐτοὶ τρεῖς ἀδελφοί,
οἱ ἄρχοντες Σερβλίας, καὶ γενάμενος ἐπικρατέστερος ὁ εἷς αὐτῶν, ὁ
96ᵛᴾ Μουντιμῆρος, καὶ θέλων μόνος | τὴν ἀρχὴν ἐπέχειν, κρατήσας παρέ-
δωκεν τοὺς δύο ἐν Βουλγαρίᾳ, μόνον τὸ παιδίον τοῦ ἑνὸς ἀδελφοῦ, 60
Γοϊνίκου, Πέτρον ὀνόματι, παρ' ἑαυτῷ κρατήσας καὶ ἐπιμελούμενος,

---

V 27 πρεσβύτας: πρεσβυτέρους coni. Bury || 29 τὴν τῶν Χριστιανῶν coni. Bekker
Bury: τὴν τῶν χρόνων P τὴν om. V edd. || 30 post Ῥωμαίων lac. ind.
Jenkins || τοῦ¹ (addendum coni. etiam Bekker): om. edd. || 30/1 τοῦ

32

Dyrrachium), therefore the emperor settled these same Serbs in these countries, and they were subject to the emperor of the Romans; and the emperor brought elders from Rome and baptized them and taught them fairly to perform the works of piety and expounded to them the faith of the Christians. And since Bulgaria was beneath the dominion of the Romans *** when, therefore, that same Serbian prince died who had claimed the emperor's protection, his son ruled in succession, and thereafter his grandson, and in like manner the succeeding princes from his family. And after some years was begotten of them Boïseslav, and of him Rodoslav, and of him Prosigoïs, and of him Blastimer; and up to the time of this Blastimer the Bulgarians lived at peace with the Serbs, whose neighbours they were and with whom they had a common frontier, and they were friendly one toward another, and were in servitude and submission to the emperors of the Romans and kindly entreated by them. But, during the rule of this same Blastimer, Presiam, prince of Bulgaria, came with war against the Serbs, with intent to reduce them to submission; but though he fought them three years he not merely achieved nothing but also lost very many of his men. After the death of prince Blastimer his three sons, Muntimer and Stroïmer and Goïnikos, succeeded to the rule of Serbia and divided up the country. In their time came up the prince of Bulgaria, Michael Boris, wishing to avenge the defeat of his father Presiam, and made war, and the Serbs discomfited him to such an extent that they even held prisoner his son Vladimer, together with twelve great boyars. Then, out of grief for his son, Boris perforce made peace with the Serbs. But, being about to return to Bulgaria and afraid lest the Serbs might ambush him on the way, he begged for his escort the sons of prince Muntimer, Borenas and Stephen, who escorted him safely as far as the frontier at Rasi. For this favour Michael Boris gave them handsome presents, and they in return gave him, as presents in the way of friendship, two slaves, two falcons, two dogs and eighty furs, which the Bulgarians describe as tribute. A short while after, the same three brothers, the princes of Serbia, fell out, and one of them, Muntimer, gained the upper hand and, wishing to be sole ruler, seized the other two and handed them over to Bulgaria, keeping by him and caring for only the son

---

Σέρβλου: τῆς Σερβλίας coni. Bekker Bury ‖ 32 ἔγγων V edd. ἔγγον P: ἔγγονος Pʸ ‖ 33 ἐγεννήθη edd.: ἐγεννήθην P ‖ 35 Βλαστήμερος edd. ‖ 35/6 Βλαστημέρου edd. ‖ 39 Βλαστημέρου edd. ‖ 41 πολεμίσας P ‖ 42 ἀπόλεσεν P ‖ Βλαστημέρου edd. ‖ 43 Μουντίμηρος Bury ‖ 44 Στρότμηρος V Στροήμηρος P: Στροήμερος Ba Be ‖ 45/6 διεκδικῆσαι: ἐκδικῆσαι edd. ‖ 46 πολεμίας P ‖ 47 ἐπτόησαν edd.: ἔπτωσαν P ἔπταισαν coni. Kyriakides ‖ Βλαδίμηρον scr. Moravcsik: Βλαστίμηρον V Βλαστιμήρων P Βλαστήμερον edd. Βλαδήμερον coni. Šafarik Rački Dümmler Grot Zlatarski ‖ 48 βοϊλάδων corr. Moravcsik: βολιάδων P edd. ‖ δώδεκα edd.: ιβ′ P ‖ δὴ: δὲ edd. ‖ 51 καθ᾽ ὁδὸν coni. Bekker: καθ᾽ ὁδοῦ edd. καθοδοῦ P ‖ 56 γούνας P ‖ ὀγδοήκοντα Moravcsik π′ P: ἐνενήκοντα Με ἐννενήκοντα Ba Be ‖ 57 αὐτοὶ om. edd. ‖ 58 γενόμενος edd. ‖ 59 Μουντίμηρος edd. ‖.

ὅστις καὶ φυγὼν ἦλθεν ἐν Χρωβατίᾳ, περὶ οὗ μετ' ὀλίγον ῥηθήσεται. Ὁ
δὲ προρρηθεὶς ἀδελφὸς ἐν Βουλγαρίᾳ, Στροΐμηρος εἶχεν υἱὸν τὸν Κλονί-
μηρον, ᾧ καὶ γυναῖκα παρέσχεν ὁ Βορίσης Βουλγάραν. Ἐξ αὐτοῦ γεν-
νᾶται ἐν Βουλγαρίᾳ ὁ Τζεέσθλαβος. Ὁ δὲ Μουντιμῆρος, ὁ τοὺς δύο 65
ἀδελφοὺς διώξας καὶ τὴν ἀρχὴν δεξάμενος, γεννᾷ υἱοὺς τρεῖς, τὸν Πριβέσθλαβον καὶ τὸν Βράνον καὶ τὸν Στέφανον, καὶ μετὰ τὸν αὐτοῦ θάνατον
διαδέχεται αὐτὸν ὁ πρῶτος υἱός, ὁ Πριβέσθλαβος. Μετὰ οὖν χρόνον
97ʳP ἕνα ἐξελθὼν | ἀπὸ Χρωβατίας ὁ προειρημένος Πέτρος, ὁ υἱὸς τοῦ Γοϊνί-
κου, διώκει ἀπὸ τῆς ἀρχῆς τὸν ἐξάδελφον αὐτοῦ, Πριβέσθλαβον μετὰ 70
τῶν δύο ἀδελφῶν, κἀκεῖνος τὴν ἀρχὴν διαδέχεται, ἐκεῖνοι δὲ φυγόντες
εἰσέρχονται ἐν Χρωβατίᾳ. Μετὰ δὲ χρόνους τρεῖς ἐλθὼν ὁ Βράνος πρὸς
156Be τὸ | πολεμῆσαι τὸν Πέτρον καὶ ἡττηθεὶς καὶ κρατηθεὶς παρ' αὐτοῦ
ἐτυφλώθη. Μετὰ δὲ χρόνους δύο φυγὼν καὶ ὁ Κλονίμηρος ἀπὸ Βουλγαρίαν, ὁ πατὴρ τοῦ Τζεεσθλάβου, καταλαμβάνει καὶ αὐτὸς καὶ εἰσέρχε- 75
ται εἰς ἓν τῶν κάστρων Σερβλίας, τὴν Δοστινίκαν, μετὰ λαοῦ πρὸς τὸ
παραλαβεῖν τὴν ἀρχήν. Τοῦτον οὖν πολεμήσας ὁ Πέτρος ἀπέκτεινεν,
97ᵛP καὶ ἐκράτησεν | ἕτερα ἔτη κ', ἄρξας ἐπὶ τῆς βασιλείας Λέοντος, τοῦ μακα-
ριωτάτου καὶ ἁγίου βασιλέως, ἔχων ὑποταγὴν καὶ δούλωσιν πρὸς αὐτόν.
Εἰρήνευσεν δὲ καὶ μετὰ Συμεών, τοῦ ἄρχοντος Βουλγαρίας, ὥστε καὶ 80
σύντεκνον αὐτὸν ἐποίησεν. Μετὰ δὲ τὸν καιρόν, ὃν αὐτὸς ὁ κύρις Λέων
ἐβασίλευσεν, παρεγένετο ὁ τότε εἰς τὸ Δυρράχιον στρατηγῶν, ὁ πρωτοσπαθάριος Λέων ὁ Ῥαβδοῦχος, ὁ μετὰ τοῦτο μάγιστρος τιμηθεὶς καὶ
λογοθέτης τοῦ δρόμου, εἰς Παγανίαν, τὴν τότε παρὰ τοῦ ἄρχοντος
Σερβλίας διακρατουμένην, πρὸς τὸ βουλευθῆναι καὶ συντυχεῖν τῷ αὐτῷ 85
ἄρχοντι Πέτρῳ περί τινος δουλείας καὶ ὑποθέσεως. Ζηλοτυπήσας δὲ
98ʳP πρὸς τοῦτο Μιχαήλ, ὁ ἄρχων τῶν Ζαχλού|μων, ἐμήνυσεν Συμεών, τῷ
Βουλγάρων ἄρχοντι, ὅτι ὁ βασιλεὺς Ῥωμαίων δεξιοῦται διὰ δώρων
τὸν ἄρχοντα Πέτρον πρὸς τὸ συνεπαρεῖν τοὺς Τούρκους καὶ ἐπελθεῖν
κατὰ Βουλγαρίας. Ἐγένετο δὲ κατὰ τὸν καιρὸν ἐκεῖνον καὶ πόλεμος 90
εἰς Ἀχελὼν μεταξὺ τῶν Ῥωμαίων καὶ τῶν Βουλγάρων. Ἐμμανὴς οὖν
157Be ἐν τούτῳ γενόμενος Συμεὼν κατὰ τοῦ ἄρχοντος Σερβ|λίας, Πέτρου,
ἀπέστειλε τὸν Σιγρίτζη Θεόδωρον καὶ τὸν Μαρμαὴν ἐκεῖνον μετὰ
φοσσάτου, ἔχοντας καὶ ἀρχοντόπουλον Παῦλον, τὸν υἱὸν Βράνου, ὃν ὁ
Πέτρος, ὁ ἄρχων Σερβλίας ἐτύφλωσεν. Δόλῳ οὖν ἐπελθόντες οἱ Βούλ- 95
98ᵛP γαροι πρὸς τὸν ἄρχοντα Σερβλίας καὶ συντεκνί|αν μετ' αὐτοῦ ποιησά-
μενοι καὶ ὅρκῳ βεβαιώσαντες μὴ παθεῖν τι παρ' αὐτῶν ἐναντίον, ἠπάτη-
σαν αὐτὸν ἐξελθεῖν πρὸς αὐτούς, ὃν καὶ παραυτα δεσμήσαντες εἰσήγαγον

V 62 ἐν Χρωβατίᾳ: εἰς Χρωβατίαν V edd. ‖ Χρωβατίᾳ] litteras χ et ωβ in ras.
scr. P¹ ‖ 63 Στροήμηρος P: Στροήμερος edd. ‖ 64 ᾧ V edd.: ὃ P ‖ 65 ὁ¹

32

of the one brother Goïnikos, Peter by name, who fled and came to Croatia, and of whom we shall speak in a moment. The aforesaid brother Stroïmer, who was in Bulgaria, had a son Klonimer, to whom Boris gave a Bulgarian wife. Of him was begotten Tzeëslav, in Bulgaria. Muntimer, who had expelled his two brothers and taken the rule, begat three sons, Pribeslav and Branos and Stephen, and after he died his eldest son Pribeslav succeeded him. Now, after one year the aforesaid Peter, son of Goïnïkos, came out of Croatia and expelled from the rule his cousin Pribeslav and his two brothers, and himself succeeded to the rule, and they fled away and entered Croatia. Three years later Branos came to fight Peter and was defeated and captured by him, and blinded. Two years after that, Klonimer, the father of Tzeëslav, escaped from Bulgaria and he too came and with an army entered one of the cities of Serbia, Dostinika, with intent to take over the rule. Peter attacked and slew him, and continued to govern for another 20 years, and his rule began during the reign of Leo, the holy emperor, of most blessed memory, to whom he was in submission and servitude. He also made peace with Symeon, prince of Bulgaria, and even made him god-father to his child. Now, after the time that this lord Leo had reigned, the then military governor at Dyrrachium, the protospatharius Leo Rhabduchus, who was afterwards honoured with the rank of magister and *office* of foreign minister, arrived in Pagania, which was at that time under the control of the prince of Serbia, in order to advise and confer with this same prince Peter upon some service and affair. Michael, prince of the Zachlumi, his jealousy aroused by this, sent information to Symeon, prince of Bulgaria, that the emperor of the Romans was bribing prince Peter to take the Turks with him and go upon Bulgaria. It was at that time when the battle of Achelo had taken place between the Romans and the Bulgarians. Symeon, mad with rage at this, sent against prince Peter of Serbia Sigritzis Theodore and the late Marmaïs with an army, and they took with them also the young prince Paul, son of Branos whom Peter, prince of Serbia, had blinded. The Bulgarians proceeded against the prince of Serbia by treachery, and, by binding him with the relationship of god-father and giving a sworn undertaking that he should suffer nothing untoward at their hands, they tricked him into coming out to them, and then on the instant bound him

---

om. edd. ‖ Τζεεσθλάβος P edd. ‖ Μουντιμήρως P: Μουντίμηρος edd. ‖ ὁ³ *om.* edd. ‖ 67 Βράνον] *litteram* β *in ras. scr.* P¹ *mg. iter.* P⁸ ‖ 68 Πριβέσθλαβος *mg.* P⁸ V edd.: Πριδέσθλαβος P ‖ 73 πολεμεῖσαι P ‖ 74 ὁ *om.* edd. ‖ 74/5 Βουλγαρίας V edd. ‖ 76 τῶν *om.* V edd. ‖ κάστρων: κάστρον V edd. ‖ *ante* Σερβλίας *add.* τῆς V edd. ‖ Δοστινίκαν: Δροστινίκαν *coni.* Skok ‖ 77 πολεμίσας P ‖ 80 ὥστε: ὅστε edd. ὅς γε *an* ὥστε? *coni.* Bekker ‖ 81 κύρης P ‖ 83 Ῥαυδοῦχος P ‖ 86 δουλείας: δουλώσεως edd. ‖ 90 *post* δὲ *add.* καὶ edd. ‖ 92 τούτω V edd.: τοῦτο P ‖ γενόμενος ἐν τούτω V edd. ‖ *ante* Συμεὼν *add.* ὁ V edd. ‖ 94 φωσσάτου P ‖ 98 παραυτὰ Be ‖

ἐν Βουλγαρίᾳ, καὶ ἀποθνήσκει ἐν φυλακῇ. Εἰσῆλθεν δὲ ἀντ' αὐτοῦ Παῦλος, ὁ υἱὸς Βράνου, καὶ ἐκράτησεν ἔτη τρία. Ὁ δὲ βασιλεύς, ὁ κύρις Ῥωμανὸς100 ἔχων ἀρχοντόπουλον ἐν τῇ πόλει Ζαχαρίαν, τὸν υἱὸν Πριβεσθλάβου, τοῦ ἄρχοντος Σερβλίας, ἀπέστειλε πρὸς τὸ γενέσθαι ἄρχοντα ἐν Σερβλίᾳ, ἀλλὰ ἀπελθὼν καὶ πολεμήσας, ἡττήθη παρὰ τοῦ Παύλου· κρατήσας γὰρ αὐτὸν παρέδωκεν τοῖς Βουλγάροις, καὶ ἐκρατεῖτο δέσμιος. Εἶτα 99ᵣP μετὰ χρόνους τρεῖς, τοῦ Παύλου ἐναν|τιωθέντος τοῖς Βουλγάροις,105 ἀπέστειλεν τὸν Ζαχαρίαν, τὸν πρότερον παρὰ τοῦ κυροῦ Ῥωμανοῦ τοῦ βασιλέως ἀποσταλέντα, καὶ διώξας τὸν Παῦλον, ἐκράτησεν αὐτὸς τὴν ἀρχὴν τῶν Σέρβλων, ὅστις πάραυτα τῶν εὐεργεσιῶν τοῦ βασιλέως Ῥωμαίων ἐπιμνησθείς, ἐγένετο κατὰ τῶν Βουλγάρων, μηδ' ὅλως θελήσας ὑποταγῆναι αὐτοῖς, ἀλλ' ὑπὸ τοῦ βασιλέως μᾶλλον Ῥωμαίων δεσπό-110 ζεσθαι. Ὥστε καὶ τοῦ Συμεὼν φοσσᾶτον κατ' αὐτοῦ ἀποστείλαντος 158Be διὰ τοῦ Μαρμαὴμ καὶ τοῦ | Σιγρίτζη {καὶ} Θεοδώρου, ὦν καὶ τὰς κεφαλὰς καὶ ἄρματα ἐκ τοῦ πολέμου ἀπέστειλε πρὸς τὸν βασιλέα Ῥωμαίων 99ᵛP ἐπινίκια (ἔτι γὰρ μεταξὺ Ῥωμαίων καὶ | τῶν Βουλγάρων μάχη ἦν), οὐδέποτε δὲ ἐπαύσατο, καθὼς καὶ οἱ πρὸ αὐτοῦ ἄρχοντες, ἀποστέλλων115 πρὸς τοὺς βασιλεῖς Ῥωμαίων, καὶ ὑποτασσόμενος καὶ δουλεύων αὐτοῖς. Πάλιν δὲ ἀπέστειλεν ἕτερον φοσσᾶτον ὁ Συμεὼν διὰ τοῦ Κνήνου καὶ τοῦ Ἡμνήκου καὶ τοῦ Ἠτζβόκλια κατὰ τοῦ ἄρχοντος Ζαχαρίου, συναποστείλας μετ' αὐτῶν καὶ Τζεέσθλαβον. Τότε ὁ μὲν Ζαχαρίας φοβηθεὶς φεύγει ἐν Χρωβατίᾳ, οἱ δὲ Βούλγαροι μηνύσαντες τοῖς ζουπάνοις ἐλθεῖν120 πρὸς αὐτοὺς καὶ παραλαβεῖν ἄρχοντα τὸν Τζεέσθλαβον καὶ δι' ὅρκου τούτους ἀπατήσαντες καὶ ἐξαγαγόντες μέχρι {τῷ} τοῦ πρώτου χωρίου 100ᵣP καὶ πάραυτα δεσμήσαντες | αὐτούς, εἰσῆλθον ἐν Σερβλίᾳ καὶ συνεπῆραν τὸν ἅπαντα λαὸν ἀπὸ μικροῦ ἕως μεγάλου, καὶ εἰσήγαγον ἕως Βουλγαρίας, τινὲς δὲ ἀποδράσαντες εἰσῆλθον καὶ ἐν Χρωβατίᾳ, καὶ ἔμεινεν125 ἡ χώρα ἔρημος. Κατὰ τὸν καιρὸν οὖν ἐκεῖνον εἰσῆλθον οἱ αὐτοὶ Βούλγαροι εἰς Χρωβατίαν μετὰ τοῦ Ἀλογοβότουρ τοῦ πολεμῆσαι, καὶ ἐσφάγησαν πάντες ἐκεῖσε παρὰ τῶν Χρωβάτων. Μετὰ δὲ χρόνους ἑπτὰ ἀπὸ τῶν Βουλγάρων φυγὼν ὁ Τζεέσθλαβος μετὰ καὶ ἑτέρων τεσσάρων, ἀπὸ Περσθλάβου εἰσῆλθεν ἐν Σερβλίᾳ, οὐχ εὗρεν δὲ εἰς τὴν χώραν, εἰ μὴ130 πεντήκοντα μόνους ἄνδρας μήτε γυναῖκας ἔχοντας, μήτε παιδία, ἀλλὰ 100ᵛP κυνηγοῦντας, καὶ διατρεφο|μένους. Μετὰ τούτων κρατήσας τὴν χώραν, 159Be ἐμήνυσεν πρὸς τὸν βασιλέα Ῥωμαίων, τὴν ἐξ | αὐτοῦ ἀντίληψιν καὶ βοήθειαν ἐπιζητῶν, ὑπισχνούμενος, δουλεύειν καὶ ὑπείκειν τῇ προστάξει

V 100 τρία edd.: γ' P ‖ κύρης P ‖ 103 πολεμίσας P ‖ 106 ἀπέστειλαν coni.
Jenkins ‖ 108 παραυτὰ Be ‖ 111 φοσσάτον P ‖ 112 καὶ² P V: eras. Pᵛ om.
Ba Be secl. Moravcsik ‖ 114 ἔτι—ἦν in parenthesi posuit Be ‖ τῶν om V.

and carried him off to Bulgaria, and he died in prison. Paul, son of Branos, took his place and governed three years. The emperor, the lord Romanus, who had in Constantinople the young prince Zacharias, son of Pribeslav, prince of Serbia, sent him off to be prince in Serbia, and he went and fought, but was defeated by Paul; who took him prisoner and handed him over to the Bulgarians and he was kept in prison. Then, three years later, when Paul had put himself in opposition to the Bulgarians, *they* sent this Zacharias, who had previously been sent by the lord Romanus the emperor, and he expelled Paul and himself took possession of the rule over the Serbs; and thereupon, being mindful of the benefits of the emperor of the Romans, he broke with the Bulgarians, being not at all wishful to be subjected to them, but rather that the emperor of the Romans should be his master. And so, when Symeon sent against him an army under Marmaïm and Sigritzis Theodore, he sent their heads and their armour from the battle to the emperor of the Romans as tokens of his victory (for the war was still going on between the Romans and the Bulgarians); nor did he ever cease, like the princes also that were before him, to send missions to the emperors of the Romans, and to be in subjection and servitude to them. Again, Symeon sent another army against prince Zacharias, under Kninos and Himnikos and Itzboklias, and together with them he sent also Tzeëslav. Then Zacharias took fright and fled to Croatia, and the Bulgarians sent a message to the 'zupans' that they should come to them and should receive Tzeëslav for their prince; and, having tricked them by an oath and brought them out as far as the first village, they instantly bound them, and entered Serbia and took away with them the entire folk, both old and young, and carried them into Bulgaria, though a few escaped away and entered Croatia; and the country was left deserted. Now, at that time these same Bulgarians under Alogobotour entered Croatia to make war, and there they were all slain by the Croats. Seven years afterwards Tzeëslav escaped from the Bulgarians with four others, and entered Serbia from Preslav, and found in the country no more than fifty men only, without wives or children, who supported themselves by hunting. With these he took possession of the country and sent a message to the emperor of the Romans asking for his support and succour, and promising to serve him and be obedient to his command, as had been the princes before him.

---

edd. || 115 δὲ *per comp. inser.* P¹ *in textum receperunt* V edd.: *omittendum coni.* Kukules || ἀποστέλλων *coni.* Kyriakides: ἀπέστελλον P edd. || 117 φοσσάτον P || 118 ʼΗτζβόκλια: ʼΗτζβούλια *coni.* Hilferding ἠτζ⟨ίργου⟩ βουλιά *coni.* Beševliev || 122 τῷ *om.* edd. *secl.* Moravcsik || 123 παραυτὰ Be || 127 ʼΑλογοβότουρ: ʼΑλοβογότουρ *coni.* Ilovajskij Tomaschek Marquart Fehér || 128 ἑπτὰ edd.: ζ′ P || 129 τεσσάρων edd.: δ′ P || 130 Πρεσθλάβου edd. || 131 πεντήκοντα edd.: ν′ P ||

αὐτοῦ, καθὼς καὶ οἱ πρὸ αὐτοῦ ἄρχοντες. Καὶ ἔκτοτε οὐ διέλιπεν ὁ135
τῶν Ῥωμαίων βασιλεὺς εὐεργετῶν αὐτόν, ὥστε καὶ ⟨οἱ⟩ εἰς Χρωβατίαν
καὶ Βουλγαρίαν καὶ ἐν ταῖς λοιπαῖς χώραις διάγοντες Σέρβλοι, οὓς ὁ
Συμεὼν διεσκόρπισεν, τοῦτο ἀκούσαντες συνήχθησαν εἰς αὐτόν. Ἀλλὰ καὶ
ἐν τῇ πόλει πολλοὶ ἀπὸ Βουλγαρίας φυγόντες εἰσῆλθον, οὓς καὶ ἐνδύσας
καὶ εὐεργετήσας ὁ βασιλεὺς τῶν Ῥωμαίων, ἀπέστειλε πρὸς τὸν Τζεέσθλα-140
101ʳP βον. Καὶ ἀπὸ τῶν πλουσίων δωρεῶν τοῦ | βασιλέως τῶν Ῥωμαίων
συστησάμενος καὶ ἐνοικίσας τὴν χώραν, ὡς τὸ πρότερον, ἐστὶν ὑποτεταγμένος δουλοπρεπῶς τῷ βασιλεῖ Ῥωμαίων, καὶ διὰ τῆς τοῦ βασιλέως
συνδρομῆς καὶ τῶν πολλῶν αὐτοῦ εὐεργεσιῶν τὴν τοιαύτην χώραν
συστήσας καὶ ἄρχων ἐν αὐτῇ βεβαιωθείς.   145
Ὅτι ὁ ἄρχων Σερβλίας ἐξ ἀρχῆς, ἤγουν ἀπὸ τῆς βασιλείας Ἡρακλείου τοῦ βασιλέως, δουλικῶς ἐστιν ὑποτεταγμένος τῷ Ῥωμαίων βασιλεῖ, καὶ οὐδέποτε τῷ ἄρχοντι Βουλγαρίας καθυπετάγη.
Ὅτι ἐν τῇ βαπτισμένῃ Σερβλίᾳ εἰσὶν κάστρα οἰκούμενα· τὸ
Δεστινίκον, τὸ Τζερναβουσκέη, τὸ Μεγυρέτους, τὸ Δρεσνεήκ, τὸ Λεσνήκ,150
101ᵛP τὸ Σαληνὲς καὶ εἰς τὸ χωρίον Βόσονα | τὸ Κάτερα καὶ τὸ Δεσνήκ.

160Be 33. Π ε ρ ὶ   τ ῶ ν   Ζ α χ λ ο ύ μ ω ν   κ α ὶ   ἧ ς   ν ῦ ν   ο ἰ κ ο ῦ σ ι
χ ώ ρ α ς.

Ὅτι ἡ τῶν Ζαχλούμων χώρα παρὰ τῶν Ῥωμαίων πρότερον
ἐκρατεῖτο, Ῥωμάνων δή φημι, οὓς ἀπὸ Ῥώμης Διοκλητιανὸς ὁ βασιλεὺς
μετῴκισεν, καθὼς καὶ εἰς τὴν τῶν Χρωβάτων ἱστορίαν εἴρηται περὶ 5
αὐτῶν. Ὑπὸ τῷ βασιλεῖ δὲ Ῥωμαίων ἡ τῶν Ζαχλούμων αὕτη χώρα
ὑπῆρχεν, ἀλλὰ παρὰ τῶν Ἀβάρων αἰχμαλωτισθεῖσα ἥ τε χώρα καὶ
ὁ ταύτης λαὸς τὸ παράπαν ἠρήμωται. Οἱ δὲ νῦν οἰκοῦντες ἐκεῖσε Ζαχλοῦμοι Σέρβλοι τυγχάνουσιν ἐξ ἐκείνου τοῦ ἄρχοντος, τοῦ εἰς τὸν βασιλέα
Ἡράκλειον προσφυγόντος. Ζαχλοῦμοι δὲ ὠνομάσθησαν ἀπὸ ὄρους οὕτω 10
102ʳP καλου|μένου Χλούμου, καὶ ἄλλως δὲ παρὰ τῇ τῶν Σκλάβων διαλέκτῳ
ἑρμηνεύεται τὸ Ζαχλοῦμοι ἤγουν 'ὀπίσω τοῦ βουνοῦ', ἐπειδὴ ἐν τῷ
τοιούτῳ χωρίῳ βουνός ἐστιν μέγας, ἔχων ἄνωθεν αὐτοῦ δύο κάστρα,
τὸ Βόνα καὶ τὸ Χλούμ, ὄπισθεν δὲ τοῦ τοιούτου βουνοῦ διέρχεται ποταμὸς καλούμενος Βόνα, ὃ ἑρμηνεύεται 'καλόν'.   15
Ὅτι ἡ γενεὰ τοῦ ἀνθυπάτου καὶ πατρικίου Μιχαήλ, τοῦ υἱοῦ
τοῦ Βουσεβούτζη, τοῦ ἄρχοντος τῶν Ζαχλούμων, ἦλθεν ἀπὸ τῶν κατοι-

---

V 136 τῶν om. edd. ‖ βασιλεὺς Ῥωμαίων edd. ‖ οἱ addendum coni. Bekker
Bury ‖ 137 διάγοντες] litteras ες in ras. scr. P¹ ‖ 142 ἐνοικήσας V edd. ‖ 150
Δεστινίκον: Δρεστινίκον coni. Skok ‖ Τζερναβουσκέη Ba Be Τζερναβρυσκέη

32, 33

And thenceforward the emperor of the Romans continually benefited him, so that the Serbs living in Croatia and Bulgaria and the rest of the countries, whom Symeon had scattered, rallied to him when they heard of it. Moreover, many had escaped from Bulgaria and entered Constantinople, and these the emperor of the Romans clad and comforted and sent to Tzeëslav. And from the rich gifts of the emperor of the Romans he organized and populated the country, and is, as before, in servitude and subjection to the emperor of the Romans; and through the co-operation and many benefits of the emperor he has united this country and is confirmed in the rule of it.

The prince of Serbia has from the beginning, that is, ever since the reign of Heraclius the emperor, been in servitude and submission to the emperor of the Romans, and was never subject to the prince of Bulgaria.

In baptized Serbia are the inhabited cities of Destinikon, Tzernabouskeï, Megyretous, Dresneïk, Lesnik, Salines; and in the territory of Bosona, Katera and Desnik.

33. Of the Zachlumi and of the country they now dwell in.

The country of the Zachlumi was previously possessed by the Romans, I mean, by those Romani whom Diocletian the emperor translated from Rome, as has been told of them in the story of the Croats. This land of the Zachlumi was beneath the emperor of the Romans, but when it and its folk were enslaved by the Avars, it was rendered wholly desolate. Those who live there now, the Zachlumi, are Serbs from the time of that prince who claimed the protection of the emperor Heraclius. They were called Zachlumi from a so-called mount Chlumos, and indeed in the tongue of the Slavs 'Zachlumi' means 'behind the mountain', since in that territory is a great mountain with two cities on the top of it, Bona and Chlum, and behind this mountain runs a river called Bona, which means 'good'.

The family of the proconsul and patrician Michael, son of Bouseboutzis, prince of the Zachlumi, came from the unbaptized who dwell on

---

coni. Šišić ‖ Μεγυρέτους: Μεγερέτους *mg.* P⁸ Μεγυρέτζυς *coni.* Skok ‖ Δρεσνεήκ: Δρεσνεὴ κ′ (=κάστρον) *coni.* Skok ‖ Λεσνήκ: Λεσνὴ κ′ (=κάστρον) *coni.* Skok ‖ 151 Βόσωνα V edd. Βόσϑνα *coni.* Šafarik ‖ τὸ³: τὰ *coni.* Bury ‖ Δεσνήκ: Λεσνήκ *coni.* Rački Δεσνὴ κ′ (=κάστρον) *coni.* Skok.
    33. 3 'Ρωμάνων edd. ‖ 4 δή Moravcsik: δέ P edd. ‖ 5 μετώκησεν P ‖ 6 τῷ *om.* edd. ‖ 8 ἐκεῖσε οἰκοῦντες edd. ‖ 8/9 Ζαχλούμοι P ‖ 9 *post* βασιλέα *add.* 'Ρωμάνων V *add.* 'Ρωμαίων edd. ‖ 10 Ζαχλούμοι P ‖ ὀνομάσϑησαν P ‖ 12 Ζαχλούμοι P ‖

33, 34, 35

κούντων άβαπτίστων εἰς τὸν ποταμὸν Βίσλας, τοὺς ἐπονομαζομένους
Λιτζίκη, καὶ ᾤκησεν εἰς τὸν ποταμόν, τὸν ἐπονομαζόμενον Ζαχλοῦμα.

161Be ῞Οτι ἐν τῷ χωρίῳ τῶν Ζαχλούμων εἰσὶν κάστρα οἰκού|μενα· τὸ 20
102ᵛP Στα|γνόν, τὸ Μοκρισκίκ, τὸ ᾿Ιοσλή, τὸ Γαλουμαήνικ, τὸ Δοβρισκίκ.

**34. Περὶ τῶν Τερβουνιωτῶν καὶ τῶν Καναλιτῶν
καὶ ἧς νῦν οἰκοῦσι χώρας.**

῞Οτι ἡ τῶν Τερβουνιωτῶν καὶ τῶν Καναλιτῶν χώρα μία ὑπάρχει.
᾿Απὸ δὲ τῶν ἀβαπτίστων Σέρβλων οἱ ἐκεῖσε οἰκοῦντες κατάγονται, ἐξ
ἐκείνου τοῦ ἄρχοντος τοῦ εἰς τὸν βασιλέα ῾Ηράκλειον προσφυγόντος 5
ἀπὸ τῆς ἀβαπτίστου Σερβλίας, μέχρι τοῦ ἄρχοντος Σερβλίας τοῦ Βλαστιμήρου. Οὗτος οὖν ὁ ἄρχων Βλαστίμηρος τῇ ἰδίᾳ θυγατρὶ δέδωκεν ἄνδρα Κράιναν, τὸν υἱὸν Βελάη, τοῦ ζουπάνου Τερβουνίας. Θέλων δὲ
οὗτος τὸν ἴδιον γαμβρὸν δοξάσαι, ὠνόμασεν αὐτὸν ἄρχοντα, ποιήσας
103ʳP αὐτὸν αὐτεξούσιον. ᾿Εξ ἐκεί|νου δὲ ὁ Φαλιμέρης ἐγεννήθη, καὶ ἀπ᾿ 10
ἐκείνου ὁ Τζουζήμερις. ῏Ησαν δὲ οἱ τῆς Τερβουνίας ἄρχοντες ἀεὶ ὑπὸ
τὸν λόγον τοῦ ἄρχοντος Σερβλίας. Τερβουνία δὲ τῇ τῶν Σκλάβων διαλέκτῳ ἑρμηνεύεται ᾿ἰσχυρὸς τόπος᾿· ἡ γὰρ τοιαύτη χώρα ὀχυρώματα
ἔχει πολλά.

῞Οτι ἐστὶν καὶ ἑτέρα χώρα ὑπὸ ταύτην τὴν χώραν Τερβουνίας, 15
Καναλή προσαγορευομένη. Τὸ δὲ Καναλή ἑρμηνεύεται τῇ τῶν Σκλάβων
162Be διαλέκτῳ ᾿ἀμαξία᾿, ἐπειδὴ διὰ τὸ εἶναι | τὸν τόπον ἐπίπεδον πάσας
αὐτῶν τὰς δουλείας διὰ ἀμαξῶν ἐκτελοῦσιν.

῞Οτι ἐν τῷ χωρίῳ Τερβουνίας καὶ τοῦ Καναλή εἰσὶ κάστρα οἰκού-
μενα· ἡ Τερβουνία, τὸ ᾿Ορμός, τὰ ῾Ρίσενα, τὸ Λουκάβεται, τὸ Ζετλήβη. 20

103ᵛP **35. Περὶ τῶν Διοκλητιανῶν καὶ ἧς νῦν οἰκοῦσι
χώρας.**

῞Οτι ἡ Διοκλείας χώρα καὶ αὐτὴ πρότερον παρὰ τῶν ῾Ρωμάνων
ἐκρατεῖτο, οὓς ἀπὸ ῾Ρώμης μετῴκισεν ὁ βασιλεὺς Διοκλητιανός, καθὼς
καὶ εἰς τὴν περὶ τῶν Χρωβάτων ἱστορίαν εἴρηται, ὑπὸ δὲ τὸν βασιλέα 5

V 18 post Βίσλας addendum καὶ coni. Laskin Iljinskij || τοὺς ἐπονομαζομένους:
τὸν ἐπονομαζόμενον Meursius Ba Be || 19 Λιτζίκη coni. Grégoire Λιτζίκη coni.
Niederle: Λινζίκη coni. Skok Διτζίκη P Δικίτζη coni. Šafarik || Ζαχλούμα
P || 21 Μοκρισκίκ: Μοκρισκί κ᾿ (=κάστρον) coni. Skok || ᾿Οσλή coni. Dvornik ||
Γαλουμαήνικ: Γαλουμσηνικ (sine acc.) coni. Rački Γαλουμαήνι κ᾿ (=κάστρον)
coni. Skok || Δοβρισκίκ: Δοβρισκὶ κ᾿ (= κάστρον) coni. Skok.

33, 34, 35

the river Visla and are called Litziki; and it settled on the river called Zachluma.

In the territory of the Zachlumi are the inhabited cities of Stagnon, Mokriskik, Iosli, Galoumaïnik, Dobriskik.

34. Of the Terbouniotes and Kanalites and of the country they now dwell in.

The country of the Terbouniotes and the Kanalites is one. The inhabitants are descended from the unbaptized Serbs, from the time of that prince who came out of unbaptized Serbia and claimed the protection of the emperor Heraclius until the time of Blastimer, prince of Serbia. This prince Blastimer married his daughter to Kraïnas, son of Belaës, 'zupan' of Terbounia. And, desiring to ennoble his son-in-law, he gave him the title of prince and made him independent. Of him was begotten Phalimer, and of him Tzouzimer. The princes of Terbounia have always been at the command of the prince of Serbia. Terbounia in the tongue of the Slavs means 'strong place'; for this country has many strong defences.

Subordinate to this country of Terbounia is another country called Kanali. Kanali means in the tongue of the Slavs 'waggon-load', because, the place being level, they carry on all their labours by the use of waggons.

In the territory of Terbounia and Kanali are the inhabited cities of Terbounia, Ormos, Rhisena, Loukabetai, Zetlibi.

35. Of the Diocletians and of the country they now dwell in.

The country of Diocleia was also previously possessed by the Romani whom the emperor Diocletian translated from Rome, as has been said in the story about the Croats, and was under the emperor of the Romans.

---

34. 1 Τερβουνιωτῶν *corr.* Moravcsik: Τερβουνιατῶν P edd. ‖ 3 Τερβουνιατῶν edd. ‖ 4/5 οἱ ἐκεῖσε οἰκοῦντες κατάγονται ἐξ ἐκείνου τοῦ ἄρχοντος τοῦ εἰς τὸν βασιλέα *coni.* Jenkins: οἱ ἐκεῖσε κατάγονται, οἱ ἐξ ἐκείνου τοῦ ἄρχοντος οἰκοῦντες τοῦ εἰς τὸν βασιλέα P edd. ‖ 6/7 Βλαστημέρου edd. ‖ 7 Βλαστήμερος edd. ‖ 8 δὲ *om.* edd. ‖ 9 ὀνόμασεν P ‖ 11 Τζουζήμερης P Τζουτζημέρης edd. ‖ 15 ἑτέρα χώρα Meursius Ba Be ἔτερα χωρία P ‖ 17 ἀμαξιά edd. ‖ 20 Ὄρμος Be ‖ Λουκάβετε V edd. Λουκάβε τε *coni.* Šafarik Λουκάβετζ *coni.* Rački.
35. 3 Διοκλῆας P Ba Be ‖ 4 μετώκησεν P ‖

35, 36

Ῥωμαίων ὑπῆρχεν. Παρὰ δὲ τῶν Ἀβάρων καὶ αὐτὴ ἡ χώρα αἰχμαλωτισθεῖσα ἠρήμωται, καὶ πάλιν ἐπὶ Ἡρακλείου,τοῦ βασιλέως ἐνῳκίσθη,
καθὼς καὶ ἡ Χρωβατία καὶ ἡ Σερβλία καὶ ἡ τῶν Ζαχλούμων καὶ ἡ
Τερβουνία καὶ τοῦ Καναλή. Διόκλεια δὲ ὀνομάζεται ἀπὸ τοῦ ἐν τῇ τοιαύτῃ
χώρᾳ κάστρου, οὗπερ ἔκτισεν ὁ βασιλεὺς Διοκλητιανός, νυνὶ δέ ἐστιν 10
104ᵣP ἐρημόκαστρον μέχρι | τοῦ νῦν ὀνομαζόμενον Διόκλεια.
    Ὅτι ἐν τῇ χώρᾳ Διοκλείας εἰσὶ μεγάλα κάστρα οἰκούμενα· τὸ
Γράδεται, τὸ Νουγράδε, τὸ Λοντοδόκλα.

163Be 36. Π ε ρ ὶ   τ ῶ ν   Π α γ α ν ῶ ν,   τ ῶ ν   κ α ὶ   Ἀ ρ ε ν τ α ν ῶ ν
    κ α λ ο υ μ έ ν ω ν,   κ α ὶ   ἧ ς   ν ῦ ν   ο ἰ κ ο ῦ σ ι   χ ώ ρ α ς.

    Ὅτι ἡ χώρα, εἰς ἣν νῦν οἰκοῦσιν οἱ Παγανοί, καὶ αὐτὴ πρότερον
παρὰ τῶν Ῥωμάνων ἐκρατεῖτο, οὓς ἀπὸ Ῥώμης ὁ βασιλεὺς Διοκλητιανὸς
μετοικίσας ἐν Δελματίᾳ ἐνῴκισεν. Οἱ δὲ αὐτοὶ Παγανοὶ ἀπὸ τῶν ἀβαπτί- 5
στων Σέρβλων κατάγονται ἐξ ἐκείνου τοῦ ἄρχοντος, τοῦ εἰς τὸν βασιλέα
Ἡράκλειον προσφυγόντος. Παρὰ δὲ τῶν Ἀβάρων καὶ αὐτὴ ἡ χώρα
αἰχμαλωτισθεῖσα ἠρήμωται, καὶ πάλιν ἐπὶ Ἡρακλείου τοῦ βασιλέως
104ᵛP ἐνῳκίσθη. | Παγανοὶ δὲ καλοῦνται διὰ τὸ μὴ καταδέξασθαι αὐτοὺς
τῷ τότε καιρῷ βαπτισθῆναι, ὅτε καὶ πάντες οἱ Σέρβλοι ἐβαπτίσθησαν. 10
Καὶ γὰρ Παγανοὶ τῇ τῶν Σκλάβων διαλέκτῳ 'ἀβάπτιστοι' ἑρμηνεύονται,
τῇ τῶν Ῥωμαίων δὲ διαλέκτῳ ἡ χώρα αὐτῶν Ἄρεντα καλεῖται, ἐξ
οὗ κἀκεῖνοι παρὰ τῶν αὐτῶν Ῥωμαίων Ἀρεντανοὶ καλοῦνται.
    Ὅτι ἐν Παγανίᾳ εἰσὶν κάστρα οἰκούμενα· τὸ Μόκρον, τὸ Βερούλ-
λια, τὸ Ὄστρωκ καὶ ἡ Σλαβίνετζα. Κρατοῦσιν δὲ καὶ ταύτας τὰς νήσους· 15
νῆσος μεγάλη ἡ Κούρκρα, ἤτοι τὸ Κίκερ, ἐν ᾗ ἔστιν καὶ κάστρον· νῆσος
ἑτέρα μεγάλη τὰ Μέλετα, ἤτοι τὸ Μαλοζεάται, ἣν ἐν ταῖς Πράξεσι τῶν
105ᵣP ἀποστόλων ὁ ἅγιος Λουκᾶς μέμνηται Μελίτην ταύτην προσαγορεύων, | ἐν
164Be ᾗ καὶ | ἔχις τὸν ἅγιον Παῦλον ἀπὸ τοῦ δακτύλου προσήψατο, ἣν καὶ
τῷ πυρὶ ὁ ἅγιος Παῦλος κατέφλεξεν· νῆσος ἑτέρα μεγάλη τὸ Φάρα· 20
νῆσος ἑτέρα μεγάλη ὁ Βράτζης. Εἰσὶ δὲ καὶ ἕτεραι νῆσοι, αἱ μὴ κρατού-
μεναι παρὰ τῶν αὐτῶν Παγανῶν· νῆσος τὰ Χώαρα, νῆσος Ἴης, νῆσος
τὸ Λάστοβον.

F   36. 18 Μελίτην — 20 κατέφλεξεν: Acta 28, 1—5.

V 6 αὕτη Be ‖ 9 ante τοῦ¹ addendum ἡ coni. Bury ‖ Διόκληα P Ba Be ‖ 10
οὗπερ: ὅπερ V edd. ‖ 11 Διόκληα P Ba Be ‖ 12 τῇ χώρᾳ] litteras ῇ et α
in ras. scr. P¹ ‖ Διόκλήας P ‖ 13 Γράδεται: Γράδεσται coni. Rački Γρά-
δετζι coni. Skok ‖ Νουγράδε: Νούιγράδε seu Νουιγράδε coni. Rački ‖

35, 36

But this country also was enslaved by the Avars and made desolate, and repopulated in the time of Heraclius the emperor, just as were Croatia and Serbia and the country of the Zachlumi and Terbounia and the country of Kanali. Diocleia gets its name from the city in this country that the emperor Diocletian founded, but now it is a deserted city, though still called Diocleia.

In the country of Diocleia are the large inhabited cities of Gradetai, Nougrade, Lontodokla.

36. Of the Pagani, also called Arentani, and of the country they now dwell in.

The country in which the Pagani now dwell was also previously possessed by the Romani whom the emperor Diocletian translated from Rome and settled in Dalmatia. These same Pagani are descended from the unbaptized Serbs, of the time of that prince who claimed the protection of the emperor Heraclius. This country also was enslaved by the Avars and made desolate and repopulated in the time of Heraclius the emperor. The Pagani are so called because they did not accept baptism at the time when all the Serbs were baptized. For 'Pagani' in the tongue of the Slavs means 'unbaptized', but in the tongue of the Romans their country is called Arenta, and so they themselves are called Arentani by these same Romans.

In Pagania are the inhabited cities of Mokron, Beroullia, Ostrok and Slavinetza. Also, they possess these islands: the large island of Kourkra, or Kiker, on which there is a city; another large island, Meleta, or Malozeatai, which St. Luke mentions in the 'Acts of the Apostles' by the name of Melite, in which a viper fastened upon St. Paul by his finger, and St. Paul burnt it up in the fire; another large island, Phara; another large island, Bratzis. There are other islands not in the possession of these same Pagani: the island of Choara, the island of Iës, the island of Lastobon.

Λοντοδόκλα: Λόντο, τὸ Δόκλα *coni.* Šafarik Λόντο, τὸ Δεόκλα *coni.* Rački Λουτοδόκλα *coni.* Skok.

36. 1 Ἀρεντανῶν: Ναρεντανῶν *coni.* Šafarik ‖ 3 αὕτη edd. ‖ 4 Ῥωμάνων *coni.* Jenkins: Ῥωμαίων P edd. ‖ 5 μετοικήσας P ‖ ἐνώκησεν P ‖ 6 εἰς: πρὸς edd. ‖ 7 αὕτη Be ‖ 12 Ἀρέντα V edd. ‖ 13 Ἀρεντανοὶ *scr.* Moravcsik: Ἀρεντάνοι P edd. ‖ 15 ἡ Σλαβίνετζα *scr.* Moravcsik εἰσλαβίνετζα P: ἡ Λαβίνετζα V edd. Λαβίνετζα *mg.* P³ Λαβρίνετζα *coni.* Novaković Λαβίνζανε *seu* Λαβίτζανε *coni.* Skok ‖ 18 Λουκᾶς P: Λούκας edd. ‖ 21 ἕτεραι P ‖ 22 Χόαρα V edd. Χόαζα *coni.* Šafarik Dümmler Rački Šišić.

37. Περὶ τοῦ ἔθνους τῶν Πατζινακιτῶν.

Ἰστέον, ὅτι οἱ Πατζινακῖται τὸ ἀπ᾽ ἀρχῆς εἰς τὸν ποταμὸν Ἀτὴλ τὴν αὐτῶν εἶχον κατοίκησιν, ὁμοίως δὲ καὶ εἰς τὸν ποταμὸν Γεήχ, ἔχοντες τούς τε Χαζάρους συνοροῦντας καὶ τοὺς ἐπονομαζομένους Οὔζους. Πρὸ ἐτῶν δὲ πεντήκοντα οἱ λεγόμενοι Οὖζοι μετὰ τῶν Χαζάρων ὁμονοή- 5
105ᵛP σαντες καὶ πόλεμον συμβαλόντες πρὸς τοὺς Πατζινακίτας, | ὑπερίσχυσαν, καὶ ἀπὸ τῆς ἰδίας χώρας αὐτοὺς ἐξεδίωξαν, καὶ κατέσχον αὐτὴν μέχρι τῆς σήμερον οἱ λεγόμενοι Οὖζοι. Οἱ δὲ Πατζινακῖται φυγόντες περιήρχοντο, ἀναψηλαφῶντες τόπον εἰς τὴν αὐτῶν κατασκήνωσιν, καταλαβόντες δὲ τὴν σήμερον παρ᾽ αὐτῶν διακρατουμένην γῆν καὶ εὑρόντες 10 τοὺς Τούρκους οἰκοῦντας ἐν αὐτῇ, πολέμου τρόπῳ τούτους νικήσαντες καὶ ἐκβαλόντες αὐτοὺς ἐξεδίωξαν, καὶ κατεσκήνωσαν ἐν αὐτῇ, καὶ δεσπόζουσιν τὴν τοιαύτην χώραν, ὡς εἴρηται, μέχρι τὴν σήμερον ἔτη πεντήκοντα πέντε.

Ἰστέον, ὅτι πᾶσα ἡ Πατζινακία εἰς θέματα ὀκτὼ διαιρεῖται, 15
106ʳP ἔχουσα καὶ μεγάλους ἄρχοντας τοσούτους. Τὰ | δὲ | θέματά εἰσιν ταῦτα·
165Be ὄνομα τοῦ πρώτου θέματος Ἠρτήμ, τοῦ δευτέρου Τζούρ, τοῦ τρίτου Γύλα, τοῦ τετάρτου Κουλπέη, τοῦ πέμπτου Χαραβόη, τοῦ ἕκτου Ταλμάτ, τοῦ ἑβδόμου Χοπόν, τοῦ ὀγδόου Τζοπόν. Κατὰ δὲ τὸν καιρόν, ὃν ἀπὸ τῆς ἰδίας χώρας οἱ Πατζινακῖται ἐξεδιώχθησαν, εἶχον ἄρχοντας 20 εἰς μὲν τὸ θέμα Ἠρτήμ τὸν Βάϊτζαν, εἰς δὲ τὸ Τζούρ τὸν Κούελ, εἰς δὲ τὸ Γύλα τὸν Κουρκοῦται, εἰς δὲ τὸ Κουλπέη τὸν Ἰπαόν, εἰς δὲ τὸ Χαραβόη τὸν Καϊδούμ, εἰς δὲ τὸ θέμα Ταλμὰτ τὸν Κώσταν, εἰς ⟨δὲ⟩ τὸ Χοπὸν τὸν Γιαζή, εἰς δὲ τὸ θέμα Τζοπὸν τὸν Βατᾶν. Μετὰ δὲ θάνατον αὐτῶν διεδέξαντο τὰς ἀρχὰς οἱ τούτων ἐξάδελφοι. Νόμος γὰρ ἐν αὐτοῖς 25
106ᵛP καὶ τύπος ἐκράτησεν παλαιὸς μὴ ἔχειν ἐξουσίαν πρὸς παῖ|δας ἢ ἀδελφοὺς αὐτῶν μεταπέμπειν τὰ ἀξιώματα, ἀλλ᾽ ἀρκεῖσθαι μόνον τοῖς κεκτημένοις τὸ καὶ μέχρι ζωῆς ἄρχειν αὐτούς, μετὰ δὲ θάνατον προχειρίζεσθαι ἢ ἐξάδελφον αὐτῶν ἢ ἐξαδέλφων παῖδας πρὸς τὸ μὴ καθόλου εἰς ἓν μέρος τῆς γενεᾶς διατρέχειν τὸ ἀξίωμα, ἀλλὰ καὶ {εἰς} τοὺς ἐκ 30 πλαγίου καὶ κληρονομεῖν καὶ ἀπεκδέχεσθαι τὴν τιμήν· ἀπὸ ξένης δὲ γενεᾶς οὐχ ὑπεισέρχεταί τις καὶ γίνεται ἄρχων. Τὰ δὲ ὀκτὼ θέματα διαιροῦνται εἰς τεσσαράκοντα μέρη, καὶ ἔχουσι καὶ ἐλάττονας ἄρχοντας.

V   37. 2 οἱ om. Be ‖ Πατζινακῖται P ‖ 3 Γεήχ] litteram ε in ras. scr. P¹ mg. iter. P ‖ 4 Χαζάρους coni. Bandurius Dankovszky Zeuss Cassel Grot Thury Marquart Manojlović Schönebaum aliique; Μαζάρους P   mg. P edd. Βαζάρους coni. Bury ‖ Οὔζους per comp. (?) P: Οὔζ V edd. Οὔζω mg. P ‖ 5 πεντήκοντα edd.: ν´ P   post πεντήκοντα excidisse πέντε coni. Pauler Bury aliique ‖ Οὖζοι per comp. (?) P: Οὔζ V edd. ‖ Χαζάρων: Μαζάρων

37

37. Of the nation of the Pechenegs.

Originally, the Pechenegs had their dwelling on the river Atil, and likewise on the river Geïch, having common frontiers with the Chazars and the so-called Uzes. But fifty years ago the so-called Uzes made common cause with the Chazars and joined battle with the Pechenegs and prevailed over them and expelled them from their country, which the so-called Uzes have occupied till this day. The Pechenegs fled and wandered round, casting about for a place for their settlement; and when they reached the land which they now possess and found the Turks living in it, they defeated them in battle and expelled and cast them out, and settled in it, and have been masters of this country, as has been said, for fifty-five years to this day. The whole of Patzinacia is divided into eight provinces with the same number of great princes. The provinces are these: the name of the first province is Irtim; of the second, Tzour; of the third, Gyla; of the fourth, Koulpeï; of the fifth, Charaboï; of the sixth, Talmat; of the seventh, Chopon; of the eighth, Tzopon. At the time at which the Pechenegs were expelled from their country, their princes were, in the province of Irtim, Baïtzas; in Tzour, Kouel; in Gyla, Kourkoutai; in Koulpeï, Ipaos; in Charaboï, Kaïdoum; in the province of Talmat, Kostas; in Chopon, Giazis; in the province of Tzopon, Batas. After their deaths their cousins succeeded to their rule. For law and ancient principle have prevailed among them, depriving them of authority to transmit their ranks to their sons or their brothers, it being sufficient for those in power to rule for their own life-time only, and when they die, either their cousin or sons of their cousins must be appointed, so that the rank may not run exclusively in one branch of the family, but the collaterals also inherit and succeed to the honour; but no one from a stranger family intrudes and becomes a prince. The eight provinces are divided into forty districts, and *these* have minor princelings over them.

---

coni. Bayer || 8 Οὔζοι P || Πατζινακίται P || 9 ἀναψηλαφῶντες edd.   ἀναψηλα-φόντες P: ἀναψηλαφοῦντες V || 10 διακρατουμένην: κρατουμένην V edd. || 12 ἐξεδίωξαν αὐτοὺς edd. || 13 τὴν τοιαύτην χώραν: τῆς τοιαύτης χώρας V edd. || τὴν²: τῆς V edd. || 14 πεντήκοντα πέντε edd.: νε΄ P   *post* ἔτη *numerum anni excidisse,* Ν̄ *autem per comp. pro* ἰνδικτιὼν *seu* ἰνδικτιῶνος *scriptum fuisse susp.* Moravcsik || 17 πρώτου V edd.: α΄ P || δευτέρου edd.: β΄ P || τρίτου edd.: γ΄ P || 18 τετάρτου edd.: δ΄ P || πέμπτου edd.: ε΄ P || Χαραβόη *corr.* Moravcsik: Χαροβόη P edd. || ἕκτου edd.: ς΄ P || 19 ἑβδόμου edd.: ζ΄ P || ὀγδόου edd.: η΄ P || 20 τῆς ἰδίας χώρας (*etiam* Bandurius): τῶν ἰδίων τόπων edd. || Πατζινακίται P || 21 Βαΐτζαν *coni.* Rásonyi   Μάιτζαν V   Μάτζαν edd. || 22 Κουρκοῦταν edd. || 22/3 Χαραβόη *corr.* Moravcsik: Χαροβόη edd.   Χαβόη P || 23 δὲ *add.* Moravcsik || 24 Βατὰν P || 27 ἀρκεῖσθαι: ἀρκεῖν *coni.* Bekker || 28 αὐτούς edd.: αὐτοῦ P || 30 τῆς *om.* edd. || εἰς *secl.* Moravcsik || 30/1 ἐκπλαγίου P: ἐκπλαγίους edd. || 32 ὀκτὼ edd.: η΄ P || 33 τεσσαράκοντα edd.: μ΄ P ||

37

'Ιστέον, ὅτι αἱ τέσσαρες τῶν Πατζινακιτῶν γενεαί, ἤγουν τὸ
166Be θέμα Κουαρτζιτζοὺρ καὶ τὸ θέμα Συρουκάλπεη καὶ τὸ | θέμα Βοροταλμὰτ 35
107ʳᴾ καὶ τὸ θέμα Βουλατ|ζοπόν, κεῖνται πέραν τοῦ Δανάπρεως ποταμοῦ
πρὸς τὰ ἀνατολικώτερα καὶ βορειότερα μέρη, ἐναποβλέποντα πρός τε
Οὐζίαν καὶ Χαζαρίαν καὶ 'Αλανίαν καὶ τὴν Χερσῶνα καὶ τὰ λοιπὰ κλίματα. Αἱ δὲ ἄλλαι τέσσαρες γενεαὶ κεῖνται ἔνθεν τοῦ Δανάπρεως ποταμοῦ πρὸς τὰ δυτικώτερα καὶ ἀρκτικώτερα μέρη, τουτέστιν τὸ θέμα 40
Γιαζιχοπὸν πλησιάζει τῇ Βουλγαρίᾳ, τὸ δὲ θέμα τοῦ κάτω Γύλα πλησιάζει τῇ Τουρκίᾳ, τὸ δὲ θέμα τοῦ Χαραβόη πλησιάζει τῇ 'Ρωσίᾳ, τὸ δὲ
θέμα 'Ιαβδιερτὶμ πλησιάζει τοῖς ὑποφόροις χωρίοις χώρας τῆς 'Ρωσίας,
τοῖς τε Οὐλτίνοις καὶ Δερβλενίνοις καὶ Λενζενίνοις καὶ τοῖς λοιποῖς
107ᵛᴾ Σκλάβοις. 'Απώκισται δὲ ἡ Πατζινακία ἐκ μὲν | Οὐζίας καὶ Χαζαρίας 45
ὁδὸν ἡμερῶν πέντε, ἐκ δὲ 'Αλανίας ὁδὸν ἡμερῶν ἕξ, ἀπὸ δὲ Μορδίας
ὁδὸν ἡμερῶν δέκα, ἀπὸ δὲ 'Ρωσίας ὁδὸν ἡμερᾶς μιᾶς, ἀπὸ δὲ Τουρκίας
ὁδὸν ἡμερῶν τεσσάρων, ἀπὸ δὲ Βουλγαρίας ὁδὸν ἡμέρας τὸ ἥμισυ, καὶ
εἰς Χερσῶνα μέν ἐστιν ἔγγιστα, εἰς δὲ τὴν Βόσπορον πλησιέστερον.
'Ιστέον, ὅτι κατὰ τὸν καιρόν, ὃν οἱ Πατζινακῖται ἀπὸ τῆς ἰδίας 50
χώρας ἐξεδιώχθησαν, θελήσει τινὲς ἐξ αὐτῶν καὶ οἰκείᾳ γνώμῃ ἐναπέμει-
ναν ἐκεῖσε, καὶ τοῖς λεγομένοις Οὔζοις συνῴκησαν, καὶ μέχρι τοῦ νῦν
εἰσιν ἐν αὐτοῖς, ἔχοντες τοιαῦτα γνωρίσματα, ὥστε διαχωρίζεσθαι
αὐτοὺς καὶ νοεῖσθαι, τίνες τε ἦσαν, καὶ πῶς αὐτοὺς ἀποσπασθῆναι τῶν
167Be ἰδίων συν|έβη· | τὰ γὰρ ἱμάτια αὐτῶν εἰσιν κόντουρα μέχρι γονάτων 55
108ʳᴾ καὶ τὰ μανίκια ἀπὸ τῶν βραχιόνων ἀποκεκομμένα, ὡς δῆθεν ἐκ τούτου
δεικνύντες, ὅτι ἀπὸ τῶν ἰδίων καὶ ὁμοφύλων ἀπεκόπησαν.
'Ιστέον, ὅτι ἔνθεν τοῦ Δανάστρεως ποταμοῦ πρὸς τὸ ἀποβλέπον
μέρος τὴν Βουλγαρίαν εἰς τὰ περάματα τοῦ αὐτοῦ ποταμοῦ εἰσὶν ἐρημό-
καστρα· κάστρον πρῶτον τὸ ὀνομασθὲν παρὰ τῶν Πατζινακιτῶν "Ασπρον 60
διὰ τὸ τοὺς λίθους αὐτοῦ φαίνεσθαι καταλεύκους, κάστρον δεύτερον τὸ
Τουγγάται, κάστρον τρίτον τὸ Κρακνακάται, κάστρον τέταρτον τὸ
Σαλμακάται, κάστρον πέμπτον τὸ Σακακάται, κάστρον ἕκτον ⟨τὸ⟩
Γιαιουκάται. 'Εν αὐτοῖς δὲ τοῖς τῶν παλαιοκάστρων κτίσμασιν εὑρίσκον-
108ᵛᴾ ται καὶ ἐκκλησιῶν | γνωρίσματά τινα καὶ σταυροὶ λαξευτοὶ εἰς λίθους 65
πωρίνους, ὅθεν καί τινες παράδοσιν ἔχουσιν, ὡς 'Ρωμαῖοί ποτε τὰς
κατοικίας εἶχον ἐκεῖσε.

V 35 Συρουκαλπέη edd. Συρουκουλπέη *coni.* Bandurius Συροκουλπέη *coni.* Németh
Σαρυκουλπέη *coni.* Marquart ‖ Βοροτάλματ edd. ‖ 36 Βουλατζοπόν P *coni.*
Marquart Németh: Βουλατζοσπόν Pˣ edd. Τζοπὸν *scr. quo deleto* Βουλατζοσπόν
iter. V¹ ‖ πέρα Ba Be ‖ 38/9 κλήματα P ‖ 39 τέσσαρες edd.: δ' P ‖
ἔνθεν (*littera* ο *erasa et* εν *in ras. scripto*) Pʸ Ba Be: ὅθεν P ὅθεν
V ‖ 41 τοῦ κάτω Γύλα: Χαβουξιγγυλὰ *coni.* Lehrberg Κουρκώτα Γύλα *coni.*

37

Four clans of the Pechenegs, that is to say, the province of Kouartzitzour and the province of Syroukalpeï and the province of Borotalmat and
the province of Boulatzopon, lie beyond the Dnieper river towards the
eastern and northern parts that face Uzia and Chazaria and Alania and
Cherson and the rest of the Regions. The other four clans lie on this side of
the Dnieper river, towards the western and northern parts, that is to say
that the province of Giazichopon is neighbour to Bulgaria, the province of
Kato Gyla is neighbour to Turkey, the province of Charaboï is neighbour
to Russia, and the province of Iabdiertim is neighbour to the tributary
territories of the country of Russia, to the Oultines and Dervlenines and
Lenzenines and the rest of the Slavs. Patzinacia is distant a five days journey
from Uzia and Chazaria, a six days journey from Alania, a ten days journey
from Mordia, one day's journey from Russia, a four days journey from
Turkey, half a day's journey from Bulgaria; to Cherson it is very near,
and to Bosporus closer still.

At the time when the Pechenegs were expelled from their country,
some of them of their own will and personal decision stayed behind there
and united with the so-called Uzes, and even to this day they live among
them, and wear such distinguishing marks as separate them off and betray
their origin and how it came about that they were split off from their own
folk: for their tunics are short, reaching to the knee, and their sleeves are
cut off at the shoulder, whereby, you see, they indicate that they have
been cut off from their own folk and those of their race.

On this side of the Dniester river, towards the part that faces Bulgaria,
at the crossings of this same river, are deserted cities: the first city is that
called by the Pechenegs Aspron, because its stones look very white; the
second city is Toungatai; the third city is Kraknakatai; the fourth city
is Salmakatai; the fifth city is Sakakatai; the sixth city is Giaioukatai.
Among these buildings of the ancient cities are found some distinctive
traces of churches, and crosses hewn out of porous stone, whence some
preserve a tradition that once on a time Romans had settlements there.

Marquart ‖ κάτω V edd.: incertum scripseritne κάτω an κάτα P ‖ 42 τοῦ
om. edd. ‖ Χαροβόη edd. ‖ 43 τοῖς ὑποφόροις χωρίοις χώρας (prima littera α ex
dimidia parte, quinta littera ι penitus erasa accentuque correcto) P^y Ba Be: ταῖς
ὑποφόροις χωρίοις χώραις P ταῖς ὑποφόροις χωρίαις, χώραις V ταῖς ὑποφόροις
χώραις Me ‖ 44 τοῖς¹ edd.: τοὺς P ‖ Οὐλτίνοις: Οὐλτίνοις coni. Šachmatov ‖ 46
πέντε edd.: ε′ P ‖ ὁδὸν² om. V edd. ‖ ἐξ edd.: ς′ P ‖ Μορδίας: Μοδίας V
Me Μηδίας coni. Meursius ‖ 47 δέκα edd.: ι′ P ‖ μίας P ‖ 48 τεσσάρων edd.:
δ′ P ‖ τὸ om. V edd. ‖ 50 Πατζινακίται P ‖ 54 αὐτοὺς¹ coni. Moravcsik:
αὐτοῖς P αὐτῶν coni. Kukules ‖ αὐτοὺς edd.: αὐτῶν P ‖ 55 κόντουρα (corr.
etiam Grégoire Psaltes) κόντευρα Be ‖ 58 Δανάστρεως coni. Westberg Laskin
Latyšev Šachmatov: Δανάπρεως P edd. ‖ 60 πρῶτον V edd.: α′ P ‖ 61
δεύτερον edd.: β′ P ‖ 62 Τουγγᾶται P ‖ τρίτον edd.: γ′ P ‖ τέταρτον edd.: δ′ P ‖
63 πέμπτον edd.: ε′ P ‖ ἕκτον edd.: ς′ P ‖ τὸ add. Moravcsik ‖ 64 Γιαιουκᾶται
P ‖ 66 πωρίνους coni. Bekker: πορίνους P Ba Be πυρίτας coni. Meursius ‖

37, 38

Ἰστέον, ὅτι καὶ Κάγγαρ ὀνομάζονται οἱ Πατζινακῖται, ἀλλ' οὐχὶ πάντες, πλὴν ὁ τῶν τριῶν θεμάτων λαός, τοῦ Ἰαβδιηρτὶ καὶ τοῦ Κουαρτζιτζοὺρ καὶ τοῦ Χαβουξιγγυλά, ὡς ἀνδρειότεροι καὶ εὐγενέστεροι τῶν 70 λοιπῶν· τοῦτο γὰρ δηλοῖ ἡ τοῦ Κάγγαρ προσηγορία.

168Be 38. Περὶ τῆς γενεαλογίας τοῦ ἔθνους τῶν Τούρκων, καὶ ὅθεν κατάγονται.

Ὅτι τὸ τῶν Τούρκων ἔθνος πλησίον τῆς Χαζαρίας τὸ παλαιὸν τὴν κατοίκησιν ἔσχεν εἰς τὸν τόπον τὸν ἐπονομαζόμενον Λεβεδία ἀπὸ τῆς τοῦ πρώτου βοεβόδου αὐτῶν ἐπωνυμίας, ὅστις βοέβοδος τὸ μὲν 5
109ʳP τῆς κλήσεως ὄνομα Λεβεδίας | προσηγορεύετο, τὸ δὲ τῆς ἀξίας, ὡς καὶ οἱ λοιποὶ μετ' αὐτόν, βοέβοδος ἐκαλεῖτο. Ἐν τούτῳ οὖν τῷ τόπῳ, τῷ προρρηθέντι Λεβεδίᾳ, ποταμός ἐστιν ῥέων Χιδμάς, ὁ καὶ Χιγγιλοὺς ἐπονομαζόμενος. Οὐκ ἐλέγοντο δὲ τῷ τότε χρόνῳ Τοῦρκοι, ἀλλὰ Σάβαρτοι ἄσφαλοι ἔκ τινος αἰτίας ἐπωνομάζοντο. Καὶ οἱ μὲν Τοῦρκοι γενεαὶ ὑπῆρχον 10 ἑπτά, ἄρχοντα δὲ εἰς αὐτοὺς εἴτε ἴδιον, εἴτε ἀλλότριόν ποτε οὐκ ἐκτήσαντο, ἀλλ' ὑπῆρχον ἐν αὐτοῖς βοέβοδοί τινες, ὧν πρῶτος βοέβοδος ἦν ὁ προρρηθεὶς Λεβεδίας. Συνῴκησαν δὲ μετὰ τῶν Χαζάρων ἐνιαυτοὺς τρεῖς, συμμαχοῦντες τοῖς Χαζάροις ἐν πᾶσι τοῖς αὐτῶν πολέμοις. Ὁ δὲ χαγάνος ἄρχων Χαζαρίας διὰ τὴν αὐτῶν ἀνδρείαν καὶ συμμαχίαν τῷ 15
109ᵛP πρώτῳ βοεβόδῳ τῶν | Τούρκων, Λεβεδίᾳ ἐπονομαζομένῳ, γυναῖκα δέδωκεν πρὸς γάμον Χαζάραν εὐγενῆ διὰ τὸ τῆς ἀνδρείας αὐτοῦ περίφημον καὶ τὸ τοῦ γένους περιφανές, ὅπως ἐξ αὐτοῦ τεκνώσῃ· ὁ δὲ Λεβεδίας
169Be ἐκεῖνος ἔκ τινος τύχης μετὰ τῆς αὐτῆς Χαζάρας οὐκ ἐπαιδοποίησεν. | Οἱ δὲ Πατζινακῖται, οἱ πρότερον Κάγγαρ ἐπονομαζόμενοι (τοῦτο γὰρ τὸ 20 Κάγγαρ ὄνομα ἐπ' εὐγενείᾳ καὶ ἀνδρείᾳ ἐλέγετο παρ' αὐτοῖς), πρὸς Χαζάρους οὖν οὗτοι κινήσαντες πόλεμον καὶ ἡττηθέντες, τὴν οἰκείαν γῆν καταλεῖψαι καὶ τὴν τῶν Τούρκων κατοικῆσαι κατηναγκάσθησαν. Ἀναμεταξὺ δὲ τῶν Τούρκων συναφθέντος πολέμου καὶ τῶν Πατζινακιτῶν, τῶν τηνικαῦτα Κάγγαρ ἐπονομαζομένων, τὸ τῶν Τούρκων φοσσᾶ- 25
110ʳP τον ἡττήθη καὶ εἰς δύο διῃρέθη | μέρη. Καὶ τὸ μὲν ἓν μέρος πρὸς ἀνατολὴν εἰς τὸ τῆς Περσίδος μέρος κατῴκησεν, οἳ καὶ μέχρι τοῦ νῦν κατὰ τὴν τῶν Τούρκων ἀρχαίαν ἐπωνυμίαν καλοῦνται Σάβαρτοι ἄσφαλοι, τὸ δὲ

V 68 καὶ om. V edd. ‖ Κάγγαρ F¹: Κάγκαρ P V F edd. Βάγκαρ hic et infra coni. Grégoire ‖ Πατζινακῖται P ‖ 69 τριῶν edd.: γ´ P ‖ Ἰαβδιηρτὶ Ba Be: Ἰαυδιηρτί P ‖ 69/70 Κουαρτζιτζοὺρ Pᵧ Ba Be: Κουαρτζιτζοῦ P V Me.

The Pechenegs are also called 'Kangar', though not all of them, but only the folk of the three provinces of Iabdierti and Kouartzitzour and Chabouxingyla, for they are more valiant and noble than the rest: and that is what the title 'Kangar' signifies.

38. Of the genealogy of the nation of the Turks, and whence they are descended.

The nation of the Turks had of old their dwelling next to Chazaria, in the place called Lebedia after the name of their first voivode, which voivode was called by the personal name of Lebedias, but in virtue of his rank was entitled voivode, as have been the rest after him. Now in this place, the aforesaid Lebedia, there runs a river Chidmas, also called Chingilous. They were not called Turks at that time, but had the name 'Sabartoi asphaloi', for some reason or other. The Turks were seven clans, and they had never had over them a prince either native or foreign, but there were among them 'voivodes', of whom first voivode was the aforesaid Lebedias. They lived together with the Chazars for three years, and fought in alliance with the Chazars in all their wars. Because of their courage and their alliance, the chagan-prince of Chazaria gave in marriage to the first voivode of the Turks, called Lebedias, a noble Chazar lady, because of the fame of his valour and the illustriousness of his race, so that she might have children by him; but, as it fell out, this Lebedias had no children by this same Chazar lady. Now, the Pechenegs who were previously called 'Kangar' (for this 'Kangar' was a name signifiying nobility and valour among them), these, then, stirred up war against the Chazars and, being defeated, were forced to quit their own land and to settle in that of the Turks. And when battle was joined between the Turks and the Pechenegs who were at that time called 'Kangar', the army of the Turks was defeated and split into two parts. One part went eastwards and settled in the region of Persia, and they to this day are called by the ancient denomination of the Turks 'Sabartoi

---

38. 4 ἔσχεν: ἐποιεῖτο V   edd. || 6 Λεβεδίας: Λαβαδίας hic et infra coni. Iljinskij || προσαγορεύετο edd. || 8 Χιδμάς: Χουμάς coni. Cassel   Χιλμάς coni. Hammer-Purgstall || ὁ V edd.: ὁ P || Χιγγιλοὺς P   V¹: Χιγγυλοὺς V F edd. || 9 Τούρκοι P || 9/10 Σάβαρτοι ἄσφαλοι scr. Moravcsik: Σαβαρτοίασφαλοι P V   Σαβαρτοιάσφαλοι V¹ F edd. Σάβαρ τουτέστι ἄσφαλοι coni. Fessler Σάβαρ ἤτοι σφάλλει et Σάβαρ ἤτοι ἄσφαλοι coni. Dankovszky Hilferding || 10 ἐπονομάζοντο P || Τούρκοι P || 11 ἑπτά edd.: ζ' P || 13 Συνώκησαν edd.: συνωκίσας P   συνοικήσας susp. Moravcsik || 14 τρεῖς: σγ' coni. Thunmann Schlözer Büdinger aliique   τ' coni. Dankovszky Marczali Zichy Grégoire aliique   σ' coni. Moravcsik   λ' seu λγ' coni. Westberg || συμμαχοῦντες: συμμαχῶν τε susp. Moravcsik || 19 Χαζάρας coni. Moravcsik: Χαζάρου P   edd. || 20 Πατζινακῖται P || 20 τοῦτο — 21 αὐτοῖς in parenthesi posuit Be || 25/6 φοσσᾶτον P || 27 κατώκισεν P || 28 Σαβαρτοιάσφαλοι edd. ||

38

ἕτερον μέρος εἰς τὸ δυτικὸν κατῴκησε μέρος ἅμα καὶ τῷ βοεβόδῳ αὐτῶν
καὶ ἀρχηγῷ, Λεβεδίᾳ, εἰς τόπους τοὺς ἐπονομαζομένους Ἀτελκούζου, 30
ἐν οἷς τόποις τὰ νῦν τὸ τῶν Πατζινακιτῶν ἔθνος κατοικεῖ. Ὀλίγου δὲ
χρόνου διαδραμόντος, ὁ χαγάνος ἐκεῖνος ἄρχων Χαζαρίας τοῖς Τούρκοις
ἐμήνυσεν τοῦ πρὸς αὐτὸν ἀποσταλῆναι Λεβεδία, τὸν πρῶτον αὐτῶν
βοέβοδον. Ὁ Λεβεδίας τοίνυν πρὸν τὸν χαγάνον Χαζαρίας ἐναφικόμενος
ἀνηρώτα τὴν αἰτίαν, δι' ἣν ἐλθεῖν πρὸς αὐτὸν αὐτὸν μετεπέμψατο. Ὁ δὲ 35
110ᵛᴾ χαγάνος | εἶπεν πρὸς αὐτόν, ὅτι· «Διὰ τοῦτό σε προσεκαλεσάμεθα, ἵνα,
ἐπειδὴ εὐγενὴς καὶ φρόνιμος καὶ ἠνδρειωμένος ὑπάρχεις καὶ πρῶτος τῶν
Τούρκων, ἄρχοντά σε τοῦ ἔθνους σου προβαλώμεθα, καὶ ἵνα ὑπείκῃς
τῷ λόγῳ καὶ τῇ προστάξει ἡμῶν.» Ὁ δὲ ἀποκριθεὶς πρὸς τὸν χαγάνον
170Βε ἀντέφησεν, ὅτι· «Τὴν περὶ ἐμέ σου σχέσιν τε καὶ | προαίρεσιν μεγάλως 40
ἐναποδέχομαι, καὶ τὴν εὐχαριστίαν ὁμολογῶ σοι προσήκουσαν, ἐπεὶ δὲ ἀδυ-
νάτως ἔχω πρὸς τὴν τοιαύτην ἀρχήν, ὑπακοῦσαι οὐ δύναμαι, ἀλλὰ μᾶλλον
ἔστιν ἕτερος ἀπ' ἐμοῦ βοέβοδος, λεγόμενος Ἀλμούτζης καὶ υἱὸν κεκτη-
μένος ὀνόματι Ἀρπαδήν· ἐκ τούτων μᾶλλον εἴτε ἐκεῖνος ὁ Ἀλμούτζης,
111ʳᴾ εἴτε ὁ υἱὸς αὐτοῦ Ἀρπαδῆς ἵνα γένηται ἄρχων, | καὶ ἔστιν ὑπὸ τὸν λόγον 45
ὑμῶν». Ἐν τούτῳ οὖν τῷ λόγῳ ἀρεσθεὶς ὁ χαγάνος ἐκεῖνος δέδωκεν
ἀνθρώπους αὐτοῦ μετ' αὐτοῦ καὶ εἰς τοὺς Τούρκους ἀπέστειλεν, οἳ καὶ
συλλαλήσαντες περὶ τούτου μετὰ τῶν Τούρκων, μᾶλλον οἱ Τοῦρκοι τὸν
Ἀρπαδῆ γενέσθαι προέκριναν ἄρχοντα, ἤπερ Ἀλμούτζη, τὸν ἑαυτοῦ
πατέρα, ὡς ἀξιολογώτερον ὄντα καὶ περισπούδαστον ἔν τε φρονήσει καὶ 50
βουλῇ καὶ ἀνδρείᾳ καὶ ἱκανὸν πρὸς τὴν τοιαύτην ἀρχήν, ὃν καὶ ἄρχοντα
κατὰ τὸ τῶν Χαζάρων ἔθος καὶ ζάκανον πεποιήκασι, σηκώσαντες αὐτὸν
εἰς σκουτάριον. Πρὸ δὲ τοῦ Ἀρπαδῆ τούτου ἄρχοντα ἕτερον οἱ Τοῦρκοι
οὐκ ἐκτήσαντο πώποτε, ἐξ οὗ καὶ μέχρι τῆς σήμερον ἐκ τῆς τούτου
111ᵛᴾ γενεᾶς ἄρχων Τουρκίας καθίσταται. Μετὰ | δέ τινας χρόνους τοῖς Τούρ- 55
κοις ἐπιπεσόντες οἱ Πατζινακῖται, κατεδίωξαν αὐτοὺς μετὰ τοῦ ἄρχοντος
αὐτῶν Ἀρπαδῆ. Οἱ οὖν Τοῦρκοι τραπέντες καὶ πρὸς κατοίκησιν γῆν
ἐπιζητοῦντες, ἐλθόντες ἀπεδίωξαν οὗτοι τοὺς τὴν μεγάλην Μοραβίαν
οἰκοῦντας, καὶ εἰς τὴν γῆν αὐτῶν κατεσκήνωσαν, εἰς ἣν νῦν οἱ Τοῦρκοι
171Βε μέχρι τῆς σήμερον κατοικοῦσιν. Καὶ ἔκτοτε πό|λεμον οἱ Τοῦρκοι παρὰ 60
τῶν Πατζινακιτῶν οὐκ ἐδέξαντο. Εἰς δὲ τὸ κατασκηνῶσαν τὸ προρρηθὲν
ἔθνος τῶν Τούρκων πρὸς ἀνατολὴν εἰς τὰ τῆς Περσίδος μέρη μέχρι τοῦ
νῦν πραγματευτὰς ἀποστέλλουσιν οὗτοι οἱ πρὸς τὸ δυτικὸν μέρος οἰκοῦν-

---

V 30 Ἀτελκούζου: Ἀτελκ Οὔζου (sine acc.) coni. Thunmann   Ἀτελ καὶ Οὔζου
(sine acc.) coni. Lehrberg Hammer-Purgstall   Ἀτελουζου (sine acc.) coni.
Roesler || 31 τά: τὸ edd. || τὸ om. edd. || 33 Λεβεδία coni. Moravcsik Λεβεδίαν

38

asphaloi'; but the other part, together with their voivode and chief Lebedias, settled in the western region, in places called Atelkouzou, in which places the nation of the Pechenegs now lives. A short while afterwards, the then chagan-prince of Chazaria sent a message to the Turks, requiring that Lebedias, their first voivode, should be sent to him. Lebedias, therefore, came to the chagan of Chazaria and asked the reason why he had sent for him to come to him. The chagan said to him: «We have invited you upon this account, in order that, since you are noble and wise and valorous and first among the Turks, we may appoint you prince of your nation, and you may be obedient to our word and our command.» But he, in reply, made answer to the chagan: «Your regard and purpose for me I highly esteem and express to you suitable thanks, but since I am not strong enough for this rule, I cannot obey you; on the other hand, however, there is a voivode other than me, called Almoutzis, and he has a son called Arpad; let one of these, rather, either that Almoutzis or his son Arpad, be made prince, and be obedient to your word.» That chagan was pleased at this saying, and gave some of his men *to go* with him, and sent them to the Turks, and after they had talked the matter over with the Turks, the Turks preferred that Arpad should be prince rather than Almoutzis his father, for he was of superior parts and greatly admired for wisdom and counsel and valour, and capable of this rule; and so they made him prince according to the custom, or 'zakanon', of the Chazars, by lifting him upon a shield. Before this Arpad the Turks had never at any time had any other prince, and so even to this day the prince of Turkey is from his family. Some years later, the Pechenegs fell upon the Turks and drove them out with their prince Arpad. The Turks, in flight and seeking a land to dwell in, came and in their turn expelled the inhabitants of great Moravia and settled in their land, in which the Turks now live to this day. And since that time the Turks have not sustained any attack from the Pechenegs. To the aforesaid nation of the Turks that settled in the east, in the regions of Persia, these Turks aforesaid who live toward the western region still send mer-

---

coni. Manojlović: χελάνδια P edd. || 34 ἐναφικόμενος: ἀφικόμενος edd. || 35 αὐτόν² *om.* edd. || 36 προσεκαλεσάμεθα edd.: προσεκαλεσώμεθα P || 37 ὑπάρχεις Ba Be: ὑπάρχῃς P || 38 προβαλώμεθα V edd.: προβαλλώμεθα (*incertum sitne* ω *an* ο) P || ὑπείκῃς edd.: ὑπήκεις P || 41 εὐχαριστίαν] εὐχαριστείαν (*prima littera a s. v. addita*) P¹ || 43 Ἀλμούτζης *coni.* Meursius Thunmann Roesler Grot: Σαλμούτζης P edd. || 44 ὁ Ἀλμούτζης P V Me: Σαλμούτζης (*spiritibus erasis et littera* ὁ *in* σ *correcta*) Pʸ || 45 ἔστιν: ἔσται *coni.* Bekker Marczali || τὸν λόγον (*coni. etiam* Bekker): τοῦ λόγου V edd. || 48 Τοῦρκοι P || 49 Ἀλμούτζη P V Me: Σαλμούτζη (*spiritu eraso et littera* σ *addita*) Pʸ Ba Be || ἑαυτοῦ: αὐτοῦ edd. || 52 συκόσαντες P || 53 Ἀρπαδῆ P || Τοῦρκοι P || 56 Πατζινακίται P || 57 Ἀρπαδῆ P || Τοῦρκοι P || 59 οἰκοῦντας: κατοικοῦντας V edd. || Τοῦρκοι P || 60 Τοῦρκοι P || παρὰ (*etiam* Bandurius): μετὰ V edd. || 61 ἐδέξαντο (*etiam* Bandurius): ἐποίησαν V edd. || 62 *post* πρὸς *add.* τὴν V edd. ||

174

38, 39, 40

112ʳP τες προρρηθέντες Τοῦρκοι, καὶ βλέπουσιν αὐτούς, καὶ ἀποκρίσεις | παρὰ
αὐτῶν πρὸς αὐτοὺς πολλάκις ἀποκομίζουσιν.   65
"Ότι ὁ τῶν Πατζινακιτῶν τόπος, ἐν ᾧ τῷ τότε καιρῷ κατώκησαν
οἱ Τοῦρκοι, καλεῖται κατὰ τὴν ἐπωνυμίαν τῶν ἐκεῖσε ὄντων ποταμῶν.
Οἱ δὲ ποταμοί εἰσιν οὗτοι· ποταμὸς πρῶτος ὁ καλούμενος Βαρούχ,
ποταμὸς δεύτερος ὁ καλούμενος Κουβοῦ, ποταμὸς τρίτος ὁ καλούμενος
Τροῦλλος, ποταμὸς τέταρτος ὁ καλούμενος Βροῦτος, ποταμὸς πέμπτος 70
ὁ καλούμενος Σέρετος.

39. Π ε ρ ὶ   τ ο ῦ   ἔ θ ν ο υ ς   τ ῶ ν   Κ α β ά ρ ω ν.

Ἰστέον, ὅτι οἱ λεγόμενοι Κάβαροι ἀπὸ τῆς τῶν Χαζάρων γενεᾶς
ὑπῆρχον. Καὶ δὴ συμβάν τινα παρὰ αὐτῶν ἀποστασίαν γενέσθαι πρὸς
112ᵛP τὴν ἀρχὴν αὐτῶν, καὶ πολέμου ἐμφυλίου καθι|στάντος, ἡ πρώτη ἀρχὴ αὐτῶν
ὑπερίσχυσεν, καὶ οἱ μὲν ἐξ αὐτῶν ἀπεσφάγησαν, οἱ δὲ ἐξέφυγον, καὶ ἦλθαν 5
καὶ κατεσκήνωσαν μετὰ τῶν Τούρκων εἰς τὴν τῶν Πατζινακιτῶν γῆν,
καὶ ἀλλήλοις συνεφιλιώθησαν, καὶ Κάβαροί τινες ὠνομάσθησαν. Ὅθεν
172Be καὶ τὴν τῶν Χαζάρων γλῶσσαν αὐτοῖς | τοῖς Τούρκοις ἐδίδαξαν, καὶ
μέχρι τοῦ νῦν τὴν αὐτὴν διάλεκτον ἔχουσιν· ἔχουσιν δὲ καὶ τὴν τῶν
Τούρκων ἑτέραν γλῶσσαν. Διὰ δὲ τὸ εἰς τοὺς πολέμους ἰσχυροτέρους 10
καὶ ἀνδρειοτέρους δείκνυσθαι τῶν ὀκτὼ γενεῶν καὶ προεξάρχειν τοῦ
πολέμου προεκρίθησαν πρῶται γενεαί. Εἷς δέ ἐστιν ἄρχων ἐν αὐτοῖς,
ἤγουν ἐν ταῖς τρισὶ γενεαῖς τῶν Καβάρων, ὅστις καὶ μέχρι τὴν σήμερον
ἔστιν.

113ʳP   40. Π ε ρ ὶ   τ ῶ ν   γ ε ν ε ῶ ν   τ ῶ ν   Κ α β ά ρ ω ν   κ α ὶ   τ ῶ ν
Τ ο ύ ρ κ ω ν.

Πρώτη ἡ παρὰ τῶν Χαζάρων ἀποσπασθεῖσα αὕτη ἡ προρρηθεῖσα
τῶν Καβάρων γενεά, δευτέρα τοῦ Νέκη, τρίτη τοῦ Μεγέρη, τετάρτη
⟨τοῦ⟩ Κουρτουγερμάτου, πέμπτη τοῦ Ταριάνου, ἕκτη Γενάχ, ἑβδόμη 5
Καρῆ, ὀγδόη Κασῆ. Καὶ οὕτως ἀλλήλοις συναφθέντες, μετὰ τῶν Τούρκων οἱ Κάβαροι εἰς τὴν τῶν Πατζινακιτῶν κατώκησαν γῆν. Μετὰ δὲ

V 64 προρρηθέντες: προειρημένοι V edd. ‖ Τοῦρκοι P ‖ ἀποκρίσεις Ba Be:
ἀποκρίσεσιν P ‖ 67 Τοῦρκοι P ‖ 69 δεύτερος edd.: β′ P ‖ Κουβοῦ: Κοβοῦ mg.
P   Κουζοῦ coni. Roesler ‖ τρίτος edd.: γ′ P ‖ 70 Τροῦλλος: Τοῦλος coni.
Roesler ‖ τέταρτος edd.: δ′ P ‖ πέμπτος edd.: ε′ P.

38, 39, 40

chants who look them up, and often bring them back official messages from them. The place of the Pechenegs, in which at that time the Turks lived, is called after the name of the local rivers. The rivers are these: the first river is that called Barouch, the second river that called Koubou, the third river that called Troullos, the fourth river that called Broutos, the fifth river that called Seretos.

39. Of the nation of the Kabaroi.

The so-called Kabaroi were of the race of the Chazars. Now, it fell out that a secession was made by them to their government, and when a civil war broke out their first government prevailed, and some of them were slain, but others escaped and came and settled with the Turks in the land of the Pechenegs, and they made friends with one another, and were called 'Kabaroi'. And so to these Turks they taught also the tongue of the Chazars, and to this day they have this same language, but they have also the other tongue of the Turks. And because in wars they show themselves strongest and most valorous of the eight clans, and are leaders in war, they have been promoted to be first clans. There is one prince among them, I mean, among the three clans of the Kabaroi, who is even to this day.

40. Of the clans of the Kabaroi and the Turks.

The first is this aforesaid clan of the Kabaroi which split off from the Chazars; the second, of Nekis; the third, of Megeris; the fourth, *of* Kourtougermatos; the fifth, of Tarianos; the sixth, Genach; the seventh, Kari; the eighth, Kasi. Having thus combined with one another, the Kabaroi dwelt with the Turks in the land of the Pechenegs. After this, at the invitation

---

39. 2 Κάβαροι edd.: Καβάροι P   *ubique sine* κ *scribendum coni.* Meursius   Βάχαροι *hic et infra coni.* Grégoire || 3 συμβάν *corr.* Moravcsik: συμβᾶσαν P edd. || 4 καθιστάντος: καταστάντος *coni.* Bekker || 5 ἦλθον edd. || 7 Κάβαροί: βάρβαροί V Me || ὀνομάσθησαν P || 8 γλῶτταν edd. || 11 ἀνδρειοτέρους edd.: ἠνδρειωτέρους P || ὀκτὼ edd.: η′ P || 13 τρισὶ edd.: τρεῖς P || τὴν: τῆς V edd.

40. 1 τῶν³ *om.* edd. || 3 ἀποσπασθεῖσα V edd.: ἀποσπαθεῖσα P || 4 δευτέρα edd.: β′ P || τρίτη edd.: γ′ P || τετάρτη edd.: δ′ P || 5 τοῦ *add.* V edd. || Κουρτυγερμάτου edd. || πέμπτη edd.: ε′ P || ἔκτη edd.: ς′ P || ἑβδόμη edd.: ζ′ P || 6 Καρή P || ὀγδόη edd.: η′ P || Κασή P || Βάχαροι V F ||

40

ταῦτα παρὰ Λέοντος, τοῦ φιλοχρίστου καὶ ἀοιδίμου βασιλέως, προσκλη-
θέντες διεπέρασαν, καὶ τὸν Συμεὼν πολεμήσαντες κατὰ κράτος αὐτὸν
ἥττησαν, καὶ ἐξελάσαντες μέχρι τῆς Πρεσθλάβου διῆλθον, ἀποκλείσαν- 10
τες αὐτὸν εἰς τὸ κάστρον τὸ λεγόμενον Μουνδράγα, καὶ εἰς τὴν ἰδίαν
113ᵛP χώραν ὑπέστρεψαν. Τῷ δὲ τότε | καιρῷ τὸν Λιούντικα, τὸν υἱὸν τοῦ
Ἀρπαδῆ εἶχον ἄρχοντα. Μετὰ δὲ τὸ πάλιν τὸν Συμεὼν μετὰ τοῦ βασιλέως τῶν Ῥωμαίων εἰρηνεῦσαι καὶ λαβεῖν ἄδειαν διεπέμψατο πρὸς
173Be τοὺς | Πατζινακίτας, καὶ μετὰ αὐτῶν ὡμοφώνησεν τοῦ καταπολεμῆσαι 15
καὶ ἀφανίσαι τοὺς Τούρκους. Καὶ ὅτε οἱ Τοῦρκοι πρὸς ταξίδιον ἀπῆλθον,
οἱ Πατζινακῖται μετὰ Συμεὼν ἦλθον κατὰ τῶν Τούρκων, καὶ τὰς αὐτῶν
φαμιλίας παντελῶς ἐξηφάνισαν, καὶ τοὺς εἰς φύλαξιν τῆς χώρας αὐτῶν
Τούρκους ἀπ' ἐκεῖσε κακιγκάκως ἀπεδίωξαν. Οἱ δὲ Τοῦρκοι ὑποστρέψαντες καὶ τὴν χώραν αὐτῶν οὕτως εὑρόντες ἔρημον καὶ κατηφανισμένην, 20
114ʳP κατεσκήνωσαν εἰς τὴν γῆν, εἰς ἣν καὶ σή|μερον κατοικοῦσιν, τὴν ἐπονο-
μαζομένην κατὰ τὴν ἀνωτέρω, ὡς εἴρηται, τῶν ποταμῶν ἐπωνυμίαν.
Ὁ δὲ τόπος, ἐν ᾧ πρότερον οἱ Τοῦρκοι ὑπῆρχον, ὀνομάζεται κατὰ τὴν
ἐπωνυμίαν τοῦ ἐκεῖσε διερχομένου ποταμοῦ Ἐτὲλ καὶ Κουζοῦ, ἐν ᾧ
ἀρτίως οἱ Πατζινακῖται κατοικοῦσιν. Οἱ δὲ Τοῦρκοι παρὰ τῶν Πατζι- 25
νακιτῶν διωχθέντες ἦλθον καὶ κατεσκήνωσαν εἰς τὴν γῆν, εἰς ἣν νῦν οἰκοῦσιν. Ἐν αὐτῷ δὲ τῷ τόπῳ παλαιά τινα ἔστιν γνωρίσματα· καὶ πρῶτον
μέν ἐστιν ἡ τοῦ βασιλέως Τραϊανοῦ γέφυρα κατὰ τὴν τῆς Τουρκίας
ἀρχήν, ἔπειτα καὶ ἡ Βελέγραδα ἀπὸ τριῶν ἡμερῶν τῆς αὐτῆς γεφύρας,
114ᵛP ἐν ᾗ καὶ ὁ πύργος ἐστὶν τοῦ ἁγίου καὶ | μεγάλου Κωνσταντίνου, τοῦ 30
βασιλέως, καὶ πάλιν κατὰ τὴν τοῦ ποταμοῦ ἀναδρομήν ἐστιν τὸ Σέρμιον
ἐκεῖνο λεγόμενον, ἀπὸ τῆς Βελεγράδας ὁδὸν ἔχον ἡμερῶν δύο, καὶ ἀπὸ
τῶν ἐκεῖσε ἡ μεγάλη Μοραβία, ἡ ἀβάπτιστος, ἣν καὶ ἐξήλειψαν οἱ Τοῦρ-
174Be κοι, |ἧς ἦρχε τὸ πρότερον ὁ Σφενδοπλόκος.
Ταῦτα μὲν τὰ κατὰ τὸν Ἴστρον ποταμὸν γνωρίσματά τε καὶ 35
ἐπωνυμίαι, τὰ δὲ ἀνώτερα τούτων, ἐν ᾧ ἐστιν ἡ πᾶσα τῆς Τουρκίας
κατασκήνωσις, ἀρτίως ἐπονομάζουσιν κατὰ τὰς {τοῦ} τῶν ἐκεῖσε ῥεόντων
ποταμῶν ἐπωνυμίας. Οἱ δὲ ποταμοί εἰσιν οὗτοι· ποταμὸς πρῶτος ὁ
Τιμήσης, ποταμὸς δεύτερος ⟨ὁ⟩ Τούτης, ποταμὸς τρίτος ὁ Μορήσης,
115ʳP ⟨ποταμὸς⟩ τέταρτος ὁ Κρίσος, καὶ πάλιν ἕτερος ποταμὸς ἡ Τί|τζα. 40

F   7 Μετὰ δὲ — 13 ἄρχοντα: cf. Georg. Mon. (cont.), ed. Bonn. p.
853, 20—855, 7; Georg. Mon. (cont.), ed. Istrin II. p. 27, 20—28, 11; Leo
Gramm., ed. Bonn. p. 267, 15—269, 4; Theod. Melit., ed. Tafel p. 186,
30—188, 2; Theoph. Cont., ed. Bonn. p. 358, 7—359, 16; Cedr., ed. Bonn. II.
p. 254, 24—256, 1; Zon. XVI. 12., ed. Bonn. III. p. 442, 17—443, 16; Leo,
Tact. XVIII. 42., ed. Migne, P. G. 107. c. 956 C—D.

40

of Leo, the Christ-loving and glorious emperor, they crossed over and fought Symeon and totally defeated him, and drove on and penetrated as far as Preslav, having shut him up in the city called Moundraga; and they went back to their own country. At that time they had Liountikas, son of Arpad, for their prince. But after Symeon was once more at peace with the emperor of the Romans and was free to act, he sent to the Pechenegs and made an agreement with them to attack and destroy the Turks. And when the Turks had gone off on a military expedition, the Pechenegs with Symeon came against the Turks and completely destroyed their families and miserably expelled thence the Turks who were guarding their country. When the Turks came back and found their country thus desolate and utterly ruined, they settled in the land where they live to-day, which is called after the above name of the rivers, as has been said. The place in which the Turks used formerly to be is called after the name of the river that runs through it, Etel and Kouzou, and in it the Pechenegs live now. But the Turks, expelled by the Pechenegs, came and settled in the land which they now dwell in. In this place are various landmarks of the olden days: first, there is the bridge of the emperor Trajan, where Turkey begins; then, a three days journey from this same bridge, there is Belgrade, in which is the tower of the holy and great Constantine, the emperor; then, again, at the running back of the river, is the renowned Sirmium by name, a journey of two days from Belgrade; and beyond lies great Moravia, the unbaptized, which the Turks have blotted out, *but* over which in former days Sphendoplokos used to rule.

Such are the landmarks and names along the Danube river; but the regions above these, which comprehend the whole settlement of Turkey, they now call after the names of the rivers that flow there. The rivers are these: the first river is the Timisis, the second river *the* Toutis, the third river the Morisis, the fourth *river* the Krisos, and again another river, the

---

V 9 πολεμίσαντες P ‖ 12 Λιούντινα Ba Be ‖ 13 'Αρπαδὴ P ‖ 14 εἰρηνεῦσαι P
V¹ F: εἰρηνεῦθαι V   εἰρηνεύεσθαι edd. ‖ 15 ὁμοφώνησεν P ‖ 16 Τοῦρκοι P ‖
17 Πατζινακίται P ‖ *post* μετὰ *add.* τοῦ edd. ‖ 18 φαμηλίας P ‖ 19 Τοῦρκοι
P ‖ 21 τὴν ἐπονομαζομένην — 22 ἐπωνυμίαν *post* κατηφανισμένην (20) *trans-
ponenda coni.* Marquart ‖ 23 Τοῦρκοι P ‖ 24 τοῦ ἐκεῖσε διερχομένου ποταμοῦ: τοῖν ἐκεῖσε διερχομένοιν ποταμοῖν *coni.* Hammer-Purgstall   τῶν ἐκεῖσε
διερχομένων ποταμῶν *coni.* Marquart ‖ 'Ετὲλ καὶ Κουζοῦ: 'Ετὲλ καὶ Οὐζοῦ
coni. Lehrberg   καὶ *omittendum coni.* Thunmann   Marquart Westberg
post 'Ετὲλ *et post* Κουζοῦ *punctum posuit* P   'Ετὲλ ποταμὸς καὶ Κουζοῦ
mg. P³ ‖ Κουζοῦ edd. ‖ 25 Πατζινακίται P ‖ Τοῦρκοι P ‖ 29 καὶ ἡ: δὲ καὶ
edd. ‖ Βελάγραδα *mg.* P⁶ edd. ‖ γέφυρας P ‖ 31 ἀναδρομήν *scr.* Moravcsik
ἀναδρομεῖν P: ἐκδρομεῖν V   ἐκδρομὴν V¹ ἐκδρομήν F edd. ‖ 32 *post* ἐκεῖνο *add.*
τὸ V edd. ‖ Βελεγράδας edd.: Βελέγραδας P Βελάγραδας *mg.* P⁶ ‖ 33/4
Τοῦρκοι P ‖ 37 ἐπονομάζουσιν: ὀνομάζουσι edd. ‖ τοῦ *om.* Bekker   *secl.*
Moravcsik   τούτων Me Ba ‖ 38 πρῶτος edd.: α' P ‖ 39 δεύτερος edd.: β' P ‖
ὁ *add.* Moravcsik ‖ τρίτος Be: γ' P ‖ 40 ποταμὸς *add.* V ‖ τέταρτος Be: δ' P ‖

178

40

Πλησιάζουσι δὲ τοῖς Τούρκοις πρὸς μὲν τὸ ἀνατολικὸν μέρος οἱ Βούλγαροι, ἐν ᾧ καὶ διαχωρίζει αὐτοὺς ὁ Ἴστρος, ὁ καὶ Δανούβιος λεγόμενος ποταμός, πρὸς δὲ τὸ βόρειον οἱ Πατζινακῖται, πρὸς δὲ τὸ δυτικώτερον οἱ Φράγγοι, πρὸς δὲ τὸ μεσημβρινὸν οἱ Χρωβάτοι. Αἱ δὲ ὀκτώ γενεαὶ τῶν Τούρκων αὗται πρὸς τοὺς οἰκείους ἄρχοντας οὐχ ὑπείκουσιν, ἀλλ' 45 ὁμόνοιαν ἔχουσιν εἰς τοὺς ποταμούς, εἰς οἷον μέρος προβάλλει πόλεμος, συναγωνίζεσθαι μετὰ πάσης φροντίδος τε καὶ σπουδῆς. Ἔχουσι δὲ κεφαλὴν πρώτην τὸν ἄρχοντα ἀπὸ τῆς γενεᾶς τοῦ Ἀρπαδῆ κατὰ ἀκολουθίαν καὶ δύο ἑτέρους, τόν τε γυλᾶν καὶ τὸν καρχᾶν, οἵτινες ἔχουσι τάξιν
115ᵛP κριτοῦ· | ἔχει δὲ ἑκάστη γενεὰ ἄρχοντα.   50
Ἰστέον, ὅτι ὁ γυλᾶς καὶ ὁ καρχᾶς οὐκ εἰσὶ κύρια ὀνόματα, ἀλλὰ ἀξιώματα.
175Be Ἰστέον, ὅτι ὁ Ἀρπαδῆς, ὁ μέγας Τουρκίας ἄρχων, ἐποίησεν | τέσσαρας υἱούς· πρῶτον τὸν Ταρκατζοῦν, δεύτερον τὸν Ἰέλεχ, τρίτον τὸν Ἰουτοτζᾶν, τέταρτον τὸν Ζαλτᾶν.   55
Ἰστέον, ὅτι ὁ πρῶτος υἱὸς τοῦ Ἀρπαδῆ, ὁ Ταρκατζοῦς ἐποίησεν υἱὸν τὸν Τεβέλη, ὁ δὲ δεύτερος υἱός, ὁ Ἰέλεχ ἐποίησεν υἱὸν τὸν Ἐζέλεχ, ὁ δὲ τρίτος υἱός, ὁ Ἰουτοτζᾶς ἐποίησεν υἱὸν τὸν Φαλίτζιν, τὸν νυνὶ ἄρχοντα, ὁ δὲ τέταρτος υἱός, ⟨ὁ⟩ Ζαλτᾶς ἐποίησεν υἱὸν τὸν Ταξίν.
Ἰστέον, ὅτι πάντες ⟨οἱ⟩ υἱοὶ τοῦ Ἀρπαδῆ ἐτελεύτησαν, οἱ δὲ 60 ἔγγονοι αὐτοῦ, ὅ τε Φαλῆς καὶ ὁ Τασῆς καὶ ὁ ἐξάδελφος αὐτῶν, ὁ Ταξίς, ζῶσιν.
Ἰστέον, ὅτι ἐτελεύτησεν ὁ Τεβέλης, καὶ ἔστιν ὁ υἱὸς αὐτοῦ ὁ
116ʳP Τερματζοῦς, ὁ ἀρτίως ἀνελθὼν φίλος | μετὰ τοῦ Βουλτζοῦ, τοῦ τρίτου ἄρχοντος καὶ καρχᾶ Τουρκίας.   65
Ἰστέον, ὅτι ὁ Βουλτζοῦς, ὁ καρχᾶς ἐστιν ὁ υἱὸς τοῦ Καλῆ, τοῦ καρχᾶ, καὶ ὅτι τὸ μὲν Καλῆ ἐστιν ὄνομα κύριον, τὸ δὲ καρχᾶς ἐστιν ἀξίωμα, ὥσπερ καὶ τὸ γυλᾶς, ⟨ὁ⟩ ἐστιν μεῖζον τοῦ καρχᾶ.

V 43 Πατζινακῖται P ‖ 44 Χρώβατοι edd. ‖ ὀκτὼ edd.: η′ P V ‖ 45 οὐχ delendum coni. Jenkins ‖ ὑπείκουσιν F: ὑπήκουσιν P V ὑπηκούουσιν Ba Be ‖ 46 ποταμούς: πολέμους coni. Marczali Jenkins ‖ προβάλλει: προσβάλλει coni. Bekker ‖ 48 Ἀρπαδῆ P ‖ 49 δύο edd.: β′ P ‖ γυλάν P ‖ καρχάν P ‖ 51 γυλᾶς P ‖ καρχάς P: καρχᾶν Be ‖ ὀνόματα κύρια edd. ‖ 53/4 τέσσαρας Be: δ′ P ‖ 54 πρῶτον edd.: α′ P ‖ δεύτερον edd.: β′ P ‖ τρίτον edd.: γ′ P ‖ 55 Ἰουτοτζάν Ba Be: Ἰουτότζαν P ‖ τέταρτον edd.: δ′ P ‖ Ζαλτάν

40

Titza. Neighbours of the Turks are, on the eastern side the Bulgarians, where the river Istros, also called Danube, runs between them; on the northern, the Pechenegs; on the western, the Franks; and on the southern, the Croats. These eight clans of the Turks do not obey their own particular princes, but have a joint agreement to fight together with all earnestness and zeal upon the rivers, wheresoever war breaks out. They have for their first chief the prince who comes by succession of Arpad's family, and two others, the gylas and the karchas, who have the rank of judge; and each clan has a prince.

Gylas and karchas are not proper names, but dignities.

Arpad, the great prince of Turkey, had four sons: first, Tarkatzous; second, Ielech; third, Ioutotzas; fourth, Zaltas.

The eldest son of Arpad, Tarkatzous, had a son Tebelis, and the second son Ielech had a son Ezelech, and the third son Ioutotzas had a son Phalitzis, the present prince, and the fourth son Zaltas had a son Taxis.

All *the* sons of Arpad are dead, but his grandsons Phalis and Tasis and their cousin Taxis are living.

Tebelis is dead, and it is his son Termatzous who came here recently as 'friend' with Boultzous, third prince and karchas of Turkey.

The karchas Boultzous is the son of the karchas Kalis, and Kalis is a proper name, but karchas is a dignity, like gylas, *which* is superior to karchas.

P ‖ 56 πρῶτος edd.: α′ P ‖ Ἀρπαδὴ P ‖ Ταρκατζοὺς P ‖ 57 δεύτερος edd.: β′ P ‖ 58 τρίτος edd.: γ′ P ‖ Ἰουτοτζάς P ‖ 59 τέταρτος edd.: δ′ P ‖ ὁ add. Moravcsik ‖ Ζαλτάς P ‖ τὸν om. edd. ‖ 60 οἱ add. edd. ‖ Ἀρπαδὴ P: Ἀρπαδᾶ edd. ‖ 61 ὁ² om. edd. ‖ Τάξις edd. ‖ 63 ὁ² om. F ‖ 64 Τερματζούς P ‖ 65 καρχὰ P ‖ 66 Βουλτζοὺς P ‖ καρχάς P ‖ ἐστιν ὁ υἱός: ἐστίν υἱὸς V υἱός ἐστι edd. ‖ 67 καρχά P ‖ Καλὴ P ‖ καρχάς P ‖ 68 γυλάς P ‖ ὁ add. edd. ‖ καρχά P.

180

41

41. Περὶ τῆς χώρας τῆς Μοραβίας.

Ἰστέον, ὅτι ὁ Μοραβίας ἄρχων, ὁ Σφενδοπλόκος, ἀνδρεῖος καὶ φοβερὸς εἰς τὰ πλησιάζοντα αὐτῷ ἔθνη γέγονεν. Ἔσχε δὲ ὁ αὐτὸς
176Be Σφενδοπλόκος τρεῖς υἱούς, καὶ τελευτῶν διεῖλεν | εἰς τρία μέρη τὴν ἑαυτοῦ χώραν, καὶ τοῖς τρισὶν υἱοῖς αὐτοῦ ἀνὰ μιᾶς μερίδος κατέλιπεν, 5 τὸν πρῶτον καταλείψας ἄρχοντα μέγαν, τοὺς δὲ ἑτέρους δύο τοῦ εἶναι ὑπὸ τὸν λόγον τοῦ πρώτου υἱοῦ. Παρήνεσεν δὲ αὐτοὺς τοῦ μὴ εἰς διάστα-
116ᵛP σιν καὶ κα|τ' ἀλλήλων γενέσθαι, παράδειγμα αὐτοῖς τοιοῦτον ὑποδείξας· ῥάβδους γὰρ τρεῖς ἐνεγκὼν καὶ συνδήσας, δέδωκεν τῷ πρώτῳ υἱῷ τοῦ ταύτας κλάσαι, τοῦ δὲ μὴ ἰσχύσαντος, πάλιν δέδωκεν τῷ δευτέρῳ, 10 ὡσαύτως καὶ τῷ τρίτῳ, καὶ εἶθ' οὕτως διαιρῶν τὰς τρεῖς ῥάβδους δέδωκεν τοῖς τρισὶ πρὸς μίαν· οἱ δὲ λαβόντες καὶ κελευσθέντες ταύτας κλάσαι, εὐθέως αὐτὰς κατέκλασαν. Καὶ διὰ τοιούτου ὑποδείγματος παρήνεσεν αὐτοὺς εἰπών, ὡς ὅτι· «Εἰ μὲν διαμένετε ἐν ὁμοψυχίᾳ καὶ ἀγάπῃ ἀδιαίρετοι, ἀκαταγώνιστοι παρὰ τῶν ἐναντίων καὶ ἀνάλωτοι γενήσεσθε· 15 εἰ δὲ ἐν ὑμῖν γένηται ἔρις καὶ φιλονικία, καὶ διαχωρισθῆτε εἰς τρεῖς
117ʳP ἀρχάς, μὴ ὑποκείμενοι τῷ πρώτῳ ἀδελφῷ, καὶ ὑπ' ἀλλήλων | ἀφανισθήσεσθε, καὶ ὑπὸ τῶν πλησιαζόντων ὑμῖν ἐχθρῶν παντελῶς ἐξολοθρευθήσεσθε.» Μετὰ δὲ τὴν τελευτὴν τοῦ αὐτοῦ Σφενδοπλόκου ἕνα χρόνον ἐν εἰρήνῃ διατελέσαντες, ἔριδος καὶ στάσεως ἐν ἑαυτοῖς ἐμπεσούσης, καὶ 20 πρὸς ἀλλήλους ἐμφύλιον πόλεμον ποιήσαντες, ἐλθόντες οἱ Τοῦρκοι τούτους παντελῶς ἐξωλόθρευσαν, καὶ ἐκράτησαν τὴν ἑαυτῶν χώραν, εἰς ἣν καὶ ἀρτίως οἰκοῦσιν. Καὶ οἱ ὑπολειφθέντες τοῦ λαοῦ διεσκορπίσθησαν, προσφυγόντες εἰς τὰ παρακείμενα ἔθνη, εἴς τε τοὺς Βουλγάρους καὶ Τούρκους καὶ Χρωβάτους καὶ εἰς τὰ λοιπὰ ἔθνη. 25

F   41. 7 Παρήνεσεν — 19 ἐξολοθρευθήσεσθε: cf. Aesopus, fab. 103., ed.
Halm; Babrius, fab. 47., ed. Schneidewin; Plutarchus, De garrulitate c.
18., ed. Bernardakis III. p. 325; Plutarchus, Regum et imperatorum
apophthegmata 174., ed. c. II. p. 8—9.

41

41. Of the country of Moravia.

The prince of Moravia, Sphendoplokos, was valiant and terrible to the nations that were his neighbours. This same Sphendoplokos had three sons, and when he was dying he divided his country into three parts and left a share apiece to his three sons, leaving the eldest to be great prince and the other two to be under the command of the eldest son. He exhorted them not to fall out with one another, giving them this example by way of illustration: he brought three wands and bound them together and gave them to the first son to break them, and when he was not strong enough, handed them on to the second, and in like manner to the third, and then separated the three wands and gave one each to the three of them; when they had taken them and were bidden to break them, they broke them through at once. By means of this illustration he exhorted them and said: «If you remain undivided in concord and love, you shall be unconquered by your adversaries and invincible; but if strife and rivalry come among you and you divide yourselves into three governments, not subject to the eldest brother, you shall be both destroyed by one another and brought to utter ruin by the enemies who are your neighbours.» After the death of this same Sphendoplokos they remained at peace for a year, and then strife and rebellion fell upon them and they made a civil war against one another and the Turks came and utterly ruined them and possessed their country, in which even now they live. And those of the folk who were left were scattered and fled for refuge to the adjacent nations, to the Bulgarians and Turks and Croats and to the rest of the nations.

V   **41.** 2 Μωραβίας P ‖ 4 τρία edd.: γ′ P ‖ 6 μέγαν edd.: μέγα P ‖ 8 καὶ om. F   *delendum coni.* Bandurius ‖ 10 ταύτας] *litteram* σ *inser.* P¹ ‖ δευτέρῳ Moravcsik   β′ P: ἑτέρῳ V edd. ‖ 14 αὐτοῖς V ‖ ὡς *om.* V edd. ‖ 16 τρεῖς edd.: γ′ P ‖ 17 πρώτῳ edd.: α′ P ‖ 20 ἑαυτοῖς: αὐτοῖς V edd. ‖ 21 Τούρκοι P ‖ 22 ἐξολώθρευσαν P ‖ ἑαυτῶν: αὐτῶν edd.

177Be 42. Γεωγραφία ἀπὸ Θεσσαλονίκης μέχρι τοῦ
Δανούβεως ποταμοῦ καὶ τοῦ κάστρου Βελε-
117ᵛP γράδας, Τουρ|κίας τε καὶ Πατζινακίας μέχρι
τοῦ Χαζαρικοῦ κάστρου Σάρκελ καὶ τῆς Ῥωσίας καὶ μέχρι τῶν Νεκροπύλων, τῶν ὄντων 5
εἰς τὴν τοῦ Πόντου θάλασσαν πλησίον τοῦ
Δανάπρεως ποταμοῦ, καὶ Χερσῶνος ὁμοῦ καὶ
Βοσπόρου, ἐν οἷς τὰ κάστρα τῶν κλιμάτων
εἰσίν, εἶτα μέχρι λίμνης Μαιώτιδος, τῆς
καὶ θαλάσσης διὰ τὸ μέγεθος ἐπονομαζομέ- 10
νης, καὶ μέχρι τοῦ κάστρου Ταμάταρχα λεγομένου, πρὸς τούτοις δὲ καὶ Ζιχίας καὶ Παπαγίας καὶ Κασαχίας καὶ Ἀλανίας καὶ Ἀβασγίας καὶ μέχρι τοῦ κάστρου Σωτηριουπόλεως.

Ἰστέον, ὅτι ἀπὸ Θεσσαλονίκης μέχρι τοῦ ποταμοῦ Δανούβεως, 15
118ʳP ἐν ᾧ τὸ | κάστρον ἐστὶν τὸ Βελέγραδα ἐπονομαζόμενον, ἔστιν ὁδὸς
ἡμερῶν ὀκτώ, εἰ καὶ μὴ διὰ τάχους τις, ἀλλὰ μετὰ ἀναπαύσεως πορεύε-
ται. Καὶ κατοικοῦσιν μὲν οἱ Τοῦρκοι πέραθεν τοῦ Δανούβεως ποταμοῦ
εἰς τὴν τῆς Μοραβίας γῆν, ἀλλὰ καὶ ἔνθεν μέσον τοῦ Δανούβεως καὶ
τοῦ Σάβα ποταμοῦ. Ἀπὸ δὲ κάτωθεν τῶν μερῶν Δανούβεως ποταμοῦ 20
τῆς Δίστρας ἀντίπερα ἡ Πατζινακία παρέρχεται, καὶ κατακρατεῖ ἡ
κατοικία αὐτῶν μέχρι τοῦ Σάρκελ, τοῦ τῶν Χαζάρων κάστρου, ἐν ᾧ
ταξεῶται καθέζονται τριακόσιοι, κατὰ χρόνον ἐναλλασσόμενοι. Ἑρμηνεύεται δὲ παρὰ αὐτοῖς τὸ Σάρκελ 'ἄσπρον ὀσπίτιον', ὅπερ ἐκτίσθη
118ᵛP παρὰ σπαθαροκανδιδάτου Πετρωνᾶ, τοῦ ἐπονο|μαζομένου Καματηροῦ, 25
178Be τὸν βασιλέα Θεόφιλον πρὸς | τὸ κτισθῆναι αὐτοῖς τὸ κάστρον τοῦτο τῶν
Χαζάρων αἰτησαμένων. Ὁ γὰρ χαγάνος ἐκεῖνος καὶ ὁ πὲχ Χαζαρίας
εἰς τὸν αὐτὸν βασιλέα Θεόφιλον πρέσβεις ἐναποστείλαντες, κτισθῆναι
αὐτοῖς τὸ κάστρον τὸ Σάρκελ ᾐτήσαντο, οἷς ὁ βασιλεύς, τῇ τούτων
αἰτήσει πεισθείς, τὸν προρρηθέντα σπαθαροκανδιδᾶτον Πετρωνᾶ μετὰ 30
χελανδίων βασιλικῶν πλωΐμων ἀπέστειλεν καὶ χελάνδια τοῦ κατεπάνω
Παφλαγονίας. Καὶ δὴ ὁ αὐτὸς Πετρωνᾶς τὴν Χερσῶνα καταλαβὼν τὰ
μὲν χελάνδια ἔλιπεν ἐν Χερσῶνι, τὸν δὲ λαὸν εἰσαγαγὼν εἰς καματερὰ

F   42. 20 Ἀπὸ δὲ — 55 καθέστηκεν: cf. Theoph. Cont. p. 122, 19—124,
5; Cedr., ed. Bonn. II. p. 129, 21—130, 13.

V   42. 4 Σάρκελ καὶ scr. Moravcsik: Σάρκελ κὲ P Σαρκελκὲ V Me Σάρκελ
(litteris κὲ erasis) Pᵛ Ba Be ‖ 5 Νεκροπύλων V edd.: Νεκροπήλων P ‖ 8
κλη's(μάτων P ‖ 10/1 ἐπονομαζομένης: καλουμένης V edd. ‖ 11 Ταμάταρχα scr.

42

42. Geographical description from Thessalonica to the Danube river and the city of Belgrade; of Turkey and Patzinacia to the Chazar city of Sarkel and Russia and to the Nekropyla, that are in the sea of Pontus, near the Dnieper river; and to Cherson together with Bosporus, between which are the cities of the Regions; then to the lake of Maeotis, which for its size is also called a sea, and to the city called Tamatarcha; and of Zichia, moreover, and of Papagia and of Kasachia and of Alania and of Abasgia and to the city of Sotirioupolis.

From Thessalonica to the river Danube where stands the city called Belgrade, is a journey of eight days, if one is not travelling in haste but by easy stages. The Turks live beyond the Danube river, in the land of Moravia, but also on this side of it, between the Danube and the Save river. From the lower reaches of the Danube river, opposite to Distra, Patzinacia stretches along, and its inhabitants control the territory as far as Sarkel, the city of the Chazars, in which garrisons of 300 men are posted and annually relieved. Sarkel among them means 'white house', and it was built by the spatharocandidate Petronas, surnamed Camaterus, when the Chazars requested the emperor Theophilus that this city should be built for them. For the then chagan and the pech of Chazaria sent envoys to this same emperor Theophilus and begged that the city of Sarkel might be built for them, and the emperor acceded to their request and sent to them the aforesaid spatharocandidate Petronas with ships of war of the imperial navy, and *sent* also ships of war of the captain-general of Paphlagonia. This same Petronas arrived at Cherson and left the ships of war at Cherson, and,

---

Moravcsik τὰ Μάταρχα P: τοῦ Μάταρχα edd. || 12/3 Παπαγίας (*secunda syllaba* πα *s. v. rubro atramento addita*) P¹ V edd.: Παγίας P || 13 Καζαχίας edd. || 16 Βελέγραδα: Βελάγραδον *mg.* P || 17 ὀκτώ edd.: η΄ P ιη΄ *coni.* Marquart || 17/8 πορεύηται Ba Be || 18 Τοῦρκοι P || 19 Μωραβίας P || εἰς τὴν τῆς Μοραβίας γῆν *post* ἔνθεν *transponendum coni.* Marquart || 22 κάστρου V edd.: κάστρων P || 23 τριακόσιοι Theoph. Cont. τ΄ *coni.* Migne Bury: τὰ P edd. || 24 ἄσπρον ὁσπίτιον: λευκὸν οἴκημα Theoph. Cont. || 25 Καματεροῦ Theoph. Cont. || 27 καὶ ὁ Theoph. Cont. *coni.* Bayer Lehrberg Marquart Bury: ὁ καὶ P edd. || 28 βασιλέα: αὐτοκράτορα Theoph. Cont. || ἐναποστείλαντες: ἀποστείλαντες edd. || 30 σπαθαροκανδιδάτον P || Πετρωνᾶ P: Πετρωνᾶν Theoph. Cont. || 31 βασιλικῶν πλωΐμων: βασιλικοπλωΐμων Theoph. Cont. || 33 χελάνδια: μακρὰς νῆας Theoph. Cont. || ἔλιπεν *coni.* Moravcsik: εὗρεν P εὗρεν edd. ὥρμισεν *coni.* Bury προσορμίσας... κατέλιπεν Theoph. Cont. || 33/4 εἰς καματερὰ καράβια: ἐν στρογγύλαις ... ναυσὶ Theoph. Cont. ||

42
καράβια, ἀπῆλθεν ἐν τῷ τόπῳ τοῦ Τανάϊδος ποταμοῦ, ἐν ᾧ καὶ τὸ κά-
119ʳP στρον | ἔμελλεν κτίσαι. Καὶ ἐπειδὴ ὁ τόπος λίθους οὐκ εἶχεν πρὸς κτίσιν 35
τοῦ κάστρου ἐπιτηδείους, καμίνιά τινα ποιησάμενος καὶ βήσσαλον ἐν
αὐτοῖς ἐγκαύσας, μετ' αὐτῶν τὴν τοῦ κάστρου κτίσιν ἐποιήσατο, ἐκ
μικρῶν τινων τῶν ἐκ τοῦ ποταμοῦ κοχλιδίων ἄσβεστον ἐργασάμενος.
Οὗτος οὖν ὁ προρρηθεὶς σπαθαροκανδιδᾶτος Πετρωνᾶς μετὰ τὸ κτίσαι
τὸ κάστρον τὸ Σάρκελ πρὸς τὸν βασιλέα Θεόφιλον εἰσελθών, εἶπεν 40
αὐτῷ, ὅτι· «Εἰ θέλῃς ὅλως τὸ τῆς Χερσῶνος κάστρον καὶ τοὺς ἐν αὐτῇ
τόπους κυρίως ἐξουσιάσαι καὶ τούτους μὴ τῆς σῆς ἐκτὸς γενέσθαι χειρός,
προβάλλου στρατηγὸν ἴδιον, καὶ μὴ τοῖς ἐκείνων καταπιστεύσῃς πρω-
119ᵛP τεύουσί τε καὶ ἄρχουσι.» Μέχρι γὰρ Θεοφίλου τοῦ | βασιλέως οὐκ ἦν
στρατηγὸς ἀπὸ τῶν ἐντεῦθεν ἀποστελλόμενος, ἀλλ' ἦν ὁ τὰ πάντα διοι- 45
κῶν ὁ λεγόμενος πρωτεύων μετὰ καὶ τῶν ἐπονομαζομένων πατέρων
179Be τῆς | πόλεως. Τοῦ οὖν βασιλέως Θεοφίλου πρὸς ταῦτα βουλευσαμένου
τὸν ὁ δεῖνα ἐξαποστεῖλαι στρατηγὸν ἢ τὸν ὁ δεῖνα, ὕστερον ἀποσταλῆναι
προέκρινεν τὸν προρρηθέντα σπαθαροκανδιδᾶτον Πετρωνᾶν ὡς † ἔμπειρα†
τοῦ τόπου γεγονότα καὶ τῶν πραγμάτων οὐκ ἀνεπιστήμονα, ὃν καὶ 50
πρωτοσπαθάριον τιμήσας, προεβάλετο στρατηγόν, καὶ εἰς Χερσῶνα
ἐξαπέστειλεν, ὁρίσας τὸν τότε πρωτεύοντα καὶ πάντας ὑπείκειν αὐτῷ,
ἐξ οὗ καὶ μέχρι τὴν σήμερον ἐπεκράτησεν ἀπὸ τῶν ἐντεῦθεν εἰς Χερσῶνα
120ʳP προβάλλεσθαι στρατηγούς. Ἀλλ' αὕτη μὲν | ἡ τοῦ Σάρκελ τοῦ κάστρου
κτίσις καθέστηκεν. Ἀπὸ δὲ τοῦ Δανούβεως ποταμοῦ μέχρι τοῦ προρρη- 55
θέντος κάστρου, τοῦ Σάρκελ ὁδός ἐστιν ἡμερῶν ξ'. Μέσον δὲ τῆς τοιαύτης
γῆς ποταμοὶ μέν εἰσιν πολλοί· δύο δὲ μέγιστοι ἐξ αὐτῶν ὅ τε Δάναστρις
καὶ ὁ Δάναπρις. Εἰσὶ δὲ ἕτεροι ποταμοί, ὅ τε λεγόμενος Συγγούλ καὶ
ὁ Ὑβὺλ ⟨καὶ⟩ ὁ Ἀλματαὶ καὶ ὁ Κοῦφις καὶ ὁ Βογοῦ καὶ ἕτεροι πολλοί.
Εἰς δὲ τὰ ὑψηλότερα τοῦ Δανάπρεως ποταμοῦ μέρη κατοικοῦσιν οἱ 60
Ῥῶς, δι' οὗ ποταμοῦ ἀποπλέοντες, πρὸς Ῥωμαίους ποιοῦνται τὴν ἄφιξιν.
Ἡ δὲ Πατζινακία πᾶσαν τὴν γῆν ⟨μέχρι⟩ τῆς τε Ῥωσίας καὶ Βοσπόρου
κατακρατεῖ καὶ μέχρι Χερσῶνος καὶ ἕως τὸ Σαράτ, Βουρὰτ καὶ τῶν
120ᵛP λ' μερῶν. Τὸ | δὲ τῆς παραλίας τῆς θαλάσσης ἀπὸ τοῦ Δανούβεως
ποταμοῦ διάστημα μέχρι τοῦ Δανάστρεως ποταμοῦ εἰσιν μίλια ρκ'. 65
Ἀπὸ δὲ τοῦ Δανάστρεως ποταμοῦ μέχρι ⟨τοῦ⟩ ποταμοῦ Δανάπρεώς
180Be εἰσιν μίλια π', ὁ χρυσὸς λεγόμενος αἰγιαλός. Ἀπὸ δὲ τὸ στόμιον ποτα|μοῦ

V 34/5 τὸ κάστρον: τὴν πόλιν Theoph. Cont. ‖ 35 κτίσαι: οἰκοδομεῖν Theoph. Cont. ‖
ἐπειδὴ: ἐπεὶ δὲ Theoph. Cont. ‖ 36 βίσαλον P   Theoph. Cont. ‖ 38 κοχλιδίων:
καχλιδίων Pᵞ Ba Be: καχλήκων Theoph. Cont. καχληκίων coni. Bekker ‖ 39 σπαθαροκανδιδᾶτος P ‖ 43 προβάλλου V edd.: προβάλου P   προβαλοῦ
coni. Bekker ‖ 46 καὶ (etiam Theoph. Cont.): om. V edd. ‖ 48 ἀποσταλῆναι:
ἀποστεῖλαι V edd. ‖ 49 σπαθαροκανδιδάτον P ‖ Πετρωνᾶ edd. ‖ ἐμπεῖρα:

42

having embarked his men on ships of burden, went off to that place on the Tanaïs river where he was to build the city. And since the place had no stones suitable for the building of the city, he made some ovens and baked bricks in them and with these he carried out the building of the city, making mortar out of tiny shells from the river. Now this aforesaid spatharocandidate Petronas, after building the city of Sarkel, went to the emperor Theophilus and said to him: «If you wish complete mastery and dominion over the city of Cherson and of the places in Cherson, and not that they should slip out of your hand, appoint your own military governor and do not trust to their primates and nobles.» For up till the time of Theophilus the emperor, there was no military governor sent from here, but all administration was in the hands of the so-called primate, with those who were called the fathers of the city. The emperor Theophilus took counsel in this matter, whether to send as military governor so-and-so or such-an-one, and at last made up his mind that the aforesaid spatharocandidate Petronas should be sent, as one who had acquired local *experience* and was not unskilled in affairs, and so he promoted him to protospatharius and appointed him military governor and sent him out to Cherson, with orders that the then primate and everyone else were to obey him; and from that time until this day it has been the rule for military governors in Cherson to be appointed from here. So much, then, for the building of the city of Sarkel. From the Danube river to the aforesaid city of Sarkel is a journey of 60 days. In this land between are many rivers: the two biggest of them are the Dniester and the Dnieper. But there are other rivers, that which is called the Syngoul and the Hybyl *and* the Almatai and the Kouphis and the Bogou and many others. On the higher reaches of the Dnieper river live the Russians, and down this river they sail and arrive at the Romans. Patzinacia possesses all the land *as far as* Russia and Bosporus and as far as Cherson and up to Sarat, Bourat and the 30 places. The distance along the sea-coast from the Danube river to the Dniester river is 120 miles. From the Dniester river to *the* river Dnieper is 80 miles, the so-called 'gold-coast'. After the

---

ἔμπειραν Theoph. Cont.V   ἔμπειρον V edd. Theoph. Cont. ἐν πείρᾳ coni. Kukules
Kyriakides ‖ 50 γεγονότα: γενόμενον V edd. ‖ καὶ² om. edd. ‖ 51 καὶ s. v. add. P¹
in textum receperunt V edd. ‖ 52 ὁρίσας: θεσπίσας Theoph. Cont.   διατάγματα
πέμψας Cedr. ‖ τὸν τότε πρωτεύοντα edd.: τόν τε πρωτεύοντα Theoph. Cont.
τῷ τότε πρωτεύοντι P ‖ 53 τὴν: τῆς V edd. ‖ 54 τοῦ Σάρκελ τοῦ κάστρου: κάστρου
Σάρκελ edd. ‖ 55 κτίσις: οἰκοδομὴ Theoph. Cont. ‖ 58 Συγγούλ: Ὑγγουλ
coni. Thunmann Brun ‖ 59 Ὕβυλ Be ‖ καὶ add. Moravcsik ‖ Κούφις P ‖
καὶ ὅ³: ὁ καὶ coni. Marquart ‖ 62 μέχρι addendum coni. Bayer Lehrberg
μεταξὺ addendum coni. Makai ‖ 63/4 τῶν λοιπῶν μερῶν coni. Lehrberg:
ἔστιν ὁδὸς ἡμερῶν... coni. Šestakov Latyšev ‖ 65 Δανάστρεως coni. Westberg
Laskin Latyšev: Δανάπρεως P edd. ‖ 66 τοῦ add. V edd. ‖ 67 δὲ om. V edd. ‖

τοῦ Δανάπρεώς εἰσι τὰ ᾿Αδαρά, κἀκεῖσε κόλπος ἐστὶν μέγας, ὁ λεγόμενος τὰ Νεκρόπυλα, ἐν ᾧ τις διελθεῖν ἀδυνατεῖ παντελῶς. Καὶ ἀπὸ
μὲν τοῦ Δανάπρεως ποταμοῦ μέχρι Χερσῶνός εἰσιν μίλια τ΄, ἐν τῷ μέσον 70
δὲ λίμναι καὶ λιμένες εἰσίν, ἐν οἷς οἱ Χερσωνῖται τὸ ἅλας ἐργάζονται.
᾿Απὸ δὲ Χερσῶνος μέχρι Βοσπόρου εἰσὶν τὰ κάστρα τῶν κλιμάτων,
121ʳP τὸ δὲ διάστημα μί|λια τ΄. Καὶ ἀπὸ Βοσπόρου τὸ τῆς Μαιώτιδος λίμνης
στόμιόν ἐστιν, ἥτις καὶ θάλασσα διὰ τὸ μέγεθος παρὰ πάντων ὀνομάζεται. Εἰς δὲ τὴν αὐτὴν Μαιώτιδα θάλασσαν εἰσρέουσιν ποταμοὶ πολλοὶ 75
καὶ μεγάλοι· πρὸς μὲν τὸ ἀρκτῷον αὐτῆς μέρος ὁ Δάναπρις ποταμός,
ἐξ οὗ καὶ οἱ ῾Ρῶς διέρχονται πρός τε τὴν μαύρην Βουλγαρίαν καὶ Χαζαρίαν
καὶ Συρίαν. ῾Ο δὲ αὐτὸς κόλπος τῆς Μαιότιδος ἔρχεται ἀντικρὺ τῶν
Νεκροπύλων, τῶν ὄντων πλησίον τοῦ Δανάπρεως ποταμοῦ, ὡς ἀπὸ
μιλίων δ΄, καὶ μίσγεται, ἐν ᾧ καὶ σοῦδαν οἱ παλαιοὶ ποιησάμενοι διεβί- 80
βασαν τὴν θάλασσαν, μέσον ἀποκλείσαντες πᾶσαν τὴν Χερσῶνος γῆν
121ᵛP καὶ τῶν κλιμάτων | καὶ τῆς Βοσπόρου γῆν, κρατοῦσαν μέχρι ͺα μιλίων ἢ
καὶ πλειόνων τινῶν. ᾿Εκ δὲ τῶν πολλῶν ἐτῶν κατεχώσθη ἡ αὐτὴ σοῦδα
καὶ εἰς δάσος ἐγένετο πολύ, καὶ οὐκ εἰσὶν ἐν αὐτῷ πλὴν δύο ὁδοί, ἐν
αἷς οἱ Πατζινακῖται διέρχονται πρός τε Χερσῶνα καὶ Βόσπορον καὶ 85
τὰ κλίματα. Εἰς δὲ τὸ ἀνατολικώτερον μέρος τῆς Μαιώτιδος λίμνης
181Be εἰσέρχονται πολλοί τι|νες ποταμοί, ὅ τε Τάναϊς ποταμός, ὁ ἀπὸ τὸ κά-
στρον Σάρκελ ἐρχόμενος, καὶ τὸ Χαράκουλ, ἐν ᾧ καὶ τὸ βερζίτικον
ἁλιεύεται, εἰσὶ δὲ καὶ ἕτεροι ποταμοί, ὁ Βὰλ καὶ ὁ Βουρλίκ, ὁ Χαδὴρ καὶ
ἄλλοι πλεῖστοι ποταμοί. ᾿Εκ δὲ τῆς Μαιώτιδος λίμνης ἐξέρχεται στό- 90
122ʳP μιον τὸ Βουρλὶκ ἐπονομαζόμενον, καὶ πρὸς τὴν τοῦ Πόντου θά|λασσαν
καταρρεῖ, ἐν ᾧ ἐστιν ἡ Βόσπορος, ἀντικρὺ δὲ τῆς Βοσπόρου τὸ Ταμάταρχα
λεγόμενον κάστρον ἐστίν. Τὸ δὲ διάστημα τοῦ περάματος τοῦ τοιούτου
στομίου ἐστὶν μίλια ιη΄. ᾿Εν δὲ τῷ μέσον τῶν αὐτῶν ιη΄ μιλίων ἐστὶ
νησίον μέγα χαμηλόν, τὸ λεγόμενον ᾿Ατέχ. ᾿Απὸ τὸ Ταμάταρχά ἐστι 95
ποταμὸς ἀπὸ μιλίων ιη΄ ἢ καὶ κ΄, λεγόμενος Οὐκρούχ, ὁ διαχωρίζων
τὴν Ζιχίαν καὶ τὸ Ταμάταρχα, ἀπὸ δὲ τοῦ Οὐκρούχ μέχρι τοῦ Νικόψεως
ποταμοῦ, ἐν ᾧ καὶ κάστρον ἐστὶν ὁμώνυμον τῷ ποταμῷ, ἔστιν ἡ χώρα
τῆς Ζιχίας· τὸ δὲ διάστημά ἐστιν μίλια τ΄. ῎Ανωθεν δὲ τῆς Ζιχίας
ἐστὶν ἡ χώρα ἡ λεγομένη Παπαγία, καὶ ἄνωθεν τῆς Παπαγίας χώρας 100
122ᵛP ἐστὶν ἡ χώρα ἡ λεγομένη Κασαχία, ἄνωθεν δὲ τῆς | Κασαχίας ὄρη τὰ
Καυκάσιά εἰσιν, καὶ τῶν ὀρέων ἄνωθέν ἐστιν ἡ χώρα τῆς ᾿Αλανίας.
῾Η δὲ τῆς Ζιχίας παράλιος ἔχει νησία, τὸ μέγα νησὶν καὶ τὰ τρία νησία·
ἔνδοθεν δὲ τούτων εἰσὶν καὶ ἕτερα νησία, τὰ καὶ ἐπινεμηθέντα καὶ παρὰ

F   80 ἐν ᾧ — 83 τινῶν: cf. Herod. IV. 3, 20; Ptolem. Geogr. III. 6, 5;
Steph. Byz. s. v. Τάφραι, etc.

42

mouth of the river Dnieper comes Adara, and there is a great gulf, called Nekropyla, where it is utterly impossible for a man to pass through. From the Dnieper river to Cherson is 300 miles, and between are marshes and harbours, in which the Chersonites work the salt. Between Cherson and Bosporus are the cities of the Regions, and the distance is 300 miles. After Bosporus comes the mouth of the Maeotic lake, which for its size everybody calls a sea. Into this same Maeotic sea run rivers many and great; on its northern side runs the Dnieper river, from which the Russians come through to Black Bulgaria and Chazaria and Syria. This same gulf of Maeotis comes opposite to, and within about four miles of, the Nekropyla that are near the Dnieper river, and joins them where the ancients dug a ditch and carried the sea through, enclosing within all the land of Cherson and of the Regions and the land of Bosporus, which cover up to 1,000 miles or even rather more. In the course of many years this same ditch has silted up and become a great forest, and there are in it but two roads, along which the Pechenegs pass through to Cherson and Bosporus and the Regions. Into the eastern side of the Maeotic lake debouch many rivers, the Tanaïs river that comes down from the city of Sarkel, and the Charakoul, in which they fish for sturgeon, and there are other rivers, the Bal and the Bourlik, the Chadir and other rivers very numerous. From the Maeotic lake debouches a mouth called Bourlik and flows down into the sea of Pontus where Bosporus is, and opposite to Bosporus is the city called Tamatarcha; the width of the strait of this mouth is 18 miles. In the middle of these 18 miles is a large, low island, called Atech. After Tamatarcha, some 18 or 20 miles from it, is a river called Oukrouch, which divides Zichia and Tamatarcha, and from the Oukrouch to the Nikopsis river, on which stands a city with the same name as the river, is the country of Zichia; the distance is 300 miles. Beyond Zichia is the country called Papagia, and beyond the country of Papagia is the country called Kasachia, and beyond Kasachia are the Caucasian mountains, and beyond the mountains is the country of Alania. Off the seaboard of Zichia lie islands, the great island and the three islands; and, closer to shore than these, are yet other islands, which have been used for pasturage

---

V 68 τὰ ᾿Αδαρά: Τάνδαρα coni. Latyšev ‖ καὶ ἐκεῖσε edd. ‖ 69 Νεκρόπυλα V edd.: Νεκρόπηλα P ‖ 70 μέσον: μέσῳ V edd. ‖ 71 οἷς: αἷς V edd. ‖ οἱ om. edd. ‖ Χερσωνῖται P ‖ 72 Βοοσπόρου P ‖ κλημάτων P ‖ 76 μὲν om. edd. ‖ 78 Συρίαν: Ζιχίαν coni. Kunik Συανίαν coni. Gibbon Μυρίαν seu Μορδίαν coni. Tomaschek ‖ 79 Νεκροπύλων V edd.: Νεκροπήλων P ‖ 80 σούδαν P ‖ 82 κλημάτων P ‖ τῆς: τὴν Ba Be ‖ ‚α: α΄ edd. ‖ 83 πλειόνων Ba Be: πλέον P ‖ σοῦδα P ‖ 85 Πατζινακίται P ‖ 86 κλήματα P ‖ 88 Χωράκουλ V edd. ‖ βερζήτικον P edd. ‖ 89 καὶ ὁ: ὁ καὶ coni. Marquart ‖ 92 ἡ: ὁ edd. ‖ τῆς: τοῦ Migne ‖ 94 μέσον: μέσῳ edd. ‖ 97 Ταματαρχά P ‖ 99 δὲ² om. edd. ‖ 102 ᾿Αλανίας] litteras ἀλανί in ras. scr. P¹ ‖ 103 Ζηχίας P ‖ νησίν P   νησὴν Pˣ: νησὶ V   νησίον edd. ‖ 104 καὶ² om. V edd. ‖ ἐπινεμηθέντα coni. Jenkins: ἐπινοηθέντα P edd. ‖

τῶν Ζιχῶν κτισθέντα, τό τε Τουργανήρχ καὶ τὸ Τζαρβαγάνιν καὶ 105
ἕτερον νησίν, καὶ εἰς τὸν τοῦ Σπαταλοῦ λιμένα ἕτερον νησίν, καὶ εἰς
182Be τὰς Πτελέας ἕτερον, ἐν ᾧ ἐν ταῖς τῶν Ἀλανῶν ἐπι|δρομαῖς οἱ Ζιχοὶ
καταφεύγουσιν. Τὸ δὲ παραθαλάσσιον ἀπὸ τῆς συμπληρώσεως τῆς
Ζιχίας, ἤτοι τοῦ Νικόψεως ποταμοῦ, ἐστὶν ἡ τῆς Ἀβασγίας χώρα μέχρι
τοῦ κάστρου Σωτηριουπόλεως· εἰσὶ δὲ μίλια τ'. 110

43. Περὶ τῆς χώρας τοῦ Ταρών.

123ʳP   Ἀλλὰ περὶ μὲν τῶν βορείων Σκυθῶν ἱ|κανῶς σοι δεδήλωται,
τέκνον ποθούμενον, ὧν ἡ γνῶσις ἐπωφελής τε καὶ εὔχρηστος ἐν καιρῷ
σοι πάντως γενήσεται· δεῖ δέ σε μηδὲ τὰ πρὸς ἀνίσχοντα ἥλιον ἀγνοεῖν,
ὅθεν ὑπήκοα πάλιν τοῖς Ῥωμαίοις ἐγένετο, ἀφ' οὗ τὸ πρῶτον τῆς τού- 5
των ἐπικρατείας ἐξέπεσον.

Πρῶτος γὰρ ὁ Κρικορίκιος ἐκεῖνος τοῦ Ταρὼν ἄρχων πρὸς τὸν
βασιλέα Ῥωμαίων ἑαυτὸν ὑπέκλινεν καὶ ὑπέταξεν, ἀλλ' ἐξ ἀρχῆς μὲν
ἐπαμφοτερίζων ἐφαίνετο, καὶ λόγῳ μὲν τὴν τοῦ βασιλέως φιλίαν προσ-
εποιεῖτο τιμᾶν, ἔργῳ δὲ τῷ τῶν Σαρακηνῶν κατάρχοντι τὰ καθ' 10
ἡδονὴν διεπράττετο, καὶ διαφόρως ἡγεμὼν ἐχρημάτισεν τῶν ἀπὸ Συρίας
123ᵛP ἐξερχομένων φοσσάτων | κατὰ τῶν ὑπηκόων θεμάτων τῷ βασιλεῖ
Ῥωμαίων, καὶ πάντα τὰ τοῖς Ῥωμαίοις ἐν ἀπορρήτῳ μελετώμενα
κατὰ τῶν ἀντιπάλων Σαρακηνῶν πρὸς Συρίαν ἐμήνυεν, καὶ λάθρα περὶ
τῶν παρ' ἡμῖν συμβαινόντων ἀεὶ πρὸς τὸν ἀμερμουμνῆν διὰ γραμμάτων 15
183Be ἐδηλοποίει, καὶ δοκεῖν μὲν ἐβούλετο | τὰ τῶν Ῥωμαίων φρονῶν, εὑρί-
σκετο δὲ μᾶλλον τὰ τῶν Σαρακηνῶν προκρίνων τε καὶ τιμῶν. Πλὴν
ἀπέστελλεν ἀεὶ δῶρα, ἅπερ τοῖς ἐκεῖσε βαρβάροις δοκεῖ τίμια, πρὸς
τὸν ἐν βασιλεῦσιν ἀοίδιμον Λέοντα, καὶ ἀντελάμβανε πλείονά τε καὶ
κρείττονα παρὰ τοῦ εὐσεβοῦς βασιλεύοντος, ὃς καὶ πολλάκις αὐτῷ προ- 20
124ʳP ετρέψατο διὰ γραμμάτων πρὸς τὴν βασι|λεύουσαν εἰσελθεῖν καὶ τὸν
βασιλέα θεάσασθαι καὶ τῶν παρ' αὐτοῦ φιλοφρονήσεων καὶ τιμῶν με-
τασχεῖν. Ὁ δὲ δεδοικώς, μὴ πρὸς λύπην καὶ σκάνδαλον τοῦ ἀμερμουμνῆ γένηται τοῦτο, προφάσεις ἐπλάττετο, καὶ τὸ μὴ δύνασθαι τὴν ἑαυτοῦ
χώραν ἔρημον τῆς ἐξ αὐτοῦ βοηθείας καταλιπεῖν, ἵνα μὴ ὑπὸ τῶν Σαρακη- 25
νῶν καταληϊσθῇ, μάτην ἐσκήπτετο.

Ὁ δὲ αὐτὸς ἄρχων τοῦ Ταρὼν κρατήσας ἐν πολέμῳ ποτὲ τοῦ
Ἀρκάικα τοὺς παῖδας, ἤγουν Κρικορίκου τοῦ πατρικίου, τοῦ πατρὸς

V 105 Ζηχῶν P ‖ Τζαρβαγάνην P: Τζαρβαγάνι V edd. ‖ 106 νησίν P   νησήν
Pˣ: νησί V νησίον edd. ‖ Σπαταλοῦ (etiam mg. P⁸): ποταμοῦ V edd. ‖
νησίν P   νησήν Pˣ: νησί V   νησίον edd. ‖ 107 Ζηχοὶ P ‖ 109 Ζηχίας P ‖
τοῦ om. edd.

42, 43

and built upon by the Zichians, Tourganirch and Tzarbaganin and another island; and in the harbour of Spalaton another island; and at Pteleai another, where the Zichians take refuge during Alan incursions. The coastal area from the limit of Zichia, that is, from the Nikopsis river, is the country of Abasgia, as far as the city of Sotirioupolis; it is 300 miles.

43. Of the country of Taron.

But concerning the northern Scyths sufficient has been made plain to you, beloved child, knowledge of which shall be all ways advantageous and useful to you in time of need; but also it is right that you should not be ignorant of the parts towards the rising sun, for what reasons they became once more subject to the Romans, after they had first fallen away from their control.

The late Krikorikios, then, prince of Taron, at first bent and submitted himself before the emperor of the Romans, but from the first he seemed double-faced, and while in word he pretended to esteem the friendship of the emperor, in fact he acted at the pleasure of the chief prince of the Saracens, and on various occasions led armies that came out of Syria against provinces subject to the emperor of the Romans, and everything that the Romans were planning in secret against their Saracen adversaries he would divulge to Syria, and would always keep the commander of the faithful informed secretly through his letters of what was going on among us; and while he wished to appear a partisan of the Roman cause, he was found, on the contrary, to prefer and favour the cause of the Saracens. However, he continually sent presents, such as appear valuable to the barbarians of those parts, to Leo, the glorious among emperors, and got in return more and better from the pious emperor, who also frequently urged him by letter to visit the imperial city and behold the emperor and partake of the bounties and honours bestowed by him. But he, fearing lest this might vex and offend the commander of the faithful, would trump up excuses, and falsely allege that it was impossible for him to leave his own country deprived of his assistance, lest it might be plundered by the Saracens.

Now, this same prince of Taron one day captured in battle the sons of Arkaïkas, that is to say, the cousins of the patrician Krikorikios, father

43. 1 Ταρῶν P ‖ 14 ἐμήνυεν: ἀνεμήνυε edd. ‖ 15 ἡμῖν Bandurius Be: ὑμῖν P ‖ ἀμερμουμνὴν P ‖ 17 τιμῶν: φρονῶν V edd. ‖ 20 εὐσεβοῦς edd.: εὐσεβοῦ P εὐσεβῶς coni. Bekker ‖ 20/1 προυτρέψατο edd. ‖ 21 καὶ om. Be ‖ 24 τὴν om. edd. ‖ 25 τῶν om. edd. ‖ 26 ἐσκήπτετο (etiam Be): ἐσκέπτετο V Me Ba ‖ 28 Κρικορίκη edd. ‖

43

τοῦ πρωτοσπαθαρίου 'Ασωτίου, τοὺς ἐξαδέλφους, εἶχε παρ' ἑαυτῷ
δεσμίους. Περὶ ὧν καὶ Συμβάτιος, ὁ τότε ἄρχων τῶν ἀρχόντων, τὸν 30
αὐτὸν μακαριώτατον βασιλέα διὰ γραμμάτων ἠξίωσεν τοῦ ἀποστεῖλαι
124ᵛP | πρὸς τὸν Ταρωνίτην καὶ ἀναλαβέσθαι σπουδάσαι τοὺς οἰκείους ἀνεψιούς,
οἵτινες ἦσαν υἱοὶ τοῦ εἰρημένου 'Αρκάϊκα, ἵνα μὴ πρὸς τὸν ἀμερμουμνῆν
ἀποσταλῶσιν· συγγενὴς γὰρ ἦν τοῦ Συμβατίου, τοῦ ἄρχοντος τῶν ἀρχόντων, Γρηγόριος ὁ πατρίκιος. Ἐπακούσας δὲ τῆς τοιαύτης τοῦ Συμβα- 35
τίου ἀξιώσεως Λέων, ὁ μακαριώτατος βασιλεύς, τὸν Σινούτην ἐκεῖνον
184Be | τὸν εὐνοῦχον ἀπέστειλε, χαρτουλάριον τηνικαῦτα τοῦ ὀξέως δρόμου
τυγχάνοντα, πρός τε τὸν ἄρχοντα τοῦ Ταρὼν τῆς τοιαύτης ἕνεκα ὑποθέσεως καὶ πρὸς τὸν 'Αδρανασήρ, τὸν κουροπαλάτην 'Ιβηρίας, διά τινας
ἑτέρας ὑποθέσεις, δοὺς αὐτῷ καὶ πρὸς ἀμφοτέρους ξενάλια τὰ ἁρμόζοντα. 40
125ʳP Διαβληθέν|τος δὲ τοῦ εἰρημένου Σινούτου παρὰ Θεοδώρου, τοῦ τῶν
'Αρμενίων ἑρμηνευτοῦ, πρὸς τὸν εἰρημένον ἀοίδιμον βασιλέα, ἐξαπεστάλη
βασιλικὸς ἀντ' αὐτοῦ ὁ πρωτοσπαθάριος Κωνσταντῖνος καὶ δομέστικος
τῆς ὑπουργίας ὁ τοῦ Λιβός, ὁ νῦν ἀνθύπατος πατρίκιος καὶ μέγας ἑταιρειάρχης, ἐνταλματικῶς ὁρισθεὶς τοῦ ἀναλαβέσθαι τὰ πρὸς τὸν ἄρχοντα 45
τοῦ Ταρών, τὸν Κρικορίκιον, ἀποσταλέντα ξενάλια, καὶ αὐτὸς μὲν πρὸς
τὸ Ταρὼν εἰσελθεῖν, τὸν δὲ Σινούτην προτρέψασθαι πρὸς τὸν 'Αδρανασήρ, τὸν κουροπαλάτην 'Ιβηρίας, κατὰ τὰ ἐνταλθέντα αὐτῷ ἀπελθεῖν.
Καταλαβὼν δὲ τὸ Ταρὼν ὁ εἰρημένος πρωτοσπαθάριος καὶ ἀποδοὺς
125ᵛP Κρικορικίῳ τὰ πρὸς αὐτὸν ἀποσταλέντα τοῦ βασιλέως δῶρα |καὶ γράμ- 50
ματα, ἀνελάβετο τὸν νόθον τοῦ Ταρωνίτου υἱόν, ὃς 'Ασώτιος ὠνομάζετο,
καὶ εἰσήγαγεν αὐτὸν πρὸς τὴν βασιλεύουσαν, ὃν ὁ βασιλεὺς τῇ τοῦ
πρωτοσπαθαρίου τιμήσας ἀξίᾳ καὶ ἱκανῶς φιλοφρονησάμενος, πρὸς
τὸν ἴδιον πατέρα διὰ τοῦ αὐτοῦ πρωτοσπαθαρίου ἀπέστειλεν. 'Αναλαβό-
μενος οὖν ὁ αὐτὸς Κωνσταντῖνος ἐκεῖθεν 'Απογάνεμ, τὸν ἀδελφὸν 55
Κρικορίκου, τοῦ ἄρχοντος τοῦ Ταρών, εἰσήγαγεν πρὸς τὸν μακάριον
185Be βασιλέα μετὰ καὶ τῶν | δύο υἱῶν τοῦ 'Αρκάϊκα, ὃν καὶ τῇ τοῦ πρωτοσπα-
θαρίου ἀξίᾳ τιμήσας ὁ βασιλεὺς καὶ φιλοφρόνως πολλάκις δεξιωσάμενος,
ἀπέστειλεν αὖθις διὰ τοῦ αὐτοῦ Κωνσταντίνου εἰς τὴν οἰκείαν χώραν
καὶ πρὸς τὸν ἴδιον ἀδελφόν. 60
126ʳP   Μετὰ δὲ ταῦτα ἐν Χαλδίᾳ ὁ εἰρημένος Κωνσταντῖνος ἐπὶ χρό|νον
ἱκανὸν διατρίψας, ἐπετράπη διὰ κελεύσεως εἰσελθεῖν ἐν τῷ Ταρὼν καὶ
ἀναλαβέσθαι Κρικορίκιον, τὸν ἄρχοντα τοῦ Ταρὼν καὶ πρὸς τὴν βασιλεύουσαν εἰσελθεῖν, ὃ καὶ ἐποίησεν. Εἰσελθόντος δὲ τοῦ αὐτοῦ Κρικορικίου ἐν τῇ θεοφυλάκτῳ πόλει καὶ τῇ τοῦ μαγίστρου καὶ στρατηγοῦ 65
Ταρὼν ἀξίᾳ τιμηθέντος, ἐδόθη αὐτῷ καὶ οἶκος εἰς κατοικίαν, ὁ τοῦ
Βαρβάρου λεγόμενος, ὁ νῦν Βασιλείου τοῦ παρακοιμωμένου οἶκος.
'Ετιμήθη δὲ καὶ ἐτησίῳ ῥόγᾳ χρυσίου μὲν δέκα λίτρας καὶ μιλιαρησίων

43

of the protospatharius Asotios, and he held them by him as prisoners. On their behalf the then prince of princes Symbatios sent letters to the same emperor, of most blessed memory, begging him to send to the Taronite and make efforts to recover these nephews of his, the sons of the said Arkaïkas, so that they might not be sent to the commander of the faithful; for the patrician Grigorios was a relative of Symbatios, the prince of princes. The emperor Leo, of most blessed memory, acceded to this request of Symbatios, and sent the late Sinoutis, the eunuch, who was then chief clerk to the foreign ministry, to the prince of Taron upon this business, and also to Adranasir, the curopalate of Iberia, on some other matters of business; and he furnished him with presents suitable to both. But when a calumnious charge was laid before the said glorious emperor against the said Sinoutis by Theodore, the Armenian interpreter, there was sent out as imperial agent in his stead the protospatharius Constantine Lips, keeper of the imperial plate, — he who is now patrician proconsul and commander of the great company, — with orders instructing him to take over the presents dispatched to the prince of Taron, Krikorikios, and himself to proceed to Taron, and to order Sinoutis to go on to Adranasir, the curopalate of Iberia, as he had been instructed to do. The said protospatharius arrived at Taron and gave to Krikorikios the gifts and letters of the emperor which had been sent to him, and took up the bastard son of the Taronite, who was called Asotios, and brought him to the imperial city; and the emperor honoured him with the rank of protospatharius and richly entertained him, and then sent him back to his father in the conduct of the same protospatharius. The same Constantine took thence Apoganem, brother of Krikorikios, prince of Taron, and brought him to the emperor, of blessed memory, together with the two sons of Arkaïkas; and him too the emperor honoured with the rank of protospatharius and many times bounteously entertained him, and sent him back again, in conduct of the same Constantine, to his country and his brother.

After this the said Constantine spent some time in Chaldia, and was then commissioned by imperial mandate to go to Taron and take Krikorikios, prince of Taron, and come to the imperial city; and this he did. When this same Krikorikios had entered the city protected of God, and had been honoured with the rank of magister and military governor of Taron, he was also given for his residence a house called the house of Barbaros, now the house of Basil the chamberlain. He was, moreover, honoured with an annual stipend of ten pounds in gold and a further ten pounds in miliaresia,

V 33 ἀμερμουμνὴν P || 46 Κρικορίκιον edd.: Γρικορίκιον P || 49 ἀποδοὺς F coni. Bekker: ἀποδιδοὺς P edd. || 51 ὀνομάζετο P || 55 ἐκεῖθεν: ἐκεῖνος edd. || post ἀδελφὸν add. τοῦ edd. || 56 Κρικορικίου Ba Be || 57 τοῦ om. edd. || 68 δέκα edd.: ι′ P || μιλιαρισίων P ||

192

43

ἑτέρας δέκα λίτρας, ὡς εἶναι τὸ πᾶν λίτρας εἴκοσι. Καὶ ἐπὶ χρόνον ἐν τῇ βασιλευούσῃ διατρίψας, καὶ διὰ τοῦ αὐτοῦ πρωτοσπαθαρίου Κων- 70 σταντίνου πάλιν πρὸς τὴν οἰκείαν διεσώθη χώραν.

126ᵛP Μετὰ δὲ ταῦτα πάλιν εἰσῆλθεν καὶ ὁ Ἀπογάνεμ πρὸς τὸν μακά- ριον βασιλέα, καὶ προεβιβάσθη παρ᾽ αὐτοῦ εἰς πατρικιότητα· ἐπετράπη δὲ καὶ εἰς γυναῖκα λαβεῖν τοῦ εἰρημένου Κωνσταντίνου θυγατέρα, καὶ ἐπὶ τῇ τοιαύτῃ προφάσει καὶ οἶκον ἐπεζήτησεν, καὶ ἔλαβεν καὶ αὐτὸς τὸν 75 τοῦ Βαρβάρου οἶκον χρυσοβουλλίου χωρίς. Καὶ φιλοφρονηθεὶς παρὰ τοῦ βασιλέως, τῷ τότε μὲν πρὸς τὴν ἰδίαν χώραν ὑπέστρεψεν πρὸς τὸ 186Be | πάλιν εἰσελθεῖν καὶ τὰ τοῦ γάμου ἀπαρτίσασθαι, ἅμα δὲ τῷ εἰς τὴν οἰκείαν χώραν διασωθῆναι μετ᾽ ὀλίγας ἡμέρας τέλει τοῦ βίου ἐχρήσατο. Ὁ δὲ τούτου ἀδελφός, Κρικορίκιος διὰ γραμμάτων αὐτοῦ ἐξῃτήσατο 80 127ʳP εἰσέρχεσθαι εἰς τὴν βασι|λεύουσαν καὶ παρὰ τῶν χειρῶν τοῦ ἁγίου βασιλέως λαμβάνειν τὴν διδομένην ῥόγαν αὐτοῦ καὶ ἐπὶ χρόνον τινὰ ἐν τῇ θεοφυλάκτῳ διατρίβειν πόλει. Καὶ ἐπὶ τούτῳ τὸν τῷ οἰκείῳ ἀδελφῷ προχειρισθέντα οἶκον εἰς κατοίκησιν λαβεῖν ἠξίου, ὃν καὶ ἐπιδέδωκεν αὐτῷ ὁ μακάριος βασιλεὺς διά τε τὸ νεωστὶ ὑποταγῆναι καὶ διὰ τὸ καὶ 85 ἄλλους ἄρχοντας τῆς ἀνατολῆς πρὸς τὸν ὅμοιον ζῆλον τῆς πρὸς Ῥω- μαίους ὑποταγῆς ἐκκαλέσασθαι· ἔγγραφον δὲ χρυσοβούλλιον δωρεὰν τοῦ τοιούτου οἴκου πρὸς αὐτὸν οὐκ ἐποίησεν.

Μετὰ δὲ χρόνους ἱκανούς, Ῥωμανοῦ τοῦ μακαρίου βασιλέως τῶν σκήπτρων τῆς βασιλείας Ῥωμαίων ἐπειλημμένου, ἀνήγαγεν ὁ αὐτὸς 90 127ᵛP Κρι|κορίκιος μὴ ἰσχύειν κρατεῖν τὸν τοῦ Βαρβάρου οἶκον, ἀλλ᾽ ἠξίου λαβεῖν ἀντ᾽ αὐτοῦ προάστειον ἐν Κελτζηνῇ, εἴτε τοῦ Τατζάτου, εἴτε ἄλλο, οἷον κελεύει ὁ βασιλεύς, ἵνα, ὅτε ἐπιδρομὴ τῶν Ἀγαρηνῶν κατὰ τῆς χώρας αὐτοῦ γένηται, ἀποστέλλειν ἐκεῖσε ἔχει τὴν οἰκείαν συγγέ- νειαν καὶ ὑπόστασιν. Ὁ δὲ βασιλεὺς τὴν ἀκριβῆ γνῶσιν τῶν πραγμάτων 95 μὴ κεκτημένος, ἐλπίζων δὲ ἀπὸ βασιλικοῦ χρυσοβουλλίου τοῦ μακαρίου Λέοντος ἔχειν τὸν Ταρωνίτην τὸν τοῦ Βαρβάρου οἶκον, δέδωκεν αὐτῷ 187Be τὸ προάστειον τοῦ Γρηγορᾶ ἐν Κελτζηνῇ, καὶ τὸν οἶκον δῆθεν | ἀντέλαβεν, χρυσοβούλλιον δὲ οὐδὲ οὗτος πρὸς αὐτὸν ἐπὶ τῷ προαστείῳ ἐποιήσατο.

128ʳP Μετὰ δὲ ταῦτα ἔγραψε πρὸς τὸν | αὐτὸν βασιλέα ὁ Τορνίκης, ὁ 100 τοῦ Ταρωνίτου ἀνεψιός, ὁ τοῦ Ἀπογάνεμ ἐκείνου υἱός, ὅτι· «Τὸν οἶκον τοῦ Βαρβάρου ὁ μακαριώτατος βασιλεὺς Λέων τῷ ἐμῷ πατρὶ ἐδωρήσατο, μετὰ δὲ τὸν τοῦ πατρός μου θάνατον — διὰ τὸ ἔτι ἀνήλικον καὶ ὀρφανὸν τυγχάνειν ἐμέ — κατ᾽ ἐξουσίαν ὁ θεῖός μου τὸν τούτου οἶκον κατεκράτη- σεν, ἀεὶ καθυπισχνούμενός μοι, ὅταν εἰς τὸν τέλειον τῆς ἡλικίας ἔλθω 105 χρόνον, ἀπολαβεῖν τὸν οἶκον τὸν πατρικόν, καὶ νῦν, ὡς ἔμαθον, δέδωκεν

43

making twenty pounds in all. After some sojourn in the imperial city, he was escorted back again to his country by this same protospatharius Constantine.

After this, Apoganem came once more to the emperor, of blessed memory, and was advanced by him to the rank of patrician; and he was also permitted to take to wife the daughter of the said Constantine, and on this ground he asked for a house as well and he too received the house of Barbaros, without a golden bull. After receiving the emperor's bounty, he then returned to his country, with intent to come again and complete the celebration of his marriage; but no sooner was he escorted back to his country than he ended his life, a few days afterwards. His brother Krikorikios sent letters asking that he might come to the imperial city and receive from the hands of the holy emperor the stipend granted to him and sojourn for some while in the city protected of God. Thereupon he proceeded to demand for his residence the house which had been set aside for his brother, and the emperor, of blessed memory, handed it over to him, both because he had lately submitted himself and in order to excite in other princes of the east a similar eagerness for submission to the Romans; but he issued no golden bull making a deed of gift of this house to him.

Several years later, when the emperor Romanus, of blessed memory, had laid hold upon the sceptre of the empire of the Romans, this same Krikorikios reported that he had not the means to keep the house of Barbaros, but demanded that he should receive in its stead a suburban estate in Keltzini, either that of Tatzates or some other, whichever the emperor directed, in order that, when the Agarenes should make an incursion into his country, he might be able to send thither his personal relatives and substance. The emperor, who did not possess an accurate knowledge of the facts, and supposed that the Taronite held the house of Barbaros in virtue of an imperial golden bull of Leo, of blessed memory, gave him the suburban estate of Grigoras in Keltzini and, of course, took back the house; but he too issued no golden bull in his favour in respect of the suburban estate.

Thereupon Tornikis, nephew of the Taronite and son of the late Apoganem, wrote to this same emperor: «The house of Barbaros was presented to my father by the emperor Leo, of most blessed memory, but after my father's death, because I was under age and an orphan, my uncle, in virtue of his authority, took possession of his house, always promising me that when I should come of age, I should take over the paternal house; and now, as I have

---

V 69 δέκα edd.: ι' P ‖ ὡς: ὥστε edd. ‖ 72 ὁ om. edd. ‖ 73 post εἰς add. τὴν edd. ‖ 84 προχειρισθέντα F: πρὸ χωρισθέντα P προχωρισθέντα V edd. προ-χαρισθέντα coni. Bekker ‖ 82 Τατζάτου (etiam V¹ F Bandurius): Πατζάτου V edd. ‖ 93 ἄλλον V edd. ‖ κελεύοι edd. ‖ 94 ἔχῃ edd. ‖ 99 οὗτος: αὐτὸς V edd. ‖ 104 ὁ om. edd. ‖ τούτου: τοῦτον Me Ba τοιοῦτον Be ‖

τὸν τοιοῦτον οἶκον ὁ ἐμὸς θεῖος τῇ βασιλείᾳ σου, καὶ ἔλαβεν εἰς ἀντισήκωσιν αὐτοῦ τὸ προάστειον τοῦ Γρηγορᾶ ἐν Κελτζηνῇ.»

Ἀπὸ δὲ τῶν τοιούτων βασιλικῶν φιλοτιμιῶν, τῶν πρὸς τὸν
128ᵛP ἄρ|χοντα τοῦ Ταρών, φθόνος ὑπεφύη καὶ ἀνεβλάστησεν πρὸς αὐτὸν παρά 110
τε τοῦ Κακικίου, τοῦ ἄρχοντος Βασπαρακά, καὶ Ἀδρανασὴρ, τοῦ κουροπαλάτου Ἰβηρίας, καὶ Ἀσωτικίου, τοῦ ἄρχοντος τῶν ἀρχόντων, οἵτινες
ἔγραψαν πρὸς τὸν βασιλέα διαγογγύζοντες, δι' ἣν αἰτίαν ὁ Ταρωνίτης
μόνος ῥόγας ἀπολαύει βασιλικῆς, αὐτῶν ἁπάντων λαμβανόντων οὐδέν.
«Τίνα γάρ — ἔλεγον — περισσοτέραν δουλείαν ἡμῶν ποιεῖται, ἢ τί 115
πλέον ἡμῶν τοὺς Ῥωμαίους ἐπωφελεῖ; Ὅθεν χρὴ ἢ καὶ ἡμᾶς ὡς ἐκεῖνον
ῥογεύεσθαι, ἢ μηδ' ἐκεῖνον ἐντὸς τῆς τοιαύτης τυγχάνειν δωρεᾶς.»
Ὁ δὲ μακάριος βασιλεὺς Ῥωμανὸς ἀντέγραψεν πρὸς αὐτοὺς μὴ παρ'
129ʳP αὐτοῦ τὴν ἐπὶ τῷ Ταρωνίτῃ γενέσθαι | ῥόγαν, ἵνα ἐπ' | αὐτῷ κεῖται
188Be καὶ ἡ ταύτης νῦν ἐκκοπή, ἀλλὰ παρὰ τοῦ μακαριωτάτου βασιλέως, καὶ 120
μὴ δίκαιον εἶναι τὰ τῶν προβεβασιλευκότων παρὰ τῶν ὕστερον ἀνατρέπε-
σθαι. Ἔγραψε δ' ὅμως πρὸς τὸν αὐτὸν Ταρωνίτην, δηλοποιῶν αὐτὸν
τὴν τῶν εἰρημένων ἀνδρῶν λύπην καὶ τὸ σκάνδαλον. Ὁ δὲ ἀνήγαγεν
μήτε χρυσόν, μήτε ἄργυρον παρέχειν δύνασθαι, ὑπισχνεῖτο δὲ ἔξωθεν
τῶν κατὰ τύπον ἀποστελλομένων ξενίων διδόναι ἱμάτια καὶ χαλκώματα, 125
μέχρι τῶν δέκα λιτρῶν συντιμώμενα, ἃ καὶ δέδωκεν μέχρι τριῶν ἢ
τεσσάρων ἐνιαυτῶν. Μετὰ δὲ ταῦτα ἀνήγαγεν μὴ δύνασθαι παρέχειν τὸ τοιοῦτον πάκτον, τὴν δὲ ῥόγαν ἢ προῖκα λαμβάνειν ἠξίου, καθὼς ἐπὶ τοῦ
129ᵛP | μακαριωτάτου βασιλέως Λέοντος, ἢ ἐκκοπῆναι αὐτήν. Ὅθεν διὰ τὸ μὴ
εἰς σκάνδαλον εἶναι τοῦ Κακικίου καὶ τοῦ κουροπαλάτου καὶ τῶν λοιπῶν 130
ἐξέκοψεν ταύτην ὁ εἰρημένος μακάριος βασιλεὺς Ῥωμανός. Παραμυθού-
μενος δὲ ὥσπερ αὐτόν, μετὰ ταῦτα τὸν τούτου υἱόν, Ἀσώτιον, ἐν τῇ
πόλει παραγεγονότα, εἰς πατρικίους ἐτίμησεν, καὶ φιλοφρονησάμενος
αὐτάρκως πρὸς τὰ ἴδια ἐξαπέστειλεν.

Τοῦ δὲ μαγίστρου Κρικορικίου τὸν βίον ἀπολιπόντος, ἀνήγαγεν 135
Τορνίκιος, ὁ τοῦ Ἀπογάνεμ υἱός, ἔρωτα ἔχειν ἐγκάρδιον εἰσελθεῖν καὶ
τὸν βασιλέα θεάσασθαι, ἐφ' ᾧ τὸν πρωτοσπαθάριον Κρινίτην καὶ ἑρμη-
νευτὴν ὁ βασιλεὺς ἐξαπέστειλεν, ὃς καὶ εἰσήγαγεν ἐν τῇ πόλει τὸν εἰρη-
130ʳP μένον Τορνίκιον, καὶ προ|ήγαγεν τὸν αὐτὸν Τορνίκιον ὁ βασιλεὺς | εἰς
189Be τὴν τῶν πατρικίων τιμήν. Προετείνετο δὲ δικαιολογίας ἐπὶ τῷ τοῦ 140
Βαρβάρου οἴκῳ, καὶ ἀκούσας, ὅτι προάστειον λαβὼν ὁ θεῖος αὐτοῦ
ἐν Κελτζηνῇ, τὴν τούτου παρεχώρησεν ἐξουσίαν, ἔλεγε μὴ δύνασθαι
τὸν θεῖον αὐτοῦ ἐπὶ τῇ πατρικῇ κληρονομίᾳ αὐτοῦ ποιεῖσθαι ἀνταλλαγήν,
καὶ ἠξίου ἢ τὸν οἶκον λαβεῖν ἢ τὸ προάστειον, εἰ δὲ μή, καὶ ἀμφότερα
παρεχώρει τῷ βασιλεῖ πρὸς τὸ μὴ ἔχειν αὐτὰ τοὺς ἐξαδέλφους αὐτοῦ. 145
Τούτου ἕνεκεν ὁ βασιλεύς, ἐπεὶ καὶ ὁ γέρων ὁ Ταρωνίτης ἐτύγχανεν

learned, my uncle has given this house to your imperial majesty, and has received in exchange for it the suburban estate of Grigoras in Keltzini.» And because of these imperial gifts bestowed on the prince of Taron, envy towards him was implanted and grew up in Kakikios, prince of Basparaka, and Adranasir, the curopalate of Iberia, and Asotikios, the prince of princes, who wrote to the emperor grumbling at the cause whereby the Taronite alone enjoyed an imperial stipend, while all of them got nothing. «For what service — they said — is he performing more than we, or in what does he help the Romans more than we do? Either, therefore, we too should be stipendiary as he is, or else he too should be excluded from this largess.» The emperor Romanus, of blessed memory, wrote back to them, that the stipend in favour of the Taronite had not been granted by him, that it should now lie with him to cut it off, but by the emperor, of most blessed memory; nor was it right that what had been done by former emperors should be undone by their successors. However, he wrote to this same Taronite informing him that the said parties were vexed and offended. He replied that he could provide neither gold nor silver, but promised to give, over and above the gifts regularly sent, tunics and bronze vessels up to ten pounds in total value, and these he did give for three or four years. But thereafter he reported that he could not provide this tribute, and demanded either that he should receive the stipend gratis as in the time of the emperor Leo, of most blessed memory, or else that it should be cut off. And so, that it might not cause offence to Kakikios and the curopalate and the rest, the said emperor Romanus, of blessed memory, cut it off. But to console him, as it were, he afterwards honoured his son Asotios, when he came to Constantinople, with patrician rank and entertained him munificently before sending him home.

On the death of the magister Krikorikios, Tornikios, son of Apoganem, reported that he heartily desired to come and behold the emperor; whereupon the emperor sent the protospatharius Krinitis, the interpreter, who brought the said Tornikios to Constantinople, and the emperor advanced the same Tornikios to the honour of patrician rank. He put forward his claims to the house of Barbaros, and, having heard that his uncle had resigned his ownership of it on receipt of a suburban estate in Keltzini, declared that his uncle had no power to effect an exchange in respect of his paternal inheritance, and demanded that he should be given either the house or the suburban estate, failing which, he was for resigning both to the emperor, so that his cousins might not have them. Therefore the emperor, since

V 110 ἀνεβλάστησεν: ἐβλάστησε edd. ‖ 111 Κακικίου (*litteris* κι *s. v. additis*) P¹ Ba Be: Κικίου V Me ‖ Βασπαρακακὰ edd. ‖ 113 διαγονγγύζοντες P ‖ 116 ἡμῶν edd.: ὑμῶν P ‖ 118 βασιλεὺς *om.* V edd. ‖ 120 μακαριωτάτου: μακαρίου V edd. ‖ *post* βασιλέως *excidisse* Λέοντος *susp.* Jenkins ‖ 122 αὐτὸν²: αὐτῷ V edd. ‖ 123 τὸ *om.* edd. ‖ 126 δέκα edd.: ι′ P ‖ 131 μακάριος: μακαριώτατος edd. ‖ 134 αὐτάρκως *scr.* Moravcsik: αὐταρκῶς P edd. ‖ 135 *ante* Κρικορικίου *add.* τοῦ edd. ‖ 140 τῷ τοῦ V edd.: τοῦ τῶ P ‖ 145 παρεχώρει: προσεχώρει edd. ‖

ἀποθανών, ἀνελάβετο τὸ προάστειον, καὶ οὐδὲ τὸν οἶκον ἀντέδωκεν, ἐπεὶ μηδὲ χρυσοβούλλιον, καθὼς ἀνωτέρω προείρηται, ἐπί τινι τούτων ἐξετέθη.

130ᵛP Μετὰ δὲ ταῦτα εἰσῆλθεν πρὸς τὴν βασιλεύουσαν Παγκράτιος 150 ἐκεῖνος, ὁ πρῶτος υἱὸς τοῦ μαγίστρου ἐκείνου Κρικορικίου τοῦ Ταρωνίτου, καὶ προεβιβάσθη παρὰ τοῦ βασιλέως εἰς τὸ τῶν πατρικίων ἀξίωμα, καὶ γέγονεν καὶ στρατηγὸς τοῦ Ταρών. Ἠιτήσατο δὲ καὶ γυναῖκα λαβεῖν ἀπὸ τῶν βασιλικῶν συγγενίδων, καὶ δέδωκεν αὐτῷ ὁ βασιλεὺς τὴν τοῦ μαγίστρου Θεοφυλάκτου ἀδελφὴν εἰς γυναῖκα. Καὶ μετὰ τὸν 155 γάμον διαθήκας ἐξέθετο, ἐν αἷς ἐδήλου, ὅτι· «Ἐάν μοι γένωνται παῖδες ἀπὸ τῆς τοιαύτης γυναικός, ἵνα ἔχουσιν τὴν ἅπασάν μου χώραν εἰς κλῆρον προγονικόν.» Καὶ ἐπὶ τούτῳ ἠτήσατο τὸν βασιλέα δοθῆναι αὐτῷ 131ʳP τὸ προάστειον τοῦ Γρηγορᾶ πρὸς | τὸ ἐν αὐτῷ τὴν πατρικίαν, τὴν τούτου 190Be γυναῖκα καθέζεσθαι, μετὰ δὲ τὴν αὐτῆς ἀποβίω|σιν εἶναι πάλιν τὸ 160 τοιοῦτον προάστειον τῆς βασιλείας αὐτοῦ. Καὶ ἐπένευσεν καὶ πρὸς τοῦτο ὁ βασιλεύς, καὶ πολλαῖς φιλοτιμίαις αὐτὸν δεξιωσάμενος, μετὰ τῆς ἰδίας γυναικὸς ἐξαπέστειλεν εἰς τὴν χώραν αὐτοῦ. Οἱ δὲ υἱοὶ τοῦ μαγίστρου Κρικορικίου, ὅ τε αὐτὸς Παγκράτιος ὁ πατρίκιος καὶ Ἀσώτιος ὁ πατρίκιος, μεγάλως παρελύπουν καὶ ἐβιάζοντο τὸν οἰκεῖον αὐτῶν ἐξάδελ- 165 φον, Τορνίκιον τὸν πατρίκιον, ὃς μὴ ὑποφέρων τὴν ἀπὸ τούτων ἐπίθεσιν, ἔγραψε πρὸς τὸν βασιλέα ἀποστεῖλαι πιστὸν ἄνθρωπον καὶ παραλαβεῖν 131ᵛP τὴν χώραν αὐτοῦ, αὐτὸν δὲ καὶ τὴν γυναῖκα καὶ τὸ παιδίον | αὐτῶν πρὸς τὸν βασιλέα εἰσαγαγεῖν. Ὁ δὲ βασιλεὺς ἀπέστειλεν τὸν πρωτοσπαθάριον Κρινίτην καὶ ἑρμηνέα πρὸς τὸ κατὰ τὴν ἀξίωσιν αὐτοῦ ἀναλαβέσθαι 170 καὶ εἰσαγαγεῖν αὐτὸν ἐν τῇ θεοφυλάκτῳ πόλει. Ὅτε δὲ τὴν τοιαύτην χώραν ὁ Κρινίτης κατέλαβεν, εὗρεν αὐτὸν ἤδη τὸν βίον ἀπολιπόντα, διαταξάμενον πρὸ τῆς τελευτῆς εἶναι πᾶσαν τὴν χώραν αὐτοῦ ὑποκειμένην τῷ βασιλεῖ Ῥωμαίων, τὴν δὲ γυναῖκα καὶ τὸ παιδίον αὐτοῦ εἰσελθεῖν πρὸς τὸν βασιλέα, ᾗ καὶ δέδωκεν ὁ βασιλεὺς εἰς κατοίκησιν, εἰσελθούσης, 175 τοῦ πρωτοσπαθαρίου Μιχαήλ, τοῦ ποτε γεγονότος κομμερκιαρίου Χαλδίας καὶ τὴν τοῦ Ψωμαθέως μονήν. Καὶ πάλιν ἀπεστάλη ὁ εἰρημένος Κρινίτης 132ʳP παρὰ τοῦ βασιλέως πρὸς | τὸ παραλαβεῖν τὴν χώραν τοῦ Ἀπογάνεμ, ἤτοι τὸ μέρος τοῦ πατρικίου Τορνικίου. Ἀνταπέστειλαν δὲ ἐκεῖθεν τοῦ 191Be Ταρωνί|του υἱοί, οἱ τοῦ ἀποθανόντος ἐξάδελφοι, ἀξιοῦντες δοῦναι τὸ 180 Οὐλνούτιν καὶ ἔχειν τὴν χώραν τοῦ ἐξαδέλφου αὐτῶν, μὴ γὰρ δύνασθαι ὅλως αὐτοὺς ζῆν, εἰ τὴν τοῦ ἐξαδέλφου αὐτῶν χώραν ὡς οἰκείαν κατάσχῃ ὁ βασιλεύς. Οἰκείᾳ δὲ ἀγαθότητι ὑπείξας ὁ βασιλεὺς τὴν αἴτησιν αὐτῶν ἐξεπλήρωσεν, καὶ δέδωκεν αὐτοῖς μὲν τὴν χώραν τοῦ Ἀπογάνεμ, τοῦ ἐξαδέλφου αὐτῶν, αὐτὸς δὲ ἀνελάβετο τὸ Οὐλνούτιν μετὰ πάσης τῆς 185

the old Taronite was now dead, resumed the suburban estate but did not give the house in exchange for it, because, as has already been stated above, no golden bull had been issued in respect of any of these transactions. After this, the late Pankratios, eldest son of that magister Krikorikios the Taronite, came to the imperial city and was advanced by the emperor to the dignity of patrician and was also made military governor of Taron. He asked that he might also be given a wife from among the ladies related to the imperial family, and the emperor gave him to wife the sister of the magister Theophylact. And after his marriage he made a will, in which he stated: «If children are born to me of this woman, they are to have all my country for their ancestral inheritance.» Thereupon he asked the emperor that he might be given the suburban estate of Grigoras for the patrician lady, his wife, to reside there, and after her death this suburban estate should revert to his imperial majesty. The emperor sanctioned this too, and after presenting him with many gifts, sent him with his wife away to his country. Now, the sons of the magister Krikorikios, this same patrician Pankratios and the patrician Asotios, greatly vexed and oppressed their cousin, the patrician Tornikios, who, finding their aggressiveness unendurable, wrote to the emperor to send a trustworthy servant and take over his country, and conduct himself and his wife and their child to the emperor. The emperor sent the protospatharius Krinitis, the interpreter, to take him and conduct him to the city protected of God, in accordance with his demand. But when Krinitis arrived in that country, he found that *Tornikios* had already departed this life, having devised before his end that all his country should be subject to the emperor of the Romans, and that his wife and his child should go to the emperor; and to her, on her arrival, the emperor gave for her residence the monastery in Psomathia of the protospatharius Michael, formerly collector of Chaldia. The said Krinitis was sent back again by the emperor to take over the country of Apoganem, that is, the portion of the patrician Tornikios. But the sons of the Taronite, the cousins of the deceased, sent back thence a demand that they should give up Oulnoutin and retain the country of their cousin, for they were quite unable to live if the emperor were to occupy their cousin's country as his own. The emperor, yielding to his own goodness of heart, fulfilled their request and gave them the country of Apoganem, their cousin, and himself took Oulnoutin with all its surrounding territory.

V 153 καὶ³ om. edd. ‖ 155/6 τὸν γάμον P¹ V edd.: τῶν γάμων (?) P ‖ 157 ἔχουσιν (littera o in ras. scripta) P¹ ἔχουσι V: ἔχωσι edd. ‖ 158 τὸν om. edd. ‖ 159 Γρηγορᾶ edd.: Γρηγορίου P ‖ 160 αὐτῆς: τοιαύτης edd. τ{οι}αύτης Migne ‖ 165 αὐτῶν] litteram ω in ras. scr. P¹ ‖ 169/70 πρωτο-σπαθάριον Κρινίτην] per comp. litteras α κρινί⸀ in ras. scr. P¹ ‖ 176 Χαλδίας ⟨οἶκον⟩ coni. Kyriakides ‖ 177 τὴν τοῦ Ψωμαθέως μονήν: τοῦ Ψωμαθέως τὴν μονήν V Me Ba Ψωμαθέως τὴν μονήν Be ‖ ἀπεστάλη V edd.: ἀπεστάλην P ‖ 181 Οὐλνούτην P edd. ‖ 185 Οὐλνούτην P edd. ‖

198

43, 44

περιχώρου αὐτοῦ. Ἡ δὲ ὅλη τοῦ Ταρὼν χώρα εἰς δύο διανεμηθεῖσα
132ᵛP ἐτύγχανεν, ἧς τὸ μὲν ἥμισυ οἱ τοῦ μαγίστρου | Κρικορικίου εἶχον υἱοί,
τὸ δὲ ἥμισυ ⟨οἱ⟩ τοῦ Ἀπογάνεμ τοῦ πατρικίου, οἱ τούτων ἐξάδελφοι.

44. Π ε ρ ὶ   τ ῆ ς   χ ώ ρ α ς   τ ο ῦ   Ἀ π α χ ο υ ν ῆ ς   κ α ὶ   τ ο ῦ
κ ά σ τ ρ ο υ   τ ο ῦ   Μ α ν ζ ι κ ί ε ρ τ   κ α ὶ   τ ο ῦ   Π ε ρ κ ρ ὶ   κ α ὶ
τ ο ῦ   Χ λ ι ά τ   κ α ὶ   τ ο ῦ   Χ α λ ι ά τ   κ α ὶ   τ ο ῦ   Ἀ ρ ζ ὲ ς   κ α ὶ
τ ο ῦ   Τ ι β ὶ   κ α ὶ   τ ο ῦ   Χ ὲ ρ τ   κ α ὶ   τ ο ῦ   Σ α λ α μ ᾶ ς   κ α ὶ   τ ο ῦ
Τ ζ ε ρ μ α τ ζ ο ῦ.   5

Ἰστέον, ὅτι πρὸ τοῦ Ἀσωτίου, τοῦ ἄρχοντος τῶν ἀρχόντων, τοῦ
πατρὸς τοῦ Συμβατίου, τοῦ ἄρχοντος τῶν ἀρχόντων, ὃν ἀπεκεφάλισεν
ὁ ἀμηρᾶς Περσίδος, ὁ Ἀποσάται, ὃς καὶ ἐποίησεν δύο υἱούς, τόν τε
Ἀσώτιον, τὸν μετ’ αὐτὸν γενόμενον ἄρχοντα τῶν ἀρχόντων, καὶ Ἀπα-
σάκιον, τὸν μετὰ ταῦτα μάγιστρον τιμηθέντα, τὰ τρία ταῦτα κάστρα 10
133ʳP τό τε Περκρὶ καὶ τὸ Χαλιὰτ καὶ τὸ Ἀρ|ζές, ὑπὸ τὴν τῆς Περσίδος ἐπι-
κράτειαν ἐτύγχανον.
192Be   Ὅτι ὁ ἄρχων ἐκαθέζετο τῶν ἀρχόντων εἰς τὴν μεγάλην Ἀρμε-
νίαν, εἰς τὸ κάστρον τὸ Κάρς, καὶ ἐπεῖχεν καὶ τὰ τρία τὰ προγεγραμμένα
κάστρα, τὸ τε Περκρὶ ⟨καὶ⟩ τὸ Χαλιὰτ καὶ τὸ Ἀρζές καὶ τὸ Τιβὶ καὶ 15
τὸ Χὲρτ καὶ τὸ Σαλαμᾶς.
    Ὅτι Ἀπελβὰρτ ἐκράτει τὸ Μανζικίερτ, καὶ ἦν ὑπὸ τὴν ἐξουσίαν
⟨Ἀσωτίου⟩, τοῦ ἄρχοντος τῶν ἀρχόντων, τοῦ πατρὸς τοῦ Συμβατίου, τοῦ ἄρχοντος τῶν ἀρχόντων. Δέδωκεν δὲ ⟨τῷ⟩ αὐτῷ Ἀπελβὰρτ
ὁ αὐτὸς Ἀσώτιος, ὁ ἄρχων τῶν ἀρχόντων, καὶ τὸ κάστρον τὸ Χλιὰτ 20
καὶ τὸ Ἀρζές καὶ τὸ Περκρί· ὁ γὰρ προρρηθεὶς Ἀσώτιος, ὁ ἄρχων
τῶν ἀρχόντων, ὁ πατὴρ τοῦ Συμβατίου, τοῦ ἄρχοντος τῶν ἀρχόντων,
133ᵛP κατεῖχεν | πάσας τὰς τῆς ἀνατολῆς χώρας. Τελευτήσαντος δὲ Ἀπελβάρτ,
κατέσχεν τὴν ἐξουσίαν αὐτοῦ ὁ ἴδιος υἱὸς αὐτοῦ, ὁ Ἀβελχαμίτ, τοῦ δὲ
Ἀβελχαμὶτ τελευτήσαντος, ἐκράτησε τὴν ἐξουσίαν αὐτοῦ ὁ πρῶτος 25
υἱὸς αὐτοῦ, ὁ Ἀποσεβατᾶς. Τοῦ δὲ Συμβατίου, τοῦ ἄρχοντος τῶν ἀρχόντων, παρὰ τοῦ Ἀποσάται, τοῦ ἀμηρᾶ Περσίδος, ἀναιρεθέντος, ἐκράτησεν αὐθεντῶς καὶ κυρίως ὡς δεσπότης καὶ αὐτοκέφαλος τό τε κάστρον
τὸ Μανζικίερτ καὶ τὰ λοιπὰ κάστρα καὶ τὰς χώρας, ὅστις καὶ ὑπετάγη
τῷ βασιλεῖ μετὰ τῶν ἑτέρων δύο ἀδελφῶν αὐτοῦ, τοῦ τε Ἀπολεσφούετ 30
καὶ τοῦ Ἀποσέλμη, διὰ τὸ διαφόρως καταπολεμηθῆναι τά τε κάστρα
καὶ πραιδευθῆναι καὶ ἀφανισθῆναι καὶ τὰς χώρας αὐτῶν παρὰ τοῦ
134ʳP δομεστίκου τῶν σχολῶν, παρέχοντες τὸν | βασιλέα Ῥωμαίων καὶ πάκτα

V 187 ἧς: καὶ Be ‖ 188 οἱ add. Be.

43, 44

The whole country of Taron was divided in two, one half of it being held by the sons of the magister Krikorikios, the other half by their cousins, *the* sons of the patrician Apoganem.

44. Of the country of Apachounis and of the city of Manzikiert and Perkri and Chliat and Chaliat and Arzes and Tibi and Chert and Salamas and Tzermatzou.

Before the time of Asotios, prince of princes, father of Symbatios, prince of princes, whom the emir of Persia Aposatai beheaded and who had two sons, Asotios, who was prince of princes after him, and Apasakios, who was afterwards honoured with the rank of magister, these three cities, Perkri and Chaliat and Arzes, were under the control of Persia.

The prince of princes had his seat in great Armenia, at the city of Kars, and held both these three cities aforementioned, Perkri *and* Chaliat and Arzes, and also Tibi and Chert and Salamas.

Apelbart possessed Manzikiert and was beneath the dominion of *Asotios*, the prince of princes, the father of Symbatios, the prince of princes. The same Asotios, prince of princes, gave to *this* same Apelbart also the city of Chliat and Arzes and Perkri: for the aforesaid Asotios, prince of princes, father of Symbatios, prince of princes, held all the countries of the east. On the death of Apelbart his son Abelchamit possessed his domain, and on the death of Abelchamit his eldest son Aposebatas possessed his domain. He, after the murder of Symbatios, prince of princes, by Aposatai, the emir of Persia, took possession, in absolute sovereignty, as an independent potentate, both of the city of Manzikiert and of the rest of the cities and the countries; and he submitted himself to the emperor together with his other two brothers, Apolesphouet and Aposelmis, after their cities and their countries had on various occasions been over-run and ravaged and destroyed by the commander-in-chief, and they paid the emperor of the Romans tribute in respect of their cities and their territories. But from the

---

44. 1 τοῦ¹: τῆς edd. ‖ 2 Μαντζικίερτ V edd. ‖ Περκρή P ‖ 3 Χλιάτ: Χαλιάτ Me *coni.* Laskin ‖ Ἀρζὲς *scr.* Moravcsik: "Αρζες P edd. ‖ 4 Τιβῆ P ‖ 7 τοῦ² edd.: καὶ P ‖ 8 ἀμηρὰς P ‖ Ἀποσάτας F edd. ‖ 11 Ἀρζές *scr.* Moravcsik: "Αρζες P "Αρσες edd. ‖ 14 Καρς (*sine acc.*) P ‖ 15 Περκρή P ‖ καὶ *add.* Moravcsik ‖ "Αρζες edd. ‖ Τιβῆ P ‖ 16 Σαλαμάς P ‖ 17 Ἀπελκάρτ edd. ‖ Μαντζικίερτ Ba Be ‖ 18 Ἀσωτίου *add.* Jenkins ‖ 19 τῷ *add.* Moravcsik ‖ 20 Χλιάτ: Χαλιάτ *coni.* Laskin ‖ 21 Ἀρζές *scr.* Moravcsik: "Αρζες P edd. ‖ Περκρή P ‖ 25 πρῶτος edd.: α' P ‖ 26 ὁ *om.* edd. ‖ Ἀποσεβατάς P ‖ 27 Ἀποσάτα edd. ‖ ἀμηρὰ P ‖ 29 Μαντζικίερτ Ba Be ‖ 30 τε *om.* edd. ‖ 33 παρέχοντες: παρέχοντος Be ‖

ὑπὲρ τῶν κάστρων καὶ τῶν χωρίων αὐτῶν. Ἀπὸ δὲ τοῦ προρρηθέντος
193Be Ἀσωτίου, τοῦ ἄρχοντος | τῶν ἀρχόντων, τοῦ πατρὸς μὲν τοῦ Συμβατίου, 35
πάππου δὲ τοῦ δευτέρου Ἀσωτίου καὶ τοῦ μαγίστρου Ἀπασακίου,
μέχρι ζωῆς τοῦ δευτέρου Ἀσωτίου, τοῦ ἄρχοντος τῶν ἀρχόντων, ὑπῆρχον τὰ τοιαῦτα τρία κάστρα ὑπὸ τὴν ἐξουσίαν τοῦ ἄρχοντος τῶν ἀρχόντων, καὶ ἐλάμβανεν ἐξ αὐτῶν πάκτα ὁ ἄρχων τῶν ἀρχόντων. Ἀλλὰ
καὶ τὸ κάστρον τοῦ Μανζικίερτ μετὰ τῆς χώρας τοῦ Ἀπαχουνῆς καὶ 40
τοῦ Κορὴ καὶ τοῦ Χάρκα ὑπὸ τὴν ἐξουσίαν καὶ ἐπικράτειαν τοῦ αὐτοῦ
ἄρχοντος τῶν ἀρχόντων ὑπῆρχεν, ἕως ὅτου Ἀποσεβατᾶς, ὁ ἀμηρᾶς τοῦ
134ᵛP Μανζικίερτ, μετὰ τῶν δύο ἀδελφῶν αὐτοῦ, τοῦ τε Ἀπο|λεσφούετ καὶ
τοῦ Ἀποσέλμη, ὑπετάγησαν τῷ βασιλεῖ, διδόντες καὶ πάκτα ὑπέρ τε
τῶν κάστρων καὶ τῶν χωρίων αὐτῶν· ἐπεὶ ⟨δὲ⟩ ὁ ἄρχων τῶν ἀρχόντων 45
δοῦλος τοῦ βασιλέως τῶν Ῥωμαίων τυγχάνει, ὡς παρ' αὐτοῦ προβαλλόμενος καὶ τὸ τοιοῦτον δεχόμενος ἀξίωμα, δηλονότι καὶ τὰ ὑπ' αὐτοῦ
δεσποζόμενα κάστρα καὶ πολιτεῖαι καὶ χωρία τοῦ βασιλέως τῶν Ῥωμαίων τυγχάνουσιν.

Ὅτι τοῦ Συμβατίου, τοῦ ἄρχοντος τῶν ἀρχόντων τῆς μεγάλης 50
Ἀρμενίας, κρατηθέντος παρὰ τοῦ Ἀποσάται, τοῦ ἀμηρᾶ Περσίδος,
καὶ ἀποκεφαλισθέντος παρ' αὐτοῦ, ἐκράτησεν ὁ Ἀποσεβατᾶς, ὁ καθεζό-
μενος εἰς τὸ κάστρον τὸ Μανζικίερτ, τὸ κάστρον τὸ Χαλιὰτ καὶ τὸ
135ʳP κάστρον τὸ Περκρὶ καὶ τὴν πολιτείαν τοῦ Ἀρ|ζές.
194Be   Ὅτι ὁ δεύτερος ἀδελφὸς τοῦ Ἀποσεβατᾶ, ὁ Ἀπολεσφούετ | καὶ 55
ὁ ἀνεψιὸς αὐτοῦ καὶ ὁ προγονός, ὁ Ἄχμετ ἐκράτησαν τὸ κάστρον τὸ
Χλιὰτ καὶ τὸ κάστρον τὸ Ἀρζὲς καὶ τὸ κάστρον τὸ Ἀλτζικέ, καὶ αὐτοὶ
ὑπετάγησαν τῷ Ῥωμαίων βασιλεῖ, καὶ ἐγένοντο ὑπὸ τὴν ἐξουσίαν αὐτοῦ
καὶ παρεῖχον καὶ πάκτα, καθὼς καὶ ὁ πρῶτος ἀδελφὸς αὐτοῦ, ὁ Ἀποσεβατᾶς, ὑπέρ τε τῶν κάστρων καὶ τῶν χωρίων αὐτῶν.   60
    Ὅτι ὁ τρίτος ἀδελφὸς τοῦ Ἀποσεβατᾶ καὶ τοῦ Ἀπολεσφούετ,
ὁ Ἀποσέλμης, ἐκράτει τὸ κάστρον τὸ Τζερματζοῦ μετὰ καὶ τῶν χωρίων
αὐτοῦ, καὶ αὐτὸς ὑπετάγη τῷ τῶν Ῥωμαίων βασιλεῖ, καὶ ἐδίδου πάκτα,
καθὼς καὶ ὁ πρῶτος ἀδελφὸς αὐτοῦ, ὁ Ἀποσεβατᾶς, καὶ ὁ δεύτερος
ἀδελφὸς αὐτοῦ, ὁ Ἀπολεσφούετ.   65
135ᵛP   Ὅτι τοῦ Ἀποσεβατᾶ τε|λευτήσαντος, ἐκράτησε τὸ κάστρον τὸ
Μανζικίερτ μετὰ τῶν χωρίων αὐτοῦ καὶ τῆς ἐπικρατείας αὐτοῦ πάσης
ὁ Ἀβδεραχείμ, ὁ υἱὸς τοῦ Ἀποσεβατᾶ, τελευτήσαντος δὲ τοῦ Ἀβδεραχείμ, ἐκράτησεν ὁ Ἀπολεσφούετ, ὁ δεύτερος ἀδελφὸς τοῦ Ἀποσεβατᾶ,
θεῖος δὲ τοῦ Ἀβδεραχείμ, τὸ κάστρον τὸ Μανζικίερτ καὶ πάσας τὰς 70

V 36 Ἀπασακίου Ba Be: Ἀπασικίου P ‖ 37 δευτέρου edd.: β' P ‖ τοῦ² om. edd. ‖
40 Μαντζικίερτ Ba Be ‖ 41 Κορῇ P ‖ τοῦ Χαρκὰ καὶ τοῦ Κορή edd. ‖ Χάρκα

44

time of the aforesaid Asotios, prince of princes, father of Symbatios and grandfather of the second Asotios and of the magister Apasakios, until the lifetime of the second Asotios, prince of princes, these three cities were under the dominion of the prince of princes, and the prince of princes received tribute from them. Moreover, the city of Manzikiert with the country of Apachounis and Kori and Charka was under the dominion and control of the same prince of princes, up till the time when Aposebatas, emir of Manzikiert, and his two brothers Apolesphouet and Aposelmis submitted themselves to the emperor and paid tribute in respect of their cities and their territories; *and* since the prince of princes is the servant of the emperor of the Romans, being appointed by him and receiving this rank from him, it is obvious that the cities and townships and territories of which he is lord also belong to the emperor of the Romans.

When Symbatios, prince of princes of great Armenia, was captured by Aposatai, the emir of Persia, and by him beheaded, Aposebatas, with his seat at the city of Manzikiert, took possession of the city of Chaliat and the city of Perkri and the township of Arzes.

The second brother of Aposebatas, Apolesphouet, and his nephew and step-son Achmet took possession of the city of Chliat and the city of Arzes and the city of Altzike, and they too submitted themselves to the emperor of the Romans and came beneath his dominion and paid tribute in respect of their cities and their territories, as did the eldest brother Aposebatas.

The third brother of Aposebatas and Apolesphouet, Aposelmis, was in possession of the city of Tzermatzou with its territories, and he too submitted himself to the emperor of the Romans and paid tribute, as did his eldest brother Aposebatas and his second brother Apolesphouet.

On the death of Aposebatas, Abderacheim, son of Aposebatas, possessed the city of Manzikiert with its territories and all its domain, and on the death of Abderacheim, Apolesphouet, second brother of Aposebatas and uncle of Abderacheim, possessed the city of Manzikiert and all the

---

scr. Moravcsik: Χαρκά P edd. ‖ 42 Ἀποσεβατάς P ‖ ἀμηράς P ‖ 43 Μανζικιερτ V Me: Μαντζικίερτ P Ba Be ‖ 45 δὲ *add.* Moravcsik γὰρ *addendum coni.* Bekker ‖ 51 Ἀποσάτα Ba Be ‖ ἀμηρά P ‖ 52 Ἀποσεβατάς P ‖ 53 Μαντζικιερτ Ba Be ‖ 54 Περκρή P ‖ Ἄρζες edd. ‖ 55 Ἀποσεβατά P ‖ Ἀπολεσφούετ edd.: Ἀπολεσφούτ P ‖ 56 Ἀχμὲτ edd. ‖ 57 Ἄρζες edd. ‖ Ἀλτζικέ *scr.* Moravcsik: Ἀλτζίκε P edd. Ἀρτζίκε *coni.* V. Laurent ‖ 59 πρῶτος *scr.* Moravcsik: α′ P *om.* V edd. ‖ ὁ² V: α′ P *om.* edd. ‖ 59/60 Ἀποσεβατάς P ‖ 61 τρίτος edd.: γ′ P ‖ Ἀποσεβατά P ‖ 62 τὸ²: τοῦ V edd. ‖ 64 πρῶτος *scr.* Moravcsik: α′ P *om.* V edd. ‖ Ἀποσεβατάς P ‖ δεύτερος Be: β′ P ‖ 66 Ἀποσεβατά P ‖ τὸ κάστρον *om.* edd. ‖ 67 Μαντζικιερτ Ba Be ‖ 68 Ἀβδηραχεὶμ edd. ‖ Ἀποσεβατά P ‖ 68/9 Ἀβδηραχεὶμ edd. ‖ 69 Ἀποσεβατά P ‖ 70 Ἀβδηραχεὶμ Ba Be ‖ Μανζικιερτ Me: Ματζικίερτ P Μαντζικιερτ Ba Be ‖

44

προρρηθείσας χώρας, καὶ αὐτοῦ τελευτήσαντος, ἐκράτησεν ὁ τρίτος
ἀδελφός, ἤγουν τοῦ ᾿Αποσεβατᾶ καὶ τοῦ ᾿Απολεσφούετ, ὁ ᾿Αποσέλμης
τό τε Μανζικίερτ καὶ πάσας τὰς προρρηθείσας χώρας.

"Οτι ὁ ᾿Αποσεβατᾶς εἶχεν υἱὸν τὸν ᾿Αβδεραχεὶμ καὶ τὸν ᾿Απελ-
μουζέ.   75

195Be   "Οτι ὁ ᾿Απολεσφούετ εἶχεν προγονὸν καὶ ἀνεψιὸν τὸν ᾿Αχάμετ,
136rP υἱὸν γὰρ οὐκ εἶχεν, ἀλλὰ τὸν ᾿Αχάμετ τὸν προγονὸν | καὶ ἀνεψιὸν αὐτοῦ
εἶχεν ἀντὶ υἱοῦ.

"Οτι ὁ ᾿Αποσέλμης εἶχεν υἱὸν τὸν ᾿Απελβάρτ, τὸν ἀρτίως κρα-
τοῦντα τὸ Μανζικίερτ.   80

"Οτι ἀποθανόντος τοῦ ᾿Αποσεβατᾶ, κατέλιπε τὸν ᾿Αβδεραχείμ,
τὸν υἱὸν αὐτοῦ ἀμηρᾶν, ὁ δὲ ἕτερος υἱὸς αὐτοῦ, ὁ ᾿Απελμουζὲ ἦν νήπιος
πάνυ, διὸ καὶ κατεφρονήθη ἐλθεῖν πρὸς τὴν τοῦ πατρὸς καὶ τοῦ ἀδελφοῦ
αὐτοῦ ἐξουσίαν.

"Οτι ὁ ᾿Αποσεβατᾶς, ὁ πρῶτος ἀδελφός, ἐκαθέζετο εἰς τὸ κάστρον 85
τὸ Μανζικίερτ, καὶ ἐκράτει, καθὼς εἴρηται, ταύτας τὰς χώρας, τό τε
᾿Απαχουνῆς καὶ τὸ Κορὴ καὶ τὸ Χάρκα, καὶ ἐδίδου τὰ ὑπὲρ αὐτῶν πάκτα
τῷ ῾Ρωμαίων βασιλεῖ, καὶ τούτου τελευτήσαντος, ἐκράτησεν ὁ υἱὸς
136vP αὐτοῦ, ὁ ᾿Αβδεραχείμ, καὶ ἐδίδου καὶ αὐτὸς τὰ προρρηθέντα | πάκτα διὰ
τὸ εἶναι, καθὼς προείρηται, νήπιον παντελῶς τὸν ἀδεδφὸν αὐτοῦ, τὸν 90
᾿Απελμουζέ.

"Οτι τοῦ ᾿Αβδεραχεὶμ τελευτήσαντος, καὶ τοῦ ἀδελφοῦ αὐτοῦ,
᾿Απελμουζὲ ὡς νηπίου καταφρονηθέντος, ἐκράτησεν τὸ κάστρον τὸ
Μανζικίερτ καὶ τὰς ὑπ᾿ αὐτῷ προρρηθείσας χώρας ὁ δεύτερος ἀδελφὸς
τοῦ ᾿Αποσεβατᾶ, ὁ προλεχθεὶς ᾿Απολεσφούετ, θεῖος δὲ τοῦ ᾿Αβδεραχεὶμ 95
καὶ τοῦ διὰ τὴν νηπιότητα καταφρονηθέντος ἀδελφοῦ αὐτοῦ, τοῦ ᾿Απελ-
μουζέ.

"Οτι τοῦ ᾿Απολεσφούετ τελευτήσαντος, ἐκράτησεν ὁ τρίτος
196Be | ἀδελφὸς τοῦ ᾿Αποσεβατᾶ, ἤγουν ὁ ᾿Αποσέλμης τὸ κάστρον τὸ Μανζι-
κίερτ μετὰ τῶν χωρίων τῶν προρρηθέντων. ῾Ο δὲ προρρηθεὶς ᾿Αχάμετ 100
ὁ καὶ ἀνεψιὸς καὶ προγονὸς τοῦ ᾿Απολεσφούετ, ἐκράτει εἰδήσει καὶ
137rP βουλήσει τοῦ ᾿Απολεσφούετ τό τε | Χλιὰτ καὶ τὸ ᾿Αρζὲς καὶ τὸ Περκρὶ·
καὶ γὰρ ὁ ᾿Απολεσφούετ υἱὸν μὴ ἔχων, καθὼς προείρηται, τοῦτον τὸν
᾿Αχάμετ, τόν τε ἀνεψιὸν καὶ προγονὸν αὐτοῦ, εἶχεν κληρονόμον πάσης
αὐτοῦ τῆς ὑποστάσεως καὶ τῶν κάστρων καὶ τῶν χωρίων αὐτοῦ.   105

"Οτι τελευτήσαντος τοῦ ᾿Αποσέλμη, ἐκράτησεν τὸ κάστρον τὸ
Μανζικίερτ ὁ υἱὸς αὐτοῦ, ὁ ᾿Απελβάρτ μετὰ καὶ τῆς περιχώρου αὐτοῦ.
῾Ο δὲ "Αχμετ ἐκράτησεν τὰ τρία κάστρα, τό τε κάστρον τὸ Χλιὰτ ⟨καὶ⟩
τὸ κάστρον τὸ ᾿Αρζὲς καὶ τὸ κάστρον τὸ ᾿Αλτζικέ.

"Οτι καὶ αὐτὸς ὁ "Αχμετ δοῦλος ἦν τοῦ βασιλέως, καθὰ καὶ 110

44

countries aforesaid, and on his death the third brother, that is, the brother of Aposebatas and Apolesphouet, Aposelmis, possessed Manzikiert and all the countries aforesaid.

Aposebatas had a son Abderacheim, and *another*, Apelmouze.

Apolesphouet had a step-son and nephew, Achamet, for he had no son, but had instead of a son Achamet, his step-son and nephew.

Aposelmis had a son Apelbart, who now possesses Manzikiert.

On the death of Aposebatas, he left Abderacheim his son to be emir, but his other son, Apelmouze, was a mere infant, and hence was passed over as unfit to enter into the authority of his father and brother.

Aposebatas, the eldest brother, had his seat at the city of Manzikiert and possessed, as has been said, these countries, Apachounis and Kori and Charka, and paid tribute in respect to them to the emperor of the Romans; and on his death his son Abderacheim ruled, and he too paid the aforesaid tribute, his brother Apelmouze being, as was said above, quite an infant.

On the death of Abderacheim, since his brother Apelmouze was passed over as an infant, the possession of the city of Manzikiert and of the aforesaid countries beneath it fell to the second brother of Aposebatas, the aforesaid Apolesphouet, uncle of Abderacheim and of his brother Apelmouze, who had been passed over because of his infancy.

On the death of Apolesphouet, the third brother of Aposebatas, that is, Aposelmis, took possession of the city of Manzikiert with the territories aforesaid. The aforesaid Achamet, who was nephew and step-son of Apolesphouet, took possession, by consent and will of Apolesphouet, of Chliat and Arzes and Perkri: for Apolesphouet, having, as was said above, no son, made Achamet, his nephew and step-son, heir of all his substance and of his cities and territories.

On the death of Aposelmis, his son Apelbart possessed the city of Manzikiert with its surrounding territory. But Achmet possessed the three cities, the city of Chliat *and* the city of Arzes and the city of Altzike.

This Achmet too was servant of the emperor, as has been said above,

V 71 τρίτος edd.: γ′ P ‖ 72 Ἀποσεβατὰ P ‖ 73 Μαντζικίερτ Ba Be ‖ 74 Ἀποσεβατὰς P ‖ υἱὸν: υἱοὺς coni. Bekker ‖ Ἀβδηραχείμ Ba Be ‖ 80 Μαντζικίερτ Ba Be ‖ 81 Ἀποσεβατὰ P ‖ Ἀβδεραχείμ V Me: Ἀβδεραχὴ P Ἀβδηραχείμ Ba Be ‖ 82 ἀμηράν P ‖ Ἀπελμουζὲ: Ἀπελμουὲζ coni. Marquart ‖ 85 Ἀποσεβατὰς P ‖ πρῶτος edd.: α′ P ‖ 86 Μαντζικίερτ Ba Be ‖ 89 Ἀβδηραχείμ Ba Be ‖ 92 Ἀβδηραχείμ Ba Be ‖ 94 Μαντζικίερτ Ba Be ‖ 95 Ἀποσεβατὰ P ‖ προλεχθείς: προρρηθείς edd. ‖ Ἀβδηραχείμ Ba Be ‖ 98 τρίτος edd.: γ′ P ‖ 99 Ἀποσεβατὰ P ‖ 99/100 Μαντζικίερτ Ba Be ‖ 100 Ἀχάμετ edd. Ἄχαμτ P ‖ 102 Ἀρζὲς scr. Moravcsik: Ἄρζες P edd. ‖ Περκρή P ‖ 104 Ἀχάμετ edd.: Ἄχαμτ P ‖ 107 Μαντζικίερτ Ba Be ‖ 108 Ἀχάμετ edd. ‖ τρία edd.: γ′ P ‖ καὶ add. Moravcsik ‖ 109 Ἄρζες Ba Be ‖ Ἀλτζικέ scr. Moravcsik: Ἀλτζίκε P edd. ‖ 110 Ἀχάμετ edd. ‖

44, 45

προείρηται, παρέχων καὶ τὰ ὑπὲρ αὐτοῦ καὶ τὰ ὑπὲρ τοῦ θείου αὐτοῦ, τοῦ Ἀπολεσφούετ, πάκτα. Ὁ δὲ Ἀπελβὰρτ μετὰ δόλου καὶ χλεύης 137ᵛP αὐτὸν ἔσφαξεν, καὶ ἀνελάβετο τὰ τρία αὐτὰ | κάστρα, τό τε κάστρον τὸ Χλιὰτ ⟨καὶ⟩ τὸ κάστρον τὸ Ἀρζὲς καὶ τὸ κάστρον τὸ Ἀλτζικέ· καὶ ταῦτα ὀφείλει ὁ βασιλεὺς ἀναλαβέσθαι ὡς ἴδια αὐτοῦ τυγχάνοντα. 115

Ὅτι ταῦτα πάντα τὰ προρρηθέντα κάστρα καὶ αἱ προρρηθεῖσαι χῶραι οὐδέποτε γεγόνασιν ὑπὸ τὴν ἐξουσίαν τῆς Περσίδος ἢ ὑπὸ τὴν ἐξουσίαν τοῦ ἀμερμουμνῆ, ἀλλ' ὑπῆρχον, καθὼς εἴρηται, ἐν ταῖς ἡμέραις 197Be τοῦ κυροῦ Λέοντος, τοῦ βασιλέως ὑπὸ τὴν ἐξου|σίαν τοῦ Συμβατίου, τοῦ ἄρχοντος τῶν ἀρχόντων, καὶ μετὰ ταῦτα ἐγένοντο ὑπὸ τὴν ἐξουσίαν 120 τῶν τριῶν ἀδελφῶν, τῶν προρρηθέντων ἀμηράδων, τοῦ τε Ἀποσεβατᾶ καὶ τοῦ Ἀπολεσφούετ καὶ τοῦ Ἀποσέλμη· καὶ ἐν ταῖς ἡμέραις αὐτῶν καὶ ἐδουλώθησαν καὶ ἐπακτώθησαν καὶ ἐγένοντο ὑπὸ τὴν ἐξουσίαν τῶν 138ʳP | βασιλέων τῶν Ῥωμαίων.

Ὅτι τὰ τρία ταῦτα κάστρα, τό τε Χλιὰτ καὶ τὸ Ἀρζὲς καὶ τὸ 125 Περκρί, εἰ κρατεῖ ὁ βασιλεύς, Περσικὸν φοσσᾶτον κατὰ Ῥωμανίας ἐξελθεῖν οὐ δύναται, ἐπειδὴ μέσον τυγχάνουσιν τῆς τε Ῥωμανίας καὶ Ἀρμενίας, καὶ εἰσὶν φραγμὸς καὶ ἀπλίκτα τῶν φοσσάτων.

45. Περὶ τῶν Ἰβήρων.

Ἰστέον, ὅτι ἑαυτοὺς σεμνύνοντες οἱ Ἴβηρες, ἤγουν οἱ τοῦ κουροπαλάτου, λέγουσιν ἑαυτοὺς κατάγεσθαι ἀπὸ τῆς γυναικὸς Οὐρίου, τῆς παρὰ τοῦ Δαυίδ, τοῦ προφήτου καὶ βασιλέως μοιχευθείσης· ἐκ γὰρ τῶν ἐξ αὐτῆς τεχθέντων παίδων τῷ Δαυὶδ ἑαυτοὺς λέγουσιν κατάγεσθαι 5 καὶ συγγενεῖς εἶναι Δαυίδ, τοῦ προφήτου καὶ βασιλέως καὶ ὡς ἐκ τούτου 138ᵛP καὶ τῆς ὑπεραγίας Θεοτόκου διὰ τὸ | ἐκ τοῦ σπέρματος Δαυὶδ ταύτην κατάγεσθαι. Διὰ τοῦτο καὶ οἱ μεγιστᾶνες τῶν Ἰβήρων ἀκωλύτως τὰς συγγενίδας αὐτῶν πρὸς γάμον ἄγουσιν, τὴν παλαιὰν οἰόμενοι φυλάττειν 198Be νομοθεσίαν· ἐξ Ἱερουσαλήμ τε λέγουσιν εἶ|ναι τὴν γέννησιν αὐτῶν, 10 καὶ ἐκ τῶν ἐκεῖσε χρηματισθῆναι κατ' ὄναρ μετελθεῖν καὶ κατοικῆσαι πρὸς τὰ μέρη Περσίδος, ἤγουν εἰς τὴν χώραν, εἰς ἣν νῦν οἰκοῦσιν. Οἱ δὲ χρηματισθέντες καὶ ἐξελθόντες ἐκ τῆς Ἱερουσαλὴμ ὑπῆρχον ὅ τε Δαυὶδ ἐκεῖνος καὶ ὁ ἀδελφὸς αὐτοῦ, Σπανδιάτης, ὅστις Σπανδιάτης ἦν ἐκ Θεοῦ λαβὼν χάρισμα, ὡς αὐτοὶ φάσκουσιν, τοῦ μὴ ἐν πολέμῳ 15

F   **45.** 3 κατάγεσθαι — 4 μοιχευθείσης: cf. II Reg. 11, 3—5; Matth. 1,
6.   6 ὡς ἐκ τούτου — 8 κατάγεσθαι: cf. The Apocryphal New Testament,
London 1820, p. 17: The Gospel of the Birth of Mary, 1, 1.   11 χρηματισθῆναι
κατ' ὄναρ: Matth. 2, 12.

V 111 αὐτοῦ²: αὐτοῦ Migne ‖ 113 αὐτὰ: αὐτοῦ edd.   *post* αὐτὰ *aliquid eras.* Pˣ ‖

44, 45

and paid tribute on his own behalf and on behalf of his uncle Apolesphouet. But Apelbart by guile and deceit slew him and took these three cities, the city of Chliat and the city of Arzes and the city of Altzike; and these the emperor should get back, as they are his property.

All these cities aforesaid and the aforesaid countries have never been beneath the dominion of Persia or beneath the dominion of the commander of the faithful, but were, as has been said, in the days of the lord Leo, the emperor, beneath the dominion of Symbatios, the prince of princes, and afterwards came beneath the dominion of the three brothers, the aforesaid emirs, Aposebatas and Apolesphouet and Aposelmis; and in their days were brought into servitude and made tributary and fell beneath the dominion of the emperors of the Romans.

If these three cities, Chliat and Arzes and Perkri, are in the possession of the emperor, a Persian army cannot come out against Romania, because they are between Romania and Armenia, and serve as a barrier and as military halts for armies.

45. Of the Iberians.

The Iberians, I mean, those who belong to the curopalate, pique themselves upon their descent from the wife of Uriah, with whom David, the prophet and king, committed adultery: for they say they are descended from the children she bore to David and are related to David, the prophet and king, and consequently to the most holy Mother of God also, inasmuch as she was by descent of the seed of David. For this reason also the great ones of the Iberians take in marriage their female relatives without impediment, believing that they are preserving the ancient ordinance; and they say that they originate from Jerusalem and were warned by an oracular dream to migrate thence and to settle over toward the region of Persia, that is to say, in the country where they live now. They who were warned by the oracle and came out of Jerusalem were the former David and his brother Spandiatis, which Spandiatis had received from God a boon, as they pretend, that in battle the sword should not touch him in any member of

---

114 καὶ add. edd. ‖ Ἄρζες Ba Be ‖ Ἀλτζίκε edd. Ἀρτζικέ coni. V. Laurent ‖ 116 αἱ s. v. add. P¹ in textum receperunt V edd. ‖ 119 τοῦ² om. V edd. ‖ 121 τριῶν edd.: γ′ P ‖ Ἀποσεβατὰ P ‖ 124 τῶν om. edd. ‖ 125 τρία edd.: γ′ P ‖ Ἀρζές scr. Moravcsik: Ἄρζες P edd. ‖ 126 Περκρή P ‖ φοσσάτον P ‖ 128 ἄπληκτα P.

45. 1 Περὶ τῶν Ἰβήρων (π̔ rubro atramento) mg. add. P¹, unde in textum receperunt V edd. ‖ 8 μεγιστάνες P ‖ 11 χρηματισθῆναι om. V edd. ‖

45

ἅπτεσθαι αὐτοῦ ξίφος εἰς οἱονδήποτε μέλος τοῦ σώματος αὐτοῦ ἄνευ
139ʳP τῆς καρδίας, ἣν καὶ διά τινος σκεπάσματος | ἐν τοῖς πολέμοις περιεφρού-
ρει. Διὰ τοῦτο καὶ ἐπτοοῦντο τοῦτον καὶ ἐδεδίεισαν οἱ Πέρσαι, ὁ δὲ
νενίκηκέ τε αὐτοὺς καὶ αὐτῶν κατεκράτησεν, καὶ τοὺς συγγενεῖς ἐνώκι-
σεν Ἴβηρας εἰς τὰς δυσκολίας, τὰς νῦν παρ' αὐτῶν κρατουμένας, ἐξ 20
ὧν καὶ κατ' ὀλίγον ἐπλατύνθησαν καὶ ηὐξήθησαν καὶ εἰς μέγα ἔθνος
ἐγένοντο. Εἶθ' οὕτως τοῦ βασιλέως Ἡρακλείου κατὰ Περσίδος ἐκστρα-
τεύσαντος, ἡνώθησαν καὶ συνεταξίδευσαν αὐτῷ, καὶ ἔκτοτε ὑπέταξαν
τῷ φόβῳ Ἡρακλείου, τοῦ βασιλέως Ῥωμαίων μᾶλλον, ἤπερ τῇ ἑαυτῶν
ἰσχύϊ καὶ δυνάμει πόλεις καὶ χώρας ἱκανὰς τῶν Περσῶν. Ἅπαξ γὰρ 25
139ᵛP τοῦ βασιλέως Ἡρακλείου τοὺς Πέρσας τροπωσαμένου καὶ εἰς τὸ | μηκέτι
εἶναι τὴν τούτων ἀρχὴν παραστήσαντος, εὐάλωτοι καὶ εὐχείρωτοι οὐ
μόνον τοῖς Ἴβηρσιν, ἀλλὰ καὶ τοῖς Σαρακηνοῖς οἱ Πέρσαι γεγόνασιν.
Διὰ δὲ τὸ κατάγεσθαι αὐτούς, ὡς αὐτοὶ λέγουσιν, ἐξ Ἱερουσαλὴμ διὰ
τὸ μεγάλην πίστιν ἔχουσιν ἐν αὐτοῖς καὶ ἐν τῷ τάφῳ τοῦ Κυρίου 30
199Be ἡμῶν {ἡ} Ἰησοῦ Χριστοῦ, καὶ κατά τινας | καιροὺς ἀφθόνως ἀποστέλ-
λουσι χρήματα τῷ πατριάρχῃ τῆς ἁγίας πόλεως καὶ τοῖς ἐκεῖσε Χριστιανοῖς. Ὁ δὲ προρρηθεὶς Δαυίδ, ὁ τοῦ Σπανδιάτου ἀδελφός, ἐγέννησεν
υἱὸν τὸν Παγκράτιον, καὶ ὁ Παγκράτιος ἐγέννησεν υἱὸν τὸν Ἀσώτιον,
καὶ ὁ Ἀσώτιος ἐγέννησεν υἱὸν τὸν Ἀδρανασή, τὸν καὶ κουροπαλάτην 35
τιμηθέντα παρὰ Λέοντος, τοῦ φιλοχρίστου βασιλέως Ῥωμαίων. Ὁ δὲ
140ʳP Σπανδιάτης, ὁ ἀδελφὸς τοῦ | προρρηθέντος Δαυίδ, ἐτελεύτησεν ἄτεκνος.
Ἀπὸ δὲ τῆς ἐξ Ἱερουσαλὴμ μετοικήσεως αὐτῶν εἰς τὴν νῦν οἰκουμένην
παρ' αὐτῶν χώραν εἰσὶν ἔτη υ' ἢ καὶ φ' μέχρι τῆς σήμερον, ἥτις ἐστὶν
ἰνδικτιῶνι ι', ἔτος ἀπὸ κτίσεως κόσμου ͵ϛυξζ' ἐπὶ τῆς βασιλείας Κωνσταν- 40
τίνου καὶ Ῥωμανοῦ, τῶν φιλοχρίστων καὶ πορφυρογεννήτων βασιλέων
Ῥωμαίων.
Ἰστέον, ὅτι ὁ φιλόχριστος καὶ πορφυρογέννητος καὶ ἀοίδιμος
βασιλεὺς Λέων ἀκούσας, ὅτι εἰς τὸν τόπον, τὸν λεγόμενον Φασιανὴν
ἐλθόντες οἱ Σαρακηνοί, τὰς ἐκεῖσε ἐκκλησίας ἐποίησαν κάστρα, ἀπέ- 45
στειλεν τὸν πατρίκιον {ὁ δεῖνα} καὶ στρατηγὸν τῶν Ἀρμενιάκων τὸν
Λαλάκωνα μετὰ τοῦ στρατηγοῦ Κολωνείας καὶ τοῦ στρατηγοῦ Μεσο-
140ᵛP ποταμίας | καὶ τοῦ στρατηγοῦ Χαλδίας, καὶ κατέστρεψαν τὰ τοιαῦτα
κάστρα, τὰς ἐκκλησίας ἐλευθερώσαντες, ληϊσάμενοι καὶ πᾶσαν τὴν
Φασιανήν, τῷ τότε καιρῷ ὑπὸ τῶν Σαρακηνῶν κρατουμένην. Καὶ εἶθ' 50
οὕτως πάλιν ἀπέστειλεν τὸν μάγιστρον Κατακαλὼν καὶ δομέστικον
τῶν σχολῶν, ὃς ἐλθὼν ἐν τῷ κάστρῳ Θεοδοσιουπόλεως καὶ τὰ πέριξ
200Be | αὐτῆς ληϊσάμενος καὶ τὴν χώραν τῆς Φασιανῆς καὶ τὰ περὶ αὐτὴν κάστρα

F   22 Εἶθ' οὕτως — 23 αὐτῷ: cf. Theoph. p. 309, 15.

his body save only in the heart, which he used to protect by a sort of covering in battles. On this account the Persians were dismayed at and feared him, and he overcame them and mastered them and settled his Iberian kinsmen in the difficult territories now possessed by them; whence by degrees they expanded and increased and grew into a great nation. Thereafter, when the emperor Heraclius marched against Persia, they united and campaigned with him, and as a result, through the dread inspired by Heraclius, emperor of the Romans, rather than by their own strength and power, they subdued a great number of cities and countries of the Persians. For once the emperor Heraclius had routed the Persians and had forcibly brought their empire to an end, the Persians were easily defeated and mastered, not by the Iberians only, but by the Saracens as well. And because they originated, as they themselves say, from Jerusalem, for this reason they are very loyal to it and to the sepulchre of our Lord Jesus Christ, and from time to time they send large sums of money to the patriarch of the holy city and to the Christians there. Now, the aforesaid David, the brother of Spandiatis, begat a son Pankratios, and Pankratios begat a son Asotios, and Asotios begat a son Adranasi, who was honoured with the rank of curopalate by Leo, the Christ-loving emperor of the Romans. But Spandiatis, the brother of the aforesaid David, died childless. And from their migration from Jerusalem to the country now inhabited by them it is 400 years, or rather 500 up to the present day, which is the 10th indiction, the year from the creation of the world 6460, in the reign of Constantine and Romanus, Christ-loving emperors of the Romans, born in the purple.

The Christ-loving and glorious emperor Leo, born in the purple, hearing that the Saracens had arrived in the place called Phasiane and had made the churches there into fortresses, sent the patrician Lalakon, military governor of the Armeniakoi, together with the military governor of Koloneia and the military governor of Mesopotamia and the military governor of Chaldia, and they destroyed these fortresses and liberated the churches and ravaged all Phasiane, at that time in the possession of the Saracens. And again afterwards he sent the magister Katakalon, the commander-in-chief, who arrived at the city of Theodosioupolis and ravaged the territory all about it, and gave up the country of Phasiane and the cities around it to the

---

V 17 σκεπάσματος: περισκεπάσματος V edd. ‖ 19 νενίκηκέ] litteras κέ in ras. scr. P¹ ‖ τε om. edd. ‖ 19/20 ἐνοίκησεν P ‖ 20 δυσκολίας: δυσχωρίας coni. Bekker ‖ 21 καὶ¹ om. Ba Be ‖ ηὐξήθησαν scr. Moravcsik: ηὐξήνθησαν P ηὐξάνθησαν edd. ‖ 29 ἐξ: ἐκ τῆς Ba Be ‖ 30 ἔχουσιν (etiam Ba): ἔχειν V Me Be ‖ 31 ἡ om. V edd. secl. Moravcsik ‖ 39 εἰσὶν a P¹ false post ι' (40) insertum huc transp. Moravcsik ‖ 40 ἔτος: ἔτη V edd. ‖ 44 τὸν¹ om. Be ‖ 46 ὁ δεῖνα per comp. P: om. edd. secl. Moravcsik ‖ 'Αρμενιακῶν edd. ‖ 51 Κατακαλὸν P ‖

45

τῷ ὁμοίῳ ὀλέθρῳ παραδούς, ὑπέστρεψεν, μεγάλην πληγὴν ἐν τούτῳ
δοὺς τοῖς Σαρακηνοῖς. Ἐπὶ δὲ τῆς βασιλείας τοῦ κυροῦ Ῥωμανοῦ, τοῦ 55
βασιλέως ὁ μάγιστρος Ἰωάννης ὁ Κουρκούας ἀπερχόμενος κατὰ τοῦ
141ʳP κάστρου Τιβίου, εἰς τὴν δίοδον αὐτοῦ ἠφάνισεν τὴν πᾶσαν χώ|ραν τῆς
Φασιανῆς, ὡς ὑπὸ τῶν Σαρακηνῶν κρατουμένην. Ἀλλὰ καὶ ὁ πατρίκιος
Θεόφιλος, ὁ ἀδελφὸς τοῦ προρρηθέντος μαγίστρου Ἰωάννου, τὸ πρῶτον
αὐτοῦ στρατηγεύοντος ἐν Χαλδίᾳ, ἐπραίδευσεν τὴν τοιαύτην χώραν 60
τῆς Φασιανῆς, ὡς καὶ τότε ὑπὸ τῶν Σαρακηνῶν δεσποζομένην. Μέχρι
γὰρ τοῦ γεγονέναι τὸν λόγον μετὰ τοὺς Θεοδοσιουπολίτας εἰς τὴν χώραν
τῆς Φασιανῆς χωρίον οὐ συνέστη, οὐδὲ εἰς τὸ κάστρον τοῦ Ἀβνίκου.
Καὶ οἱ Ἴβηρες πάντοτε εἶχον ἀγάπην καὶ φιλίαν μετὰ τῶν Θεοδοσιουπολιτῶν καὶ τῶν Ἀβνικιωτῶν καὶ μετὰ τῶν Μανζικιερτῶν καὶ μετὰ 65
πᾶσαν τὴν Περσίδα, ἀλλ᾽ ἐν Φασιανῇ οὐδέποτε ἐπεκτήσαντο χωρία.
141ᵛP   Ὅτι πολλάκις ὁ κύρις Λέων, ὁ βασιλεὺς | καὶ ὁ κύρις Ῥωμανὸς
καὶ αὐτὴ ἡ βασιλεία ἡμῶν ἐπεζήτησεν τὸ κάστρον τὸ Κετζέον τοῦ ἀναλαβέσθαι αὐτὸ καὶ εἰσαγαγεῖν ταξάτους πρὸς τὸ μὴ ἐκεῖθεν σιταρχεῖσθαι
τὴν Θεοδοσιούπολιν, ἐξασφαλιζόμενοι πρός τε τὸν κουροπαλάτην καὶ 70
τοὺς ἀδελφοὺς αὐτοῦ τοῦ — μετὰ τὸ παραληφθῆναι τὴν Θεοδοσιούπο-
201Be λιν — ἀνα|λαβέσθαι αὐτοὺς τὸ τοιοῦτον κάστρον, ἀλλ᾽ οὐκ ἠνέσχοντο
οἱ Ἴβηρες τοῦτο ποιῆσαι διὰ τὴν ἀγάπην τῶν Θεοδοσιουπολιτῶν, καὶ
διὰ τὸ μὴ πορθηθῆναι τὸ κάστρον Θεοδοσιούπολιν, ἀλλ᾽ ἀντεδήλωσαν
τὸν κύριν Ῥωμανὸν καὶ τὴν βασιλείαν ἡμῶν, λέγοντες, ὅτι· «Εἰ τοῦτο 75
ποιήσωμεν, ἀτιμία ἔχομεν γενέσθαι εἰς τοὺς γείτονας ἡμῶν, οἷον εἰς
142ʳP τὸν μάγιστρον καὶ {εἰς τὸν} ἐξουσιαστὴν Ἀβασγίας καὶ εἰς | τὸν Βασπαρα-
κανίτην καὶ εἰς τοὺς ὑπερεξάρχοντας τῶν Ἀρμενίων, καὶ εἰπεῖν ἔχουσιν,
ὅτι ὁ βασιλεὺς ἀπίστους ἔχει τοὺς Ἴβηρας, τόν τε κουροπαλάτην καὶ
τοὺς ἀδελφοὺς αὐτοῦ, καὶ οὐ πιστεύει αὐτοῖς, καὶ διὰ τοῦτο ἀνελάβετο 80
⟨τὸ⟩ κάστρον ἐξ αὐτῶν, ἀλλὰ μᾶλλον ἂς ἀποστείλῃ ὁ βασιλεὺς τουρμάρχην ἢ βασιλικόν τινα, καὶ ἂς καθέζηται εἰς τὸ κάστρον τοῦ Κετζέου,
καὶ ἂς θεωρῇ.» Καὶ ἐδέξαντο διὰ κελεύσεως, ὅτι· «Τί ὄφελος ἢ τουρμάρχην ἢ βασιλικὸν ἀποστεῖλαι; Πάντως ἐὰν εἰσέλθῃ εἴτε τουρμάρχης,
εἴτε βασιλικός, μετὰ δέκα ἢ δώδεκα ἀνθρώπων ἔχει εἰσελθεῖν, καὶ 85
καθέζεσθαι ἔχει εἰς τὸ ἀπλίκτον, ὃ παρ᾽ ὑμῶν λάβῃ· καὶ ἐπεὶ πολλαί
εἰσιν ὁδοί, αἱ εἰσάγουσαι εἰς τὸ κάστρον Θεοδοσιουπόλεως, οὐ δύναται
142ᵛP ἀπὸ τοῦ | κάστρου βλέπειν τὰ εἰσερχόμενα καρβάνια εἰς τὸ κάστρον
Θεοδοσιουπόλεως· δύνανται δὲ εἰσέρχεσθαι καρβάνια ἐν Θεοδοσιουπόλει τῇ νυκτί, ἐκείνων μηδὲν νοούντων.» Ἀλλ᾽ οὖν διὰ τὸ μὴ θέλειν 90
τοὺς Ἴβηρας πορθηθῆναι τὴν Θεοδοσιούπολιν, ἀλλὰ μᾶλλον σιταρ-

45

like destruction, and returned after inflicting thereby a great blow upon the Saracens. And in the reign of the lord Romanus, the emperor, the magister John Kourkouas, marching against the city of Tibi, utterly devastated in his passage the whole country of Phasiane, since it was in the possession of the Saracens. Moreover, the patrician Theophilus also, brother of the aforesaid magister John, when he was for the first time military governor of Chaldia, plundered this country of Phasiane, because then too it was controlled by the Saracens. For by the time that terms had been agreed with the Theodosioupolitans, no village had been left standing in the country of Phasiane, or about the city of Abnikon either. And the Iberians always maintained loving and friendly relations with the men of Theodosioupolis and Abnikon and Manzikiert and with all Persia, but in Phasiane they never acquired any territories.

The lord Leo, the emperor, and the lord Romanus and our own imperial majesty several times asked for the city of Ketzeon, so that we might take it over and introduce garrisons, in order to stop Theodosioupolis from being revictualled thence, assuring the curopalate and his brothers that, after Theodosioupolis had been taken, they should have this city back; but the Iberians did not consent to do this, out of their love for the Theodosiou-politans and in order that the city of Theodosioupolis might not be taken, and declared in answer to the lord Romanus and to our imperial majesty, saying: «If we do this, we shall become dishonoured in the eyes of our neighbours, such as the magister the ruler of Abasgia and the Basparakanite and the potentates of the Armenians, and they will say that 'the emperor holds the Iberians, the curopalate and his brothers, for faithless and does not trust them, and that is why he has taken over *the* city from them'; but let the emperor rather send a lieutenant-general or some imperial agent, and let him take up his quarters in the city of Ketzeon and let him watch.» And they were instructed by imperial mandate, to this effect: «What is the use of our sending either lieutenant-general or imperial agent? Even if he enters, whether he be lieutenant-general or imperial agent, he will enter with ten or a dozen men and will take up his quarters in the lodgings which you will provide for him; and since the roads leading to the city of Theo-dosioupolis are many, he cannot from the city see the caravans entering the city of Theodosioupolis; and caravans may enter Theodosioupolis by night, and they none the wiser.» And so, then, because the Iberians did not wish that Theodosioupolis should be taken, but rather that it should be

---

V 55 τοῦ¹ *om.* edd. || τοῦ² *om.* edd. || 65 Μαντζικιερτῶν Ba Be || 67 κύρης¹ P || κύρης² P || 75 κύρην P || εἰ] *in ras. scr.* P¹ || 76 ποιήσομεν edd. || 77 εἰς τὸν *secl.* Jenkins || 81 τὸ *add.* edd. || ἀς (*sine acc.*) P || 82 ἀς (*sine acc.*) P || καθέζηται edd.: καθέζεται P || τὸ *om.* edd. || Κετζέου edd.: Κετζέος P || 83 ἀς (*sine acc.*) P || θεωρῇ Be: θεωρεῖ P || 85 δέκα edd.: ι′ P || δώδεκα edd.: ιβ′ P || 86 ἀπλήκτον P || ὑμῶν: ὑμῖν edd. || λάβῃ edd.: λάβει P ||

202Be χεῖσθαι, τούτου ἕνεκα οὐχ ὑπήκουσαν, καὶ δέδωκαν τὸ κά|στρον τὸ
Κετζέον, καίτοι καὶ ὅρκον ἔγγραφον δεχόμενοι τοῦ — μετὰ τὸ παραληφθῆναι τὴν Θεοδοσιούπολιν — ἀποστραφῆναι αὐτοῖς τὸ τοιοῦτον κάστρον.

Ὅτι οὐδέποτε ἠβουλήθησαν οἱ Ἴβηρες πραιδεῦσαι ἢ αἰχμαλωτίσαι 95
τὰ πέριξ τοῦ κάστρου Θεοδοσιουπόλεως ἢ τὰ χωρία αὐτοῦ ἢ εἰς τὸ
κάστρον τοῦ Ἀβνικίου ἢ τὰ περὶ αὐτὸ χωρία ἢ εἰς τὸ κάστρον Μανζικίερτ
143ʳP καὶ | εἰς τὴν αὐτοῦ ἐπικράτειαν.

Ὅτι καθὼς ἐνίσταται ὁ κουροπαλάτης περὶ τῶν χωρίων τῆς
Φασιανῆς, ἐπιζητῶν ὅλην τὴν Φασιανὴν καὶ τὸ κάστρον τοῦ Ἀβνίκου, 100
προφασιζόμενος χρυσοβούλλια ἔχειν τοῦ μακαρίου βασιλέως, τοῦ κυροῦ
Ῥωμανοῦ καὶ τῆς ἡμετέρας βασιλείας, ὧν καὶ τὰ ἴσα πρὸς ἡμᾶς ἀπέστειλεν διὰ τοῦ Ζουρβανέλη πρωτοσπαθαρίου, τοῦ ἀζάτου αὐτοῦ,
ταῦτα ἐπισκεψάμενοι εὕρομεν αὐτὸν μηδεμίαν βοήθειαν ἔχοντα. Τὸ μὲν
γὰρ χρυσοβούλλιον τοῦ πενθεροῦ ἡμῶν περιέχει ὑποσχέσθαι τὸν αὐτὸν 105
κουροπαλάτην, ὡς δι' ὅρκου ἐβεβαίωσεν αὐτὸν οἰκείᾳ χειρὶ ἐγγραψάμε-
νος, τοῦ διαμεῖναι ἐν τῇ πίστει τῆς ἡμετέρας βασιλείας καὶ τοῖς μὲν
143ᵛP ἐχθροῖς ἡμῶν ἀντιμάχεσθαι, | τοὺς δὲ φίλους ὑπερασπίζεσθαι καὶ τὴν
ἀνατολὴν ὑπόσπονδον ποιῆσαι τῇ βασιλείᾳ ἡμῶν καὶ κάστρα χειρώ-
σασθαι καὶ μεγάλα πρὸς θεραπείαν ἡμῶν ἔργα ποιήσασθαι, καὶ ὑπεσχέθη 110
αὐτῷ παρὰ τοῦ πενθεροῦ ἡμῶν, ἵνα, ἐὰν φυλάξῃ τὴν τοιαύτην πιστὴν
203Be δούλωσιν καὶ εὐγνωμοσύνην, διαμείνῃ ἀμετασάλευτος | καὶ αὐτὸς καὶ
οἱ τοῦ γένους αὐτοῦ ἐν τῇ τούτου ἀρχῇ καὶ ἐξουσίᾳ· καὶ οὐ μεταστήσει
τὰ ὅρια τῶν τόπων αὐτοῦ, ἀλλὰ κατὰ τῶν πρώην βασιλέων τὰ σύμφωνα
στέρξει, καὶ οὐχὶ περαιτέρω ὑπερβήσεται, καὶ ὅτι οὐδὲ κωλύσει αὐτὸν 115
καταστρέψαι τὴν Θεοδοσιούπολιν καὶ τὰ λοιπὰ κάστρα τῶν ἐχθρῶν,
144ʳP κἄν τε δι' αὐτοῦ μόνου πολιορκηθήσονται, κἄν τε δι' | αὐτοῦ τοῦ στρατο-
πέδου ἡμῶν. Ταῦτα μὲν τὰ κεφάλαια περιέχουσιν τὰ χρυσοβούλλια,
ἐξ ὧν οὐδεμίαν βοήθειαν ὁ κουροπαλάτης ἔχει· τὸ μὲν γὰρ τοῦ πενθεροῦ
ἡμῶν διαγορεύει, ὅτι οὐ παρασαλεύσομεν αὐτὸν ἐκ τῶν παλαιῶν ὁρίων 120
τῆς χώρας αὐτοῦ, καὶ ὅτι, ἐὰν δυνηθῇ εἴτε καὶ μόνος, εἴτε καὶ μετὰ
τοῦ στρατοπέδου ἡμῶν, πολιορκήσει καὶ καταστρέψει τὴν Θεοδοσιούπολιν καὶ τὰ λοιπὰ κάστρα τῶν ἐχθρῶν, οὐχὶ δὲ κατασχεῖν αὐτὰ εἰς τελείαν
δεσποτείαν καὶ κυριότητα· τὸ δὲ τῆς βασιλείας ἡμῶν περιέχει, ἵνα,
ὅσους ἂν τόπους δυνηθῇ καὶ αὐτὸς καὶ ὁ ἀνεψιὸς αὐτοῦ, ὁ μάγιστρος 125
144ᵛP Ἀδρανασέ, ἐξ οἰκείας δυνάμεως καθυποτάξαι τῶν Ἀγαρηνῶν, | ἢ ἀπὸ
τοῦ νῦν καθυποτάξει, κατέχει ἐπὶ δεσποτείᾳ καὶ κυριότητι. Καὶ ἐπεὶ
οὔτε ἐξ οἰκείας δυνάμεως τὴν Θεοδοσιούπολιν κατεστρέψατο, οὔτε τὸ

V 95 ἐβουλήθησαν edd. ‖ 97 Ἀβνίκου edd. ‖ Μαντζικίερτ Ba Be ‖ 100 ἐπιζητῶν
edd.: ἐπεζήτων P ‖ 101 χρυσοβούλλια edd.: χρυσοβούλλιον P ‖ 105 πεμθεροῦ

45

revictualled, for this reason they did not obey and give up the city of Ketzeon, although they received a sworn promise in writing that after the capture of Theodosioupolis this city should revert to them.

The Iberians never consented to raid or take prisoners in the environs of the city of Theodosioupolis or in its territories, or in the city of Abnikion or the territories about it, or in the city of Manzikiert or the area controlled by it.

Whereas regarding the territories of Phasiane the curopalate persists in his demand for all Phasiane and the city of Abnikon, and alleges that he has golden bulls of the emperor the lord Romanus, of blessed memory, and of our imperial majesty, copies of which he sent us by the hand of Zourbanelis the protospatharius, his 'azat', we examined these and found that they gave him no help. For, first, the golden bull of our father-in-law embodies a promise of this same curopalate, as he assured him on his oath and inscribed it with his own hand, that he will abide in loyalty to our imperial majesty, and fight against our foes and protect our friends, and subdue the east to our imperial majesty, and reduce cities and do great works for our comfort; and on the part of our father-in-law a promise was made to him that, if he continues in this loyal servitude and gratitude, he shall remain unshaken, both he and those of his family, in his rule and dominion; and *the emperor* will not move the boundaries of his territories, but will be content with the agreements made by former emperors and will not push beyond them; nor will he stop *the curopalate* from destroying Theodosioupolis and the rest of the cities of the enemy, whether he lays siege to them with his own unaided strength or with the assistance of this our army. Such are the main points contained in the golden bulls, and from them the curopalate gets no help: for that of our father-in-law lays it down that we will not disturb him from the ancient boundaries of his country, and that, if he can, whether by himself or with our army, he shall lay siege to and destroy Theodosioupolis and the rest of the cities of the enemy, but not so as to hold them in absolute sovereignty and lordship; while that of our own imperial majesty includes a provision that all the places of the Agarenes which both he and his nephew, the magister Adranase, may be able by their own power to reduce, or shall in future reduce, he shall hold as sovereign lord. And since by his own power he subdued neither Theodosioupolis nor

---

P ‖ 108 τοὺς δὲ φίλους *corr.* Moravcsik: τοῖς δὲ φίλοις P edd. ‖ 111 αὐτῷ *corr.* Tomašić: αὐτοῖς P edd. ‖ πεμθεροῦ P ‖ πιστὴν: πίστιν edd. ‖ 113 μεταστήση F ‖ 115 στέρξει Be: στέρξη P   στέρξη Me Ba ‖ οὐχὶ *om.* edd. ‖ *post* περαιτέρω *add.* μὴ edd. ‖ ὑπερβήσηται F ‖ 116 τὴν *bis* P ‖ 117 δι᾽ αὐτοῦ: διὰ τοῦ αὐτοῦ Me Ba   τοῦ *secl.* Be ‖ 119 πεμθεροῦ P ‖ 120 παρασαλεύομεν V edd. ‖ 122 καταστρέψει V edd.: καταστρέψη P ‖ 126 ᾽Αδρανασέ *scr.* Moravcsik: ᾽Αδρανασαὶ P   ᾽Αδρανασὴ edd. ‖ 127 κατέχη edd. ‖

Ἀβνίκιον, οὔτε τὸ Μαστάτον, οὐκ ὀφείλει ταῦτα κατέχειν, ὡς ὄντα
ἔνθεν τοῦ Ἔραξ ποταμοῦ, ἤτοι τοῦ Φάσιδος, διότι τὸ μὲν κάστρον τοῦ 130
Ἀβνίκου μέχρι τοῦ νῦν ἦν αὐτεξούσιον καὶ αὐτοδέσποτον, ἔχον ἴδιον
ἀμηρᾶν, καὶ πολλάκις ὁ λαὸς τῆς βασιλείας ἡμῶν ἐπραίδευσεν αὐτό,
204Be ἀλλὰ καὶ ὁ πρωτο|σπαθάριος Ἰωάννης καὶ στρατηγὸς ὁ Ἀρραβωνίτης
καὶ ὁ πατρίκιος Θεόφιλος καὶ ἀρτίως στρατηγὸς Θεοδοσιουπόλεως, καὶ
οἱ λοιποὶ στρατηγοὶ μεγάλην πραῖδαν καὶ αἰχμαλωσίαν εἰς αὐτὸ ἠργά-135
145ʳᴾ σαντο, κατακαύσαντες τὰ χωρία αὐτοῦ, μὴ|δέποτε τοῦ κουροπαλάτου
πραιδεύσαντος αὐτό. Καὶ ἡνίκα ἠφανίσθησαν τὰ τούτου χωρία παρὰ
τῆς βασιλείας ἡμῶν, ὑπεισῆλθον οἱ Ἴβηρες, καὶ κατεκράτησαν αὐτά,
πειρώμενοι ἐκ τούτου τὸ κάστρον κρατῆσαι. Ὁ δὲ ἀμηρᾶς πολλάκις
μηνυθεὶς παρὰ τοῦ πατρικίου Θεοφίλου καὶ στρατηγοῦ καὶ ἰδών, ὅτι 140
οὐδαμόθεν ἔχει ἐλπίδα ζωῆς, ὑπετάγη καὶ κατένευσεν γενέσθαι δοῦλος
τῆς βασιλείας ἡμῶν, δοὺς τὸν υἱὸν αὐτοῦ ὅψιδα. Τὸ δὲ Μαστάτον ὑπῆρχεν
τῶν Θεοδοσιουπολιτῶν, καὶ ἡνίκα ὁ μάγιστρος Ἰωάννης ἐπολιόρκησεν
τὴν Θεοδοσιούπολιν ἑπτὰ μῆνας, διὰ τὸ μὴ δύνασθαι παραλαβεῖν αὐτὴν
ἀποστείλας λαόν, παρέλαβεν τὸ αὐτὸ κάστρον τὸ Μαστάτον, καὶ εἰσήγα-145
145ᵛᴾ γεν | ἐν αὐτῷ τὸν πρωτοσπαθάριον Πετρωνᾶν τὸν Βόϊλαν, τὸν τότε
ὄντα κατεπάνω Νικοπόλεως. Ὁ δὲ μάγιστρος Παγκράτιος συνταξιδεύ-
σας τῷ αὐτῷ μαγίστρῳ ἐν Θεοδοσιουπόλει, ἡνίκα ἔμελλεν ἀναχωρεῖν,
παρεκάλεσεν, ἵνα δώσῃ αὐτῷ τὸ τοιοῦτον κάστρον, ποιήσας ἔγγραφον
ὅρκον πρὸς αὐτὸν τοῦ ἐπικρατεῖν αὐτὸ καὶ μηδέποτε τοῦτο τοῖς Σαρα-150
κηνοῖς ἐπιδοῦναι. Καὶ διὰ τὸ εἶναι αὐτὸν καὶ Χριστιανὸν καὶ δοῦλον τῆς
βασιλείας ἡμῶν, πιστεύσας τῷ ὅρκῳ αὐτοῦ, δέδωκεν αὐτὸ τὸν εἰρημένον
Παγκράτιον, ὁ δὲ πάλιν ἀπεχαρίσατο αὐτὸ τοῖς Θεοδοσιουπολίταις.
205Be Καὶ ἡνίκα παρελήφθη ἡ Θεοδοσιούπολις, | ὑπεισελθόντες οἱ Ἴβηρες
ἐκράτησαν αὐτό, διότι οὔτε τὸ τοιοῦτον κάστρον τὸ Μαστάτον, οὔτε τοῦ 155
146ʳᴾ Ἀβνίκου ἔχουσιν ἐξουσίαν | ἐπιζητεῖν. Ἀλλ᾽ ἐπειδὴ ὁ κουροπαλάτης
πιστὸς καὶ ὀρθὸς δοῦλος καὶ φίλος ἡμῶν ἐστιν, διὰ τὴν αὐτοῦ παράκλη-
σιν ἵνα γένηται σύνορον τῆς Φασιανῆς ὁ ποταμὸς ὁ Ἔραξ, ἤτοι ὁ Φᾶσις,
καὶ τὰ μὲν ἀριστερὰ μέρη, τὰ πρὸς τὴν Ἰλλυρίαν, κατέχωσιν οἱ Ἴβηρες,
τὰ δὲ δεξιά, ὅσα εἰσὶν πρὸς τὴν Θεοδοσιούπολιν, κἄν τε κάστρα, κἄν τε 160
χωρία εἰσίν, ὦσιν ὑπὸ τὴν βασιλείαν ἡμῶν, τοῦ ποταμοῦ δηλονότι σύνορον ἀμφοτέρων ὑπάρχοντος, καθὼς καὶ ζῶν ὁ μακάριος Ἰωάννης ὁ
Κουρκούας περὶ τούτου ἐρωτηθεὶς ἐξεῖπεν συμφέρον εἶναι τὸν ποταμὸν
σύνορον. Τὸ μὲν γὰρ ἀκριβὲς δίκαιον οὐδεμίαν ἐξουσίαν παρέχει τῷ
κουροπαλάτῃ, εἴτε εἰς τὰ ἔνθεν τοῦ ποταμοῦ, εἴτε εἰς τὰ ἐκεῖθεν δια-165
146ᵛᴾ κράτησιν ἔχειν, διότι τὰ τοιαῦ|τα πάντα χωρία τῶν Θεοδοσιουπολιτῶν

V 129 Ἀβνίκου edd. ‖ Μαστάτον V² edd.: Ναστάτον P V F ‖ ὀφείλει Be:
ὀφείλῃ P ὀφείλῃ Me Ba ‖ 132 ἀμηρᾶν P ‖ 135/6 εἰργάσαντο Be ‖

45

Abnikion nor Mastaton, he has no right to hold them, lying as they do on
this side of the Erax or Phasis river; because the city of Abnikon, on the
one hand, has hitherto been independent and self-governing, under its own
emir, and several times the army of our imperial majesty has raided it,
yes, and the protospatharius John Arrhabonitis, the military governor, and
the patrician Theophilus, who is now military governor of Theodosioupolis,
and the rest of the military governors have taken great plunder and many
prisoners in it, and burnt its villages, while the curopalate has never raided
it at all. And when these villages had been utterly devastated by our imperial
majesty, the Iberians crept in and took possession of them, and tried
thereafter to possess themselves of the city. But the emir, after being several
times warned by the patrician and military governor Theophilus, and seeing that he had no hope of survival from any quarter, submitted himself and consented to become the servant of our imperial majesty, and gave
his son as a hostage. Mastaton, on the other hand, belonged to the Theodosioupolitans; and when the magister John had besieged Theodosioupolis
seven months, because he was unable to take it he sent some men and took
this same city of Mastaton and introduced into it the protospatharius
Petronas Boïlas, who was then captain-general of Nicopolis. And the magister Pankratios, who had joined the campaign of this same magister at
Theodosioupolis, when *the latter* was about to retire, begged him to give
him this city, and made him an oath in writing that he would retain it and
never give it up to the Saracens. He, as the said Pankratios was a Christian
and servant of our imperial majesty, trusted to his oath and gave it him,
and he gave it back again to the Theodosioupolitans. And when Theodosioupolis was taken, the Iberians crept in and took possession of *Mastaton;*
for these reasons they have no authority to demand either this city of Mastaton
or that of Abnikon. But since the curopalate is our faithful and upright
servant and friend, at his request let the frontier of Phasiane be the river
Erax or Phasis, and let the Iberians possess the parts on the left hand side
towards Illyria, and all the parts on the right towards Theodosioupolis,
whether cities or villages, be beneath our imperial majesty, the river, that
is to say, forming the frontier between the two, just as in his lifetime John
Kourkouas, of blessed memory, when asked about this, declared that it was
best for the river to be the frontier. Strict justice does not allow the curopalate
any authority to exercise control either on this side of the river or on the
other, since all these villages of the Theodosioupolitans were enslaved and

---

139 ἀμηρᾶς P ‖ 140 ἰδὼν edd.: ἰδῶς P ‖ 141 οὐδαμόθεν: οὐδαμῶς edd. ‖ δοῦλος
γενέσθαι edd. ‖ 143 Θεοδοσιουπολίτων P ‖ 149 δώσῃ edd.: δώσει P ‖ 152/3
τὸν εἰρημένον Παγκράτιον: τῷ εἰρημένῳ Παγκρατείῳ edd. ‖ 155 τὸ τοιοῦτον
κάστρον τὸ Μαστάτον: τοῦ τοιούτου κάστρου τοῦ Μαστάτου edd. ‖ 159 Ἰλλυρίαν:
Ἰβηρίαν coni. Brosset Laskin ‖ κατέχωσιν edd. κατέχουσιν P ‖ 162 ὅ² om.
edd. ‖ 163 Κουρκοῦας P ‖ 166 Θεοδοσιουπολίτων P ‖

214

45, 46

τὰ στρατεύματα τῆς βασιλείας ἡμῶν ἠχμαλώτισαν καὶ ἐπυρπόλησαν,
καὶ οὐδέποτε χωρὶς ἡμετέρου λαοῦ Ἴβηρες ἐξῆλθον καὶ ἐπραίδευσαν
Θεοδοσιούπολιν, ἀλλ' ἀεὶ φίλους εἶχον αὐτούς, καὶ ἐπραγματεύοντο μετ'
αὐτῶν, καὶ τῷ μὲν στόματι ἤθελον πορθηθῆναι τὴν Θεοδοσιού-170
πολιν, τῇ δὲ καρδίᾳ οὐδαμῶς ἐβούλοντο παραληφθῆναι αὐτήν. Ἀλλ'
ἡ βασιλεία ἡμῶν, ὡς εἴρηται, διὰ τὴν πρὸς τὸν κουροπαλάτην ἀγάπην
ἠθέλησεν γενέσθαι τὸν ποταμὸν τὸν Ἔραξ, ἤτοι τὸν Φᾶσιν σύνορον
ἀμφοτέρων, καὶ ὀφείλουσιν ἀρκεῖσθαι εἰς τὴν τοιαύτην διακράτησιν καὶ
μηδὲν πλέον ἐπιζητεῖν.   175

206Be 46. Π ε ρ ὶ   τ ῆ ς   γ ε ν ε α λ ο γ ί α ς   τ ῶ ν   Ἰ β ή ρ ω ν   κ α ὶ   τ ο ῦ
κ ά σ τ ρ ο υ   Ἀ ρ δ α ν ο υ τ ζ ί ο υ.

147rP   Ἰστέον, ὅτι ὁ Παγκράτιος καὶ ὁ Δαυὶδ ὁ Μάμπαλις, ὃ ἑρμηνεύεται
'πανάγιος', ὑπῆρχον υἱοὶ τοῦ μεγάλου Συμβατίου, τοῦ Ἴβηρος. Καὶ
ἔλαχεν τὸ Ἀρδανούτζι εἰς κληρονομίαν τῷ Παγκρατίῳ, τῷ δὲ Δαυὶδ 5
ἔλαχεν ἑτέρα χώρα. Ὁ δὲ Παγκράτιος ἐποίησεν υἱοὺς τρεῖς, τὸν Ἀδρα-
νασέρ, τὸν Κουρκένιον καὶ τὸν πατρίκιον Ἀσώτιον, τὸν καὶ Κισκάσην,
καὶ διεμέρισεν αὐτοὺς τὴν χώραν αὐτοῦ, καὶ ἔλαχεν τὸ Ἀρδανούτζι τῷ
υἱῷ αὐτοῦ, Κουρκενίῳ, κἀκείνου τελευτήσαντος ἀτέκνου, εἴασεν αὐτὸ
τῷ ἀδελφῷ αὐτοῦ, Ἀσωτίῳ, τῷ καὶ Κισκάσῃ. Ὁ δὲ πατρίκιος Ἀσώτιος, 10
ὁ καὶ Κισκάσης, ἐπῆρεν γαμβρὸν εἰς θυγατέρα αὐτοῦ τὸν Κουρκένην
ἐκεῖνον, τὸν μάγιστρον, ὅστις δυναστεύσας ἀφείλετο ἐκ τοῦ πενθεροῦ
147vP αὐτοῦ Ἀσω|τίου τὸ Ἀρδανούτζι κατὰ τυραννίδα, καὶ δέδωκεν αὐτῷ
εἰς ἀντισήκωσιν τό τε Τυρόκαστρον καὶ τὴν ποταμίαν τοῦ Ἀτζαρά,
τὴν οὖσαν σύνορον Ῥωμανίας εἰς Κώλωριν. Εἶχεν δὲ γυναῖκα ὁ πατρί- 15
κιος Ἀσώτιος, ὁ καὶ Κισκάσης, τὴν ἀδελφὴν τοῦ μαγίστρου Γεωργίου
καὶ ἐξουσιαστοῦ Ἀβασγίας. Καὶ ὅτε ἐγένοντο κατ' ἀλλήλων ὅ τε μάγιστρος Κουρκένιος καὶ ὁ μάγιστρος Γεώργιος καὶ ἐξουσιαστὴς Ἀβασγίας,
διὰ τὸ συναγωνίζεσθαι τὸν πατρίκιον Ἀσώτιον τοῦ ἐξουσιαστοῦ Ἀβασγίας δυνηθεὶς ὁ Κουρκένιος ἀφείλετο καὶ τὴν ἀντισήκωσιν, ἣν δέδωκεν 20
αὐτῷ ὑπὲρ τοῦ Ἀρδανουτζίου, καὶ ἐδίωξεν αὐτόν, καὶ ἀπῆλθεν εἰς
207Be Ἀβασγίαν. Τελευτήσαντος δὲ τοῦ μαγίστρου | Κουρκενίου, κα|τελείφθη
148rP τὸ Ἀρδανούτζι τῇ γυναικὶ αὐτοῦ, τῇ τοῦ πατρικίου Ἀσωτίου, τοῦ
⟨καὶ⟩ Κισκάση, θυγατρὶ ὡς πατρικὸν αὐτῆς. Ὅτε δὲ διεμέριζον τὴν
χώραν τοῦ μαγίστρου Κουρκενίου μεθ' ὅπλων, ὅ τε Ἀσώτιος ὁ κουρο- 25
παλάτης καὶ ὁ μάγιστρος Γεώργιος, ὁ ἐξουσιαστὴς Ἀβασγίας καὶ ὁ

_____

V 169 εἶχον] litteras εἶχ in ras. scr. P¹ ‖ 173 Ἔραξ (littera ι erasa) Pʸ
Meursius Ba Be: Ἱέραξ P V ‖ 174 ὀφείλουσιν edd.: ὀφείλωσιν P.

45, 46

burnt by the armies of our imperial majesty, and never without our army did the Iberians come out and raid Theodosioupolis, but always maintained friendship with them and traded with them; and while they said they wished Theodosioupolis to be taken, in their hearts they by no means desired its capture. However, our imperial majesty, for our love of the curopalate, as has been said, has consented that the river Erax, or Phasis, shall be the frontier between the two, and they must be content with retaining this much, and demand nothing more.

46. Of the genealogy of the Iberians and of the city of Ardanoutzi.

Pankratios and David the Mampalis, which means 'all-holy', were sons of the elder Symbatios the Iberian. Ardanoutzi fell to the inheritance of Pankratios, and other country fell to David. Pankratios had three sons, Adranaser, Kourkenios and the patrician Asotios, called Kiskasis, and he divided his country among them, and Ardanoutzi fell to his son Kourkenios, who, dying childless, left it to his brother Asotios, called Kiskasis. The patrician Asotios, called Kiskasis, married his daughter to the late magister Kourkenis, who, having grown great, revolted, and deprived his father-in-law Asotios of Ardanoutzi, and gave him in exchange Tyrokastron and the river region of Atzaras, which forms the frontier of Romania at Kolorin. Now, the patrician Asotios, called Kiskasis, had to wife the sister of the magister George, ruler of Abasgia. And when the magister Kourkenios and the magister George, ruler of Abasgia, fell out with one another, the patrician Asotios took the side of the ruler of Abasgia, and for that reason Kourkenios, gaining the upper hand, deprived him even of what he had given him in exchange for Ardanoutzi, and expelled him, and he departed to Abasgia. On the death of the magister Kourkenios, Ardanoutzi was left to his wife, the daughter of the patrician Asotios, called Kiskasis, as her father's heiress. Now when Asotios the curopalate and the magister George, ruler of Abasgia, and the magister Pankratios, brother of the aforesaid curopalate, were dividing up the country of the magister Kourkenios by

---

46. 2 Ἀδρανουτζίου edd. ‖ 3 *post* Δαυὶδ *add.* καὶ edd. *omittendum coni.* Brosset ‖ *post* ὅ³ *addendum* καὶ *coni.* Marquart ‖ 5 Ἀρδανούτζη P: Ἀδρανούτζη edd. ‖ 6 τρεῖς V edd.: γ′ P ‖ 8 αὐτοῖς V edd. ‖ Ἀρδανούτζι Moravcsik: Ἀδρανούτζη P edd. ‖ 12 πεμθεροῦ P ‖ 13 Ἀρδανούτζη P: Ἀδρανούτζη Ba Be ‖ 15 *ante* Ῥωμανίας *add.* τῆς edd. ‖ Κόλωρην P ‖ 20 ἀφείλετο V edd.: ἀφείλατο P ‖ 21 Ἀρδανουτζίου Moravcsik: Ἀδρανούτζίου P edd. ‖ 23 Ἀρδανούτζη P: Ἀδρανούτζη edd. ‖ 24 καὶ add. Moravcsik ‖

μάγιστρος Παγκράτιος, ὁ ἀδελφὸς τοῦ προρρηθέντος κουροπαλάτου,
ἦλθον εἰς συμβίβασιν, καὶ ἐπῆρεν ἕκαστος τὸ πλησιάζον αὐτῷ. Τὸ δὲ
᾿Αρδανούτζιν ἐπλησίαζεν τῷ Συμβατίῳ, τῷ τοῦ προρρηθέντος Δαυὶδ
υἱῷ. Τότε ἐκράτησαν πάντες τὴν γυναῖκα τοῦ μαγίστρου Κουρκενίου, 30
ἤγουν τὴν θυγατέρα τοῦ πατρικίου ᾿Ασωτίου, τοῦ καὶ Κισκάση, λέγοντες, ὡς ὅτι· «Σὺ γυνὴ οὖσα οὐ δύνασαι κρατεῖν τὸ κάστρον.» Τότε δέ-
148ᵛP δωκεν ὁ Συμ|βάτιος εἰς ἀντισήκωσιν τοῦ κάστρου χωρία τῇ γυναικί, καὶ
ἀνελάβετο τὸ τοιοῦτον κάστρον τὸ ᾿Αρδανούτζιν.

᾿Ιστέον, ὅτι ἡ συγγένεια τῶν τοιούτων ᾿Ιβήρων τοῦτον ἔχει τὸν 35
τρόπον. Τοῦ Δαυὶδ ἡ μήτηρ καὶ τοῦ ᾿Αδρανασὲ τοῦ κουροπαλάτου,
τοῦ πατρὸς τοῦ ἀρτίως ᾿Ασωτίου τοῦ κουροπαλάτου, ὑπῆρχον δύο
ἀδελφῶν παιδία, ἤγουν ἐξαδέλφαι. Εἶχεν δὲ Συμβάτιος, ὁ τοῦ Δαυὶδ
υἱός, γυναῖκα τὴν θυγατέρα τοῦ μαγίστρου Παγκρατίου, τοῦ πατρὸς
τοῦ ᾿Αδρανασῆ, τοῦ ἀρτίως μαγίστρου, καὶ τελευτησάσης, ἔλαβεν ὁ 40
᾿Αδρανασῆ τὴν ἀδελφὴν τοῦ Συμβατίου, τοῦ υἱοῦ τοῦ Δαυίδ.

149ʳP
208Be
῞Οτι τὸ κάστρον τὸ ᾿Αρδανούτζιν ἐστὶν ὀχυρὸν πάνυ, ἔχει δὲ καὶ
ῥαπάτιν μέγα ὡς χωρόπολιν, καὶ αἱ πραγματεῖαι | τῆς | τε Τραπεζοῦντος
καὶ τῆς ᾿Ιβηρίας καὶ τῆς ᾿Αβασγίας καὶ ἀπὸ πάσας τὰς χώρας τὰς ᾿Αρ-
μενικὰς καὶ τῆς Συρίας ἐκεῖσε ἀφικνοῦνται, ἔχει δὲ καὶ κομμέρκιον ἐκ 45
τῶν τοιούτων πραγματειῶν ἄπειρον. ῾Η δὲ χώρα τοῦ κάστρου ᾿Αρδα-
νουτζίου, ἤτοι τὸ ᾿Αρζῦν ἐστιν καὶ πολλὴ καὶ εὔφορος, καὶ ὑπάρχει
κλειδὶν τῆς τε ᾿Ιβηρίας καὶ ᾿Αβασγίας καὶ τῶν Μισχιῶν.

῞Οτι ὁ μακάριος βασιλεύς, ὁ κύρις ῾Ρωμανὸς ἀπέστειλεν τὸν
πατρίκιον Κωνσταντῖνον καὶ δρουγγάριον τοῦ πλωΐμου, τῷ τότε καιρῷ 50
πρωτοσπαθαρίου καὶ μαγγλαβίτου τυγχάνοντος, δεδωκὼς αὐτῷ καὶ
ἱμάτιον μαγιστράτου πρὸς τὸ ποιῆσαι τὸν Κουρκένιον τὸν ῎Ιβηρα μάγιστρον. Μετὰ δὲ τὸ ἐξελθεῖν τὸν πατρίκιον Κωνσταντῖνον καὶ δρουγγά-
149ᵛP ριον τοῦ | πλωΐμου μέχρι Νικομηδείας εἰσῆλθεν ὁ μοναχὸς ᾿Αγάπιος
ὁ τοῦ Κυμινᾶ, ὃς ἦν τῷ τότε καιρῷ εἰς τὴν ἁγίαν πόλιν εὐχῆς ἕνεκα. 55
Καὶ διερχομένου αὐτοῦ τὴν ᾿Ιβηρίαν, κατήντησεν εἰς τὸ κάστρον τὸ
᾿Αρδανούτζιν. Καὶ εἶχεν ὁ πατρίκιος ᾿Ασώτιος, ὁ καὶ Κισκάσης καλούμενος, ἔχθραν μετὰ τοῦ γαμβροῦ αὐτοῦ, τοῦ Κουρκένη, καὶ ἐλάλησεν
εἰς τὸν μοναχὸν ᾿Αγάπιον, ὅτι· «᾿Ενορκῶ σε εἰς τὸν Θεὸν καὶ εἰς τὴν
δύναμιν τοῦ τιμίου καὶ ζωοποιοῦ σταυροῦ, ἵνα ἀπέλθῃς ἐν τῇ πόλει, καὶ 60
εἴπῃς τὸν βασιλέα, ἵνα ἀποστείλῃ καὶ παραλάβῃ τὸ κάστρον μου καὶ
ἔχῃ ὑπὸ τὴν ἐξουσίαν αὐτοῦ.» ῾Ο δὲ μοναχὸς ᾿Αγάπιος εἰσελθὼν ἐν
τῇ πόλει, διηγήσατο τὸν βασιλέα, ὅσα ἐλάλησεν πρὸς αὐτὸν ὁ πατρί-

---

V 29 ᾿Αδρανούτζιν edd. ‖ 32 ὡς om. V edd. ‖ 33 ἀντισήκωσιν: συνάντησιν V
edd. ‖ 34 τοιοῦτο V edd. ‖ ᾿Αδρανούτζιν edd. ‖ 36 Τοῦ Δαυὶδ: τοῦ Συμβατίου

46

force of arms, they came to an accommodation and each took what was next to him. And Ardanoutzi lay next to Symbatios, son of the aforesaid David. Then all of them seized on the widow of the magister Kourkenios, that is, the daughter of the patrician Asotios, called Kiskasis, and said to her: «You, as a woman, cannot possess the city.» Then Symbatios gave the woman territories in exchange for the city, and took the city of Ardanoutzin. These Iberians are related to one another in the following manner. The mother of David and the mother of Adranase the curopalate, father of the present curopalate Asotios, were the children of two brothers, that is to say, they were first cousins. Symbatios, the son of David, had to wife the daughter of the magister Pankratios, father of Adranasi who is now magister, and after her death Adranasi married the sister of Symbatios, son of David.

The city of Ardanoutzin is very strongly defended, and has moreover a considerable suburban area like a provincial city, and the commerce of Trapezus and of Iberia and of Abasgia and from the whole country of Armenia and Syria comes to it, and it has an enormous customs revenue from this commerce. The country of the city of Ardanoutzin, the 'Arzyn', is both extensive and fertile, and it is a key of Iberia and Abasgia and of the Mischians.

The emperor the lord Romanus, of blessed memory, sent the patrician Constantine, the lord admiral, who was at that time protospatharius and lictor, with a tunic of the magistracy in order to make Kourkenios the Iberian a magister. When the patrician Constantine, the lord admiral, had reached Nicomedeia, the monk Agapios of Kyminas came on the scene, who had at that time been visiting the holy city to fulfil a vow. In his passage through Iberia he had come to the city of Ardanoutzin. The patrician Asotios, called Kiskasis, at feud with his son-in-law Kourkenios, had spoken thus to the monk Agapios: «I adjure you, by God and by the power of the honourable and life-giving Cross, to go to Constantinople and tell the emperor to send and take over my city, and have it beneath his dominion.» The monk Agapios came to Constantinople and related to the emperor all that the patrician

---

seu ⟨Συμβατίου τοῦ υἱοῦ⟩ τοῦ Δαβὶδ coni. Brosset Laskin ‖ Ἀδρανασὴ edd. ‖ 40 Ἀδρανασή edd. ‖ 42 Ἀδρανούτζιν Ba Be ‖ ὀχυρόν ἐστι πάνυ V edd. ‖ 43 ῥαπάτην P ‖ μέγα V edd.: μέγαν P ‖ χωρόπολιν: χωρόπουλον sive χωριόπουλον coni. Meursius ‖ 44 τῆς² om. V edd. ‖ πάσας τὰς χώρας τὰς Ἀρμενικὰς: πάσης τῆς χώρας τῆς Ἀρμενίας edd. ‖ 46/7 Ἀρδανουτζίου Moravcsik: Ἀδρανουζίου P Ἀδρανουτζίου edd. ‖ 47 Ἀρζήν edd. ‖ 48 κλειδὴν P ‖ Μισχιῶν: Μοσχιῶν coni. Meursius Bandurius Laskin ‖ 49 κύρης P ‖ 50 Κωνσταντῖνον per comp. P: Κώνσταντα edd. ‖ 51 πρωτοσπαθαρίου καὶ μαγγλαβίτου τυγχάνοντος: πρωτοσπαθαρίῳ καὶ μαγγλαβίτῃ τυγχάνοντι coni. Brosset ‖ 52 μαγιστράτου edd.: μαγιστράτον P ‖ 53 Κωνσταντῖνον per comp. P: Κώνσταντα edd. ‖ 55 Κυμηνὰ P ‖ καιρῷ: χρόνῳ edd. ‖ 57 Ἀδρανούτζιν edd. ‖ 62 ἔχη edd.: ἔχει P ‖

218

46

κιος | 'Ασώτιος, ὁ καὶ Κισκάσης. Τοῦ δὲ προρρηθέντος πατρι|κίου
Κωνσταντίνου καὶ δρουγγαρίου τοῦ πλωΐμου ἐν Νικομηδείᾳ τυγχάνον- 65
τος διὰ τὴν προρρηθεῖσαν τῆς προβολῆς τοῦ μαγίστρου τοῦ Κουρκένη
Ἴβηρος ὑπόθεσιν, ἐκ προστάξεως τοῦ βασιλέως ἐδέξατο πιττάκιον τοῦ
πατρικίου Συμεών, τοῦ πρωτοασηκρῆτις, ὡς ὅτι· «Κελεύει ὁ βασιλεὺς
ἡμῶν ὁ ἅγιος καταλιπεῖν σε πάσας σου τὰς δουλείας καὶ ἀπελθεῖν ἐν
συντομίᾳ πρὸς τὸν πατρίκιον 'Ασώτιον, τὸν καὶ Κισκάσην λεγόμενον, 70
καὶ παραλαβεῖν τὸ κάστρον αὐτοῦ τὸ 'Αρδανούτζιν, ἐπειδὴ διὰ τοῦ
μοναχοῦ 'Αγαπίου ἐδηλοποίησεν τὸν βασιλέα ἡμῶν τὸν ἅγιον τοῦ ἀπο-
150ᵛP σταλῆναι πιστὸν ἄνθρωπον καὶ οἰκεῖον τοῦ παραλαβεῖν | τὸ κάστρον
αὐτοῦ τὸ 'Αρδανούτζιν· καὶ ἀπερχομένου σου ἐν Χαλδίᾳ, ἀναλαβοῦ
ἄρχοντας χρησίμους, οὓς ἐπίστασαι εἶναι ἠνδρειωμένους καὶ πιστούς, 75
καὶ εἴσελθε καὶ κράτησον τὸ τοιοῦτον κάστρον.» Τοῦ δὲ πατρικίου
Κωνσταντίνου καὶ δρουγγαρίου τοῦ πλωΐμου ἀπελθόντος ἐν Χαλδίᾳ
καὶ ἀναλαβομένου τουρμάρχας χρησίμους καὶ ἄρχοντας καὶ λαὸν μέχρι
τῶν τ', εἰσῆλθεν ἐν 'Ιβηρίᾳ, καὶ ἐκράτησεν αὐτὸν ὁ μακάριος Δαυίδ,
ὁ ἀδελφὸς 'Ασωτίου, τοῦ ἀρτίως κουροπαλάτου, λέγων πρὸς αὐτόν· 80
«Ποῦ ἀπεστάλης παρὰ τοῦ βασιλέως, καὶ τί δουλείαν ὀφείλεις ἐκτελέσαι,
ὅτι τοσοῦτον λαὸν ἐπιφέρῃ μετὰ σεαυτοῦ;» 'Εσκέπτοντο γὰρ διὰ τὸ
151ʳP ἀποθανεῖν 'Αδρανασὲ τὸν κουροπαλάτην, ὅτι μήπως | ὁ βασιλεὺς τὸν
Κουρκένιον ὀφείλει τιμῆσαι κουροπαλάτην, ἐπειδὴ ἀναμεταξὺ οἱ τοῦ
'Αδρανασὲ τοῦ κουροπαλάτου παῖδες, τοῦ πατρὸς αὐτῶν τελευτήσαντος, 85
210Be φιλονικίας τινὰς ἔσχον μετὰ τοῦ ἐξαδέλ|φου αὐτῶν. Διὰ τὸ καὶ τὸν
πρῶτον ἄνθρωπον αὐτοῦ ἀπολῦσαι μετὰ μεγάλου κανισκίου τὸν Κουρκένιον πρὸς τὸν βασιλέα, ἐξαιτούμενον τὸ κουροπαλατίκιν ἢ τὸ μαγιστρᾶτον, ὑπέλαβον οἱ τέσσαρες ἀδελφοί, ἤγουν οἱ τοῦ 'Αδρανασὲ τοῦ κουροπαλάτου παῖδες, ὅτι διὰ τὸ ποιῆσαι τὸν Κουρκένιον κουροπαλάτην ἀπέρχεται 90
ἐκεῖσε. 'Ο δὲ πατρίκιος Κωνσταντῖνος ἀπελογήσατο, ὅτι· «Διὰ τὸ μέλλειν
με τιμῆσαι τὸν Κουρκένιον μάγιστρον ἐπιφέρομαι καὶ τὸν τοσοῦτον
151ᵛP λαόν.» Καὶ ἀπελθόντος | τοῦ αὐτοῦ πατρικίου Κωνσταντίνου εἰς τὴν
χώραν τοῦ Κουρκενίου, ἐτίμησεν αὐτὸν μάγιστρον καὶ ἀποχαιρετίσας
αὐτὸν * * *, ὅτι· «'Απέρχομαι εἰς τὸν Δαυὶδ τὸν μάγιστρον.» Εἶχεν 95
δὲ ὁ αὐτὸς πατρίκιος Κωνσταντῖνος καὶ πρὸς τὸν Δαυὶδ κέλευσιν ἀπὸ
τοῦ βασιλέως καὶ ξένια. Καὶ εἰσῆλθεν εἰς τὸ κάστρον τοῦ πατρικίου
'Ασωτίου, τοῦ καὶ Κισκάση, εἰς τὸ 'Αρδανούτζιν, καὶ δέδωκεν αὐτῷ
τὴν πρὸς αὐτὸν τοῦ βασιλέως κέλευσιν οὐ περὶ τοῦ κάστρου 'Αρδανουτζίου
περιέχουσάν τι, ἀλλὰ περὶ ἑτέρων ὑποθέσεων. Εἶπεν δὲ πρὸς αὐτὸν ὁ 100

V 65 Κωνσταντίνου *per comp.* P: Κώνσταντος edd. ‖ 67 ἐδέξατο: ἔλαβε τὸ
edd. ‖ 68 πρωτοασηκρίτης *per comp.* P: ἀσηκρῆτις edd. ‖ 71 'Αρδανούτζιν F

46

Asotios, called Kiskasis, had said to him. The aforesaid patrician Constantine, the lord admiral, who was at Nicomedeia on the aforesaid business of appointing Kourkenios the Iberian to be magister, received by command of the emperor a missive of the patrician Symeon, the head of the imperial chancellery, which said: «Our holy emperor commands that you leave all you are engaged upon and go in haste to the patrician Asotios, called Kiskasis, and take over his city of Ardanoutzin, since he has declared to our holy emperor, by the mouth of the monk Agapios, that a trustworthy and familiar servant should be sent to take over his city of Ardanoutzin; go, then, to Chaldia and take some capable officers, whom you know to be brave and trustworthy, and enter and take possession of this city.» The patrician Constantine, the lord admiral, went to Chaldia and took capable lieutenant-generals and officers and men to the number of 300, and entered Iberia and fell into the hands of David, of blessed memory, brother of Asotios who is now curopalate, who said to him: «Whither have you been sent by the emperor and what task are you to perform, that you bring so many men along with you?» For they suspected that, now Adranase the curopalate was dead, the emperor must be about to honour Kourkenios with the rank of curopalate; because, in the mean time, the sons of the curopalate Adranase had, after their father's death, had certain quarrels with their cousin. And since Kourkenios had dispatched his chief man with a large gift to the emperor, requesting that he might be made curopalate or magister, the four brothers, that is, the sons of Adranase the curopalate, assumed that *the patrician Constantine* came thither to create Kourkenios curopalate. But the patrician Constantine put them off by saying: «Because I am about to honour Kourkenios with the rank of magister I bring with me so many men.» And the patrician Constantine went off to the country of Kourkenios and honoured him with the rank of magister, and, bidding him farewell, *said:* «I am going to David the magister.» For this same patrician Constantine had for David also a mandate and presents from the emperor. And he entered Ardanoutzin, the city of the patrician Asotios, called Kiskasis, and gave him the imperial mandate addressed to him, which contained nothing about the city of Ardanoutzin, but was about other matters. But

'Αρδανούζην P: 'Αδρανούτζιν edd. || 72/3 ἀποσταλῆναι: ἀποστεῖλαι edd. || 74 'Αδρανούτζιν edd. || 77 Κωνσταντίνου *per comp.* P: Κώνσταντος edd. || 79 τῶν *om.* edd. || 81 τί: τίνα edd. || ὀφείλεις edd.: ὀφείλης P || 82 τὸ Be το (*sine acc.*) P: τοῦτο V Me Ba || 83 *post* τὸν¹ *add.* καὶ edd. || 84 ὀφείλη edd. || 87 πρῶτον V edd.: α' P || αὐτοῦ *om.* V edd. || ἀπολῦσαι: ἀποστεῖλαι V edd. || 88 κουροπαλατίκην P || 88/9 μαγιστράτον P || 89 τέσσαρες edd.: δ' P || οἱ² *om.* V edd. || 90 *ante* παῖδες *add.* οἱ V edd. || 91 Κωνσταντῖνος *per comp.* P: Κώνστας edd. || 93 Καὶ ἀπελθόντος — 95 μάγιστρον *post* ξένια (97) *transp.* edd. || 93 Κωνσταντίνου *per comp.* P: Κώνσταντος edd. || 95 *lac. ind.* εἶπεν *aut aliquid simile excidisse coniciens* Moravcsik || 96 Κωνσταντῖνος *per comp.* P: Κώνστας edd. || 98 'Αδρανούτζιν edd. || 99 'Αρδανουτζίου Moravcsik: 'Αδρανουτζίου P edd. ||

46

πατρίκιος Κωνσταντῖνος, ὅτι· «Κἂν μὲν ἡ κέλευσις οὐδὲν περιέχει περὶ τοῦ κάστρου Ἀρδανουτζίου, ἀλλ᾽ οὖν τοῦ μοναχοῦ Ἀγαπίου πρὸς τὸν
152ʳP βασιλέα εἰσελθόντος καὶ ἀναγγείλαντος αὐτόν, ὅσα καὶ | παρήγγειλας
αὐτὸν περὶ τοῦ κάστρου Ἀρδανουτζίου, διὰ τοῦτο καὶ ἀπέστειλέν με,
ὅπως παραλάβω τὸ κάστρον καὶ εἰσαγάγω ἐν αὐτῷ, ὅνπερ περιφέρομαι105
λαόν.» Καὶ ἐπειδή, καθὰ προείρηται, εἶχεν ἔχθραν ὁ πατρίκιος Ἀσώτιος,
211Be ὁ καὶ Κισκάσης, μετὰ τοῦ γαμβροῦ αὐτοῦ, | τοῦ Κουρκένη, προεθυμήθη
δοῦναι τὸ κάστρον αὐτοῦ μᾶλλον τὸν βασιλέα. Ὁ δὲ πατρίκιος Κωνσταντῖνος εἶχεν παρ᾽ ἑαυτῷ φλάμμουλα, καὶ ἐπιδέδωκεν τῷ πατρικίῳ Ἀσωτίῳ, τῷ καὶ Κισκάσῃ. Ὁ δὲ βαλὼν αὐτὸ εἰς κοντάριον, ἐπιδέδωκεν110
τῷ πατρικίῳ Κωνσταντίνῳ εἰπών, ὅτι· «Ἐπίστησον αὐτὸ ἄνωθεν εἰς
τὸ τεῖχος, ἵνα γνῶσιν πάντες τοῦ βασιλέως εἶναι ἀπὸ τῆς σήμερον
152ᵛP ἡμέρας τὸ τοιοῦτον κάστρον.» Καὶ τοῦτο | ποιήσας ὁ πατρίκιος Κων-
σταντῖνος καὶ τὸ φλάμμουλον ἐπιστήσας ἄνωθεν τοῦ τείχους καὶ τοὺς
βασιλεῖς τῶν Ῥωμαίων κατὰ τὸ εἰωθὸς εὐφημήσας, πᾶσιν ἐγένετο115
γνωστόν, ὅτι τὸ κάστρον τὸ Ἀρδανούτζιν ἀπεχαρίσατο ὁ πατρίκιος
Ἀσώτιος, ὁ καὶ Κισκάσης, τὸν βασιλέα. Ὁ οὖν Δαυίδ, ὁ μέγας, τὴν
ἑαυτοῦ χώραν οὐκ ἐδίδου τὸν βασιλέα, κἂν τάχα συνορῇ τὴν τοῦρμαν
τοῦ Ἀκαμψῆ καὶ τῇ Μουργούλῃ. Ὁ οὖν πατρίκιος Κωνσταντῖνος ἀνήγαγε
πρὸς τὸν βασιλέα, ἐξαποστείλας δύο ἀναφοράς, τὴν μὲν μίαν περιέχουσαν,120
ὅπως ἐτίμησεν τὸν Κουρκένην μάγιστρον, καὶ ὅπως ὁ Κουρκένιος ἀπεδέ-
ξατο τὸ μαγιστρᾶτον, καὶ εὐφήμησεν τὸν βασιλέα, τὴν δὲ ἑτέραν περιέχουσαν περὶ τοῦ κάστρου Ἀρδανουτζίου, καὶ ὅπως τοῦτο παρέλαβεν
153ʳP | παρὰ τοῦ πατρικίου Ἀσωτίου, τοῦ καὶ Κισκάση, καὶ ὅτι μεγάλην διαφο-
ρὰν καὶ ἔχθραν ἔχουσιν πρὸς ἀλλήλους ὅ τε πατρίκιος Ἀσώτιος μετὰ125
τοῦ γαμβροῦ αὐτοῦ, τοῦ μαγίστρου Κουρκενίου, καὶ ἵνα ἀποστείλῃ ὁ
212Be βα|σιλεὺς βοήθειαν τοῦ ταξατεῦσαι τὸ τοιοῦτον κάστρον, καὶ ὅτι, εἰ
ἐνδέχεται, ἔλθῃ καὶ ὁ δομέστικος τῶν σχολῶν. Ταῦτα ἰδόντες οἱ Ἴβηρες,
ὅ τε μάγιστρος Κουρκένιος καὶ ὁ μάγιστρος Δαυίδ, ὁ ἀδελφὸς τοῦ κουροπαλάτου Ἀσωτίου, ἔγραψαν πρὸς τὸν βασιλέα, ὅτι· «Εἰ τοῦτο κατα-130
δέξηται ἡ βασιλεία σου, καὶ εἰσέλθῃ μέσον τῆς χώρας ἡμῶν, ἐξερχόμεθα
τῆς δουλώσεως τῆς βασιλείας σου, καὶ γινόμεθα μετὰ τῶν Σαρακηνῶν,
153ᵛP ἐπειδὴ ἔχειν ἔχομεν μετὰ τῶν Ῥωμαί|ων μάχας καὶ πολέμια, καὶ βιαζό-
μενοι κινῆσαι ἔχομεν φοσσάτον κατά τε τοῦ κάστρου Ἀρδανουτζίου
καὶ τῆς χώρας αὐτοῦ καὶ αὐτῆς τῆς Ῥωμανίας.» Ταῦτα καὶ διὰ τῶν135

V 101 Κωνσταντῖνος per comp. P: Κώνστας edd. ‖ 102 Ἀρδανουτζίου Moravcsik: Ἀδρανουτζίου P edd. ‖ 103 παρήγγειλας V edd.: παρείγγειλας
(litteris ει in ras. scriptis) P¹ ‖ 104 Ἀρδανουτζίου Moravcsik: Ἀδρανουτζίου P edd. ‖ 108/9 Κωνσταντῖνος per comp. P: Κώνστας edd. ‖ 109

46

the patrician Constantine said to him: «Although the mandate contains nothing about the city of Ardanoutzin, none the less the monk Agapios came to the emperor and reported to him all that you had bidden him about the city of Ardanoutzin, and therefore *the emperor* has sent me, to take over the city and introduce into it the men I bring along with me.» And since, as has been said above, the patrician Asotios, called Kiskasis, was at feud with his son-in-law Kourkenios, he had made up his mind the rather to give his city to the emperor. The patrician Constantine had with him standards and he gave *one* to the patrician Asotios, called Kiskasis. He put it upon a pike and gave it to the patrician Constantine, saying: «Set it up on top of the wall, that all may know that from this day this city belongs to the emperor.» The patrician Constantine did so and set the standard on top of the wall and made the customary salutations of the emperors of the Romans, so that it became known to all that the patrician Asotios, called Kiskasis, had made a present of the city of Ardanoutzin to the emperor. Now, the elder David made no offer of his country to the emperor, notwithstanding it marched with the county of Akampsis and with Mourgouli. So then the patrician Constantine reported to the emperor in two dispatches, the one containing the news of how he had honoured Kourkenios with the rank of magister, and of how Kourkenios had accepted the magistracy and saluted the emperor; and the other containing news about the city of Ardanoutzin, and of how he had taken it over from the patrician Asotios, called Kiskasis, and that the patrician Asotios and his son-in-law the magister Kourkenios had a great quarrel and feud with one another, and that the emperor should send succour for the garrisoning of this city, and that, should it be possible, the commander-in-chief should also come. When the Iberians, the magister Kourkenios and the magister David, brother of the curopalate Asotios, saw what was done, they wrote to the emperor: «If your imperial majesty approves this and enters our country, then we put off our servitude to your imperial majesty and make common cause with the Saracens, since we shall have fighting and hostilities with the Romans and shall, perforce, move an army against the city of Ardanoutzin and its country, and against Romania itself.» *The emperor*, having learnt

---

φλάμουλα P ‖ 110 βαλὼν: λαβὼν V edd. ‖ *post* κοντάριον *add.* περιέθηκε καὶ V edd. ‖ 111 Κωνσταντίνῳ *per comp.* P V Me: Κώνσταντι Ba Be ‖ 113/4 Κωνσταντίνος *per comp.* P V Me: Κώνστας Ba Be ‖ 114 φλάμουλλον P ‖ 116 'Αδρανούτζιν edd. ‖ 118 τούρμαν P ‖ 119 'Ακαμψὴ P ‖ Μουργούλη Be: Μούργουλη P ‖ Κωνσταντίνος *per comp.* P V Me: Κώνστας Ba Be ‖ 121 Κουρκένιον edd. ‖ 122 μαγιστράτον P ‖ 123 'Αρδανουτζίου Moravcsik: 'Αδρανουτζίου P edd. ‖ 124 καὶ Κισκάση V edd.: Κεκισκάση P ‖ 126 τοῦ² *om.* edd. ‖ 129 *post* Δαυὶδ *add.* καὶ edd. ‖ 134 φοσσάτον P ‖ 'Αρδανουτζίου Moravcsik: 'Αδρανουτζίου P edd. ‖ 135 αὐτοῦ *coni.* Moravcsik: αὐτῶν P edd. ‖

46

γραμμάτων τῶν προρρηθέντων ἀρχόντων ἀναμαθὼν καὶ παρὰ τῶν ἀποσταλέντων παρ' αὐτῶν ἀνθρώπων ἀκηκοὼς καί πτοηθείς, μήπως γένωνται μετὰ τῶν Σαρακηνῶν καὶ ἐξαγάγωσι τὰ τῆς Περσίας φοσσᾶτα κατὰ 'Ρωμανίας, ἠρνήσατο λέγων, ὅτι· «Οὐκ ἔγραψα τὸν πρωτοσπαθάριον Κωνσταντῖνον καὶ μαγγλαβίτην περὶ τοῦ τοιούτου κάστρου καὶ 140 τῆς χώρας αὐτοῦ τοῦ παραλαβεῖν αὐτήν, ἀλλ' ἐξ οἰκείας ὡς εἰπεῖν ἀφροσύνης τοῦτο ἐποίησεν.» Καὶ ταῦτα εἶπεν ὁ βασιλεύς, τελείως ἀπο-
154ʳP θεραπεῦσαι τούτους βουλόμενος, καὶ ἐδέξατ|ο ὁ αὐτὸς πρωτοσπαθάριος Κωνσταντῖνος καὶ μαγγλαβίτης κέλευσιν μετὰ ὕβρεων καὶ ἀπειλῶν περιέχουσαν· «Τίς διωρίσατό σοι τοῦτο ποιῆσαι; Ἀλλὰ μᾶλλον ἔξελθε 145
213Be ἐκ τοῦ κάστρου, καὶ ἀναλαβοῦ Ἀσώτιον, τὸν υἱὸν τοῦ τελευ|τηκότος Ἀδρανασέ, τοῦ κουροπαλάτου, καὶ εἰσάγαγε αὐτὸν ἐνταῦθα, ὅπως τιμήσωμεν αὐτὸν τὴν τοῦ πατρὸς αὐτοῦ ἀξίαν τοῦ κουροπαλάτου.» Ταῦτα δεξάμενος ὁ πατρίκιος Κωνσταντῖνος, κατέλιπεν τὸν πατρίκιον Ἀσώτιον, τὸν καὶ Κισκάσην, εἰς τὸ ἑαυτοῦ κάστρον, τὸ Ἀρδανούτζιν, 150 κἀκεῖνος ἐξελθὼν ἀπήει πρὸς τὸν Δαυίδ, τὸν μέγαν, καὶ ἐπιδέδωκεν αὐτῷ, ἥνπερ εἶχεν πρὸς αὐτὸν κέλευσιν, καὶ ὑπέστρεψεν, καὶ εἰσῆλθεν
154ᵛP εἰς Ἰβηρίαν, καὶ εὗρεν ἐπὶ τὸ αὐτὸ | συνηθροισμένους τόν τε μάγιστρον Κουρκένιον καὶ τὸν μάγιστρον Δαυίδ, τὸν ἀδελφὸν Ἀσωτίου τοῦ κουροπαλάτου. Καὶ ἤρξαντο φιλονικεῖν καὶ κατονειδίζειν τὸν πατρίκιον Κων- 155 σταντῖνον, λέγοντες, ὅτι· «Κρυπτὸς ἄνθρωπος καὶ κακὸς τυγχάνεις, ὅτι οὐκ ἐφανέρωσας ἡμᾶς περὶ τοῦ κάστρου Ἀρδανουτζίου, ὅτι μέλλεις τοῦτο κρατῆσαι» καὶ ὅτι· «Οὐ συμφέρει τοῦτο κρατεῖσθαι παρὰ τοῦ βασιλέως, ἡμεῖς γὰρ καὶ περὶ τῆς τοιαύτης ὑποθέσεως ἀνηγάγομεν πρὸς τὸν βασιλέα, καὶ ἐδεξάμεθα μηδαμῶς γινώσκειν τὸν βασιλέα περὶ 160 τῆς ὑποθέσεως ταύτης, ἀλλὰ σὲ τοῦτο ποιῆσαι διὰ τὴν ἀγάπην τοῦ πατρικίου Ἀσωτίου, τοῦ καὶ Κισκάση.» Ὁ δὲ πατρίκιος Κωνσταντῖνος
155ʳP προσαπολογησάμενος τούτοις | τὰ εἰκότα, ἀνελάβετο Ἀσώτιον, τὸν υἱὸν Ἀδρανασὲ τοῦ κουροπαλάτου, καὶ εἰσήγαγεν αὐτὸν ἐν τῇ πόλει, καὶ ἐτιμήθη παρὰ τοῦ βασιλέως κουροπαλάτης. 165

Τί δὲ καὶ περὶ τῶν ἔν τισι καιροῖς μεταξὺ 'Ρωμαίων καὶ διαφόρων ἐθνῶν συμβεβηκότων; Ἄξιον γάρ, φίλτατε υἱέ, μηδὲ τὴν περὶ τούτων
214Be μνήμην διαφυγεῖν σε, ἵν' ἐν ὁμοίοις | καιροῖς, τῶν αὐτῶν προσπιπτόντων, εἴη σοι εὐχερὴς ἡ ἐπανόρθωσις διὰ τῆς προγνώσεως.

F   168 ἐν ὁμοίοις — 169 προγνώσεως: cf. Thucyd. I. 22, 4.

V 138 φοσσάτα P ‖ 140 Κωνσταντῖνον *per comp.* P Me: Κώνσταντα Ba Be ‖ καὶ¹: τὸν edd. ‖ 144 Κωνσταντῖνος *per comp.* P Me: Κώνστας Ba Be ‖ 145 διορίσατο

46

of these things through the letters of the aforesaid princes and having
heard them from their envoys, and being terrified lest perchance they
might make common cause with the Saracens and lead out the armies of
Persia against Romania, denied it, saying: «I did not write to the protospatharius Constantine, the lictor, about this city and its country, telling
him to take it over, but out of his own folly, so to say, he has done this.»
So spoke the emperor in his desire to give them all satisfaction; and
this same protospatharius Constantine, the lictor, received a mandate
couched in terms of insult and menace: «Who instructed you to do this?
Come you, the rather, out of the city and take Asotios, son of the late Adranase the curopalate, and conduct him hither, so that we may honour him
with his father's rank of curopalate.» On receipt of these orders, the patrician
Constantine abandoned the patrician Asotios, called Kiskasis, in his city
of Ardanoutzin, and himself took leave and departed to the elder David
and gave him the mandate which he had for him, and returned and entered
Iberia and found, met together in one place, the magister Kourkenios
and the magister David, brother of Asotios the curopalate. And they began
to quarrel with and to heap abuse upon the patrician Constantine, saying:
«You are a sly and evil fellow in not revealing to us, concerning the city
of Ardanoutzin, that you were about to take possession of it», and, «It is
not the emperor's policy to possess himself of it, for we ourselves reported
to the emperor on this affair and have received a reply that the emperor
knows nothing whatsoever about this affair, but that you have done this
out of love of the patrician Asotios, called Kiskasis.» The patrician Constantine made a reasonable defence to these charges, and took Asotios, son of
Adranase the curopalate, and conducted him to Constantinople, and he
was honoured by the emperor with the dignity of curopalate.

But what of events which have taken place at various times
between the Romans and different nations? For it is worth while, my dearest
son, that record of these things also should not escape you, in order that,
should the same things come about on similar occasions, you may by fore-
knowledge find a ready remedy.

P ‖ 146 τετελευτηκότος edd. ‖ 149 Κωνσταντῖνος *per comp.* P Me: Κώνστας
Ba Be ‖ 150 καὶ Κισκάσην V¹ edd.: Κεκισκάσην P V ‖ Ἀρδανούτζιν Morav-
csik: Ἀδρανούτζιν P edd. ‖ 151 ἀπῄει edd.: ἀπείη P ‖ μέγαν edd.: μέγα
P ‖ 152 ἥνπερ εἶχεν: ἦν περιεῖχε edd. ‖ 155/6 Κωνσταντῖνον *per comp.* P Me:
Κώνσταντα Ba Be ‖ 156 τυγχάνεις Ba Be: τυγχάνης P ‖ 157 Ἀρδανουτζίου
Moravcsik: Ἀδρανουτζίου P edd. ‖ μέλλεις Be: μέλλης P ‖ 158 Οὖ *om.* edd. ‖
162 καὶ Κισκάση V edd.: Κεκισκάση P ‖ Κωνσταντῖνος *per comp.* P Me: Κώνστας
Ba Be ‖ 163 προσαπολογισάμενος P ‖ 164 Ἀδρανασὴ edd. ‖ 166 Τί: Ἴσθι Be
Migne ‖ 167 τὴν περὶ: περὶ τὴν Be.

224

47. Περὶ τῆς τῶν Κυπρίων μεταναστάσεως ἔχει
ἡ ἱστορία τάδε.

Τῆς νήσου ἀλωθείσης ὑπὸ τῶν Σαρακηνῶν καὶ ἐπὶ ἑπτὰ ἔτεσιν
ἀοικήτου μεινάσης, καὶ τοῦ ἀρχιεπισκόπου Ἰωάννου μετὰ τοῦ λαοῦ
155ʳP αὐτοῦ πρὸς τὴν βασιλεύουσαν καταλαβόντος, ἐγένετο οἰκονο|μία παρὰ 5
τοῦ βασιλέως Ἰουστινιανοῦ ἐν τῇ ἁγίᾳ ἕκτῃ συνόδῳ τοῦ τὴν Κύζικον
παραλαβεῖν μετὰ τῶν ἐπισκόπων αὐτοῦ καὶ τοῦ λαοῦ τῆς νήσου καὶ
ποιεῖσθαι καὶ χειροτονίας, ἡνίκα ἂν λείψῃ ἐπίσκοπος, πρὸς τὸ μὴ δια-
πεσεῖν τὴν αὐθεντίαν καὶ τὰ δίκαια τῆς Κύπρου (καὶ γὰρ καὶ αὐτὸς
ὁ Ἰουστινιανὸς ὁ βασιλεὺς Κύπριος ἦν, καθὼς καὶ παρὰ τῶν παλαιῶν 10
Κυπρίων ὁ λόγος μέχρι τῆς σήμερον ἐπεκράτησεν), ὥστε καὶ ὡρίσθη
ἐν τῇ ἁγίᾳ ἕκτῃ συνόδῳ χειροτονεῖν τὸν ἀρχιεπίσκοπον Κύπρου τὸν
τῆς Κυζίκου πρόεδρον, καθὼς ἐν τῷ λθ΄ κεφαλαίῳ τῆς αὐτῆς ἁγίας
ἕκτης συνόδου ἀναγέγραπται.

Μετὰ δὲ ἑπτὰ ἔτη θελήσει Θεοῦ ἐκινήθη ὁ βασιλεὺς πάλιν οἰκίσαι 15
156ʳP τὴν Κύπρον, καὶ ἀπέστειλεν | πρὸς τὸν ἀμερμουμνῆν τοῦ Βαγδὰδ τρεῖς
τῶν ἐνδόξων Κυπρίων, αὐτόχθονας τῆς αὐτῆς νήσου τυγχάνοντας, τοὺς
λεγομένους Φαγγουμεῖς, μετὰ καὶ βασιλικοῦ τινος ἀγχίνου τε καὶ ἐνδό-
215Be ξου, γράψας | τῷ ἀμερμουμνῇ, ἵνα τὸν ἐν Συρίᾳ ὄντα λαὸν τῆς νήσου
Κύπρου ἀπολύσῃ εἰς τὸν ἴδιον τόπον. Καὶ ὑπακούσας ὁ ἀμερμουμνῆς 20
τῇ τοῦ βασιλέως γραφῇ, ἀπέστειλε κατὰ πάσας τὰς Συρίας ἐνδόξους
Σαρακηνούς, καὶ ἐπεσώρευσεν πάντας τοὺς Κυπρίους καὶ διεπέρασεν
εἰς τὸν ἴδιον τόπον. Ἀπέστειλεν δὲ καὶ ὁ βασιλεὺς βασιλικόν, καὶ διεπέρασεν καὶ τοὺς ἐν Ῥωμανίᾳ οἰκήσαντας, ἤγουν ἔν τε τῇ Κυζίκῳ καὶ τῷ
156ᵛP Κιβυρραιωτῶν καὶ τῷ Θρακησίων, καὶ ἐνῳκίσθη | ἡ νῆσος. 25

48. Κεφάλαιον λθ΄ τῆς ἁγίας ἕκτης συνόδου, τῆς
ἐν τῷ Τρούλλῳ τοῦ μεγάλου παλατίου γεγονυίας.

Τοῦ ἀδελφοῦ καὶ συλλειτουργοῦ ἡμῶν Ἰωάννου, τοῦ τῆς Κυπρίων
νήσου προέδρου, ἅμα τῷ οἰκείῳ λαῷ ἐπὶ τὴν Ἑλλησπόντιον ἐπαρχίαν —

F   48. 3 Τοῦ ἀδελφοῦ — 21 χειροτονηθήσεται: Canon XXXIX. VII. Conc.
ed. Mansi XI. c. 961. = ed. Ralles—Potles II. p. 395.

V   47. 1/2 ἔχει ἡ ἱστορία τάδε: ἡ ἱστορία ὧδε πως ἔχει V ‖ 4 ἀοικήτου
(littera ν erasa) Pˣ V edd.: ἀνοικήτου P ‖ 9 καὶ γὰρ — 11 ἐπεκράτησεν
in parenthesi posuit Be ‖ 10 ὁ² om. edd. ‖ Κυπρίος P ‖ 11 ὁρίσθη P ‖ 13 λθ΄

47. Of the migration of the Cypriots the story is as follows.

When the island was captured by the Saracens and remained un-inhabited seven years, and the archbishop John came with his folk to the imperial city, a dispensation was made by the emperor Justinian in the holy sixth synod that he, with his bishops and the folk of the island, should take over Cyzicus and should make his appointments whenever a bishopric should fall vacant, to the end that the authority and rights of Cyprus might not be interrupted (for the emperor Justinian himself also was a Cypriot, as from the Cypriots of olden days the tale has persisted unto this day); and so it was ordained in the holy sixth synod that the archbishop of Cyprus should appoint the president of Cyzicus, as it is recorded in the 39th chapter of the same holy sixth synod.

But after seven years, by God's will the emperor was moved to populate Cyprus again, and he sent to the commander of the faithful of Bagdad three of the illustrious Cypriots, natives of the same island, called Phangoumeis, in charge of an imperial agent both intelligent and illustrious, and wrote to the commander of the faithful asking him to dismiss the folk of the island of Cyprus that were in Syria to their own place. The commander of the faithful obeyed the emperor's epistle, and sent illustrious Saracens to all the parts of Syria and gathered together all the Cypriots and carried them over to their own place. And the emperor, for his part, sent an imperial agent and carried over those who had settled in Romania, that is, at Cyzicus and in the Kibyrrhaiote and Thrakesian *provinces*, and the island was populated.

48. Chapter 39 of the holy sixth synod, held in the Domed Hall of the Great Palace.

Whereas our brother and fellow-minister John, president of the isle of the Cypriots, because of the barbarian assaults and to the end that they

Ba Be: τθ′ P ‖ 15 ἑπτὰ edd.: ζ′ P ‖ οἰκίσαι Be: οἰκεῖσαι P οἰκῆσαι V Me Ba ‖ 16 ἀμερμουμνὴν P ‖ 19 ἀμερμουμνὴ P ‖ ἐν om. Be ‖ 20 ἀπολύσῃ Be: ἀπολύσει P ‖ 21 πάσας τὰς Συρίας: πάσης τῆς Συρίας Be πάσας τῆς Συρίας Me Ba ‖ 25 Κιβυρραιωτῶν edd.: Κιβυρρωτῶν P ‖ Θρακησίων corr. Moravcsik: Θρακήσιν P Θρακησίῳ edd. ‖ ἐνοικίσθη P.
48. 2 Τρούλλῳ P ‖ γεγονυίας: γενομένης V edd. ‖ 3 Κυπρίων Mansi Ralles-Potles: Κυπρίου P Κύπρου Be Ralles-Potles in apparatu ‖ 4 'Ελλη-σπόντιον Meursius Be Mansi Ralles-Potles: 'Ελίσπονδον P ‖ 5 τὰς βαρβαρικὰς

48

διά τε τὰς βαρβαρικὰς ἐφόδους, διά τε τὸ τῆς ἐθνικῆς ἐλευθερωθῆναι 5
δουλείας καὶ καθαρῶς τοῖς σκήπτροις τοῦ Χριστιανικωτάτου κράτους
ὑποταγῆναι — τῆς εἰρημένης μεταναστάντος νήσου προνοίᾳ τοῦ φιλαν-
θρώπου Θεοῦ καὶ μόχθῳ τοῦ φιλοχρίστου καὶ εὐσεβοῦς ἡμῶν βασιλέως,
συνορῶμεν, ὥστε ἀκαινοτόμητα διαφυλαχθῆναι τὰ παρὰ τῶν ἐν Ἐφέσῳ
157ʳP τὸ πρότερον συνελθόντων θεοφόρων πατέρων τῷ θρόνῳ τοῦ προ|γεγραμ- 10
216Be μένου ἀνδρὸς παρασχεθέντα προνόμια, | ὥστε τὴν νέαν Ἰουστινιανού-
πολιν τὸ δίκαιον ἔχειν τῆς Κωνσταντινέων πόλεως καὶ τὸν ἐπ' αὐτῇ
καθιστάμενον θεοφιλέστατον ἐπίσκοπον πάντων προεδρεύειν ⟨τῶν⟩
τῆς Ἑλλησποντίων ἐπαρχίας καὶ ὑπὸ τῶν οἰκείων ἐπισκόπων χειροτο-
νεῖσθαι κατὰ τὴν ἀρχαίαν συνήθειαν (τὰ γὰρ ἐν ἑκάστῃ ἐκκλησίᾳ ἔθη 15
καὶ οἱ θεοφόροι ἡμῶν πατέρες παραφυλάττεσθαι διεγνώκασιν), τοῦ
τῆς Κυζικηνῶν πόλεως ἐπισκόπου ὑποκειμένου τῷ προέδρῳ τῆς εἰρημένης Ἰουστινιανουπόλεως, μιμήσει τῶν λοιπῶν ἁπάντων ἐπισκόπων τῶν
ὑπὸ τὸν λεχθέντα θεοφιλέστατον πρόεδρον Ἰωάννην, ἀφ' οὗ, χρείας
157ᵛP καλούσης, καὶ ὁ τῆς αὐτῆς Κυζικηνῶν πόλεως ἐπίσκοπος | χειροτονη- 20
θήσεται.

Ἐπεὶ δὲ καὶ τὰ περὶ ἐθνῶν οὕτως ἀκριβῶς σοι διετυπώσαμεν
καὶ προεξεθέμεθα, δίκαιον μὴ μόνον περὶ τῶν ἐν τῇ καθ' ἡμᾶς πολιτείᾳ,
ἀλλὰ καὶ περὶ πάσης τῆς τῶν Ῥωμαίων ἀρχῆς κατά τινας χρόνους
καινοτομηθέντων σαφῆ κεκτῆσθαί σε τὴν εἴδησιν, ὡς ἂν ἡ περὶ τῶν 25
ἐγγυτέρω καὶ οἰκείων γνῶσις πλέον τῶν ἄλλων ἐν σοὶ διαμένουσα ποθει-
νότερον ἀναδείξῃ πρὸς τὸ ὑπήκοον.

Ἰστέον, ὅτι ἐπὶ Κωνσταντίνου, υἱοῦ Κωνσταντίνου, τοῦ καὶ
Πωγωνάτου καλουμένου, Καλλίνικός τις ἀπὸ Ἡλιουπόλεως Ῥωμαίοις
217Be προσφυγών, τὸ διὰ τῶν σιφώνων ἐκφερόμενον πῦρ | ὑγρὸν κατεσκεύασεν, 30
δι' οὗ καὶ τὸν τῶν Σαρακηνῶν στόλον ἐν Κυζίκῳ Ῥωμαῖοι κατέφλεξαν-
158ʳP τες | τὴν νίκην ἤραντο.

F   28 Ἰστέον — 32 ἤραντο: cf. Theoph. p. 354, 13—17; Leo Gramm., ed.
Bonn. p. 160, 6—10; Theod. Melit., ed. Tafel p. 110, 14—18; Cedr., ed.
Bonn. I. p. 765, 11—15; Zon. XIV. 20., ed. Bonn. III. p. 223, 16—224,4.

48

might be free from slavery to the infidel and be subject unfeignedly to the sceptre of his most Christian majesty, hath with his own folk migrated from the said isle to the province of Hellespont, by the providence and mercy of God and by the labour of our Christ-loving and pious emperor; we do resolve: that the privileges accorded unto the throne of the aforesaid by the fathers inspired of God at their sometimes meeting in Ephesus shall be preserved uninjured; that the new Justinianoupolis shall have the right of the city of the Constantinians; and that the most pious bishop who is set over it shall preside over all *the bishops* of the province of Hellespont, and shall be appointed by his own bishops, according to the ancient custom (for our fathers inspired of God have resolved that the practices in each church are to be preserved), the bishop of the city of the Cyzicenes being subject to the president of the said Justinianoupolis in like manner as are all the rest of the bishops under the said most pious president John, by whom as need shall arise the bishop also of the same city of the Cyzicenes shall be appointed.

But now that we have thus accurately formulated and set before you the matters concerning foreign nations, it is right that you should be certainly informed about reforms introduced, not only in the affairs of our city, but at various times over all the empire of the Romans, to the end that knowledge of things closer at hand and domestic may abide with you preeminently and may show you more worthy of affection to your subjects.

In the time of Constantine, son of Constantine, called Pogonatus, one Callinicus fled from Helioupolis to the Romans and manufactured the liquid fire which is projected through the tubes, by the aid of which the Romans gutted the fleet of the Saracens at Cyzicus, and gained the victory.

V Ba Be Mansi Ralles-Potles: τοῦ βαρβαρικοῦ P ‖ ἐθνικῆς edd. Mansi Ralles-Potles: ἐθνηκοὺς P ‖ 6 τοῖς σκήπτροις edd. Mansi Ralles-Potles: τοῖς Κύπροις P ‖ 7 μετανασταντος edd.: μεταστάντος P Mansi Ralles-Potles *in apparatu* ‖ 11 παρασχεθέντα προνόμια edd. Mansi Ralles-Potles: πραχθέντα προνοία P ‖ 12 Κωνσταντινέων πόλεως: Κωνσταντινουπόλεως Me Mansi Ralles-Potles ‖ 13 τῶν *add.* Ba Be Mansi Ralles-Potles ‖ 14 Ἑλλησποντίων Ba Be Mansi Ralles-Potles: Ἑλισπόντων P ‖ 15 τὰ γὰρ — 16 διεγνώκασιν *in parenthesi posuit* Be ‖ 15 ἔθη Ba Be Mansi Ralles-Potles: ἔθνη P ‖ 19 ἀφ': ὑφ' Mansi Ralles-Potles ‖ 24 πάσης τῆς V edd.: πᾶσι τῇ P ‖ ἀρχῆς V edd.: ἀρχὴ P ‖ 28 Κωνσταντίνου² F: Κωνσταντίου P V F¹ edd. ‖ 30 σιφόνων P ‖ πῦρ ὑγρὸν: πῦρ θαλάσσιον Theoph.

49

49. Ὁ ζ η τ ῶ ν, ὅ π ω ς τ ῇ τ ῶ ν Π α τ ρ ῶ ν ἐ κ κ λ η σ ί ᾳ ο ἱ
Σ κ λ ά β ο ι δ ο υ λ ε ύ ε ι ν κ α ὶ ὑ π ο κ ε ῖ σ ϑ α ι ἐ τ ά χ ϑ η-
σ α ν, ἐ κ τ ῆ ς π α ρ ο ύ σ η ς μ α ν ϑ α ν έ τ ω γ ρ α φ ῆ ς.

Νικηφόρος τὰ τῶν Ῥωμαίων σκῆπτρα ἐκράτει, καὶ οὗτοι ἐν τῷ
ϑέματι ὄντες Πελοποννήσου ἀπόστασιν ἐννοήσαντες, πρῶτον μὲν τὰς 5
τῶν γειτόνων οἰκίας τῶν Γραικῶν ἐξεπόρϑουν καὶ εἰς ἁρπαγὴν ἐτίϑεντο,
ἔπειτα δὲ καὶ κατὰ τῶν οἰκητόρων τῆς τῶν Πατρῶν ὁρμήσαντες πόλεως,
τὰ πρὸ τοῦ τείχους πεδία κατέστρεφόν τε καὶ ταύτην ἐπολιόρκουν, μεϑ'
ἑαυτῶν ἔχοντες καὶ Ἀφρικοὺς Σαρακηνούς. Ἐπεὶ δὲ χρόνος ἱκανὸς
158ᵛP διῆλϑεν, καὶ σπάνις τῶν ἀναγκαίων τοῖς ἔνδοϑεν τοῦ τείχους | γίνεσϑαι 10
ἤρξατο, ὕδατός τε καὶ τροφῶν, βουλὴν βουλεύονται εἰς συμβιβάσεις τε
ἐλϑεῖν καὶ λόγους ἀπαϑείας λαβεῖν καὶ τηνικαῦτα τὴν πόλιν ὑποτάξαι
αὐτούς. Ἐπεὶ οὖν ὁ τηνικαῦτα στρατηγὸς ὑπῆρχεν πρὸς τὴν ἄκραν τοῦ
ϑέματος ἐν κάστρῳ Κορίνϑου, καὶ προσδοκία ἦν τοῦ παραγενέσϑαι
αὐτὸν καὶ καταπολεμῆσαι τὸ ἔϑνος τῶν Σκλαβήνων, ὡς καὶ πρώην 15
καταμηνυϑέντος αὐτοῦ περὶ τῆς καταδρομῆς αὐτῶν παρὰ τῶν ἀρχόντων, ἐβουλεύσαντο οἱ τοῦ κάστρου οἰκήτορες πρότερον ἀποσταλῆναι
218Be σκοπὸν εἰς τὰ ἀνατολικώτερα τῶν ὀρέων καὶ ἀπο|σκοπεῦσαι καὶ γνῶναι,
εἰ ἄρα παραγίνεται ὁ στρατηγός, παραγγείλαντες καὶ σημεῖον δεδωκότες
159ʳP τῷ ἀποσταλμένῳ, ἵνα, εἰ | μὲν ἴδοι ἐρχόμενον τὸν στρατηγόν, ἐν τῇ 20
ὑποστροφῇ αὐτοῦ κλίνῃ τὸ φλάμμουλον, ὅπως γνῶσιν τὴν ἔλευσιν τοῦ
στρατηγοῦ, εἰ δὲ μή γε, κατέχειν ὀρϑὸν τὸ φλάμμουλον πρὸς τὸ μὴ
ἔχειν αὐτοὺς προσδοκίαν ⟨τοῦ⟩ τοῦ λοιποῦ παραγίνεσϑαι τὸν στρατηγόν.
Τοῦ οὖν σκοποῦ ἀπελϑόντος καὶ μαϑόντος μὴ παραγίνεσϑαι τὸν στρατηγόν,
ὑπέστρεφεν ὀρϑὸν κατέχων τὸ φλάμμουλον. Καὶ δὴ τοῦ Θεοῦ εὐδοκή- 25
σαντος διὰ πρεσβειῶν τοῦ ἁγίου ἀποστόλου Ἀνδρέου, τοῦ ἵππου ὀλισϑή-
σαντος καὶ τοῦ ἐπιβάτου ὑποπεπτωκότος, ἔκλινεν τὸ φλάμμουλον, καὶ
οἱ τοῦ κάστρου οἰκήτορες ἰδόντες τὸ γεγονὸς σημεῖον καὶ νομίσαντες
ἐξ ἅπαντος παραγίνεσϑαι τὸν στρατηγόν, ἤνοιξαν τὰς πύλας τοῦ κάστρου,
159ᵛP καὶ ἐξῆλϑον | ϑαρσαλέοι κατὰ τῶν Σκλαβήνων, καὶ εἶδον τὸν πρωτόκλη- 30
τον ἀπόστολον ὀφϑαλμοφανῶς ἵππῳ ἐπικαϑήμενον καὶ δρόμῳ ἐπερχό-
μενον κατὰ τῶν βαρβάρων· καὶ δὴ τρέψας τούτους κατὰ κράτος καὶ
διασκορπίσας καὶ ἀπελάσας πόρρω τοῦ κάστρου φυγάδας ἐποίησεν. Οἱ
δὲ βάρβαροι ἰδόντες καὶ καταπλαγέντες καὶ ἔκϑαμβοι γεγονότες ἐπὶ
τῇ κατ' αὐτῶν κραταιᾷ ἐπελεύσει τοῦ ἀηττήτου καὶ ἀκαταγωνίστου 35
ὁπλίτου καὶ στρατηγοῦ καὶ ταξιάρχου καὶ τροπαιούχου καὶ νικηφόρου

F   49. 4 Νικηφόρος — 75 αὐτούς: cf. Synodalis epistola patriarchae Nicolai
III Grammatici, ed. Migne, P. G. 119. c. 877 D—880 A. = ed. Ralles—Potles,
V. p. 72.

49

49. He who enquires how the Slavs were put in servitude and subjection to the church of Patras, let him learn from the present passage.

Nicephorus was holding the sceptre of the Romans, and these *Slavs* who were in the province of Peloponnesus decided to revolt, and first proceeded to sack the dwellings of their neighbours, the Greeks, and gave them up to rapine, and next they moved against the inhabitants of the city of Patras and ravaged the plains before its wall and laid siege to itself, having with them African Saracens also. And when a considerable time had gone by and there began to be dearth of necessaries, both water and foodstuffs, among those within the wall, they took counsel among themselves to come to terms of composition and to obtain promises of immunity and then to surrender the city to their yoke. And so, as the then military governor was at the extremity of the province in the city of Corinth, and it had been expected that he would come and defeat the nation of the Slavenes, since he had received early intelligence of their assault from the nobles, the inhabitants of the city resolved that a scout should first be sent to the eastern side of the mountains and spy out and discover if the military governor were in fact coming, and they instructed and gave a signal to their envoy, that if he were to see the military governor coming, he should on his way back dip the standard, so they might know of the coming of the military governor, but if not, to hold the standard erect, so they might for the future not expect the military governor to come. So the scout went off and found that the military governor was not coming, and began to come back, holding the standard erect. But, as it pleased God through the intercession of the holy apostle Andrew, the horse slipped and the rider fell off and dipped the standard, and the inhabitants of the city, seeing the signal given and believing that the military governor was coming undoubtedly, opened the gates of the city and sallied forth bravely against the Slavenes; and they saw the first-called apostle, revealed to their eyes, mounted upon a horse and charging upon the barbarians, yea, and he totally routed them and scattered them and drave them far off from the city and made them to flee. And the barbarians saw and were amazed and confounded at the violent assault upon them of the invincible and unconquerable warrior and captain and marshal, the triumphant and victorious first-called apostle Andrew,

---

V   **49.** 2 Σκλαβοί edd. ‖ 5 τὰς V edd.: τοῦ P ‖ 8 κατέστρεφόν τε: κατεστρέ-φοντο V edd. ‖ 9 ante Σαρακηνούς add. καὶ edd. ‖ 13 αὐτοῖς V edd. ‖ 15 Σκλαβηνῶν Be Σκλαβινῶν Me Ba ‖ 18 σκοπὸν edd.: σκοποὺς P ‖ 20 ἀπεσταλ-μένῳ edd. ‖ 21 κλίνη Ba Be; κλήνει P ‖ φλάμουλον P ‖ 22 φλάμουλον P ‖ 23 τοῦ add. Moravcsik ‖ 25 φλάμουλον P ‖ 27 φλάμουλον P ‖ 28 ἰδόντες edd.: ἰδότες P ‖ 30 Σκλαβηνῶν edd. ‖ 34 ἰδόντες V edd.: εἰδότες P ‖ καὶ² om. edd. ‖

49

πρωτοκλήτου ἀποστόλου Ἀνδρέου, ἐταράχθησαν, ἐσαλεύθησαν, τρόμος
ἐπελάβετο αὐτούς, καὶ προσέφυγον εἰς τὸν πάνσεπτον ναὸν αὐτοῦ.
160ʳP   Τοῦ οὖν στρατηγοῦ μετὰ τὸ τρόπαιον ἐν τῇ τρίτῃ ἡμέρᾳ καταλα-
219Be βόντος καὶ τὴν νίκην τοῦ ἀποστόλου μα|θόντος, κατεμήνυσεν τῷ βασι- 40
λεῖ Νικηφόρῳ τήν τε ἔφοδον τῶν Σκλαβήνων καὶ τὴν προνομὴν καὶ
αἰχμαλωσίαν καὶ ἀφανισμὸν καὶ τὴν λεηλασίαν καὶ τἄλλα δεινά, ὅσα
καταδραμόντες ἐποίησαν εἰς τὰ μέρη τῆς Ἀχαΐας, ἔτι δὲ καὶ τὴν πολυήμε-
ρον πολιορκίαν καὶ τὴν κατὰ τῶν οἰκητόρων τοῦ κάστρου διηνεκῇ ἐπίθεσιν, ὡσαύτως καὶ τὴν ἐπισκοπὴν καὶ συμμαχίαν καὶ τὸ τρόπαιον καὶ 45
τὴν κατὰ κράτος νίκην, τὴν γενομένην παρὰ τοῦ ἀποστόλου, καὶ ὡς
160ᵛP ὀφθαλμοφανῶς ὡράθη ἐπιτρέχων καὶ διώκων | τοὺς πολεμίους κατὰ
νῶτον καὶ τροπούμενος αὐτούς, ὡς καὶ αὐτοὺς τοὺς βαρβάρους αἰσθέσθαι
τὴν τοῦ ἀποστόλου πρὸς ἡμᾶς ἐπισκοπὴν καὶ συμμαχίαν, καὶ διὰ τοῦτο
προσφυγεῖν αὐτοὺς εἰς τὸν σεβάσμιον ναὸν αὐτοῦ. Ὁ δὲ βασιλεὺς ταῦτα 50
ἀναμαθὼν παρεκελεύσατο οὕτως· «Ἐπεὶ καὶ τὸ τρόπαιον καὶ ἡ κατὰ
κράτος νίκη παρὰ τοῦ ἀποστόλου γέγονεν, ὀφειλόμενον καθέστηκεν
πᾶσαν τὴν ἐκστρατείαν τῶν πολεμίων καὶ τὰ λάφυρα καὶ τὰ σκῦλα
αὐτῷ ἀποδοθῆναι.» Καὶ διωρίσατο αὐτούς τε τοὺς πολεμίους μετὰ
πάσης τῆς φαμιλίας καὶ συγγενείας καὶ πάντων τῶν προσηκόντων 55
αὐτοῖς, ἔτι δὲ καὶ πάσης τῆς ὑπάρξεως αὐτῶν, ἀφορισθῆναι εἰς τὸν ναὸν
161ʳP τοῦ | ἀποστόλου ἐν τῇ μητροπόλει Πατρῶν, ἐν ᾗ ὁ πρωτόκλητος καὶ
μαθητὴς τοῦ Χριστοῦ τὸν τῆς ἀθλήσεως διήνυσεν ἀγῶνα, δεδωκὼς
περὶ αὐτῶν καὶ σιγίλλιον ἐν τῇ αὐτῇ μητροπόλει.
     Ταῦτα οἱ πρεσβύτεροι καὶ ἀρχαιότεροι ἀνήγγειλαν, παραδόντες 60
220Be ἀγράφως χρόνῳ τε καὶ βίῳ τοῖς ὕστερον, ὅπως | ἂν κατὰ τὸν προφήτην
γνῷ γενεὰ ἡ ἐρχομένη τὸ γεγονὸς θαῦμα διὰ πρεσβειῶν τοῦ ἀποστόλου,
καὶ ἀναστήσονται καὶ ἀπαγγελοῦσιν αὐτὸ τοῖς υἱοῖς αὐτῶν, ἵνα μὴ
ἐπιλάθωνται τῶν εὐεργεσιῶν, ὧν ἐποίησεν ὁ Θεὸς διὰ πρεσβειῶν τοῦ
ἀποστόλου. Ἔκτοτε δὲ οἱ ἀφορισθέντες Σκλαβῖνοι ἐν τῇ μητροπόλει 65
καὶ τοὺς στρατηγοὺς καὶ τοὺς βασιλικοὺς καὶ πάντας τοὺς ἐξ ἐθνῶν
161ᵛP ἀποστελλομένους πρέσβεις | ὡς ὁμήρους διατρέφουσιν, ἔχοντες ἰδίους
καὶ τραπεζοποιοὺς καὶ μαγείρους καὶ πάντας τοὺς παρασκευάζοντας
τὰ τῆς τραπέζης βρώματα, τῆς μητροπόλεως εἰς ταῦτα μηδὲν καινοτο-
μουμένης, ἀλλ' αὐτοὶ οἱ Σκλαβῖνοι ἀπὸ διανομῆς καὶ συνδοσίας τῆς 70
ὁμάδος αὐτῶν ἐπισυνάγουσιν τὰς τοιαύτας χρείας. Ἐποίησεν δὲ καὶ
σιγίλλιον Λέων, ὁ ἀείμνηστος καὶ σοφώτατος βασιλεύς, λεπτομερῶς

F   62 γνῷ — 64 εὐεργεσιῶν: Psalm. 77, 6—7, cf. Psalm. 21, 31.

49

and were thrown into disorder and shaken, and trembling gat hold upon them and they fled for refuge in his most sacred temple.

Now when the military governor arrived on the third day after the rout and learnt of the victory of the apostle, he reported to the emperor Nicephorus upon the onset of the Slavenes and the foraging and enslaving and destroying and the plundering and all the other horrors which in their incursion they had inflicted on the regions of Achaea; and also upon the siege of many days and the sustained assault on the inhabitants of the city; and in like manner upon the visitation and aid in battle and the rout and the total victory won by the apostle, and how he had been seen revealed to their eyes charging upon and pursuing the rear of the foe and routing them, so that the barbarians themselves were aware that the apostle had visited us and was aiding us in the battle, and therefore had fled for refuge to his hallowed temple. The emperor, learning of these things, gave orders to this effect: «Since the rout and total victory were achieved by the apostle, it is our duty to render to him the whole expeditionary force of the foe and the booty and the spoils.» And he ordained that the foemen themselves, with all their families and relations and all who belonged to them, and all their property as well, should be set apart for the temple of the apostle in the metropolis of Patras, where the first-called and disciple of Christ had performed this exploit in the contest; and he issued a bull concerning these matters in that same metropolis.

These things the older and more ancient narrated, handing them down in unwritten tradition to them who lived in the after time, so that, as the prophet says, the coming generation might know the miracle wrought through the intercession of the apostle, and might rise up and declare it to their sons, that they might not forget the benefits done by God through the intercession of the apostle. And from that time the Slavenes who were set apart in the metropolis have maintained like hostages the military governors and the imperial agents and all the envoys sent from foreign nations, and they have their own waiters and cooks and servants of all kinds who prepare foods for the table; and the metropolis interferes in none of these matters, for the Slavenes themselves collect the necessary funds by apportionment and subscription among their unit. And Leo, too, the ever-memorable and most wise emperor, issued a bull containing a detailed

---

V 39 τρίτη edd.: γ' P ‖ 41 Σκλαβηνῶν edd. ‖ 45 τὸ om. edd. ‖ 47 ὁράθη P ‖ 48 ὡς: ὥστε edd. ‖ αἴσθεσθαι V edd.: αἴθεσθαι P αἴδεσθαι coni. Jenkins ‖ 50 αὐτοῦ ναόν V edd. ‖ 53 ἐκστρατιὰν P ‖ 55 φαμηλίας P ‖ 59 σιγίλλον Be ‖ αὐτῇ] litteram ῇ in ras. scr. P¹ ‖ 63 ἀναστήσονται F Ba Be: ἀναστήσωνται P ‖ 64 ὧν: ἃς V ‖ 65 Σκλαβηνοὶ edd. ‖ 70 Σκλαβηνοὶ edd. ‖ 72 σοφώτατος: ἀοίδιμος edd.

232

49, 50

περιέχον τό, τί ὀφείλουσιν παρέχειν οἱ αὐτοὶ ἐναπογραφόμενοι τῷ μητρο-
πολίτῃ, καὶ μὴ ἀπαργυρίζεσθαι παρ' αὐτοῦ ἢ ἄλλως πως κατ' ἐπίνοιαν
ἄδικον ζημιοῦσθαι αὐτούς. 75

50. Π ε ρ ὶ τ ῶ ν ἐ ν τ ῷ θ έ μ α τ ι Π ε λ ο π ο ν ν ή σ ο υ Σ κ λ ά -
β ω ν, τ ῶ ν τ ε Μ η λ ι γ γ ῶ ν κ α ὶ 'Ε ζ ε ρ ι τ ῶ ν κ α ὶ π ε ρ ὶ
162ʳP τ ῶ ν τ ε λ ο υ μ έ ν ω ν π α ρ' | α ὐ τ ῶ ν π ά κ τ ω ν, ὁ μ ο ί ω ς
κ α ὶ π ε ρ ὶ τ ῶ ν ο ἰ κ η τ ό ρ ω ν τ ο ῦ κ ά σ τ ρ ο υ Μ α ΐ ν η ς κ α ὶ
τ ο ῦ π α ρ' α ὐ τ ῶ ν τ ε λ ο υ μ έ ν ο υ π ά κ τ ο υ. 5

'Ιστέον, ὅτι οἱ τοῦ θέματος Πελοποννήσου Σκλάβοι ἐν ταῖς ἡμέραις
221Be τοῦ βασιλέως Θεοφίλου καὶ τοῦ υἱοῦ αὐτοῦ, | Μιχαήλ, ἀποστατήσαντες
γεγόνασιν ἰδιόρρυθμοι, ληλασίας καὶ ἀνδραποδισμοὺς καὶ πραίδας καὶ
ἐμπρησμοὺς καὶ κλοπὰς ἐργαζόμενοι. 'Επὶ δὲ τῆς βασιλείας Μιχαήλ, τοῦ
υἱοῦ Θεοφίλου, ἀπεστάλη ὁ πρωτοσπαθάριος Θεόκτιστος, οὗ τὸ ἐπίκλην 10
ὁ τῶν Βρυεννίων, στρατηγὸς ἐν τῷ θέματι Πελοποννήσου μετὰ δυνάμεως καὶ ἰσχύος πολλῆς, ἤγουν Θρακῶν καὶ Μακεδόνων καὶ τῶν λοιπῶν
162ᵛP δυτικῶν θεμάτων τοῦ πολεμῆ|σαι καὶ καθυποτάξαι αὐτούς. Καὶ πάντας
μὲν τοὺς Σκλάβους καὶ λοιποὺς ἀνυποτάκτους τοῦ θέματος Πελοποννήσου ὑπέταξε καὶ ἐχειρώσατο, μόνοι δὲ οἱ 'Εζερῖται καὶ οἱ Μηλιγγοὶ 15
κατελείφθησαν ὑπὸ τὴν Λακεδαιμονίαν καὶ τὸ "Ελος. Καὶ ἐπειδὴ ὄρος
ἐστὶν ἐκεῖσε μέγα καὶ ὑψηλότατον, καλούμενον Πενταδάκτυλος, καὶ
εἰσέρχεται ὥσπερ τράχηλος εἰς τὴν θάλασσαν ἕως πολλοῦ διαστήματος,
διὰ δὲ τὸ εἶναι τὸν τόπον δύσκολον κατῴκησαν εἰς τὰς πλευρὰς τοῦ
αὐτοῦ ὄρους, ἐν μὲν τῷ ἑνὶ μέρει οἱ Μηλιγγοί, ἐν δὲ τῷ ἑτέρῳ μέρει 20
οἱ 'Εζερῖται. Καὶ ὁ μὲν προρρηθεὶς πρωτοσπαθάριος Θεόκτιστος καὶ
στρατηγὸς Πελοποννήσου δυνηθεὶς καὶ τούτους καθυποτάξαι, ἐξέθετο
163ʳP τοῖς μὲν Μηλιγγοῖς νομίσματα ξ', | τοῖς δὲ 'Εζερίταις νομίσματα τ',
ἅτινα καὶ ἐτέλουν, αὐτοῦ στρατηγοῦντος, καθὼς παρὰ τῶν ἐντοπίων
διασώζεται μέχρι τῆς σήμερον ἡ τοιαύτη φήμη. 'Επὶ δὲ τῆς βασιλείας 25
τοῦ κυροῦ 'Ρωμανοῦ, τοῦ βασιλέως, στρατηγῶν ὁ πρωτοσπαθάριος
222Be 'Ιωάννης ὁ Πρωτεύων εἰς | τὸ αὐτὸ θέμα ἀνήγαγεν πρὸς τὸν αὐτὸν
κύριν 'Ρωμανὸν περί τε τῶν Μηλιγγῶν καὶ τῶν 'Εζεριτῶν, ὅτι ἀποστατή-
σαντες οὐ πείθονται οὔτε τῷ στρατηγῷ, οὔτε βασιλικῇ κελεύσει ὑπείκουσιν, ἀλλ' εἰσὶν ὥσπερ αὐτόνομοι καὶ αὐτοδέσποτοι, καὶ οὔτε παρὰ τοῦ 30
στρατηγοῦ δέχονται ἄρχοντα, οὔτε συνταξιδεύειν αὐτῷ ὑπείκουσιν,
οὔτε ἄλλην τοῦ δημοσίου δουλείαν ἐκτελεῖν πείθονται. Καὶ μέχρι τοῦ

V   50. 2 Μηλιγγῶν scr. Moravcsik: Μιλήγγων P Me   Μιλιγγῶν Ba Be || 4 post account of what these same persons who are ascribed to the metropolitan are liable to provide, and forbidding him to exploit them or in any other way to hurt them unjustly at his whim.

50. Of the Slavs in the province of Peloponnesus, the Milingoi and Ezeritai, and of the tribute paid by them, and in like manner of the inhabitants of the city of Maïna and of the tribute paid by them.

The Slavs of the province of Peloponnesus revolted in the days of the emperor Theophilus and his son Michael, and became independent, and plundered and enslaved and pillaged and burnt and stole. And in the reign of Michael, the son of Theophilus, the protospatharius Theoctistus, surnamed Bryennius, was sent as military governor to the province of Peloponnesus with a great power and force, viz., of Thracians and Macedonians and the rest of the western provinces, to war upon and subdue them. He subdued and mastered all the Slavs and other insubordinates of the province of Peloponnesus, and only the Ezeritai and the Milingoi were left, towards Lacedaemonia and Helos. And since there is there a great and very high mountain called Pentadaktylos, which runs like a neck a long distance out into the sea, and because the place is difficult, they settled upon the flanks of this same mountain, the Milingoi in one part, and in the other part the Ezeritai. The aforesaid protospatharius Theoctistus, the military governor of Peloponnesus, having succeded in reducing these too, fixed *a tribute of* 60 nomismata for the Milingoi, and of 300 nomismata for the Ezeritai, and this they used to pay while he was military governor, as this report of it is preserved to this day by the local inhabitants. But in the reign of the lord Romanus the emperor, the protospatharius John Proteuon, military governor in this same province, reported to the same lord Romanus concerning both Milingoi and Ezeritai, that they had rebelled and neither obeyed the military governor nor regarded the imperial mandate, but were practically independent and self-governing, and neither accepted a head man at the hand of the military governor, nor heeded orders for military service under him, nor would pay other dues to the treasury. While his

κάστρου add. τοῦ edd. ‖ Μαΐνης scr. Moravcsik: Μαινῆς P Μαϊνῆς edd. ‖ 5 τοῦ παρ' αὐτῶν τελουμένου πάκτου: τῶν παρ' αὐτῶν τελουμένων πάκτων edd. ‖ 11 Βροιενίων P ‖ 15 Ἐζερεῖται P ‖ Μιληγγοὶ P edd. ‖ 16 Ἕλος P ‖ 19 δὲ om. Be ‖ 20 Μιληγγοὶ P edd. ‖ 20 μέρει² om. edd. ‖ 22 ἐξέθετο (etiam Bandurius): ἐπέθετο edd. ‖ 23 Μιληγγοῖς P Ba Be   Μιλιγγοί mg. P⁸ ‖ 27 εἰς τὸ αὐτό: ἐν τῷ αὐτῷ Be ‖ θέμα V Me: θέματι P Ba Be ‖ 28 κῦρην P ‖ Μηλίγγων P   Μιληγγῶν Ba Be ‖

50

163^vP ἀνελθεῖν τὴν ἀναφορὰν αὐτοῦ | συνέβη προβληθῆναι τὸν πρωτοσπαθά-
ριον Κρινίτην τὸν Ἀροτρᾶν στρατηγὸν ἐν Πελοποννήσῳ, τῆς δὲ ἀνα-
φορᾶς τοῦ πρωτοσπαθαρίου Ἰωάννου καὶ στρατηγοῦ Πελοποννήσου 35
τοῦ Πρωτεύοντος καταλαβούσης καὶ κατ' ἐνώπιον τοῦ βασιλέως τοῦ
κυροῦ Ῥωμανοῦ ἀναγνωσθείσης καὶ περιεχούσης τὴν ἀποστασίαν τῶν
προρρηθέντων Σκλάβων καὶ τὴν πρὸς τὰς βασιλικὰς προστάξεις δυσπεί-
θειαν ἢ μᾶλλον ἀπείθειαν, ἐδέξατο ὁ αὐτὸς πρωτοσπαθάριος Κρινίτης,
ἵνα, ἐπεὶ εἰς τοσαύτην ἤλασαν ἀποστασίαν καὶ ἀπείθειαν, ἐκστρατεύσῃ 40
κατ' αὐτῶν καὶ καταπολεμήσῃ καὶ ὑποτάξῃ καὶ ἐξολοθρεύσῃ αὐτούς.
Ἀρξάμενος οὖν πολεμεῖν αὐτοὺς ἀπὸ μηνὸς Μαρτίου καὶ κατακαύσας
164^rP τὰ θέρη αὐτῶν καὶ ληϊσάμενος πᾶσαν τὴν | γῆν αὐτῶν, ἔσχεν αὐτοὺς
ἀνθισταμένους καὶ ἀντέχοντας μέχρι μηνὸς Νοεμβρίου, ἀπὸ τότε δὲ
ἰδόντες τὴν ἑαυτῶν ἐξολόθρευσιν, ἠτήσαντο λόγον καὶ τοῦ ὑποταγῆναι 45
αὐτοὺς καὶ τυχεῖν συμπαθείας, ὑπὲρ ὧν πρώην ἐπλημμέλησαν. Ὁ οὖν
223Be προρρηθεὶς πρωτοσπαθάριος | καὶ στρατηγὸς ὁ Κρινίτης ἐξέθετο αὐτοῖς
πάκτα πλείονα, ὧν ἐτέλουν, τοῖς μὲν Μηλιγγοῖς ἀπὸ τῶν ξ' νομισμάτων,
ὧν πρότερον ἐτέλουν, νομίσματα φμ', ὡς εἶναι τὸ πᾶν πάκτον αὐτῶν
νομίσματα χ', τοῖς δὲ Ἐζερίταις ἀπὸ τῶν τ' νομισμάτων, ὧν πρότερον 50
ἐτέλουν, ἕτερα νομίσματα τ', ὡς εἶναι τὸ πᾶν πάκτον αὐτῶν νομίσματα
χ', ἅτινα καὶ ἀπήτησεν καὶ εἰσεκόμισεν ὁ αὐτὸς πρωτοσπαθάριος Κρινίτης ἐν τῷ θεοφυλάκτῳ κοιτῶνι. Τοῦ δὲ πρωτοσπαθαρίου Κρινίτου ἐν
164^vP τῷ θέματι μετατεθέντος | Ἑλλάδος, καὶ τοῦ πρωτοσπαθαρίου Βάρδα
τοῦ Πλατυπόδη προβληθέντος στρατηγοῦ ἐν Πελοποννήσῳ, καὶ τῆς 55
ἀταξίας γεναμένης καὶ στάσεως παρὰ αὐτοῦ τοῦ πρωτοσπαθαρίου
Βάρδα τοῦ Πλατυπόδη καὶ τῶν ὁμοφρόνων αὐτοῦ πρωτοσπαθαρίων καὶ
ἀρχόντων, καὶ τὸν πρωτοσπαθάριον Λέοντα τὸν Ἀγέλαστον ἀποδιωξάν-
των ἀπὸ τοῦ θέματος, καὶ εὐθέως γενομένης καὶ τῆς τῶν Σκλαβησιάνων
ἐπιθέσεως κατὰ τοῦ αὐτοῦ θέματος, ἀπέστειλαν οἱ αὐτοὶ Σκλάβοι, 60
οἵ τε Μηλιγγοὶ καὶ οἱ Ἐζερῖται, πρὸς τὸν κύριν Ῥωμανόν, τὸν βασιλέα,
ἐξαιτούμενοι καὶ παρακαλοῦντες τοῦ συμπαθηθῆναι αὐτοῖς τὰς προσθή-
κας τῶν πάκτων καὶ τελεῖν αὐτούς, καθὼς καὶ πρότερον ἐτέλουν.
Ἐπεὶ δέ, καθὼς προείρηται, εἰσῆλθον οἱ Σκλαβησιάνοι ἐν τῷ θέματι
165^rP | Πελοποννήσου, δεδιὼς ὁ βασιλεύς, ἵνα μὴ καὶ αὐτοὶ προστεθέντες τοῖς 65
Σθλάβοις παντελῆ ἐξολόθρευσιν τοῦ αὐτοῦ θέματος ἐργάσωνται, ἐποίη-
σεν αὐτοῖς χρυσοβούλλιον τοῦ τελεῖν αὐτοὺς πάκτα, ὡς καὶ πρότερον,
224Be | τοὺς μὲν Μηλιγγοὺς ξ' νομίσματα, τοὺς δὲ Ἐζερίτας ⟨νομίσματα⟩ τ'.
Αὕτη οὖν ἐστιν ἡ αἰτία τῆς προσθήκης καὶ τῆς ἐκκοπῆς τῶν πάκτων
τῶν τε Μηλιγγῶν καὶ τῶν Ἐζεριτῶν.   70

50

report was on its way, it happened that the protospatharius Krinitis Arotras was appointed military governor in Peloponnesus, and when the report of the protospatharius John Proteuon, military governor of Peloponnesus, arrived and was read in the presence of the emperor, the lord Romanus, and was *found* to contain *news of* the revolt of the aforesaid Slavs and of their reluctant obedience, or, more properly, their disobedience to the imperial commands, this same protospatharius Krinitis was instructed, since they had gone so far in revolt and disobedience, to march against them and defeat and subdue and exterminate them. And so, beginning his war upon them in the month of March and burning down their crops and plundering all their land, he kept them to defence and resistance until the month of November, and then, seeing that they were being exterminated, they begged to negotiate for their submission and pardon for their past misdoings. And so the aforesaid protospatharius Krinitis, the military governor, fixed upon them tributes greater than they had been paying: upon the Milingoi 540 nomismata on top of the 60 nomismata which they had paid before, so that their total tribute was 600 nomismata, and upon the Ezeritai another 300 nomismata on top of the 300 nomismata they had paid before, so that their total tribute was 600 nomismata, which this same protospatharius Krinitis exacted and conveyed to the *Treasury of the* Bedchamber guarded of God. But when the protospatharius Krinitis was transferred to the province of Hellas and the protospatharius Bardas Platypodis was appointed military governor in Peloponnesus, and disorder and strife were aroused by this same protospatharius Bardas Platypodis and by protospatharii and nobles who took his part, and they expelled the protospatharius Leo Agelastos from the province, and straight away the Slavesians made an attack upon this same province, then these same Slavs, both Milingoi and Ezeritai, sent to the lord Romanus, the emperor, requesting and praying that the increments to their tribute should be forgiven them, and that they should pay what they had paid before. And since, as has been said above, the Slavesians had entered the province of Peloponnesus, the emperor, fearing lest they might join forces with the Slavs and bring about the total destruction of this same province, issued for *the latter* a golden bull providing that they should pay as before, the Milingoi 60 nomismata, and the Ezeritai 300 *nomismata*. Such, then, is the cause of the increase of the tribute of the Milingoi and Ezeritai, and of its remission.

V 38 τὴν *om.* edd. ‖ 41 καταπολεμήσῃ Ba Be: καταπολεμίσει P   καταπολεμήσει V ‖ ὑποτάξῃ Ba Be: ὑποτάξει P ‖ ἐξολοθρεύσει V ‖ 42 αὐτούς: αὐτὸς Me ‖ 45 καὶ *om.* V edd. ‖ 46 αὐτοὺς *scr.* Moravcsik: αὐτοῖς P(?) V edd.: αὐτ᾿ς (*inter* τ *et* ς *duabus litteris erasis*) Pᵛ ‖ 48 Μιληγγοῖς Ba Be ‖ 55 Πλατοιπόδη P ‖ 56 γενομένης edd. ‖ 59 Σκλαβισιάνων P: Σκλαβησιανῶν edd. ‖ 61 Μιληγγοὶ edd. ‖ κύρην P ‖ 64 ʼΕπεὶ δέ: ʼΕπειδὴ Migne ‖ Σκλαβισιάνοι P: Σκλαβησιανοὶ edd. ‖ 66 Σκλάβοις edd. ‖ 67 τοῦ τελεῖν αὐτούς: ἵνα τελῶσι τὰ V edd. ‖ 68 Μιληγγοὺς edd. ‖ νομίσματα² *add.* edd. ‖ 70 τε *om.* edd. ‖ Μιληγγῶν edd. ‖ ʼΕζερίτων P ‖

50

'Ιστέον, ότι οἱ τοῦ κάστρου Μαΐνης οἰκήτορες οὐκ εἰσὶν ἀπὸ τῆς γενεᾶς τῶν προρρηθέντων Σκλάβων, ἀλλ' ἐκ τῶν παλαιοτέρων 'Ρωμαίων, οἳ καὶ μέχρι τοῦ νῦν παρὰ τῶν ἐντοπίων "Ελληνες προσαγορεύονται διὰ τὸ ἐν τοῖς προπαλαιοῖς χρόνοις εἰδωλολάτρας εἶναι καὶ προσκυνητὰς τῶν εἰδώλων κατὰ τοὺς παλαιοὺς "Ελληνας, οἵτινες ἐπὶ τῆς βασιλείας 75
165ᵛP τοῦ ἀοιδίμου Βασιλείου | βαπτισθέντες Χριστιανοὶ γεγόνασιν. Ὁ δὲ τόπος, ἐν ᾧ οἰκοῦσιν, ἐστὶν ἄνυδρος καὶ ἀπρόσοδος, ἐλαιοφόρος δέ, ὅθεν καὶ τὴν παραμυθίαν ἔχουσιν. Διάκειται δὲ ὁ τοιοῦτος τόπος εἰς ἄκραν τοῦ Μαλέα, ἤγουν ἐκεῖθεν τοῦ Ἐζεροῦ πρὸς τὴν παραθαλασσίαν. Διὰ δὲ τὸ τελείως ὑποτεταγμένους εἶναι αὐτοὺς καὶ ἄρχοντα παρὰ τοῦ στρα- 80 τηγοῦ δέχεσθαι καὶ πειθαρχεῖν καὶ ὑπείκειν ταῖς τοῦ στρατηγοῦ προσ- τάξεσιν παρέχουσιν πάκτον ἐκ παλαιτάτου χρόνου νομίσματα υʹ.

'Ιστέον, ὅτι ἡ Καππαδοκίας στρατηγὶς τὸ παλαιὸν τοῦρμα ἦν τῆς τῶν 'Ανατολικῶν στρατηγίδος.

'Ιστέον, ὅτι ἡ Κεφαλληνίας στρατηγίς, ἤγουν τὰ νησία, τοῦρμα 85 ἦν τὸ παλαιὸν τῆς στρατηγίδος Λαγουβαρδίας, ἐπὶ δὲ Λέοντος, τοῦ
225Be φιλοχρίστου δεσπότου, γέγονεν στρατηγίς.
166ʳP 'Ιστέον, ὅτι ἡ Κα|λαβρίας στρατηγὶς δουκᾶτον ἦν τὸ παλαιὸν τῆς στρατηγίδος Σικελίας.

'Ιστέον, ὅτι ἡ τοῦ Χαρσιανοῦ στρατηγὶς τοῦρμα ἦν τὸ παλαιὸν 90 τῆς τῶν 'Αρμενιάκων στρατηγίδος.

'Ιστέον, ὅτι ἐπὶ Λέοντος, τοῦ φιλοχρίστου δεσπότου, ἀπὸ τοῦ θέματος τῶν Βουκελλαρίων εἰς τὸ Καππαδοκῶν θέμα μετετέθησαν ταῦτα τὰ βάνδα, ἤτοι ἡ τοποτηρησία Βάρετας, ἡ τοποτηρησία Βαλβαδώνας, ἡ τοποτηρησία "Ασπονας καὶ ἡ τοποτηρησία 'Ακαρκοῦς, καὶ ἀπὸ τοῦ 95 θέματος τῶν 'Ανατολικῶν εἰς τὸ Καππαδοκῶν θέμα μετετέθησαν ταῦτα τὰ βάνδα, ἤτοι ἡ τοποτηρησία τῆς Εὐδοκιάδος, ἡ τοποτηρησία τοῦ 'Αγίου 'Αγαπητοῦ, ἡ τοποτηρησία 'Αφραζείας, καὶ ἐγένοντο ταῦτα τὰ ἑπτὰ βάνδα, ἤτοι τὰ τῶν Βουκελλαρίων τέσσαρα καὶ τρία τῶν 'Ανατολικῶν,
166ᵛP τοῦρμα | μία, ἡ νῦν τὰ Κόμματα λεγομένη. 100

'Ιστέον, ὅτι ἐπὶ Λέοντος, τοῦ φιλοχρίστου δεσπότου, ἀπὸ τοῦ θέματος τῶν Βουκελλαρίων εἰς τὸ θέμα Χαρσιανοῦ μετετέθησαν ταῦτα τὰ βάνδα, ἤτοι ἡ τοποτηρησία τοῦ Μυριοκεφάλου, ἡ τοποτηρησία τοῦ Τιμίου Σταυροῦ καὶ ἡ τοποτηρησία Βερινουπόλεως, καὶ ἐγένοντο τοῦρμα ἡ νῦν Σανίανα λεγομένη. Καὶ ἀπὸ τοῦ θέματος τῶν 'Αρμενιάκων εἰς τὸ 105 τοῦ Χαρσιανοῦ θέμα μετετέθησαν ταῦτα τὰ βάνδα, ἤτοι ἡ τοῦ Κωμοδρό- μου τοποτηρησία, ἡ τοποτηρησία Τάβιας, καὶ εἰς τὴν τοῦρμαν τοῦ Χαρσιανοῦ τὴν εἰρημένην προσετέθησαν. 'Απὸ δὲ τοῦ Καππαδοκῶν
226Be εἰς τὸ τοῦ Χαρσιανοῦ θέμα ταῦτα τὰ | βάνδα μετετέθησαν, ἤτοι ἡ τοῦρμα Κασῆς ἐξ ὁλοκλήρου καὶ ἡ τοποτηρησία Νύσσης μετὰ τῆς Καισαρείας. 110

50

The inhabitants of the city of Maïna are not of the race of the aforesaid Slavs, but of the ancient Romans, and even to this day they are called 'Hellenes' by the local inhabitants, because in the very ancient times they were idolaters and worshippers of images after the fashion of the ancient Hellenes; and they were baptized and became Christians in the reign of the glorious Basil. The place where they live is waterless and inaccessible, but bears the olive, whence their comfort is. This place is situated on the tip of Malea, that is, beyond Ezeron towards the coast. Seeing that they are perfectly submissive and accept a head man from the military governor, and heed and obey the commands of the military governor, they have paid from very ancient times a tribute of 400 nomismata.

The province of Cappadocia was of old a county of the province of the Anatolikoi.

The province of Kephallenia, or the Islands, was of old a county of the province of Lombardy, but became a province in the time of Leo, the Christ-loving sovereign.

The province of Calabria was of old a duchy of the province of Sicily.

The province of Charsianon was of old a county of the province of the Armeniakoi.

In the time of Leo, the Christ-loving sovereign, the following hundreds were transferred from the province of the Boukellarioi to the province of the Cappadocians, viz., the garrison of Bareta, the garrison of Balbadona, the garrison of Aspona and the garrison of Akarkous; and from the province of the Anatolikoi to the province of the Cappadocians were transferred the following hundreds, viz., the garrison of Eudokias, the garrison of Haghios Agapitos, the garrison of Aphrazeia; and these seven hundreds, that is, the four of the Boukellarioi and three of the Anatolikoi, became one county, now called the Kommata.

In the time of Leo, the Christ-loving sovereign, the following hundreds were transferred from the province of the Boukellarioi to the province of Charsianon, viz., the garrison of Myriokephalon, the garrison of Timios Stauros and the garrison of Berinoupolis, and they became the county now called Saniana. And from the province of the Armeniakoi to the province of Charsianon were transferred the following hundreds, viz., the garrison of Komodromos, the garrison of Tabia, and were added to the said county of Charsianon. From the province of the Cappadocians to the province of Charsianon the following hundreds were transferred, viz., the county of Kasi in toto and the garrison of Nyssa with Caesarea.

V 79 τὴν om. Be ‖ 82 ἐκ παλαιτάτου edd.: ἔκπαλαι τὰ τοῦ P ‖ 83 post ἡ add. τῆς edd. ‖ 86 Λογουβαρδίας Ba Be ‖ 88 Καλαβρίας V edd.: Καλαβρία P ‖ δουκάτον P ‖ 90 τούρμα P ‖ 91 'Αρμενιακῶν Be ‖ 94 Βαλβαδῶνας P: Βαλβαδῶνος V edd. ‖ 85 'Ακαρκοὺς P ‖ 98 ἑπτὰ edd.: ζ' P ‖ 99 τέσσαρα edd.: δ' P ‖ τρία edd.: γ' P ‖ 100 τούρμα P ‖ 105 Σανιάνα edd. ‖ 'Αρμενιακῶν edd. ‖ 106/7 Κομοδρόμου P ‖ 107 Ταβίας V edd. ‖ τούρμαν P ‖ 109 τούρμα P ‖ 110 Νύσης P ‖

167ʳP   Ἰστέον, ὅτι τοῖς παρελ|θοῦσιν χρόνοις τὸ τοῦ Χοζάνου θέμα
ὑπὸ τῶν Σαρακηνῶν ἦν, ὁμοίως καὶ τὸ τοῦ Ἀσμοσάτου θέμα καὶ αὐτὸ
ὑπὸ τῶν Σαρακηνῶν ἦν. Τὸ δὲ Χανζὶτ καὶ ἡ Ῥωμανόπολις κλεισοῦραι
τῶν Μελιτηνιατῶν ὑπῆρχον. Καὶ ἀπὸ τοῦ ὄρους τοῦ Φατιλάνου πάντα
τὰ ἐκεῖθεν τῶν Σαρακηνῶν ὑπῆρχον, τὸ δὲ Τεκῆς ἦν τοῦ Μανουήλ. 115
Ἡ δὲ Κάμαχα ἡ τοῦρμα ἄκρα Κολωνείας ἦν, ἡ δὲ τῆς Κελτζηνῆς τοῦρμα
ὑπὸ τὴν Χαλδίαν ἦν. Ἡ δὲ Μεσοποταμία τῷ τότε καιρῷ θέμα οὐκ ἦν.
Λέων δέ, ὁ φιλόχριστος καὶ ἀείμνηστος βασιλεύς, τὸν Μανουὴλ ἐκεῖνον
ἀπὸ τοῦ Τεκῆς μετὰ λόγου ἐξήγαγεν, καὶ ἐν τῇ πόλει αὐτὸν εἰσήγαγεν,
καὶ πρωτοσπαθάριον πεποίηκεν. Ἔχει δὲ ὁ αὐτὸς Μανουὴλ υἱοὺς τέσσα- 120
ρας, τὸν Παγκρατούκαν, τὸν Ἰαχνούκαν, τὸν Μουδάφαρ καὶ τὸν Ἰωάννην.
167ᵛP Καὶ τὸν μὲν Παγκρα|τούκαν ὁ βασιλεὺς ἱκανᾶτον πεποίηκεν καὶ μετὰ
τοῦτο στρατηγὸν εἰς τοὺς Βουκελλαρίους, τὸν δὲ Ἰαχνούκαν εἰς Νικόπο-
λιν στρατηγὸν ἐποίησεν, τὸν δὲ Μουδάφαρ καὶ τὸν Ἰωάννην ἐν Τραπε-
ζοῦντι δέδωκεν γῆν βασιλικήν, ἅπαντας ἀξιώμασιν τιμήσας καὶ δοὺς 125
αὐτοῖς εὐεργεσίας πολλάς. Καὶ ἐποίησεν θέμα τὴν Μεσοποταμίαν, καὶ
τὸν Ὀρέστην ἐκεῖνον τὸν Χαρσιανίτην στρατηγὸν προεβάλετο, καὶ τότε
δέδωκεν τὴν τῆς Καμάχας τοῦρμαν ὑπὸ τὸ θέμα εἶναι τῆς Μεσοποταμίας,
227Be εἶθ' | οὕτως καὶ τὴν Κελτζηνῆς τοῦρμαν ὑπὸ τὸ θέμα καὶ αὐτὴν Μεσο-
ποταμίας ἐποίησεν. Ἀρτίως δὲ ταῦτα πάντα γεγονότα ὑπὸ τὴν τῶν 130
Ῥωμαίων ἐξουσίαν, εἰς τὸ Μεσοποταμίας θέμα ἐπὶ Ῥωμανοῦ δεσπότου
168ʳP προσετέθη ἥ τε Ῥωμανόπολις καὶ τὸ | Χανζίτ.

Ἰστέον, ὅτι ἐπὶ Λέοντος, τοῦ φιλοχρίστου δεσπότου, ἡ Λάρισσα
τοῦρμα τῆς Σεβαστείας ἦν, τὸ δὲ Κυμβαλαῖος ἦν τοῦρμα τοῦ Χαρσιανοῦ,
τὸ δὲ Συμπόσιον ἦν ἐρημία πρὸς τὰ μέρη τῆς Λυκανδοῦ παρακείμενον. 135
Καὶ ἐπὶ τῆς βασιλείας Λέοντος, τοῦ φιλοχρίστου δεσπότου, Εὐστάθιος
ὁ τοῦ Ἀργυροῦ ἀπὸ τῆς ἐξορίας ἀνακληθεὶς εἰς τὸ Χαρσιανὸν στρατηγὸς
προεχειρίσθη, ὁ δὲ Μελίας εἰς τὴν Μελιτηνὴν ἔτι πρόσφυγος ἦν, καὶ
ὁ Βαασάκιος μετὰ τῶν δύο ἀδελφῶν αὐτοῦ, τοῦ τε Κρικορίκη καὶ τοῦ
Παζουνῆ, ἀλλὰ καὶ ὁ Ἰσμαὴλ ὁ Ἀρμένιος ἐκεῖνος, οἵτινες καὶ πρὸς 140
αὐτὸν καὶ τὸν προρρηθέντα Ἀργυρὸν ἔγραψαν διὰ τοῦ χρυσοβούλλου
λόγον λαβεῖν καὶ ἐξελθεῖν καὶ τὸν μὲν Βαασάκιον καὶ τοὺς ἀδελφοὺς
168ᵛP αὐτοῦ | εἰς Λάρισσαν καθεσθῆναι καὶ ὀνομασθῆναι μὲν τὸν Βαασάκιον
Λαρίσσης κλεισουριάρχην, ὅπερ καὶ γέγονεν, τὸν δὲ Ἰσμαὴλ κλεισουριάρχην
εἰς τὸ Συμπόσιον, ὃ καὶ γέγονεν, τὸν δὲ Μελίαν εἰς Εὐφράτειαν εἰς τὰ 145
Τρυπία εἰς τὴν ἐρημίαν γενέσθαι τουρμάρχην, ὅπερ καὶ ἐγένετο. Ἐξελθόν-
των δὲ τῶν Μελιτηνιατῶν καὶ τὸν Ἰσμαὴλ ἐκεῖνον ἀνελόντων, ἔμενεν τὸ

F   120 Ἔχει — 126 Μεσοποταμίαν: cf. De Them. p. 31, 1—5 (= ed. Pertusi
p. 73, IX 3—6).

50

In past times the province of Chozanon was beneath the Saracens and in like manner the province of Asmosaton also was beneath the Saracens. Chanzit and Romanopolis were frontier passes of the Melitenians. And from the mountain of Phatilanon all beyond belonged to the Saracens; Tekis belonged to Manuel. Kamacha was the extreme county of Kolonia, and the county of Keltzini was under Chaldia. Mesopotamia was not a province at that time. But Leo, the Christ-loving and ever-memorable emperor, brought the late Manuel out of Tekis upon a promise of *immunity*, and brought him to Constantinople and made him protospatharius. This same Manuel has four sons, Pankratoukas, Iachnoukas, Moudaphar and John. Pankratoukas the emperor made commander of the Hicanati and thereafter military governor of the Boukellarioi, and Iachnoukas he made military governor of Nicopolis, and to Moudaphar and John he gave crown land at Trapezus, and he honoured them all with dignities and conferred on them many benefits. And he made Mesopotamia a province and appointed the late Orestes, the Charsianite, to be military governor of it, and then gave the county of Kamacha to be under the province of Mesopotamia, and thereafter put the county of Keltzini also beneath the province of Mesopotamia. All these being now beneath the dominion of the Romans, in the time of the sovereign Romanus Romanopolis and Chanzit were added to the province of Mesopotamia.

In the time of Leo, the Christ-loving sovereign, Larissa was a county of Sebasteia, and Kymbalaios was a county of Charsianon, and Symposion was a desert adjacent to the region of Lykandos. And in the reign of Leo, the Christ-loving sovereign, Eustathius Argyrus was recalled from banishment and appointed military governor of Charsianon, while Melias was still a refugee at Melitene, as was Baasakios with his two brothers Krikorikios and Pazounis, and also the late Ismael the Armenian; these wrote to *the emperor* and to the aforesaid Argyrus, asking that they might receive a promise of *immunity* in form of a golden bull and might come out, and that Baasakios and his brothers might have their seat at Larissa and Baasakios be named frontier warden of Larissa, which was done; and that Ismael should be frontier warden of Symposion, which was done; and that Melias should be made lieutenant-general of Euphrateia, of the Trypia, *and* of the Desert, and that was done. But since the Melitenians came out and did away

---

V 113 κλησοῦραι P: κλεισοῦρα edd. || 114 Μελιτινιατῶν] *litteras* νιατ *in ras. scr.* P¹ || 115 ὑπῆρχεν edd. || 116 τούρμα P || Κελτζινῆς P || τούρμα P || 118 ἀείμνηστος: ἀοίδιμος edd. || 120 "Εχει: εἶχε *coni.* Jenkins || 121 Ἰαχνοῦκαν P || 122 ἱκανάτον P || 123 Ἰαχνοῦκαν P || 128 τούρμαν P || 129 Κελτζινῆς P || τούρμαν P || *post* αὐτὴν *add.* τῆς edd. || 130/1 ἐξουσίαν τῶν Ῥωμαίων edd. || 134 Κυμβαλαίος P   Κυμβαλαιὸς edd. || 135 Λικανδοῦ P || 138 προεχειρίσθη *coni.* Moravcsik: παρεχωρίσθη P   ἐχωρίσθη edd. || 143 τὸν μὲν Be || 144 κλησουριάρχην P || 145 Εὐφράτιαν P || 147 Μελιτινιατῶν P ||

Συμπόσιον ἔρημον. Τοῦ δὲ Βαασακίου, ὅτι προδοσίαν μελετᾷ, διαβλη-
228Be θέν|τος καὶ ἐξορισθέντος, πάλιν ὑπὸ τῆς Σεβαστείας ἡ Λάρισσα τοῦρμα
ἐγένετο, στρατηγοῦ προβληθέντος ἐκεῖσε τοῦ Ἀργυροῦ Λέοντος, τοῦ150
υἱοῦ Εὐσταθίου, τοῦ μετὰ ταῦτα μαγίστρου γεγονότος καὶ δομεστίκου
169ʳP τῶν σχολῶν. Ὁ δὲ Μελίας εἰς Εὐφράτειαν καθεζόμενος, ὁ|πότε καὶ
προεβλήθη Κωνσταντῖνος ὁ Δοὺξ εἰς τὸ Χαρσιανόν, κατῆλθεν οὗτος ὁ
προρρηθεὶς Μελίας, καὶ τὸ παλαιὸν κάστρον τὴν Λυκανδὸν ἐκράτησεν,
καὶ ἔκτισεν αὐτὸ καὶ ὠχυροποίησεν, καὶ ἐκεῖσε ἐκαθέσθη, καὶ ὠνομάσθη155
παρὰ Λέοντος, τοῦ φιλοχρίστου βασιλέως, κλεισοῦρα. Καὶ μετὰ τοῦτο
διεπέρασεν ἀπὸ Λυκανδοῦ εἰς τὸ ὄρος τῆς Τζαμανδοῦ, κἀκεῖσε τὸ νῦν
ὂν κάστρον ἔκτισεν, καὶ ὡσαύτως κἀκεῖνο κλεισοῦρα ἐκαλεῖτο. Ἐκράτησεν δὲ καὶ τὸ Συμπόσιον, ποιήσας αὐτὸ τουρμαρχᾶτον. Ἐπὶ δὲ Κωνσταντίνου, τοῦ φιλοχρίστου δεσπότου, τοῦ τὸ πρῶτον, συνούσης αὐτῷ160
καὶ Ζωῆς τῆς μητρὸς αὐτοῦ, γέγονεν ἡ Λυκανδὸς στρατηγίς, καὶ πρῶτος
Λυκανδοῦ στρατηγὸς ὠνομάσθη ὁ πατρίκιος Μελίας, δηλονότι τῷ τότε
169ᵛP καιρῷ αὐτοῦ κλεισουράρχου ἐν Λυ|κανδῷ τυγχάνοντος. Ὁ δὲ αὐτὸς
Μελίας — διά τε τὴν συνοῦσαν αὐτῷ πρὸς τὸν βασιλέα τῶν Ῥωμαίων
πίστιν καὶ τὰς πολλὰς καὶ ἀπείρους αὐτοῦ κατὰ Σαρακηνῶν ἀνδραγαθίας165
— μετέπειτα μάγιστρος ἐτιμήθη.
    Ἰστέον, ὅτι ἡ Ἄβαρα τοῦρμα ἦν ὑπὸ τὸ θέμα Σεβαστείας, ἐπὶ δὲ
Ῥωμανοῦ δεσπότου γέγονεν κλεισοῦρα.
229Be   Ἰστέον, ὅτι τύπος ἐκράτησεν παλαιὸς τὸν κατεπάνω Μαρ|δαϊτῶν
Ἀτταλείας παρὰ τοῦ βασιλέως δηλονότι προβάλλεσθαι, διὸ καὶ παρὰ170
Λέοντος, τοῦ μακαριωτάτου βασιλέως, κατεπάνω προεβλήθη Σταυράκιος
ὁ Πλατὺς ἐπονομαζόμενος, ὃς χρόνους μὲν διέπρεψεν ἱκανούς, οὐχὶ
καλῶς δὲ καὶ τὰ τέλη διέθηκεν. Τοῦ γὰρ πρωτοσπαθαρίου Εὐσταθίου
170ʳP καὶ ἀσηκρῆτις ἐν τῷ τῶν Κιβυρραιωτῶν θέματι | ἐκ προσώπου
ἀποσταλέντος, φθόνοι τινὲς ἀναμεταξὺ τούτων καὶ μάχαι γεγόνασιν· ὅ τε175
γὰρ Σταυράκιος ὁ Πλατὺς εἰς τὸν πατρίκιον Ἡμέριον καὶ λογοθέτην
τοῦ δρόμου θαρρῶν, ὡς ἅτε παρ’ αὐτοῦ εἰς τὸν βασιλέα μεσιτευθείς,
τῷ ἐκ προσώπου Εὐσταθίῳ ἀντέπιπτεν, καὶ μάλιστα ἐναντίως εἶχεν,
ἐν οἷς αὐτὸν ἑώρα ἔξω τοῦ δέοντός τι διαπραττόμενον ἢ καὶ προστάττοντα,
ὅ τε δὲ πάλιν ὁ ἐκ προσώπου Εὐστάθιος πρὸς τὸ Σταυράκιον διέκειτο180
ἐχθρωδῶς, καὶ πολλὰς κατ’ αὐτοῦ ἐπιθέσεις καὶ μηχανὰς ἐπλάττετο.
Ὅθεν αἰτίας ὁ προρρηθεὶς Εὐστάθιος κατὰ τοῦ Σταυρακίου ἀνήγαγεν,
ὡς· «Τὸ τῶν Κιβυρραιωτῶν θέμα δύο στρατηγοὺς ἔχειν οὐ δύναται,
δηλονότι ἐμὲ καὶ Σταυράκιον, τὸν κατεπάνω Μαρδαϊτῶν, ἀλλὰ γὰρ ἐμοῦ

V 152 καὶ om. V edd. || 154 Μελείας P || Λικανδὸν P || 155 ὀνομάσθη P ||
156 κλεισούρα P || 157 Λικανδοῦ P || 159 τουρμαρχάτον P || 160 τοῦ τὸ:

with that Ismael, Symposion remained deserted. And when Baasakios was accused of plotting treachery and exiled, Larissa became once more a county under Sebasteia, and Leo Argyrus, son of Eustathius, was appointed military governor there, he who afterwards became magister and commander-in-chief. But Melias had his seat at Euphrateia, and when Constantine Dux had been appointed in Charsianon, this Melias aforesaid came down and took possession of the ancient city of Lykandos and built it up and fortified it and took his seat there, and it was named a frontier pass by Leo, the Christ-loving emperor. After this he crossed from Lykandos to the mountain of Tzamandos and there built the city which is there now, and similarly this too was designated a frontier pass. And he took possession of Symposion also and made it into a county. And in the first reign of Constantine the Christ-loving sovereign, when his mother Zoë was associated with him, Lykandos became a province, and the first military governor to be nominated was the patrician Melias, who was, of course, at that time frontier warden of Lykandos. And this same Melias, both for the loyalty that was in him toward the emperor of the Romans and for his many and infinite feats of daring against the Saracens, was afterwards honoured with the rank of magister.

Abara used to be a county under the province of Sebasteia, but in the time of the sovereign Romanus it became a frontier pass.

By old-established rule the captain-general of the Mardaïtes of Attalia was appointed of course by the emperor; and therefore by Leo, the emperor, of most blessed memory, Stauracius, surnamed Platys, was appointed captain-general, who gave splendid service for several years, but disposed things ill at his ending. For when the protospatharius Eustathius, of the imperial chancellery, was sent as deputy *military governor* to the province of the Kibyrrhaiotai, certain jealousies and broils arose between them: and sometimes Stauracius Platys, who relied upon the patrician Himerius, the foreign minister, as one who had been his intermediary with the emperor, would fall foul of the deputy Eustathius and indeed flatly oppose him in matters where he saw him acting or giving orders beyond his competence; and sometimes, on the other hand, the deputy Eustathius would be at odds with Stauracius and would devise many assaults and artful accusations against him. For this reason the aforesaid Eustathius reported unfavourably on Stauracius, saying: «The province of the Kibyrrhaiotai cannot have two military governors, me, that is, and Stauracius, captain-general of the

---

τοῦτο edd.   τὸ *coni.* Bekker ‖ 161 Λιχανδὸς P ‖ 162 Λιχανδοῦ P ‖ ὀνομάσθη
P ‖ Μελίας P V edd.: Μελείας (*littera* ε *rubro atramento addita*) P⁸ *mg.* P⁸ ‖
163 κλεισουριάρχου Ba Be ‖ Λιχανδῶ P ‖ 164 Μελίας P V edd.: Μελείας
(*littera* ε *rubro atramento addita*) P⁸ *mg.* P⁸ ‖ 172 διέπρεψεν: διέτριψεν Be ‖
ἰχανούς V edd.: ἰχανῶς P ‖ 174 ἀσηκρίτης P ‖ 178 ἐκ προσώπου Ba Be:
ἐκπροσώπου P   ἐκπροσώπῳ Pˣ V ‖ 183 Κιβυρραιωτῶν edd.: Κιβυρρωτῶν P ‖
184 *post* καὶ *add.* τὸν edd. ‖

242

50

170ᵛP προ|στάττοντος καὶ διοικεῖν ἐθέλοντος, ἄλλα ποιεῖν ὁ κατεπάνω Μαρ-185
δαϊτῶν βούλεται, καὶ αὐτεξούσιος ὢν τὰ αὐτῷ δοκοῦντα μανικῶς δια-
πράττεται.» Ἀνήγαγεν δὲ καὶ ἄλλας ψευδολογίας τινάς, καὶ πολλὰς
μηχανὰς καιʼ αὐτοῦ συνερράψατο, τὰς μὲν πιθανῶς συνθείς, τὰς δὲ
συκοφαντικῶς τε καὶ μανικῶς ἀναπλασάμενος. Καὶ οὗτος δηλονότι τῷ
230Be πατρικίῳ Ἡμερίῳ καὶ λογοθέτῃ | τοῦ δρόμου θαρρῶν ταῦτα ἔγραψεν, 190
ἐπειδὴ τῷ τότε καιρῷ φίλος Εὐσταθίου μᾶλλον ἦν ὁ πατρίκιος Ἡμέριος,
ἤπερ Σταυρακίου, κἂν ὕστερον ἐχθρανθέντες ἀμφότεροι ἔχθρας ἀνάμεστοι
καὶ μανίας πλήρεις γεγόνασιν. Τὴν οὖν τοιαύτην ἀναφορὰν Εὐσταθίου
δεξάμενος ὁ βασιλεὺς καὶ τῇ αἰτήσει τοῦ πατρικίου Ἡμερίου πεισθείς,
171ʳP | δέδωκεν τὴν τοῦ τοιούτου κατεπάνω ἐξουσίαν τῷ πρωτοσπαθαρίῳ 195
Εὐσταθίῳ καὶ ἐκ προσώπου. Τοῦ δὲ μακαρίου βασιλέως τὸν βίον ἀπὸ
τῶν κάτω πρὸς τὰ ἄνω μεταλλαχότος, Ἀλέξανδρος, ὁ ἀδελφὸς αὐτοῦ,
τῆς αὐτοκράτορος ἀρχῆς ἐγκρατὴς γεγονώς, ὡς πάντας τοὺς ὑπὸ τοῦ
μακαρίου βασιλέως καὶ ἀδελφοῦ αὐτοῦ προβληθέντας ἔν τισιν ἀρχαῖς
διεδέξατο, χαιρεκάκοις καὶ κακοβούλοις ἀνδράσιν πεισθείς, οὕτω δὴ καὶ 200
τὸν προρρηθέντα Εὐστάθιον διεδέξατο, καὶ ἀντʼ αὐτοῦ πεποίηκεν ἕτερον.
Ὁ γὰρ Χασὲ ἐκεῖνος, ὁ ἐκ Σαρακηνῶν τῷ γένει ὁρμώμενος, Σαρακηνὸς
δὲ τῷ ὄντι τῇ γνώμῃ καὶ τῷ τρόπῳ καὶ τῇ λατρείᾳ διατελῶν, ὁ τοῦ
πατρικίου Δαμιανοῦ δοῦλος, ἐπεὶ πολλὴν παρρησίαν εἶχεν τῷ τότε καιρῷ
171ᵛP ὁ πρωτοσπαθάριος | οὗτος Χασὲ πρὸς τὸν κύριν Ἀλέξανδρον, τὸν βασιλέα, 205
ὡσαύτως καὶ ὁ πρωτοσπαθάριος Νικήτας, ὁ ἀδελφὸς τοῦ Χασέ, ὁ καὶ
τῶν Κιβυρραιωτῶν στρατηγὸς γεγονὼς παρὰ αὐτοῦ τοῦ κυροῦ Ἀλεξάν-
δρου βασιλέως, ὁ Νικήτας οὖν οὗτος, ὁ ἀδελφὸς τοῦ προρρηθέντος Χασέ,
τὸν βασιλέα ᾐτήσατο, ὅτι· «Ὡς ἀρχαῖόν σου φίλον εὐεργετεῖν με πρέπον
231Be ἐστίν, ἓν δὲ πρὸς τὴν βασιλείαν σου αἴτημα ἔχω, | καὶ δίκαιόν ἐστιν 210
εἰσακοῦσαί μου». Τοῦ δὲ βασιλέως διαπορουμένου καὶ ἀντερωτῶντος,
τί ἂν εἴη τοῦτο τὸ αἴτημα, καὶ ὅπερ ἐάν ἐστιν, ὑπακοῦσαι ὑποσχομένου,
ὁ προρρηθεὶς Νικήτας ᾐτήσατο, ὅτι· «Τὸν υἱόν μου, αἰτοῦμαι, ἵνα ποιήσῃ
ἡ βασιλεία σου κατεπάνω τῶν Μαρδαϊτῶν Ἀτταλείας», οὗτινος ὁ βασι-
172ʳP λεὺς τῇ αἰτήσει πεισθείς, ἐπὶ προε|λεύσεως εἰσαγαγὼν ἐπὶ τοῦ Χρυσο-215
τρικλίνου τὸν υἱὸν τοῦ πρωτοσπαθαρίου Νικήτα, τὸν σπαθαροκανδιδᾶτον
Ἀβέρκιον, προεβάλετο αὐτὸν κατεπάνω τῶν Μαρδαϊτῶν Ἀτταλείας,
καθὼς καὶ ὁ μακάριος Λέων ὁ βασιλεὺς πρότερον Σταυράκιον τὸν Πλατὺν
ἐπονομαζόμενον. Καὶ ὁ ἐξ ἀρχῆθεν παλαιὸς ἔχων τύπος, καθὼς ἐν
ἀρχαῖς εἴρηται, ὑπὸ τοῦ βασιλέως προβάλλεσθαι τὸν κατεπάνω Μαρ-220
δαϊτῶν.

V 188 συνθείς] litteras in ras. scr. P¹ ‖ 189 οὗτος (littera ω partim erasa
accentuque correcto) Pˣ V edd.: οὕτως P ‖ 191 ἐπεὶ δὴ P: Ἐπὶ δὲ edd. ‖

Mardaïtes; for while I give one set of orders and try to administer them, the captain-general of the Mardaïtes will do something different, and being his own master acts wildly as he sees fit.» He reported other false charges besides, and concocted many artful accusations against him, composing some that had an air of probability and inventing others that were calumnious and wild. These things he wrote down, relying of course upon the patrician Himerius, the foreign minister. And at that time the patrician Himerius was more friendly with Eustathius than with Stauracius, though afterwards the two fell out and became full of enmity and replete with fury. The emperor, then, received this report of Eustathius and, acceding to the request of the patrician Himerius, gave the authority of this captain-general to the protospatharius Eustathius, the deputy. But when the emperor, of blessed memory, exchanged the things below for the things above, Alexander his brother took the position of senior emperor, and as he superseded all who had been appointed to any commands by the emperor his brother, of blessed memory, being thereto persuaded by malicious and foolish men, so he superseded the aforesaid Eustathius also, and made another in his stead. For the late Chase, who sprang from the race of the Saracens and continued a true Saracen in thought and manners and religion, the slave of the patrician Damian, this protospatharius Chase had at that time great freedom of intercourse with the lord Alexander the emperor, as had also the protospatharius Niketas, the brother of Chase, who was made military governor of the Kibyrrhaiotai by this lord Alexander the emperor; this Niketas, then, brother of the aforesaid Chase, made a request to the emperor, saying: «As I am your old friend, it is fitting you should do me a favour; and I have a thing to request of your imperial majesty, and it is right that you should grant it to me.» The emperor being taken by surprise and asking in his turn what this request might be and promising to grant it whatever it was, the aforesaid Niketas made his request, saying: «I request that your imperial majesty should make my son captain-general of the Mardaïtes of Attalia»; and the emperor, acceding to his request, on the occasion of a procession introduced into the Chrysotriclinus the son of the protospatharius Niketas, the spatharocandidate Abercius, and appointed him captain-general of the Mardaïtes of Attalia, just as Leo the emperor, of blessed memory, had previously appointed Stauracius, surnamed Platys. It is the old rule, established from the beginning, as was said at the start, that the captain-general of the Mardaïtes is appointed by the emperor.

192 ἐχθρανθέντες Be: ἔχθραν θέντες P ‖ 193 Εὐσταθίου] litteras σταθ in ras. scr. P¹ ‖ 196 καὶ: τῷ edd. ‖ ἐκ προσώπου Ba Be: ἐκπροσώπω P ‖ Τοῦ δὲ μακαρίου βασιλέως Be: τῶ δὲ μακαρίω βασιλεῖ P ‖ 198 ὡς Meursius Be: ὃς P ‖ 205 κῦριν P ‖ 207 τοῦ αὐτοῦ V edd. ‖ 208 ante βασιλέως add. τοῦ edd. ‖ 213 ποιήσῃ Ba Be ποιήσῃ V Me: ποιήσει P ‖ 216 σπαθαροκανδιδάτον P ‖

50

Ἰστέον, ὅτι ἐπὶ βασιλέως τοῦ Θεοφίλου παρακοιμώμενος γέγονεν Σχολαστίκιος ὀστιάριος, ἐπὶ δὲ Μιχαήλ, υἱοῦ Θεοφίλου, παρακοιμώμενος Δαμιανὸς πατρίκιος, καὶ μετὰ τοῦτον ἐπὶ τοῦ αὐτοῦ γέγονεν παρακοιμώμενος Βασίλειος, ὁ φιλόχριστος βασιλεύς. Ἐπὶ δὲ Βασιλείου, τοῦ φιλο- 225
172ᵛP χρίστου δεσπότου, παρακοιμώμενος | οὐ γέγονεν δι' ὅλης τῆς αὐτοῦ βασιλείας. Ἐπὶ δὲ Λέοντος, τοῦ φιλοχρίστου δεσπότου, παρακοιμώμενος γέγονεν Σαμωνᾶς ὁ πατρίκιος, καὶ μετὰ τοῦτον ἐπὶ τοῦ αὐτοῦ βασιλέως γέγονεν Κωνσταντῖνος πατρίκιος. Ἐπὶ δὲ Ἀλεξάνδρου βασιλέως γέγονεν
232Be παρακοιμώμενος πατρίκιος Βαρβᾶτος, ἐπὶ δὲ | Κωνσταντίνου, τοῦ 230 φιλοχρίστου δεσπότου, γέγονεν πάλιν Κωνσταντῖνος πατρίκιος, ὁ προρρηθεὶς ἐπὶ Λέοντος δεσπότου, ἐπὶ δὲ Ῥωμανοῦ δεσπότου Θεοφάνης πατρίκιος, ἐπὶ δὲ Κωνσταντίνου πάλιν τὸ δεύτερον γέγονεν Βασίλειος πατρίκιος.

Ἰστέον, ὅτι ἐπὶ Λέοντος, τοῦ φιλοχρίστου καὶ ἀειμνήστου βασι- 235 λέως, ἦν ὁ Κτενᾶς ἐκεῖνος γέρων, κληρικὸς πάνυ πλούσιος, ὅστις ἦν καὶ δομέστικος εἰς τὴν Νέαν Ἐκκλησίαν, ὑπῆρχεν δὲ τεχνίτης εἰς τὸ ἆσμα,
173ʳP οἷος τῷ τότε καιρῷ ἕτερος οὐκ ἦν. Ὁ δὲ αὐτὸς Κτενᾶς τὸν πατρί|κιον Σαμωνᾶν ἐδυσώπησεν, τῷ τότε καιρῷ παρακοιμωμένου αὐτοῦ ὄντος, μεσιτεῦσαι αὐτὸν εἰς τὸν βασιλέα τοῦ γενέσθαι πρωτοσπαθάριον καὶ 240 φορεῖν ἐπικούτζουλον καὶ προέρχεσθαι εἰς τὸν Λαυσιακὸν καὶ καθέζεσθαι ὡς πρωτοσπαθάριον καὶ ρογεύεσθαι αὐτὸν λίτραν μίαν καὶ ὑπὲρ τῆς τοιαύτης ἀντιλήψεως δοῦναι τῷ βασιλεῖ λίτρας τεσσαράκοντα. Ὁ δὲ βασιλεὺς οὐκ ἠνέσχετο τοῦτο ποιῆσαι, λέγων τῶν ἀδυνάτων τυγχάνειν, καί· «Εἰς μεγάλην ἀδοξίαν τῆς βασιλείας μου κληρικὸν γενέσθαι πρω- 245 τοσπαθάριον.» Ἀκούσας δὲ ὁ αὐτὸς Κτενᾶς παρὰ τοῦ πατρικίου Σαμωνᾶ ταῦτα, προσέθηκεν εἰς τὰς τεσσαράκοντα λίτρας καὶ σχολαρίκια ζυγὴν μίαν, ἐκτιμηθεῖσαν λίτρας δέκα καὶ τραπεζίου ἀσήμιν ἔνζωδον διάχρυσον ἀνάγλυφον, ἐκτιμηθὲν καὶ αὐτὸ λίτρας δέκα. Καὶ δυσωπηθεὶς ὁ βασι-
173ᵛP λεὺς τῇ παρακλήσει | τοῦ πατρικίου Σαμωνᾶ καὶ παρακοιμωμένου, 250
233Be ἀνελάβετο τὰς τεσσαράκοντα τοῦ | χρυσίου λίτρας καὶ τὴν ζυγὴν τὰ σχολαρίκια καὶ τοῦ τραπεζίου τὸ ἀνάγλυφον καὶ διάχρυσον ἀσήμιν, ὡς γενέσθαι τὸ πᾶν δόμα τοῦ αὐτοῦ Κτενᾶ λίτρας ἑξήκοντα. Τότε ἐποίησεν αὐτὸν ὁ βασιλεὺς πρωτοσπαθάριον, καὶ ἐρογεύθη τῷ καιρῷ ἐκείνῳ λίτραν μίαν. Ἔζησεν δὲ ὁ αὐτὸς Κτενᾶς μετὰ τὸ τιμηθῆναι αὐτὸν πρωτοσπα- 255 θάριον ἔτη δύο καὶ ἐτελεύτησεν· ἐρογεύθη δὲ τὰ δύο ἔτη ἀνὰ λίτραν μίαν.

50

In the time of the emperor Theophilus, Scholasticius the door-keeper was chamberlain, and in the time of Michael, son of Theophilus, the patrician Damian was chamberlain and after him, in the same reign, Basil, the Christ-loving emperor, was chamberlain. In the time of Basil, the Christ-loving sovereign, there was no chamberlain during all his reign. In the time of Leo, the Christ-loving sovereign, the patrician Samonas was chamberlain, and after him, in the time of the same emperor, the patrician Constantine. In the time of Alexander the emperor, the patrician Barbatus was chamberlain; and in the time of Constantine, the Christ-loving sovereign, the patrician Constantine, mentioned before in the time of the sovereign Leo, was *chamberlain* again; and in the time of the sovereign Romanus, the patrician Theophanes; and in the second reign of Constantine, the patrician Basil.

In the time of Leo, the Christ-loving and ever-memorable emperor, lived the late Ktenas, an aged cleric of great wealth, who was precentor of the New Church and was skilled in singing as was no other at that time. This same Ktenas besought the patrician Samonas, who was at that time chamberlain, to intercede for him with the emperor so that he might be made protospatharius and wear the shirt and go in procession to the Lausiacus and take his seat as protospatharius and receive a stipend of one pound, and in respect of this remuneration might give the emperor forty pounds. But the emperor could not bring himself to do this, saying that it was out of his power, and «to the great disgrace of my imperial majesty if a cleric becomes protospatharius». On hearing this from the patrician Samonas, this same Ktenas added to the forty pounds a pair of ear-rings valued at ten pounds, and a silver table with animals on it in gold relief, also valued at ten pounds. And the emperor, besought by the request of the patrician Samonas, the chamberlain, took the forty pounds of gold and the pair of ear-rings and the table with its gold on silver relief work, so that the total gift of the same Ktenas amounted to sixty pounds. Then the emperor made him protospatharius, and he received a stipend on that occasion of one pound. After being honoured with the rank of protospatharius this same Ktenas lived two years and then died; and he received a stipend of one pound for each of the two years.

τοῦ edd. ‖ 233 πάλιν *om.* edd. ‖ δεύτερον edd.: β′ P ‖ 243 τεσσαράκοντα edd.: σαράκοντα P ‖ 244 τοῦτο Meursius Ba Be: τοῦτον P ‖ 247 τεσσαράκοντα edd.: μ′ P ‖ 248 δέκα edd.: ι′ P ‖ τραπεζίου P V Ba Be: τραπέζιον Pᵞ ‖ ἀσίμην P ‖ ἔνζωδον Be: ἔνζοδον (*littera* ζ *in ras. scripta*) P¹ Ba   ἔνδοξον V ‖ 249 δέκα edd.: ι′ P ‖ 251 τεσσαράκοντα edd.: μ′ P ‖ 252 ἀσίμην P ‖ 253 λίτρας V edd.: λίτραι P ‖ ἑξήκοντα edd.: ξ′ P ‖ 256 δύο¹ edd.: β′ P.

51

51. Περὶ τοῦ, τίνι τρόπῳ γέγονεν τὸ βασιλικὸν δρομώνιον, καὶ περὶ τῶν πρωτοκαράβων τοῦ αὐτοῦ δρομωνίου, καὶ ὅσα περὶ τοῦ πρωτοσπαθαρίου τῆς φιάλης.

Ἰστέον, ὅτι μέχρι τῆς βασιλείας Λέοντος, τοῦ ἀοιδίμου καὶ σοφω- 5
174rP τάτου βασιλέως, οὐκ ἦν βασιλικὸν δρομώνιον, | ἐν ᾧ εἰσήρχετο ὁ βασιλεύς,
ἀλλ' εἰς ῥούσιον ἀγράριον εἰσήρχετο, πλὴν ἐπὶ Βασιλείου, τοῦ φιλοχρίστου
δεσπότου, ὅτε ἀπῆλθεν ὁ αὐτὸς βασιλεὺς εἰς τὰ θέρμα τῆς Προύσης,
καὶ πάλιν ὅτε ἀπῆλθεν θεάσαθαι τὸ γεφύριον τοῦ Ῥηγίου, δηλονότι τῇ
κελεύσει αὐτοῦ καὶ προνοίᾳ κτιζόμενον, εἰς δρομώνιον εἰσῆλθεν, καὶ 10
ἕτερον δρομώνιον ἠκολούθει ὄπισθεν. Οἱ δὲ ἐν αὐτῷ εἰσελθόντες ἐλάται
ὑπῆρχον ἀπὸ τοῦ βασιλικοῦ ἀγραρίου καὶ ἀπὸ τῶν Στενιτῶν πλωΐμων.
234Be Τὸ γὰρ παλαιὸν εἶχεν καὶ τὸ Στε|νὸν χελάνδια βασιλικοπλώϊμα μέχρι
τῶν δέκα. Ἐπεὶ δὲ ὁ μακάριος βασιλεὺς ὅλα τὰ πλείονα αὐτοῦ μεταστασίματα εἰς τὰς Πηγὰς ἐποίει διὰ τὸ καὶ ὑπ' αὐτοῦ κτισθῆναι τὰ τοιαῦτα 15
174vP παλάτια, ὁμοίως καὶ | εἰς τὸ Ἕβδομον καὶ εἰς τὴν Ἱερείαν καὶ εἰς τὸν
Βρύαν, εἰσήρχετο εἰς ἀγράριον κατὰ τὸν παλαιὸν τύπον. Ὅτε δὲ εἰς
μακρότερον ἀπῄει πρόκενσον, οἷον εἰς τὰ θέρμα τῆς Προύσης καὶ εἰς
ἐπιτήρησιν τοῦ Ῥηγίου τῆς γεφύρας, εἰσῄει, καθὼς προείρηται, εἰς
δρομώνιον, καὶ ἠκολούθει ἕτερον δρομώνιον διὰ τὸ καὶ πλείονας ἄρχοντας 20
εἰσέρχεσθαι μετὰ τοῦ βασιλέως καὶ τοὺς ὑπολοίπους εἰς τὸ δεύτερον
δρομώνιον. Ὁ δὲ ἀοίδιμος καὶ σοφώτατος Λέων ὁ βασιλεὺς φιλοτιμό-
τερόν πως πρὸς τοὺς μαγίστρους καὶ πατρικίους καὶ οἰκείους συγκλητι-
κοὺς διακείμενος καὶ θέλων ἀεὶ τούτοις συγχαίρεσθαι, λογισάμενος μὴ
ἐπαρκεῖν εἰς ὑποδοχὴν πλειόνων ἀρχόντων τὸ ἀγράριον, ἐποίησεν δρο- 25
175rP μώνιον, καὶ δὴ ἀπαύστως εἰσήρχετο ἐν αὐτῷ, ὅπου δ' ἂν | ἐβούλετο
ἀπελθεῖν. Συνήρχοντο δὲ μετ' αὐτοῦ, οἵους ἂν ἐβούλετο τῶν ἀρχόντων,
ἀπό τε μαγίστρων καὶ πατρικίων. Κατὰ τύπον γὰρ ἐν τῷ ἀγραρίῳ οὐδεὶς
ἕτερος εἰσήρχετο μετὰ τοῦ βασιλέως, εἰ μὴ ὁ δρουγγάριος τῆς βίγλης
καὶ ὁ δρουγγάριος τοῦ πλωΐμου καὶ ὁ λογοθέτης τοῦ δρόμου καὶ ὁ 30
ἑταιρειάρχης καὶ ὁ μυστικὸς καὶ ὁ τῶν δεήσεων, καὶ ὅτε παρῆν ἐν τῇ
πόλει, καὶ ὁ δομέστικος τῶν σχολῶν καὶ ὁ παρακοιμώμενος καὶ ὁ πρωτο-
235Be βεστιάριος καὶ ἐκ τῶν κοιτωνιτῶν, οὓς ἂν ἐκέλευσεν ὁ | βασιλεύς. Δι'
οὖν τὸν τρόπον τοῦτον ἐποίησεν Λέων, ὁ ἀοίδιμος καὶ σοφώτατος βασιλεύς, τὸ δρομώνιον, καὶ μετά τινα καιρὸν ἐποίησεν καὶ ἕτερον δρομώνιον, 35
ὃ καὶ δεύτερον προσηγορεύθη καὶ ἀκόλουθος ὠνομάσθη. Καὶ γὰρ εἰς

V   **51.** 3 δρομωνίου edd.: δρόμωνος P ‖ 8 ἀπῆλθεν corr. Jenkins: ἐπῆλθεν
P edd. ‖ 9 Ῥιγίου P ‖ 10 κτιζόμενον edd.: κτιζομένου P ‖ 12 Στενίτων P ‖
13 καὶ om. edd. ‖ βασιλικοπλώϊμα: βασιλικὰ πλώϊμα edd. ‖ 14 δέκα edd.:

51

51. Why the imperial galley came to be made, and of the steersmen of this same galley, and all about the protospatharius of the basin.

Until the reign of Leo, the glorious and most wise emperor, there was no imperial galley for the emperor to embark in, but he used to embark in a scarlet barge; except that, in the time of the Christ-loving sovereign Basil, when this same emperor visited the hot baths of Prousa, and again when he went to inspect the bridge of Rhegion that was, of course, being built by his mandate and providence, he embarked in a galley, and another galley followed behind. And the rowers who embarked in it were taken from the imperial barge and from the sailors of the Stenon. For of old the Stenon too had up to ten ships of war of the imperial navy. But since the emperor, of blessed memory, on most of his progresses always went to Pegai because of the palace he had built there, and in like manner to Hebdomon and to Hiereia and to Bryas, he used to embark in a barge, according to the old rule. But when he was going on a longer progress, to the hot baths of Prousa, for example, and to inspect the bridge of Rhegion, he would embark, as was said above, in a galley, and another galley would follow, so that more nobles could embark with the emperor, and the rest in the second galley. But the glorious and most wise Leo, the emperor, who was rather more hospitably inclined towards magisters and patricians and familiars of senatorial rank, and who always wished them to share his pleasure in this, reckoned that the barge was inadequate for the reception of a larger number of nobles, and constructed a galley, and would invariably embark in it wherever he desired to go. And there would go with him whomsoever he might desire of the nobles, both of magisters and patricians. For in the barge it used to be the rule that none other embarked with the emperor except the colonel of the watch and the lord admiral and the foreign minister and the commander of the company and the private secretary and the secretary of the pleas and, when he was present in Constantinople, the commander-in-chief also, and the chamberlain and the master of the wardrobe and of the gentlemen of the bed-chamber whomsoever the emperor commanded. For this reason, then, Leo, the glorious and most wise emperor, constructed the galley, and, some while after, he constructed another galley as well, which was known as the 'second' and christened 'Attaché'. For this emperor, of blessed memory, would go on distant

---

ι' P || 14/5 μεταστασήματα P || 16 Ἱερείαν Moravcsik: Ἱερίαν Ba Be Εἱρίαν P Me ᾽Ηρία Meursius || 16 τὸν: τὴν edd. || 17 Βροίαν P || post εἰς¹ add. τὸ edd. || 19 γέφυρας P || 20 διὰ τὸ coni. Bekker: διότι P edd. || 21 δεύτερον edd.: β' P || 24 τούτοις coni. Jenkins; τοῦτο P edd. || 31 παρῆν] παρεῖν (littera ει in ras. scripta) P¹ || 33 κοιτωνίτων P edd. || 36 δεύτερον edd.: β' P || ἀκολούθως V edd. || ὀνομάσθη P ||

248

51

175ʳP μακρόκενσα | ἀπήει ὁ μακάριος οὗτος βασιλεύς, οἷον εἰς Νικομήδειαν,
εἰς τὸν Ὄλυμπον, εἰς τὰ Πύθια, καὶ διὰ τοῦτο ἐπετηδεύσατο τὰ δύο
δρομώνια εἰς ὑπηρεσίαν καὶ ἀνάπαυσιν αὐτοῦ τε καὶ τῶν ἀρχόντων
αὐτοῦ. Πολλάκις γὰρ ἐξερχομένου αὐτοῦ εἰς τὰ πλησίον πρόκενσα, 40
τὴν μίαν οὐσίαν κατελίμπανεν εἰς τὸν ἱππόδρομον πρὸς φύλαξιν τοῦ
παλατίου διὰ τὸ τὸ τάγμα τοῦ ἀριθμοῦ κατὰ τὸν ἐπικρατήσαντα παλαιὸν
τύπον μετὰ τοῦ δομεστίκου τῶν σχολῶν ταξιδεύειν, καὶ ἐναπομένοντες
εἰς τὸν ἱππόδρομον ⟨οὐ⟩ συνεξιοῦσι κατὰ τύπον τοῖς βασιλεῦσιν εἰς
τὰ πρόκενσα.   45
      Ὅτι ἐξ ἀρχῆς καὶ ἄνωθεν βασιλικὸν ὀφφίκιον ἦν τῷ πρωτο-
σπαθαρίῳ τῆς φιάλης· οὗτος δὲ ὁ πρωτοσπαθάριος τῆς φιάλης ἐπεκράτει
176ʳP καὶ εἶχεν ὑπ' αὐτὸν πάντας τοὺς ἐλάτας | τῶν βασιλικῶν ἀγραρίων,
ῥουσίων τε καὶ μαύρων, ἄνευ τῶν ἀγραρίων τῆς αὐγούστης· τὰ γὰρ
ἀγράρια τῆς αὐγούστης, τά τε ῥούσια καὶ μαῦρα, ἐπεκράτει καὶ ἐξου- 50
σίαζεν ὁ τῆς τραπέζης τῆς αὐγούστης. Ἐπὶ δὲ τῆς βασιλείας Λέοντος,
τοῦ ἀοιδίμου καὶ σοφωτάτου βασιλέως, καινουργηθέντα τὰ δρομώνια
236Be κελεύσει βασιλικῇ, εἶχεν ὁ αὐτὸς πρωτοσπαθάριος τῆς φιάλης | καὶ τῶν
τοιούτων δρομωνίων τοὺς ἐλάτας ὑπὸ τὴν ἑαυτοῦ ἐξουσίαν. Ὁ οὖν προρρηθεὶς πρωτοσπαθάριος τῆς φιάλης καθ' ἑκάστην ἡμέραν καὶ καθ' 55
ἑκάστην δείλην ἀπὸ παλαιοῦ τύπου κατήρχετο καὶ ἐκαθέζετο ἐν τῇ
φιάλῃ (διὰ τοῦτο γὰρ καὶ ἐλέγετο πρωτοσπαθάριος τῆς φιάλης), καὶ
τὰς ἀναμεταξὺ δίκας τῶν ἐλατῶν τῶν τε ἀγραρίων καὶ τῶν δρομωνίων,
176ᵛP τῶν παρ' αὐτοῦ ἐξουσιαζομένων, ἔκρινεν καὶ κατὰ τὸ δί|καιον ἐδίκαζέν
τε καὶ ἐδιοίκει. Καὶ ἡνίκα παρὰ τὸ δέον εὕρισκέν τινα ἢ ἐργαζόμενον 60
ἢ τινα ἀδικοῦντα ἢ εἰς τὴν ἰδίαν δουλείαν βαγεύοντα, τοῦτον διὰ μαγγλα-
βίων σφοδρῶν ἐπεξήρχετο. Καὶ καθ' ὃν εἴρηται τρόπον, πάντες οἱ τῶν
δρομωνίων ἐλάται καὶ οἱ τῶν τοῦ βασιλέως ἀγραρίων, τῶν τε ῥουσίων
καὶ τῶν μαύρων, ὑπὸ τὴν χεῖρα καὶ τὴν ἐφορείαν ὑπῆρχον τοῦ πρωτοσπαθαρίου τῆς φιάλης. Τὰ δὲ τῆς αὐγούστης ἀγράρια, τά τε ῥούσια καὶ 65
μαῦρα, ὑπὸ τὴν χεῖρα καὶ τὴν ἐφορείαν ὑπῆρχον τοῦ τῆς τραπέζης τῆς
αὐγούστης, δηλονότι τὸν λόγον τῶν ἀγραρίων τούτων ποιοῦντος τοῦ
τῆς τραπέζης οὐχὶ πρὸς τὴν αὐγοῦσταν, ἀλλὰ πρὸς τὸν βασιλέα. Ἐπὶ
δὲ Λέοντος, τοῦ ἀοιδίμου καὶ σοφωτάτου βασιλέως, ἦν πρωτοσπαθάριος
177ʳP τῆς | φιάλης ὁ πρωτοσπαθάριος Ἰωάννης, οὗ τὸ ἐπίκλην ὁ Θαλάσσων, 70
καὶ μετ' αὐτὸν γέγονεν ὁ πρωτοσπαθάριος ὁ Ποδάρων, καὶ μετ' ἐκεῖνον
ὁ πρωτοσπαθάριος Λέων ὁ Ἀρμένης, ὁ τοῦ πρωτοσπαθαρίου Ἀρσενίου
237Be καὶ μαγγλαβίτου πατήρ. Οὗτοι δέ, ὅ τε ὁ πρωτο|σπαθάριος ὁ Ποδάρων
καὶ ὁ πρωτοσπαθάριος Λέων ὁ Ἀρμένης, πρωτελάται γεγόνασιν τοῦ
πατρικίου Νάσαρ καὶ δρουγγαρίου τοῦ πλωΐμου, καὶ ἐπὶ Βασιλείου, 75

51

progresses, to Nicomedeia, for instance, to Olympus, to Pythia, and therefore he had the two galleys specially made for the service and recreation of himself and his nobles. For when he went out on a short progress, he used often to leave one of the complements behind in the hippodrome to guard the palace; because the brigade of the Arithmos, according to the old rule which has grown into force, goes out on active service under the commander-in-chief and they, *this complement*, stay behind in the hippodrome and do *not* go out on progress with the emperors in the ordinary way.

From time immemorial the protospatharius of the basin has been an imperial appointment; and this protospatharius of the basin used to control and have beneath him all the oarsmen of the imperial barges, both scarlet and black, except for the barges of the Augusta: for the barges of the Augusta, both scarlet and black, were controlled by and under the authority of the master of the Augusta's table. In the reign of Leo, the glorious and most wise emperor, when the new galleys were constructed by imperial mandate, this same protospatharius of the basin had beneath his authority the oarsmen of these galleys also. Now, the aforesaid protospatharius of the basin would by ancient rule go down every day in the afternoon and take his seat in the basin (for which reason he was called the protospatharius of the basin), and would judge cases arising between the oarsmen, both of the barges and of the galleys, over whom he had authority, and would give sentence and administer according to the law. And whenever he found anyone acting beyond his competence or wronging another or remiss in his own work, he would punish him with a sound cudgelling. And, as has been said, all the oarsmen of the galleys and of the emperor's barges, both scarlet and black, were beneath the hand and the supervision of the protospatharius of the basin. But the barges of the Augusta, both scarlet and black, were beneath the hand and the supervision of the master of the Augusta's table, though of course the master of the table accounted for these barges not to the Augusta, but to the emperor. In the time of Leo, the glorious and most wise emperor, the protospatharius John, surnamed Thalasson, was protospatharius of the basin, and after him the protospatharius Podaron, and after him the protospatharius Leo Armenius, father of the protospatharius Arsenius, the lictor. These, the protospatharius Podaron and the protospatharius Leo Armenius, had been chief oarsmen of the patrician Nasar, the lord admiral, and in the time of Basil, the Christ-loving sovereign, were

---

V 42 τὸ² om. edd. ‖ 42/3 κατὰ τὸν ἐπικρατήσαντα παλαιὸν τύπον: κατὰ τὸν παλαιὸν τύπον ἐπεκράτησαν V ‖ 43 ἐναπομένοντες (*etiam* V¹): ἐναπομένοντος V Me ‖ 44 οὐ *add.* Moravcsik ‖ 56 δείλην V edd.: δήλης P ‖ 58 ἐλάτων P ‖ 60 ἢ ⟨μὴ⟩ ἐργαζόμενον *coni.* Kyriakides ‖ 61/2 μαγλαβίων P ‖ 62 ἐπεξήρχετο F Be: ὑπεξήρχετο P ‖ καθ' ὃν edd.: καθὰ P ‖ 63 τε om. edd. ‖ 64 ἐφορίαν P: θεωρίαν edd. ‖ 66 χεῖρα F edd.: χεῖραν P ‖ ἐφορίαν P ‖ 68 αὐγούσταν P ‖ 70 πρωτοσπαθάριος om. edd. ‖ 73 ὁ³ om. Ba Be ‖ 74 πρωτοσπαθάριος om. Ba Be ‖

51

τοῦ φιλοχρίστου δεσπότου, ἀνῆξαν ἀπὸ τοῦ πλωΐμου, καὶ γεγόνασιν
πρωτελάται τοῦ ἀγραρίου τοῦ βασιλέως, ἐπὶ δὲ τῆς βασιλείας Λέοντος,
τοῦ ἀοιδίμου καὶ σοφωτάτου βασιλέως, ἡνίκα καὶ τὰ δρομώνια ἐποίησεν,
διὰ τὴν ἀνδρείαν αὐτῶν καὶ τὴν ἐμπειρίαν τῆς θαλάσσης ἐποίησεν αὐτοὺς
πρωτοκαράβους. Καὶ περιστάσεως γενομένης, εἰσήγαγεν ὁ βασιλεὺς 80
177ᵛᴾ τῶν δύο δρομωνίων τοὺς ἐλάτας μετὰ τῶν δύο πρωτοκα|ράβων τοῦ
πρώτου δρομωνίου εἰς χελάνδια πλώϊμα, δοὺς αὐτοῖς ἐξόπλισιν πολλὴν
καὶ ἀναγκαίαν, οἷον σκουτάρια, δόρκας, κλιβάνια κάλλιστα καὶ ἄλλα,
ὅσα ἐπιδέονται πλώϊμοι στρατιῶται ἐπιφέρεσθαι, καὶ ἀνελάβετο αὐτοὺς
ὁ πατρίκιος Εὐστάθιος καὶ δρουγγάριος τοῦ πλωΐμου μετὰ τοῦ βασιλικοῦ 85
στόλου, καὶ ἀπῄει κατὰ τῶν ἐναντίων. Τοῦτο δὲ ὅλον ἐποίησεν ὁ βασιλεὺς
διὰ τὸ ἀποβλέπειν τὸν πατρίκιον Εὐστάθιον καὶ δρουγγάριον τοῦ πλωΐμου
πρὸς πόλεμον τῶν ἐναντίων. Καὶ ἀντ' ἐκείνων ἐκυβέρνα τὸ βασιλικὸν
δρομώνιον Μιχαὴλ ὁ γέρων καὶ ⟨Μιχαὴλ⟩ ὁ συνετὸς ἐκεῖνος, ὄντων αὐτῶν
τῷ τότε καιρῷ πρωτελατῶν. Οἱ δὲ ἐλαύνοντες εἰς τὰ δρομώνια ἕως τῆς 90
178ʳᴾ ἐλεύσεως τῶν βασιλικῶν ἐλατῶν ὑπῆρχον Στενῖται ἐκ τῶν | οὐσιῶν
τοῦ Στενοῦ. Ὅτε δὲ ὑπέστρεψαν ἐκ τοῦ ταξιδίου, πάλιν ἦσαν εἰς τὴν
ἰδίαν δουλείαν, καθὼς καὶ προϋπῆρχον. Τότε οἰονεὶ φιλοτιμούμενος
ὁ βασιλεὺς τὸν πρωτοσπαθάριον τὸν Ποδάρωνα διὰ τὸ ἀνδραγαθῆσαι
238Bₑ αὐτὸν καὶ εὐδοκιμῆσαι | ὑπὲρ πάντας εἰς τὸν πόλεμον καὶ μαρτυρηθῆναι 95
καὶ παρὰ τοῦ πατρικίου Εὐσταθίου καὶ δρουγγαρίου τοῦ πλωΐμου
ἕτερον τοιοῦτον μὴ εἶναι εἰς τὸ πλώϊμον ἐπί τε ἀνδρείᾳ καὶ διεγέρσει
καὶ ταῖς λοιπαῖς ἀρεταῖς καὶ μάλιστα τῇ πρὸς τὸν βασιλέα εὐνοίᾳ καὶ
ὀρθῇ πίστει, δέδωκεν αὐτῷ καὶ τὴν ἐξουσίαν τοῦ πρωτοσπαθαρίου τῆς
φιάλης. Διὰ δὲ τὸ εἶναι αὐτὸν ἀγράμματον προστάξει τοῦ βασιλέως 100
κατήρχετο κριτὴς ἀπὸ τοῦ ἱπποδρόμου, καὶ συνεκαθέζετο μετὰ αὐτοῦ
178ᵛᴾ ἐν τῇ φιάλῃ, καὶ ἔκρινεν τοὺς ἐλάτας. | Τὰ δὲ αὐγουστιατικὰ ἀγράρια,
καθὼς προείρηται, ἐπεκράτει ὁ τῆς τραπέζης τῆς αὐγούστης. Μετὰ
τοῦτο δὲ προεβάλετο ὁ βασιλεὺς τόν τε Ποδάρωνα καὶ τὸν Λέοντα τὸν
Ἀρμένην τοποτηρητὰς τοῦ βασιλικοῦ πλωΐμου, πρωτοκαράβους δὲ τοῦ 105
δρομωνίου αὐτοῦ προεβάλετο τὸν Μιχαὴλ ἐκεῖνον τὸν γέροντα, πρωτελά-
την τῷ τότε καιρῷ τοῦ δρομωνίου τυγχάνοντα, δευτεροελάτην δὲ γεγονότα τοῦ ἀγραρίου Βασιλείου, τοῦ φιλοχρίστου δεσπότου, καὶ τὸν
ἕτερον Μιχαήλ, οὗ τὸ ἐπίκλην ὁ Βαρκαλᾶς, ὅστις ἦν πρότερον εἰς τὸ
πλώϊμον πρωτελάτης τοῦ δρουγγαρίου Εὐσταθίου καὶ πατρικίου, ὅτε 110
ἐπέρασεν τοὺς Τούρκους, καὶ κατεπολέμησεν τὸν Συμεών, τὸν ἄρχοντα
Βουλγαρίας. Οὗτος οὖν ὁ Συμεών, ὁ ἄρχων Βουλγαρίας, μαθὼν τὴν τοῦ
179ʳᴾ πλω|ΐμου πρὸς τὸν ποταμὸν ἄφιξιν, καὶ ὅτι μέλλει τὸ πλώϊμον τοὺς
Τούρκους κατ' αὐτοῦ περάσαι, ἐποίησεν λέσας, ἤτοι πλοκοὺς ἰσχυροὺς
πάνυ καὶ στερεμνίους, ὥστε μὴ δύνασθαι τοὺς Τούρκους ἀντιπερνᾶν, 115

51

promoted from the navy and became chief oarsmen of the barge of the emperor; and in the reign of Leo, the glorious and most wise emperor, when he constructed the galleys, he made them steersmen for their bravery and seamanship. And when a crisis arose, the emperor seconded the oarsmen of the two galleys, together with the two steersmen of the first galley, to ships of war of the navy, giving them much needful equipment, such as shields, leather targes, very fine coats of mail and everything else that naval personnel require to take with them; and the patrician Eustathius, the lord admiral, took them with the imperial fleet and went off against the enemy. All this the emperor did because the patrician Eustathius, the lord admiral, was intending to engage the enemy. And in their stead the imperial galley was steered by Michael the elder and the late *Michael* the clever, who were at that time chief oarsmen. And pending the return of the imperial oarsmen, those who rowed the galleys were Stenites from the complements of the Stenon. But when they returned from the campaign, they resumed the same employment that they had been in before. Then the emperor, to reward, as it were, the protospatharius Podaron because of the bravery he had shown and because he had approved himself above all others in the battle and had received a personal testimonial from the patrician Eustathius, the lord admiral, that there was in the navy none other like him for bravery and energy and the other virtues, and particularly for affection and upright loyalty toward the emperor, gave to him the authority of the protospatharius of the basin. But because he was illiterate, by order of the emperor a judge from the hippodrome used to go down and take his seat with him in the basin and judge the oarsmen. But the barges of the Augusta, as has been said before, were in the control of the master of the Augusta's table. After this, the emperor appointed Podaron and Leo Armenius to be vice-admirals of the imperial navy, and as steersmen of his galley he appointed the late Michael the elder, who was at that time chief oarsmen of the galley, and had been second oarsman of the barge of Basil, the Christ-loving sovereign, and the other Michael, surnamed Barkalas, who had previously served in the navy as chief oarsmen of the lord admiral, the patrician Eustathius, when he carried the Turks across and defeated Symeon, prince of Bulgaria. Now this Symeon, prince of Bulgaria, on learning that the navy had arrived in the river, and that the navy was about to carry over the Turks against him, constructed mantlets or wicker fencing, very strong and tough, so that the Turks might not be able to cross over, and by this device the Turks were

---

V 88 τῶν P¹ V edd.: τὸν P ‖ 89 *post* καὶ *alterum* Μιχαὴλ *addendum coniecit* Moravcsik ‖ ὁ² *om.* V edd. ‖ αὐτῶν: αὐτῷ V Me ‖ 90 πρωτελάτων P ‖ 91 ἐλάτων P ‖ Στενεῖται P ‖ 97 πλώϊμον] *litteras* πλω *in ras. scr.* P¹ ‖ 98 *post* τῇ *add.* τὸν P *del.* P¹ ‖ 100 δὲ: τε edd. ‖ 101 ἀπὸ: ἐπὶ *coni.* Zachariä v. Lingenthal ‖ 102 αὐγουστιακὰ V edd. ‖ 106 δρομωνίου] *litteras* μων *in ras. scr.* P¹ ‖ 107 τοῦ *om.* edd. ‖ 109 ὁ *om.* edd. ‖ 111 κατεπολέμισεν P ‖ 114 πλοκὰς V edd. ‖ ‖ ἰσχυρὰς Ba Be ‖ 115 ἀντιπερᾶν V edd. ‖

252

51

239Be | δι' ἣν ἐπίνοιαν καὶ ἐκωλύθησαν οἱ Τοῦρκοι τὸ πρῶτον περᾶσαι. Ὁ οὖν
προρρηθεὶς Μιχαὴλ ὁ Βαρκαλᾶς μετὰ καὶ ἄλλων δύο πλωΐμων ἀναλαβόμενοι τὰ σκουτάρια καὶ σπαθία αὐτῶν, ἀνδρείῳ καὶ ῥωμαλέῳ ὁρμήματι
ἐκπηδήσαντες τοῦ χελανδίου, κατέκοψαν τὰς λέσας, ἤτοι τοὺς πλοκούς,
καὶ ἤνοιξαν τὸν πόρον τοὺς Τούρκους. Τοῦτον οὖν τὸν Βαρκαλᾶν οἱ 120
Τοῦρκοι ἰδόντες καὶ τὸ ἀνδρεῖον αὐτοῦ ὑπερθαυμάσαντες, ὅτι μόνος τῶν
δύο προπορευόμενος πλωΐμων πρῶτος κατέκοψεν τὸν πλοκόν, θαυμά-
179ᵛP σαντες εἶπον, ὅτι | τοῦτον ἔπρεπεν ὀνομάζεσθαι πατρίκιον καὶ εἶναι
κεφαλὴν τοῦ πλωΐμου. Τὴν οὖν τοῦ Βαρκαλοῦ ἀνδρειότητα ἀκούσας ὁ
βασιλεύς, ἐποίησεν αὐτὸν δευτεροελάτην εἰς τὸ βασιλικὸν δρομώνιον. 125
Εἶθ' οὕτως τοῦ Ποδάρωνος καὶ τοῦ Λέοντος γενομένων τοποτηρητῶν,
προεβλήθη ὁ Μιχαὴλ ὁ γέρων καὶ οὗτος ὁ Βαρκαλᾶς πρωτοκάραβοι τοῦ
δρομωνίου.

Ὅτι ὁ προρρηθεὶς Λέων ὁ Ἀρμένης, ὁ πατὴρ τοῦ πρωτοσπαθαρίου
Ἀρσενίου καὶ μαγγλαβίτου, τοῦ τελευτήσαντος, τελευτᾷ τοποτηρητὴς 130
ὢν εἰς τὸ πλώϊμον, ὁ δὲ πρωτοσπαθάριος ὁ Ποδάρων μετά τινας χρόνους
προεβλήθη στρατηγὸς ἐν τῷ θέματι τῶν Κιβυρραιωτῶν.

Ὅτι τοῦ Ποδάρωνος γεγονότος τοποτηρητοῦ, προεβλήθη πρωτοσπαθάριος τῆς φιάλης ὁ πρωτοσπαθάριος Θεοφύλακτος ὁ Βιμβιλίδης,
180ʳP ἀνεψιὸς τυγχάνων τοῦ | πρωτοσπαθαρίου Ἰωάννου, οὗ τὸ ἐπίκλην 135
240Be Θαλάσσων, καὶ διήρκεσεν ἐν ἔτεσί τισιν | τῆς πρώτης αὐτοκρατορίας
Κωνσταντίνου, τοῦ πορφυρογεννήτου καὶ φιλοχρίστου δεσπότου. Τούτου
οὖν τελευτήσαντος, — διὰ τὸ ὑπεργηρᾶσαι τὸν προρρηθέντα Μιχαὴλ τὸν
γέροντα καὶ ἐν πολλῶν ἐτῶν περιόδοις διατρίψαι ἐν τῇ τοῦ πρωτοκαρά-
βου ὑπουργίᾳ — ἐτιμήθη τῇ τοῦ πρωτοσπαθαρίου ἀξίᾳ καὶ προεβλήθη 140
καὶ πρωτοσπαθάριος τῆς φιάλης. Καὶ εἰσερχομένου τοῦ βασιλέως ἐν
τῇ φιάλῃ ἐν τῷ δρομωνίῳ καὶ ἀπιόντος εἴτε ἐν προκένσῳ, εἴτε ἀλλαχοῦ,
ἵστατο ὁ καλὸς ἐκεῖνος γέρων καὶ ἀείμνηστος κατὰ τὴν τῆς θαλάσσης
ἐμπειρίαν μέσον τοῦ δρομωνίου, προθυμοποιῶν καὶ προτρεπόμενος τοὺς
180ᵛP τοῦ δρομωνίου ἐλάτας γενναιότερον καὶ ἀνδρικώτερον ἐλαύνειν τε | καὶ 145
κωπηλατεῖν, ἅμα δὲ καὶ τοῖς τότε πρωτοκαράβοις ὑποτιθέμενος κατὰ
τὴν δυσκρασίαν καὶ πνεῦσιν τῶν ἀνέμων τὴν βασίλειον ναῦν πηδαλιουχεῖν
τε καὶ κυβερνᾶν. Τούτου οὖν τελευτήσαντος, — διὰ τὸ νήπιον τυγχάνειν
τὸν βασιλέα καὶ τὸ ἀδιάκριτον τοῦ πατρικίου Κωνσταντίνου καὶ παρακοιμωμένου — γέγονεν ὁ Θεόδοτος ἐκεῖνος πρωτοκάραβος, τῷ τότε 150
καιρῷ πρωτελάτης ὤν, τιμηθεὶς κατὰ διαφόρους καιροὺς κανδιδᾶτος,
στράτωρ, σπαθάριος, σπαθαροκανδιδᾶτος καὶ μετὰ ταῦτα πρωτοσπαθάριος καὶ πρωτοσπαθάριος τῆς φιάλης, ὃς ἦν γαμβρὸς τοῦ προρρηθέντος Μιχαήλ, τοῦ γέροντος. Οὐδὲ γὰρ ἀπὸ παλαιοῦ τύπου ποτὲ ἐγεγό-
νει ἢ ἐτιμήθη πρωτοκάραβος τοῦ βασιλέως πρωτοσπαθάριος, ἀλλ' οὐδὲ 155

at first prevented from crossing. So the aforesaid Michael Barkalas and two other sailors took up their shields and swords, and leaping down from the warship with a brave and powerful rush, cut down the mantlets or wicker fences and opened the passage for the Turks. The Turks, who watched this Barkalas and exceedingly admired his bravery because he, by himself, advancing in front of the two sailors, was first to cut down the fencing, said in their admiration that this man ought to be named patrician and be head of the navy. So the emperor, on hearing of the bravery of Barkalas, made him second oarsman in the imperial galley. Thereafter, when Podaron and Leo became vice-admirals, Michael the elder and this Barkalas were appointed steersmen of the galley.

The aforesaid Leo Armenius, father of the late protospatharius Arsenius, the lictor, died a vice-admiral of the navy; but the protospatharius Podaron was after some years appointed military governor in the province of the Kibyrrhaiotai.

When Podaron became vice-admiral, the protospatharius Theophylact Bimbilidis was appointed protospatharius of the basin, who was nephew of the protospatharius John, surnamed Thalasson, and he lasted during a few years of the first reign of Constantine the Porphyrogenitus, the Christ-loving sovereign. On his death, since Michael the elder aforesaid was grown very old indeed and had given many long years of service as steersman, he was honoured with the rank of protospatharius and was also appointed protospatharius of the basin. And when the emperor embarked on the galley in the basin and set out either upon a progress or somewhere else, that good old man, ever memorable for his seamanship, would take his stand amidships of the galley, inspiring und urging the oarsmen of the galley to pull and row more bravely and manfully, and at the same time instructing the steersmen of the day how to manage the rudders and steer the imperial vessel when the winds were blowing distemperately. Well, he died; and, owing to the infancy of the emperor and the indiscretion of the patrician and chamberlain Constantine, the late Theodotus, at that time chief oarsmen, was made steersman, and was at sundry times honoured with the ranks of candidate, strator, spatharius, spatharocandidate, and afterwards protospatharius and protospatharius of the basin; he was son-in-law of the aforesaid Michael the elder. For by ancient rule a steersman of the emperor had never been made, or honoured with the

241Be
181ʳP σπαθαροκανδιδᾶτος, ἀλλ' | ἢ κανδιδᾶτος ἢ στράτωρ | ἢ τὸ πολὺ σπαθάριος. Ἐπὶ δὲ Λέοντος, τοῦ ἀοιδίμου καὶ σοφωτάτου βασιλέως, οὗτος μόνος ὁ Μιχαὴλ ἐτιμήθη σπαθάριος καὶ μετὰ ταῦτα σπαθαροκανδιδᾶτος. Διὰ δὲ τὸ νήπιον τυγχάνειν τὸν βασιλέα, καθὼς εἴρηται, καὶ τὸ ἀδιάκριτον τοῦ πατρικίου Κωνσταντίνου καὶ παρακοιμωμένου γεγόνασιν οἱ 160 πρωτοκάραβοι σπαθαροκανδιδᾶτοι, καὶ οὗτος ὁ Μιχαὴλ πρωτοσπαθάριος. Τοῦ δὲ βασιλέως τοῦ κυροῦ Ῥωμανοῦ ἀνελθόντος ἐν τῷ παλατίῳ καὶ τῆς βασιλείας, οὐκ οἶδ' ὅπως εἰπεῖν, ἐγκρατοῦς γενομένου, τὸν μὲν Θεόδοτον διὰ τὴν πρὸς Κωνσταντῖνον, τὸν φιλόχριστον δεσπότην καὶ βασιλέα, εὔνοιαν οὐ μόνον διεδέξατο, ἀλλὰ καὶ τὴν διὰ δαρμοῦ καὶ κουρᾶς 165 ἐπεξῆλθε τιμωρίαν, καὶ ἐν διηνεκεῖ παρέπεμψεν ἐξορίᾳ, ἐν ᾗ καὶ τῷ 181ᵛP τέλει τοῦ βίου ἐχρήσατο, | ἐάσας τὸν σὺν αὐτῷ πρωτοκάραβον Κωνσταντῖνον ἐκεῖνον τὸν Λωρικᾶτον διὰ τὸ διὰ φόβον εὐνοϊκῶς διακεῖσθαι πρὸς αὐτὸν καὶ ὅρκῳ ἰδιοχείρῳ ἐξαρνησάμενον τὴν πρὸς τὸν βασιλέα Κωνσταντῖνον εὔνοιαν καὶ ἀγάπην, ὃν πρῶτον μὲν σπαθαροκανδιδᾶτον 170 ἐτίμησεν, καὶ πρῶτον πρωτοκάραβον ποιήσας καὶ πρωτοσπαθάριον τῆς φιάλης προβαλόμενος, μετ' ὀλίγον καὶ πρωτοσπαθάριον ἐτίμησεν. Οὗτος οὖν δι' ὑπομνήσεως τοῦ κληρικοῦ Ἰωάννου καὶ κατὰ συγχώρησιν Θεοῦ ῥέκτωρος γεγονότος, ὑπέθετο τῷ μακαρίτῃ βασιλεῖ, τῷ κυρῷ Ῥωμανῷ, ὅτι «Ὁ πρωτοσπαθάριος Θεοφύλακτος καὶ τῆς τραπέζης τῆς 175
242Be αὐγούστης, ἐπεὶ προβολὴ καὶ ἀντίληψίς τῆς | μητρὸς τοῦ βασιλέως τυγχάνει καὶ αὐτοῦ τοῦ βασιλέως, ἀνάγκη καὶ πρὸς τοὺς ἰδίους δεσπότας
182ʳP καὶ εὐεργέ|τας προσπαθεῖν. Καὶ τίς ἡ χρεία τὸν λαὸν τῶν ἀγραρίων τῆς φιάλης ἐν δυσὶν ἐξουσίαις διαιρεῖσθαι; Δύναται γὰρ ὁ τῆς τραπέζης τῆς αὐγούστης τῇ πρὸς τὸν βασιλέα καὶ τὴν αὐγοῦσταν εὐνοίᾳ κρατού- 180 μενος, ἐξαπατῆσαι τοὺς ὑπ' αὐτοῦ κρατουμένους αὐγουστιατικοὺς ἀγραριώτας, πολλάκις δὲ καὶ τοὺς τῶν δρομωνίων ἐλάτας, καὶ μελετήσουσίν τινα ἐπανάστασιν κατὰ τῆς βασιλείας σου.» Ταῦτα εἰπὼν πείθει τὸν κακὸν ἐκεῖνον καὶ σκολιὸν ῥέκτωρα καὶ δι' αὐτοῦ τὸν βασιλέα. Εὔκολον γὰρ ἡ κουφότης καὶ ἀδιάκριτος γνώμη πρὸς ἅπαν τὸ κακούργως λεγό- 185 μενον καὶ ὑποτιθέμενον ἀποπλανᾶσθαι καὶ ἐκκυλίεσθαι. Καὶ εἰπὼν
182ᵛP πείθει καὶ πείσας, δίδοται αὐτῷ καὶ ἡ τῶν αὐγου|στιατικῶν ἀγραρίων ἐξουσία. Καὶ ἔκτοτε ἐπεκράτησεν τὸ τὸν πρωτοκάραβον τοῦ βασιλικοῦ δρομωνίου ἐπέχειν καὶ ἐξουσιάζειν πάντας τοὺς ἐλάτας τῶν τε δρομωνίων

V 156 σπαθαροκανδιδάτος P ‖ κανδιδάτος P ‖ 158 σπαθαροκανδιδάτος P ‖ 159 νήπιον — καὶ τὸ om. Be ‖ 160 καὶ om. V edd. ‖ 161 σπαθαροκανδιδάτοι P ‖ 163 ἐγκρατοῦς edd.: ἐγκρατῶς P ‖ 165 ⟨οὐ⟩ διεδέξατο coni. Meursius ‖ 166 ἐπεξῆλθε corr. Jenkins: ὑπεξῆλθε P edd. ‖ παρέπεμπεν V edd. ‖ 168 φόβου

51

rank of protospatharius, or even of spatharocandidate, but was either a candidate or a strator, or at the most, a spatharius. And in the time of Leo, the glorious and most wise emperor, this Michael alone was honoured with the rank of spatharius and subsequently of spatharocandidate. But owing, as has been said, to the infancy of the emperor and to the indiscretion of the patrician Constantine, the chamberlain, steersmen became spatharocandidates, and this Michael a protospatharius . But when the emperor lord Romanus ascended into the palace and, somehow or other, possessed himself of the throne, he superseded Theodotus because of his affection for Constantine, the Christ-loving sovereign and emperor, and not only that but he punished him with flogging and tonsuring and dismissed him to perpetual banishment, in which he came to the end of his life; but his colleague in the steersmanship, the late Constantine Loricatus, *the emperor lord Romanus* let be, because *Loricatus* was affectionately disposed towards him through fear and had renounced, by an oath written in his own hand, his affection and love toward the emperor Constantine; him *the emperor lord Romanus* first honoured with the rank of spatharocandidate, and, after making him first steersman and appointing him protospatharius of the basin, honoured him shortly afterwards with the rank of protospatharius. Now, this man, by means of a memorial to the cleric John, whom God had allowed to become rector, put before the emperor, of blessed memory, the lord Romanus, this suggestion: «The protospatharius Theophylact, master of the Augusta's table, since he is an appointment and a support of the mother of the emperor and of the emperor himself, must necessarily be in sympathy with his own masters and benefactors. Besides, what need is there for the men of the barges of the basin to be divided between two authorities ? For the master of the Augusta's table, governed by his affection towards the emperor and the Augusta, may mislead the sailors of the barges of the Augusta, who are under his control, and perhaps even the oarsmen of the galleys, and they will plan a rising against your imperial majesty.» With these words he won over that evil and crooked rector, and through him the emperor. For it is easy for a light head and indiscreet heart to be seduced and fall towards every malicious word and hint. He spoke and won them over, and, having won them over, was given the authority over the barges of the Augusta also. And since then it has become the rule for the steersman of the imperial galley to have charge of and exercise authority

edd. ‖ 169 ἐξαρνησάμενον edd.: ἐξαρνησαμένου P ‖ 170 σπαθαροκανδιδάτον P ‖ 174 ῥέκτωρος scr. Moravcsik: ῥαίκτωρος (litteris αι in ras. scriptis) P¹ V edd. ‖ βασιλεῖ, τῷ: τῷ βασιλεῖ Be ‖ 180 τὴν αὐγούσταν Moravcsik: τὴν αὐγούστην edd. τῇ αὐγούστῃ P ‖ 182 μελετήσουσίν coni. Moravcsik: μελετήσωσίν P μελετήσωσί edd. ‖ 184 ῥέκτωρα scr. Moravcsik: ῥαίκτωρα P edd. ‖ 188 τὸν πρωτοκάραβον Meursius Ba Be: τῶν πρωτοκαράβων P ‖

51, 52

βασιλικῶν τε καὶ αὐγουστιατικῶν ἀγραρίων καὶ εἶναι καὶ πρωτο- 190
σπαθάριον τῆς φιάλης.

Ἰστέον, ὅτι ἐπὶ Λέοντος, τοῦ φιλοχρίστου καὶ ἀειμνήστου βασιλέως, ἐγένετο ἀπὸ τῶν τῆς δύσεως θεμάτων λογαρίου ἀπαίτησις διὰ τοῦ
πρωτοσπαθαρίου Λέοντος καὶ γεγονότος στρατηγοῦ τοῦ Τζικάνη ἐκ
τῶν αἱρουμένων μὴ ταξιδεύειν.   195

Ἰστέον, ὅτι καὶ πάλιν ἐπὶ τοῦ αὐτοῦ φιλοχρίστου καὶ ἀειμνήστου
243Be Λέοντος ἐγένετο ἀπὸ τῶν τῆς δύσεως θεμάτων | λογαρίου ἀπαίτησις
διὰ τοῦ μαγίστρου Ἰωάννου τοῦ Ἐλαδᾶ, τῷ τότε πατρικίου αὐτοῦ ὄντος.

183ʳP   Ἰστέον, ὅτι καὶ πάλιν ἐπὶ Ῥωμανοῦ δεσπότου, βουληθέντος
ταξιδεῦσαι τοὺς Πελοποννησαίους ἐν Λαγουβαρδίᾳ, τοῦ πρωτοσπαθαρίου 200
Ἰωάννου τοῦ Πρωτεύοντος ἐν Πελοποννήσῳ τότε στρατηγοῦντος,
ᾑρετίσαντο οἱ αὐτοὶ Πελοποννησαῖοι μὴ ταξιδεῦσαι, ἀλλὰ δοῦναι ἱππάρια
χίλια ἐστρωμένα καὶ χαλινωμένα καὶ λογάριον κεντηνάριον ἕν, ἅπερ
καὶ μετὰ πολλῆς προθυμίας παρέσχον.

52. Ἡ γενομένη ἀπαίτησις τῶν ἱππαρίων ἐν τῷ
θέματι Πελοποννήσου ἐπὶ Ῥωμανοῦ δεσπότου,
καθὼς προείρηται.

Ὁ μητροπολίτης Κορίνθου ἱππάρια τέσσαρα· ὁ μητροπολίτης
Πατρῶν ἱππάρια τέσσαρα· οἱ ἐπίσκοποι πάντες τοῦ θέματος ἀνὰ ἱππά- 5
ρια δύο· οἱ πρωτοσπαθάριοι ἀνὰ ἱππάρια τρία· οἱ σπαθαροκανδιδᾶτοι
183ᵛP ἀνὰ ἱππάρια δύο· | οἱ σπαθάριοι, οἱ στράτωρες ἀνὰ ἱππαρίου ἑνός· τὰ
βασιλικὰ καὶ πατριαρχικὰ μοναστήρια ἀνὰ ἱππάρια δύο· τὰ τῶν ἀρχιεπισκοπῶν, μητροπόλεων καὶ ἐπισκοπῶν μοναστήρια ἀνὰ ἱππάρια δύο·
244Be τὰ ἄπορα μοναστήρια σύνδυο ἱππάριον ἕν. Οἱ δὲ ἔχοντες βα|σιλικὰ 10
ἀξιώματα, πλώϊμοι, κογχυλευταί, χαρτοποιοὶ ἱππάρια οὐ δεδώκασιν.

Ἰστέον, ὅτι καὶ πᾶς ὁ στρατὸς Πελοποννήσου ἀπῃτήθησαν ὑπὲρ
τοῦδε τοῦ ταξιδίου ἀνὰ νομίσματα πέντε, οἱ δὲ παντελῶς ἄποροι σύνδυο
νομίσματα πέντε, ἐξ ὧν συνέστη καὶ τὸ προρρηθὲν διὰ χαράγματος
κεντηνάριον ἕν.   15

V 192 ἀειμνήστου καὶ φιλοχρίστου edd. ‖ 200 Πελοποννησέους P: Πελοποννησίους
F¹ edd. ‖ Λογουβαρδίᾳ Ba Be ‖ 102 Πελοποννησέοι P: Πελοποννήσιοι F
edd. ‖ μὴ s. v. add. P¹ in textum receperunt V edd. ‖ 204 καὶ om. V
edd. ‖ προθυμίας] litteras θυμ in ras. scr. P¹.

51, 52

over all the oarsmen, both of the imperial galleys and of the barges of the Augusta, and to be also protospatharius of the basin.

In the time of Leo, the Christ-loving and ever-memorable emperor, a demand was made from the provinces of the west, through the protospatharius Leo Tzikanes, the ex-military governor, for ready money from those who opted against military service.

And again, in the time of the same Christ-loving and ever-memorable Leo, ready money was demanded from the provinces of the west, through the magister John Eladas, who was then patrician.

And again in the time of the sovereign Romanus, who desired the Peloponnesians to do military service in Lombardy, the protospatharius John Proteuon being then military governor in Peloponnesus, these same Peloponnesians opted against military service, but to give *instead* a thousand horses, with saddles and bridles, and one hundred pounds in ready money, and these they supplied with great readiness.

52. D e m a n d   m a d e   f o r   h o r s e s   i n   t h e   p r o v i n c e   o f   P e l o-
p o n n e s u s   i n   t h e   t i m e   o f   t h e   s o v e r e i g n   R o m a n u s,
a s   s t a t e d   a b o v e.

The metropolitan of Corinth, four horses; the metropolitan of Patras, four horses; all the bishops of the province, two horses each; the protospatharii, three horses each; the spatharocandidates, two horses each; the spatharii, the strators, one horse each; the imperial and patriarchal monasteries, two horses each; the archiepiscopal, metropolitan and episcopal monasteries, two horses each; the monasteries without means, one horse between two. Holders of imperial dignities, sailors, purple-fishers, parchment-makers did not provide horses.

A demand was made for five nomismata per head from the whole military force of Peloponnesus in respect of this military service, and from those absolutely without means of five nomismata from every two, and from this was made up the aforesaid one hundred pounds in coined money.

---

52. 4 τέσσαρα edd.: δ′ P ‖ 5 τέσσαρα edd.: δ′ P ‖ 6 τρία edd.: γ′ P ‖ σπαθαροκανδιδάτοι P ‖ 7 στράτορες P ‖ 8/9 ἀρχιεπισκοπῶν coni. Moravcsik: ἀρχιεπισκόπων P edd. ‖ 9 ἐπισκόπων edd. ‖ 10 σὺν δύο P ‖ 11 κονχυλευταὶ P ‖ 13 πέντε scr. Moravcsik: ε′ P edd. ‖ σὺν δύο P ‖ 14 πέντε scr. Moravcsik: ε′ P edd.

53. Ἱστορία περὶ τοῦ κάστρου Χερσῶνος.

Βασιλεύοντος Διοκλητιανοῦ ἐν Ῥώμῃ, ἐν δὲ τῇ Χερσωνιτῶν
184ʳP στεφανηφοροῦντος καὶ πρωτεύοντος Θεμιστοῦ, τοῦ Θεμιστοῦ, | Σαυρό-
ματος, ὁ ἐκ τῶν Βοσποριανῶν, Κρισκορόνου δὲ παῖς γενόμενος, συναθροί-
σας Σαρμάτας τοὺς τὴν Μαιώτιδα λίμνην οἰκοῦντας, ἐστρατοπεδεύσατο 5
κατὰ Ῥωμαίων, καὶ καταλαβὼν ⟨τὴν⟩ τῶν Λαζῶν χώραν καὶ πολεμήσας
τοὺς ἐκεῖσε, φθάζει καὶ ἕως τοῦ Ἅλυος ποταμοῦ. Μαθὼν δὲ τοῦτο ὁ
βασιλεὺς Διοκλητιανός, πορθεῖσθαι τὴν τῶν Λαζῶν χώραν καὶ τὴν
Ποντικήν, ἀπέστειλεν ἐκεῖσε στρατὸν ἀντιπαρατάξασθαι Σαρμάταις
βουλόμενος. Ἦν δὲ ἔξαρχος τοῦ στρατοῦ Κώνστας τριβοῦνος, καὶ καταλα- 10
βὼν τὸν Ἅλυν ὁ Κώνστας σὺν τῷ στρατῷ, ἐκαθέσθη ἐκεῖσε, κωλύων
Σαρμάτας ἀντιπερᾶσαι τὸν Ἅλυν. Καὶ μὴ δυναμένου αὐτοῦ ἀντιπαρατά-
245Be ξασθαι αὐτούς, | ἐβουλεύετο καθ᾽ ἑαυτὸν ὁ | Κώνστας μηδαμῶς ἄλλως
184ᵛP δύνασθαι τοὺς Σαρμάτας ἐκδιῶξαι, εἰ μήτι γε τῶν πλησιοχώρων τῆς
Βοσποριανῶν καὶ τῆς Μαιώτιδος λίμνης τινὰς κατ᾽ αὐτῶν ἐκπεμφθῆναι 15
εἰς πόλεμον καὶ τὰς τούτων φαμιλίας ἐκπορθῆσαι, ὅπως ταῦτα ἀκούσας
ὁ Σαυρόματος ὑποστρέψῃ ἐκ τοῦ πολέμου, καὶ ταῦτα μηνῦσαι τῷ βασιλεῖ,
ἐφ᾽ ᾧ τε ἀποστεῖλαι κατὰ τῶν Χερσωνιτῶν καὶ τούτους διεγεῖραι κατὰ
τῶν Σαρματῶν, ὡς πλησιοχώρων αὐτῶν ὄντων, καὶ πολεμῆσαι τὰς
αὐτῶν φαμιλίας πρὸς τὸ τὸν Σαυρόματον ἀκούσαντα τὸ τάχος ὑποστρέψαι 20
ἐκ τοῦ πολέμου. Ὁ δὲ βασιλεὺς Διοκλητιανὸς ταῦτα ἀκούσας, ἀπέστειλεν
185ʳP | εὐθέως κατὰ τῶν Χερσωνιτῶν, προτρεπόμενος συμμαχῆσαι αὐτῷ καὶ
ἀπελθόντας τὴν Βοσποριανῶν καὶ Σαρματῶν χώραν ἐκπορθῆσαι καὶ
τὰς τούτων φαμιλίας αἰχμαλωτίσαι. Στεφανηφοροῦντος δὲ τότε καὶ
πρωτεύοντος τῆς Χερσωνιτῶν Χρήστου, τοῦ Παπίου, οἱ Χερσωνῖται 25
τοῖς τοῦ βασιλέως ῥήμασιν ἀσμένως ὑπακούσαντες, ἐμηχανῶντο λοιπόν,
ποίῳ τρόπῳ δυνηθεῖεν τήν τε τοῦ Σαυρομάτου πόλιν Βόσπορον καὶ τὰ
τῆς Μαιώτιδος καστέλλια παραλαβεῖν. Καὶ συναθροίσαντες τοὺς τῶν
πλησιοχώρων καστελλίων ἄνδρας καὶ κατασκευάσαντες ἄρματα πολεμικὰ
καὶ ἐνθέντες ἐν αὐτοῖς τὰς λεγομένας χειροβολίστρας, παρεγένοντο κατὰ 30
185ᵛP | τὴν Βοσποριανῶν πόλιν, καὶ ποιήσαντες ἐγκρύμματα διὰ τῆς νυκτὸς
246Be ὀλιγοστοὶ προσῆψαν τὸν πόλεμον τῇ πόλει, | καὶ τειχομαχήσαντες ἀπὸ
ὄρθρου ἕως ὥρας τρίτης, ἐτεκμήραντο τοῦ φυγεῖν, μὴ προδείξαντες

V   53. 4 Κρισκορόνου coni. Bekker: Κρίσκων. Ὅρου P   Κρισκωνόρου Be ‖
5 τούς om. edd. ‖ ἐστρατ{οπεδ}εύσατο Migne ‖ 6 τὴν add. Be ‖ πολεμίσας
P ‖ 8 ante πορθεῖσθαι addendum καὶ coni. Jenkins ‖ 11 ἐκαθέσθη: κατέστη
Be ‖ 13 αὐτοῖς edd. ‖ ἄλλως V edd.: ἄλλος P ‖ 14 μήτοι P ‖ 16 φαμηλίας
P ‖ ἐκπορθῆσαι F ἐκπορθεῖσαι P V: ἐκπορθεῖσθαι edd. ‖ 17 Σαυρόματος scr.

53

53. Story of the city of Cherson.

When Diocletian was emperor in Rome, and Themistus, son of Themistus, was chief magistrate and primate in the country of the Chersonites, Sauromatus the Bosporian, son of Criscoronus, gathered together the Sarmatians who dwelt on the Maeotic lake and marched against the Romans, and, having occupied *the* country of the Lazi and defeated those who were there, arrived as far as the Halys river. The emperor Diocletian, learning this, that the country of the Lazi and the Pontic land were being laid waste, sent thither an army with intent to oppose the Sarmatians. The commander of the army was Constans the tribune, and Constans, having reached the Halys with the army, sat down there and prevented the Sarmatians from crossing the Halys. And being unable himself to oppose them, Constans resolved in his own mind that in no other way could he expel the Sarmatians except perhaps if some of the neighbours of the Bosporians and of the Maeotic lake were sent out to make war upon them and plunder their families, in order that Sauromatus might hear of it and retire from the war; and to communicate this in a message to the emperor, so that *the emperor* should send to the Chersonites and rouse them against the Sarmatians, their neighbours, and to attack their families, so that Sauromatus, when he heard of it, might speedily retire from the war. Hearing this, the emperor Diocletian at once sent to the Chersonites bidding them to join him in the war and to go and plunder the country of the Bosporians and Sarmatians and take their families captive. The chief magistrate and primate of the country of the Chersonites was at that time Chrestus, son of Papias, and the Chersonites willingly obeyed the words of the emperor and therefore set about devising in what manner they might be able to capture the city of Sauromatus, Bosporus, and the forts of the Maeotis. They gathered together the men of the neighbouring forts and constructed military waggons and placed in them the so-called arbalests, and they arrived at the city of the Bosporians and, after laying an ambush while it was night, a handful of them joined battle at the city; and having fought at the wall from dawn till the third hour, they made a show of flight, not

---

Moravcsik: Σαυρομάτος P   Σαυρομάτας edd. ‖ ὑποστρέψῃ Ba Be: ὑποστρέ-
(ψῃ?) *per comp.* P   ὑποστρέψῃ V Me ‖ μηνῦσαι *coni.* Jenkins: μηνύσῃ
edd. μηνύσει P ἐμήνυσε *coni.* Bekker ‖ 18 ἀποστεῖλαι *coni.* Bekker: ἀπέστειλε
P edd. ‖ καὶ τούτους διήγειρεν *bis* P ‖ διεγεῖραι coni. Bekker: διήγειρεν P
διήγειρε edd. ‖ 19 Σαρματῶν Migne: Σαρμάτων P edd. ‖ 20 φαμηλίας P ‖
Σαυρομάταν edd. ‖ 23 ἀπελθόντας Be: ἀπελθόντες   P ‖ Σαρματῶν Migne:
Σαρμάτων P edd. ‖ 24 φαμηλίας P ‖ αἰχμαλωτίσαι] *litteras* αἴχμα *in ras. scr.*
P¹ ‖ 25 *post* Χερσωνιτῶν *add.* χώρας V edd. ‖ Χρίστου P ‖ 32 ὀλίγιστοι Be ‖
33 προδείξαντες *corr.* Moravcsik: προσδείξαντες P   *coni.* Bekker: προσ-
δέξαντες edd. ‖

53

τὰς ἐν τοῖς ἄρμασι κατασκευασμένας χειροβολίστρας. Καὶ δὴ τῶν ἐν τῇ
Βοσπόρῳ νομισάντων ὡς δι' ὀλιγότητα ἡττημένους φεύγειν τοὺς Χερσω- 35
νίτας, καταθαρρήσαντες ἑαυτῶν ἐξήεσαν πρὸς δίωξιν αὐτῶν. Οἱ δὲ
Χερσωνῖται ἠρέμα, φησί, φεύγοντες ταῖς χειροβολίστραις τοὺς διώκον-
τας ἀνήλισκον Βοσποριανούς, ἀναστάντες δὲ καὶ οἱ ἐνεδρεύοντες Χερσω-
186ʳP νῖται, καὶ περικυκλώσαντες τοὺς Βοσποριανούς, πάντας αὐτοὺς | κατέσφα-
ξαν, καὶ ὑποστρέψαντες κατέλαβον τὴν Βόσπορον, ὁμοίως δὲ καὶ τὰ πρὸς 40
τὴν Μαιώτιδα λίμνην καστέλλια καὶ πάσας τὰς φαμιλίας ⟨τῶν⟩
Σαυρομάτων, καὶ ἐκαθέζοντο ἐν τῇ Βοσπόρῳ, μηδένα τοῦ λοιποῦ κατα-
σφάζοντες, πλὴν τῶν πολεμησάντων, καὶ ἐχόμενοι Βοσπόρου, ἐφύλαττον
αὐτήν. Ἡμερῶν δέ τινων διαγενομένων, λέγει Χρῆστος, ὁ τοῦ Παπίου
ταῖς τῶν Σαυρομάτων γυναιξίν, ὅτι· «Ἡμεῖς οὐκ εἴχαμεν χρείαν ὑμᾶς 45
πολεμεῖν, ἀλλ' ἐπειδὴ ὁ Σαυρόματος ἀπῆλθεν τὴν τῶν Ῥωμαίων χώραν
πορθῆσαι, τούτου χάριν προτραπέντες ἡμεῖς παρὰ τοῦ βασιλέως Ῥω-
186ᵛP μαίων, ὡς ὑπήκοοι αὐτοῦ ὄντες, ἐπο|λεμήσαμεν ὑμᾶς. Ἐὰν οὖν θέλετε
ζῆσαι ἐν τῇ πόλει ὑμῶν, δεῦτε ἀποστείλωμεν πρέσβεις πρὸς τὸν κύριον
ὑμῶν, Σαυρόματον, ἐφ' ᾧ τε αὐτὸν ποιῆσαι εἰρήνην μετὰ τῶν Ῥωμαίων 50
ἐπ' ὄψεσι τῶν πρέσβεων ἡμῶν καὶ ἀναχωρῆσαι τῶν ἐκεῖσε, καὶ ἡμεῖς
247Be ἀφίομεν ὑμᾶς, | καὶ ἀπερχόμεθα ἐν τῇ πόλει ἡμῶν, οὕτω μέντοι, προπέμ-
ποντος Σαυρομάτου ἐνταῦθα τοὺς πρέσβεις ἡμῶν καὶ μετὰ τῶν ἰδίων
ἀνθρώπων μηνύοντος ἡμῖν τὰ τῆς εἰρήνης, καὶ οὕτως ἀφίομεν ὑμᾶς
καὶ ἀναχωροῦμεν· εἰ δὲ καὶ δοκιμάσῃ Σαυρόματος δόλῳ τινὶ ἔρχεσθαι, 55
ὡς νομίζων ἡμᾶς ἐνταῦθα συγκλεῖσαι καὶ πολεμῆσαι, καὶ γνῶμεν τοῦτο
διὰ τῶν σκουλκατώρων ἡμῶν, πάντας ὑμᾶς ἀπὸ μικροῦ ἕως μεγάλου
187ʳP κατασφάξομεν, καὶ οὕτως | ἀναχωροῦμεν τῶν ἐντεῦθεν. Καὶ τί τὸ λοιπὸν
Σαυρομάτῳ ὄφελος, τῆς φαμιλίας αὐτοῦ πάσης καὶ τῆς πόλεως ἀπολλυ-
μένης;» Αἱ δὲ γυναῖκες Σαυρομάτου ταῦτα ἀκούσασαι, σπουδαίως τοῦτο 60
γενέσθαι παρεσκεύασαν. Καὶ δὴ ἀποστέλλουσιν οἱ Χερσωνῖται μετὰ
Βοσποριανῶν καὶ ἰδίους πέντε πρέσβεις πρὸς Σαυρόματον, μηνύοντες
αὐτῷ τὰ γενόμενα καὶ λεχθέντα. Καὶ δὴ τῶν πρέσβεων καταλαβόντων
τὸν Σαυρόματον κατὰ τοὺς τοῦ Ἅλυος ποταμοῦ τόπους, ἀνήγγειλαν
αὐτῷ πάντα τὰ γενόμενα κατὰ τῶν Βοσποριανῶν παρὰ τῶν Χερσωνιτῶν. 65
Ὁ δὲ ἐν πολλῇ στενώσει γενόμενος, ὡς δῆθεν, φησί, βουλόμενος τοὺς
187ᵛP τῶν Χερσωνιτῶν | πρέσβεις ἐκ τῆς ὁδοιπορίας ἀναπαῦσαι, λέγει αὐτοῖς·
«Ἐπειδὴ κοπωμένοι ἐστέ, θέλω ὑμᾶς ὀλίγας ἡμέρας ἀναπαῆναι, καὶ
εἶθ' οὕτως πάντα τὰ ὑφ' ὑμῶν λεχθέντα ποιήσω· *** ἐντεῦθεν ἀπέλθατε

V 34 κατεσκευασμένας Ba Be ‖ τῇ Ba Be: τῶ P ‖ 41 φαμηλίας P ‖ τῶν
add. edd. ‖ 42 Σαυροματῶν V edd. ‖ 43 Βοσπόρου: τὴν Βόσπορον edd. ‖
44 Χρίστος P ‖ 45 Σαυροματῶν edd. ‖ εἴχαμεν: ἔχομεν edd. ‖ 48 θέλητε

53

having exposed the arbalests they had made, that were in their waggons. Those in Bosporus of course supposed that the Chersonites had been beaten owing to their small numbers and were in flight, and, with complete confidence in themselves, they sallied forth to pursue them. But the Chersonites, as it appears, retiring gradually, destroyed the pursuing Bosporians with the arbalests, and the Chersonites besides who lay in ambush started up and surrounded the Bosporians and put them all to the sword, and, returning, captured Bosporus and in like manner also the forts on the Maeotic lake and all the families of *the* Sarmatians; and they took up their quarters in Bosporus, putting none to the sword thereafter save those who had fought, and they held on to Bosporus and guarded it. After some days interval, Chrestus, son of Papias, said to the women of the Sarmatians: «We ourselves had no need to make war upon you, but since Sauromatus has gone off to ravage the country of the Romans, we, being for this reason bidden by the emperor of the Romans, whose subjects we are, have made war on you. So now, if you would live in your city, come, let us send envoys to your lord Sauromatus, so that he may conclude peace with the Romans in sight of our envoys and withdraw from those parts, and we will leave you and go off to our city; but only when Sauromatus so escorts our envoys hither and sends us with his own men the news of the peace, then so will we leave you and withdraw; but if Sauromatus so much as tries to proceed by any trickery, believing he may cut us off here and attack us, and we get to know of it through our scouts, we will put all of you, both small and great, to the sword and so withdraw hence. And what good will Sauromatus get of it hereafter, if all his family and the city are destroyed?» Hearing this, the women of Sauromatus made preparations to carry it out with alacrity. And with the Bosporians the Chersonites sent to Sauromatus five envoys of their own, to inform him of what had been done and said. Well, when the envoys reached Sauromatus, in the region of the Halys river, they reported to him all that had been done against the Bosporians by the Chersonites. He was in great perturbation, and, pretending to desire, as it appears, that the envoys of the Chersonites should take rest after their journey, said to them: «Since you are fatigued, I desire you to rest yourselves a few days and then I will do all that you have said; *** go

---

edd. ‖ 49 ἀποστείλωμεν Moravcsik ἀποστείλομεν P: ἀποστέλλωμεν edd. ‖ 51 ἐπ' ὄψεσιν edd.: ἐφόψεσι P ‖ 52 ἀφίομεν scr. Moravcsik: ἀφίωμεν P ἀφίεμεν Be ἀφίημεν Me Ba ‖ 53 Σαυρομάτου coni. Bekker: Σαυρόματος P edd. ‖ 54 μηνύοντος coni. Moravcsik: μηνύων P edd. ‖ ἀφίομεν scr. Moravcsik: ἀφίωμεν P edd. ‖ 57 σκουλκατόρων edd. ‖ 59 φαμηλίας P ‖ 60 Σαυρωμάτου P ‖ 62 πέντε edd.: ε' P ‖ Σαυρώματον P ‖ 64 Σαυρώματον P ‖ 65 Χερσωνίτων P ‖ 67 Χερσωνίτων P ‖ 68 κοπομένοι P: κοπώμενοι edd. ‖ 69 ὑμῶν V edd.: ἡμῶν P ‖ post ποιήσω lac. coni. Jenkins ‖ ἀπέλθετε edd. ‖

πρὸς τοὺς Ῥώμης, καὶ μάθετε παρ' αὐτῶν καὶ πείθεσθε, ὅτι ἀληθεύω 70
ὑμῖν καὶ οὐ ψεύδομαι.» Τῶν δὲ Χερσωνιτῶν ἀπελθόντων πρὸς Κώνσταν
248Be | μετὰ καὶ πρέσβεων τοῦ Σαυρομάτου, ἐπύθοντο τὰ μεταξὺ αὐτῶν γενό-
μενα, ἀνήγγειλαν δὲ τῷ Κώνστᾳ καὶ πάντα τὰ ὑπ' αὐτῶν κατὰ τὴν
Βοσπορϊανῶν καὶ τὴν Μαιώτιδα λίμνην γενόμενα, καὶ τό, πῶς τὰς
φαμιλίας Σαυρομάτου παρέλαβον, καὶ ὅτι τῇ ἀνάγκῃ ταύτῃ εἰς εἰρήνην 75
188ʳᴾ ἦλθεν ὁ Σαυρόματος. | Ἀκούσας δὲ ταῦτα ὁ Κώνστας πάνυ ἐλυπήθη, καὶ
λέγει τοῖς Χερσωνίταις· «Καὶ τί μοι τὸ ὄφελος λοιπὸν τῆς ὑμετέρας
συμμαχίας, ἀφ' ἧς ἐγὼ ἐποίησα πάκτα δοῦναι αὐτοῖς χρυσίον τοσοῦτον;»
Λέγουσιν αὐτῷ οἱ Χερσωνῖται· «Μὴ λυπηθῇς, δέσποτα, καὶ ἐὰν θέλῃς,
ἡμεῖς ἀναλύομεν τὸ περὶ τῆς δόσεως πάκτον». Λέγει αὐτοῖς ὁ Κώνστας· 80
«Καὶ πῶς δυνατόν;» Λέγουσιν αὐτῷ οἱ Χερσωνῖται· «Δήλωσον καὶ
αὐτὸς τῷ Σαυρομάτῳ, ὅτι· Τὰ μὲν ἤδη μεταξὺ ἡμῶν γενόμενα πάκτα
κεκράτηνται· ἐπεὶ οὖν τῇ αἰτίᾳ τῇ σῇ κἀγὼ ἀναλώματα καὶ ζημίας
πολλὰς ἐποίησα σὺν τῷ στρατῷ ἀπὸ Ῥώμης ἕως τῶν ὧδε, δός μοι καὶ
188ᵛᴾ σὺ ταῦτα, κἀγώ σοι ἀποδίδωμι τὰς φαμιλίας σου | πάσας καὶ τὴν πόλιν 85
σου.'» Περιχαρὴς δὲ γενόμενος ὁ Κώνστας ἐμήνυσεν ταῦτα τῷ Σαυρομάτῳ. Ὁ δὲ Σαυρόματος ἀκούσας καὶ λυπηθεὶς σφόδρα, μηνύει τῷ
Κώνστᾳ λέγων, ὅτι· «Οὐ θέλω δοῦναι τίποτ' οὖν, οὐδὲ λαβεῖν, ἀλλὰ
μόνον ἀπόστειλόν μοι τοὺς Χερσωνίτας, ἵνα τῶν ἐντεῦθεν ἀναχωρήσω.»
Λέγουσιν οἱ Χερσωνῖται τῷ Κώνστᾳ· «Μὴ ἀπολύσῃς ἡμᾶς, ἕως ἂν πάντας 90
249Be τοὺς αἰχμαλώτους ἀπολάβῃς.» Τότε μηνύει ὁ | Κώνστας τῷ Σαυρομάτῳ
λέγων, ὅτι· «'Απόστειλόν μοι πάντας, οὓς ἔχεις, αἰχμαλώτους, καὶ ἀπολύω
τοὺς Χερσωνίτας.» Ὁ δὲ Σαυρόματος ταῦτα ἀκούσας, ἄκων καὶ μὴ
βουλόμενος ἀπέλυσεν ἅπαντας, οὓς εἶχεν, αἰχμαλώτους ἕως ἑνός. Ἀπολα-
189ʳᴾ βὼν οὖν ὁ Κώνστας ἅπαν|τας τοὺς πραιδευθέντας, δύο τῶν Χερσωνιτῶν 95
πρέσβεις κατασχὼν παρ' ἑαυτῷ, τοὺς ἄλλους ἀπέστειλεν πρὸς τὸν Σαυρόματον, ὅστις Σαυρόματος παραλαβὼν αὐτοὺς προαπέστειλεν ἐκ τῆς
τῶν Λαζῶν χώρας μετὰ καὶ τῶν ἰδίων ἀνθρώπων πρὸς τὸ παραδοῦναι
αὐτοὺς τήν τε Βόσπορον καὶ τὰς φαμιλίας αὐτῶν. Αὐτὸς δὲ ⟨ὁ⟩ Σαυρόματος τὴν πορείαν μετὰ τοῦ ἔθνους αὐτοῦ ἐν καταστάσει ἐποιεῖτο πρὸς 100
τὸ †ἀθροίλους† τοὺς Χερσωνίτας παραδοῦναι τὰς φαμιλίας καὶ ἀναχωρῆσαι. Οἱ δὲ Χερσωνῖται τοὺς οἰκείους πρέσβεις ὑποδεξάμενοι ἐν τῇ Βοσπόρῳ, καὶ μεμαθηκότες τὰ γενόμενα ἅπαντα ὑπὸ Κώνσταντος καὶ τοῦ
Σαυρομάτου, παρέδωκαν τοῦ Σαυρομάτου ἄνθρωπον τήν τε Βόσπορον
189ᵛᴾ καὶ | τὰ τῆς Μαιώτιδος καστέλλια καὶ τὰς φαμιλίας πάσας ἀβλαβεῖς, 105

V 70 Ῥώμης: Ῥωμαίους F ‖ 71 οὐ: μὴ edd. ‖ Κώνσταντα edd. ‖ 72 Σαυρωμάτου
P ‖ ἐποίθοντο P ‖ 73 τὴν (etiam Bandurius): τῶν V edd. ⟨τὴν⟩ τῶν coni.
Bekker ‖ 75 φαμηλίας P ‖ Σαυρωμάτου P ‖ 76 Σαυρώματος P ‖ 82 Σαυρωμάτω

53

hence to the men of Rome and learn of them and be persuaded that my words to you are truth and that I do not lie.» The Chersonites went off to Constans together with envoys of Sauromatus, and learnt what had gone on between them, and reported to Constans all that had been done by them in the country of the Bosporians and at the Maeotic lake, and how they had captured the families of Sauromatus, and that Sauromatus had through this necessity been brought to make peace. On hearing this, Constans was quite cast down, and said to the Chersonites: «And what good, then, is your alliance to me, now that I have made agreements to give them so much gold?» The Chersonites said to him: «Be not cast down, my lord: if you wish, we will dissolve the agreement for your payment.» Constans said to them: «How is it possible?» The Chersonites said to him: «Do you, for your part, thus declare to Sauromatus: 'The agreements already made between us hold good; and now, since on your account I too have incurred expenses and great losses on my way hither from Rome with the army, do you, for your part, pay me these, and I will give you back all your families and your city'.» Constans was overjoyed and sent this message to Sauromatus. Sauromatus, when he heard it, was exceedingly downcast, and sent to Constans a message saying: «I will neither pay nor take anything at all; do you but send me the Chersonites, that I may withdraw hence.» The Chersonites said to Constans: «Do not dismiss us until you get back all the prisoners.» Then Constans sent a message to Sauromatus saying: «Send me all whom you hold prisoners, and I will dismiss the Chersonites.» Sauromatus, when he heard it, unwillingly and against his desire dismissed all the prisoners whom he held, to the last one of them. So then Constans, having got back all those who had been taken in the forays, kept with him two envoys of the Chersonites and sent the others to Sauromatus, and Sauromatus received them and sent them on ahead out of the country of the Lazi, together with some of his own men, to whom might be handed over Bosporus and their families. Sauromatus himself put his march with his nation in train, so that the Chersonites might *honestly* hand over the families and withdraw. The Chersonites, having received their own envoys in Bosporus and having learnt all that had been done by Constans and Sauromatus, handed over to Sauromatus' agent both Bosporus and the forts of the Maeotis and all the families, unharmed, and came in peace to the country

P ‖ 84 τῶν om. edd. ‖ 85 φαμηλίας P ‖ 86/7 Σαυρωμάτω P ‖ 87 Σαυρώματος P ‖ 91 Σαυρωμάτω P ‖ 92 post οὕς add. ἂν V edd. ‖ 93 Χερσωνίτας] litteras χερσωνιτα in ras. scr. P¹ ‖ Σαυρωμάτος P ‖ 94 post οὕς add. ἂν edd. ‖ 95 Χερσωνίτων P ‖ 96/7 Σαυρώματον P ‖ 97 Σαυρώματος P ‖ 99 αὐτοῖς edd. ‖ φαμηλίας P ‖ ὁ add. Moravcsik ‖ 99/100 Σαυρώματος P 101 ἀθροίλους intra cruces posuit inter ἀθροι et λους aliquid excidisse coniciens Moravcsik: ἀδόλως coni. Jenkins ἀθρόους ὅλους vel ἀθρόως ὅλας coni. Kyriakides ἀθρόως ὅλας coni. Dujčev ἀθορύβους coni. Trypanis ‖ φαμηλίας P ‖ 103 γενόμενα edd.: γινόμενα P ‖ 104 Σαυρωμάτου P ‖ Σαυρωμάτου P ‖ ἄνθρωπον per comp. P: ἀνθρώπῳ Ba Be ‖ 105 φαμηλίας P ‖

53

καὶ κατέλαβον ἐν εἰρήνῃ τὴν Χερσωνιτῶν. Ὁ δὲ Κώνστας, ἀναχωρήσαν-
τος τοῦ Σαυρομάτου ἐκ τῶν Ῥωμαϊκῶν τόπων, καὶ αὐτὸς ἀνέζευξεν
ἐπὶ τὴν Ῥώμην, καὶ ἀνήγγειλεν πάντα τῷ βασιλεῖ τὰ ὑπὸ τῶν Χερσωνιτῶν γενόμενα, προσαγαγὼν καὶ τοὺς δύο αὐτῶν πρέσβεις, οὕστινας
ἰδὼν ὁ βασιλεὺς καὶ φιλοφρόνως ἀποδεξάμενος καὶ τὰ μέγιστα εὐχαριστή-110
σας, εἶπεν αὐτοῖς· «Τί θέλετε παράσχω ὑμῖν τε καὶ τῇ πόλει ὑμῶν
250Be ὑπὲρ τῆς τοιαύτης εὐνοίας τε καὶ | συμμαχίας;» Οἱ δὲ εἶπον τῷ βασιλεῖ,
ὅτι· «Ἡμεῖς, δέσποτα, οὐδὲν ἕτερον θέλομεν, εἰ μήτι γε τοῦτο μόνον
αἰτοῦμεν, ἐφ᾽ ᾧ τε δεξιὰς ἐλευθερίας καὶ ἀτελείας παρασχέσθαι ἡμῖν
190ʳP ὑπὸ | τοῦ κράτους ὑμῶν.» Ὁ δὲ βασιλεὺς ἀσμένως ὑποκύψας τῇ αἰτήσει115
αὐτῶν, ἀφθόνως παρέσχεν αὐτοῖς τὰς τοιαύτας τῆς ἐλευθερίας τε καὶ
ἀτελείας δεξιάς, ἀποστείλας αὐτοὺς μετὰ καὶ δώρων πλείστων κατὰ
τὴν Χερσωνιτῶν, ὡς γνησίους ὄντας αὐτοὺς ὑπηκόους τῆς Ῥωμαίων
βασιλείας. Ὁ δὲ Κώνστας μεγάλως καὶ αὐτὸς ὑποδεχθεὶς παρὰ τοῦ
βασιλέως Διοκλητιανοῦ, ὡς ἀνδρείως παραταξάμενος κατὰ τὸν τῶν120
Σαυρομάτων πόλεμον καὶ περιφανὴς καὶ ἔνδοξος γενόμενος, μετ᾽ ὀλίγον
τινὰ χρόνον τῆς Ῥωμαίων ἀνεδείχθη βασιλείας, Διοκλητιανοῦ ἐπὶ τὴν
Νικομήδειαν ἐπαναγαγόντος.

Κώνστα δὲ τελευτήσαντος, ἐν Ῥώμῃ ἐβασίλευσεν Κωνσταντῖνος,
190ᵛP | ὁ υἱὸς αὐτοῦ, καὶ ἐρχομένου αὐτοῦ ἐπὶ τὸ Βυζάντιον, ἀντιστάσεως αὐτῷ125
ὑπό τινων ἐν τῇ Σκυθίᾳ γενομένης, ὑπεμνήσθη τὸ ὑπὸ τοῦ πατρὸς
αὐτοῦ, Κώνστα λεχθὲν περὶ τῆς τῶν Χερσωνιτῶν εὐνοίας τε καὶ συμμαχίας, καὶ ἀπέστειλεν κατὰ τὴν τῶν Χερσωνιτῶν πρέσβεις, ἐφ᾽ ᾧ τε
ἐλθεῖν αὐτοὺς κατὰ τὴν τῶν Σκυθῶν χώραν καὶ μαχήσασθαι τοῖς ἀνθε-
στηκόσιν αὐτῷ. Στεφανηφοροῦντος δὲ τότε καὶ πρωτεύοντος τῆς Χερσωνι-130
τῶν Διογένους, τοῦ Διογένους, οἱ Χερσωνῖται τὴν κέλευσιν ἀσμένως
πειθαρχήσαντες, πάσῃ σπουδῇ κατασκευάσαντες τά τε πολεμικὰ ἄρ-
251Be ματα καὶ τὰς χειροβολίστρας, καταλαμβάνουσι | τὸν Ἴστρον ποταμὸν
191ʳP καὶ τοῦτον περάσαντες, ἀντεπαρατάξαντο τοῖς ἀνθεστηκόσιν, καὶ ἐ|τρο-
πώσαντο αὐτούς. Μαθὼν δὲ ὁ βασιλεὺς τὴν ὑπ᾽ αὐτῶν γενομένην τροπήν,135
ἐκέλευσεν αὐτοὺς κατὰ τὴν ἐνεγκαμένην ἀπιέναι, τοὺς δὲ τούτων πρωτεύοντας προσκαλεσάμενος κατὰ τοῦ Βυζαντίου καὶ εὐχαριστήσας τὰ
μέγιστα, ἔφη αὐτοῖς· «Ἐπειδὴ καὶ νῦν εὐνοϊκῶς ὑπὲρ ἡμῶν ἐκάμετε,
καθὼς καὶ ἐπὶ τῶν εὐσεβῶν προγόνων τῆς ἡμετέρας θειότητος, ἰδοὺ καὶ
ἡμεῖς ἐπικυροῦντες τὰς ἤδη ἐπ᾽ ἐλευθερίᾳ καὶ ἀτελείᾳ δοθείσας ὑμῖν ἐν140
τῇ Ῥωμαίων ἐκ τῆς ἡμετέρας βασιλείας δεξιάς, παρέχομεν ὑμῖν καὶ
ἡμεῖς ἀνδριάντα χρυσοῦν μετὰ καὶ χλαμύδος βασιλικῆς καὶ φιβλατούρας
καὶ στέφανον χρυσοῦν πρὸς εὐπρέπειαν τῆς ὑμετέρας πόλεως μετὰ καὶ
191ᵛP ἐγγράφου ἡ|μῶν ἐλευθερίας καὶ ἀτελείας ὑμῶν τε καὶ τῶν πλωΐμων
ὑμῶν, καὶ πρὸς τὴν γνησιότητα τῆς ὑμῶν εὐνοίας δίδομεν ὑμῖν καὶ145

53

of the Chersonites, Constans, too, on the withdrawel of Sauromatus from the Roman territories, himself set out for Rome, and reported to the emperor all that had been done by the Chersonites; and he brought their two envoys also, whom the emperor saw and bounteously entertained and thanked most gratefully, and then said to them: «What will you that I should grant to you and your city in return for this affection and alliance?» They said to the emperor: «We, my lord, wish for nothing else, but request this one thing only, that your majesty should grant us pledges of freedom and immunity from tribute.» The emperor gladly acceded to their request and ungrudgingly granted them these pledges of freedom and of immunity from tribute, and sent them to the country of the Chersonites with very many gifts besides, as true subjects of the empire of the Romans. Constans too was grandly entertained by the emperor Diocletian for his brave support in the war of the Sarmatians, and became noble and illustrious and after a short while was proclaimed emperor of the Romans, when Diocletian had retired to Nicomedeia.

On the death of Constans, his son Constantine became emperor at Rome, and when he came to Byzantium, and certain of those in Scythia revolted against him, he called to mind what had been said by his father Constans concerning the affection of the Chersonites and their alliance, and he sent envoys to the country of the Chersonites, with instructions that they should go to the country of the Scythians and fight those who had revolted against him. The chief magistrate and primate of the Chersonites was at that time Diogenes, son of Diogenes, and the Chersonites gladly obeyed the imperial mandate and with all zeal constructed the military waggons and the arbalests and arrived at the Ister river and, having crossed it, arrayed themselves against the rebels and routed them. The emperor, learning of the victory won by them, bade them go back to their country, but their primates he invited to the city of Byzantium and, after thanking them most gratefully, he said to them: «Since now too you have laboured loyally on our behalf, as in the time of the pious forbears of our divine majesty, see, we too do ratify the pledges of freedom and immunity from tribute already granted to you in the city of the Romans by our imperial government; and for our part we give you besides a golden statue with imperial cloak and clasp and a golden crown, for the beautifying of your city, and thereto our charter of freedom and immunity from tribute for you and for your sailors; and, for the purity of your affection, we give you also golden

---

V 107 Σαυρωμάτου P ‖ 116 τε *om.* edd. ‖ 121 Σαυρωμάτων P   Σαυρομάτων Migne ‖ 122 ἀνεδείχθη (*coni. etiam* Bekker): ἀνεδέχθη edd. ‖ 127 λεχθὲν V edd.: λεχθήσει (*littera* θ *in ras. scripta*) P¹ ‖ 129 αὐτοὺς *om.* edd. ‖ 130 τῆς edd.: τῇ P ‖ 134 ἀντιπαρετάξαντο Migne ‖ 142 ἀνδρίαντα P ‖

53

δακτυλίους χρυσοῦς, ἐκτυποῦντας τὰς ἡμετέρας εὐσεβεῖς εἰκόνας, δι᾽ ὧν τὰς κατὰ καιρὸν μελλούσας ἀποστέλλεσθαι ἡμῖν παρ᾽ ὑμῶν ἀναφοράς τε καὶ δεήσεις σφραγίζοντες ταύτας, γνωρίμους ἡμῖν ἀποδείκνυτε τοὺς ἑαυτῶν πρέσβεις, πρὸς ἐπὶ τούτοις δὲ παρέχομεν ὑμῖν καθ᾽ ἕκαστον ἔτος νεῦρόν τε καὶ κάνναβον, σίδηρόν τε καὶ ἔλαιον ὑπὲρ κατασκευῆς 150 τῶν βαλλιστρῶν ὑμῶν, καὶ δίδομεν ὑμῖν πρὸς ἀποτροφὴν ὑμῶν χιλίας ἀννώνας, ἐφ᾽ ᾧ τε εἶναι ὑμᾶς βαλλισταρίους, λεγόμενον, ὡς τὰς τοιαύτας

252Be
192ʳP σιτήσεις τε καὶ συνη|θείας πάσας καθ᾽ ἕκαστον ἔτος τῶν | ἐντεῦθεν μέλλομεν ὑμῖν ἀποστέλλειν κατὰ τὴν Χερσωνιτῶν.» Οἱ δὲ Χερσωνῖται τὰς τοιαύτας εἰληφότες ἀννώνας, εἰς ἑαυτούς τε καὶ τὰ τούτων τέκνα 155 διαμερίσαντες, τὸν ἀριθμὸν συνεστήσαντο· διὰ τὸ καὶ ἕως τοῦ νῦν τὰ τούτων τέκνα κατὰ τῶν γονέων τῆς στρατείας συμπλήρωσιν ἐν τῷ ἀριθμῷ κατατάσσονται. Ἐφοδίοις δὲ καὶ δώροις πλείστοις τότε τιμηθέντων ὑπὸ τοῦ θεοφιλοῦς βασιλέως Κωνσταντίνου, τοῦ τε Διογένους καὶ τῶν σὺν αὐτῷ, κατέλαβον τὴν Χερσωνιτῶν ἀποκομίζοντες καὶ τὰς θείας 160 φιλοτιμίας.

Μετὰ δὲ χρόνους τινὰς τοῦ ταῦτα γεγονέναι Σαυρόματος, ὁ ἔγγονος Σαυρομάτου, τοῦ Κρισκορόνου, τοῦ πολεμήσαντος τὴν Λαζικήν, συν-
192ᵛP αθροί|σας πόλεμον ἐκ τῆς Μαιώτιδος λίμνης, ἐπανέστη τοῖς Χερσωνίταις, βουλόμενος, φησίν, τὴν τῆς αἰχμαλωσίας ὕβριν τοῦ οἰκείου πάππου 165 ἐκδικῆσαι, τὴν παρ᾽ αὐτῶν ἐπὶ Διοκλητιανοῦ τοῦ βασιλέως γενομένην. Μεμαθηκότες δὲ τοῦτο οἱ Χερσωνῖται, στεφανηφοροῦντος τότε καὶ πρωτεύοντος τῆς Χερσῶνος Βύσκου, τοῦ Σουπολίχου, ἀντιπαραταξάμε-νοι καὶ αὐτοὶ ὑπήντησαν τῷ Σαυρομάτῳ ἔξω ἐν τοῖς τοῦ λεγομένου Καφᾶ τόποις, καὶ πολεμήσαντες μετὰ αὐτοῦ, τοῦ Θεοῦ τοῖς Χερσωνίταις 170 βοηθοῦντος, ἐνίκησαν τὸν Σαυρόματον καὶ ἐδίωξαν, θήσαντες καὶ ὁροθεσίας ἐν τῷ αὐτῷ λεγομένῳ Καφᾶ, ἐν ᾧ τόπῳ πολεμήσαντες τὸν

253Be
193ʳP Σαυρόματον | ἐνίκησαν, ἐν ᾧ καὶ ὅρκους ἐπετέλεσεν ὁ αὐτὸς Σαυ|ρόματος καὶ οἱ σὺν αὐτῷ ὑπολειφθέντες τοῦ μηκέτι αὐτοὺς χάριν πολέμου ὑπερ-βαίνειν τὰς μεταξὺ αὐτῶν τεθείσας ὁροθεσίας, ἀλλ᾽ ἕκαστον αὐτῶν 175 τοὺς ἰδίους ἔχειν τόπους πρὸς τὰς τεθείσας ὁροθεσίας. Καὶ οὕτως ἀνε-χώρησεν ἐπὶ τὴν Βόσπορον ⟨ὁ⟩ Σαυρόματος, καὶ οἱ Χερσωνῖται εἰς τὰ ἴδια.

Καὶ δὴ τούτων οὕτως γενομένων, πάλιν μετὰ χρόνους τινὰς ἕτερος Σαυρόματος ἀναστὰς καὶ σὺν αὐτῷ πλῆθος ἀνδρῶν ἐκ τῆς Μαιώτιδος 180 λίμνης, παρετάξαντο πόλεμον κατὰ τῶν Χερσωνιτῶν, καὶ παρελθὼν τὰς μεθ᾽ ὅρκου τεθείσας ὁροθεσίας ἐν τῷ Καφᾶ ὑπὸ τοῦ πρώτου γενο-

---

V 146 χρυσοὺς P ‖ 147 ἡμῖν] litteram η in ras. scr. P¹ ‖ 150 κάνναβον P ‖ 151 βαλιστρῶν P ‖ 152 βαλισταρίους P ‖ ⟨τὸ⟩ λεγόμενον coni. Kyriakides ‖ 156 διὰ τὸ: δι᾽ αὐτὸ coni. Bekker ‖

rings expressing the likenesses of our pious selves, wherewith you are to seal reports and petitions which shall from time to time be sent from you to us, and thus make your envoys known to us; and besides, in addition to these, we grant you annually cord and hemp, iron and oil, for the manufacture of your bows, and we give you for your sustenance a thousand military rations, so that you may be bowmen (*as they are called*): so that all these provisions and regular grants we shall send you every year from here to the country of the Chersonites.» The Chersonites, receiving these rations, divided them out among themselves and their sons and so made up the brigade, and that is why, even to this day, their sons are «enrolled in the brigade», to fill up the number of their parents' levy. Diogenes and those with him were then honoured with a multitude of supplies and gifts by Constantine, the emperor beloved of God, and came to the country of the Chersonites, bringing back the gifts conferred by his divine majesty.

Some years after these events had taken place, Sauromatus, grandson of Sauromatus the son of Criscoronus who had attacked Lazike, gathered together a warlike power from the Maeotic lake and rose against the Chersonites, desiring, it appears, to avenge the insult of the captivity done to his grandfather by them in the time of Diocletian the emperor. The Chersonites, Byscus, son of Supolichus, being at that time chief magistrate and primate of Cherson, learnt of this and on their side arrayed themselves in opposition and met Sauromatus outside, in the region of Kapha, so-called, and they fought with him, and, God aiding the Chersonites, defeated Sauromatus and drove him off; and they set up boundary-stones in that same Kapha by name, in the place where they had fought and defeated Sauromatus, and there this same Sauromatus and those that were left with him swore oaths in due form that they would never more pass for purposes of war beyond the boundary-stones set up between them, but that each of them should keep to his own places on his side of the boundary-stones set up. And so they withdrew, Sauromates to Bosporus, and the Chersonites to their own homes.

When this had been done, once more after some years another Sauromatus rose up and with him a multitude of men from the Maeotic lake, and they drew up their force against the Chersonites, and, crossing over the boundary-stones set up in Kapha by the first Sauromatus with an oath that

---

157 συμπληρῶσιν P ‖ 159 τε edd.: τότε P ‖ 169 ἀποκομίσαντες edd. ‖ 162 Σαυρώματος P ‖ 163 Σαυρωμάτου P ‖ πολεμίσαντος P ‖ 167 Μεμαθηκότες: μαθόντες V edd. ‖ Χερσωνίται P ‖ 169 Σαυρωμάτω P ‖ 170 Καφά P ‖ πολεμίσαντες P ‖ 171 Σαυρώματον P ‖ 172 πολεμήσαντες] *litteras* λεμη *in ras. scr.* P¹ ‖ 173 Σαυρώματον P ‖ ᾧ *edd.*: οἷς P ‖ Σαυρώματος P ‖ 174 αὐτούς Meursius Ba Be: αὐτοῖς P ‖ 177 ὁ *add.* edd. ‖ Σαυρώματος P ‖ Χερσωνίται P ‖ 180 Σαυρώματος P ‖ 181 παρετάξατο edd. ‖ ‖ Χερσωνίτων P ‖ 182 τῷ V edd.: τῇ P ‖ Καφά P ‖

μένου Σαυρομάτου τοῦ μηδένα ποτὲ ἐπιχειρῆσαι τῶν Βοσποριανῶν
193ᵛP πολέμου χάριν ταύτας ὑπερβῆναι, οὗτος ὁ Σαυρόματος | ὑπερέβη, ὡς οἷα
βουλόμενος τὴν μετὰ βίας αὐτῷ ἀφαιρεθεῖσαν γῆν ἐκδικῆσαι καὶ ἀπολα-185
βεῖν. Καὶ δὴ ἐν τοῖς τότε καιροῖς στεφανηφοροῦντος καὶ πρωτεύοντος
τῆς Χερσωνιτῶν Φαρνάκου, τοῦ Φαρνάκου, ἀντεπαρατάξαντο καὶ οἱ
Χερσωνῖται τῷ Σαυρομάτῳ, καὶ ἀπαντήσαντες ἀλλήλους ἐν τοῖς τοῦ
προειρημένου Καφᾶ τόποις, ἔστησαν ἑκάτερα τὰ μέρη ἐν τοῖς ὄρεσιν.
Ὁ δὲ Σαυρόματος ὢν μέγας τὴν ἡλικίαν ἐθάρρησεν ἑαυτῷ, καὶ ἐμε-190
γαλαύχει κατὰ τῶν Χερσωνιτῶν φρυαττόμενος, θαρρῶν ἅμα καὶ ἐπὶ τῷ
ἀπείρῳ πλήθει, τῷ μετ' αὐτοῦ ὄντι. Ὁ δὲ Φαρνάκος μικρὸς ἦν τῇ ἡλικίᾳ
κατὰ τὸν Σαυρόματον, καὶ ἰδὼν τὸ πλῆθος τοῦ Σαυρομάτου, ἐσκέψατο
194ʳP μετὰ τοῦ ἰδίου | στρα|τοῦ, ἐφ' ᾧ τε μονομαχῆσαι αὐτὸν μετὰ τοῦ Σαυρο-
254Be μάτου καὶ μὴ ἄπειρον πλῆθος ἀπολέσθαι. Καὶ δὴ σκέψεως τοιαύτης 195
γενομένης, δηλοῖ ὁ Φαρνάκος τὸ πλῆθος τοῦ Σαυρομάτου λέγων, ὅτι·
«Τίς χρεία ἐστὶν τοσούτου ὄχλου γενέσθαι ἀπώλειαν; Οὐ γὰρ ὑμεῖς
οἰκείᾳ προαιρέσει πρὸς τὸν πόλεμον ἐτράπητε, ἀλλὰ Σαυρόματος ὑμᾶς
προετρέψατο. Θελήσατε οὖν τοῦτον ἀναγκάσαι τοῦ μονομαχῆσαι μετ'
ἐμοῦ, καὶ ἐὰν διὰ τοῦ Θεοῦ δυνηθῶ αὐτόν, ὑμεῖς ἀναχωρεῖτε εἰς τὰ ἴδια 200
ἀβλαβῶς, καὶ αὐτὸς καὶ ἡ πόλις αὐτοῦ ὑπέπεσάν μοι, εἰ δὲ καὶ δυνηθῇ με
αὐτός, καὶ οὕτως ὑμεῖς ἀναχωρεῖτε εἰς τὰ ἴδια, καὶ αὐτὸς ἐπέβη ἐν τοῖς
194ᵛP ἐμοῖς.» Ὁ δὲ ὄχλος τῶν Σαυρομάτων | ἡδέως τοῦτο ἀποδεξάμενος
προετρέψατο τὸν Σαυρόματον μονομαχῆσαι μετὰ τοῦ Φαρνάκου. Ὁ οὖν
Σαυρόματος μαθὼν μικρὸν πάνυ ὄντα τῇ ἡλικίᾳ τὸν Φαρνάκον, ἑαυτὸν 205
δὲ ὑπερμεγέθη, ἐχάρη ἐπὶ τούτῳ, πεποιθὼς τῇ οἰκείᾳ δυνάμει καὶ οἷς
ἐκέχρητο ὅπλοις κατατεθωρακισμένος. Καὶ τούτων οὕτως δοξάντων,
λέγει ὁ Φαρνάκος τῷ ἰδίῳ στρατῷ, ὅτι· «Ὅταν κατέλθω διὰ τοῦ Θεοῦ
εἰς τὸ μονομαχῆσαι, καὶ ἴδητε, ὅτι ὁ Σαυρόματος τὰ νῶτα αὐτοῦ ἔχει
πρὸς ὑμᾶς καὶ τὴν ὄψιν πρὸς τοὺς ἰδίους, ἐγὼ δὲ τὴν ὄψιν μου πρὸς 210
ὑμᾶς καὶ τὰ νῶτά μου πρὸς τοὺς ἐναντίους, ἅπαντες ὑμεῖς βάλετε μίαν
κραυγὴν καὶ μόνον λέγοντες τὸ ἆ, ἆ, καὶ μὴ δευτερώσητε ἐπὶ τῇ κραυγῇ.»
195ʳP Καὶ δὴ | κατελθόντων αὐτῶν ἀμφοτέρων ἐν τῷ πεδίῳ πρὸς τὴν μονομα-
χίαν καὶ τρακτευόντων ἑαυτούς, καὶ τοῦ Φαρνάκου γενομένου εἰς τὸ τοῦ
255Be Σαυρομάτου μέρος καὶ τοῦ Σαυρομάτου εἰς | τὸ τοῦ Φαρνάκου, ἔδωκεν 215
ὁ τοῦ Φαρνάκου στρατὸς μίαν φωνήν, τὸ ἆ, ἆ. Ὁ δὲ Σαυρόματος τῆς τοιαύτης
φωνῆς ἀκούσας περιεστράφη ἰδεῖν ἐναγώνιος, τίς ἡ γενομένη κραυγὴ

V 183 Σαυρωμάτου P || 184 Σαυρώματος P || 187 ἀντεπαρετάξαντο V ἀντιπαρε-
τάξαντο Ba Be || 188 Σαυρωμάτω P || ἀλλήλοις edd. || 189 Καφὰ P || 190
Σαυρωμάτος P || 191 Χερσωνίτων P || 192 Φάρνακος edd. || 193 Σαυρώματον
P || ἰδὼν edd.: ἰδὼς P || Σαυρωμάτου P || 194 Σαυρωμάτου P || 196 Φάρνακος

53

none of the Bosporians should ever attempt to pass beyond them for purposes of war, this Sauromatus passed beyond them, as desiring to avenge and recover the land forcibly taken from him. In those times the chief magistrate and primate of the country of the Chersonites was Pharnacus, son of Pharnacus, and the Chersonites on their side arrayed themselves against Sauromatus, and they met one another in the region of the aforesaid Kapha, and each side took up position on the mountains. Sauromatus, being of huge stature, had confidence in himself and boasted insolently over the Chersonites, confiding also at the same time in the infinite multitude that was with him. But Pharnacus was of small stature compared to Sauromatus, and, seeing the multitude of Sauromatus, resolved with his own army that he should fight in single combat with Sauromatus, to avoid the destruction of an infinite multitude. This resolution having been made, Pharnacus made a declaration to the multitude of Sauromatus, saying: «What need is there of the destruction of so great a throng? For you have not resorted to war of your own choice, but Sauromatus has bidden you to it. Do you, then, urge him to fight in single combat with me, and if by God's aid I overpower him, do you withdraw unharmed to your own homes, and he and his city shall have fallen beneath me; but if he overpowers me, in this case also you withdraw to your own homes, and he shall have become master over mine.» The throng of the Sarmatians accepted this with joy, and told Sauromatus to fight in single combat with Pharnacus. So Sauromatus, learning that Pharnacus was quite small in stature, while he himself was gigantic, was delighted at this, for he trusted in his own strength and in his armour, by which he was completely protected. This being so resolved upon, Pharnacus said to his army: «When I go down with God's aid to the single combat, and you see that Sauromatus has his back towards you and his face towards his own men, while I have my face towards you and my back towards the enemy, do you all raise one shout, saying simply 'Ah! Ah!', and after the shout, do not repeat it.» And so, when both had gone down to the plain for the single combat, and were manoeuvring about one another, and Pharnacus had taken the ground of Sauromatus and Sauromatus that of Pharnacus, the army of Pharnacus gave one shout, 'Ah! Ah!'. Sauromatus, hearing this shout, turned about in the action to see what cry was raised in the army of

---

edd. ‖ τὸ πλῆθος: τῷ πλήθει V edd. ‖ τοῦ om. edd. ‖ Σαυρωμάτου P ‖ 198 Σαυρώματος P ‖ 199 ἀναγκάσαι: παρακαλέσαι V edd. ‖ 201 με V edd.: μοι P ‖ 203 Σαυρωμάτων P   Σαυρομάτων edd. ‖ 204 Σαυρώματον P ‖ 205 Σαυρώματος P ‖ Φάρνακον edd. ‖ 208 Φάρνακος edd. ‖ 209 ἴδητε Be: ἴδεται P ‖ Σαυρώματος P ‖ ἔχει (etiam Migne) εἶχε edd. ‖ 211 βάλλετε F edd. ‖ 212 δευτερώσητε V edd.: δευτερώσεται P ‖ 215 Σαρωμάτου P   Σαυρωμάτου V ‖ τοῦ om. edd. ‖ Σαυρωμάτου P ‖ Φαρνάκου] litteram υ s. v. add. P[1] ‖ 216 Σαυρώματος P ‖

ἐν τῷ τοῦ Φαρνάκου στρατῷ. Ἐν δὲ τῷ περιστρέψαι τὸν Σαυρόματον τὴν ἑαυτοῦ ὄψιν εἰς τὰ ὀπίσω διηνοίχθη μικρὸν τὸ τοῦ κασσιδίου αὐτοῦ πέταλον, καὶ εὐθέως ἐπιδραμὼν ὁ Φαρνάκος ἔδωκεν τῷ κοντῷ τὸν 220 Σαυρόματον καὶ ἀνεῖλεν αὐτόν. Πεσόντος δὲ τοῦ Σαυρομάτου, κατελθὼν ὁ

195ᵛP Φαρνάκος | τοῦ ἵππου, ἀπεκεφάλισεν αὐτόν, καὶ γενόμενος ἐγκρατὴς τοῦ πολέμου, τὸ μὲν πλῆθος τῆς Μαιώτιδος ἀπέλυσεν, τοὺς δὲ τῆς Βοσπόρου αἰχμαλώτους λαβὼν καὶ τὴν γῆν αὐτῶν ἀφελόμενος, ἐν Κυβερνικῷ ἄνω τῆς τῶν Χερσωνιτῶν ὁροθεσίας ἔστησεν, ἄχρι τεσσαράκοντα καὶ μόνον 225 μιλίων γῆν αὐτοῖς ἐάσας, αἵτινες ὁροθεσίαι ἕως τοῦ νῦν διαμένουσιν, αἱ δὲ εἰρημέναι πρῶται ὁροθεσίαι ἐν Καφᾷ εἰσιν ἀποκείμεναι. Ὀλίγους δέ τινας κατασχὼν παρ' ἑαυτῷ τῶν Βοσποριανῶν ὁ Φαρνάκος γεωργῶν ἕνεκα, τοὺς ἄλλους ἅπαντας οἴκτου ἀξιώσας ἀπέλυσεν κατὰ τῶν Βοσπορια- νῶν ἀπελθεῖν, οἵτινες ἀπολυθέντες ὑπὸ τοῦ Φαρνάκου, ὑπὲρ τῆς τοιαύτης 230

196ʳP εὐεργεσίας καὶ φιλαν|θρωπίας αὐτοῦ τῆς εἰς αὐτοὺς γενομένης στήλην αὐτῷ ἤγειραν ἐν τῇ Βοσπόρῳ. Ἔκτοτε οὖν λοιπὸν ἡ τῶν Σαυρομάτων ἐν τῇ Βοσπόρῳ βασιλεία κατελύθη.

Τούτων δὲ οὕτως γενομένων, Λαμάχου στεφανηφοροῦντος καὶ
256Be πρωτεύοντος τῆς τῶν Χερσωνιτῶν, Ἀσάνδρου δὲ τῆς Βο|σποριανῶν 235 βασιλεύοντος, κακίᾳ πολλῇ μεμεστωμένοι οἱ Βοσποριανοὶ κατὰ τῶν Χερσωνιτῶν καὶ μηδαμῶς δυνάμενοι τῇ πονηρίᾳ ἠρεμεῖν, ἔσπευδον ἀεὶ τρόπῳ τινὶ τὴν ἀνταμοιβὴν τῶν αἰχμαλωσιῶν τοῖς Χερσωνίταις ἀποδοῦ- ναι. Καὶ δὴ μεμαθηκότες ἔχειν θυγατέρα μονογενῆ τὴν Γυκίαν, ἔχοντος δὲ καὶ τοῦ Ἀσάνδρου υἱούς, ἐμηχανῶντο ἐπιγαμβρείαν ποιήσασθαι, 240

196ᵛP ὅπως διὰ τούτου ἀδεῶς ἐπιβαί|νοντες τῇ Χερσωνιτῶν ἀμύνασθαι. Καὶ δὴ ἀποστέλλουσι πρέσβεις κατὰ τὴν Χερσωνιτῶν παρακαλοῦντες· «Ἐὰν οἴδαμεν, ὅτι ἀγάπη ἀληθὴς μεταξὺ ἡμῶν ἐστιν, καὶ ἀδόλως πρὸς ἀλλήλους ἔχομεν, ἐπιγαμβρεύσωμεν ἑαυτοῖς, καὶ δότε ἡμῖν εἰς νύμφην τὴν θυγατέρα Λαμάχου, τοῦ πρώτου ὑμῶν, ἕνεκεν τοῦ υἱοῦ Ἀσάνδρου, 245 τοῦ κυρίου ἡμῶν, ἢ λάβετε αὐτὸν αὐτόθι εἰς γαμβρόν, καὶ οἴδαμεν, ὅτι πιστὰ ἔχομεν εἰς ἀλλήλους, τοῦ υἱοῦ τοῦ βασιλέως ὄντος μεθ' ὑμῶν.» Λέγουσιν αὐτοῖς οἱ Χερσωνῖται, ὅτι· «Ἡμεῖς πρὸς ὑμᾶς θυγατέρα ἡμῶν δοῦναι οὐκ ἀνεχόμεθα, εἰ δὲ ἐκ τῶν υἱῶν Ἀσάνδρου, τοῦ βασιλέως ὑμῶν, θέλετε δοῦναι ἡμῖν εἰς γαμβρόν, δεχόμεθα, οὕτω μέντοι, μὴ 250

197ʳP δυναμένου ἔτι τοῦ υἱοῦ Ἀσάνδρου, | τοῦ ἐρχομένου πρὸς ἡμᾶς ἐπιγαμβρεύ- σασθαι, καιρῷ ποτε ἢ χρόνῳ πειραθῆναι τοῦ ὑποστρέψαι κατὰ τὴν τῶν Βοσποριανῶν χάριν ἐπισκέψεως ἢ προσηγορίας τοῦ οἰκείου πατρός,

---

V 218 ἐν τῷ τοῦ Φαρνάκου στρατῷ   om. Ba Be || Σαυρώματον P || 220 Φάρνακος edd. || 221 Σαυρώματον P || Σαυρωμάτου P || 222 Φάρνακος edd. || 224 Κυβερνικῷ: Κιμμερικῷ coni. Laskin || 225 τῆς V edd.: τοῦ P || μόνον V edd.

53

Pharnacus. And as Sauromatus turned his face to the rear, the plating of his helmet opened a crack, and at once Pharnacus charged upon him and smote Sauromatus with his lance and slew him. When Sauromatus had fallen, Pharnacus got down from his horse and cut off his head, and, having won the battle, dismissed the multitude of the Maeotis, but took prisoner them of Bosporus and took away their land and set up boundary-stones in Kybernikon, beyond the country of the Chersonites, leaving to the Bosporians land up to forty miles only, and these boundary-stones remain to this day, and the said first boundary-stones in Kapha are laid aside. Pharnacus, keeping by him some few of the Bosporians to do agricultural work, in pity dismissed all the rest, to go to *the country* of the Bosporians, and they, dismissed by Pharnacus, erected a column to him in Bosporus for the beneficence and mercy which he had shown towards them. From that time, then, the rule of the Sauromati in Bosporus was ended.

These events, then, fell out so; but when Lamachus was chief magistrate and primate of the country of the Chersonites and Asander was king of the country of the Bosporians, the Bosporians, being replete with much malice against the Chersonites and wholly unable to rest from wickedness, were still eager how they might pay back the recompense of the captivities upon the Chersonites. And so, learning that *Lamachus* had an only daughter, Gykia, while Asander had sons, they set about contriving the conclusion of a marriage alliance, in order that thereby they might safely gain a footing in the country of the Chersonites and take vengeance on it. And so they sent envoys to the country of the Chersonites, with this request: «If we know that sincere love exists between us, and if our relations one toward another are without guile, let us make for ourselves a marriage alliance, and do you give us the daughter of Lamachus, your first man, to be bride of the son of Asander our lord, or else receive him on your side as son-in-law, and we shall know that we have faith one toward another when the king's son is among you.» The Chersonites said to them: «We cannot consent to giving our daughter to you; but if from among the sons of Asander your king you would like to give us a son-in-law, we accept, but on such terms that the son of Asander who comes to us to be allied in marriage shall no longer have in his power ever at any time or season to attempt to return to the country of the Bosporians for the purpose of visiting or greeting his

---

μόνων P ‖ 226 ἕως: μέχρι V edd. ‖ 227 ὁροθεσίαι] litteras οθ in ras. scr.
P¹ ‖ Καφὰ P ‖ 228 Φάρνακος edd. ‖ γεωργῶν: γεωργιῶν coni. Bekker ‖
232 Σαυρωμάτων P Σαυρομᾰτᾶν Migne ‖ 234 Τούτων] litteram T rubro atramento scriptam eras. et novam litteram T in ras. scr. P¹ ‖ 235 Χερσωνίτων
P ‖ 244 ἐπιγαμβρεύσωμεν V: ἐπιγαμβρεύσομεν P edd. ‖ 247 βασιλέως ὄντος
(coni. etiam Bekker): βασιλεύοντος edd. ‖ 251 ἐρχομένου: ἀρχομένου Ba Be ‖

εἰ δὲ τοῦτο βούλεται, πάντως, ὅτι τῇ ὥρᾳ ἀποθνήσκει.» Τῶν δὲ πρέσβεων ἀπολυθέντων καὶ καταλαβόντων τὴν Βοσποριανῶν καὶ ταῦτα 255
257Be ἀναγγελλόντων, ἀπέστειλεν πάλιν | ὁ ᾿Ασάνδρος πρέσβεις, λέγων τοῖς Χερσωνίταις, ὅτι· «᾿Εὰν ἀληθῶς λέγετε καὶ πιστοποιεῖτέ με, ὅτι Λάμαχος ἀνέχεται ζεῦξαι τὴν θυγατέρα αὐτοῦ τῷ μειζοτέρῳ μου υἱῷ, ἀποστελῶ ὑμῖν αὐτὸν ἐκεῖνον αὐτόθι ἐπιγαμβρεύσασθαι.» ῾Ην δὲ Λάμαχος τοῖς τότε καιροῖς, ὡς λόγος, πλούτῳ πολλῷ κομῶν ἔν τε χρυσίῳ καὶ ἀργυρίῳ, 260
197ᵛP παισί ⟨τε⟩ καὶ παιδίσκαις καὶ | ἀλόγοις διαφόροις καὶ κτήμασι πολλοῖς, καὶ τέσσαρσι δὲ ῥεγεῶσι τὸν οἶκον αὐτοῦ ἐπικρατεῖν ἐν πλάτει καὶ μήκει ἕως κάτω τῶν λεγομένων Σωσῶν, ἐν οἷς καὶ ἰδίαν πύλην εἶχεν ἐν τῷ τείχει καὶ τέσσαρας πυλεῶνας μεγάλους εἰς τὴν εἴσοδον καὶ τὴν ἔξοδον σὺν ἑτέροις δὲ παραπυλίοις σεμνοῖς, ὥστε εἰσερχομένων τῶν ἀλόγων 265 αὐτοῦ ἐν τῇ πόλει, ἑκάστην ἀγέλην ζώων, ἵππων τε καὶ φορβάδων, βοῶν τε καὶ δαμάλεων, προβάτων τε καὶ ὄνων καὶ δι᾿ ἰδίας πύλης εἰσιέναι καὶ εἰς ἰδίαν στάσιν ἀπιέναι. Παρεκάλεσαν οὖν οἱ Χερσωνῖται τὸν Λάμαχον, ἐφ᾿ ᾧ τε ἐπιγαμβρεύσασθαι αὐτὸν τὸν τοῦ ᾿Ασάνδρου υἱόν. Τοῦ δὲ Λαμάχου ἐπινεύσαντος τῇ παρακλήσει αὐτῶν, ἦλθεν ὁ τοῦ ᾿Ασάνδρου 270
198ʳP υἱὸς | ἐν τῇ Χερσῶνι, καὶ ἔγημεν τὴν Γυκίαν. Καὶ διετοῦς μικροῦ χρόνου διαγενομένου, ἐτελεύτησεν ὁ Λάμαχος· ἡ γὰρ μήτηρ τῆς Γυκίας προτελευτήσασα ἦν. ῾Η οὖν Γυκία μετὰ τὴν τοῦ ἐνιαυτοῦ περαίωσιν τῆς τοῦ πατρὸς ταφῆς, τῆς ἐνιαυσιαίας ἡμέρας ἐνστάσης, τὴν μνήμην θέλουσα φαιδρῦναι τοῦ ἰδίου πατρός, στεφανηφοροῦντος τότε καὶ πρωτεύοντος 275
258Be τῆς Χερσῶνος Ζή|θου, τοῦ Ζήθονος, παρεκάλεσεν τοῖς προύχουσι τῆς πόλεως, ἐφ᾿ ᾧ τε ἄνευ ὕβρεως ἀνεχθῆναι αὐτοὺς τοῦ λαβεῖν παρ᾿ αὐτῆς σὺν παντὶ τῷ δήμῳ οἶνόν τε καὶ ἄρτους καὶ ἔλαιον, κρέα τε καὶ ὄρνεα καὶ ὄψα, καὶ εἴ τι ἕτερον πρὸς τὴν τῆς εὐφρασίας χρείαν, πρὸς τὸ τὴν
198ᵛP ἡμέραν τῆς μνήμης τοῦ Λαμάχου ἅπαντας τοὺς | πολίτας σὺν γυναιξὶν 280 καὶ τέκνοις καὶ πάσῃ τῇ φαμιλίᾳ αὐτῶν εὐφρανθῆναι καὶ ἀγάλλεσθαι, ἕκαστον ἐν τῷ ἰδίῳ ῥεγεῶνι καὶ δημοσίᾳ χορεύειν καὶ ἔργου τινὸς τὸ σύνολον μὴ ἅψασθαι, συνταξαμένη τοῖς πολίταις ἐν ὅρκῳ, ἐφ᾿ ᾧ τε ἅπαντα τὸν χρόνον τῆς ζωῆς αὐτῆς οὕτω τὰ τῆς εὐφρασίας καθ᾿ ἕκαστον χρόνον διδόναι αὐτοῖς ἐν τῇ αὐτῇ τοῦ Λαμάχου μνήμῃ. Τούτων δὲ οὕτως 285 γενομένων ⟨καὶ⟩ ἐν ὅρκῳ ὑπ᾿ αὐτῆς παγιωθέντων, ὁ ταύτης ἀνήρ, ὁ τοῦ ᾿Ασάνδρου υἱός, ἔχων ἐν κρυπτῷ τὸν δόλον καὶ ἐπιζητῶν καιρὸν προδοσίας, ἀκούσας ταῦτα ⟨τὰ⟩ παρὰ τῆς Γυκίας λεχθέντα καὶ ἐν ὅρκῳ παγιωθέντα, ἐθαύμασε μὲν καὶ ἐπήνεσεν τὴν Γυκίαν ἐπὶ τῇ ἐνόρκῳ συντάξει, ὡς γνησίως περὶ τοὺς γονεῖς ἔχουσαν, συνθέμενος δὲ καὶ 290

V 254 βούλεται coni. Bekker: βούλει P edd.   ‖   260 ἀργυρίῳ V edd.: ἀργύρω
P ‖ 261 παισί edd.: παῖδες P ‖ τε add. V edd. ‖ 263 Σωσῶν Moravcsik:
Σουσῶν P edd.   ‖   264 τέσσαρας Ba Be τεσσάρας Pᵛ: τέσσαρσι P V Me ‖

53

father, and if he shall resolve to do this, surely he dies that hour.» The envoys were dismissed and reached the country of the Bosporians and reported this, and Asander once more sent envoys, saying to the Chersonites: «If you speak truly, and assure me that Lamachus consents to yoke his daughter with my eldest son, that same son will I send there to you, to be joined in marriage.» Lamachus in these days, as it appears, prided himself upon much wealth, in gold and silver, male and female slaves, and cattle of various kinds and many estates, and his mansion occupied ground far and wide in four wards, as far as to below the so-called Sosae, in which it had its own gate in the wall and four main gate-ways for ingress and egress, together with other small side-entrances, so that when his cattle entered the city, each herd of beasts, stallions and mares, cows and heifers, sheep and asses, came in through its own gate, and went to its own stabling. The Chersonites, therefore, begged Lamachus that this son of Asander might be his son-in-law. Lamachus granted their request, and the son of Asander came to Cherson and married Gykia. And after the space of about two years, Lamachus died; the mother of Gykia had died before him. So, after the lapse of a year, when the anniversary of her father's burial was near, Gykia, wishing to keep bright the memory of her father, begged the leading men of the city, the chief magistrate and primate of Cherson being Zethus, son of Zethon, that they would kindly consent, together with all the populace, to receive from her wine and loaves of bread and oil, flesh and game and fish, and anything else needed to make merry, to the end that upon this day of the commemoration of Lamachus all the citizens, with their wives and children and all their families, should feast and rejoice, each in his own ward, and dance in the streets and completely abstain from any work; and she promised the citizens upon oath that each year of her life she would in the same way give them the means of merry-making at this same commemoration of Lamachus. This being so arranged *and* confirmed by her upon oath, her husband, the son of Asander, who was plotting in secret and looking for an occasion of treachery, when he heard what Gykia had said and confirmed on oath, admired and congratulated Gykia upon the sworn convenant, as one showing a truly filial spirit towards her parents, and consented himself also, as it appears, to rejoice and pour

---

πυλεῶνας: πυλαιῶσι V ‖ μεγάλους: μεγάλοις V Me ‖ 265 σὺν P^y Ba Be: καὶ P V Me ‖ 267 τε¹ *om.* Be ‖ πύλας edd. ‖ 269 ἐπιγαμβρεύσεσθαι edd. ‖ 271 Γυκίαν: γυναῖκα V edd. ‖ 276 τῆς Χερσῶνος edd.: τὴν Χερσῶνα P ‖ 277 ἄνευ ὕβρεως: ἐνιαυσιαίως *coni.* Jenkins ‖ ἀνεχθῆναι *coni.* Kukules: ἀναχθῆναι P edd. συναχθῆναι *coni.* Bekker ‖ 281 φαμηλία PV ‖ 283 συνταξαμένη edd.: συνταξαμένης P ‖ 286 καὶ *add.* Be ‖ 288 τὰ *add.* edd. ‖ 289 μὲν *om.* edd. ‖

199ʳP αὐτός, | φησί, χαίρειν καὶ σπένδειν ἐπὶ τῇ τοιαύτῃ συντάξει. Καὶ μετὰ
τοῦτο παρελθούσης τῆς μνήμης καὶ τῆς εὐφρασίας, δηλοῖ τοῖς ἐν Βοσπόρῳ δι' οἰκείου παιδὸς λέγων αὐτοῖς, ὅτι· «Εὖρον μέθοδον, δι' ἧς
ἀκόπως τὴν Χερσῶνα μέλλομεν παραλαβεῖν· ὑμεῖς οὖν ἐκ διαλειμμάτων
ἀποστέλλετέ μοι δέκα ἢ δώδεκα νεωτέρους χρησίμους ἐκτὸς τῶν ἐν 295
259Be τῷ καράβῳ ἐλαυ|νόντων ὡς δῆθεν ξένιά μοι πέμποντες, ἐν Συμβόλῳ δὲ
παραβαλλόντων τῶν ἐρχομένων καράβων ὑμῶν καὶ ἐκεῖ μενόντων,
ἐμοῦ δὲ πέμποντος καὶ δι' ἵππων φέροντος τοὺς ἐρχομένους νεωτέρους
ἐν τῇ πόλει καὶ τὰ πεμπόμενα.» Καὶ δὴ τῷ τρόπῳ τούτῳ ἐπὶ διετῇ χρό-
199ᵛP νον ἐκ τοῦ κατὰ μέρος ἐρχομένων τῶν Βοσποριανῶν μετὰ τῶν ξε|νίων 300
πρὸς τὸ μὴ γνωσθῆναι τῇ πόλει τὸν δόλον ἔφερε μὲν αὐτοὺς πεζικῶς ἐκ
τοῦ Συμβόλου ὁ τοῦ Ἀσάνδρου υἱός, καὶ μετὰ ἡμέρας τινὰς πάλιν ἐπὶ
πάντων πρὸς ἑσπέραν ἀπέλυεν αὐτούς, φησίν, ἐπὶ τὰ ἔξω ὡς δῆθεν
βραδέστερον διὰ τὴν ὥραν. Οἱ δὲ ἐξερχόμενοι ἐκ τῆς χώρας ἄχρι τριῶν
μιλίων, σκοτίας βαθείας γενομένης, ὑπέστρεφον καὶ ἤρχοντο ἐν τῷ 305
λεγομένῳ Λιμῶνι, καὶ ἐκεῖθεν διὰ καράβου ἔφερεν αὐτοὺς ἐν ταῖς Σώσαις, καὶ διὰ τοῦ παραπυλίου, οὗ εἶχεν ἐν τῷ τείχει, εἰσέφερεν αὐτοὺς
ἐν τῷ οἴκῳ αὐτοῦ, μηδενὸς εἰδότος, εἰ μήτι γε τριῶν παίδων αὐτοῦ
Βοσποριανῶν καὶ μόνων πιστικῶν αὐτοῦ ὄντων, ἑνὸς μὲν τοῦ ἐν Συμβόλῳ
200ʳP ἀπερχομένου καὶ μηνύοντος ἀναχωρεῖν τοὺς | καράβους, ἄλλου δὲ τοῦ 310
ὑποστρέφοντος τοὺς Βοσποριανοὺς καὶ φέροντος ἐν Λιμῶνι, ἑτέρου δὲ
τοῦ ἐκ Λιμῶνος μετὰ καράβου ἀποκομίζοντος ἐν ταῖς Σώσαις καὶ
ἀποκαθιστῶντος ἐν τῷ τοῦ Λαμάχου οἴκῳ, καὶ δι' ὧν ἐπέτρεφεν αὐτοὺς
ἐν ταῖς ἀποθήκαις αὐτοῦ, μήτε τῆς Γυκίας εἰδούσης τὸν δόλον, προσδο-
κῶν, καθὰ εἴρηται, κατὰ τὴν ἐνιαυσιαίαν ἡμέραν τῆς τοῦ Λαμάχου 315
260Be μνή|μης, τῆς πόλεως πάσης εὐφραινομένης τε καὶ ἀποκοιμωμένης,
αὐτὸν τὴν νύκτα ἐπαναστῆναι μετὰ τῶν Βοσποριανῶν τε καὶ οἰκείων
καὶ ἐμπρῆσαι τὴν πόλιν καὶ πάντας κατασφάξαι. Συναχθέντων δὲ ἐν τῷ
διετεῖ χρόνῳ ἐν τῷ τῆς Γυκίας οἴκῳ ἄχρις διακοσίων Βοσποριανῶν, καὶ
200ᵛP τῆς μνήμης τοῦ Λαμάχου ἤδη λοιπὸν | ἐγγιζούσης, ἐγένετο παιδίσκην 320
τῆς Γυκίας κουβικουλαρέαν, πάνυ αὐτῇ οὖσαν προσφιλεστάτην, πταίσα-
σαν ἀπὸ ὄψεως αὐτῆς γενέσθαι καὶ ἀποκλεισθῆναι αὐτήν. Ἐν ᾧ δὲ
οἴκῳ ἀπεκλείσθη ἡ παιδίσκη, ὑποκάτωθεν αὐτοῦ ἦσαν οἱ Βοσποριανοὶ
ἐπιτρεφόμενοι. Τῆς δὲ παιδίσκης καθεζομένης καὶ νηθούσης τὸ λίνον,
ἐγένετο τὸ σφοντύλιν τῆς ἀτράκτου αὐτῆς ἐκπεσεῖν καὶ κυλισθὲν εἰσελ- 325

V 291 σπενδεῖν P ‖ 295 δέκα edd.: ι' P ‖ δώδεκα edd.: ιβ' P ‖ 296 Συμβόλῳ
scr. Moravcsik: συμβόλῳ edd. ‖ 302 Συμβόλου scr. Moravcsik: συμβόλου
edd. ‖ 304 τριῶν edd.: γ' P ‖ 305 σκοτείας P: σκοτιᾶς edd. ‖ γενομένης
V edd.: γινομένης P ‖ 306 Λιμῶνι coni. Meursius: λίμνω P λίμνῳ V edd. ‖
306/7 Σώσαις P ‖ 307 οὗ: ὃ edd. ‖ 308 τριῶν scr. Moravcsik γ' P: τρεῖς

53

a libation on this covenanted occasion. Afterwards, when the commemoration and merry-making had gone by, he made a declaration to those in Bosporus, through his confidential slave, and said to them: «I have found a means whereby we shall take Cherson without trouble; do you, therefore, send to me at intervals ten or twelve serviceable young fellows, in addition to the rowers of the ship, on the pretext that you are sending me presents, and let your ships that come hither put in at Symbolon and wait there, and I will escort and convey on horseback to the city the youths who come and the *presents* that are sent.» And so, in this manner, over a period of two years the Bosporians came, a few at a time, bringing the presents in order that the plot might not become known to the city, and the son of Asander conveyed them on foot from Symbolon, and then again a few days later, in sight of all, towards evening he would, as it appears, send them off outside the city, of course at as late an hour as he could. They would go out of the city a distance of three miles, and then, when it was pitch dark, would turn about and come to the so-called Limon, and thence he would convey them by boat to Sosae, and, through the side-gate which he had in the wall, would introduce them into his mansion; none being privy save three Bosporian slaves of his, who were his only confidants, one of whom used to go to Symbolon and give the word for the ships to depart, another would turn the Bosporians about and convey them to Limon, and the other would carry them by boat from Limon to Sosae and return them to the mansion of Lamachus; and by the agency of these *three slaves* he maintained them in his magazines, without even Gykia's being aware of the plot; and he expected, as has been said, on the anniversary of the commemoration of Lamachus, while all the city was making merry or had gone to sleep, to start up in the night with the Bosporians and his own slaves, and burn the city and put everyone to the sword. Now when, during the space of two years, as many as two hundred Bosporians had been collected in Gykia's mansion, and the commemoration of Lamachus was then already approaching, it fell out that a girl slave of Gykia, a chamber-maid, of whom she was exceedingly fond, committed some fault and was banished from her company and shut up. The room in which the girl slave was shut up had beneath it the Bosporians who were being kept there. It happened that, while the girl slave was sitting and spinning flax, the weight fell off her

---

V edd. ‖ *ante* παίδων *add.* τῶν V edd. ‖ 309 *ante* Βοσποριανῶν *add.* τῶν edd. ‖ μόνον V edd. ‖ πιστικῶν: πιστῶν V edd. ‖ 311 Λειμῶνι Migne ‖ 312 Λειμῶνος Migne ‖ Σώσαις P ‖ 313 ἀπέτρεφεν edd. ‖ 315 ἐνιαυσίαν edd. ‖ 317 νύκτα V edd.: νύκταν P ‖ 319 διακοσίων Be: σ΄ P ‖ 321 κουβικουλαρέαν Moravcsik: κουβικουλαρίαν *coni.* Bekker κουβουκλαρέαν P edd. κουβουκλαρίαν Migne ‖ οὖσαν V edd.: οὖση P ‖ προσφιλεστάτην *corr.* Moravcsik: προσφιλέστατον P edd. ‖ 324 ἐπιτρεφόμενοι *corr.* Moravcsik: ἀποτρεφόμενοι P edd. ‖ 325 αὐτῆς *om.* V edd. ‖ ἐκπεσεῖν: πεσεῖν V edd. ‖ κυλισθὲν edd.: κυλισθέντα P ‖

θεῖν εἰς βαθυτάτην ὀπὴν πρὸς τὸν τοῖχον. Ἡ δὲ ἀναστᾶσα πρὸς τὸ
ἐπᾶραι αὐτό, ὁρᾷ αὐτὸ ἐν βαθυτάτῃ ὀπῇ ὄν, καὶ μὴ δυναμένης αὐτῆς
ἐκσπάσαι αὐτὸ διὰ τὸ βάθος, ἠναγκάσθη ἐκ τοῦ πάτου τοῦ πρὸς τὸν
τοῖχον ἀνασπάσαι ἕνα βήσσαλον πρὸς τὸ τοῦτο ἐπᾶραι, καὶ ὁρᾷ διὰ τῆς
201ᴿᴾ ὀπῆς κάτω ἐν τῷ ὑπο|γέῳ οἴκῳ τὸ πλῆθος τῶν ὄντων ἀνδρῶν. Καὶ 330
ἰδοῦσα εὐφυῶς πάλιν ἀπέθετο ἐν τῷ τόπῳ τὸ βήσσαλον πρὸς τὸ μὴ γνωσθῆναι τοῖς κάτω, καὶ λαθραίως ἀποστείλασα μίαν τῶν παίδων, προσεκαλεῖτο τὴν κυρίαν αὐτῆς τοῦ ἐλθεῖν πρὸς αὐτήν, ὀφείλουσάν τι ἀναγ-
καῖον ἀκοῦσαι καὶ ἰδεῖν. Ἡ δὲ Γυκία ὑπὸ τοῦ Θεοῦ κατανυγεῖσα ἀπῆλθεν
261Βε πρὸς τὴν παι|δίσκην, καὶ εἰσελθούσης αὐτῆς κατὰ μόνας ἐν τῷ οἰκήματι 335
καὶ κλεισάσης τὴν θύραν, πεσοῦσα ἡ παιδίσκη πρὸς τοὺς πόδας αὐτῆς,
εἶπεν· «Δέσποινα, ἐξουσίαν ἔχεις ⟨εἰς⟩ τὴν ἀχρείαν σου δούλην· πλὴν
βούλομαι τῇ κυρίᾳ μου ξένον τι καὶ παράδοξον πρᾶγμα δεῖξαι.» Ἡ δὲ
Γυκία εἶπεν αὐτῇ· «Ἀφόβως εἰπὲ καὶ δεῖξον, τί τὸ τοιοῦτον;» Ἡ δὲ παι-
201ᵛᴾ δίσκη | ἀπαγαγοῦσα αὐτὴν πρὸς τὸν τοῖχον καὶ εὐφυῶς ἐπάρασα τὸ βήσσα- 340
λον λέγει αὐτῇ· «Ὁρᾷς διὰ τῆς ὀπῆς, δέσποινα, τὸν κάτω κρυπτόμενον
ὄχλον τῶν Βοσποριανῶν;» Ἡ δὲ Γυκία ἰδοῦσα καὶ ἐκπλαγεῖσα ἐπὶ τῷ
πράγματι ἔφη· «Οὐκ ἀργὸν τὸ σκέμμα τοῦτο.» Καὶ λέγει τῇ παιδίσκῃ·
«Πῶς εὗρες τὸ πρᾶγμα τοῦτο;» Ἡ δὲ παιδίσκη λέγει· «Πάντως, δέσποινα, ὅτι ἐκ θελήματος Θεοῦ ἔπεσεν τὸ σφοντύλιν ἐκ τῆς ἀτράκτου 345
μου, καὶ κυλισθὲν εἰσῆλθεν ἐν τῇ ὀπῇ ταύτῃ καὶ, μὴ δυναμένης μου αὐτὸ
ἐπᾶραι, ἠναγκάσθην τὸ βήσσαλον ἀνασπάσαι, καὶ τότε εἶδον αὐτούς.»
Ἡ δὲ ἐκέλευσεν τῇ παιδίσκῃ ἀποθέσθαι τὸ βήσσαλον εὐφυῶς ἐν τῷ τόπῳ
202ᴿᴾ αὐτοῦ, καὶ ἐπιλαβομένη αὐτῆς καὶ περιπλακεῖσα κατεφί|λησε γνησίως,
καὶ εἶπεν αὐτῇ· «Μηδὲν πτοηθῇς, τέκνον, συγκεχώρηταί σου τὸ πταῖσμα, 350
ὁ γὰρ Θεὸς ἠθέλησέ σε πταῖσαι, ἵνα τὸν δόλον ἡμῖν φανερώσῃ· βλέπε
οὖν, ὅσῃ δυνάμει φυλάξαι τὸ πρᾶγμα, καὶ μὴ τολμήσῃς τινὶ τὸ σύνολον
τοῦτο θαρρῆσαι.» Καὶ λοιπὸν εἶχεν αὐτὴν διόλου μεθ' ἑαυτῆς πλέον τοῦ
226Βε πρώτου ὡς πιστικὴν αὐτὴν οὖσαν. Καὶ προσκαλεσα|μένη ἡ Γυκία δύο
τινὰς τῶν συγγενῶν αὐτῆς, πιστικοὺς αὐτῇ ὄντας πάνυ, λέγει αὐτοῖς 355
ἐν τοῖς ἰδιάζουσιν· «Ἀπελθόντες συναγάγετε καθ' ἑαυτοὺς ἐν μυστηρίῳ
τοὺς πρωτεύοντας καὶ εὐγενεῖς τῆς πόλεως, καὶ ἐκλεξάσθωσαν τρεῖς
ἄνδρας πιστικούς, δυναμένους φυλάξαι μυστήριον καὶ πρᾶγμα ποιῆσαι,
202ᵛᴾ καὶ πιστοποιήσουσιν | αὐτοὺς οἱ πάντες ἐνόρκως πρὸς τὸ καὶ αὐτοὺς ἐμὲ
πληροφορῆσαι, ἐν οἷς μέλλω ἐπερωτᾶν αὐτούς, καὶ ἀποστειλάτωσαν 360
αὐτοὺς πρός με ἐν μυστηρίῳ, καὶ ἔχω αὐτοῖς ἀναγκαῖόν τι καὶ ὠφέλιμον
τῇ πόλει θαρρῆσαι, μόνον διὰ τάχους ποιήσατε, ὃ λέγω ὑμῖν.» Ἀπελθόντων δὲ τῶν συγγενῶν αὐτῆς καὶ ἐν μυστηρίῳ ταῦτα τοῖς πρωτεύουσιν

53

spindle and rolled and dropped into a very deep crevice by the wall. Getting up to recover it, she saw it lying in a very deep crevice, and, being unable owing to the depth to pluck it out, she was forced to pluck up a brick from the floor by the wall in order to recover it, and she saw through the crevice down below in the basement room the multitude of men who were there. When she had seen, she deftly put the brick back again in its place in order not to reveal herself to those below, and sent in secret one of the servants and invited her mistress to come to her, for there was something needful for her to hear and see. Gykia, pricked on by God, went to the slave girl, and when she entered the room alone and closed the door, the girl slave fell at her feet and said: «Lady, yours is the power *over* your unworthy slave: but I would show to my mistress a matter strange and unlooked-for.» Gykia said to her: «Fear not: speak and show what this is.» The girl slave led her to the wall and, deftly raising the brick, said to her: «Do you see, lady, through the crevice the throng of Bosporians in hiding below ?» Gykia looked and was astonished at the affair, and said: «This is a serious plot!» And she said to the girl slave: «How did you find out this matter ?» The girl slave said: «Surely, lady, by the will of God, the weight fell off my spindle and rolled and dropped into this crevice, and as I was unable to recover it I was forced to pluck up the brick, and then I saw them.» She bade the girl slave put the brick back deftly in its place, and then she caught her in her arms and embraced her and kissed her in earnest, and said to her: «Fear nothing, child; your fault is forgiven you, for God willed you to err, so that He might reveal the plot to us; see, now, that you do all you can to keep the matter close, and do not venture to entrust it to anybody at all.» And for the future she kept her wholly with herself as her confidante, even more than at first. Then Gykia summoned two of her relations, who were very much in her confidence, and said to them in private: «Go and collect together on their own in secret the primates and nobles of the city, and let them choose out three men in whom they confide, men who can keep a secret and do a deed, and let them all upon oath assure these men that they will satisfy me in what I am about to ask of them, and let them send them to me in secret, and I will confide to them a thing necessary and advantageous for the city; only do with speed what I tell you.» Her relations went off and told this in secret to the

---

V 328 τοῦ² *om.* edd. ‖ 329 βίσαλον P ‖ 331 βίσαλον P ‖ 333 ὀφείλουσάν edd.: ὀφείλουσά P ‖ 337 εἰς *addendum coni.* Bekker ‖ 339 καὶ δεῖξον: δεῖξον· καὶ edd. ‖ 340/1 βίσαλον P ‖ 345 σφοντύλην P ‖ 346/7 αὐτὸ ἐπᾶραι: ἐπᾶραι αὐτὸ Be ‖ 347 ἠναγκάσθην F edd.: ἠναγκάσθη P ‖ βίσαλον P ‖ 348 βίσαλον P ‖ 352 τολμήσῃς Ba Be: τολμήσεις P ‖ 353 πλέον edd.: πλὴν P ‖ 354 πιστικὴν: πιστὴν V edd. ‖ αὐτήν: αὐτῇ *coni.* Bekker ‖ 355 πιστικοὺς: πιστοὺς V edd. ‖ 356 συναγάγετε: συνάγετε edd. ‖ 357 ἐκλεξάτωσαν edd. ‖ 358 πιστικούς: πιστούς V edd. ‖

εἰρηκότων, εὐθέως ἐξελέξαντο τρεῖς ἄνδρας, οὓς ᾔδεσαν αὐτοὶ πιστοὺς
εἶναι, καὶ πιστοποιήσαντες αὐτοὺς πάντες ἐν ὅρκῳ, ὅτι εἴ τι συνθῶνται 365
τῇ Γυκίᾳ εἴτε ποιῆσαι, εἴτε δοῦναι, μὴ ἀκυρῶσαι τοὺς λόγους αὐτῶν,
ἀλλ᾽ εἰς πέρας ἀγαγεῖν τὰ ὑπ᾽ αὐτῶν συνταττόμενα αὐτῇ. Τούτων δὲ
πρὸς τὴν Γυκίαν ἐν μυστηρίῳ ἀπελθόντων, ἐδέξατο αὐτούς, καὶ λέγει
203ʳᴾ αὐτοῖς· «Δύνα|σθέ με πληροφορῆσαι ἐν ὅρκῳ, περὶ ὧν μέλλω ἐπερωτᾶν
ὑμᾶς, ὅτι ποιεῖτε ταῦτα;» Οἱ δὲ εἶπον αὐτῇ· «Ναί, κυρία, ἑτοίμως ἔχο- 370
μεν, περὶ ὧν μέλλεις ἡμῖν ἐπιζητεῖν, πληροφορῆσαί σε, ὅτι εἰς πέρας
ἄγονται οἱ λόγοι σου». Τότε λέγει αὐτοῖς ἡ Γυκία· «Πληροφορήσατέ με,
ὅτι ἂν ἀποθάνω, ἐν μέσῳ τῆς πόλεώς με θάπτετε, καὶ λέγω ὑμῖν τὸ
263Bе μυστήριόν μου· | ἰδοὺ βαρὺ ὑμῖν τίποτε οὐκ ἐπιζητῶ.» Οἱ δὲ ἄνδρες
ἀκούσαντες τοῦτο, μετὰ πάσης προθυμίας ἐπληροφόρησαν αὐτὴν ἐν 375
ὅρκῳ, λέγοντες, ὅτι· «Ἐὰν τελευτήσῃς, ἐν μέσῳ τῆς πόλεώς σε θάψομεν
καὶ οὐκ ἐξάξομέν σε ἔξω τῶν τειχῶν.» Ἡ δὲ Γυκία πεισθεῖσα τοῖς
ὅρκοις αὐτῶν λέγει αὐτοῖς· «Ἐφ᾽ οἷς ἐπληροφορήσατέ με, κἀγὼ λοιπὸν
203ᵛᴾ ἐμφαίνω ὑμῖν τὸ μυστήριόν μου· ἰδοὺ | εἰδέναι ὑμᾶς θέλω, ὅτι ὁ ἀνήρ
μου τὸ ἔμφυτον κακὸν τῆς πόλεως αὐτοῦ ἔχων, τὸ τοῦ δόλου καὶ φθόνου 380
καθ᾽ ἡμῶν, ὄχλον ἐκ τοῦ κατὰ μέρος Βοσπορανῶν ἐν κρυφῇ εἰσαγαγὼν
ἐν τῷ οἴκῳ μου, ἄχρις διακοσίων ψυχῶν ἐνόπλων διατρέφει, ἐμοῦ μὴ
εἰδυίας τὸ πρᾶγμα· ἀλλ᾽ ὁ Θεὸς νῦν διὰ προφάσεως ἐφανέρωσέν μοι
αὐτό. Αὐτὸς οὖν ταύτην ἔχει τὴν σκέψιν, ἐφ᾽ ᾧ τε, φησίν, εἰς τὴν μνήμην
τοῦ πατρός μου διδούσης μου τὴν εὐφρασίαν τῇ πόλει, καὶ εὐφρανθέντων 385
ὑμῶν καὶ ἀποκοιμωμένων, αὐτὸν τὴν νύκτα ἐπαναστῆναι μετὰ τῶν
συνόντων αὐτῷ Βοσπορανῶν τε καὶ οἰκείων, καὶ βαλεῖν ἐμπρησμὸν ἐν
τοῖς οἴκοις ὑμῶν καὶ κατασφάξαι πάντας ὑμᾶς. Ἰδοὺ λοιπὸν φθάζει καὶ ἡ
204ʳᴾ μνήμη τοῦ πατρός μου, καὶ δέον μέν ἐστι πρὸς τὸν | ὅρκον μου δοῦναι
ὑμῖν κατὰ τὸ ἔθος τὰ τῆς εὐφρασίας, πάντα γὰρ ἑτοίμως ἔχω. Θελήσατε 390
οὖν πάντες προσδραμεῖν χαίροντες καὶ ζητῆσαι καὶ λαβεῖν πάντα προ-
θύμως πρὸς τὸ μήπω νοῆσαι αὐτόν, ὅτι ἔγνωμεν τὸ πρᾶγμα, καὶ ἄφνω
ἐμφύλιος πόλεμος γένηται. Θελήσατε οὖν καὶ δημοσίως κατὰ τὸ ἔθος
264Bе εὐφραίνεσθαι, συμμέτρως δέ, καὶ χορεύειν ἐν ταῖς πλα|τείαις, ἑτοιμάσατε
δὲ ἕκαστος ἐν τοῖς οἴκοις ὑμῶν ξύλα τε καὶ φορτία καὶ δᾷδας στεγνὰς 395
πρὸς τό, μισοποιούντων ὑμῶν τὰς εὐφρασίας καὶ τοὺς χορούς, δόξασθαι
πρὸς ἀνάπαυσιν ὑμῶν ἀπιέναι, καὶ ἐμοῦ δὲ ταχέστερον μισοποιησάσης
καὶ κελευούσης ἀσφαλισθῆναι τοὺς πυλεῶνάς μου, ὑμεῖς εὐθέως ἐν
204ᵛᴾ ἡσυχίᾳ πολλῇ σὺν παι|σὶ καὶ παιδίσκαις ὑμῶν πανοικὶ παρενέγκαντες
τὰ ξύλα καὶ φορτία καὶ δᾷδας, παράθετε αὐτὰ ἐν τοῖς πυλεῶσί μου καὶ 400

V 364 αὐτοὶ V edd.: αὐτοὺς P ‖ 367 ἀγαγεῖν Ba Be: ἀγάγαι P ‖ 369 ἐν ὅρκῳ
πληροφορῆσαι edd. ‖ 371 μέλλεις V edd.: μέλλῃς P ‖ 372 ἄγονται V edd. ‖

53

primates, and they immediately chose out three men, in whom they knew they could confide, and all on their oaths assured them that, if they should covenant with Gykia to do or to give anything, they would not go back on their words, but would carry out to the end what they promised to her. These men went in secret to Gykia, who received them and said to them: «Are you able to satisfy me on oath concerning these things that I am about to ask of you, that you will do them?» They said to her: «Yes, lady, we will readily satisfy you concerning what you are about to require of us, that your words shall be carried out to the end.» Then Gykia said to them: «Satisfy me that if I die, you will bury me in the middle of the city, and I will tell you my secret; see, I do not require anything at all burdensome of you.» The men, on hearing this, with all readiness satisfied her upon oath, saying: «If you die, we will bury you in the middle of the city and will not carry you outside the walls.» Gykia believed their oaths, and said to them: «In view of the satisfaction you have given me, I on my part will now discover my secret to you; see now, I would have you know that my husband, who has the congenital vice of his city, that of plotting and envy against us, has introduced secretly into my mansion a throng of Bosporians, a few at a time, as many as two hundred souls, armed, and maintains them, I being in ignorance of the affair; but now God has found an occasion to reveal it to me. This, then, is his plan, that, so it appears, when at the commemoration of my father I provide the merry-making to the city and you have made merry and are gone to sleep, he will start up in the night with the Bosporians that are with him, and with his own slaves, and will set fire to your houses and put you all to the sword. See, now, my father's commemoration approaches, and I must, in accordance with my oath, give you as usual the means of merry-making, for I have all ready therefor. Do you, then, all run up joyfully and ask for and take everything eagerly, so that he may not yet realise that we have got to know of the affair, and a civil war suddenly break out. Resolve, therefore, to make merry publicly as usual, though moderately, and to dance in the squares, but let each of you make ready in his house timber and faggots and dry torches, so that when you break off the merry-makings and dances you may appear to go off to take your rest, and I for my part will break them off rather early and order my doors to be made fast, and then you, very quietly, with your male and female slaves and all your households, must at once bring along the timber and faggots and torches and pile them

382 διαχοσίων Be: σ′ P ‖ 384 ἔχει edd.: ἔχειν P ‖ 385 πόλει V edd.: πόλεως P ‖ 386 καὶ om. V edd. ‖ 390 post ἔθος add. μου V edd. ‖ 392 μήπω V edd.; μήπως P ‖ 396 μισοποιούντων: hic et infra cum σ duplicato scribendum censuit Kukules ‖ ὑμῶν Be: ἡμῶν P ‖ τὰς edd.: τῆς P V ‖ τοὺς χορούς edd.: τῶν χωρῶν P ‖ δόξασθαι edd.: δόξεται P ‖ 397 δὲ: δὴ Migne ‖ 399 παισὶ Ba Be: παῖδες P ‖ παρενεγκόντες Be ‖ 400 αὐτά: ταῦτα edd. ‖

παραπυλίοις καὶ κύκλῳ τῆς οἰκίας πάσης, ἐπιχέοντες καὶ ἔλαιον τοῖς
ξύλοις πρὸς τὸ τάχιον ἀφθῆναι, καὶ ἡνίκα ἐξέλθω ἐγὼ καὶ εἴπω ὑμῖν,
εὐθέως βάλετε τὴν πυράν, καὶ ὑμεῖς δὲ ἐν ὅπλοις παραστήκετε κύκλῳ
τῆς οἰκίας, ἵνα ὅπου τινὰς θεωρήσετε ἐκπηδῶντας ἐκ τοῦ οἴκου διὰ
θυρίδος, τούτους κατασφάζητε. Ἀπελθόντες οὖν τὸ μυστήριον τοῦτο 405
λαλήσατε καὶ ἑτοιμάσατε πάντα, ἃ εἶπον ὑμῖν.» Οἱ δὲ πολῖται ταῦτα
ἀκούσαντες ἀπὸ τῶν τριῶν ἀνδρῶν, ἐποίησαν πάντα ἐν συντομίᾳ κατὰ
205ʳP τὸν λόγον τῆς Γυκίας. Ἐνστάσης δὲ τῆς μνημοσύνου ἡμέρας, | ὡς δῆθεν
χαιρομένη ἡ Γυκία μετεπέμψατο τοὺς τῆς πόλεως ἄνδρας, προτρεπομένη
τοῦ λαβεῖν αὐτοὺς τὰ τῆς εὐφρασίας. Συνέτρεχε δὲ καὶ ὁ ἀνὴρ αὐτῆς ἐπὶ 410
τοῦτο, καὶ παρεκάλει πλεῖον οἶνον δοθῆναι αὐτοὺς ἐπὶ τῇ εὐφρασίᾳ. Οἱ
δὲ πολῖται ἀσμένως πάντα δεξάμενοι εὐφραίνοντο, καθὼς παρηγγέλθη-
σαν, καὶ ἐχόρευον τὴν πᾶσαν ἡμέραν, φθασάσης δὲ τῆς ἑσπέρας, ἤρξαντο
265Be μισοποιεῖν οἱ | πολῖται καὶ ἀπιέναι ἐν τοῖς οἴκοις αὐτῶν τοῦ ἀναπαῆναι,
εὐφραίνοντο δὲ πανοικί. Καὶ ἡ Γυκία ἐν τῷ οἴκῳ αὐτῆς προτρεπομένη 415
πάντας τοὺς αὐτῆς ἀδεῶς πίνειν πρὸς τὸ μεθυσθέντας αὐτοὺς τάχιον
κοιμηθῆναι, μόνον ταῖς κουβικουλαρίαις αὐτῆς παρήγγειλεν τοῦ νήφειν,
205ᵛP καὶ ἑαυτὴν τοῦ οἴνου | ἐφύλαττεν. Εὑρηκυῖα γὰρ ποτήριον πορφυροῦν
δέδωκεν τῇ κουβικουλαρέᾳ αὐτῆς, τῇ τὸ πρᾶγμα εἰδούσῃ, καὶ παρήγγειλεν αὐτῇ ἐν αὐτῷ αὐτὴν κιρνᾶν σὺν ὕδατι. Ὁ δὲ ἀνὴρ αὐτῆς θεωρῶν 420
τὸ πορφυροῦν ποτήριον, οὐχ ὑπενόει σὺν ὕδατι αὐτὴν πίνειν. Τῆς δὲ
ἑσπέρας φθασάσης, καὶ τῶν πολιτῶν, ὡς ἤδη εἶπον, μισοποιησάντων,
λέγει τῷ ἀνδρὶ αὐτῆς ἡ Γυκία· «Εὐφρανθέντων ἡμῶν, δεῦρο λοιπὸν
ἀναπαυθῶμεν καὶ ἡμεῖς.» Ὁ δὲ ἀνὴρ αὐτῆς ἀκούσας μᾶλλον ἐχάρη, καὶ
ἔσπευσεν τοῦ κοιμηθῆναι· οὐ γὰρ ἠδύνατο ἀφ' ἑαυτοῦ εἰπεῖν τοῦτο, 425
μήπως ὑπόνοιαν δῷ τῇ γυναικί, περὶ οὗ ἐβουλεύετο δόλου. Κελεύει οὖν
ἡ Γυκία ἀσφαλισθῆναι τοὺς πυλεῶνας καὶ πάντα τὰ παραθύρια καὶ
206ʳP ἐνεχθῆναι αὐτῇ τὰς κλεῖς κατὰ τὸ ἔθος. | Καὶ τούτου γενομένου, λέγει
ἐν τῷ λεληθότι τῇ πιστῇ αὐτῆς κουβικουλαρέᾳ, τῇ τὸν δόλον εἰδούσῃ,
ὅτι· «Θέλησον σὺν ταῖς λοιπαῖς κουβικουλαρέαις εὐφυῶς ἐπᾶραι πάντα 430
τὰ κόσμιά μου καὶ τὸ χρυσίον, καὶ εἴ τι χρήσιμον δύνασθε ἐγκολπίσασθαι,
καὶ ἑτοιμάσατε ἑαυτάς, ἵνα, ὅταν εἴπω ὑμῖν, ἀκολουθήσητέ μοι.» Αἱ δὲ
266Be ποιήσασαι κατὰ τὴν κέλευσιν αὐτῆς ἦσαν ἔτοι|μαι. Τοῦ δὲ ἀνδρὸς αὐτῆς
δῆθεν ἀνακλιθέντος τοῦ ἐκ συντόμου κοιμηθῆναι ⟨καὶ⟩ διὰ τάχους
αὐτὸν πάλιν ἀναστῆναι πρὸς ἐπιβουλὴν τῆς πόλεως, ἡ δὲ Γυκία παρέσυρεν 435

V 401 ἐπιχέαντες edd. ‖ 402 ἀφθῆναι edd.: αὐθῆναι P ‖ 403 βάλετε: λάβετε
V edd. ‖ παρεστήκετε edd. ‖ 404 θεωρήσητε V edd. ‖ 406 λαλήσαται] secundam
litteram α in ras. scr. P¹ ‖ 407 τριῶν edd.: γ´ P ‖ συντομίᾳ edd.: συντόμως P ‖ 412
ηὐφραίνοντο Ba Be ‖ 414 τοῦ: εἰς τὸ edd. ‖ 415 εὐφραίνοντο V Me: ηὐφραίνοντο Ba

53

up in my doorways and side-gates and all round the house, pouring oil
also upon the timbers so that they may catch the sooner, and when I come
out and give you the word, set fire to them at once, and yourselves stand
by armed around the house, so that where you see any jumping out of the
house through a window, you may put them to the sword. Go now, and
tell this secret, and make ready all that I have told you.» When they heard
these things from the three men, the citizens hastily did all in accordance
with the word of Gykia. When the commemoration day was upon them,
Gykia, with an appearance of enjoyment, sent for the men of the city and
told them to take the means of merry-making. And her husband, too,
helped in this and begged that more wine should be given them for the
merry-making. The citizens gladly took everything and began to make
merry, as they had been ordered, and danced all the day; but when evening
had come the citizens began to break off, and to go off to their houses to
take their rest. And they made merry with all their households. Gykia
in her house urged all her people to drink freely in order that they might
get drunk and sleep the sooner, only enjoining upon her chamber-maids
to be sober, and she herself abstained from wine. For she had found a purple
goblet and gave it to her chamber-maid, who was in the secret, and instructed
her to pour water into it for her. Her husband, seeing the purple goblet,
did not suspect that she was drinking water out of it. When evening had
come, and the citizens, as I have already said, had broken off the merry-
making, Gykia said to her husband: «We have made merry; come, now
let us too take our rest.» Hearing this, her husband was only too glad, and
hastened to go to sleep; for he could not have said this himself, in case
he might give his wife a hint of the plot he was hatching. So Gykia ordered
the gates to be made fast and all the windows, and the keys to be brought
to her as usual. When this was done, she said aside to her confidential
chamber-maid, the one who knew of the plot: «You, with the rest of the
chamber-maids, are deftly to remove all my jewelry and gold, and anything
else of use that you can carry in your bosoms, and make yourselves ready,
so that when I give you the word, you may follow me.» They did as she
bade them, and were ready. Her husband was of course lying down in order
to take a hasty nap *and* to get up again in a short while for his treachery
against the city; but Gykia avoided going to sleep until all their house-

---

Be εὐφραίνετο P ‖ 416 αὐτῆς Migne ‖ 417 κουβικουλαρέαις coni. Jenkins ‖ αὐτῆς
edd. ‖ 418 ἑαυτὴν coni. Bekker: ἑαυτῇ P   ἑαυτὴ edd. ‖ Εὐρηκυῖα: εὑροῦσα V
edd. ‖ 419 κουβικουλαρίᾳ Migne ‖ 421 ὑπενόει V edd.: ὑπενόειν P ‖ 424 Ὁ δὲ: ὁ
δὴ ὁ edd. ‖ 425 ἔσπευσεν: ἔπεσε edd. ‖ 429 κουβικουλαρίᾳ Migne ‖ 430 κουβικουλαρέαις (litteris βι in ras. scriptis) P V Ba Be: κουβικουλαρίαις Migne ‖ 431
ἐγκολπίσασθαι Meursius Ba Be: ἐγκαλωπήσασθαι P ‖ 432 ἀκολουθήσητέ coni.
Bekker: ἀκολουθήσατε P edd. ‖ 434 συντόμου edd.: σύντομον P ‖ 434 καὶ add.
Jenkins Kukules ‖

τοῦ καθευδῆσαι, ἕως ἂν πᾶσα ἡ φαμιλία αὐτῶν ἐκοιμήθη. Ὁ δὲ ἀνὴρ
αὐτῆς ἐκ τοῦ πολλοῦ πότου ἀφύπνωσεν. Ἡ δὲ Γυκία ἰδοῦσα τοῦτον
206ᵛP κοιμηθέντα, εὐφυῶς τὸν κοιτῶνα | τῷ κλειδίῳ ἠσφαλίσατο, ἀποκλείσασα
τὸν ἄνδρα καὶ κατελθοῦσα ἐκ τοῦ οἴκου σὺν ταῖς κουβικουλαρέαις αὐτῆς,
ἐξελθοῦσα τῶν παραπυλίων ἡσύχως καὶ κλείσασα, εὐθέως ἐπέτρεψεν 440
τοὺς τῆς πόλεως διὰ τάχους βληθῆναι τὸ πῦρ κύκλῳ τοῦ οἴκου. Βληθέν-
τος δὲ τοῦ πυρός, καὶ τοῦ οἴκου ἀναφθέντος, εἴ πού τις τῶν ἔσωθεν ὄντων
ἠδυνήθη ἐκπηδῆσαι ἢ ἑαυτὸν ῥίψαι, ὑπὸ τῶν πολιτῶν κατεσφάγη. Τοῦ
δὲ οἴκου παντὸς καὶ τῶν ἐν αὐτῷ ἕως ἐδάφους καταφλεχθέντων, διέσωσεν
ὁ Θεὸς τὴν Χερσωνιτῶν πόλιν ἐκ τῶν ἐπιβούλων Βοσποριανῶν. Ἡ δὲ 445
Γυκία, βουλομένων τῶν πολιτῶν τὴν καταφλεχθεῖσαν αὐτῆς οἰκίαν
207ʳP ὀρύξαι καὶ καθᾶραι τὸν τόπον πρὸς οἰκοδομήν, οὐκ εἴασεν, ἀλλὰ μᾶλ|λον
ἐπέτρεψεν πάσῃ τῇ πόλει φέρειν ἕκαστον αὐτῶν καὶ ἐκχύνειν αὐτόθι τὴν
πᾶσαν αὐτῶν κοπρίαν πρὸς τὸ ἐν αὐτοῖς καταχωσθῆναι τὴν πᾶσαν
αὐτῆς οἴκησιν, ὡς πρὸς ἐπιβουλὴν τῆς πόλεως γενομένην· διὸ καὶ ἐκλήθη 450
ὁ τόπος Λαμάχου Σκοπὴ ἕως τῆς σήμερον.

Τούτων οὖν ἁπάντων οὕτως γενομένων, ἰδόντες οἱ Χερσωνῖται τὴν
267Be τοιαύτην ἄπειρον ὑπὸ τῆς Γυκίας εἰς αὐτοὺς μετὰ Θεὸν | γενομένην
εὐεργεσίαν, καὶ ὅτι οὐδενὸς τῶν αὐτῆς τὸ σύνολον ἐφείσατο, ἀλλὰ τὴν
σωτηρίαν τῆς πόλεως προετιμήσατο, ὑπὲρ τῆς τοιαύτης μισθαποδοσίας 455
δύο χαλκοῦς ἀνδριάντας πρὸς τιμὴν αὐτῆς ἐν τῇ πλατείᾳ τῆς πόλεως
207ᵛP ἀνήγειραν, νεάζουσαν αὐτὴν τῇ ἡλικίᾳ | δεικνύοντες, καθ᾽ ὃν καιρὸν
ἦν τότε συμβαίνουσα, ἐν τούτοις δεικνύοντες καὶ τὴν αὐτῆς ἄφατον
εὐεργεσίαν καὶ στοργὴν περὶ τοὺς πολίτας, ὅτι καὶ ἐν ἡλικίᾳ νέα οὖσα
οὕτως ἐφρόνησεν τὴν ἰδίαν πατρίδα μετὰ Θεὸν περισῶσαι. Ἐν μὲν γὰρ 460
τῇ μιᾷ στήλῃ σωφρόνως αὐτὴν κεκαλλωπισμένην στήσαντες καὶ τὰ τῆς
ἐπιβουλῆς τοῦ οἰκείου ἀνδρὸς τοῖς πολίταις ἐμφαίνουσαν, ἐν δὲ τῇ ἑτέρᾳ
ἐναγώνιον αὐτὴν καὶ ἐπαμυνομένην κατὰ τῶν τῆς πόλεως ἐπιβούλων
ἀποδεικνύοντες, ἐν οἷς καὶ ἐπέγραψαν ἐν τῇ τοῦ ἀνδριάντος αὐτῆς βάσει
ἅπασαν τὴν ὑπ᾽ αὐτῆς μετὰ Θεὸν γενομένην τοῖς πολίταις εὐεργεσίαν. 465
208ʳP Εἴπερ μέλλει τις εἶναι φιλόκαλος, τῆς αὐτῆς συ|νεχῶς κατὰ καιρὸν τὴν
βάσιν ἀποσμήχει πρὸς τὴν τῶν ἐν αὐτῇ γενομένων ἀνάγνωσίν τε καὶ
ὑπόμνησιν τῶν ὑπ᾽ αὐτῆς γενομένων, ἔλεγχον δὲ τῶν ἐπιβούλων Βοσποριανῶν.

Μετὰ δὲ χρόνους τινάς, στεφανηφοροῦντος καὶ πρωτεύοντος 470
τῆς Χερσωνιτῶν Στρατοφίλου, τοῦ Φιλομούσου, πάνυ σοφωτάτη οὖσα ἡ
Γυκία καὶ θέλουσα δοκιμάσαι τοὺς Χερσωνίτας καὶ γνῶναι, εἰ ἄρα

F   450 διὸ καὶ — 451 σήμερον: cf. Matth. 27, 8.

53

hold was sleeping, and her husband was soundly off after his deep potations. Gykia, seeing him asleep, deftly made fast the bed-chamber with the key, shutting her husband in, came down from the house with her chamber-maids, went quietly out of the side-gates and locked them, and at once gave the word to them of the city to light the fire quickly all round the house. The fire was lit and the house caught, and if any of those within managed to jump or throw himself out, he was slain by the citizens. The whole house, with those in it, was gutted to the foundation, and God preserved the city of the Chersonites from the treacherous Bosporians. When the citizens wished to dig into her gutted house and to clear the site for building, Gykia would not allow it, but rather bade all the city bring, each one of them, and empty out on that spot all their ordures, so that her whole dwelling might be buried deep in them, inasmuch as it had served for treachery against the city; and so unto this day the place has been called the Spy-tower of Lamachus.

All these things having so fallen out, the Chersonites, seeing the infinite benefits that Gykia had, under God, conferred upon them, and that she had not spared anything of her own at all, but had put first the salvation of the city, erected in payment for this service she had done them two bronze statues to her honour in the city square, representing her as young in years, as then, at that time, she was, and therein showing her ineffable benefits and affection toward the citizens, in that at her tender age she had shown such wisdom for the preservation, under God, of her own fatherland. For upon one column they set her soberly adorned and discovering to the citizens the tale of her husband's treachery, and upon the other they represented her in action and fighting against the betrayers of the city; and thereto, upon the base of her statue, they also inscribed all the benefits which she had, under God, conferred upon the citizens. And if any would be a lover of virtue, he regularly scours from time to time the base of the same, so that what is there written may be read and there may be a reminder of what she did, and a refutation of the treacherous Bosporians.

And after some years, when the chief magistrate and primate of the country of the Chersonites was Stratophilus, son of Philomusus, Gykia, who had most excellent wit, desired to put the Chersonites to the proof

V 436 φαμηλία P ‖ 439 κουβικουλαρίαις Migne ‖ 441 τοὺς: τοῖς edd. ‖ βληθῆναι: ἐμβληθῆναι V edd. ‖ 442 ἔσεωθεν P ‖ 443 ἠδυνήθη ἐκπηδῆσαι: ἐκπηδῆσαι ἐδυνήθη edd. ‖ 448 πάσῃ V edd.: πᾶσιν P ‖ τῇ om. edd. ‖ πόλει V edd.: πύλη P ‖ ἐκχύνειν scr. Moravcsik ἐκχύνην P: ἐκχέειν edd. ‖ 452 οὕτως om. V edd. ‖ 454 αὐτῆς Migne ‖ 455 τῆς¹: τὴν Ba Be ‖ 456 χαλκοὺς P ‖ 459 οὖσα] litteram α in ras. scr. P¹ ‖ 461 κεκαλλωπισμένην F Be: καὶ καλωπισμένην P ‖ 464 ἀνδριάντος P ‖ 467 ἀποσμήχει edd.: ἀποσμίχην P ‖ γενομένων: γεγραμμένων coni. Bekker ‖ 471 τῆς: τῶν V edd. ‖

ἀληθῶς μέλλουσιν τὴν τοῦ ὅρκου ὑπόσχεσιν ἐκπληροῦν καὶ θάπτειν αὐτὴν
ἐν μέσῳ τῆς πόλεως, συλλογισαμένη μετὰ τῶν παιδισκῶν αὐτῆς, ἐποίη-
268Be σεν ἑαυτὴν | τινα ἀηδιζομένην καὶ ἀποθανοῦσαν. Καὶ κηδεύσασαι αὐτὴν 475
αἱ παιδίσκαι, ἐμήνυσαν τοῖς πολίταις λέγουσαι, ὅτι· «Ἡ κυρία ἡμῶν
208ᵛP ἐτελεύτησεν, καὶ ἐν ποίῳ τόπῳ μέλλει θά|πτεσθαι, ὑποδείξατε ἡμῖν.»
Οἱ δὲ Χερσωνῖται ἀκούσαντες, ὅτι τέθνηκεν ἡ Γυκία, σκεψάμενοι καθ᾽
ἑαυτούς, οὐκέτι τὸ ἱκανὸν τοῦ ὅρκου ἔσπευσαν ποιῆσαι, ὥστε ἐν μέσῳ τῆς
πόλεως αὐτὴν ταφῆναι, ἀλλὰ ἄραντες αὐτὴν ἐξήνεγκαν ἔξω τῆς πόλεως 480
θάψαι. Ἀποτεθέντος δὲ τοῦ κραββάτου πρὸς τὸ μνῆμα, ἀνακαθίσασα ἡ
Γυκία καὶ περιβλεψαμένη πάντας τοὺς πολίτας, λέγει· «Αὕτη ὑμῶν ἐστιν
ἡ μεθ᾽ ὅρκου ὑπόσχεσις; Οὕτως ἀληθεύετε περὶ πάντων; Ἄβαλε λοιπὸν
τῷ πιστεύοντι Χερσωνίτῃ πολίτῃ.» Οἱ δὲ Χερσωνῖται ἰδόντες τὴν ὑπ᾽
αὐτῆς γενομένην αὐτῶν χλεύην, αἰσχυνθέντες μεγάλως ἐπὶ τῷ γεγονότι 485
τῆς παραβασίας πράγματι, παρεκάλουν αὐτὴν πολλὰ τοῦ ἡσυχάσαι καὶ
209ʳP παραχωρῆσαι αὐτοῖς | τὸ πταῖσμα καὶ μὴ ἐπὶ πλεῖον ὀνειδίζειν αὐτοῖς.
Λοιπὸν δευτέροις ὅρκοις αὐτὴν ἐπιστώσαντο, ὥστε μηκέτι ἔξω τῆς
πόλεως θάψαι αὐτήν, ἀλλ᾽ ἐν μέσῳ τῆς πόλεως, ὃ δὴ καὶ ἐποίησαν. Καὶ
γὰρ αὐτῆς ζώσης ἔτι, ἐν ᾧ τόπῳ ᾑρετίσατο, τὴν σορὸν αὐτῆς ἐστήσαντο, 490
καὶ ἀνδριάντα χαλκοῦν καὶ ἕτερον ἤγειραν, καὶ τοῦτον χρυσώσαντες
ἔστησαν πρὸς τῇ ταφῇ αὐτῆς πρὸς περισσοτέραν πίστωσιν.
269Be   Ἰστέον, ὅτι ἔξω τοῦ κάστρου Ταμάταρχα πολλαὶ πηγαὶ ὑπάρ-
χουσιν ἄφθαν ἀναδιδοῦσαι.
    Ἰστέον, ὅτι ἐν Ζιχίᾳ πρὸς τὸν τόπον τῆς Πάγης, τῆς οὔσης εἰς 495
τὸ μέρος τῆς Παπαγίας, ἐν ᾧ κατοικοῦσι Ζιχοί, ἐννέα πηγαὶ εἰσὶν ἄφθαν
ἀναδιδοῦσαι, πλὴν οὐχ ὁμοχροοῦσιν τῶν ἐννέα πηγῶν τὰ ἔλαια, ἀλλὰ τὰ
209ᵛP μὲν ἐξ αὐτῶν | εἰσιν ἐρυθρά, τὰ δὲ ξανθά, τὰ δὲ μελανώτερα.
    Ἰστέον, ὅτι ἐν Ζιχίᾳ ἐν τῷ τόπῳ τῷ καλουμένῳ Πάπαγι, ἐν ᾧ
καὶ πλησίον ἔστι χωρίον ἐπονομαζόμενον Σαπαξί, ὃ ἑρμηνεύεται ᾽κονιορ- 500
τός᾽, ἔστιν ἐκεῖσε βρύσις ἄφθαν ἀναδιδοῦσα.
    Ἰστέον, ὅτι καὶ ἑτέρα βρύσις ἔστιν ἐκεῖσε ἄφθαν ἀναδιδοῦσα ἐν
τῷ χωρίῳ τῷ καλουμένῳ Χαμούχ. Τὸ δὲ Χαμοὺχ ἔστιν ὄνομα τοῦ
συστησαμένου ἀρχαίου ἀνδρὸς τὸ χωρίον· τὸ οὖν χωρίον ἐκεῖνο διὰ τοῦτο
ἐκλήθη Χαμούχ. Ἀπέχουσι δὲ οἱ τοιοῦτοι τόποι ἀπὸ τῆς θαλάσσης 505
ὁδὸν ἰδιοκαβάλλου ἡμέρας μιᾶς.
    Ἰστέον, ὅτι ἐν τῷ θέματι Δερζηνῆς πλησίον τοῦ χωρίου τοῦ Σαπι-
κίου καὶ τοῦ χωρίου τοῦ ὀνομαζομένου Ἐπισκοπείου, ἔστιν πηγὴ ἄφθαν
ἀναδιδοῦσα.

V 473 μέλλωσι edd. ‖ ἐκπληροῦν V edd.: ἐκπληρῦν P ‖ 474 συλλογισαμένη
V¹ F edd.: συλλογήσασα P ‖ παιδισκῶν Migne: παιδίσκων P edd. ‖ 475 ἑαυτήν

53

and to know whether in fact they would fulfil the sworn promise and bury her in the middle of the city; and having concerted with her girl slaves, she made herself as one who was weary of life and had died. Her girl slaves laid her out on the bier and sent a message to the citizens, saying: «Our lady has died, and do you point out to us in what place she is to be buried.» The Chersonites, when they heard that Gykia was dead, turned the matter over in their minds and were no longer eager to fulfil the oath that she should be buried in the middle of the city, and they took her up and bore her outside the city to bury her. But when the bier was set down at the tomb, Gykia sat up and looked about on all the citizens and said: «Is this your sworn promise ? Is this your truth in all your dealings ? Woe to him, then, who puts faith in a Chersonite citizen !» The Chersonites, seeing the mock she had made of them, were greatly ashamed of their conduct in breaking their word, and earnestly besought her to be appeased and to pardon their transgression and to rail upon them no more. And so they gave their word to her with a renewal of their oaths that thereafter they would not bury her outside the city, but in the middle of the city, and so they did. And while she was still alive, they set up her coffin in the spot that she chose, and erected yet another bronze statue and gilded it and set it upon her tomb for greater assurance.

Outside the city of Tamatarcha are many wells yielding naphtha.

In Zichia, near the place called Pagi, which is in the region of Papagia and is inhabited by Zichians, are nine wells yielding naphtha, but the oils of the nine wells are not of the same colour, some of them being red, some yellow, and some blackish.

In Zichia, in the place called Papagi, near which is a village called Sapaxi, which means 'dust', there is a spring yielding naphtha.

There is there yet another spring yielding naphtha, in the village called Chamouch. Chamouch is the name of the man of olden times who founded the village: for this reason that village was called Chamouch. These places are distant from the sea a journey of one day without changing horses.

In the province of Derzene, near the village of Sapikion and the village called Episkopion, is a well yielding naphtha.

---

edd.: αὐτήν P ‖ 478 Χερσωνίται P ‖ 480 *post* πόλεως² *add.* αὐτὴν V edd. ‖ 481 θάψαι: ταφῆναι V edd. ‖ κραβάτου P ‖ 483 ἄβαλαι Pᵛ: ἄβαλα P ἀβάλα V edd. ‖ 486 παραβάσεως V edd. ‖ 491 ἀνδρίαντα P ‖ χαλκοῦν (*coni. etiam* Bekker): χαλκὸν edd. ‖ 494 ἄφθαν: νάφθαν *coni.* Latyšev ‖ 495 Ζηχία P ‖ εἰς: πρὸς edd. ‖ 496 Ζηχοὶ P ‖ 497 ὁμοχροοῦσι Meursius Ba Be: ὁμοχρυοῦσιν P ‖ ἐννέα edd.: θ′ P ‖ 499 Ζηχία P ‖ 500/1 κονιορτός V edd.: κορνιοτὸς P ‖ 507 τοῦ *coni.* Jenkins: τὰ P edd. ‖ 508 Ἐπισκοπίου P edd. ‖

53

210ʳP Ἰστέον, ὅτι ἐν τῷ θέματι τοῦ Τζιλιάπερτ ὑπὸ | τὸ χωρίον τὸ 510
Σρεχιαβαρὰξ ἔστιν ἐκεῖσε πηγὴ ἄφθαν ἀναδιδοῦσα.

Ἰστέον, ὅτι εἰ ἀντάρωσί ποτε οἱ τοῦ κάστρου Χερσῶνος, ἢ ἐναντία
τῶν βασιλικῶν κελεύσεων βουληθῶσι διαπράξασθαι, ὀφείλουσιν τηνικαῦτα, ὅσα εὑρεθῶσιν ἐν τῇ πόλει Χερσωνίτικα καράβια, μετὰ τοῦ γόμου
270Be αὐτῶν εἰσκομίζεσθαι, οἱ | δὲ ναῦται καὶ ἐπιβάται Χερσωνῖται ἵνα δε- 515
σμεύωνται καὶ ἐναποκλείωνται εἰς τὰ ἐργαλεῖα, εἶθ᾽ οὕτως ὀφείλουσιν
ἀποσταλῆναι τρεῖς βασιλικοί· εἷς μὲν ἐν τῇ παραλίᾳ τοῦ θέματος τῶν
Ἀρμενιάκων, ἕτερος δὲ ἐν τῇ παραλίᾳ τοῦ θέματος Παφλαγονίας καὶ
ἄλλος ἐν τῇ παραλίᾳ τοῦ θέματος τῶν Βουκελλαρίων, ἵνα πάντα τὰ
Χερσωνίτικα καράβια κρατῶσιν, καὶ τὸν μὲν γόμον καὶ τὰ καράβια 520
210ᵛP εἰσκομίζωσιν, | τοὺς δὲ ἀνθρώπους δεσμεύωσι καὶ ἐναποκλείωσιν εἰς
δημοσίους φυλακάς, καὶ ἀναγάγωσι περὶ τούτων, καὶ ὡς ἂν δέξωνται.

Πρὸς τούτοις ἵνα οἱ τοιοῦτοι βασιλικοὶ κωλύωσι καὶ τὰ Παφλαγονικὰ
καὶ Βουκελλαρικὰ πλοῖα καὶ πλαγίτικα τοῦ Πόντου τοῦ μὴ διαπερᾶν
ἐν Χερσῶνι μετὰ σίτου ἢ οἴνου ἢ οἰασδήποτε χρείας ἢ πραγματείας. 525
Εἶθ᾽ οὕτως ὀφείλει δέξασθαι καὶ ὁ στρατηγὸς τοῦ κόψαι καὶ τὰς δέκα
λίτρας, τὰς διδομένας ἀπὸ τοῦ δημοσίου εἰς τὸ κάστρον Χερσῶνος, καὶ τὰς
δύο τοῦ πάκτου, καὶ τηνικαῦτα ἀναχωρῆσαι ἀπὸ Χερσῶνος τὸν στρατηγὸν καὶ ἀπελθεῖν ἐν ἑτέρῳ κάστρῳ καὶ καθεσθῆναι ἐκεῖσε.

Ὅτι ἐὰν οὐ ταξιδεύσωσιν οἱ Χερσωνῖται εἰς Ῥωμανίαν, καὶ 530
211ʳP πιπράσκωσι τὰ | βυρσάρια καὶ τὰ κηρία, ἅπερ ἀπὸ τῶν Πατζινακιτῶν
πραγματεύονται, οὐ δύνανται ζῆσαι.

Ὅτι ἐὰν μὴ ἀπὸ Ἀμινσοῦ καὶ ἀπὸ Παφλαγονίας καὶ τῶν Βουκελλαρίων καὶ ἀπὸ τῶν πλαγίων τῶν Ἀρμενιάκων περάσωσι γεννήματα,
οὐ δύνανται ζῆσαι οἱ Χερσωνῖται. 535

V 510 τὸ χωρίον om. Be || 512 εἰ] in ras. scr. P¹ || 514 Χερσωνιτικὰ edd. ||
516 ἐναποκλείωνται edd.: ἐναποκλείονται P || 518 Ἀρμενιακῶν V edd. || 520
Χερσωνίτικα scr. Moravcsik: Χερσωνιτικὰ P edd. || 524 πλαγιτικὰ edd. || 525
πραγματείας: πράγματος V edd. || 534 Ἀρμενιακῶν V edd. || 535 Χερσω-
νῖται P.

53

In the province of Tziliapert, below the village of Srechiabarax, there is a well yielding naphtha.

If ever the men of the city of Cherson revolt or decide to act contrary to the imperial mandates, then all Chersonite ships at Constantinople must be impounded with their cargoes, and Chersonite sailors and passengers must be arrested and confined in the gaols; and then three imperial agents must be sent: one to the coast of the province of the Armeniakoi, another to the coast of the province of Paphlagonia, and another to the coast of the province of the Boukellarioi, in order to take possession of all Chersonite ships, and to impound the cargo and the ships, and to arrest the men and confine them in public prisons, and to report upon these matters and as they may be instructed. Moreover, these imperial agents must forbid the Paphlagonian and Boukellarian merchant-ships and coastal vessels of Pontus to cross to Cherson with grain or wine or any other needful commodity or merchandise. Then, the military governor too must be instructed to sequestrate the ten pounds granted by the treasury to the city of Cherson and also the two pounds of tribute, and then the military governor must withdraw from Cherson and go to another city and take up residence there.

If the Chersonites do not journey to Romania and sell the hides and wax that they get by trade from the Pechenegs, they cannot live.

If grain does not pass across from Aminsos and from Paphlagonia and the Boukellarioi and the flanks of the Armeniakoi, the Chersonites cannot live.

INDEX OF PROPER NAMES

Passages are cited by chapter and line in the chapter. P, in such citations, stands for «Proem».

Abbreviation: *Byzantinoturcica* = Gy. Moravcsik, *Byzantinoturcica* II. *Sprachreste der Türkvölker in den byzantinischen Quellen*, Budapest, 1943 (2nd ed., Berlin, 1958).

Μεγυρέτους (τό), city in Serbia 32/150.

Μέκε, Mecca: τοῦ Μέκε 15/4.

Μελετᾶ, deserted city in Dalmatia: — 29/292.

Μέλετα (τά), island off Dalmatia 30/110; νῆσος ἑτέρα μεγάλη τὰ Μέλετα, ἤτοι τὸ Μαλοζεάται, ἣν ...ὁ ἅγιος Λουκᾶς μέμνηται, Μελίτην ταύτην προσαγορεύων 36/16—18.

Μελίας, patrician and magister 50/138, 145, 152, 154, 162, 164.

Μελίτη cf. Μέλετα.

Μελιτηνή (ἡ), city in Asia Minor 50/138; Μελιτηνιᾶται (οἱ) 50/114, 147.

Μελιτηνιᾶται cf. Μελιτηνή.

Μένανδρος, dramatist 23/25.

Μεσημβρία (ἡ), Mesembria 9/102.

Μεσοποταμία, province 45/47, 50/117, 126, 128, 129, 131.

Μηλιγγοί, Milingoi 50/2, 15, 20, 23, 28, 48, 61, 68, 70 [Μιληγγοί variant in P].

Μιληγγοί cf. Μηλιγγοί.

Μιλινίσκα (ἡ), city in Russia: τὴν Μιλινίσκαν 9/6.

Μιρόσθλαβος, prince of the Croats: Μιροσθλάβου (gen.) 31/77.

Μισχιοί, Mischians 46/48.

Μιχαήλ, 1. emperor (II): Μιχαὴλ ὁ Τραυλός 22/41, 29/61.
2. emperor (III) 50/7, 9, 223.
3. prince of the Zachlumi 32/87, 33/16.
4. protospatharius and collector 43/176.
5. chief oarsman, spatharocandidate, protospatharius of the basin 51/89, 106, 127, 138, 154, 158, 161.
6. cf. Βαρκαλᾶς, Βορίσης.

Μοάμεδ cf. Μουάμεθ 2.

Μοκρισκίκ (τό), city in the territory of the Zachlumi 33/21.

Μοκρός (ὁ), zupania of Pagania 30/106, 107.

Μόκρον (τό), city in Pagania 36/14.

Μομψουεστία (ἡ), city in Asia Minor 22/20.

Μοραβία, Moravia 41/1, 2, 42/19; ἡ μεγάλη Μοραβία 13/5, 38/58; ἡ μεγάλη Μοραβία, ἡ ἀβάπτιστος 40/33.

Μορδία, Mordia 37/46.

Μορήσης (ὁ), river in the country of the Turks (= Magyars) 40/39.

Μουάμεθ, 1. prophet 17/2, 21/50, 51, 69; Μουχούμετ 14/1, 2, 11, 15/2, 5, 7; Μουάμεθ, ὃν οἱ Ἄραβες καλοῦσι Μουχούμετ 16/10; Μουάμεθ, ἤτοι τοῦ Μουχούμετ 25/58, 60.
2. chief of the Arabs: Μοάμεδ 22/64.

Μουδάφαρ, son of Manuel protopatharius 50/121, 124.

Μούνδαρος, son of Zinaros (= Nizaros) 14/5, 6.

Μουνδράγα, city in Bulgaria: κάστρον τὸ λεγόμενον — 40/11.

Μουντιμῆρος, prince of the Serbs 32/43, 52, 59, 65.

Μουράν, city of the Venetians: κάστρον — 27/93.

Μουργούλη (ἡ), county in the province of Chaldia: τῇ Μουργούλη 46/119.

Μούσελ (τό), emirate 25/73.

Μουχλώ, chief of the Croats 30/64.
— Cf. *Byzantinoturcica* p. 177 (2nd ed. p. 203).

Μουχούμετ cf. Μουάμεθ 1.

Μυριοκέφαλον (τό), garrison in the province of Charsianon: τοποτηρησία Μυριοκεφάλου 50/103.

Μωσῆς, Moses 17/8.

Ναπρεζή cf. Στρούκουν.

Ναρσῆς, patrician 27/15, 17, 19, 27, 32.

Νάσαρ, patrician and lord admiral 51/75.

Νέα Ἐκκλησία (ἡ), church in the imperial palace at Constantinople 50/237.

Νεάπολις (ἡ), Naples 27/4, 10, 49, 51, 58, 59, 60, 60, 67.

Νεασήτ cf. Ἀειφόρ.

Νέκη(ς), clan of the Turks (= Magyars): δευτέρα τοῦ Νέκη 40/4. — Cf. *Byzantinoturcica* p. 182 (2nd ed. p. 210).

Νεκρόπηλα cf. Νεκρόπυλα.

Νεκρόπυλα (τά), gulf near the Dnieper river 42/5, 69, 79 [Νεκρόπηλα everywhere P].

Νεμογαρδάς, city in Russia: τοῦ Νεμογαρδάς 9/4.

Νεόκαστρον, city of the Venetians: κάστρον — 27/92.

GLOSSARY

The Glossary contains 1. words which occur in *D. A. I.* only (these are marked with an asterisk), 2. words peculiar to Byzantine civilization, 3. words of the Postclassical and Byzantine periods, 4. uncommon ancient words or ancient words used in an altered sense in the Byzantine period, 5. words of foreign origin.

Passages are cited by chapter and line in the chapter. P, in such citations, stands for «Proem».

Abbreviation: *Byzantinoturcica* = Gy. Moravcsik, *Byzantinoturcica* II. *Sprachreste der Türkvölker in den byzantinischen Quellen*, Budapest, 1943 (2nd ed. Berlin 1958).

ἄβαλε 53/483.

ἀβάπτιστος 13/116, 29/69, 71, 75, 81, 82, 30/74, 31/4, 6, 83, 32/2, 5, 33/18, 34/4, 36/5, 11, 40/33.

ἀγάπη 30/75, 41/14, 45/64, 73, 172, 46/161, 51/170, 53/243.

ἄγγελος 13/33, 50, 77, 79, 14/20.

ἀγγούριον 29/261.

ἁγιάζω 21/89.

ἅγιος, 9/72, 82, 88, 13/35, 36, 39, 48, 49, 59, 78, 84, 98, 112, 113, 118, 130, 131, 141, 168, 19/9, 21/5, 67, 125, 22/71, 73, 74, 74, 77, 27/81, 84, 29/23, 235, 236, 241, 241, 244, 245, 262, 269, 276, 277, 278, 279, 282, 30/48, 88, 31/36, 49, 32/79, 36/18, 19, 20, 40/30, 43/81, 45/32, 46/55, 69, 72, 47/6, 12, 13, 48/1, 49/26, 50/97.

ἀγράμματος 13/150, 51/100.

ἀγράριον (~ Latin *agrariensis, agrarius?*) 51/7, 12, 17, 25, 28, 48, 49, 50, 58, 63, 65, 67, 77, 102, 108, 178, 187, 190.

*ἀγραριώτης (~ Latin *agrariensis, agrarius ?*) 51/181.

ἀδιαίρετος 41/15.

ἀδιάκριτος 51/149, 159, 185.

ἀείμνηστος 29/89, 95, 49/72, 50/118, 235, 51/143, 192, 196.

ἀειπάρθενος 21/124.

ἀζάτος (~ Armenian *azat*): ἀζάτου (gen.) 45/103. — Cf. De thematibus, ed. Pertusi p. 75/7; N. Adontz, *Byzantion*, 13 (1938), p. 161.

ἀηδίζομαι 53/475.

ἄθλησις 49/58.

αἵρεσις 14/28, 17/14.

αἱρετίζομαι 51/202, 53/490.

αἱρετικός 13/138.

αἰχμαλωσία 29/21, 116, 45/135, 49/42, 53/165, 238.

αἰχμαλωτεύω 30/28.

αἰχμαλωτίζω 29/226, 33/7, 35/6, 36/8, 45/95, 167, 53/24.

αἰχμάλωτος 13/159, 21/16, 53/91, 92, 94.

αἰών P/48, 13/88, 88, 27/35, 36.

ἀκαθαίρετος 19/7.

ἀκαινοτόμητος 48/9.

ἀκαταγώνιστος 41/15, 49/35.

ἀκαταμάχητος 15/10.

ἀκέραιος 29/269.

ἀκμήν 29/142, 30/70.

ἀκολουθία 40/48.

ἄκρα 49/13, 50/78, 116.

ἀκυρῶ 13/137, 53/366.

ἅλας (τό) 42/71.

ἀληθινός 6/9.

ἁλιεύω 42/89.

ἀλλάγιον 29/22, 32.

ἀλλόπιστος 13/116.

ἄλογον 7/12, 17, 29/129, 53/261, 265.

ἀμαξία 34/17.

ἀμερμουμνῆς (~ Arabic *amīr al-mūminīn*) 25/56, 64, 80, 84, 43/15, 33, 47/16, 19, 20; ἀμερμουμνῆ (gen.) 25/74, 78, 43/23, 44/118.

ἀμετασάλευτος 45/112.

*ἀμηραδία (~ Arabic *amīr*) 25/67, 68, 68, 69, 69, 70, 70, 71, 71, 72, 72, 73, 73, 76; ἀμηραδίας..., ἤτοι στρατηγίδας 25/66.
ἀμηραῖος (~ Arabic *amīr*) 21/102. — Cf. Theophanes, ed. de Boor p. 335₁₃ etc.
ἀμηρᾶς (~ Arabic *amīr*) 21/41, 25/75, 79, 82, 83, 44/8, 27, 42, 51, 82, 45/132, 139; ἀμηράδων (pl. gen.) 44/121. — Cf. *Byzantinoturcica* p. 71—72 (2nd ed. 66—69).
ἀμηρεύω (~ Arabic *amīr*) 18/4, 21/36. — Cf. Theophanes, ed. de Boor p. 336₂₈ etc.
ἀμφίασις 30/52.
ἀνά cf. Grammatical Notes.
ἀναβλαστῶ 43/110.
ἀνάγλυφος 50/249, 252.
ἀνάγω 43/90, 123, 127, 135, 46/119, 159, 50/27, 182, 187, 53/522.
ἀναδείκνυμι (= proclaim) 53/122.
ἀναδρομή 40/31.
ἀναζεύγνυμι 53/107.
ἀνάθεμα 13/125.
ἀναθεματίζω 13/54, 88, 140.
ἀναίδην cf. ἀνέδην.
ἀνακλίνομαι 53/434.
ἀνάκρασις 13/177 [ἀνάκρισην P].
ἀνακύπτω 27/21.
ἀναμανθάνω 13/105, 30/40, 46/136, 49/51.
ἀναμέσον 21/85.
ἀνάμεστος 50/192.
ἀναμεταξύ 38/24, 50/175, 51/58.
ἀναπλάσσομαι 50/189.
ἀναρρύομαι 13/160.
ἀνατολή 27/79, 38/26, 62, 43/86, 44/23, 45/109.
ἀνατολικός 37/37, 40/41, 42/86, 49/18.
ἀνατροπεύς 13/142.
ἀναφορά 46/120, 50/33, 34, 193, 53/147.
ἀναφωνῶ 14/32.
ἀναψηλαφῶ 37/9.
ἀνδραγάθημα 26/5.
ἀνδραγαθῶ 51/94.
ἀνδρειῶ: ἠνδρειωμένος 15/8, 38/37, 46/75.
ἀνεγείρω 53/457.
ἀνέδην 7/9 [ἀναίδην P].
ἀνεκδίκητος 13/97.
ἀνέχομαι 13/97, 45/72, 50/244, 53/249, 258, 277; cf. Grammatical Notes.
ἀνήκω 6/7, 51/76.
ἀνήλικος 43/103.

ἄνθραξ 13/64.
ἀνθύπατος 33/16, 43/44.
ἀνίσχυρος 22/20.
ἀννῶνα (~ Latin *annona*) 53/152, 155.
ἀνταλλαγή 43/143.
ἀνταμοιβή 53/238.
ἀνταποκρίνομαι 21/98.
ἀνταποστέλλω 43/179.
ἀνταρσία 22/42, 25/9.
ἀντεισέρχομαι 22/7.
ἀντιδηλῶ 29/166, 45/74.
ἀντίληψις 51/176.
ἀντιμηνύω 27/19.
ἀντίπερα 42/21.
ἀντιπερῶ 29/101, 51/115, 53/12; cf. Grammatical Notes.
ἀντιπίπτω 29/138, 50/178.
ἀντισήκωσις 43/107, 46/14, 20.
ἀντιστρέφω 13/47.
ἀνυπόδετος 26/50.
ἀνυπότακτος 50/14.
ἀνυψῶ P/38.
ἀνώτερος 40/36.
ἀξία 13/86, 38/6, 43/53, 58, 66, 46/148, 51/140.
ἀξίωμα 37/27, 30, 40/52, 68, 43/152, 44/47, 50/125, 52/11.
ἀοίδιμος 13/189, 29/73, 83, 89, 30/127, 127, 40/8, 43/19, 42, 45/43, 50/76, 51/5, 22, 34, 52, 69, 78, 157.
ἀπάθεια 49/12.
ἀπαίτησις 51/193, 197, 52/1.
ἀπαιτῶ 4/7, 50/52, 52/12.
ἀπαραποίητος 13/112.
ἀπαργυρίζω 49/74.
ἀπάρτι 29/273; cf. ἰὰμ ἔρα.
ἀπαρτίζομαι 43/78.
ἀπεκδέχομαι 37/31.
ἀπεμπολῶ cf. Grammatical Notes.
ἀπηνῶς 29/244.
ἄπιστος 13/106, 143, 45/79.
ἀπλίκτον (~ Latin *applicatus*) 44/128, 45/86 [ἀπλήκτον, ἄπληκτα P].
ἀπλοϊκός 1/9.
ἁπλός cf. Grammatical Notes.
ἀπό cf. Grammatical Notes.
ἀποβιῶ 17/2, 21/35.
ἀποβίωσις 43/160.
ἀποθεραπεύω 46/142.
ἀποκαθιστῶ cf. Grammatical Notes.
ἀποκεφαλίζω 44/7, 52, 53/222.
ἀποκηρύττω 13/54, 140.
ἀποκινῶ 9/20, 23, 80, 92.

ἀποκρημνίζω 9/29.
ἀποκρισιάριος 1/19, 21, 29/70, 172, 177,
    180.
ἀποκτέννω 17/17, 21/45.
ἀποπεραίνομαι 9/103.
ἀπόρθητος 19/7.
ἀποσκαλώνω 9/90.
ἀποσκοπεύω 49/18.
ἀποσμήχω 53/467.
ἀποστασία 39/3, 50/37, 40.
ἀπόστολος 27/85, 31/36, 36/18, 49/26,
    31, 37, 40, 46, 49, 52, 57, 62, 65.
ἀποσυνάγομαι 9/22, 28/44.
*ἀποσώστης 7/11.
ἀποτροφή 53/151.
ἀποχαιρετίζω 46/94.
ἀποχαρίζομαι 45/153, 46/116.
ἀπρόσοδος 50/77.
ἀπώλεια 29/151, 169, 53/197.
ἀριθμός 51/42, 53/156, 158.
ἀρκτικός 37/40.
ἀρκτῷος 42/76.
ἄρματα (τά) (~ Latin arma) 32/113.
ἄρμενον 9/85.
ἀρνητής 29/96.
*ἀρχιδιάκων 29/232, 262.
ἀρχιεπισκοπή 52/8.
ἀρχιεπίσκοπος 31/23, 47/4, 12.
ἀρχιερεύς 13/56.
ἀρχοντία 27/2, 30/98, 100. — Cf. Nice-
    phorus patriarcha, ed. de Boor p.
    40₂₃; De cerimoniis, ed. Bonn. p. 635₃.
ἀρχοντόπουλος 32/94, 101. — Cf. Anna
    Comnena VII. 7., ed. Leib II. p.
    108₁₂ etc.
ἄρχων 8/29, 9/5, 106, 13/90, 101, 29/66,
    76, 79, 127, 136, 142, 149, 153, 154,
    155, 165, 196, 30/73, 77, 78, 84, 87,
    90, 141, 142, 31/21, 25, 43, 44,58,
    60, 62, 76, 32/30, 33, 40, 42, 45,52,
    58, 80, 84, 86, 87, 88, 89, 92, 95,
    96, 102, 102, 115, 118, 121, 135,
    145, 146, 148, 33/9, 17, 34/5, 6, 7,
    9, 11, 12, 36/6, 37/20, 32, 33, 38/11,
    15, 32, 38, 45, 49, 51, 53, 55, 56,
    39/12, 40/13, 45, 48, 50, 58, 65,
    41/2, 42/44, 43/7, 27, 38, 45, 56,
    63, 86, 110, 111, 46/75, 78, 136,
    49/16, 50/31, 58, 80, 51/20, 25, 27,
    39, 111, 112; μέγας ἄρχων 37/16,
    40/53, 41/6; ἄρχων τῶν ἀρχόντων
    43/30, 34, 112, 44/6, 7, 9, 13, 18,
    19, 20, 21, 22, 26, 35, 37, 38, 39,

42, 45, 50, 120. — Cf. K. Amantos,
    Ἱστορία τοῦ βυζαντινοῦ κράτους II.,
    (Athènes, 1947), p. 428.
ἄς 45/81, 82, 83.
ἀσάλευτος P/33.
ἄσβεστος 42/38.
ἀσηκρῆτις (~ Latin a secretis) 50/174.
ἀσήμιν 28/42, 50/248, 252.
ἄσπρος 30/72, 31/4, 83, 32/3, 6, 42/24.
ἄστεπτος 26/19.
ἀσύγκριτος 17/20.
ἀσυνάρτητος 22/65.
ἀσφαλίζομαι 1. (= give surety, confirm)
    13/68, 22/15.
    2. (make fast [the doors]) 53/398,
    427, 438.
*ἄσφαλος 38/10, 28.
ἄτεκνος 45/37, 46/9.
ἀττικίζω 1/11.
αὐγοῦστα (~ Latin augusta) 51/49, 50,
    51, 65, 67, 68, 103, 176, 180, 180.
αὐγουστιατικός (~ Latin augusta) 51/
    102, 181, 187, 190. — Cf. De ceri-
    moniis, ed. Bonn. p. 423₂₀.
αὐθεντία 47/9.
αὐθεντῶς 44/28. — Cf. Eustathius metro-
    polita, Opuscula, ed. Tafel p. 40₅₁,
    ₅₄, 164₂₈.
αὐτεξούσιος 30/77, 34/10, 45/131, 50/186.
αὐτοδέσποτος 30/88, 45/131, 50/30.
αὐτοκέφαλος 29/62, 66, 87, 44/28.
αὐτοκρατορία 51/136.
αὐτοκράτωρ 13/161, 21/9, 25/47, 50/198.
αὐτόνομος 6/11, 30/88, 50/30.
αὐτός 1. ἐπὶ τὸ αὐτό 27/46, 46/153.
    2. cf. Grammatical Notes.
αὐτουργός 29/211.
αὐχένιον 9/85.
ἀφανισμός 3/4, 49/42.
ἄφατος 53/458.
ἀφέλεια 29/59, 85.
ἀφηνιάζω 29/65.
ἄφθα 53/494, 496, 501, 502, 508, 511.
ἀφίημι cf. Grammatical Notes.
ἀφυπνῶ 53/437.
ἄχραντος 21/125.
βαγεύω (~ Latin vagor ?) 51/61.
βαλλιστάριος (~ Latin ballistarius)
    53/152.
βαλλίστρα (~ Latin ballista) 53/151.
βαλτώδης (~ Slavic *bolto) 28/4. — Cf.
    Anna Comnena VIII. 3., ed. Leib
    II. p. 135₂₄.

βάνδον (~ Latin *bandum*) 50/94, 97, 99, 103, 106, 109.
βαπτίζω 29/69, 72, 74, 76, 83, 84, 30/89, 31/24, 31, 34, 35, 68, 71, 86, 32/28, 149, 36/10, 10, 50/76; cf. Grammatical Notes.
βάπτισμα 30/88.
βάρβαρος 43/18, 49/32, 34, 48; cf. Index of Proper Names.
βαρβαρικός 48/5.
βασανίζω 29/244.
βασιλεία 1. (rule, reign, kingdom, empire, throne) P/9, 36, 40, 22/6, 30, 32, 35, 82, 25/25, 28, 26/37, 29/54, 59, 65, 72, 88, 31/58, 32/78, 146, 43/90, 45/40, 55, 50/9, 25, 75, 136, 227, 51/5, 51, 77, 163, 53/119, 122, 233.
2. (= imperial majesty) 8/27, 43/107, 161, 45/68, 75, 102, 107, 109, 124, 132, 138, 142, 152, 161, 167, 172, 46/131, 132, 50/210, 214, 245, 51/183, 53/141.
βασίλειον 13/150, 27/6.
βασίλειος P/48, 13/26, 124, 152, 165, 51/147.
βασιλεύουσα 2/16, 43/21, 52, 63, 70, 81, 150, 47/5.
βασιλεύς Tit./2, 2, 4, P/5, 48, 1/2, 16, 4/3, 7, 9, 5/4, 7, 6/4, 7/13, 8/19, 25, 11/4, 5, 13/32, 45, 49, 51, 57, 61, 68, 77, 89, 101, 107, 109, 109, 114, 121, 126, 130, 146, 147, 149, 162, 21/10, 15, 46, 122, 22/4, 10, 14, 17, 23, 43, 80, 81, 25/12, 14, 33, 27/12, 68, 28/6, 11, 11, 36, 29/3, 7, 12, 54, 62, 70, 74, 83, 87, 89, 95, 97, 104, 106, 106, 108, 116, 170, 171, 174, 176, 180, 186, 188, 189, 198, 207, 212, 238, 242, 252, 30/15, 127, 128, 131, 31/8, 10, 12, 16, 17, 19, 21, 27, 28, 33, 59, 59, 32/9, 10, 16, 18, 19, 22, 25, 26, 27, 31, 38, 79, 88, 100, 107, 108, 110, 113, 116, 133, 136, 140, 141, 143, 143, 147, 147, 33/4, 6, 9, 34/5, 35/4, 5, 7, 10, 36/4, 6, 8, 40/8, 13, 28, 31, 42/26, 28, 29, 40, 44, 47, 43/8, 9, 12, 19, 22, 31, 36, 42, 50, 52, 57, 58, 73, 77, 82, 85, 89, 93, 95, 100, 102, 113, 118, 120, 129, 131, 137, 138, 139, 145, 146, 152, 154, 158, 162, 167, 169, 169, 174,

175, 175, 178, 183, 183, 44/30, 33, 44, 46, 48, 58, 63, 88, 110, 115, 119, 124, 126, 45/4, 6, 22, 24, 26, 36, 41, 44, 56, 67, 79, 81, 101, 114, 46/49, 61, 63, 67, 68, 72, 81, 83, 88, 97, 99, 103, 108, 112, 115, 117, 118, 120, 122, 127, 130, 142, 159, 160, 160, 165, 47/6, 10, 15, 21, 23, 48/8, 49/40, 50, 72, 50/7, 26, 36, 61, 65, 118, 122, 156, 164, 170, 171, 177, 194, 196, 199, 205, 208, 209, 211, 214, 218, 220, 222, 225, 228, 229, 235, 240, 243, 244, 249, 254, 51/6, 6, 8, 14, 21, 22, 29, 33, 34, 37, 44, 52, 63, 68, 69, 77, 78, 80, 86, 94, 98, 100, 104, 125, 141, 149, 155, 157, 162, 165, 169, 174, 176, 177, 180, 184, 192, 53/8, 17, 21, 26, 47, 108, 110, 112, 115, 120, 135, 159, 166, 247, 249; μέγας βασιλεύς 13/83, 141, 168, 22/79.
βασιλεύω P/43, 48, 1/23, 13/33, 81, 188, 21/47, 25/54, 26/6, 71, 27/6, 8, 29/277, 32/82, 43/20, 53/2, 124, 236.
βασιλικά (τά) 30/16.
βασιλικοπλώϊμος 51/13.
βασιλικός 1/23, 8/11, 17, 24, 13/41, 165, 21/114, 29/111, 42/31, 43/96, 109, 114, 154, 50/29, 38, 125, 51/1, 6, 12, 46, 48, 53, 85, 88, 91, 105, 125, 188, 190, 52/8, 10, 53/142, 513.
βασιλικός (ὁ) 7/2, 3, 12, 8/2, 7, 10, 13, 16, 29/74, 43/43, 45/82, 84, 85, 47/18, 23, 49/66, 53/517, 523.
βασιλίς 27/14, 27.
βασίλισσα 27/23.
βδέλυγμα 19/8.
βερζίτικον (~ Bulgarian?) 42/88. — Cf. *Byzantinoturcica* p. 88 (2nd ed. p. 89).
βήσσαλον (Latin *bessalis*) 29/246, 42/36, 53/329, 331, 340, 347, 348, [βήσαλον everywhere P].
βίγλα (~ Latin *vigilia*) 9/49, 50, 29/175, 51/29; cf. δρουγγάριος.
βλαττίον (~ Latin *blatta*) 6/8.
*βοάνος (~ Turkish *ban*?) 30/93; βοεάνου (gen.) 31/78. — Cf. *Byzantinoturcica* p. 178 (2nd ed. p. 204).
*βοεάνος cf. βοάνος.
*βοέβοδος (~ Slavic *vojevoda*) 38/5, 5, 7, 12, 12, 16, 29, 34, 43. — Cf. *Byzantinoturcica* p. 91 (2nd ed. p. 93).

βοϊλᾶς (~ Bulgarian *boila*): βοϊλάδων (pl.
       gen.) 32/48 [βολιάδων P]. — Cf.
       Byzantinoturcica p. 91 (2nd ed. p. 93).
βουνός P/37, 33/12, 13, 14.
βραδύς: βραδέστερον 53/304.
βράσμα 9/62.
βρύσις 53/501, 502.
βυρσάριον 53/531.
γειτνιάζω 1/25.
γενεαλογοῦμαι 14/2.
γενική 23/25, 30, 31.
γενικός 14/3.
γέννημα 53/534.
γεφύριον 29/259, 51/9.
γεωγραφία 42/1.
γίνομαι: γενάμενος 32/58, 50/56.
γλῶσσα 29/82, 265, 39/8, 10.
γνησιότης 53/145.
γοῦνα (~ Slavic *guna*) 32/56. — Cf. De
       cerimoniis, ed. Bonn. p. 381$_{11, 18}$.
γράμματα (τά) 4/10, 29/221, 43/15, 21,
       31, 50, 80, 46/136.
γραφικός 14/17.
*γυλᾶς (~ Hungarian *yila* ~ *g'ila*) 40/49,
       51, 68.—Cf. *Byzantinoturcica* p. 109.
       (2nd ed, p. 115).
γύναιον 4/12.
γύρα 9/107,
γυρόθεν 9/75.
δαρμός 51/165.
δάσος 42/84.
δέησις: ὁ τῶν δεήσεων 51/31.
δειλανδρῶ 29/206.
δεξιοῦμαι 32/88, 43/58, 162.
δέσμιος 29/165, 30/43, 32/48, 104, 43/30.
δεσμῶ 32/98, 123.
δέσποινα 21/124, 53/337, 341, 344.
δεσποτεία 45/124, 127,
δεσπότης 26/68, 72, 44/28, 50/87, 92,
       101, 131, 133, 136, 160, 168, 226,
       227, 231, 232, 232, 51/8, 76, 108,
       137, 164, 177, 199, 52/2, 53/79, 113.
δεσποτικός 13/38, 63.
*δευτεροελάτης 51/107, 125.
δευτερῶ 53/212.
δέχομαι (= be instructed, receive a
       reply) 45/83, 46/160, 50/39, 53/522,
       526.
δηλοποιῶ 8/25, 26/23, 27/33, 29/94,
       43/16, 122, 46/72.
δῆμος 13/171, 53/278.
δημόσιον 27/13, 18, 50/32, 53/527.
δημόσιος 22/69, 53/522.

δημοσίως 53/393.
δημοτελής 13/38.
διαβάζω 2/21.
διάβημα P/32.
διαγογγύζω 43/113.
διαδέχομαι (= supersede) 50/200, 201,
       51/165.
διαίρω: διηρμένον 1/11.
διάκονος 13/46, 31/23.
διακράτησις 29/14, 45/165, 174.
διακρατῶ 22/48, 32/85, 37/10.
διάλεκτος 25/18, 27/69, 29/80, 218, 264,
       272, 31/7, 32/12, 33/11, 34/12, 17,
       36/11, 12, 39/9.
διαμερίζομαι 27/7.
διαμεριμνῶ 1/7. — Cf. Genesius, ed.
       Bonn. p. 64$_{16}$; Constantinus Porphy-
       rogenitus, Narratio de imagine Edes-
       sena, cap. VIII., ed. Migne, P. G.
       113. c. 129$_D$ = E. Dobschütz,
       Christusbilder, (Leipzig, 1899), Bei-
       lage II. B, p. 49**.
διαπρέπω 50/172.
διασκορπίζω 32/138, 41/23, 49/33.
διάσωσις 32/51. — Cf. De cerimoniis,
       ed. Bonn. p. 683$_{13}$.
διασώστης 7/5, 7.
διαταγή 13/155, 169.
διάταξις 13/60, 111, 141, 158.
διατάσσομαι 43/173.
διατυπῶ 48/22.
διαφόρως 43/11, 44/31.
διάχρυσος 50/248, 252.
*διβάρια (τά) 28/42.
διδάσκω cf. Grammatical Notes.
δίδωμι cf. Grammatical Notes.
διεγείρω 21/39, 71, 53/18.
διέγερσις 51/97.
διεκδικῶ 27/26, 32/45.
διέπω 16/5, 25/35.
διερμηνεύω 13/200.
διευθύνω 27/26.
διήγημα 26/4.
διηρμένον cf. διαίρω.
δικαίωμα P/44.
διογκῶ 1/11.
διορίζομαι 13/35, 51, 46/145, 49/54.
διχόνοια 31/78.
διωρία 22/44.
διώροφος 29/254.
δοκιμάζω 53/55, 472.

δομέστικος (~ Latin *domesticus*) 50/237; δομέστικος τῆς ὑπουργίας 43/43; δομέστικος τῶν σχολῶν 44/33, 45/51, 46/128, 50/151, 51/32, 43.
δοξάζω P/48, 34/9.
δόρκα 26/31, 51/83. — Cf. Hesychius s. v. δόρκαι.
δουκᾶτον (~ Latin *ducatus*) 28/47, 49, 50/88.
δουλεία 6/4, 7, 12, 8/20, 13/27, 166, 29/25, 179, 185, 32/86, 34/18, 43/115, 46/69, 81, 48/6, 50/32, 51/61, 93.
δουλεύω 25/53, 32/116, 134, 49/2.
δούλη 53/337.
δουλικός 32/13.
δουλικῶς 31/59, 32/147.
δουλοπρεπῶς 32/143.
δοῦλος 21/6, 22/13, 28/36, 32/12, 16, 44/46, 110, 45/141, 151, 157, 50/204.
δουλῶ 44/123.
δούλωσις 29/215, 30/132, 32/37, 79, 45/112, 46/132.
δούξ (~ Latin *dux*) 27/60, 77, 94, 28/45, 46.
δρομικός 29/279.
δρόμος cf. λογοθέτης, χαρτουλάριος.
δρομώνιον 51/2, 3, 6, 10, 11, 20, 20, 22, 25, 35, 35, 39, 52, 54, 58, 63, 78, 81, 82, 89, 90, 106, 107, 125, 128, 142, 144, 145, 182, 189, 189.
δρουγγάριος (~ Latin *drungarius*) 51/110; δρουγγάριος τοῦ πλωΐμου 29/97, 99, 46/50, 53, 65, 77, 51/30, 75, 85, 87, 96; δρουγγάριος τῆς βίγλης 51/29.
δυσδιέξοδος 9/42, 103.
δυσκολία 45/20.
δύσκολος 50/19.
δυσκρασία 51/147.
δυσπείθεια 50/38.
δυσσεβής 14/2.
δυσωπῶ 29/187, 50/239, 249.
δυτικός 13/4, 37/40, 38/29, 63, 40/43, 50/13.
δωροφορῶ P/38.
ἐγγίζω 53/320.
ἔγγονος 22/37, 81, 40/61, 53/162; ἔγγων 32/32.
ἔγγραφος 21/13, 22/16, 43/87, 45/93, 149, 53/144.
ἔγγων cf. ἔγγονος.
ἐγείρω 26/36, 29/252, 53/232, 491.
ἐγκάρδιος 43/136.

ἐγκολπίζομαι 53/431 [ἐγκαλωπήσασθαι P].
ἔγκριτος 13/145.
ἔγκρυμμα 29/38, 53/31.
ἐγχόρηγος 29/247.
*ἐγχυλιάζω 29/250.
ἑδράζω P/32.
ἐθνικός 13/96, 31/40, 48/5.
εἴδησις 44/101, 48/25.
εἰδωλολάτρης 50/74.
εἴδωλον 50/75.
εἰκονίζω 29/280.
εἰκονομάχος 13/138.
εἴλημα 29/254.
εἰληματικός 29/243, 252, 271, 282, 284.
εἰμί, εἶμι cf. Grammatical Notes.
εἰς cf. Grammatical Notes.
εἰσήγησις 13/124.
εἰσκομιδή 27/19, 21, 22.
εἰσκομίζω 27/18, 21, 50/52, 53/515, 521.
εἰσφέρω 53/307.
ἐκγόνη 13/148. — Cf. Malalas, ed. Bonn. p. 413₉ = Chronicon Paschale, ed. Bonn. p. 613₁₆.
ἔκγονος 21/28, 28, 111, 111.
ἐκδικῶ 13/67, 53/166, 185.
ἐκεῖθεν (= beyond) 8/34, 28/21, 29/16, 18, 33, 30/21, 24, 62, 31/5, 32/3, 45/165, 50/79.
ἐκεῖνος (= μακαρίτης) 13/32, 32/93, 38/32, 42/27, 43/7, 36, 101, 152, 45/14, 46/12, 50/118, 127, 140, 236, 51/89, 106, 150, 168.
ἔκθαμβος 49/34.
ἐκκλησία 13/35, 40, 48, 50, 54, 55, 59, 84, 98, 113, 127, 139, 144, 154, 172, 19/6, 7, 22/72, 27/42, 45, 37/65, 45/45, 49, 48/15, 49/1; cf. Index of Proper Names (Νέα Ἐκκλησία).
ἐκκλησιαστικός 13/168.
ἐκκοπή 43/120, 50/69.
ἐκκόπτω 43/129, 131.
ἐκ προσώπου cf. πρόσωπον.
ἐκστρατεία 49/53.
ἐκτιμῶ 50/248, 249.
ἐκχύνω 53/448.
ἐλαιοφόρος 50/77.
ἐλαιών 30/111.
ἐλάτης 51/11, 48, 54, 58, 63, 81, 91, 102, 145, 182, 189.
ἐλευθερία 29/181, 53/114, 116, 140, 144.
ἐλευθερός 6/11.
ἐλευθερῶ 45/49, 48/5.
ἔλευσις 49/21, 51/91.

*ἐμβλήσκομαι 9/56. — Cf. ἐκβλήσκεσθαι
Theophanes, ed. de Boor p. 184₁₀;
ἔμβλησαν Phrantzes, ed. Papado-
poulus p. 141₂₆.
ἐμπορευτικός 31/88.
ἐμπόριον 27/93, 96, 31/55.
ἔμπορος 20/9.
ἐμπρησμός 50/9, 53/387.
ἐν cf. Grammatical Notes.
ἐναγώνιος 53/217, 463.
ἐναλλαγή 29/221.
ἐναποβλέπω 37/37.
ἐναπογράφω 13/112, 49/73.
ἐναποδέχομαι 38/41. — Cf. Ioannes
Chrysostomus, Homilia in Gene-
sim XLIV., ed. Migne, P. G. 54.
c. 406 [= 447ₑ].
ἐναποδιώκω 31/11. — Cf. Μηναῖα τοῦ
ὅλου ἐνιαυτοῦ, Σεπτέμβριος ΙΓ´, Θεοτο-
κίον, vol I. (ἐν Ῥώμῃ, 1888), p. 150.
ἐναποκλείω 29/244, 53/516, 521.
ἐναπολαμβάνω 29/14.
ἐναπομένω 37/51, 51/43.
*ἐναπονεύω 29/60.
*ἐναποπλέω 9/57.
*ἐναποστέλλω 42/28.
ἐναποφέρομαι 29/7.
*ἐναποφράσσω 28/26.
*ἐναφικνοῦμαι 38/34.
ἐνδότερος 14/9, 22/63.
ἐνεγκαμένη 53/136. — Cf. Constantinus
Porphyrogenitus, Narratio de ima-
gine Edessena, cap. XXIV., ed.
Migne, P. G. 113. c. 445ᴅ = ed.
E. Dobschütz, Christusbilder, (Leipzig, 1899), Beilage II B, p. 75**;
Cecaumenus, ed. Vasiljevskij—
Jernstedt p. 39; Vita Niconis τοῦ
Μετανοεῖτε, ed. Sp. Lampros,
Νέος Ἑλληνομνήμων, 3 (1906), p. 135;
Vita Theodori Studitae, ed. Migne,
P. G. 99. c. 320ᴀ; Anna Comnena
V. 3., ed. Leib II. p. 16₃₀.
ἔνζῳδος 50/248.
ἔνθεν (= on this side) 29/19, 37/39,
58, 42/19, 45/130, 165.
ἔνθεσμος 13/162.
ἐνιαυσιαῖος 53/274, 315.
ἐνόρδινος (~ Latin ordo) 22/26.
ἐνορκῶ 46/59.
ἔνστασις 29/154.
*ἐνταλματικῶς 43/45.
ἐνυπόστατος 13/36.

ἐνώπιον P/44, 50/36.
ἐξαδέλφη 46/38.
ἐξάδελφος 32/70, 37/25, 29, 29, 40/61,
43/29, 145, 165, 180, 181, 182, 185,
188, 46/86.
ἐξαποστέλλω 13/34, 29/74, 42/48, 52,
43/42, 134, 138, 163, 46/120.
ἐξάρτισις 9/16.
ἔξαρχος 53/10.
ἐξασφαλίζομαι 13/84, 45/70.
ἐξισχύω 11/13.
ἐξοδιάζω 27/17.
ἐξολόθρευσις 50/45, 66.
ἐξολοθρεύω 41/18, 22, 50/41.
ἐξορία 50/137, 51/166.
ἐξόριστος 29/143.
ἐξουθενῶ 13/173.
ἐξουσιάζω 13/167, 29/196, 42/42, 51/50,
59, 189.
ἐξουσιαστής 45/77, 46/17, 18, 19, 26.
ἐξουσιαστικός 13/153.
ἐξουσιοκράτωρ 10/4, 11/3, 9. — Cf. De
cerimoniis, ed. Bonn. p. 679₄.
ἐξυφαίνω 27/30.
ἐπαίρω 13/52, 26/58, 46/11, 28, 53/327,
329, 340, 347, 430.
*ἐπαιχμαλωτίζω 30/122.
ἐπάνω 29/218, 251, 254, 283.
ἐπαρχία 24/3, 48/4, 14.
ἐπέλευσις 49/35.
ἐπί cf. αὐτός, πρός.
ἐπιβάτης 49/27, 53/515.
ἐπιγαμβρεία 53/240.
ἐπιγαμβρεύω 53/244, 251, 259, 269.
ἐπιθεσπίζω 31/51.
ἐπίκλην 21/11, 29/98, 50/10, 51/70, 109,
135.
ἐπικούτζουλον 50/241.
ἐπιληπτικός 14/19.
ἐπιληψία 14/18.
ἐπινίκια (τά) 32/114.
ἐπισκοπεῖον 29/240.
ἐπισκοπή 1. (= visitation) P/41, 49/45,
49.
          2. (= bishopric) 52/9.
ἐπίσκοπος 19/4, 27/64, 30/89, 31/23,
47/7, 8, 48/13, 14, 17, 18, 20, 52/5.
ἐπισυνάγω 9/8, 22/37, 49/71.
ἐπισωρεύω 47/22.
ἐπιτήρησις 51/19.
*ἐπιφορτῶ 21/65.
ἐπωφελής 43/3.
ἔρα cf. ἰάμ.

ἐργαλεῖον 53/516.
ἐρημόκαστρον (~ Latin *castrum*) 27/62, 29/290, 30/111, 35/11, 37/59.
ἐρήμωσις 19/8.
ἑρμηνεύς 43/170.
ἑρμηνευτής 43/42, 137.
ἐστρωμένος cf. στρώννυμι.
ἑταιρειάρχης 51/31; μέγας ἑταιρειάρχης 43/44.
ἑταιρίζομαι 25/29.
εὐαγγέλιον 26/51.
εὐδοκῶ 49/25.
εὐθεῖα 23/30, 31, 32.
εὔκαιρος 22/47.
εὐλαβής 21/88, 90, 93, 31/45, 47.
εὐλογῶ P/8.
εὐνοῦχος 43/37.
εὐφραίνομαι 53/281, 316, 385, 394, 412, 415, 423.
εὐφρασία 53/279, 284, 292, 385, 390, 396, 410, 411.
εὐχαριστία 38/41.
εὐχαριστῶ 53/110, 137.
ἐφαπλῶ 13/42.
ἐφορεία 51/64, 66.
ἐχθραίνομαι 50/192.
ἐχθρωδῶς 50/181.
ἔχω cf. Grammatical Notes.
ἕως cf. Grammatical Notes.

ζάκανον (~ Slavic *zakon*) 8/17, 38/52. — Cf. Suidas s. v. δατόν; P. Kretschmer, *Archiv für slavische Philologie*, 27 (1905), p. 232; S. B. Psaltes, *Grammatik der byzantinischen Chroniken*, (Göttingen, 1913), pp. 36—37.
*ζουπανία (~ Slavic *župan*) 30/91, 105, 106.
ζουπάνος (~ Slavic *župan*) 29/67, 32/120, 34/8. — Cf. *Byzantinoturcica* p. 121 (2nd ed. p. 131).
ζυγή 50/247, 251.
ζῶ cf. Grammatical Notes.
ζωοποιός 46/60.

ἠνδρειωμένος cf. ἀνδρειῶ.
ἦτον cf. ἰὰμ ἔρα. — Cf. Grammatical Notes.
ἡττῶ 5/9, 40/10.

θεϊκός 13/60.
θεῖος 13/133, 19/5, 26/51, 53/160.
θειότης 53/139.
θέλημα 53/345.
θέλησις 21/82, 37/51, 47/15.
θέμα 27/1, 47, 29/224, 293, 30/1, 12,

13, 116, 32/11, 37/15, 16, 17, 21, 23, 24, 32, 35, 35, 35, 36, 40, 41, 42, 43, 69, 43/12, 49/5, 14, 50/1, 6, 11, 13, 14, 27, 54, 59, 60, 64, 66, 93, 93, 96, 96, 102, 102, 105, 106, 109, 111, 112, 117, 126, 128, 129, 131, 167, 174, 183, 51/132, 193, 197, 52/2, 5, 53/507, 510, 517, 518, 519.
θεματίζω 16/1. — Cf. Cedrenus, ed. Bonn. p. 497₁₈.
θεμάτιν 16/8.
θεόπτης 17/8.
θεός cf. Index of Proper Names.
θεοστεφής Tit./4.
θεοτόκος cf. Index of Proper Names.
θεοφιλής 48/13, 19, 53/159.
θεοφόρος 48/10, 16.
θεοφύλακτος 1/21, 8/1, 43/65, 83, 171, 50/53.
θέρμα (τά) 51/8, 18. — Cf. Ph. Kukules, Ἐπετηρὶς Ἑταιρείας Βυζαντινῶν Σπουδῶν, 11 (1935), p. 202.
θηλυκόν 23/25.
θλίψις 32/49.
θρησκεία 17/7.
θριαμβεύω 22/8.
θυσιαστήριον 13/40.

ἰὰμ ἔρα (~ Latin *iam era*): ἰὰμ ἔρα, ὅπερ ἑρμηνεύεται 'ἀπάρτι ἦτον' 29/273.
ἰδιάζω: ἐν τοῖς ἰδιάζουσιν 53/356.
*ἰδιοκάβαλλος (~ Latin *caballus*) 53/506.
*ἰδιοκρατῶ 25/75.
ἰδιόρρυθμος 25/79, 84, 29/66, 50/8.
ἴδιος 26/17.
ἰδιόχειρον 31/35.
ἰδιόχειρος 51/169.
ἱερεύς 29/74, 31/22, 34.
ἱερός 13/41, 113.
ἱκανᾶτος 50/122.
ἵνα cf. Grammatical Notes.
ἰνδικτιών (~ Latin *indictio*) 16/6, 27/54, 29/234, 45/40.
ἱππάριον 51/202, 52/1, 4, 5, 5, 6, 7, 7, 8, 9, 10, 11.
ἱπποδρομία 22/8.
ἱπποδρόμιον 9/68, 31/28.
ἱππόδρομος 51/41, 44.
ἱστορία 13/31, 21/35, 23/6, 25/1, 33/5, 35/5, 47/2, 53/1.
ἱστορικός (ὁ) 21/31, 33.
ἱστῶ cf. Grammatical Notes.
καβαλλαρικόν (~ Latin *caballarius*) 31/71, 79, 82, 85.

καβαλλικεύω (~ Latin *caballico*) 15/10.

καδῆς (~ Arabic *qāḍī*): οἵους ἐκεῖνοι λέγουσι καδῆς, τουτέστιν πιστοὺς καὶ ἡγιασμένους 21/89. — Cf. *Byzantinoturcica* p. 133 (2nd ed. p. 145).

καθαμαξεύω 1/8.

καθεξῆς 25/77, 32/33.

καθιστῶ cf. Grammatical Notes.

καθολικός 13/113.

καθομιλῶ 1/12.

καθυπισχνοῦμαι 43/105.

καθυποτάσσω 15/8, 31/60, 32/148, 45/ 126, 127, 50/13, 22.

καθυπουργῶ 1/22.

καινοτομῶ P/24, 13/175, 48/25, 49/69.

κακιγκάκως 13/65, 40/19. — Cf. Ed. Kurtz, *Byzantinische Zeitschrift*, 3 (1894), pp. 152—155; 8 (1899), pp. 157—158.

κακοπιστία 25/19.

καλλιγραφία 1/10.

*καλοκαιρίζω 8/35.

καλοκαίριον 29/267.

καλύβιον 28/10.

καμάρα 29/243, 252.

καματερός 42/33.

καμελαύκιον: (~ Latin *camellaucium*) τὰ στέμματα, ἃ παρ' ὑμῶν καμελαύκια ὀνομάζεται 13/29; τὰ στέμματα, ἅπερ ὑμεῖς καμελαύκια λέγετε 13/34. — Cf. A. A. Papadopulos, Ἐπετηρὶς Ἑταιρείας Βυζαντινῶν Σπουδῶν, 5 (1928), pp. 293—299.

καμηλεύω 14/13. — Cf. Georgius Monachus, ed. de Boor p. 698[10]; Theophanes, ed. de Boor p. 333[25].

καμίνιον 42/36.

κάμπος (~ Latin *campus*) 29/47.

κανδιδᾶτος (~ Latin *candidatus*) 51/151, 156.

κανίσκιον 46/87.

κάνναβος 53/150.

κανονίζω 22/77.

κανών 13/144, 167, 16/1.

καράβιον 29/91, 114, 42/34, 53/514, 520, 520.

κάραβος 53/296, 297, 306, 310, 312.

καρβάνιον (~ Persian *kārvān*) 45/88, 89.—Cf. Praecepta Nicephori, cod. Monac. gr. 452. fol. 127ʳ.

*καρχᾶς (~ Hungarian *qarχa > karχa*) 40/49, 51, 65, 66, 67, 67, 68. — Cf. *Byzantinoturcica* p. 139 (2nd ed. p. 155).

κασσίδιον (~ Latin *cassis*) 53/219.

καστέλλιον (~ Latin *castellum*) 27/96, 30/95, 53/28, 29, 41, 105.

κάστρον (~ Latin *castrum*) 7/6, 9/6, 8, 21, 11/1, 2, 26/13, 19, 21, 27/38, 38, 39, 40, 42, 43, 44, 50, 64, 73, 73, 73, 74, 74, 76, 79, 80, 80, 82, 82, 82, 82, 83, 83, 84, 84, 85, 85, 86, 86, 86, 86, 87, 87, 87, 87, 91, 91, 91, 92, 92, 92, 93, 93, 95, 28/9, 29/8, 11, 26, 26, 29, 46, 49, 61, 86, 91, 92, 92, 93, 100, 101, 110, 112, 114, 115, 118, 118, 138, 153, 161, 175, 190, 197, 200, 217, 223, 224, 225, 227, 230, 235, 236, 237, 241, 245, 246, 251, 253, 254, 255, 256, 258, 260, 261, 263, 266, 266, 268, 272, 274, 274, 275, 287, 293, 30/14, 18, 19, 51, 98, 115, 121, 132, 133, 134, 134, 135, 136, 136, 138, 31/29, 30, 55, 55, 68, 32/76, 149, 33/13, 20, 34/19, 35/10, 12, 36/14, 16, 37/60, 61, 62, 62, 63, 63, 40/11, 42/2, 4, 8, 11, 14, 16, 22, 26, 29, 34, 36, 37, 40, 41, 54, 56, 72, 87, 93, 98, 110, 44/2, 10, 14, 15, 20, 28, 29, 31, 34, 38, 40, 45, 48, 53, 53, 54, 56, 57, 57, 60, 62, 70, 85, 93, 99, 105, 106, 108, 108, 109, 109, 113, 113, 114, 114, 116, 125, 45/45, 49, 52, 53, 57, 63, 68, 72, 74, 81, 82, 87, 88, 88, 92, 94, 96, 97, 97, 100, 109, 116, 123, 130, 139, 145, 149, 155, 160, 46/2, 32, 33, 34, 42, 46, 56, 61, 71, 73, 76, 97, 99, 102, 104, 105, 108, 113, 116, 123, 127, 134, 140, 146, 150, 157, 49/14, 17, 28, 29, 33, 44, 50/4, 71, 154, 158, 53/1, 493, 512, 527, 529.

*καταγνώμη 13/173.

κατάγομαι 14/4, 26/4, 31/5, 32/3, 34/4, 36/6, 38/2, 45/3, 5, 8, 29.

καταδέχομαι 13/146, 36/9, 46/130.

καταθαρρῶ 53/36.

κατακολουθῶ 13/155.

κατακυριεύω 25/63.

κατάλευκος 37/61.

καταληϊζομαι 28/7, 43/26.

καταντῶ 26/13, 46/56.

κατανύσσω 53/334.

καταπολαύω 2/15.

καταρτίζω 9/11.

κατάρτιον 9/85.

κατάρχων 43/10.

κατασκήνωσις 32/10, 20, 37/9, 40/37.
κατάστασις 13/115, 145; ἐν καταστάσει 53/100.
καταστρατεύω 25/48.
κατατολμῶ 13/102.
καταφανίζω 40/20.
κατεπάνω 27/70, 42/31, 45/147, 50/169, 171, 184, 185, 195, 214, 217, 220. — Cf. A. N. Jannaris, *Byzantinische Zeitschrift*, 10 (1901), pp. 204—207.
κατευοδῶ P/40.
κατηχούμενα (τά) 29/283.
κατοικία 37/67, 42/22, 43/66.
κατονειδίζω 46/155.
κέλευσις 8/24, 29/111, 31/19, 43/62, 45/83, 46/96, 99, 101, 144, 152, 50/29, 51/10, 53, 53/131, 433, 513.
κεντηνάριον (~ Latin *centenarium*) 51/ 203, 52/15.
κερατάριον 28/26, 30.
κεφάλαιον 13/11, 45/118, 47/13, 48/1.
κηρίον 53/531.
κλειδίον 53/438; κλειδίν 46/48.
κλεισούρα 29/29, 41, 44, 50/113, 156, 158, 168.
κλεισουράρχης 50/163; κλεισουριάρχης 50/144, 144.
κλεισουριάρχης cf. κλεισουράρχης.
κληρικός 8/23, 50/236, 245, 51/173.
κλιβάνιον (~ Latin *clibanum*) 15/12, 51/83.
κλίματα (τά), 1/28, 10/5, 8, 11/8, 10, 12, 37/38, 42/8, 72, 82, 86 [κλήματα everywhere P]. — Cf. S. P. Šestakov, Памятники христианскаго Херсона III, (Moskva, 1908), pp. 69—71; V. G. Vasiljevskij, Журналъ Министерства Народнаго Просвѣщенія, 185 (1876), Іюнь, pp. 419—425 = Труды II. 1. (Sanktpeterburg), 1909, pp. 195—201; F. Westberg, Византійскій Временникъ, 15 (1908), pp. 255—257; E. Honigmann, *Die sieben Klimata und die* πόλεις ἐπίσημοι, (Heidelberg, 1929).
κογχυλευτής 52/11.
κοινόβιον 22/74.
κοινωφελής 13/166.
κοιτών 1. (= resting-place, bed-chamber) 29/242, 53/438.
 2. (= treasury) 50/53.
κοιτωνίτης 51/33.

κομμερκιάριος (~ Latin *commerciarius*) 43/176.
κομμέρκιον (~ Latin *commercium*) 46/45.
*κονδοῦρα 31/53, 73, 74, 74, 80, 81, 88 [κοντοῦρα variant in P].
κοντάριον 9/35, 46/110.
*κοντοβεύομαι 9/35.
κοντός 53/220.
κοντοῦρα cf. κονδοῦρα.
κόντουρος 37/55. — Cf. Michael Psellus, ed. Sathas, *Bibl. gr. medii aevi* V, p. 532—536; O. Schissel, *Glotta*, 22 (1934), pp. 286—289; K. Amantos, Ἑλληνικά, 8 (1935), pp. 269—270; Ph. Kukules, Ἐπιστημονικὴ Ἐπετηρὶς τῆς Φιλοσοφικῆς Σχολῆς τοῦ Πανεπιστημίου Ἀθηνῶν, 1935—1936, p. 119; H. Grégoire, *Annuaire de l'Institut de philologie et d'histoire orientales et slaves*, 5 (1937), p. 450.
κοπρία 53/449.
κοπῶ 53/68; cf. Grammatical Notes.
κοσμήτης 29/251.
κοσμικός 1/7, 31/46,
κόσμιον 53/431.
κουβικουλαρέα (~ Latin *cubicularia*) 53/321, 419, 429, 430, 439; κουβικουλαρία 53/417.
κουρά 51/165.
κουράν (~ Arabic *qur'ān*) 25/80. — Cf. *Byzantinoturcica* p. 146 (2nd ed. p. 163).
κουροπαλάτης 43/39, 48, 111, 130, 45/2, 35, 70, 79, 99, 106, 119, 136, 156, 165, 172, 46/25, 27, 36, 37, 80, 83, 84, 85, 89, 90, 129, 147, 148, 154, 164, 165.
*κουροπαλάτικιν 46/88.
κουρσεύω (~ Latin *cursor*) 1/27.
κουφότης 51/185.
κοχλίας 29/284 [κοχλίας (gen.) P].
κοχλίδιον 42/38.
κράββατος 53/481.
κραταιός 49/45.
κράτος 1. (= majesty) 48/6.
 2. (= state) 53/115.
κρατῶ (= cover space) 9/87, 42/82. — Cf. F. Dölger, *Beiträge zur Geschichte der byzantinischen Finanzverwaltung besonders des 10. und 11. Jahrhunderts*, (München, 1927), p. 87—88; *Sechs byzantinische Praktika des 14. Jahr-*

hunderts für das Athoskloster Iberon, (München, 1949), p. 123.
κροτῶ 25/50.
κρυφῇ: ἐν κρυφῇ 53/381.
κτηνοτροφῶ 14/8.
κτίσις 1. (= building) 42/35, 37, 55.
  2. (= creation) 16/7, 21/1, 22/62, 27/54, 45/40.
κτίσμα 37/64.
κυκλόθεν 27/77.
κύκλῳ 29/267, 53/401, 403, 441.
κυλίω 29/124, 53/325, 346.
κυνηγῶ 29/152, 32/132.
κυρία 1. (= lordship) P/5.
  2. (= lady, mistress) 53/333, 338, 370, 476.
κύριος P/3, 39, 13/43, 21/84, 22/57, 59, 29/197, 45/30, 53/49, 246; κύρις 13/147, 149, 170, 32/81, 100, 45/67, 67, 75, 46/49, 50/28, 61, 205; κυρός 13/148, 192, 32/106, 44/119, 45/55, 101, 50/26, 37, 207, 51/162, 174; cf. Index of Proper Names.
κύριος: κύριον ὄνομα 40/51, 67.
κυριότης 45/124, 127.
κύρις, κυρός cf. κύριος.
κυρίως 42/42, 44/28.
κωπηλατῶ 51/146.
λαλῶ 29/147, 209, 46/58, 63, 53/406.
λανθάνω: ἐν τῷ λεληθότι 53/429.
λαξευτός 37/65.
λαῦ (~ Dalmatian lau): λέγεται 'Ρωμαϊστὶ 'ὁ κρημνὸς λαῦ' 29/219. — Cf. P. Skok, Zeitschrift für Ortsnamenforschung, 4 (1928), p. 214.
λαύρα 22/73.
λεηλασία 49/42, 50/8.
λείψανον 27/81, 29/10.
λεπτομερῶς 49/72.
λέσα (~ Slavic lěsa): λέσας, ἤτοι πλοκούς 51/114, 119. — Cf. Cedrenus, ed. Bonn. II. p. 591₂₀.
λιθάριον 9/47.
λίτρα 28/42, 43/68, 69, 69, 126, 50/242, 243, 247, 248, 249, 251, 253, 254, 256, 53/527.
λογάριον 51/193, 197, 203.
λογοθέτης: λογοθέτης τοῦ δρόμου 32/84, 50/176, 190, 51/30.
λόγῳ 7/10, 10.
μαγγλάβιον (~ Latin manuclavium) 51/61.
μαγγλαβίτης (~ Latin manuclavium) 46/51, 140, 144, 51/73, 130.

μαγίσδιον (~ Arabic masjid) 21/114. — Cf. Byzantinoturcica p. 161 (2ⁿᵈ ed. p. 182).
μαγιστρᾶτον (~ Latin magistratus) 46/52, 88, 122.
μαγιστριανός (~ Latin magistrianus) 22/15, 17.
μάγιστρος (~ Latin magister) 32/83, 43/65, 135, 151, 155, 163, 187, 44/10, 36, 45/51, 56, 59, 77, 125, 143, 147, 148, 46/12, 16, 17, 18, 22, 25, 26, 27, 30, 39, 40, 52, 66, 92, 94, 95, 121, 126, 129, 129, 153, 154, 50/151, 166, 51/23, 28, 198.
μαθηματικός (ὁ) 16/2.
μακάριος 17/1, 21/35, 22/1, 81, 29/73, 32/78, 43/31, 36, 56, 72, 85, 89, 102, 118, 120, 129, 131, 45/101, 162, 46/49, 79, 50/171, 196, 199, 218, 51/14, 37.
μακαρίτης 51/174.
μακρόθεν 28/13.
*μακρόκενσον (~ Latin [pro]cessus) 51/37.
μάμμη 26/69, 72.
μανιάκιον 25/81.
μανίκιον (~ Latin manica) 37/56.
μαρκήσιος (~ Latin marchensis) 26/42.
μάρτυρ 23/34.
μάρτυρος 23/34.
μάρτυς (= martyr) 29/262, 278.
μαστρομίλης (~ Latin magister militum): μαστρομίλης ἑρμηνεύεται τῇ 'Ρωμαίων διαλέκτῳ 'κατεπάνω τοῦ στρατοῦ' 27/69. — Cf. De cerimoniis, ed. Bonn. p. 690₂₃.
μαῦρος 12/1, 2, 42/77, 51/49, 50, 64, 66.
μεγαλεπήβολος P/11 [μεγαλεπίβολος P].
μεγαλοφυής P/28.
μέγας (= old, elder) 21/32, 26/2, 3, 15, 17, 70, 46/4, 117, 151.
μεγιστᾶνες (οἱ) 30/17, 45/8.
μέναυλο(ς) (~ Latin venabulum): τοῦ μεναύλου 26/33. — Cf. Theophanes, ed. de Boor p. 221₃.
μέρος: ἐκ τοῦ κατὰ μέρος 53/300, 381.
μεσιτεύω 50/177, 240.
μέσον 9/27, 30, 34, 26/31, 29/236, 30/139, 42/19, 56, 70, 81, 94, 44/127, 46/131, 51/144.
μεσουρανῶ 29/268.
μετά cf. Grammatical Notes.
μετάμελος 32/18.
μεταστασίματα (τά) 51/14.

*μεταφθείρω 29/220.

μέχρι cf. Grammatical Notes.

μήκοθεν 28/50, 30/108, 31/88.

*μητρόθειος 22/79.

μητρόπολις 27/80, 49/57, 59, 65, 69, 52/9.

μητροπολίτης 49/73, 52/4.

μιαιφονία 22/76.

μιλιαρήσιον (~ Latin *miliarensis*): μιλιαρησίων (pl. gen.) 43/68.

μίλιον (~ Latin *milium*) 9/53, 26/14, 20, 27/77, 29/30, 265, 42/65, 67, 70, 73, 80, 82, 94, 94, 96, 99, 110, 53/226, 305.

μισθαποδοσία 53/455.

μισθαποδότης 29/202.

μισθωτεύομαι 14/11. — Cf. Georgius Monachus, ed. de Boor p. 698₈.

μισοποιῶ (~ Latin *missus*) 53/396, 397, 414, 422.

μνημόσυνον 29/144.

μνημόσυνος 53/408.

μοναστήριον 22/72, 26/9, 52/8, 9, 10.

μοναχός 14/22, 29/278, 46/54, 59, 62, 72, 102.

μονή 22/78, 43/177.

μονοκράτωρ 26/5.

μονόξυλον 9/2, 3, 11, 17, 22, 32, 43, 51, 54, 60, 84, 95, 112.

μυστικός (ὁ) 51/31.

ναός 13/40, 19/10, 27/84, 29/236, 241, 270, 278, 279, 282, 283, 283, 49/38, 50, 56.

νεόκαστρον (~ Latin *castrum*) 27/41, 28/48; cf. Index of Proper Names.

νερόν 9/62.

νηπιότης 44/96.

νησίον 9/27, 41, 78, 27/72, 28/49, 50, 29/258, 285, 287, 288, 288, 289, 42/95, 103, 103, 50/85; νησίν 42/103, 106, 106.

νοήμων 1/5.

νόμισμα 22/12, 30/134, 134, 135, 135, 136, 136, 137, 138, 141, 142, 50/23, 23, 48, 49, 50, 50, 51, 51, 68, 68, 82, 52/13, 14.

νόμῳ 4/4.

νουνεχῶς P/9.

νωθρότης 29/59, 85.

ξενάλιον 7/9, 43/40, 46. — Cf. De cerimoniis, ed. Bonn. p. 461₉ etc.

ξενιάζω 31/63, 64. — Cf. Ph. Kukules, Βυζαντινῶν βίος καὶ πολιτισμός Β΄, I. p. 12.

ὁδηγῶ P/43.

οἴγω cf. Grammatical Notes.

οἶδα cf. Grammatical Notes.

οἰκοδομή 53/447.

οἰκονομία 47/5.

ὀλιγοστός 22/37, 53/32.

ὀλιγωρῶ 14/21. — Cf. Georgius Monachus, ed. de Boor p. 699₁; Theophanes, ed. de Boor p. 334₉.

ὁλοσχερῶς 22/36.

ὁμάς 49/71.

ὁμόπιστος 13/161.

ὁμόφρων 50/57.

ὁμοφωνῶ 40/15.

ὁμοχροῦ 53/497.

ὁμοψυχία 41/14.

ὀπτασία 14/20.

ὅρασις 17/20.

ὀρθόδοξος 13/137, 21/10.

*ὀρθόπλωρα 9/48.

ὁρίζω 26/47, 29/141, 42/52, 43/45, 47/11; ὡρισμένος 9/48.

ὁρισμός 31/32.

ὁρκίζω 29/199.

ὁροθεσία 53/172, 175, 176, 182, 225, 226, 227.

ὅσιος 25/1.

ὁσπίτιον (~ Latin *hospitium*) 42/24.

ὁστιάριος (~ Latin *ostiarius*) 50/223.

οὐά (~ Arabic *wa*) 14/33; τὸ δὲ 'οὐά' ἀντὶ τοῦ 'καί' συνδέσμου τιθέασιν 14/34.

οὐσία 51/41, 91. — Cf. De cerimoniis, ed. Bonn. p. 579₁, 614₁₉, 657₃, 664₇ etc.

ὀφθαλμοφανῶς 49/31, 47.

ὀφφίκιον (~ Latin *officium*) 51/46.

ὄχθη 9/37.

ὄχλησις 28/38.

ὀχυροποιῶ 50/155.

ὄψης (~ Latin *obses*) 7/5, 6, 10, 8/13, 14, 45/142; ὁμήρους, ἤτοι ὄψιδας 1/21.

ὄψις: ἐπ᾽ ὄψεσι 53/51. — Cf. Theophanes, ed. de Boor p. 10₂₈ etc.; Preisigke, *Wörterbuch der griechischen Papyrusurkunden* II. p. 217.

παγιδεύω 29/194.

παγιῶ 22/25, 53/286, 289. — Cf. Menander fr. 3., Excerpta de legationibus, ed. de Boor I, p. 181₂₂; Theophanes, ed. de Boor p. 364₈.

παιδάριον 4/12.

παιδίον 8/31, 30/27, 32/52, 60, 131, 43/168, 174, 46/38.

παιδοποιῶ 38/19.

*πακτιώτης (~ Latin *pactum*) 9/9, 109. — Cf. A. Eck, *Annuaire de l'Institut de philologie et d'histoire orientales*, 2 (1934), pp. 343—349.

πακτιωτικός (~ Latin *pactum*) 9/21.

πάκτον (~ Latin *pactum*) 21/14, 27/18, 28/39, 40, 30/133, 31/65, 32/57, 43/128, 44/33, 39, 44, 59, 63, 87, 89, 112, 50/3, 5, 48, 49, 51, 63, 67, 69, 82, 53/78, 80, 82, 528. — Cf. I. Dujčev, *Annales de l'Institut Kondakov*, 10 (1938), p. 147—150.

πακτῶ (~ Latin *pactum*) 44/123.

παλαιόκαστρον (~ Latin *castrum*) 37/64.

παλάτιον (~ Latin *palatium*) 26/36, 59, 29/9, 102, 237, 239, 253, 31/28, 48/2, 51/16, 42, 162.

πάμφαυλος 29/188.

πανάγιος 46/4.

πανοικί 53/399, 415.

πάνσεπτος 49/38.

παντοκράτωρ cf. Index of Proper Names.

πάντοτε 25/83, 45/64.

πάπας 26/12, 27/16, 29/105, 107, 31/33, 39, 49, 51.

παραβασία 53/486.

παράβασις 13/97.

παραβάτης 13/92, 124, 142.

παραβλάπτω 2/4, 12, 13/10.

παραδειγματίζω 13/88.

παράδεισος 14/30, 17/17, 18.

παράδοσις 13/168, 37/66.

παραθαλάσσιον 42/108.

παραθύριον 53/427.

παρακαθίζω 19/3, 26/46, 28/21, 28, 29/93, 112.

παρακλάδιον 9/93.

παράκλησις 45/157, 50/250, 53/270.

παρακοιμώμενος 43/67, 50/222, 223, 224, 226, 227, 230, 239, 250, 51/32, 149, 160.

παρακύπτω 9/69.

παράληψις 30/6.

*παραμόνιμον 29/24. — Cf. παραμονή Theophanes, ed. de Boor p. 376₂₆.

παραπύλιον 53/265, 307, 401, 440.

παρασαλεύω 45/120.

παραστέλλω 22/21.

παραστήκω 53/403.

παρασύρω 53/435.

πάραυτα 32/98, 108, 123.

παράφρων 14/29.

παρεμβολή 21/86.

παροξυνόμενος 23/33.

παρρησιαστικός 13/20.

πάσχα 29/22, 23.

πάτος 29/281, 53/228.

πατριάρχης 13/45, 58, 64, 70, 89, 45/32.

πατριαρχικός 52/8.

πατριαρχῶ 13/128.

πατρικία (~ Latin *patricia*) 43/159.

πατρίκιος (~ Latin *patricius*) 25/27, 27/9, 9, 10, 15, 17, 27, 32, 59, 60, 29/97, 99, 33/16, 43/28, 35, 44, 133, 152, 164, 165, 166, 179, 188, 45/46, 58, 134, 140, 46/7, 10, 15, 19, 23, 31, 50, 53, 57, 63, 64, 68, 70, 76, 91, 93, 96, 97, 101, 106, 108, 109, 111, 113, 116, 119, 124, 125, 149, 149, 155, 162, 162, 50/162, 176, 190, 191, 194, 204, 224, 228, 229, 230, 231, 232, 234, 238, 246, 250, 51/23, 28, 75, 85, 87, 96, 110, 123, 149, 160, 198.

πατρικιότης (~ Latin *patricius*) 43/73.

πατρικόν 46/24.

πατροπαράδοτος 13/157.

πεζικόν 31/72, 80, 82, 85.

πελεκᾶνος 9/47.

*πέλλα (Latin *pala* ?) 9/18.

πέπερις (-ιν ?) 6/8.

πέραθεν 42/18.

πέραμα 9/66, 68, 28/21, 26, 37/59, 42/93.

περιήγησις P/21, 13/199.

περίπλους 23/28.

περίστασις 13/51, 51/80.

περιτομή 17/11.

περίφημος 38/17.

περίχωρος (ἡ) 18/4, 30/11, 120, 43/186, 44/107.

πέταλον 53/220.

πετεινός 9/74, 77.

πετζιμέντα (τά) (~ Latin *impedimentum*) 9/56. — Cf. De cerimoniis, ed. Bonn, p. 474₃.

πέχ (~ Turkish *bäg*) 42/27. — Cf. *Byzantinoturcica* p. 214 (2ⁿᵈ ed. p. 250).

πηγνύω cf. Grammatical Notes.

πηδαλιουχῶ 1/8, 51/147.

πινακίδιον 25/80.

πιστικός 53/309, 354, 355, 358.

πίστις (= faith) 32/29.
πιστοποιῶ 53/257, 359, 365.
πίστωσις 53/492.
πιττάκιον 46/67.
*πλαγίτικος 53/524.
πλάνη 14/28.
πλάσσω: ὁ πλάσας (= Creator) P/32.
πλατεῖα 53/394, 456.
πληθύνω 29/230.
πλημμυρῶ 9/28.
πληροφορία 29/151.
πληροφορῶ 13/80, 29/135, 144, 53/360, 369, 371, 372, 375, 378.
πλοκός 51/114, 119, 122.
πλώϊμον 29/98, 100, 46/50, 54, 65, 77, 51/30, 75, 76, 85, 87, 96, 97, 105, 110, 113, 113, 124, 131; cf. δρουγγάριος.
πλώϊμος 42/31, 51/82, 84.
πλώϊμος (ὁ) 51/12, 117, 122, 52/11, 53/144.
πλώρᾳ 9/34.
πνεῦμα 29/270.
πνεῦσις 51/147.
πόλις 1. (= Constantinople) 1/22, 2/16, 8/1, 13/81, 21/125, 29/172, 32/101, 139, 43/65, 83, 133, 138, 171, 46/60, 63, 164, 50/119, 51/32, 53/514; cf. βασιλεύουσα.
   2. ἁγία πόλις (= Jerusalem) 21/5, 67, 22/72, 45/32, 46/55.
πολιτεία 1. (= state, polity) P/23, 13/175, 21/53, 123.
   2. (= township) 44/48, 54.
*πολύδια: τὰ πολύδια, ὃ λέγεται γύρα 9/107. — Cf. K. Nevolin, Финнскій Вѣстникъ, 20 (1847), No. 8., pp. 1—10 (= Сборникъ сочиненій, S. Peterburg, 1870, pp. 521—527); N. Lavrovskij, Журналъ Министерства Народнаго Просвѣщенія, 166 (1873), Мартъ, pp. 113—121; S. Gedeonov, Варяги и Русь II. (S. Peterburg, 1876), pp. 546—547; P. Jurčenko, Чтенія въ Имп. Обществѣ Исторіи и Древностей россійскихъ при Московскомъ Университетѣ, 1877, II., pp. 1—14; S. Vvedenskij, Извѣстія Общества археологіи, исторіи и этнографіи при Казанскомъ Университетѣ, 22 (1906), pp. 149—163; L. Niederle, *Slavia*, 7 (1928—29), pp. 979—980;

N. Popov, *Byzantinoslavica*, 3 (1931), pp. 92—96; *D. A. I.* Commentary, pp. 59—60.
πολυέραστος 13/195.
πολυήμερος 49/43.
πολύς: τὸ πολύ 51/156.
πολυώδυνος 9/103.
πόρτα (~ Latin *porta*) 30/53, 54.
πορφυρογέννητος Tit./4, 26/67, 45/41, 43, 51/137.
ποταμία 46/14.
πραγματεία 2/18, 46/43, 46, 53/525.
πραγματεύομαι 6/3, 14/13, 45/169, 53/532.
πραγματευτής 38/63.
πραῖδα (~ Latin *praeda*) 29/21, 35, 30/30, 45/135, 50/8.
πραιδεύω (~ Latin *praedor*) 2/3, 5/12, 10/6, 13/10, 29/47, 31/86, 44/32, 45/60, 95, 132, 137, 168, 53/95.
πραιτώριον (~ Latin *praetorium*) 21/114, 27/58.
πράνδιον (~ Latin *brandeum*) 6/8. — Cf. Theophanes, ed. de Boor p. 232₉; Eparchicon Biblion IX. 6., ed. Zepos p. 382.
πράσινος 29/280.
πρεσβεία 49/26, 62, 64.
πρεσβύτεροι 31/23, 49/60.
πριγκιπᾶτον (~ Latin *principatus*) 27/2, 53.
προβάλλομαι (= appoint) 21/42, 29/76, 38/38, 42/43, 51, 54, 44/46, 50/33, 55, 127, 150, 153, 170, 171, 199, 217, 220, 51/104, 106, 127, 132, 133, 140, 172.
προβάλλω (= break out sc. of war) 40/46.
προβασιλεύω 43/121.
πρόβατον 2/6, 53/267.
προβιβάζω 43/73, 152.
προβολή 46/66, 51/176.
πρόγνωσις 46/169.
προγονικός 13/136, 43/158.
προγονός 44/56, 76, 77, 101, 104.
προεδρεύω 48/13.
πρόεδρος 47/13, 48/4, 17, 19.
προέλευσις 13/46, 50/215.
προεξάρχω 39/11.
προθυμοποιῶ 51/144.
πρόκενσον (~ Latin *processus*) 51/18, 40, 45, 142.
προκτίζω 29/274.

προμνημονεύω 13/126.
προνόμιον 48/11.
προπάλαιος 50/74.
προπορεύομαι 51/122.
πρός cf. Grammatical Notes.
προσαναπαύω 9/83.
*προσαποκινῶ 29/28.
προσαπολογοῦμαι 46/163.
προσευχή 14/33.
προσηγορία 1. (= denomination, title) 32/11, 37/71.
    2. (= greeting) 53/253.
πρόσκρουσις 13/184.
προσκυνητήριον 19/11.
προσκυνητής 50/74.
προσονομάζω 14/34.
προσπαθῶ 51/178.
προσρίπτω 30/82.
πρόσταγμα 13/38, 53.
πρόσταξις 29/145, 31/17, 32/134, 38/39, 46/67, 50/38, 81, 51/100.
προστρίβομαι 13/136.
προσυμφωνῶ 6/6.
προσφεύγω 28/13, 31/10, 32/9, 31, 33/10, 34/5, 36/7, 41/24, 48/30, 49/38, 50.
πρόσφυγος cf. πρόσφυξ.
πρόσφυξ 31/9; πρόσφυγος 50/138.
πρόσωπον: ὁ ἐκ προσώπου 50/174, 178, 180, 196.
προτελευτῶ 53/272.
πρόφημι 29/84.
προφήτης 14/3, 24, 16/10, 17/13, 19/9, 45/4, 6, 49/61.
πρωτελάτης 51/74, 77, 90, 106, 110, 151. — Cf. De cerimoniis, ed Bonn. p. 577₁₋₃ (πρωτοελάτης).
πρωτεύω 53/3, 25, 130, 168, 186, 235, 275, 470; πρωτεύων 42/43, 46, 52, 53/136, 357, 363.
πρωτοασηκρῆτις (~ Latin a secretis) 46/68.
πρωτοβεστιάριος (~ Latin vestiarius) 51/32.
πρωτοκάραβος 51/2, 80, 81, 105, 127, 139, 146, 150, 155, 161, 167, 171, 188.
πρωτόκλητος 49/30, 37, 57.
πρῶτος 53/245.
πρωτοσπαθάριος 29/233, 32/82, 42/51, 43/29, 43, 49, 53, 54, 57, 70, 137, 169, 176, 45/103, 133, 146, 46/51, 139, 143, 50/10, 21, 26, 33, 35, 39, 47, 52, 53, 54, 56, 57, 58, 120, 173, 195, 205, 206, 216, 240, 242, 245,

254, 255, 51/70, 71, 72, 72, 73, 74, 94, 129, 131, 134, 135, 139, 140, 152, 155, 161, 172, 175, 194, 200, 52/6; πρωτοσπαθάριος τῆς φιάλης 51/3, 46, 47, 53, 55, 57, 64, 69, 99, 133, 141, 153, 171, 190.
πυκτεύω 29/177.
πυλεών 53/264, 398, 400, 427.
πῦρ: πῦρ ὑγρόν 13/73, 48/30.
πώρινος 37/66.
ῥαίκτωρ cf. ῥέκτωρ.
*ῥαπάτιν (~ Arabic rabaḍ) 46/43. — Cf. E. Honigmann, Byzantion, 10 (1935), pp. 148—149.
ῥεγεών (~ Latin regio) 53/262, 282.
ῥέκτωρ (~ Latin rector) 51/174, 184. [ῥαίκτωρ everywhere P].
ῥηγᾶτον (~ Latin regatus) 26/6, 25, 55, 28/18, 41. — Cf. Eustathius, De Thessalonica a Latinis capta, ed. Bonn. p. 417₄.
ῥήξ (~ Latin rex) 26/1, 2, 3, 7, 7, 16, 45, 57, 59, 63, 66, 69, 28/17, 20, 23, 27, 31, 33, 38, 46, 29/105, 107, 117, 119, 122, 132, 133, 143, 146, 152, 152, 154, 162, 163, 165, 169; μέγας ῥήξ 30/74.
ῥιζιμαῖος 9/27. — Cf. Praktikon a. 1301, ed. F. Dölger, Sechs byzantinische Praktika des 14. Jahrhunderts für das Athoskloster Iberon, (München, 1949), p. 52₄₃₃; Narratio de Sancta Sophia, ed. N. Bǎnescu, Ἐπετηρὶς Ἑταιρείας Βυζαντινῶν Σπουδῶν, 3 (1926), p. 150₁₉.
ῥιπτάριον 28/32. — Cf. Leo, Tactica V. 3,. ed. Migne, P. G. 107. c. 711C etc.
ῥόγα (~ Latin erogatio, roga) 43/68, 82, 114, 119, 128.
ῥογεύω (~ Latin erogo) 7/17, 43/117, 50/242, 254, 256.
ῥοδωτός 15/12. — Cf. cod. Vindob. theol. gr. 244. f. 201ʳ, ed. A. Delatte, Miscellanea Giov. Mercati III, (Roma, 1946), p. 496; Liddell-Scott, Greek-English Lexicon s. v.
ῥούσιος 51/7, 49, 50, 63, 65.
σάββατον 29/23, 30/48.
σαγῆνα (~ Latin sagena) 30/108, 31/52, 72, 73, 80, 81, 87. — Cf. Mauricius, Tactica, ed. Scheffer p. 347₁.
σαγίον (~ Latin sagum) 13/41.

σαγίττα (~ Latin *sagitta*) 9/69, 75.
σαρκικός 17/18.
σεβάσμιος 49/50.
σεμνός 53/265. — Cf. E. Dawes—N. H.
  Baynes, *Three Byzantine Saints*,
  (Oxford, 1948), pp. 74, 75.
*σέρβυλα: 'σέρβυλα' ἡ κοινὴ συνήθεια
  τὰ δουλικά φησιν ὑποδήματα 32/13;
  cf. τζερβουλιανός.
σηκῶ 38/52.
σημέντον (~ Latin *segmentum*) 6/8.
σιγίλλιον (~ Latin *sigillum*) 49/59, 72.
σιταρχῶ 45/69, 91.
σίτησις 53/153.
σκαλώνω (~ Latin *scala*) 9/31, 48, 95. —
  Cf. Nicephorus Uranus, Tactica, ed.
  A. Dain, *Naumachica* (Paris, 1943),
  p. 78₅, etc.
σκάνδαλον 43/23, 123, 130.
σκαρμός (~ Latin *scalmus*) 9/18. — Cf.
  Leo, Tactica XIX. 5., ed. A. Dain,
  Naumachica, (Paris, 1943), p. 19₂₇.
σκαρφίον 9/77. — Cf. *Journal of Hellenic
  Studies* 30 (1910), p. 99.
σκαφίδιον 9/17.
σκέμμα 53/343.
σκληρύνομαι 30/80.
σκορπίζω 30/37.
σκουλκάτωρ (~ Latin *sculcator*) 53/57.
σκουτάριον (~ Latin *scutum*) 38/53,
  51/83, 118.
σκυλίον 32/56.
σοῦδα (~ Latin *suda*) 42/80, 83. — Cf.
  F. Dölger, Der Titel des sog. Suidaslexikons, *Sitzungsberichte der Bayer.
  Akad. d. Wiss.*, Philos.-hist. Abt.
  1936. H. 6, München 1936; H. Grégoire, *Byzantion*, 11 (1936), pp. 777—
  778; 12 (1937), pp. 295—300; A.
  Dain, *Annuaire de l'Institut de philologie et d'histoire orientales et slaves*,
  5 (1937), pp. 233—241; F. Dölger,
  Byzantinische Zeitschrift, 38 (1938),
  pp. 36—57.
σπαθάριος 51/152, 156, 158, 52/7.
σπαθαροκανδιδᾶτος (~ Latin *candidatus*)
  42/25, 30, 39, 49, 50/216, 51/152, 156,
  158, 161, 170, 52/6.
σπαθίον 27/45, 51/118.
σπάνιος 7/9.
σπλαγχνίζομαι 29/97.
σταδιασμός P/21, 13/200.

σταυρός 37/65, 46/60, 50/104; cf. Index
  of Proper Names.
στεγνός 53/395.
στέμμα 13/26, 28, 34, 44, 59, 63, 126.
στενοχωρῶ 26/47.
στενῶ 29/264, 265.
στένωσις 53/66.
στερεά 27/90.
στεφανηφορῶ 53/3, 24, 130, 167, 186,
  234, 275, 470.
στέφω 13/68, 70, 26/12, 23.
στοιχῶ 13/157, 20/2, 21/83, 22/15.
στόμιον 9/81, 86, 98, 42/67, 74, 90, 94.
*στρατηγίς 25/66, 50/83, 84, 85, 86, 87,
  88, 89, 90, 91, 161.
στρατηγός (= military governor) 13/95,
  101, 30/125, 128, 130, 131, 32/19,
  42/43, 45, 47, 51, 54, 43/65, 153,
  45/46, 47, 47, 48, 133, 134, 135,
  140, 49/13, 19, 20, 22, 23, 24, 29, 39,
  66, 50/11, 22, 29, 31, 34, 35, 47, 55,
  80, 81, 123, 124, 127, 137, 150, 162,
  183, 207, 51/132, 194, 53/526, 528;
  στρατηγῶν 32/82, 50/24, 26, 51/201.
στρατηγῶν cf. στρατηγός.
στράτωρ (~ Latin *strator*) 51/152, 156,
  52/7.
στρώννυμι: ἐστρωμένος 51/203.
συγγενίς 13/165, 43/154, 45/9.
συγγραφή 29/56.
συγκλητικός 51/23.
σύγκλητος 13/57, 25/41; σύγκλητος βουλή
  13/171.
συγκοπή 29/281. — Cf. Scriptores ori-
  ginum Constantinopolitanarum, ed.
  Preger I. p. 145₂₂; Theophanes
  Continuatus, ed. Bonn. p. 143₂₃.
συγχαίρομαι 51/24.
συγχώρησις 26/52, 51/173.
συγχωρῶ 53/350.
συκοφαντικῶς 50/189.
συλλαλῶ 38/48.
συλλειτουργός 48/3.
συμβίβασις 46/28, 49/11.
σύμβιος 29/201.
συμβίωσις 13/182.
συμπάθεια 50/46.
συμπαθῶ 17/22, 50/62; cf. Grammatical
  Notes.
συμπενθερία 30/74.
συμπενθεριάζω 13/107, 114, 143, 148.
συμπλήρωμα 29/266.

συμπλήρωσις 42/108, 53/157.
συμφιλιοῦμαι 39/7.
σύμφωνον 45/114.
συμψευδομαρτυρῶ 14/22. — Cf. Georgius
Monachus, ed. de Boor II. p. 699₁.
*συναλλάγιον 13/120, 134.
συναναστρέφομαι 14/16.
συνάντησις 26/46.
σύνδεσμος 14/35.
συνδιατριβή 13/182.
συνδίδωμι 30/59; cf. Grammatical Notes.
συνδοσία 49/70.
συνδρομή 32/144.
συνειστρέχω 30/56.
συνεπαίρω 32/89, 123; cf. Grammatical
Notes.
συνεπαμύνομαι 29/105, 162.
συνέργεια 22/51.
συνετίζω P/13, 32.
συνήθεια 1. (= usage, colloquial) 29/275,
32/13.
2. (= regular grant) 53/153.
συνιστῶ 13/120.
σύνοδος 47/6, 12, 14, 48/1.
συνοικέσιον 13/180.
συνομιλία 13/182.
συνορίτης 32/37.
σύνορον 30/9, 114, 32/53, 45/158, 161,
164, 173, 46/15.
συνορῶ (-άω) 48/9.
συνορῶ (-έω) 31/6, 37/4, 46/118.
συνταξιδεύω 45/23, 147, 50/31 [-ταξειδ-
everywhere P]
σύνταξις 53/290, 291.
συντάσσομαι 53/283.
συντεχνία 32/96.
σύντεχνος 26/55, 32/81.
συντιμῶ 43/126.
συντομία: ἐν συντομίᾳ 46/70, 53/407 [ἐν
συντόμως P].
σύντομος: ἐκ συντόμου 53/434 [ἐκ σύντομον P].
συρράπτομαι 50/188.
σύρω 9/15, 53.
σφάζω 21/76, 76.
σφοντύλιν 53/325, 345.
σφραγίζω 53/148.
σχέσις 38/40.
σχολαρίκιον 50/247, 252. — Cf. diploma,
ed. M. I. Gedeon, Byzantinische Zeitschrift, 5 (1896), p. 115₆.
σχολή cf. δομέστικος.
σωφρονισμός 13/193.

*ταξατεύω (~ Latin taxatus) 46/127.
ταξατιών (~ Latin taxatio) 22/28.
ταξᾶτος (~ Latin taxatus) 45/69.
ταξειδεύω, ταξείδιον cf. ταξιδεύω, ταξίδιον.
ταξεώτης 30/34, 47, 42/23.
ταξίαρχος (ταξιάρχης?) 49/36.
ταξιδεύω 51/43, 195, 200, 202, 53/530
[ταξειδ- everywhere P].
ταξίδιον 30/28, 30, 40/16, 51/92, 52/
13 [ταξειδ- everywhere P].
τεκνῶ 38/18.
τετραπέδικος 29/247. — Cf. Gregorius
Nyssenus, Epistola XXV., ed. Migne,
P. G. 46. c. 1097c.
*τζερβουλιανός: ἡ κοινὴ συνήθεια...
φησιν... 'τζερβουλιανοὺς' τοὺς τὰ
εὐτελῆ καὶ πενιχρὰ ὑποδήματα φοροῦντας 32/14. — Cf. Praecepta
Nicephori, ed. Kulakovskij, p. 1₂₀
= cod. Monac. gr. 452. fol. 109ᵛ
(τζερβούλια); S. B. Psaltes, Grammatik der byzantinischen Chroniken,
(Göttingen, 1913), p. 74; Ph. Kukules Ἐπιστημονικὴ Ἐπετηρὶς τῆς
Φιλοσοφικῆς Σχολῆς τοῦ Πανεπιστημίου Ἀθηνῶν 1935—1936, p. 124.
τζυκανιστήριον (~ Persian čougān) 9/27.
— Cf. Ph. Kukules, Ἐπετηρὶς Ἑταιρείας Βυζαντινῶν Σπουδῶν, 13 (1937),
p. 114; C. Diem, Asiatische Reiter-
spiele, (Berlin, 1942²), pp. 111, 260;
A. Pagliaro, Un gioco persiano alla
corte di Bizanzio, Studi Bizantini e
Neoellenici, 5 (1939), pp. 521—524.
τίποτε 53/88, 374.
τοιοῦτος cf. Grammatical Notes.
τόλμημα 13/67.
τόνος 23/33.
τοξεία 28/32.
τοποτηρησία 50/94, 94, 95, 95, 97, 97,
98, 103, 103, 104, 107, 107, 110.
τοποτηρητής 51/105, 126, 130, 133.
τοῦρμα (~ Latin turma) 46/118, 50/83,
85, 90, 100, 104, 107, 109, 116, 116,
128, 129, 134, 134, 149, 167.
*τουρμαρχᾶτον (~ Latin turma) 50/159.
τουρμάρχης (~ Latin turma) 45/81, 83,
84, 46/78, 50/146.
τρακτεύω (~ Latin tracto) 53/214.
τράπεζα 1. ἁγία τράπεζα 13/39, 49, 84,
131; ἱερὰ τράπεζα 13/42, 113.

2. ὁ τῆς τραπέζης 51/51, 66, 68, 103, 175, 179.

τραπέζιον 50/248, 252.

τραπεζοποιός 49/68.

τριάς cf. Index of Proper Names.

τριβοῦνος (~ Latin *tribunus*) 53/10.

τριετία 32/41.

τριώροφος 29/255.

τροπαιοῦχος 49/36.

τροποῦμαι (= deceive) 14/20. — Cf. Theophanes, ed. de Boor p. 334₇ etc.

τροπῶ 2/23, 45/26, 49/48, 53/134.

τύπος 13/22, 67, 22/26, 27/19, 29/68, 37/26, 43/125, 50/169, 219, 51/17, 28, 43, 44, 56, 154.

ὑλογραφία 29/280. — Cf. Theophanes, ed. de Boor p. 443₂₅.

ὕπαρξις 49/56.

ὕπατος 25/28.

ὑπεισέρχομαι 37/32, 45/138, 154.

ὑπεράγιος 45/7.

ὑπερασπίζω P/31, 45/108.

ὑπερβόρειος 25/16.

ὑπεργηρῶ 51/138.

*ὑπερεξάρχων 45/78.

ὑπερθαυμάζω 51/121.

ὑπερισχύω 30/67, 86, 37/6, 39/5.

ὑπερνικῶ 5/9.

*ὑπερούσιος (= wealthy) 14/27.

*ὑπερπολεμῶ 27/26.

ὑπήκοος 17/16, 43/5, 12, 53/48, 118.

ὑπηρεσία 51/39.

ὑπηρέτης 13/46.

ὑπόγεως 53/330.

ὑπόθεσις 13/111, 29/129, 32/86, 43/38, 40, 46/67, 100, 159, 161.

ὑποκάτωθεν 53/323.

ὑποκλίνω 43/8.

ὑπόκρημνος 29/227.

ὑποκύπτω 53/115.

ὑπομάσθιον 30/81.

ὑπόσπονδος 26/8, 45/109.

ὑπόστασις 43/95, 44/105. — Cf. F. Dölger, *Beiträge zur Geschichte der byzantinischen Finanzverwaltung besonders des 10. und 11. Jahrhunderts*, (München, 1927), p. 153.

ὑποταγή 29/215, 30/131, 32/37, 79, 43/87.

ὑποτάσσω P/17, 1/6, 27/47, 29/72, 140, 161, 30/69, 79, 31/59, 32/27, 40, 110, 116, 142, 147, 43/8, 85, 44/29,

44, 58, 63, 45/23, 141, 48/7, 49/12, 50/15, 41, 45, 80.

ὑπότροπος 27/45.

ὑπουργία 13/27, 51/140; cf. δομέστικος.

ὑπόφορος 30/132, 37/43.

ὕφαλος 9/69.

ὑψῶ 29/126.

φαλκώνιον (~ Latin *falco*) 32/55.

φαμιλία (~ Latin *familia*) 27/37, 29/4, 40/18, 49/55, 53/16, 20, 24, 41, 59, 75, 85, 99, 101, 105, 281, 436.

φενακίζω: πεφενακισμένος 14/29.

φέρω cf. ἐνεγκαμένη.

φημί: φησί(ν) 53/37, 66, 165, 291, 303, 384.

φθάζω 9/69, 29/207, 53/7, 388.

φιάλη 51/4, 57, 102, 142, 179; cf. πρωτοσπαθάριος τῆς φιάλης.

*φιβλατοῦρα (~ Latin *fibulatorium*) 53/142.

φίλος (ὁ) (= 'friend' *sc.* diplomatic) 8/18, 9/69, 40/64, 45/108, 157.

φιλοτιμία 1/23, 43/109, 162, 53/161.

φιλοτιμοῦμαι 22/16, 51/93.

φιλοφρόνησις 31/66, 43/22.

φιλοφρονοῦμαι 43/53, 76, 133.

φιλόχριστος 26/68, 72, 29/70, 45/36, 41, 43, 48/8, 50/87, 92, 101, 118, 133, 136, 156, 160, 225, 225, 227, 231, 235, 51/7, 76, 108, 137, 164, 192, 196.

φιμοῦμαι P/29.

φλάμμουλον (~ Latin *flammula*) 29/39, 42, 30/44, 46/109, 114, 49/21, 22, 25, 27 [φλάμου- everywhere P].

φορβάς 53/266.

φορτίον 53/400.

φορτῶ 20/9.

φοσσᾶτον (~ Latin *fossatum*) 11/12, 15/9, 9, 30/49, 55, 85, 32/94, 111, 117, 38/25, 43/12, 44/126, 128, 46/134, 138.

φοσσατικῶς (~ Latin *fossatum*) 30/45.

φραγμός (= barrage) 2/19, 9/24, 26, 36, 38, 39, 41, 44, 45, 45, 47, 47, 53, 55, 57, 60, 61, 64, 65.

φράσις 1/11.

φρυάττομαι 53/191.

φύλακος 23/31.

φύλαξις 40/18, 51/41.

φύλαρχος 14/25.

φωλεύω 9/46.

φωταγωγός 29/257.

χαγάνος (~ Turkish *qaɣan*) 13/134, 38/15, 32, 34, 36, 39, 46, 42/27.— Cf. *Byzantinoturcica* p. 279—280 (2nd ed. pp. 332—334).

χαιρέκακος 50/200.

χαίρω 29/169, 53/291, 391; χαίρομαι 53/206, 409, 424.

χαλινῶ 51/203; cf. Grammatical Notes.

χάραγμα 52/14.

χαρέριον (Arabic *ḥarir*) 6/8. — Cf. Eparchicon Biblion IX. 6., ed. Zepos p. 382.

χαρίζομαι 13/53.

χάρισμα 45/15.

χαρτοποιός 52/11.

χαρτουλάριος (~ Latin *chartularius*): χαρτουλάριος τοῦ ὀξέως δρόμου 43/37.

*χειροβολίστρα 53/30, 34, 37, 133. — Cf. De cerimoniis, ed. Bonn. p. 670₁ (χειροτοξοβολίστρων).

χειροτονία 47/8.

χειροτονῶ 21/51, 47/12, 48/14, 20.

χελάνδιον 8/2, 8, 10, 12, 15, 29/98, 42/31, 31, 33, 51/13, 82, 119.

χλεύη 44/112, 53/485.

χοῦς P/46.

χρεωποιοῦμαι 8/19. — Cf. Gregentius, Homeritarum leges, ed. Migne, P. G. 86, 1. c. 612c.

χρῆμα 4/6, 13/15, 26/8, 27/20, 29/121, 45/32.

χρηματίζω 13/109, 16/11, 20/3, 21/116, 43/11, 45/11, 13.

χριστιανικός, χριστιανός cf. Index of Proper Names.

χρονικόν 17/1, 21/1.

χρονογράφος 22/1.

χρόνος (= year) 1/19, 16/3, 21/93, 22/61, 25/26, 28/17, 40, 42, 29/32, 30/67, 79, 85, 31/43, 32/33, 68, 72, 74, 105, 128, 38/55, 41/19, 43/89, 50/172, 51/131, 53/162, 179, 285, 470.

χρυσοβούλλιον (~ Latin *bulla*) 43/76, 96, 99, 148, 45/101, 105, 118, 50/67.

χρυσοβούλλιος (~ Latin *bulla*) 43/87.

χρυσόβουλλον (~ Latin *bulla*) 50/141.

χρυσός cf. Grammatical Notes.

χύμα 13/14.

χωρίον (= village) 32/122, 45/63, 136, 137, 161, 166, 53/500, 503, 504, 504, 507, 508, 510. — Cf. F. Dölger, *Beiträge zur Geschichte der byzantinischen Finanzverwaltung besonders des 10. und 11. Jahrhunderts*, (München, 1927), p. 126.

χωρόπολις 46/43. — Cf. Michael Attaliota, ed. Bonn. p. 148₈.

ψευδοκατηγορία 25/42.

ψευδολογία 50/187.

ψευδοπροφήτης 17/3.

ψευδώνυμος 14/23.

ψυχάριον 9/52, 32/55.

ψωμίον 9/75.

ὡρισμένος cf. ὁρίζω.

ὠτίον 26/49.

GRAMMATICAL NOTES

Since *D. A. I.* contains many linguistic phenomena which diverge from classical usage and illustrate the mediaeval and modern development of the language, we think it necessary to summarize here the most noteworthy demotic characteristics of the language of *D. A. I.*

Words and names cited without indication of chapter and line occur in the Glossary and Index.

Orthography:

νδ ~ ντ: κονδοῦρα, σφοντύλιν.
Cf. Critical Introduction, pp. 18—19, 36, 37.

Accentuation:

ἀντίπερα, ἀπάρτι, αὐθεντῶς, θέρμα, κύρις, λάβε **27/24**, μήκοθεν, πάραυτα, ῎Αβαρεις, ᾿Αρκάϊκα (gen.) ᾿Αρμενιάκοι, ῎Ασπονας (gen.), Δανούβιν (acc.), Μάσαλμα (gen.), Πάρθικος, Πελοποννησαῖοι, ῾Ραούσι(ν), Τάβιας (gen.), Τετραγγούριν, Χερσωνίτικος; cf. below, Substantives ending in -ιν.
Cf. Critical Introduction, p. 18.

Substantives:

nom. -ας (-ᾶς); acc. -α (-ᾶ): Βόρενα, Λεβεδία, Λιούντικα, Νικήτα, Πετρωνᾶ, Ποργᾶ;

nom. -ᾶς; plur. gen. -άδων: ἀμηράδων, βοϊλάδων;

nom. -ης (-ής, -ῆς); acc. -η (-ή -ῆ), gen. -η (-ῆ): ἀμερμουμνῆ, ᾿Αδρανασή, ᾿Αδρανασῆ, ᾿Αλμούτζη, ᾿Αποσέλμη, ᾿Αρπαδή, ᾿Αρπαδῆ, Βεριγγέρη, Βουσεβούτζη, Γιαζή, Ζουρβανέλη, Καλῆ, Καρῆ, Κασῆ, Κισκάση, Κουρκένη, Κρασημέρη, Κρικορίκη, Μεγέρη, Νέκη, Παζουνῆ, Πλατυπόδη, Σιγρίτζη, Τεβέλη, Τερπημέρη;

nom. -ός (< -ιος): κυρός;

nom. -ις (< -ιος): κύρις, Δανούβιν (acc.);

nom. -ίν, -ιν (< -ίον, -ιον): ἀσήμιν, θεμάτιν, κλειδίν, κουροπαλατίκιν, νησίν, ῥαπάτιν, σφοντύλιν, ᾿Αρδανούτζι(ν), Οὐλνούτιν, ῾Ραούσι(ν), Τετραγγούριν, Τζαρβαγάνιν;

nom. -ί; gen. -ί: Τιβί;

nom. -ιμον; plur. nom. -ίματα: μετασταίματα;

nom. -ις; gen. -ι: Δάναπρι, Δάναστρι.

Adjectives:

nom. -ος, -η, -ον (~ -ος, -ον): ἕτοιμαι (plur. nom.) **53/433**, ὁμοφύλαις (plur. dat.) **14/24**;

nom. -ος (< -ής): ἄσφαλοι (? plur. nom.) **38/10, 28**;

nom. -ός (< -οῦς): ἁπλός **23/33**, χρυσός **42/67**;

comparative: βραδέστερον **53**/304, μειζοτέρῳ **53**/258, μελανώτερα **53**/498, πλη-σιέστερον **37**/49, ταχέστερον **53**/397, τάχιον **53**/402, 416;

congruence: εὐεργεσιῶν καὶ φιλοτιμιῶν, τῶν ἐπαξίων πάντων **1**/23, γυναικῶν …παρόντων **17**/20.

Numerals:

ἔνας (< εἷς) ἕνα βήσσαλον **53**/329.

Pronouns:

αὐτός (= this) passim, e. g.: **2**/11, **5**/5, **9**/63, **13**/75, **14**/11, **27**/73, **28**/11, **29**/245, **32**/81, **40**/27, **44**/19;

ὁ αὐτός (= the same, the said, the aforementioned) passim, e. g.: **8**/9, **9**/104, **16**/8, **18**/4, **31**/8, **32**/10, **38**/19, **41**/3, **42**/32, **43**/27, **44**/20, **49**/59, **50**/39, **51**/8, **53**/173; τό (= αὐτό): διὰ τὸ **45**/30, **53**/156;

ὁ τοιοῦτος (= this, the said) passim, e.g.: **1**/25, **2**/22, **4**/7, **6**/7, **8**/14, **9**/36, **11**/9, **13**/6, 118, **15**/6, **29**/32, 68, 246, **30**/18, 132, **31**/24, 47, **32**/23, 144, **33**/14, **34**/13, **35**/9, **38**/51, **42**/93, **43**/88, 157, **44**/38, **45**/48, 155, **46**/35, 140, **50**/78, 195, **51**/54, **53**/216, 505, 523:

οἱοσδήποτε: τὸ οἱονδήποτε **13**/82, τοῦ οἱουδήποτε **13**/122, τὸν οἱονδήποτε **25**/38; οἱοσοῦν: ὁ οἱοσοῦν **13**/89, 102;

ὁ δεῖνα: τὸν ὁ δεῖνα **42**/48, 48;

τίς: τί δουλείαν **46**/81.

Prepositions:

ἀνά + gen.: **29**/248, 248, **31**/73, 74, 74, **41**/5, **52**/7;

ἀπό + acc.: **9**/5, 6, 96, 106, **26**/25, 42, **31**/55, **32**/74, **42**/67, 87, 95, **46**/44;

εἰς + acc. (= in, into, on, at, by, among, about) passim, e. g.: **6**/4, **7**/6, **9**/10, 60, **13**/174, **15**/9, **16**/9, **21**/17, **22**/63, **25**/80, **26**/24, **27**/39, **28**/22, **29**/288, **30**/16, 103, **31**/29, **32**/82, **33**/5, **35**/5, **37**/21, 59, **38**/30, **39**/10, **40**/46, **42**/86, **44**/14, **45**/57, 165, **46**/55, **50**/78, 137, **51**/92, 131, **53**/214, 264;

ἐν + dat. (= to, into, at, upon) passim, e. g.: **1**/21, **7**/2, **8**/4, **9**/3, **13**/98, **21**/56, **22**/37, **26**/9, **27**/7, **28**/14, **29**/118, 157, **30**/76, **32**/50, 120, 139, **42**/34, **43**/62, 171, **45**/89, **46**/60, 79, **50**`53, 174, **51**/26, 142, **53**/52, 266, 311, 387, 414, 525;

[ἐν + acc. in P: **29**/235, 245, 261, 268, 275, **32**/92, **51**/139; cf. S. G. Kapsomenakis, *Voruntersuchungen zu einer Grammatik der Papyri der nachchristlichen Zeit*, (München, 1938), pp. 111—112];

ἕως + acc.: **21**/55, **22**/48, **42**/63;

μετά + acc. (= with): **25**/23, **29**/4, **30**/75, **45**/62, 65;

μέχρι + acc.: **37**/13, **39**/13, **42**/53;

πρὸς ἐπί: πρὸς ἐπὶ τούτοις **53**/149; cf. D. Tabachovitz, *Museum Helveticum*, 3 (1945), pp. 160—161.

Prepositional adverbs:

with gen.: ἀναμέσον, ἀναμεταξύ, ἀντίπερα, ἐκεῖθεν, ἔνθεν, ἐνώπιον, ἐπάνω, κύκλῳ, λόγῳ, μέσον, μήκοθεν, νόμῳ, πέραθεν, ὑποκάτωθεν.

Verbs:

-άω ~ -έω: ἀπεμπολοῦσιν 9/16, ἔζουν 30/121;
-ῶ ~ -νῶ: ἀντιπερνᾶν 51/115;
augment: ἀνάλωσεν 13/99, ἀντεπαρατάξαντο 53/134, 187, ἀπέλασαν 32/25, ἐδιοίκει
51/60 [cf. P: P/35, 13/35, 51, 170, 21/20, 64, 25/5, 26/47, 64, 71, 27/13, 17, 31, 65,
29/28, 141, 233, 30/17, 46, 62, 32/42, 33/10, 34/9, 38/10, 39/7, 40/15, 41/22, 43/51,
45/19, 46/145, 47/11, 25, 49/47, 50/155, 162, 51/36];
reduplication: ἀποσταλμένῳ 49/20, βαπτισμένος 31/31, 68, 71, 86, 32/149,
κατασκευασμένας 53/34, κοπωμένοι 53/68, μεταμέλημαι 29/167, τελευτηκότος 46/146,
χαλινωμένα 51/203 [cf. P: 1/12];
aorist: ἁλωθείσης 47/3, ἀναπαῆναι 53/68, 414, ἀνεχθῆναι 53/277, ἀπέλθατε
53/69, ἐπιπέσαντες 30/28, εἴχαμεν 53/45, ἦλθαν 39/5, καθευδῆσαι 53/436, συμπαθηθῆναι
50/62, συνεπαρεῖν 32/89, ὑπέπεσαν 53/201;
εἰσαγάγω 21/100 [εἰσαγαγὸν P], ἐκβάλω 21/96 [ἔκβαλων P]; cf. S. B. Psaltes, *Grammatik der byzantinischen Chroniken*, (Göttingen, 1913), p. 244; N. Bănescu, *Die Entwicklung des griechischen Futurums von der frühbyzantinischen Zeit bis zur Gegenwart*, (Bukarest, 1915), pp. 72—74; L. Radermacher, *Koine* [Akademie der Wissenschaften in Wien, Philos.-hist. Kl. Sitzungsberichte, 224. Bd. 5. Abh.], (Wien, 1947), p. 64;
imperative: μὴ κοιμᾶσαι 9/25;
ἅς: ἂς ἀποστείλη 45/81, ἂς καθέζηται 45/82 [καθέζεται P], ἂς θεωρῇ 45/83 [θεωρεῖ P];
γίνομαι: γενάμενος 32/58, 50/56;
διδάσκω + dat.: 1/13, 39/8;
δίδωμι: ἀντέδωκαν 32/55, δέδωκαν 45/92, παρέδωκαν 53/104, συνέδωκαν 30/59;
εἰμί: ἦτον 29/273;
εἶμι: συνεξιοῦσι 51/44;
ἔχω: ἔχης εἰδέναι P/26, ἔχεις ἀποκρούεσθαι 13/76, κλῶσαι ἔχω 27/29, ἀποστέλλειν
ἔχει 43/94, ἔχομεν γενέσθαι 45/76, εἰπεῖν ἔχουσιν 45/78, ἔχει εἰσελθεῖν 45/85, καθέζεσθαι
ἔχει 45/86, ἔχειν ἔχομεν 46/133, κινῆσαι ἔχομεν 46/134;
ἡττῶ 5/9, 40/10;
ἵημι: ἀφίομεν 53/52, 54, ἀφίησεν 26/34;
ἱστῶ (< ἵστημι): ἀποκαθιστῶντος 53/313, ἱστῶσιν 21/42, καθιστᾷ P/5, παραστήκετε 53/403, συνιστᾶν 13/120;
οἴγω (< οἴγνυμι): ἀνοιγομένου 9/12;
οἶδα: εἰδούσης 53/314, εἰδούση 53/419, 429 [οἶδα ~ εἶδον in P: 45/140, 49/28,
34, 53/193; cf. S. G. Kapsomenakis, *Voruntersuchungen zu einer Grammatik der Papyri
der nachchristlichen Zeit*, (München, 1938), p. 91]; cf. Critical Introduction, p. 36;
πηγνύω (< πήγνυμι): πηγνύουσι 9/74.

Use of the cases:

acc. instead of dat.: 26/60, 28/45, 29/140, 30/124, 31/84, 32/17, 43/122, 44/33, 45/
75, 152, 46/8, 61, 63, 72, 104, 108, 117, 118, 139, 157, 49/13, 50/124, 51/120, 53/13, 99, 104,
188, 196, 220, 411, 441;
εἰς + acc. instead of dat. passim, e. g.: 9/16, 13/85, 21/103, 26/39, 46/59, 49/56,
53/155, 527.

Negation:

μηδὲν θαυμάσῃς 1/10, οὐδὲν οὐκ ἐποίησαν 30/37, οὐ θέλω δοῦναι τίποτ' οὖν 53/88,
μηδὲν πτοηθῆς 53/350, βαρὺ ὑμῖν τίποτε οὐκ ἐπιζητῶ 53/374.

Use of the tenses:

ἵνα + pres. ind.: **13**/54, 86, 87, **30**/130, **31**/41, 42, **43**/94, 119, 157, **45**/127 [cf. P: **13**/82, **45**/159, **46**/62, **53**/516]; cf. Critical Introduction, p. 35.

ἵνα + pres. opt.: **13**/125, **46**/169;

ἵνα + fut. ind.: **21**/84 [cf. P: **29**/140, **45**/149, **47**/20, **50**/41, 213].

Genitivus absolutus:

instead of participium coniunctum: 8/7, **27**/75, **28**/20, **29**/44, 89, 111, 173, 174, 195, 196, **42**/47, **43**/64, 66, 175, **46**/51, 56, 74, 77, 78, 93, **49**/24, 27, 40, **50**/163, 239, **51**/40, 162, 163, 198, **53**/12, 71, 158, 346.

Nominativus absolutus:

14/17, 23, 24, 26, **25**/8, **26**/27, 28, **29**/32, **31**/15, **32**/46, **38**/48, **41**/21, **46**/113, 114, 115, **50**/130, **51**/52, 187.

INDEX OF SOURCES AND PARALLEL PASSAGES

I. BIBLE

Ezechiel
40, 2 : P/36—37

Daniel
9, 27 : 19/8—9

Zacharias
9, 15 : P/31

Evangelium Matthaei
1, 6 : 45/3—4
2, 12 : 45/11
5, 14 : P/37—38
24, 15 : 19/8—9
27, 8 : 53/450—451

Acta Apostolorum
4, 13 : 13/150
7, 54 : 29/210
28, 1—5 : 36/18—20

Epistola ad Galatas
1, 15 : P/35

Epistola ad Timotheum
II. 4, 1 : 29/203

Epistola Ioannis
II. 8 : 29/203

Epistola Iacobi
1, 17 : P/4—5

Apocalypsis
20, 9 : 13/98—99

Evangelium Apocryphum
(ed. London, 1820)
p. 17 : 45/6—8

II. ANCIENT AUTHORS

Aesopus
(ed. Halm)
fab. 103 : 41/7—19

Apollodorus
(ed. Jacoby, F. Gr. Hist. II B.)
fr. 324; p. 119 : 23/2—4

Apollonius Dyscolus
(ed. Schneider)
p. 47 : 23/30—36

Aristophanes
(ed. Kock, C. A. Fr. I.)
fr. 550, 551; p. 531 : 23/20—22

Artemidorus
(ed. Stiehle, Philologus XI.)
fr. 21; p. 203 : 23/11—17
fr. 22; p. 203 : 23/22—24

Asinius Quadratus
(ed. Jacoby, F. Gr. Hist. II A.)
fr. 2; p. 448 : 23/36—38

Athenaeus
(Dipnosophistae, ed. Kaibel)
I. 44 b; p. 102, 15—19 : 23/40—44

Babrius
(ed. Schneidewin)
fab. 47 : 41/7—19

Charax
(ed. Jacoby, F. Gr. Hist. II A.)
fr. 3.; p. 483 : 24/9—13
fr. 26, 27; p. 488 : 24/4—8

Cratinus
(ed. Kock, C. A. Fr. I.)
fr. 101; p. 46 : 23/39

Dionysius Periegetes
(ed. Müller, G. G. M. II.)
v. 69; p. 108 : 23/26—27
v. 282; p. 117 : 23/20

(Pseudo-) Draco
(De metris, ed. Herrmann)
p. 99 : 21/61—62

Habro
(ed. Berndt, Berl. Phil. Wochenschrift
XXXV.)
p. 1454 : 23/38

Herodianus
(ed. Lentz)
I. p. 76, 29—30 : **23**/18
I. p. 196, 22—29 : **23**/30—36, 38, 39
II. p. 854, 1—9 : **23**/30—36, 38, 39

Herodorus
(ed. Jacoby, F. Gr. Hist. I.)
fr. 2 a; p. 215 : **23**/4—11

Herodotus
IV. 3, 20 : **42**/80—83

Homerus
Ilias II. 672 : **23**/35
Ilias II. 867 : **23**/35
Odyssea VIII. 492 : **13**/104

Marcianus
(Periplus, ed. Müller, G. G. M. I.)
II. 7; p. 544 : **23**/28—30

Menander
(ed. Kock, C. A. Fr. III.)
fr. 79; p. 25 : **23**/25

Parthenius
(ed. Martini, Mythographi Graeci II.
1. suppl.)
fr. 10; p. 17 : **23**/18

Plutarchus
(ed. Bernardakis)
De garrulitate c. 18; III. p. 325 : **41**/ 7—19
Regum et imperatorum apophthegmata
174; II. p. 8—9 : **41**/7—19.

Ptolemaeus
Geogr. III. 6, 5 : **42**/80—83

Simonides
(ed. Diehl, A. L. Gr. II.² 5.)
fr. 165; p. 143 : **21**/61—62

Strabo
XIV. 2, 5; p. 652 : **21**/61—62

Thucydides
I. 22, 2 : **46**/168—169

III. BYZANTINE AUTHORS

Achmes
(Oneirocriticon, ed. Drexl)
p. 212, 20 : **21**/81—82

Basilius
(Paraenesis, ed. Migne, P. G. 107.)
c. XL D : **29**/123—126

Cedrenus
(ed. Bonn.)
I. 717, 7—17 : **16**/6—9
I. p. 738, 3—739, 15 : **14**/2—28, **17**/2—10
I. p. 739, 15—17, 22 : **17**/10—11, 14—23
I. p. 744, 9—21 : **14**/31—36
I. p. 746, 8—15 : **19**/2—11
I. p. 755, 1—5, 8—18 : **20**/3—10, **21**/51—
62, 64—65
I. p. 764, 18—20 : **20**/11—12
I. p. 765, 11—15 : **48**/28—32

I. p. 765, 19—766, 6 : **21**/4—16
I. p. 770, 22—24 : **21**/46—48
I. p. 771, 4—15, 18—21 : **22**/9—26
II. p. 129, 21—130, 13 : **42**/20—55
II. p. 218, 22—219, 3 : **29**/56—69
II. p. 219, 4—220, 8 : **29**/88—116
II. p. 220, 9—221, 7 : **29**/70—79, 88—116
II. p. 221, 8—225, 8 : **29**/116—216
II. p. 254, 24—256, 1 : **40**/7—13

Concilia
(ed. Mansi = Ralles-Potles)
Canon XIV. IV. Conc. (VII. c. 364 =
II. p. 251) : **13**/142—145
Canon XXXIX. VII. Conc. (XI. c. 961
= II. p. 395) : **48**/3—21
Canon LXXII. VII. Conc. (XI. c. 976 =
II. p. 471) : **13**/142—145

Constantinus Porphyrogenitus
De cerimoniis (ed. Bonn. = ed. Vogt.)
p. 5, 2—4 = I. p. 2, 15—17 : **1/8**—13
p. 456, 3—4 : **1/4**
p. 456, 4—5 : **30/2**
p. 690, 23 (scholion) : **27/69**—70

De thematibus (ed. Bonn.)
p. 31, 1—5 (= ed. Pertusi p. 73, IX. 3—6) :
50/120—126
p. 61, 11—62, 18 (= ed. Pertusi p. 97,
18—98, 42) : **29/88**—116

Eparchicon biblion
(ed. Zepos)
IX. 6; p. 382 : **6/8**—9

Excerpta cod. Bruxellensis II 4836
(ed. Davreux, Byzantion X.)
p. 99 : **16/6**—9

Excerpta cod. Harl. 5624
(ed. Lampros, Νέος Ἑλληνομνήμων XV.)
p. 358—359 : **17/2**—10
p. 359 : **14/2**—28, **17/14**—23
p. 362 : **14/31**—36
p. 363 : **18/1**—6

Georgius Monachus
(ed. de Boor)
p. 697, 13—699, 10 : **14/2**—28
p. 699, 10 (apparatus) : **14/28**—31
p. 700, 5—6 : **17/10**—11
p. 706, 1—13 : **14/31**—36
p. 765, 8—14 : **13/61**—66

Georgius Monachus (cont.)
(ed. Bonn. = ed. Istrin)
p. 905, 19—907, 5 = II. p. 56, 8—34 :
13/147—149
p. 913, 6—8 = II. p. 60, 6—8 : **13/147**—
149
p. 917, 11—18 = II. p. 62, 15—21 : **26/**
66—72
p. 853, 20—855, 7 = II. p. 27, 20—28,
11 : **40/7**—13

Leo Grammaticus
(ed. Bonn.)
p. 152, 20—153, 3 : **16/6**—9
p. 153, 4—154, 7 : **14/2**—28
p. 160, 6—10 : **48/28**—32
p. 267, 15—269, 4 : **40/7**—13

Leo Sapiens
(Tact., ed. Migne, P. G. 107.)
XVIII. 42; c. 956 C—D : **40/7**—13
XVIII. 101, c. 969 A—B : **29/82**—84
XVIII. 112—115; c. 972 D—973 B : **15/**
10—14

Lydus
(De magistratibus, ed. Wuensch)
II. 13; p. 68, 23—24 : **6/9**

Menander
(ed. de Boor, Exc. de leg.)
fr. 3; p. 177, 12—34 : **29/123**—126

Nicephorus
(ed. de Boor)
p. 32, 23—33, 6 : **21/4**—16
p. 36, 16—17 : **22/22**—26
p. 39, 12—14 : **22/27**—29
p. 53, 10—54, 1 : **21/116**—125

Nicolaus III Grammaticus
(Synodalis epistola, ed. Migne, P. G.
119 = Ralles—Potles)
c. 877 D—890 A = V. p. 72 : **49/4**—75

Notitiae epsicopatuum
(ed. Parthey)
No. 3, 754; p. 130 : **9/72**

Procopius
(ed. Haury)
De bello Vand. I. 2—4; p. 320, 18—322,
4, 311, 5—313, 1, 317, 9—20, 322,
4—326, 4 : **25/3**—55

Socrates
Hist. eccl. VII. 43 : **13/98**—99

Stephanus Alexandrinus
(ed. Usener)
I. p. 3—16, II. p. 15—22 : **16/1**—5

Stephanus Byzantius
(ed. Meineke)
s. v. Ἰβηρίαι : **23/2**—44
s. v. Ἰσπανίαι : **24/2**—13
s. v. Τάφραι : **42/80**—83

(Pseudo-) Symeon
(ed. Bonn.)

p. 695, 3—697, 2 : **29**/116—216

Theodosius Melitenus
(ed. Tafel)

p. 105, 24—106, 21 : **14**/2—28
p. 110, 14—18 : **48**/28—32
p. 186, 30—188, 2: **40**/7—13

Theophanes
(ed. de Boor)

p. 93, 31—95, 25 : **25**/3—55
p. 273, 14—27 : **29**/123—126
p. 309, 15 : **45**/22—23
p. 333, 1—334, 19 : **14**/2—28, **17**/2—10
p. 334, 17—27 : **14**/28—31, **17**/14—23
p. 336, 4—8, 14—16, 28—29 : **18**/1—6
p. 337, 13—17 : **18**/1—6
p. 339, 15—24 : **19**/2—11
p. 343, 17—20, 24—28, 30—31 : **20**/2—5, **21**/51—54
p. 344, 12—15 : **20**/5—7
p. 345, 8—11, 16—18 : **20**/3—5, 7—10, **21**/54—57, 64—65
p. 346, 20—25 : **20**/12—13, **21**/65—69
p. 346, 20—347, 4 : **21**/16—23, 71—74
p. 347, 26—28 : **21**/16—23, 71—74, 106—110
p. 353, 14—16 : **20**/11—12
p. 354, 13—17 : **48**/28—32
p. 355, 1—25 : **20**/12—13, **21**/4—16
p. 356, 15—17 : **21**/35—37
p. 360, 13—17 : **21**/35—37
p. 360, 27—361, 3 : **21**/38—46
p. 361, 15—16, 26—28 : **21**/46—48, **22**/6—9
p. 363, 1—20 : **22**/9—22
p. 364, 4—7 : **22**/22—26
p. 368, 15 : **22**/29—31
p. 369, 26 : **22**/29—31
p. 370, 6—8 : **22**/27—29, 35—36
p. 371, 19 : **22**/31—32
p. 374, 14—16, 25, 28 : **22**/32—35
p. 374, 28—375, 13 : **22**/6—9
p. 384, 15—19 : **22**/48—49
p. 386, 20—27 : **21**/112—113, 115, **22**/48—51
p. 395, 13—396, 23 : **21**/116—125
p. 396, 23—24 : **22**/52—53
p. 398, 5 : **22**/52—53
p. 401, 4—8, 13—14 : **22**/52—54

p. 402, 19 : **22**/54—55
p. 403, 12—13, 24—25 : **21**/23—30, **22**/36—39, 53—55
p. 421, 7—10 : **22**/55—56
p. 424, 12—16 : **21**/23—30
p. 425, 13—15 : **21**/23—30
p. 426, 1—7 : **21**/23—30, **22**/36—39
p. 429, 15 : **22**/56—57
p. 448, 28 : **22**/57—59
p. 449, 1, 4—8 : **22**/57—59
p. 453, 25—30 : **13**/61—66
p. 461, 7, 10 : **22**/59—60
p. 465, 27—30 : **22**/59—61
p. 484, 5—19 : **22**/62—76

Theophanes continuatus
(ed. Bonn.)

p. 73, 13—76, 7 : **22**/40—48
p. 74, 21—22 : **27**/33—34
p. 122, 19—124, 5 : **42**/20—55
p. 288, 18—289, 2 : **29**/56—69
p. 289, 2—290, 23 : **29**/88—116
p. 291, 1—292, 13 : **29**/70—79
p. 292, 14—294, 2 : **29**/88—116
p. 294, 3—297, 23 : **29**/116—216
p. 358, 7—359, 16 : **40**/7—13
p. 414, 1—415, 9 : **13**/147—149
p. 422, 10—13 : **13**/147—149
p. 431, 11—19 : **26**/66—72
p. 474, 1—7 : **22**/40—48

Theophylactus Simocatta
(ed. de Boor)

p. 243, 10—244, 17 : **29**/123—126

Vita Sophronii
(ed. Papadopulos-Kerameus)

p. 144 : **19**/8—9

Vita Theophanis
(ed. de Boor)

p. 30, 11—12 : **22**/77—78

Zonaras
(ed. Bonn. III.)

XIV. 19; p. 219, 7—10 : **20**/7—10, **21**/64—65
XIV. 20; p. 223, 16—224, 4 : **48**/28—32
XIV. 20; p. 224, 11—225, 7 : **21**/4—16
XV. 1; p. 252, 9—253, 6 : **21**/116—125
XVI. 9; p. 425, 1—429, 6 : **29**/70—79, 88—216
XVI. 12; p. 442, 17—443, 16 : **40**/7—13